THE CONTEMPORARY INTERNATIONAL ECONOMY: A READER SECOND EDITION

The Contemporary International Economy: A Reader

Second Edition

Edited by John Adams

St. Martin's Press
New York

Library of Congress Card Catalogue Number: 84-51147

Manufactured in the United States of America
98765
fedcb
For information, write St. Martin's Press, Inc.
175 Fifth Avenue, New York, NY 10010

cover design: Darby Downey
text design: Frank Sloan

ISBN: 0-312-16672-9

Acknowledgments

I. TRADE PATTERNS AND THE NATIONAL ECONOMY

"The Greeks Have a Word for Bananas But Lack Bananas" by Barry Newman. Reprinted by permission of *The Wall Street Journal* © Dow Jones & Company, Inc., 1983. All Rights Reserved.

"Trade and the Structure of American Industry" by J. Michael Finger. Reprinted from volume no. 460 of THE ANNALS of The American Academy of Political & Social Science. THE ANNALS © 1982 by The American Academy of Political & Social Science.

"New Theories of Trade Among Industrial Countries" by Paul Krugman. Reprinted by permission of the American Economic Association from *American Economic Review,* May 1983, Vol. 73, No. 2, pp. 343–347.

"Linking Up to Distant Markets: South to North Exports of Manufactured Consumer Goods" by Donald B. Keesing. Reprinted by permission of the American Economic Association from *American Economic Review,* May 1983, Vol. 73, No. 2, pp. 338–342.

II. MULTILATERAL TRADE NEGOTIATIONS

"The Tokyo Round of Multilateral Trade Negotiations" by Robert E. Baldwin. Reprinted from Robert E. Baldwin, *The Multilateral Trade Negotiations: Toward Greater Liberalization?* Special Analysis, 1979, pp. 1–2 and 8–30, by permission of the American Enterprise Institute; and from Robert E. Baldwin, *Beyond the Tokyo Round Negotiations,* Thames Essay No. 22 (London: Trade Policy Research Centre, 1979), pp. 22–23, by permission.

"Statement on U.S. Aims at the World Trade Minister's Meeting: One Industry's View" by the Semiconductor Industry Association. Reprinted from the U.S. Approach to 1982 Meeting of World Trade Ministers on the GATT, Hearing Before the Subcommittee on International Trade of the Committee on Finance, United States Senate, Ninety-Seventh Congress, Second Session, March 1, 1982, Washington, D.C.

Acknowledgments and copyrights continue at the back of the book on pages 546–548, which constitute an extension of the copyright page.

Preface

This collection of readings is designed for introductory courses in international economics, international business, and international relations. It may also be used in the first graduate courses in these fields. The book's primary aim is to make it easier for students and other interested persons to learn what economists currently have to say about international economic problems. It simplifies instructors' jobs by placing at their disposal a set of readings that constructively and imaginatively supplements their lectures and standard textbooks.

Assembling such a collection required devoting many hours to reviewing hundreds of articles from scores of publications. At times it seemed easier to write a chapter on a given topic than to continue a frustrating line of search for a satisfactory article. Fortunately, significant problems quickly attract the attention of the best economic minds. In fact, a frequent achievement of these minds is to identify new problems and make the rest of us conscious of them so that analysis and policy-making can proceed. With the keen anticipation of a child looking for Easter eggs, I did persevere in all the searches and this anthology is the result.

When I compiled the first edition of this reader I naively thought that I would draw most heavily on writers who simplified, distilled, and summarized the writings of those economists who worked on the frontiers. I learned then, and my experience this time reconfirmed, something I suspect many students (and perhaps even their teachers) would not guess: that the best and most creative economists are also very commonly the finest and most lucid writers. To a great extent, therefore, these assembled readings exemplify new ideas and adroit exposition by their initial proponents. Not all are easily read, but this is because the economics and politics of the international economic system are complex. Excepting some specialized documents, the selections in this collection portray the dimensions of significant issues arising in the operation of the contemporary international economy, introduce fresh ideas, and suggest imaginative reforms. Together they take the reader to the current boundaries of international economic thought.

Six years have elapsed since the first edition was published. The broadening integration of the American economy into the world economy is no longer a novelty. Every American—farmer, worker, businessman, consumer, government official—is involved everyday with aspects of the network of international economic relations: prices, investments, travel, deals, consumer products, negotiations with foreign governments.

In 1985, the main question is no longer whether the United States will become more fully involved in an emerging global economy. What has now become evident is that the many dimensions of the links that have emerged since the late 1970s have created a number of problems of adjustment. Key American industries such as steel, textiles, and automobiles are experiencing substantial and sometimes fatal pressure from foreign competition. American businesses are now truly transnational with much of their productive capacity sited in other lands and a large portion of their profits flowing from foreign operations. This change may or may not affect investment and job creation in the United States.

Coping with the interplay of foreign economic and domestic policy increasingly absorbs the time of officials in the executive branch and representatives in Congress. Agriculture is a case in point. The policymaking process is complicated by the special interest backlash from workers and businesses hurt by foreign competition. This backlash has been strengthened by the very difficult world economic climate of the early 1980s when severe recession, high rates of unemployment, excessive inflation, and very high interest rates prevailed in most developed economies.

European nations, and to some degree the United States, have been compelled by internal political forces to become more guarded in their espousal of freer trade and more open monetary movements. The Japanese have continued to manage their trade, currency, and industrial policies in ways that often confound the wishes of their trading partners for more access to the Japanese market. Smaller Third World nations such as Taiwan and Korea are now major factors in world trade, with Mexico, Pakistan, and the Middle East playing larger roles. The extraordinarily large debts of some important Third World and Eastern European countries generate concern about massive defaults and international monetary collapse. There is now sufficient experience with floating exchange rates to permit considered judgements about their effectiveness in this period of international economic stress. The acute poverty of many poor peoples of South Asia and Sub-Saharan Africa persists as a sobering reminder of the failure of international economic relations—trade, investment, and aid—to bring rising incomes and rapid technological progress to *all* nations.

In view of these developments since 1979, this edition is organized around the theme of the integration of the American economy into the global economy. The problems associated with that integration have inspired new thinking about international trade connections and about international financial linkages. An important element has been the emergence of political forces in the United States hostile to, or guarded about, further extensions of economic integration, at least at its present pace. In order to continue to make a strong case for wider and more liberal international commercial and financial participation, economists have had to consider and respond to the fears that give rise to negative political reactions.

The readings that follow are grouped under six headings: Trade Patterns and the National Economy, Multilateral Trade Negotiations, The United States in the World Economy: Issues of the 1980s, The International Monetary System: Operation and Management, The Multinational Corporation in the International Economy, and Rich Country–Poor Country Relationships. Each of these sections is introduced by a brief comment.

A major contrast between this and the first edition is that there are more readings on trade and trade policy: 15 instead of 11. This demonstrates the explosion of concern about the domestic economic effects of freer trade and their political consequences. In contrast, I have reduced the number of papers covering international finance, the multinational corporation, and the position of the developing nations from 28 to 18.

While there is scarcely agreement that the international monetary system is working perfectly, the old debate over the desirability of shifting from a system of fixed to more flexible rates has become less intense. The role of the multinational corporation in the international economy has been pretty thoroughly examined by critics and enthusiasts with little new now being said on either side. Similarly, the rich nation–poor nation dialogue (or lack of dialogue) about the New International Economic Order has settled into a conventional mold. As the global economy has passed into a time of turbulence in the 1980s, both rich and poor nations have become more selfishly absorbed with their own immediate successes and failures in coping with the dimensions of international economic integration. Great power rivalry centered on the substantial deterioration of relations between the United States and the Soviet Union, and insurrections within the smaller powers and some nasty neighborhood wars, have vastly complicated the march of mankind to global conciliation and concord.

To summarize the chief difference in tone between the first and second editions, I would say the first edition embodied many noble hopes: that freer trade based on a rather simple comparative advantage rationale could be easily implemented, with much benefit to participating nations, firms, and workers; that a free or flexible exchange rate system would make it easier for nations to manage their monetary and fiscal policies, and hence better control internal unemployment and inflation; that multinational corporations would, for good or ill depending upon one's perspective, expand operations vigorously across the Third World; and that a new and more just international economic order would be at least partially instituted, thereby bringing more equal roles for all nations and a more equal sharing of world economic opportunity. The second edition does not reflect the abandonment of these hopes. What it does mirror is a much greater appreciation of the complexities of achieving global economic integration and its political ramifications. There is a political awareness in my new choices that was lacking in some earlier writings. This realism may become a basis for deeper and clearer thinking about international economic policy-making and lead to more skilled policy formulation and implementation, both domestically and internationally. Proper policies can then serve as the instruments for continued progress in the international economy. If this view is correct, then that progress will be manifested in freer movements of goods, persons, and ideas, and in wider economic integration among nations and peoples everywhere.

I want to thank the authors of the articles for acceding to my requests to use their works. It is a great pleasure to be able to present this collection of exceptional papers to a new generation of readers. Ellen Magenheim, a graduate student at the University of Maryland, helped me find and choose the articles and I thank her for her diligence and effervescence. Another Maryland graduate student, Carolyn Chapman, aided me in tying up difficult loose ends in the final stages; my great appreciation to her. Gail Ifshin, a Maryland graduate student who served in 1983–84 on the staff of the Council of Economic Advisers, called my attention to desirable selections; thanks to her, too.

After helping me do the first edition while she was an undergraduate student at Maryland, Orit Frenkel received a master's degree from the University of Michigan and now works in the Office of the United States Trade Representative. In addition to this role and pursuing a doctoral degree at Johns Hopkins, she provided advice on selections for the second edition. My colleague at Maryland, Arvind Panagariya, gave me sage counsel. Ed Tower of Duke University and two anonymous readers made extremely useful assessments of my initial choices and suggested some papers I had not seen. Marie Speake helped with word processing and typing at her usual high level of perfection.

Lastly, I dedicate this book to my children, Jennifer, Lara, and Michael. Their lives will be transformed beyond my comprehension by things only foreshadowed here.

John Adams

Contents

I. Trade Patterns and the National Economy

The fundamental issue in international trade theory is how the national economy and the world economy are related through patterns of international trade. Trade theory explains why a country exports certain products and imports others and traces the effects of trade on the pattern of domestic production.

The theory of comparative advantage demonstrates that gains of specialization arise within an international division of labor. In this model's simple form, trade between two countries in two commodities is analyzed. Following the Heckscher-Ohlin argument, specialization in an export commodity is attributable to a nation's factor proportions. Countries are assumed to have different endowments of land, labor, and capital, and each nation will specialize in exporting goods that require in production more of the factors the country has in relative abundance.

When David Ricardo devised the theory of comparative advantage, he used a now famous example. He said that England should import wine from Portugal, where sun and soil were conducive of grape production, and export cloth, which its labor and machinery could produce economically. He employed wry humor to ridicule the foolishness of the English attempting to use hothouses and other extraordinary means to produce costly grapes to brew their own wine at home.

Although Ricardo developed his theories in 1817, his lessons still have not been fully absorbed in the 1980s. A good case in point is the peculiar one of Greek bananas. In the first selection in this section, Barry Newman equals Ricardo's wry humor in his account of the effects on the Grecian economy of a prohibition halting imports of bananas. Consumers cannot buy the bananas they yearn for at reasonable prices; smuggling erupts; apple producers rejoice and form a lobby to continue the barring of bananas; and the few Greek banana farmers are making big money. And, yes, there is even a call for growing bananas in Greek greenhouses.

The second reading is by J. Michael Finger. He examines adjustment problems arising from the growing integration of the United States economy into the world economy. He points out that those workers and industries threatened by imports find it relatively easy to command the attention of politicians and policymakers. In contrast, consumers and exporters have difficulty articulating their interests and pressing for reduced barriers to trade.

The usual textbook production possibilities curve presentation of comparative advantage makes it appear that rather large amounts of labor and other factors must be shifted from import-competing to exporting industries. Finger points out that such movements are really rather minute. Much of the opposition to relaxation of barriers to imports may stem from increased competition, which forces down excessive profits and wages in affected industries. Few, if any, jobs will be lost in these industries if owners and workers are willing to accept lower and fairer returns. Where labor reallocation is needed, adjustment assistance may have some very limited role, but Finger believes that maintaining full employment with sound macroeconomic policies is probably the best way to ease adjustment stresses caused by an expanding trade sector.

The principle of comparative advantage is very convincing and easy to grasp when we are talking about such commodities as wine and cloth or wheat and steel. Exports of these items are clearly dependent upon particular national endowments of climate, soils, machinery, and labor. Yet, when we look around us we find that many broad categories of imports and exports overlap. We import small automobiles and export large automobiles. We import certain kinds of cloth and clothing, but export others. In addition, our factor proportions are at least crudely the same as those of our major trading partners, Japan and Western Europe.

Paul Krugman mentions a number of current explanations of overlapping trade patterns. He develops two of the newer theories in some depth: the theory of intraindustry trade and the theory of technological competition. He says that the standard factor proportions argument accounts well enough for a nation's broad pattern of industrial specialization. But trade within a given industry category—that is, intraindustry trade—is to be explained by the existence of increasing returns to scale. Within an industry, nations specialize in a few items which they produce under conditions of economies of scale. The theory of technological competition has not been well developed as yet, but contains some fascinating implications. If, for example, manufactured exports depend upon nations' capacities to create and exploit technological advantages, which yield lower costs or better products, there may be gains to protection. Some nations, notably Japan, are trying to target industries where their research and development efforts can surpass those of the United States. Since this new theory opens up possibilities for national gains from protection usually denied by conventional comparative cost models, its several lines of analysis will require considerable exploration.

The final paper shifts attention away from the United States and the developed countries to rising Third World exporters like Korea and

Taiwan. Successful middle income countries must not only worry about their own internal economic transformation towards export industries but also consider how successfully to join their economies with those of the rich countries where they find their major markets. A miscalculation could have disastrous consequences for continuing their economic success. Keesing stresses an often neglected facet of international trade: the importance of accurate information about foreign consumers' changing tastes and about marketing channels. Sound anticipation of demand permits these emerging economies to participate in intraindustry trade and enjoy economies of scale. Without reliable information flows and good marketing arrangements, a nation's comparative advantage in production will remain latent or underexploited.

1. The Greeks Have a Word For Banana But Lack Bananas

Barry Newman

Are there no bananas in Olympia?

Yes.

Are there no bananas in Thebes? Yes. In Corinth? Yes. In Sparta, Marathon, Delphi? Yes, yes, yes.

Are there no bananas on Crete?

That depends on your definition of banana. Little green pods do grow on that Greek island, on scorched, drooping plants that look as though they want to be banana trees. They are called bananas (the Greek word for banana is pronounced banana), but they don't taste much like bananas—or, at least, that's what people say. A foreigner can't easily get a taste of a ripe Cretan banana. They are all sold secretly, on the black market. To buy a banana anywhere in Greece, you need a connection.

All over the world, people take bananas for granted. A bunch of bananas off the boat from Panama isn't exactly what dreams are made of, right? Well, in this country, dreams *are* made of bananas. Alien bananas are contraband in Greece. For Greeks, a sweet, yellow, pulpy Panamanian banana is the forbidden fruit.

A GENEROUS TIP

"Greece no banana," says the taxi driver at the Athens airport, ecstatically accepting an exotic beauty as a tip. A traveler has just slipped through customs with a bunch in a brown paper bag, defying a five-pound limit. The driver tenderly places his in the glove compartment. "I show it to my grandson," he says.

It has been 12 years now since the last banana boat sailed away from Piraeus. There are children in Greece today who don't even know what

Barry Newman is a staff reporter with *The Wall Street Journal*. He is currently assigned to London.

a banana is. Greece was a dictatorship in 1971, and dictatorships sometimes do strange things. The one in Greece outlawed the traffic in foreign bananas.

The head of internal security, Col. Stelios Pattakos, gave the order. He was born on Crete, a bone-dry island, and was friendly toward some farmers there who had it in their heads to try growing a fruit native to equatorial jungles. The colonel got rid of the competition. Still, the Cretan crop was so puny it couldn't satisfy a 50th of the Greek passion for bananas. The price went up. The government imposed controls. And then the banana peddlers went underground.

When the dictatorship collapsed in 1974, Col. Pattakos was sentenced to life imprisonment for non-banana-related offenses. Democracy returned—but bananas didn't. Bureaucrats do strange things, too.

A banana avalanche, they determined, would hurt the Greek apple business. Everybody would suddenly stop eating apples and start eating bananas. It didn't do any good to argue that comparing apples and bananas was like comparing apples and oranges. So Col. Pattakos got life, and the Greek people got life without bananas.

A THWARTED IMPORTER

One man, on his own, has borne the greatest burden of bananalessness. His name is Myron Mauricides. He has short gray hair and a thick neck that cranes forward when he walks. He stoops. He wears crushed cord jackets. He looks like Jack Lemmon in one of his more exasperated roles.

Mr. Mauricides is the head of the Association of Greek Banana Importers.

When he is presented with a banana during lunch at an Athens cafe, Mr. Mauricides's eyes go limpid with nostalgia. "Ah, smell," he says, taking a whiff and hiding the thing under his napkin. "You know, after the war, people used to bring nylons. Then it was Scotch. Now they bring bananas."

For 23 years, until 1962, Mr. Mauricides was a middleman on 42nd Street in New York. He fixed up American companies with Greek distributors. Then he thought, "If I can get accounts for other people, why not get one for myself?" So he got the Bristol-Myers account and moved back to Greece.

Mr. Mauricides did well, so well that Bristol-Myers moved to Greece, too, and put him out of business. "I snooped around for something else," he says. "Bananas looked good."

Thus, Myron Mauricides became the first person to sell boxed bananas to the Helenes. "We had a boat coming in once a week, like clockwork," he says. Then the junta struck and bananas were finished. "There isn't much more to talk about," Mr. Mauricides says, "except 12 years of frustration."

Only once since the onset of prohibition have Greeks plumbed the joys of the true banana. For three wild months in 1978, while a freethinking minister looked the other way, they ate through an entire year's supply—50,000 tons. That is 300 million bananas, 33 for every man, woman and child: Nobody knew if he would ever see a banana again.

After the binge, some truckers began to smuggle bananas in from Germany. One was caught and thrown into jail, and that was the end of that. For a time, Yugoslavian tourists took to sneaking into the country with bags full of bananas. They made a killing and went home loaded with blue jeans. Then Greece imposed the five-pound limit. Yugoslavian tourists were forced to surrender their bananas at the border, or else eat them on the spot.

"Can you imagine the scene?" says Mr. Mauricides. "Somebody should make a Broadway musical out of this!"

Intent on breaking the apple lobby, Mr. Mauricides proposed that the government allow bananas into the country and then impose a banana tax. "They tax liquor. Why not bananas?" he asks. "Listen, the government could take in $120,000 a day on this. Why not turn the banana to your advantage? Why not squeeze the banana for all its worth?"

The government won't bite. (It won't comment, either.)

Now Mr. Mauricides is in court. He requested an import permit. The government denied it. He sued. A judge found for bananas. But the case is sensitive. So it has been sent up to the Council of State, the highest administrative court in the land.

Greek banana policy is at issue in the Common Market, too. Greece is a member, but it won't let in Common Market bananas. Where do bananas grow in the Common Market? In Martinique and Guadeloupe; those are Caribbean islands, but in France they are considered as French as Champagne. The Common Market banana case appears destined for the European Court of Justice.

Myron Mauricides has finished his fish. For dessert he orders fruit salad: a dish of sliced apples and oranges. Mr. Mauricides takes a bite. His lips curl as if it were a mouthful of quicklime. Stealthily, he slips his smuggled gift from under his napkin and cuts it into the salad. He tastes, and smiles. "An apple," he says, "is no substitute for a banana."

But can a Cretan banana stand in for a Chiquita? The way to find out is to eat one. An exhaustive search of Athens fails to turn up a clandestine banana pusher. The alternative is a voyage to Crete and a long drive to the village of Arvi, on the island's south coast, where the Cretan banana was born.

The road to Arvi, corrugated by a grader, would probably puree a truckload of Chiquitas. It winds down to the sea out of a desiccated mountain, past patches of stunted banana trees toasting in the summer sun.

Arvi has a street, a hotel, a cafe. It has a store that sells seeds and bug killer. Dimitrias Hatzakis and Yiorgos Spanakis are in there one morning, drinking coffee. Mr. Spanakis runs the store. Mr. Hatzakis grows bananas.

"Let me tell you about the climate here," says Mr. Hatzakis, who is fat and bald and who used to be in construction. "This is the only place in Greece that the sparrows don't leave in winter."

"We have the smallest rainfall in the country, though, unfortunately for the bananas," says Mr. Spanakis, stroking his mustache. He has decorated his shop with cactus plants.

"Bananas need humidity," Mr. Hatzakis says. "It's our only problem."

Neither the corrugated road nor perpetual drought has prevented prosperity from making its way here. The banana growers of Arvi, Mr. Hatzakis boasts, are the richest farmers in Greece.

"When a smuggler offers four times the official price," he says, "you have to look at the practical side of bananas." But you don't want to be caught selling at four times the official price, so "we write out false receipts," says Mr. Spanakis.

"If they start importing, that will be the end of us here," Mr. Hatzakis says. He has a better idea: government money to build greenhouses. Production would shoot up, prices would come down, and the Greeks would be in banana heaven. Mr. Hatzakis has a few greenhouses already, and he offers a tour of them.

Set up on the mountainside, they are covered with soft plastic and fed by black rubber hoses that look like errant sea snakes. Inside, the heat is equatorial, and the air is thick with moisture and the sweet smell of mulch. The trees are tall and full; water beads on their leaves. The fruit, though small, appears to have true banana potential.

"We could compete with imports," Mr. Hatzakis says. "Just give us 10 more years."

Would it be possible to taste one of his hothouse bananas?

"Oh, you won't find any here," he says, emerging into the sunlight. "We ship them green. We don't have ripe bananas in Arvi."

2. Trade and the Structure of American Industry

J. MICHAEL FINGER

Over the past few decades the U.S. economy has indeed become more "international." In 1980, almost eight percent of the goods and services consumed were imported, as compared with four percent in the early 1960s. This internationalization has produced stresses and has mandated adjustments that are, from one point of view, problems, and from another point of view, opportunities.

Expanding trade is more often—or at least more loudly—described as a problem than as an opportunity. For example, a labor union official, testifying before the United States Congress, suggested that unless the growth of imports was controlled, the United States would eventually become "a nation of hamburger stands." This is a graphic way to express the widespread concern that U.S. industries, paying American wages, cannot expect to compete with manufacturers in low-wage countries and must either go out of business or move their production facilities abroad. Expanding trade, this view suggests, will cause the U.S. manufacturing sector to disappear, leaving only service sector jobs—in hamburger stands and that sort of thing.

Perhaps in no area of public policy are half-truths and misinformation as abundant, influential, and even institutionalized as in the area of trade policy. The information to which the concern about becoming a nation of hamburger stands refers, the increase of imports is, of course, a truth. But the missing half of the story is that we now export eight percent of the goods and services we produce, as compared with four percent 20 years ago. As to trade with low-income countries, it is true that U.S. manufactured imports from low-wage countries have increased tremendously, in volume almost fivefold over the 1970–80 decade, or in value by almost $25 billion. Yet at the same time, U.S. exports to these countries have increased by 50 percent more—by almost $37 billion. On the global scale, while developing country exports of manufactured goods to industrial countries more than doubled in

J. Michael Finger is a senior economist on the World Bank's Development Policy Staff.

volume, the increase of industrial countries' manufactured exports to developing countries was three times larger.[1] To cut off the U.S. manufacturing sector from trade, particularly from trade with the developing countries, would isolate it from a market that is expanding more rapidly—in net, not just gross terms—than the U.S. market and other industrial country markets. Far from retarding the U.S. industrial sector, trade with the low-income countries makes a significant contribution to the vitality of this sector.

The fear that a country will come to import everything and export nothing is one of the trade policy's most common misconceptions. If firms and individuals from the United States sell less and less in foreign countries while buying more and more from them, they will soon run out of the foreign currencies needed to buy goods in foreign countries. Or, before that, their attempts to buy foreign currency for dollars will push up the dollar price of foreign currencies, making foreign goods more expensive to Americans, whose incomes are earned in dollars, and American goods less expensive to foreigners, whose incomes are earned in foreign currencies. Unless the government intervenes, normal price adjustments will maintain balance between exports and imports and will prevent a country from becoming an importer of everything and an exporter of nothing.

Thus both common sense and the facts of the matter indicate that increased trade with the rest of the world is not immiserizing.

ADJUSTMENT TO INCREASED TRADE

Capitalizing on the opportunity that increased trade provides requires two kinds of adjustment. One of these is familiar—the shifting of resources from activities that are performed more efficiently abroad to sectors in which the domestic economy has a comparative advantage. And as markets become international, the market power of national firms is eroded. Particularly at the policy level, the need to adjust to this change is more often ignored than discussed.

Moving Resources

Though the proportion of total U.S. production that enters into international trade has doubled in the past 25 years, the amount of shifting of resources from industry to industry that this has entailed has been minimal. For one reason, the doubling of the trade ratio has involved only 4 percentage points of gross national product (GNP) spread over more than 20 years, while total employment in the U.S. economy has increased by more than three percent per year. And a large proportion of the increase of trade has involved intra- rather than inter-industry specialization. . . . Adjustment has been primarily a matter of eliminating certain product lines and expanding others. The U.S. textile industry—though not the apparel industry—has, by adjusting its product mix toward the more sophisticated products using more technologically advanced production methods, regained parity with foreign producers, so that U.S. exports of textiles are now considerably larger than imports. Furthermore, the proportion of intraindustry trade in the growth of a trade has been less in the textiles sector than in many others. In machinery and capital goods, for example, more than three-fourths of the post–World War II expansion of trade has involved intraindustry specialization, rather than the contraction of one industry and the expansion of another.

As to actual magnitudes, relevant evidence may be taken from U.S. Labor Department estimates of the impact of the balanced reductions of trade barriers agreed to by the United States and by our trading partners at the Tokyo Round of international negotiations.[2] Of the 297 U.S. manufacturing industries affected, only 30 have estimated net changes of employment of more than one-half of one percent of their initial level. And in only three small industries (pottery products, artificial flowers, and lace goods), accounting among them for less than one-tenth of one percent of U.S. manufactured output, will increased trade cause employment to decline by as much as five percent.

Reduction of Market Power

Internationalization has brought forward another sort of adjustment issue—one which is more a question of adjustment within industries than of a resource transfer between industries. Industries such as auto and steel have long been highly concentrated domestically and have been protected from foreign competition by tariffs and location. . . . Differences in highway systems and in gasoline prices led to significant differentiation between American autos and autos produced for European and Japanese markets, which insulated American producers from international competition over the major part of their product line. As tariffs were reduced throughout the 1950s and 1960s, nearly every country's industrial sector was growing rapidly, and domestic capacity in basic industries such as steel was always strained to keep up with domestic demand. This left producers with little incentive to compete for foreign markets.

However, the growth of world trade in industrial products, excess capacity stemming from lower industrial country growth rates than were expected when present capacity was installed, and rising energy prices in the United States have intensified across-border competition for markets. In determining the market power of producers, the relevant definition of market is now international, not domestic. Though the number of producers located in a country may have changed very little, the number that compete for the market in that country has increased considerably.

The changes that adjustment to greater competition within industries demands do not necessarily include a net transfer of resources out of such industries. This erosion of the market power of national firms calls less for changes in the structure of production between industries than for changes in the structure of distribution. As . . . [exemplified by] the steel and auto industries, until they were exposed to international competition, profit rates were high. Wage rates continue to be much higher than in other industries. With the market power of such industries diminished by international competition, the market will no longer support the tradition of rates of return higher than in other industries. Much of the clamor for import relief for such sectors is, implicitly, pressure on the government to defend that tradition.

Policies aimed at assisting people to transfer from one industry to another are not appropriate for such industries. In opportunity cost terms, that is, when resources are valued at what they would earn in other industries, the United States is not a high cost producer.[3] The need here is not to shift resources to higher productivity, and ultimately higher-paying alternatives, but to persuade them to accept the lower rates of return—the rates enjoyed in other industries—required by the loss of their market power.

The Overtaking of The American Economy

A final element in our current trade situation comes less from the internationalization of the American economy than from the overtaking of it by other economies. Theory suggests that the mix of traded goods will constantly change. As countries at lower stages of development expand their capacity, their exports of simpler manufactures whose technologies they have mastered will expand, allowing them to buy larger volumes of capital goods and other sophisticated manufactured goods from the industrial countries. Over time, the pattern of trade between the industrial and the more advanced developing countries should become more and more like trade among the industrial countries—intraindustry trade within the more sophisticated industries, based on product-line economies of scale rather than on industrywide differences in technology between countries. The next tier of developing countries, just beginning on the path to industrialization, would become the world's supplier of simpler manufactures.

In the early 1960s the United States was further along this path than any other country, and our manufactured exports were based in large part on our huge capital stock and our technological advantage over the rest of the world. It is, however, well known that for two decades the U.S. rate of investment has been lower than rates in most other industrialized and many developing countries. The share of GNP allocated to investment in new plants and equipment has been three times as large in Japan, and in a number of Asian developing countries, as in the United States. A low overall rate of investment shows up in specifics such as our aging steel capacity and a stock of machine tools in place with a higher average age than in any other industrial country except the United Kingdom. As a result, the composition of our exports is changing—a smaller share for machinery based on technological advantage and a larger one for agricultural exports based on abundant farmland. Viewed only from the perspective of export composition, our economy is moving back toward the nineteenth century.

POLICY CONSIDERATIONS

Being overtaken by the rest of the world may be embarrassing, but it is not a failing. It might be quite sensible for American society to choose to consume more than 90 percent of our output and to invest a proportion that is, by the numbers of many other countries, quite small.

One senses, however, some reluctance to live with the implications of this choice, particularly with its trade implications. Relatively slow growth implies relatively large changes in the composition of U.S. imports and exports and therefore relatively large shifts of resources from one sector to another. Ascribing these stresses to "unfair" foreign competition has considerable political appeal.

Adjustment Policy

Shifts of resources contribute to the total output and the overall efficiency of the economy, but often come in conflict with another social objective. Many of the programs and policies that influence the flexibility of the industrial structure were not established with adjustment as their primary objective. They arose from the twentieth-century liberal concern with so-called economic security or, more particularly, from concern at a policy level with the side effects of economic growth. The general objective of these policies was to minimize the dislocations, and to offset the income losses embedded in the responses of economies to changes of consumer tastes and of modes of production. But the discomfort of remaining in a declining sector and the potential gains from shifting to an advancing one are the incentives by which a market economy shifts resources from one use to another, and these shifts play a major role in economic growth. Thus these policies have often tended to compromise the capacity of the economy to adjust and grow.[4]

Discussion of adjustment policy has tended to concentrate sequentially on two questions: (1) how to shift resources from lower to higher productivity uses and (2) how to choose and promote industries with high growth potential and strong positions in international trade.

Policy analysts have tended first to look for policies that serve the economic security and the growth-efficiency objective simultaneously, that is, to try to find a way to avoid trading one constituency against another. The "golden path," however, has not been found. Reviewers have more or less unanimously agreed that public policy to promote economic security has often sought to delay the transfer of resources, or at least it has had that effect.[5]

Thus answers to the first question did not produce a golden path to security—a path that had no costs in terms of growth and efficiency. Indeed, it was generally found that "the greatest contribution to rapid reallocation has probably been the pursuit of full employment and a generally high level of demand."[6]

To promote adjustment through growth, one obviously has to promote growth, and this can be approached in either a macro or a micro context. In macro terms, growth involves the allocation of a larger share of GNP to investment and research. It obviously reduces short-run consumption possibilities. An alternative approach, which might be described as "economic growth on the cheap," is suggested by the second policy question listed previously—how to pick industries with high growth potential and promote them, that is, how to transfer resources to winners and away from losers without increasing the total amount of resources devoted to research and investment.

Japan is frequently given as the prime example of the effectiveness of picking and promoting industrial winners. The attraction of the Japanese model apparently is that it offers a costless solution to the problem of lagging economic growth: by having government direct or induce the available amount of savings to the "right" industries, the growth rate of aggregate output that a given savings rate produces will be increased. On careful examination, however, this interpretation does not fit the Japanese case very well. Several major growth industries—for example, autos and radio and television receivers—were not picked by the Japanese government. Investment in Japan was no more growth efficient than elsewhere, in the sense that a percentage point of GNP devoted to investment did not buy more growth in Japan than it did in other countries. There were simply more percentage points of investment in Japan. With an abundance of capital available, the usual response of the Japanese government to pressures generated by tax advantages or other incentives for particular industries was to extend those advantages to yet other industries. Aggressive entrepreneurs and a very high savings rate—not its bureaucracy—are the secrets to Japan's success. The Japanese government has looked good not because it has rationed capital skillfully but because it has not had to ration capital.[7]

One frequently hears that the key to successful adjustment policy is indicative planning. The government should develop a scientifically precise, long-run plan identifying which industries will expand and which will contract and then implement that plan. The objection that it is not easy to predict which industries will—or should, on efficiency grounds—expand or contract is met by the suggestion that policy concentrate on a few extreme cases, the obvious winners and losers. A look at recent trade statistics would provide preliminary lists, and professional analytical studies of these industries would then produce the final determinations. The needed technical expertise is available on government staffs or can be hired.

Apart from the technical questions, our open political system requires that such determinations be enforced and defended at a political level. But at that level technical evidence is not a secure basis for a political sorting of those industries that will receive public support and those that must fend for themselves. Those who lose at a technical level are free to appeal that decision at a political level, as was the case recently when the U.S. International Trade Commission determined that imports were not a major cause of injury to the U.S. automobile industry. Even if the government has a solid technical case—in the sense that impartial, trained experts would agree that the government's decision is correct—it may not be able to make its case stick at the political level. At that level of public debate, the relevant audience will not be competent to evaluate conflicting technical arguments.

Such a government decision, if it is to stick politically, must rely for its defense on the competence of the technical staff that furnished the data for the decision, that is, on the expertise of the government's witnesses. In the United States, there is a tradition of disrespect for public officials, and the last two presidents elected have run against the federal bureaucracy. It would thus be impossible for a president to defend an industrial plan by pointing out that it was developed by the same bureaucracy that he indicated during his election campaign as bloated and incompetent.

In the U.S. political system, economic distress seems to be a stronger political force than economic potential. Our industrial policy has tended to be a sequence of rescue programs for firms in trouble, always with the intention of putting the distressed firm back on its feet, rather than of transferring resources to other uses, and usually adorned with accusations of unfair practices by the foreign competition.

In this setting, trade policy can hardly aspire to more than a minimization of the number of such programs and the degree to which they distort trade. Defending the openness of our economy will thus continue to involve the tedious job of identifying the protective impact of industry and other programs, calculating the costs of such protection, and attempting to bring this information to bear on the relevant decisions, which may themselves be difficult to identify.

Administrative Mechanisms

Some trade questions are decided through formal decision mechanisms. But on these, as on other trade issues, the benefits from trade tend to be widely dispersed among many users and consumers while the costs fall on a smaller group of producers that compete with imports. For this and other reasons, the policy mechanisms tend to reflect the mercantilist presumption that exports are the gains from trade and imports the costs. Thus in so-called escape clause cases—the question of restricting auto imports from Japan is a recent example—the U.S. International Trade Commission is required to investigate injury to domestic producers from import competition. The law requires no such investigation of gains to users of imports—to other producers who use the imported good as an input, or to consumers of a finished good. Indeed, in framing its recommendations for the president, the International Trade Commission is precluded by law from considering user or consumer gains from trade.

The dumping and countervailing duty mechanisms are similarly biased toward the interests of producers who compete directly with imports. The legal objective of these mechanisms is to police the fairness of trade practices employed by foreigners when they sell in the U.S. market. The mechanisms pursue that objective by restricting imports—in design, from unfair exporters only. They are, therefore, economic instruments with the power to restrict imports, and they will, the simple idea of greed suggests, attract those with an interest in having imports restricted. This will include not only firms and industries beset by unfair competition but more generally those least favorably situated vis-à-vis their foreign competitors' costs. Pressures from such interests have brought about changes in the details of the dumping and the countervailing duty mechanisms. They have come over time to put more severe limits on the trade practices foreign sellers may employ in the U.S. market than parallel parts of domestic antitrust law places on domestic firms. They tend also to concentrate on foreign versus domestic costs rather than on the nature of the trade practices that foreign firms employ.[8]

While calculation and publication of the costs of production will surely influence the political climate, this climate has little impact on those structured decisions. Legislation would be needed to build this information into the decision mechanisms through which trade policy is administered.

The government might find political, and not just economic, merits in institutional changes that allow them to judge these formalized trade questions in the light of overall costs and benefits. Under present arrangements, the technical commissions and offices that investigate trade complaints may take up only the interests of producers who compete with imports. As a result, consumer groups have no alternative but to go over the heads of such officials and apply pressure on politicians. As consumer interests have become more vocal, trade disputes have tended to escalate into higher-level disputes than they might have if, at the lower levels, a technical outlet were provided for consumer as well as for producer interests.

Though our administrative trade policy mechanisms are slanted toward protection, they have been used with restraint. In the five years from 1975–79, only 2.2 percent of U.S. manufactured imports were granted relief under the antidumping and countervailing duty statutes, and only 3.8 percent under the escape clause.[9] The expansion of trade was much greater than the spread of protection, even in this 1975–79 period, when there was much talk of the rise of the "new protectionism." The U.S. market remains the most open of the major industrial country markets.

NOTES

1. World Bank, *World Development Report 1981* (New York: Oxford University Press, 1981), p. 31.
2. Thomas Bayard and James Orr, *Trade and Employment Effects on Tariff Reductions Agreed to in the MTN.* Economic Discussion Paper 1, U.S. Department of Labor, Bureau of International Labor Affairs, April 1980.
3. On this point see R. G. Anderson and M. E. Kreinin, "Labor Costs in the American Steel and Auto Industries," *The World Economy*, 4: 199–208 (June 1981).
4. The best review of those policies is Martin Wolf, *Adjustment Policies and Problems in Developed Countries.* World Bank Staff Working Paper 349, 1979.
5. Goran Ohlin, "Introduction," in Organization for Economic Co-operation and Development, *Adjustment for Trade: Studies on Industrial Adjustment Problems and Policies* (Paris: Author, 1975), p. 11.
6. Ibid.
7. For an extended discussion and references, see J. M. Finger, *Industrial Country Policy and Adjustment to Imports from Developing Countries.* World Bank Staff Working Paper 470, July 1981.
8. J. M. Finger, H. K. Hall, and D. R. Nelson, "The Political Economy of Administered Protection." *American Economic Review*, June 1982.
9. J. M. Finger, "The Industry-Country Incidence of 'Less than Fair Value' Case in U.S. Import Trade," in *Export Diversification and the New Protectionism*, eds. Werner Baer and Malcolm Gillis (Champaign: University of Illinois Bureau of Economic and Business Research for the National Bureau of Economic Research, 1981), pp. 260–79.

3. New Theories Of Trade Among Industrial Countries

PAUL KRUGMAN

Most students of international trade have long had at least a sneaking suspicion that conventional models of comparative advantage do not give an adequate account of world trade. This is especially true of trade in manufactured goods. Both at the macro level of aggregate trade flows and at the micro level of market structure and technology, it is hard to reconcile what we see in manufactures trade with the assumptions of standard trade theory.

In particular, much of the world's trade in manufactures is trade between industrial countries with similar relative factor endowments; furthermore, much of the trade between these countries involves two-way exchanges of goods produced with similar factor proportions. Where is the source of comparative advantage?

Furthermore, most manufacturing industries are characterized by at least some degree of increasing returns (especially if we include dynamic scale economies associated with *R&D* and the learning curve). Not coincidentally, most manufacturing industries are also imperfectly competitive to at least some extent. Can a model which assumes constant returns, exogenous technology, and perfect competition give adequate guidance for trade policy in these industries?

In response to these questions, many economists have proposed alternatives to conventional trade theory. The alternatives include the "product cycle" view, with the stress on endogenous innovation and the diffusion of technology; the arguments of many observers that much trade among industrial countries is based on scale economies rather than comparative advantage; and the common argument that a protected home market can promote exports. Until recently, however, none of these alternatives was presented in a form which economists would properly call a model: that is, a formal structure in which macro behavior is derived from micro motives. This lack of formalization

Paul Krugman is Professor of Economics at Massachusetts Institute of Technology.

essentially barred alternatives to comparative advantage, however plausible, from the mainstream of international economics.

In the last five years or so, however, there has been a significant change. A number of theorists have begun to apply methods drawn from the theory of industrial organization to international trade, to produce a new genre of trade models. These models offer a new way of looking at trade—and particularly at manufactures trade among the industrial countries.

A characteristic feature of the new models is that they often rely on very special assumptions. This is probably inevitable: given the inherent complexity of the world once the great simplifying device of constant returns is dropped, only special assumptions will yield tractable analysis. In spite of the specialness of individual models, however, the new literature on trade is starting to give rise to concepts which look more general than the particular models used to illustrate them. The purpose of this paper is to sketch out two such concepts which I believe are important and more general in application than the particular models in which they have been expressed. The first is the theory of "intraindustry" trade, a view which incorporates scale economies as well as comparative advantage as major causes of trade and gains from trade. The second is the (less well developed) theory of technological competition, which may begin to shed some light on the dynamics of international competition in research-intensive industries.

I. THE THEORY OF INTRAINDUSTRY TRADE

It has long been known as a theoretical point that increasing returns can be an alternative to comparative advantage for the explanation of trade. It has also been suspected by many economists that scale economies do in fact play a major role in manufactures trade among the industrial countries—perhaps more important than differences in factor endowments. The problem in making this more than just a wise remark has been the difficulty of introducing scale economies into formal models of trade.

The traditional way of doing this is to assume that increasing returns are wholly external to firms. The models which result from this assumption, however, have never had much influence. External economies are too vague and unmeasurable to be an appealing explanation of trade patterns. To have the right "feel," it appears, a formalization of the role of scale economies must lay its stress on internal economies of scale—and this, until recently, was not something trade theorists knew how to do.

In the last few years, however, a relatively coherent view of the role of scale economies in trade has finally emerged. This view—which we might rather grandly call the "theory of intraindustry trade"—was developed by a number of authors who found in recent developments in monopolistic competition theory the modelling techniques needed.

The basic idea of the theory is extremely simple. We distinguish between two kinds of trade: interindustry trade based on comparative advantage, and intraindustry trade based on economies of scale. The *industrial* structure of the country's production will be determined by its factor endowments. Within each industry, however, there is assumed to be a wide range of potential products, each produced under conditions of increasing returns. Because of these scale economies, each country will produce only a limited subset of the products in each industry, with the pattern of *intraindustrial* specialization—which country produces what—essentially arbitrary.

The implications for the trade pattern are straightforward and empirically plausible. Each country will be a *net* exporter in industries in which it has a comparative advantage, just as conventional theory suggests. Because of intraindustry specialization, however, each country will import some products even in industries in which it is a net exporter, and vice versa; that is, there will be intraindustry as well as interindustry trade. Furthermore, the more similar countries are in their factor endowments, the less different their industrial structures will be, and hence the more their trade will have an intraindustry character.

If the theory of intraindustry trade is so simple, why is it a new development? The answer is in part that it is not: the basic story just described may be found in many informal discussions of trade in the 1960's. A formal model of intraindustry trade, however, must deal with the problem of market structure. The existence of unexhausted economies of scale means that markets cannot be perfectly competitive. They could, however, be characterized by Chamberlinian monopolistic competition, and in fact the product differentiation-cum-scale economies story seems to dovetail very naturally with this approach. Notice that we need not believe that Chamberlinian equilibrium is actually a realistic description of the world. The point is that it is a useful *device* for closing the model, and is in some sense less unrealistic in this context than perfect competition. Thus a number of economists, including Avinash Dixit and Victor Norman, Kelvin Lancaster, Elhanan Helpman, Wilfred Ethier, and myself (1981) have presented Chamberlinian models which formalize the story just described. These models differ in detail, but bear a strong family resemblance to one another, justifying us in referring to a "theory."

The theory of intraindustry trade, then, provides a neat explanation of the empirical puzzles posed by manufactures trade among the industrial countries. It explains both why similar countries trade so much, and why so much of their trade is two-way exchanges of similar products. It also provides some interesting new insights into the effects of trade on welfare and income distribution. Traditional models have very strong distributional effects; even though trade liberalization may potentially make everyone better off, the movement of the income distribution is always enough to insure that the real income of scarce factors of production falls. If there are increasing returns to scale, however, this need not be the case. Scale economies produce some extra gains, in the form of longer production runs and a greater variety of products. If changes in the income distribution are not too large—if, for example, trade liberalization takes place between countries with similar relative factor endowments—the advantages of a larger market can outweigh the distributional effects of trade. This means that the distributional effects of trade may depend on its causes. If scale economies are relatively unimportant and countries differ substantially in factor endowments, we have the conventional Stolper-Samuelson result that scarce factors lose from trade. If, on the other hand, scale economies are important and factor endowments are similar, all factors gain from trade.

But when would these conditions hold? The situation of significant scale economies combined with weak comparative advantage is precisely that of trade in manufactured goods among industrial countries. If we believe that trade liberalization is easiest when nobody gets hurt, this may help explain why the great trade liberalization of the postwar period has focused on manufactures trade between advanced nations.

II. THE THEORY OF TECHNOLOGICAL COMPETITION

The theory of intraindustry trade seems to suggest that trade in manufactured goods among industrial countries is a benign thing, less likely to cause adjustment problems than other trade, and hence easier to liberalize. Another strand in recent theory, however, suggests that in some manufacturing sectors—specifically, those where *R&D* play a crucial role—there may be a strong temptation for countries to engage in protectionist or interventionist policies.

Here again the basic concept is quite simple. I adopt a more partial view than in the last section, focusing on a single industry; I assume that in the industry there are only two firms, one domestic and one foreign. Suppose these firms can compete technologically, investing in *R&D* to lower their costs, develop new products, or both. The amount they spend on *R&D* determines their position in a later competition in actual product markets. It is possible to envision a variety of particular models of this type: the *R&D* may apply to product or process improvement, it may be certain or uncertain in its results, product development may have a winner-take-all aspect or leave room for second prizes, and so on. But for a wide variety of particular models,

Figure 1

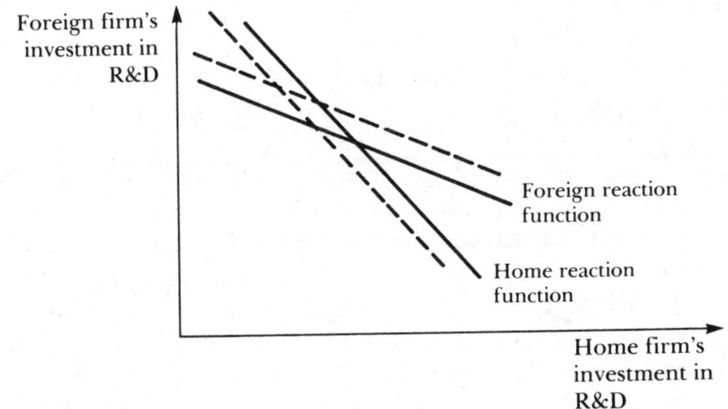

the basic technological competition will be summarizeable by a diagram like Figure 1. Each firm's optimal investment in *R&D* will be declining in the other's investment, as indicated by the two reaction functions; the noncooperative equilibrium will be where the schedules cross.

I should note as an aside that a similar analysis might also be applied where technology is improved, not through formal *R&D*, but through learning by doing. The technological competition would then take the form of willingness to accept low initial earnings to move faster down the learning curve; the qualitative character of the results would probably be much the same.

As in the case of intraindustry trade models, the simplicity here is in some respects misleading. To derive these schedules explicitly requires analysis of a kind that has only recently become well understood, through the work of such authors as Dixit. We must solve the model backwards: first deriving the post-*R&D* equilibrium conditional on the levels of *R&D* expenditure, then using the results of this analysis to derive the relationship of expected profits to *R&D*, which allows us to draw the reaction functions. Thus behind the simplicity of the figure lies a complex competitive process. I have drawn the diagram with "nice" properties: the curves slope downwards, there is a unique equilibrium, and it will be stable under plausible adjustment schemes. To show that the curves actually have these properties, or to find the restrictions on parameters necessary to insure that they do, will be far from trivial.

Suppose, however, that we assume that technological competition in some industries can actually be reasonably well represented in this way. We can then use the diagram to think about a subject which is central to debate over trade policy but virtually untouched by trade theorists. This is the effect of trade policy on technology. What I have in mind, in particular, is the argument that a protected home market can give a country's high technology firms an advantage which eventually gives them an edge in export markets as well.

It seems clear from Figure 1 that this argument does make a good deal of sense. Suppose that the foreign government denies the home firm access to part or all of its market. What this denial of access will do in a variety of particular models is to raise the expected return to a marginal dollar of *R&D* by the foreign firm, lower the expected marginal return to *R&D* by the domestic firm. Thus the reaction functions will shift in the directions indicated by the dotted lines. Foreign *R&D* will be greater than it would otherwise have been; domestic *R&D* will be less. Because the foreign firm's relative technological position is improved, it may well increase its share of unprotected as well as protected markets. In other words, import protection will turn out to be a form of export promotion.

Is this desirable from the point of view of the foreign government? Recent work by Barbara Spencer and James Brander suggests that it may be, although *R&D* subsidy is probably a better policy. As they point out, in imperfectly competitive markets there is some monopoly rent for which firms are competing. Government action may enable domestic firms to seize a larger share of these rents than they would otherwise be able to get.

Introducing technological competition into trade theory, then, does seem to give some justification for the kinds of industrial policies which Japan is accused of following. Or at any rate, it offers support for the idea that protecting *R&D*–intensive industries may really be a beggar-thy-neighbor policy, not simply a beggar-thyself policy, which conventional theory would suggest. This by no means clinches the case for protectionism, but it gives some reason to be more worried about foreign targeting of high technology industries than about other trade-distorting practices.

This paper has sketched out two new approaches to trade among industrial countries, based on the recent emergence of a literature which applies concepts from industrial organization theory to international trade. Of the two, the theory of intraindustry trade is a relatively finished product, while the theory of technological competition is still in a rough state. Both are, I hope, of some use for thinking about issues—including important policy issues—which cannot be handled by traditional theory.

REFERENCES

Brander, James and Spencer, Barbara, "Strategic Commitment with *R&D*: The Symmetric Case," mimeo., 1982.

Dixit, Avinash, "The Role of Investment in Entry-Deterrence," *Economic Journal*, March 1980, *90*, 95–106.

——— and Norman, Victor, *Theory of International Trade*, Oxford University Press, 1980.

Ethier, Wilfred, "National and International Return to Scale in the Modern Theory of International Trade," *American Economic Review*, June 1982, *72*, 389–405.

Helpman, Elhanan, "International Trade Under Economies of Scale and Imperfect Competition: A Chamberlin-Heckscher-Ohlin Model," *Journal of International Economics*, August 1981, *11*, 305–40.

Krugman, Paul, "Intraindustry Specialization and the Gains from Trade," *Journal of Political Economy*, October 1981, *89*, 959–73.

———, "Import Protection as Export Promotion," in Henrik Kierzkowski, ed., *Monopolistic Competition in International Trade*, Oxford University Press, 1984.

Lancaster, Kelvin, "Intra-Industry Trade Under Perfect Monopolistic Competition," *Journal of International Economics*, May 1980, *10*, 151–75.

Spencer, Barbara and Brander, James, "International *R&D* Rivalry and Industrial Strategy," mimeo., 1982.

4. Linking Up to Distant Markets: South to North Exports of Manufactured Consumer Goods

DONALD B. KEESING

Finished consumer goods have emerged as the most important category of manufactured goods exported from developing to developed countries; they now make up at least half the total. This is a trade in products ready to be sold in stores on the other side of the world. The products exported are mostly labor intensive, ranging from clothes and shoes to transistor radios, digital watches, or the latest television games.

Trade in finished consumer goods has grown astonishingly. From 1970 to 1980, OECD imports of goods in categories consisting mainly of manufactured consumer goods increased in nominal value 14.55

Donald Keesing is an economist with the World Bank. The views expressed in this paper are his own, and not those of the World Bank which, however, supported the research under project RPO 671–68, "Key Institutions and Expansion of Manufactured Exports." Principal consultants were Lawrence H. Wortzel and Camilo Jaramillo.

TABLE 1. Exports to OECD in Sixteen Categories Consisting Mainly of Consumer Goods, by Region of Origin, 1980

	HONG KONG, TAIWAN (CHINA), AND REPUBLIC OF KOREA	OTHER EAST, SOUTHEAST OR SOUTH ASIA	LATIN AMERICA AND CARIBBEAN	AFRICA, MIDDLE EAST, AND OCEANIA
Sixteen Categories as Percent of Region's Manufactured Exports to OECD	61.6	32.3	18.0	15.6
Region's Percent Share of Developing Economy Exports to OECD				
Fifteen categories other than apparel	77.4	14.1	7.7	0.8
Apparel	65.9	23.9	5.8	4.4
Sixteen categories of mainly consumer goods	71.7	19.0	6.8	2.6
Other manufactured goods	34.6	30.8	23.9	10.7
Total manufactured goods	50.7	25.7	16.4	7.2

Source: Computed from OECD, *Trade by Commodities, Market Summaries: Imports, January–December, 1980.*

times while total manufactured imports from developing countries increased 10.84 times. (These comparisons exclude Australia and New Zealand, which were not OECD members in 1970). Using the UN index of the unit value of developed country exports of manufactured goods as a deflator, the "real" growth rate for all manufactured goods was 14.0 percent a year over the decade. For finished consumer goods, real growth averaged 17.4 percent. For finished consumer goods other than apparel, the growth rate averaged 20.4 percent a year. In apparel, where export opportunities were increasingly curtailed by quotas, growth averaged 15 percent a year.

The most successful developing economies in exporting finished consumer goods have been Hong Kong, Taiwan (China), and the Republic of Korea. As Table 1 shows, in 1980 these three economies exported slightly over half of the manufactured goods shipped from developing economies to OECD countries. They enjoyed a larger share of the market for sixteen categories of consumer goods—close to 72 percent. Other Asian countries supplied another 19 percent, while 7 percent came from Latin America and the Caribbean.

The United States is the leading market for these same sixteen categories, buying 46 percent, compared to 14 percent shipped to Germany, 8.5 percent to the United Kingdom, and 36 percent to the European Community as a whole in 1980.

Most of these finished consumer goods are made by developing economy firms—enterprises started, owned, and managed by people from the developing economies, usually entrepreneurs who started small, often quite recently. Such firms are especially dominant in apparel, footwear, and other simple products. As Gerald Helleiner's research on "related party transactions" in the United States helps to show, large shares of products such as radios, watches, television sets, cameras, or passenger cars are made by developed country "multinationals." On an overall basis, however, at least 80 percent of all finished consumer goods appear to be made by developing economy firms.

Developing economy firms have thus succeeded remarkably in linking up their production with the needs and fast-changing demands of stores and customers thousands of miles away. In research at the World Bank, through interviews and consultant papers, we have been exploring the institutional arrangements and the marketing aspects of this trade to learn how this linking is achieved. Here in sketch form are a few of the findings.

Although some developing economy manufacturers distribute their own products (more on this later), most exports of finished consumer goods are made to buyers' orders. Production is not begun until the exporting enterprise receives an order complete with a letter of credit or equivalent commitment to pay for the goods. The buyer specifies in full detail the design of the product, the materials to be used, the numbers and sizes to be made, and such other matters as the way the product will be labeled, packed and shipped. Designs and requirements change from order to order. In many of the same industries, production to buyers' orders is common also in developed countries. Developing economy firms are expected to achieve comparable standards.

Manufactured consumer goods are generally shipped already packaged and labeled, ready to be put straight onto the retailer's counter or clothesrack, or handed in a box to the customer. (Garments are often shipped in a specified assortment of sizes and colors; furniture is usually shipped knocked-down to be assembled in the retail store.) The developing economy manufacturing enterprise is expected to put together the entire package complete with documentation. Buyers care about all the details, including, for example, the accessories, printed labels, and packaging.

The buyer is responsible for marketing and distribution in the country of destination. Thus he takes the risks that the product will not sell as hoped. The buyer and the exporting enterprise each take risks that the product will not be made on schedule, or will have to be rejected because of defects when inspected prior to packing, or will prove defective when sold to retail customers. The buyer risks losing customers and business while the exporting enterprise risks not being paid and not getting further orders.

The most important categories of buyers are importers and retailers. Firms known almost universally as importers are really importer-wholesalers. They tend to specialize in a rather narrow range of products. The bigger importers buy in large volume, often in several continents. To supply retailers they carry a large inventory based on their own (not necessarily original) designs. Their success depends on anticipating market trends and, at the same time, holding down costs wherever possible, not least by seeking out low-cost sources of supply.

The search for low-cost suppliers often leads importers into developing economies where the industry lacks export experience. Importers and other buyers who open up this trade commonly provide advice and teaching to exporting enterprises as necessary on practically all aspects of the business, while at first supervising every step. As the enterprise learns, a stable relationship evolves through which the importer recovers the investment in teaching. Importers also buy from experienced firms. An importer can give large orders and live with delayed delivery because of a large inventory. Interviews suggest, however, that importers in many lines of business bargain hard and squeeze their manufacturers' prices down as much as possible. They also tend to be quick to move on to new sources of supply or new varieties of merchandise, and will desert an established buying relationship over a small rise in costs if there is a good alternative source.

Retailers, especially large chain stores, do much of their buying directly. The proportion bought varies by product: it is high in most garments, for example, but low in footwear. As buyers, retailers generally shun direct buying from unreliable or inexperienced suppliers. They move in to cut out the middleman, however, once the exporting enterprise has become good at its tasks and requires only moderate supervision.

Retailers from different types of stores have different objectives. Some stores sell merchandise with little styling but low prices; they search for bargains or suppliers with very low costs. Others are concerned about quality, styling, and punctual delivery to fit into their merchandise plans for a coming season. These retailers are usually willing to offer prices at least a few percent higher than those paid by importers, though goods made in developing economies are often sold as low price or bargain items. Retailers known for quality merchandise seldom quibble over price, but seek to develop long-term relationships with exporting enterprises that can meet their needs.

A third important category of buyers are manufacturers or ertswhile manufacturers from developed countries, who still design their own products and market them under their established brand names, but subcontract the actual production (or part of it) to be competitive with imports. Like the better quality retailers, manufacturer-buyers are generally concerned to achieve reliable quality and stable relationships.

Practically all buyers including retailers and manufacturers are prepared to help experienced enterprises make new and difficult orders; thus supervision is given for adjustments in production to make a new design. In addition, buyers provide much useful advice and information in placing orders and in their routine visits to check quality control and to inspect the product.

Eventually exporting enterprises become adept at meeting buyers' needs. The learning process is usually far from easy, however, even with advice and supervision from buyers. During this process, inexperienced enterprises find themselves exposed to large risks, not least financial, and survive precariously; many suffer losses from mistakes or failures; many must invest added funds to keep going; some must look for new buyers.

The enterprises that survive acquire experience in manufacturing a variety of designs, and in some cases a succession of products. Learning to make entirely new items is sometimes necessary for survival in face of changing demand. Some enterprises make profits, expand, and diversify into additional products as they gain experience.

Skills are gained that are attractive to buyers. Many an enterprise comes to know exactly what is required in exporting to each of its major markets, for example, styling and sizes and documentation, and is ready to put together the whole package reliably with a minimum of instructions and assistance. Such entrepreneurs acquire the ability to study a sample of a product, or a set of specifications, and quickly translate it into a suitable production process using equipment and labor on hand in the enterprise, perhaps not only to make the product but to "knock off" copies quickly. Some enterprises learn to make high-priced, high-quality versions of products, using more expensive materials and designs. Some become expert in quality control.

Exporting enterprises also acquire valuable experience in the marketing part of their business. This involves attracting or finding suitable buyers and inducing them to place orders. Fundamentally, the enterprise tries to sell its production capacity and capabilities. By satisfying buyers, it builds a regular business with them, which may lead it to have full order books and a roster of regular customers.

Attracting buyers is made simpler by the circumstance that each category of buyers puts much effort into finding promising suppliers in economies known for low costs and export-oriented policies. Buyers try to learn what they can about the capabilities of any enterprise that might serve as a supplier, including what it has been making and for whom. Even so, a new buyer typically comes to visit the enterprise before placing an order. Usually the management welcomes visitors in a showroom displaying attractive items the firm has made. A new buyer is likely to want to see the plant in operation as well. In his visit a buyer seeks to assess the firm's management; when he discusses what he wants made and how, he must be reassured that the firm can do the job. The firm in turn must decide which orders to accept; usually it has a minimum size limit.

Exporting enterprises frequently take the initiative in contacting buyers and trying to interest them in placing orders. Often this requires travel. Many of the managers interviewed traveled at least once a year to major developed country markets, visiting actual and potential buyers, while enriching their knowledge of the business in other ways as well.

Managers and sales personnel ordinarily travel overseas with samples of items their firm has made. Frequently these are based on designs made for other buyers—usually a design is exclusive only for the one market so that it can be offered to customers elsewhere. In other cases, designs are copied from samples bought abroad or from pictures in magazines. Buyers nevertheless appear to judge firms partly by their sense of what is an attractive design or the latest style, made well. Some enterprises producing mainly to order send their designers abroad to improve their skills. The most experienced and successful firms in various products offer a choice of styling to their customers, and play an active role in helping the buyer select a design. However, developing economy firms that specialize in design—as do many small Hong Kong garment firms—seem to enjoy little financial success.

Together with firms that manufacture for export, exporting enterprises also include trading companies that organize production for export by smaller firms or handicraft workers. A buyer deals mainly with the trading company, though he may be allowed to supervise its subcontractor. Large trading companies, which are now being promoted in many developing economies by special incentives, help to provide active marketing abroad, maintain offices there, and approach wholesalers and retailers in search of orders.

Some exports from developing countries are made, not to buyers' orders, but on the basis of production for inventory with sale by manufacturers' representatives—usually nationals of the importing country, working on commission or directly for the developing economy manufacturer. This sort of distribution is limited, as a rule, to large firms making standardized products in only a few basic designs and sizes.

Products distributed directly by firms from Brazil included towels, T-shirts, jeans, and men's robes in cotton terrycloth. Furniture manufacturers from more than one country have been found to have their own distribution subsidiaries. Some of the television set manufacturers from Taiwan (China) and Korea have begun to sell through American sales representatives, although with only limited success. Distribution by manufacturers has also been encountered exceptionally in other products, including radios, watches, and electric fans. Most of the products distributed in this way are also commonly made to buyers' orders.

One large Korean firm has its own wholesale distribution in the United States, even though its products—mainly shirts and other garments, but also leather shoes—come in many designs and sizes. When interviewed in 1978, from its warehouses in New Jersey and Los Angeles it invoiced to 600 stores. In shirts it offered customers a choice of 40 patterns, though much of its output (6 million shirts per month) continued to be made to buyers' orders. The firm promoted by having 1,500–2,500 people travel each year to visit customers.

No developing economy brand or product line was being advertised to households or individual consumers in developed countries, at the time of our East Asian interviews. All sales by manufacturers through their representatives or distributors were made to retailers or wholesalers in the country of destination, frequently with a choice of brand names. However, many developing economy firms vigorously promoted their own brands and product lines at home and, in some cases, in other developing economies.

For developing countries trying to export, our findings confirm the importance of measures that improve incentives and reduce costs. Buyers know what prices they can pay and are ready to switch to competing sources of supply elsewhere in the world. Thus only where exchange rates and policies bring about low costs—above all of labor and high quality materials—will buyers place orders and teach new suppliers. Orders are given by preference in economies with easy, duty-free access to imported inputs, since this makes it much easier to get together on time a complete, packaged product and to move on to new designs or materials. Experience has shown that much tends to go wrong when exports are ordered in economies with inward-looking policies: export orders are neglected or refused because of higher returns in the domestic market, inputs are not delivered, costs rise and cease to be competitive, etc.

These findings are also a reminder that export responses to policies depend on people, and thus on the information conveyed and expectations created. Policy changes begin to be successful when they cause buyers to change their perceptions and shift their search to a new country. Results also depend on persuading entrepreneurs, local or foreign, to try to export from the country. Since buyers and entrepreneurs do not think exactly like economists, we may not be the best source of advice on their responses to policy measures.

REFERENCE

Helleiner, Gerald K., *Intra-firm Trade and the Developing Countries*, New York: St. Martin's Press, 1981.

II. Multilateral Trade Negotiations

One message of the first set of readings is that a nation's willingness to move in the direction of freer trade depends upon the balance of internal political forces. In very simple terms, the political strength of groups supporting that movement must exceed that of groups resisting it. In general, those who favor liberalizing trade are those who will benefit directly and significantly from the expansion of exports: businesses and workers in export-oriented industries. Consumers will gain from a rise in imports but their interests are often weakly represented. Import concessions will be resisted by businessmen and workers in import-threatened industries.

A simple rule for national conduct would seem to be: expand exports while restricting imports. This would satisfy export-oriented interests while not disturbing import-competing interests; consumers are not likely to be organized enough to make much of a fuss. During the period of mercantilism in the seventeenth and eighteenth centuries, most important nations consistently pursued such policies. They competed aggressively with each other for trading spheres and colonial markets. Some nations, including the United States, face a resurgence of calls for pursuit of neomercantilist policies in the 1980s.

The fallacy of mercantilism hinges on the obvious fact that one nation's exports are another nation's imports. As nations restrict one another's imports, they are squeezing one another's exports and lowering the total level of international trade.

Overcoming natural tendencies towards mercantilistic restrictions on imports can be attained only when there exists an understanding, shared among many nations, that all will work towards joint removal of barriers to trade. At the international level, a nation will normally lower its barriers to imports only when its trading partners are making similar concessions. Trade negotiations are therefore inherently reciprocal and interactive. Since trade patterns are often not simply bilateral but involve complex triangular and multilateral exchanges, negotiations are usually best held with the fullest possible participation of the international community of nations.

The international framework in which modern multilateral trade negotiations take place is institutionalized in the General Agreement on Tariffs and Trade (GATT). At periodic meetings representatives of major and minor trading nations assemble to engage in immensely intricate discussions over mutual reductions in barriers to trade. The most-favored-nation principle, a cornerstone of these international trade arrangements, grants equal terms of access to all potential suppliers when concessions are negotiated between any single nation and another. This principle thus generalizes within the group of nations any bilateral concessions. It has, however, been much vitiated by many exceptions, one of which is the preferential access to rich country markets granted certain developing country exports.

Important GATT sessions of the last twenty-five years have been the Kennedy Round, 1962–67, the Tokyo Round, 1973–79, and the meeting of GATT ministers in Geneva in 1982. To prepare for the Kennedy and Tokyo Rounds the United States had to enact domestic legislation that enabled its negotiators to bargain flexibly to attain the necessary agreements. The U.S. stance for the Kennedy Round was embodied in the Trade Expansion Act of 1962, while the Trade Reform Act of 1974 guided American participation in the Tokyo Round. The strong national commitment to trade liberalization that undergirded these two acts arose from the preponderant dominance of internal political forces favoring freer trade, as opposed to antifree trade interests. In the 1980s, however, American and other national commitments to freer trade are weaker and the Geneva meeting made little headway.

The two purposes of this set of readings are (1) to report on the nature of GATT negotiations from 1960 into the mid–1980s and (2) to explain why the strong momentum in the direction of greater liberalization has slowed.

The paper by Robert Baldwin that opens this section summarizes the state of affairs at the end of the Tokyo Round. A problem that had arisen by the late 1970s was that the most obvious and unwise tariff barriers to trade had been removed or reduced. The remaining barriers to trade were thus predominantly nontariff barriers. Some of these had been created as a way around GATT strictures against tariffs. Nontariff barriers take many forms: quotas, including "voluntary" quotas; export subsidies; complicated labeling or sanitary standards; time-consuming customs procedures; requirements that the national government and the army buy from domestic suppliers. Many nations have adopted "escape clauses" that permit them to opt out of GATT agreements when imports are judged severely to threaten a domestic industry. Baldwin's essay illustrates well how tortuous negotiations are for identification and removal of these nontariff restraints.

The Geneva GATT meeting of 1982 was preceded in the United States by preparatory hearings and discussions in Congress. The purpose was to permit various interests to air their views and to develop a national consensus about the United States stance. Economists, members of the executive branch, and representatives of business, labor, and consumer groups testified.

Two readings are provided to capture the flavor of this interesting and revealing process. The first is a statement by the Semiconductor Industry Association.The United States has a clear, technologically-based comparative advantage in semiconductor exports. Our industry faces a number of foreign restrictions on its exports and is frustrated by them. The industry's testimony is therefore a classic affirmation of the importance of an American commitment to freer trade. Indeed, the document goes beyond endorsement of the free trade position to urge freedom of movement of investment funds and ideas. The semiconductor industry opposed policies now pursued in Europe, Japan, and the developing nations that are restricting entry of American semiconductor products and American investors.

This ringing advocacy of more liberal trade policies is followed by a protectionist statement from a representative of American labor. The labor spokesman argues that previous GATT concessions have cost Americans jobs and have not had beneficial economic effects. He argues that foreign nations have taken advantage of the overeagerness of the United States to reduce its trade barriers and have not lowered their own barriers equivalently. The American government has not, he says, acted vigorously to use the "safeguard" (or "escape") clauses to reduce the damaging impact of imports on U.S. industry and jobs. No more liberalization should occur, it is argued, until the effects of previous concessions are more clearly ascertained and until foreign governments show more enthusiasm for receiving exports of American goods and services.

In the following article Jeffrey Schott reports on the results of the GATT ministers' meeting. Despite a renewed general pledge of adherence to more liberal trade policies, the session generated little progress on specifics and did not seriously consider a number of pressing new issues. Whether the pessimistic tone of Schott's report will be justified by events as they unfold in the last half of the decade remains to be established. The economic recovery after 1983 has somewhat eased pressures for trade restrictions. In mid–1984 the United States and Japan reached some important agreements on trade access to each other's markets and the United States achieved at least partial entry into Japan's financial services sector. Perhaps international negotiations over matters of mutual interest and concern will not be as intractable as Schott believes.

The last paper in this section is a comprehensive overview of the state of multilateral negotiations in the mid–1980s. Aho and Bayard argue that long-run structural changes in the world economy, such as the rise of newly industrialized countries and higher energy prices, are reducing the prospect for further success in trade liberalization discussions. They are concerned that continued slow economic growth, in conjunction with high unemployment, will gravely reduce nations' willingness to remove barriers to trade, to services exchange, and to the entry of foreign investment and technology. The leadership of the United States is called for, but America's own domestic problems and its diminished role in the international economy make assuming a leadership role more difficult.

If there is anything optimistic to be said, to counter the pessimistic concerns of Schott and Aho and Bayard, it is that there is now vast awareness of the dangers of a relapse into mercantilism. Multilateral negotiations are still active, ongoing, and candid. Nations have not yet turned inward, closing their doors to external contacts. It is widely understood that protrade forces must be rallied in defense of liberal ideals and that the actions of selfish antitrade groups must be countered with effective argument and by trying to meet their legitimate fears with appropriate adjustment measures (such as labor retraining). Guarded optimism for continued progress in multilateral trade negotiations in the late 1980s may be a more realistic sentiment.

5. The Tokyo Round of Multilateral Trade Negotiations

ROBERT E. BALDWIN

INTRODUCTION

As the Multilateral Trade Negotiations (also known as the Tokyo Round) draw to a conclusion, the U.S. Congress faces a significant choice; it can either accept or reject without amendment a proposed set of rules of "good" behavior in international commerce that will shape the conduct of international trade for at least the rest of this century.* The rules were drawn up in more than five years of negotiations aimed both at further cutting tariffs and at reducing or eliminating nontariff impediments to and distortions of international trade. Ministers of the ninety-nine nations involved agreed in the inaugural Tokyo Declaration that where the reduction or elimination of such nontariff impediments was not appropriate they should at least be brought "under more effective international discipline."

The emphasis on nontariff distortions of trade makes the current negotiating round different from the six previous trade-liberalizing exercises held since World War II within the framework of the General Agreement on Tariffs and Trade (GATT). Earlier negotiations focused primarily on reducing tariffs. The last multilateral effort, the so-called Kennedy Round lasting from 1962 to 1967, cut import duties in the major industrial nations by an average of 35 percent for dutiable manufactures and 20 percent for agricultural products. As a result, the average duty for dutiable manufactured goods declined to only about 10 percent in the United States, the European Community, and Japan by the conclusion of the Kennedy Round cuts. This is in contrast to a

* The proposed codes were approved by Congress in the Trade Agreements Act of 1979. Most other industrial countries also promptly approved the codes, but, as of July 1980, only a few developing countries had signed them.

Robert Baldwin is Professor of Economics at the University of Wisconsin, Madison.

U.S. tariff level for dutiable imports of nearly 60 percent in 1931. Further tariff reductions of about 33 percent for all participants are scheduled as part of the agreements reached in the Tokyo Round negotiations.

The most significant part of these agreements, however, is the series of detailed codes spelling out permissible and nonpermissible "good" behavior by governments in almost all areas where nontariff measures have threatened the basic trade-liberalizing objective of the GATT. Consideration of these codes is especially timely not merely because the negotiations have just ended but also because, unlike tariff reductions, the codes must be approved by both houses of Congress before they can be implemented. The implementing bill will not only approve the agreements and any administrative actions needed to implement them but will repeal and amend any existing laws that must be changed for them to take effect. In accordance with the 1974 Trade Act, no amendments to the implementing bill will be permitted in either the House or Senate, and the bill must be voted on no more than ninety legislation days from its introduction in Congress. According to present plans, the President will submit the implementing bill to Congress in May.

The purpose of this analysis is to assist in evaluating the results of the Tokyo Round, especially the package agreement on nontariff measures. This package covers subsidies and countervailing duties, antidumping practices, government procurement policies, valuation and licensing practices, technical barriers to trade (standards), differential and more favorable treatment for developing countries, safeguard actions for balance of payments and developmental purposes, and dispute settlement and surveillance procedures under the GATT. The negotiators failed to reach agreement on codes covering safeguards against injurious imports and commercial counterfeiting, but the hope is that final agreement on these subjects will be reached within a few months.* Moreover, the participants agreed to reassess in the near future the GATT provisions relating to export restraints. In addition, specific agreements have been reached with regard to steel, aircraft, certain agricultural products, and several nontariff measures of only bilateral interest. The following analysis will describe the measures or practices that have led to the desire for improved codes, the nature of the agreed upon or proposed codes and how they differ from existing GATT rules, and finally a brief evaluation of each. After appraising the mechanisms established to secure compliance with the different nontariff codes, the various other agreements concluded will be examined more closely, including the tariff-cutting formula that has been adopted. . . .

* As of July 1980, no agreement on a safeguards code had been reached, and the short-run prospects for such an agreement were not favorable.

THE NONTARIFF AGREEMENTS

Subsidies and Countervailing Duties

Two trends of recent years have been especially important in focusing attention on the potential trade-distorting effects of subsidies. One is the increasing economic intervention by governments in order to redistribute income toward various groups that the electorate regards as "socially deserving," while the other is the growing degree of openness and interdependence among the major trading nations. As a result, there are many more types of government subsidies than when the GATT was first adopted, and any given subsidy is now likely to have a more direct effect on trade than in the late 1940s.

Selective subsidies that affect production activities, that is, those that are not merely lump-sum income transfers, tend to misallocate economic resources and thereby reduce the potential output of the international community unless the subsidies serve to offset other economic distortions that cannot be eliminated or handled by better means. There are, in fact, a number of circumstances where subsidies can be justified on this ground. For example, some types of socially desirable research may not take place if a firm fears that the results will become freely available to its competitors and make it impossible to recoup the costs of undertaking the research. Similarly, the stickiness of wages along with imperfections of capital markets may justify temporary subsidies to particular regions or specific industries. But if the reason for the subsidy is to promote economic efficiency and growth, the subsidy should be only temporary. However, one may wish to assist a particular group simply on equity grounds or for some other noneconomic reason. Moreover, various political or social factors may prevent the government from providing direct income grants that do not distort production. In these circumstances international political and economic problems often arise because distorting production may produce not just temporary but permanent income losses to citizens of other countries.

Article III of the GATT explicitly permits "the payment of subsidies exclusively to domestic producers." However, Article XVI requires that members who maintain a subsidy "which operates directly or indirectly to increase exports . . . or reduce imports . . . shall notify the Contracting Parties . . . of the estimated effects of the subsidization."[1] If "it is determined that serious prejudice to the interests of any contracting party is caused or threatened by such subsidization," the country granting the subsidy, "shall, upon request, discuss . . . the possibility of limiting the subsidization." In 1955 a section added to the article stated that any subsidy on the export of a nonprimary product resulting "in the sale of such product for export at a price lower than the comparable price charged . . . in the domestic market" should cease after January 1958 or "the earliest, practicable date thereafter." At the insistence of the United States export subsidies on primary products, that is, agricultural products and minerals, were not prohibited, although they were not to give a member "more than an equitable share of world export trade" in the affected product.

While open and direct export subsidy of manufactured goods by the advanced industrial countries has been kept to a minimum since the late 1950s, various indirect subsidies have developed that the new code tries to control more effectively. First it strengthens the GATT condemnation of government export subsidies on nonprimary products by stating flatly that they should not be granted. This ban is also extended to minerals. More important, by eliminating the requirement that export subsidies result in a lower sales price abroad than at home, it recognizes that under conditions of imperfect competition export subsidies need not always result in dual pricing. An updated list of export subsidies is also provided that includes such measures as currency retention schemes, internal freight rates more favorable for export goods than for domestic products, and special tax, credit, and insurance-rate breaks for exporters. However, export tax benefits such as those provided when U.S. firms form a Domestic International Sales Corporation (DISC) may still be permitted under these latter rules, and the financing of exports at only slightly more than the government's borrowing rate will definitely still be allowed.

In carrying out their wide-ranging efforts for income redistribution and full employment, governments provide extensive domestic subsidies for specific industries, for example, coal, steel, shipping and shipbuilding, textiles, aircraft, and electronics; for specific regions, such as depressed areas; and even for broad product sectors and activities, for example, manufacturing, agriculture, education, health services, and research. The subsidizing means include favorable tax treatment (tax holidays and deferrals, accelerated depreciation, investment credits), below-market borrowing privileges, the payment of fringe benefits, production subsidies, wage subsidies, lump-sum payments, and the sale of government-owned services at favorable rates. It does not take an economist to appreciate that domestic firms receiving this kind of assistance are able to compete more effectively against foreign imports and also in export markets.

As already noted, Article XVI of the GATT provides for consultation only if a member believes another's subsidies are seriously prejudicing its interests. An alternative route for settling such disputes is the use of Article XXIII, which relates to "nullification or impairment" of benefits accruing under the General Agreement. If a contracting party considers that any of these benefits is being nullified or impaired, it can, after the failure of bilateral consultations, have the matter referred to the contracting parties as a whole. Over time the procedure has evolved of appointing a working party or panel of experts to investigate the dispute and report on the merits of the alleged nullification or impairment in terms of the Articles of Agreement. After receiving the report the contracting parties can, if they deem the circumstances warrant it, authorize one of the parties to suspend concessions it has granted to the offending party. The use of the panel or working party to settle disputes has been infrequent, however. Between 1948 and 1977 only thirty-five disputes of all types reached this state, and their frequency has diminished sharply in recent years.[2]

The greater use of domestic subsidies in most industrial countries other than the United States coupled with the vagueness of existing GATT provisions covering subsidies and the inadequate mechanism for dispute settlement prompted the United States to press in the Tokyo Round negotiations for substantial changes in the rules on domestic subsidies. The code that has evolved explicitly recognizes the right of signatories to use domestic subsidies "for the promotion of social and economic policy objectives," including the elimination of industrial, economic, and social disadvantages of specific regions, and restructuring of certain sectors adversely affected by trade and other economic policies, the maintenance of employment, and the encouragement of research and development programs. It also lists means of subsidization (with the implication that they are legitimate and need not be temporary) to meet these objectives, such as government financing of commercial enterprises, government provision of operational services to these enterprises, governmental financing of research, and various fiscal incentives to private firms. The code also explicitly recognizes, however, that domestic subsidies may cause or threaten to cause serious prejudice, especially when they adversely affect "the conditions of normal competition," and the signatories agree to seek to avoid causing such injury. Moreover, the dispute settlement mechanism is improved for both export and domestic subsidies. If consultations with other members fail to satisfy a signatory who believes another nation's domestic subsidy causes injury to its own domestic industry, nullification or impairment of its GATT benefits, or serious prejudice to its interests, the dispute can be referred to a committee of signatories of the code for conciliation. If the matter remains unresolved, any signatory involved can request that the committee appoint a panel of experts to present its findings concerning the rights and obligations of the parties involved. The committee may then authorize appropriate countermeasures based on the panel's report.

For countries that subsidize more extensively than the United States, the incentive to agree to tighter controls over both export and domestic subsidies is to obtain an "injury clause" in the U.S. countervailing duty law. Countervailing duties are discriminatory levies on imported goods permitted under the GATT (Article VI) to offset any government subsidy on the "manufacture, production or export of any merchandise" if the effect of the subsidy is "to cause or threaten material injury" to a domestic industry. Imposing countervailing duties to handle the problem of foreign subsidies is quite different from utilizing the provisions of Articles XVI and XXIII. The countervailing-duty route can be used only against subsidized imports, since imposing import duties obviously does not offset a country's loss of an export market because of foreign subsidies. More important, the decision whether to countervail is made entirely by the importing country according to its established procedures. Other countries have been concerned for many years because U.S. procedures do not require proof of material injury before countervailing duties can be imposed on subsidized imports. However, U.S. negotiators agreed to accept the normal GATT requirement that material injury must be caused or threatened before countervailing can take place. Nevertheless, provisional countervailing measures can be taken after a preliminary finding that a subsidy exists and there is sufficient evidence of injury. The criteria listed in the code for determining injury also specify that the effects of the subsidy on the volume of imports as well as their price must be taken into consideration.

One might conclude from the language of the subsidies/countervailing duty code that the United States will not receive any benefits that do not already exist in the various GATT articles dealing with subsidies, even though the country is giving up its right to countervail without proof of material injury and may be implicitly accepting the legitimacy of many domestic subsidies of other countries. A more appropriate view, in my opinion, is that the code represents a potentially significant accomplishment that may enable the international community to control in a realistic manner the trade-distorting effects of domestic subsidies, particularly those that reduce the exports of another country. The United States has never literally enforced its own subsidy and countervailing duty law; to do so would create an administrative nightmare and lead to such extensive retaliation that our international economic and political position would be jeopardized. On the other hand, the various provisions of the GATT that apply to subsidies, especially to domestic subsidies, are vague and scattered throughout the document. Moreover, the dispute settlement mechanism under Article XXIII is more a means of resolving unusual situations not covered by the specific articles of the agreement than a regular procedure for settling ordinary disputes that arise in the operation of trade policies. Consequently, it has been difficult to find a sensible intermediate position between countervailing against every trivial foreign subsidy and ignoring all but the most flagrant trade-distorting subsidies. The introduction of an injury clause into U.S. law coupled with the creation of a dispute settlement committee for subsidies alone may enable us to attain such a position. The word "may" is used because the key to the code's success is how effective the dispute settlement and enforcement mechanism will be. Since this issue applies to all the codes, it will be considered later in this [selection].

Anti-Dumping Practices

One of the few areas of progress on nontariff measures in the Kennedy Round was agreement on a code dealing with anti-dumping practices. The United States signed the document as an Executive Agreement, but the Congress strongly objected to the fact that it was never submitted to that body for approval. A law was passed directing the International Trade Commission to ignore the new code in making its decisions on whether injury occurred as a result of dumping. The new anti-dumping agreement reached in the Tokyo Round affords an opportunity to eliminate this highly unsatisfactory state of affairs, since it will be part of the package submitted to Congress for approval and the implementing bill will contain any necessary changes in U.S. law.

The new agreement on the implementation of anti-dumping practices under Article VI of GATT differs from the previous one mainly in two respects: the determination of injury and the establishment of a dispute settlement mechanism. The impetus for revision of the anti-dumping code was the desire to make its injury provisions consistent with those negotiated in the code on subsidies and countervailing duties. Like those in the latter code, the provisions of the new agreement specify that both the volume of dumped imports and their effect on prices in domestic markets be considered in determining injury. The illustrative list of factors to consider in examining the impact of dumping on the industry concerned is made consistent with the subsidies code, as is the provision cautioning that demonstrated injury under the code must be caused by dumped imports rather than other economic factors. Both the subsidies/countervailing duties and anti-dumping codes state in footnotes that "injury" is to mean material injury to a domestic industry. However, the revised U.S. anti-dumping law to be submitted as part of the implementing bill apparently will simply specify that injury not be "immaterial" rather than use the phrase "material injury."

Although a committee on anti-dumping practices had been established under the old code, its purpose had been merely to facilitate periodic consultations among members on matters relating to the administration of anti-dumping systems. The new agreement makes the powers of the committee similar to those of committees established under the other nontariff codes. It can perform a conciliation role in disputes, appoint panels to examine the matters under dispute, and authorize retaliatory actions.

Safeguards

Article XIX of the General Agreement permits member countries to withdraw or modify a concession (such as a tariff reduction) previously granted "if, as a result of unforeseen developments," a product is being imported in such increased quantities "as to cause or threaten serious injury to domestic producers." But consultations with exporting countries must take place prior to or immediately after the withdrawal or modification and, if equivalent concessions on other products are not agreed upon, these exporting countries can withdraw some of their own concessions.

These "escape clauses" or safeguards have not worked well in recent years. Most of the major industrial trading nations have entered into various bilateral agreements with other countries outside the GATT framework, whereby these other countries "voluntarily" agree to limit their exports of particular products. This procedure permits the importing country to discriminate against the exports of one or more countries and does not involve the granting of offsetting concessions by the importing nation. The exporting nations have not complained of "nullification and impairment" under Article XXIII because of the threat of even more severe restriction if the matter gets into the hands of national legislators.

A draft code under consideration attempts to bring the various types of safeguards back within the GATT framework and to spell out in more detail the procedures each country must follow in carrying out such actions. On the latter point the code sets forth (as the relevant U.S. law does) a list of indicators to be considered in determining serious injury and also specifies that safeguard measures should be only temporary and progressively liberalized. A committee on safeguard measures, composed of the signatories to this code, is also established for surveillance and dispute settlement. Whether a country will have the right to restrict imports from only a few sources—that is, to discriminate against certain countries—and whether "voluntary" export restraints and "orderly" marketing agreements will be allowed under Article XIX is still under discussion. Reportedly, the European Community [EC] is strongly urging that selective discrimination be permitted. The developing countries, on the other hand, are vigorously opposing the proposal, since they believe it will be used mainly against them for both economic and political purposes.

The most-favored-nation principle (MFN), that is, nondiscrimination among countries with respect to trade policies, has already been so widely breached that it is somewhat hard to become concerned about a limited policy of selectivity. For example, the European Community discriminates against nonmembers such as the United States. The EC also gives special preferential treatment to the former colonies of its members as well as to several other states. Both of these actions are permitted under current GATT rules. There are other customs unions and free trade areas in the world, including, for example, the arrangement between the United States and Canada on automobiles and automobile parts. The granting of tariff preferences to the developing countries and the fact that the new codes will discriminate against nonsignatories are further indications that the most-favored-nation principle is widely violated in actual price.

More important than the MFN principle is whether economic adjustments occur in the injured industry so that the import restrictions are in fact only temporary. Unless solid evidence of adjustment efforts is required, the same conditions justifying the initial relief are likely to persist for years. Under these circumstances it is difficult, as experience with textiles indicates, not to find some way of continuing the import relief. If pressures were exerted on industries that resulted in the gradual movement of resources out of these sectors into more productive lines, the matter of temporary discrimination would not seem so significant. Unfortunately neither U.S. law nor GATT rules deal effectively with the adjustment problem.

Government Procurement

Purchasing policies by governments are excluded from the GATT principle of nondiscrimination under Article III. But favoritism toward domestic producers in government nonmilitary purchasing has increasingly irritated exporters as government purchases have escalated in recent years. The United States discriminates against foreign exporters on the basis of the so-called Buy American Act of 1933.[3] It has been implemented by generally giving U.S. producers a 6 percent price preference over foreigners. However, small firms and those in depressed areas receive a 12 percent price preference, and the Defense Department gives U.S. producers a 50 percent preference on all nonmilitary purchases. Many states and municipalities in the United States also have purchasing rules that openly discriminate against foreigners. Other countries do not have such explicitly discriminating legislation, but this does not mean that they do not favor their domestic producers over foreign bidders. A study of the share of domestic purchases in total nonmilitary spending by governments suggests that by using various administrative means other nations are every bit as discriminatory as the United States.[4]

Stating in a code that governments should not discriminate against foreign products or suppliers in their purchasing policies is obviously merely a first step. Discrimination is the result not only of deliberate efforts to favor local producers but also of ignorance on the part of purchasing agents who are reluctant to spend the time and take the risks involved in purchasing from foreign suppliers. Consequently, it is necessary for nations to establish administrative procedures that enable foreigners to learn about and participate in bidding opportunities, meet the required specifications, find out why any bid was rejected, and have access to a dispute settlement mechanism. In short, the entire procurement process must be made more open or transparent so that discrimination is made more difficult. The new government procurement code in the Tokyo Round attempts to do this. It contains detailed rules relating to such matters as describing the technical specifications for a product, publishing notices of bidding opportunities, qualifying as a possible supplier, determining the time allocated for submitting bids, awarding contracts, furnishing knowledge about bids, and reviewing complaints.

The code is clearly in the interest of the United States. The governments of most other industrial countries own or control a much larger part of secondary and tertiary economic activities than does the U.S. government. Moreover, the purchases of these industries often involve the type of high technology capital goods for which the United States has a competitive production advantage. While opportunities for trade worth as much as $20 billion a year could open up in foreign government purchasing markets now closed to U.S. exporters, there are still several important government agencies and classes of products excluded from the general provisions of the code. For example, most countries exclude telecommunications equipment, and the U.S. Defense Department omits such items as textiles, shoes, and specialty steel from its list of eligible products.

Customs Valuation and Licensing

Two other areas where administrative practices sometimes restrict trade needlessly are valuing imports for the assessment of customs duties and issuing import licenses. The United States has nine different methods of determining customs value and has been severely criticized by foreign countries who charge that these methods are not applied in a uniform manner.

In addition, foreign governments argue that one of the nine methods, the so-called American selling price (ASP) is blatantly unfair. In the Tariff Act of 1922 some congressmen succeeded in raising the level of protection on a particular group of products of special interest to them not by raising the *rates* at which imports were taxed (since this would have made these rates embarrassingly high) but by raising the *base* on which the rates were levied.[5] Specifically, the duty was levied on the value of similar products produced in the United States rather than, as usual, on the export value of the items themselves. Suppose, for example, the selling price of a unit of some benzenoid chemical produced in the United States is $150, while the export value of the same commodity produced in Germany is $90. If a 40 percent tariff is levied on the American selling price, the duty is $60, whereas if levied on the export value, it is only $36. Under the ASP system the landed price of the foreign-produced chemical will, when transport costs are included, exceed the price of its American substitute. However, under the usual method of valuing imports, the foreign product will be cheaper if the various costs of shipping the product to the United States do not exceed $24, that is, $150 minus $90 minus $36. One of the few nontariff items negotiated in the Kennedy Round was the elimination of the ASP system, but Congress failed to accept this part of the package. If the new code on customs valuation is accepted by Congress, however, the ASP system will be abolished.

The new code sets out five methods of determining customs value. The first is the primary method, while the others are secondary methods to be followed in sequence if the primary method fails. The primary method values imports at their transaction value, that is "the price actually paid or payable for the goods when sold for export to the country of importation" plus certain costs and expenses incurred with respect to the imported goods that are not included in the price paid. Examples of these are selling commissions, brokerage fees, packing costs, royalties and license fees, and "assists," such as the plans or various tools that help the importer use or sell the product.

If the customs value cannot be ascertained under the primary method, the next method is to ascertain the transaction value of identical goods exported to the same country at or about the same time as the goods under consideration. The third method is to use the transaction value of similar (rather than identical) goods exported to the same country at the same time. Failing the existence of adequate information for this procedure, the importer can request that either the value be deduced from the unit price at which identical or similar goods imported at the same time are resold in the country of importation less appropriate transportation costs, profit margins, and the like, or be computed from material, manufacturing, and other costs and margins in the country of exportation. Both a committee on customs valuation consisting of the parties to the agreement and a technical committee on customs valuation under the auspices of the Customs Cooperation Council are established to facilitate dispute settlement. The customs valuation committee can request the technical committee to examine a disputed matter or create a panel for this purpose.

The transactions-value method is similar to the actual-value method that is cited in Article VII of the GATT as the preferred way of valuing imports for customs purposes. However, the growing practices of providing various services and assets free of charge or at reduced cost along with the product makes it necessary to elaborate how to calculate this value. Article VII merely states that, when the actual value cannot be determined, the value should be "based on the nearest ascertainable equivalent of such value." Spelling out in detail just what these other valuation methods are and the order in which they should be followed should go far in reducing the irritations of traders over customs valuation procedures.

Since U.S. exporters often complain that foreign customs officials arbitrarily increase the value of American products as well as that foreign customs procedures are uncertain, the new code deserves the support of Congress. Elimination of ASP is a concession in the technical sense of the word, but presumably this will be taken into account in determining the overall balance of concessions with other countries. As a customs valuation method, however, it deserves to be abolished, since it is deceitful in its purpose and grants a particular set of producers protective privilege that may no longer be warranted. Alternative, more transparent means for assistance exist, if these producers are being seriously injured or threatened with injury by imports.

Many countries, mainly developing nations, have import licensing systems for such purposes as facilitating the allocation of scarce foreign exchange. However, the red tape involved in obtaining these licenses sometimes makes them significant barriers to trade. An important licensing code, similar to those proposed for government procurement and customs valuation, tries to minimize any trade-distorting effects by specifying that the rules for submitting import-licensing applications be published, that the forms and procedures be as simple as possible, and that licenses not be refused for minor documentation errors or variations in value, quantity, or weight of the licensed product.

A section on automatic import licensing, that is, a system under which licenses are granted freely, states that import licensing should continue only "as long as the circumstances which gave rise to its introduction prevail" and that properly completed applications should be approved immediately on receipt or at least within a maximum of ten working days. In order to prevent discrimination among countries when licenses are not automatically issued, signatories agree to furnish information upon request concerning the past allocation by country and to publish the rules for applying for licenses as far in advance as possible of the opening date of submission. The period of license validity is not to be so short as to preclude imports, and governments are not to discourage the full utilization of quotas. In addition to dealing with other licensing technicalities that sometimes distort trade, the code establishes a committee on import licensing to facilitate consultation and the settling of disputes.

Since 38 percent of U.S. industrial exports now go to developing countries, the reduction in delays and frustrations on the part of

American exporters that this code promises should also be very much appreciated by the Congress.

Technical Barriers to Trade (Standards) and Commercial Counterfeiting

The customs valuation and import licensing problems faced by exporters and importers are often child's play when compared with those arising from the many product standards with which these traders must contend. In customs valuation and import licensing, clearly identifiable governmental authorities issue regulations and make decisions. But product requirements relating to health, safety, environmental protection, national security, technology, packaging, marking and labeling, and the like are set out in many different places within the government and the private sector and are often difficult to discover by potential exporters or importers.

The standards code agreed upon by the negotiators states that technical regulations and certification procedures shall not be formulated or applied in a manner that creates obstacles to international trade or discriminates against the products of particular countries. To carry out these goals a series of procedures is agreed upon. When framing new standards and certification rules governments are to publish notices of this intent, provide copies of the proposed rules upon request, and allow enough time before their adoption for interested parties to comment upon them. Each adherent to the code shall ensure that "an enquiry point exists which is able to answer all reasonable enquiries from interested parties" regarding any technical regulation or certification system. Moreover, the signatories agree upon request to advise other members, especially the developing countries, on how best to meet their technical regulations.

There are two levels of obligations in carrying out these and other provisions in the code. For technical regulations and certification procedures set by central governments, the signatories "shall ensure that" these agencies comply with the code. For the various rules formulated by regional, state, local, and private organizations, the code requires its adherents to "take such reasonable means as may be available to them" to ensure compliance.

While encouraging the harmonization of standards among nations, the code is not intended to interfere with the right of countries to adopt rules that meet their particular goals in areas such as health, safety, and environmental protection. The dispute settlement mechanism is similar to that in the other codes. First, a member must enter into bilateral discussions if requested by another signatory. If the dispute is not resolved in these consultations, the matter can be referred to the committee on technical barriers to trade that is established under the code, which can then appoint technical expert groups or panels to consider the issues, consult with the disputants, and make recommendations or rulings on the matter. The committee reviews the finding of these groups and can authorize retaliatory actions.

Like the other technical codes, the one on standards represents a valuable attempt to reduce needless distortions of international trade. Furthermore, since the process of making rules and regulations is already more open in the United States than in many other countries, the efforts to publicize this process and to disseminate more widely knowledge about such rules is very much in U.S. interests.

With regard to trademarks and trade names U.S. negotiators have argued, not that rules and regulations are sometimes needlessly trade-distorting, but that more rules and regulations are needed to prevent "unfair" trade. Foreign producers sometimes affix the trademark or trade name of another firm on their products without permission. The United States has proposed discouraging this commercial counterfeiting by requiring that such merchandise be detained or seized at the time of importation, if the appropriate authorities are requested to do so by the person having the right to the protection of the trademark and trade name. Steps also would be taken to settle disputes and to prevent the misuse of this procedure to block imports. The reaction of other countries to the U.S. proposal has led to optimism that an agreement in this area can be reached within a few months.

Special and Differential Treatment for Developing Countries

Not only have the developing countries been accorded more favorable treatment in the tariff field by means of tariff preferences and exclusion from the full reciprocity requirement, but they have also been given special privileges in the various codes dealing with nontariff trade barriers. In the subsidies code, for example, developing countries are excluded from the ban on export subsidies, provided they agree "to reduce or eliminate export subsidies" when these are inconsistent with their "competitive needs." If they agree to this provision, other countries cannot take countervailing actions against their export subsidies in accordance with Article VI of GATT. However, developing country signatories also agree that their export subsidies shall not be used in a manner that causes adverse effects to the trade or production of another signatory, and action against these subsidies can be taken by resorting to the panel procedure under Articles XVI and XXIII. Similarly, the government procurement code permits developing countries to negotiate the exclusion of certain entities or products from the rules, while the safeguards code being considered contains a provision whereby the developed countries agree to make an effort to avoid safeguard actions on products of special interest to the developing nations. In addition to these special provisions, a general "enabling clause" has been agreed upon that provides a firmer legal basis for continuing tariff preferences and more favorable treatment with regard to nontariff trade barriers. Since this modifies the basic most-favored-nation principle set forth in Article I of the GATT, it was negotiated in the so-called Framework on GATT Reform Group. The clause merely states: "Notwithstanding the provisions of Article I in the General Agreement, contracting parties may accord differential and more favorable treatment to developing countries, without according such treatment to other contracting parties." This applies to tariffs, nontariff measures, regional or global arrangements among developing countries for reducing or eliminating tariffs, and special treatment for the least developed of the developing nations. The developed countries further agree not to expect reciprocal reductions in tariffs and nontariff barriers by the developing countries in trade negotiations if these are inconsistent with the developmental, financial, and trade needs of the latter countries. The text also contains the following clause dealing with the "graduation" of the developing countries to fuller GATT responsibilities:

> Less developed contracting parties expect that their capacity to make contributions or negotiated concessions or take mutually agreed upon action under the provisions and procedures of the General Agreement would improve with the progressive development of their economies and improvement in their trade situation and they would accordingly expect to participate more fully in the framework of rights and obligations under the General Agreement.

There is, however, no mechanism to determine when a developing country has reached the stage when it should assume these greater responsibilities. It has not been determined whether the text covering these points should appear as a new GATT article or be adopted by the members as a declaration or decision.

Safeguards for Balance of Payments and Development Purposes

Another issue considered by the Framework Group was measures taken for balance of payments and development purposes. The phrasing of Article XII dealing with restrictions to safeguard the balance of payments implies that, while quantitative controls over imports are permissible for this purpose, an import surcharge is not. However, countries have in fact quite often used this method, which most economists think is less distorting than quantitative restrictions. The declaration on the subject recognizes this fact and states that countries should use measures that are the least disruptive of trade. The signatories also declare their conviction that restrictive trade measures are in general an inefficient means of maintaining or restoring balance of payments equilibrium. The developing countries are also permitted in

Article XVIII of the GATT to restrict imports for another purpose, namely, to implement their development programs. However, the provisions of the article are complex and quite stringent. The declaration broadens the reasons for taking such actions and makes them less difficult to meet.

Dispute Settlement and Surveillance Procedures for the Various Codes

Each of the major codes provides for a committee composed of the code's signatories to facilitate the settlement of disputes that have failed to be resolved through consultations between the disputants. Although the mechanisms differ somewhat from code to code, each committee elects its own chairman and can establish a panel of experts of from three to five members to review the facts of the case and make such findings as will assist the committee in making recommendations or giving rulings. The committee or a panel can also play a conciliating role in the dispute. Preference is given to government officials in selecting panel members from lists of qualified persons supplied by the signatories. After receiving the panel report the committee itself makes recommendations to the parties involved or rules on the matter. If the recommendations are not followed, the committee can take further appropriate action including, for example, the authorization of appropriate countermeasures. Some of the codes also specify that the committee keep under surveillance any matter on which it has made a recommendation or ruling.

In addition to the provisions in each code on dispute settlement, an Understanding Regarding Notification, Consultation, Dispute Settlement and Surveillance was agreed upon in the GATT Reform Group "with a view of improving and refining" the mechanism under Articles XXII (on consultation) and XXIII (on nullification or impairment). Under these articles the contracting parties (the entire GATT membership) rather than any committee appoint panels or working groups, receive the panel reports, make recommendations and rulings, and keep relevant matters under surveillance. The director-general proposes the composition of any panel to the contracting parties for approval. According to the understanding, members of a panel should "preferably be governmental." Moreover, while a panel "should make an objective assessment of the matter before it, including an objective assessment of the facts of the case and the applicability of and conformity with the General Agreement," it should make only such other findings as will assist the contracting parties in making recommendations or rulings "if so requested." Besides stating that the contracting parties shall keep under surveillance any matter on which they have made a recommendation or rule, the understanding includes a provision committing them "to conduct a regular and systematic review of developments in the trading system."

In evaluating the prospects for enforcing the various codes, it is necessary to consider why the panel procedure has not worked as well in recent years as in GATT's first decade. Hudec points out that the fundamental reason is the breakdown in substantive consensus about GATT rules: some members feel that certain rules are no longer valid and that certain important trade problems are not covered in the document.[6] The main purpose of negotiating new codes has been to amplify and modify the older GATT rules in order to meet these objections. Even if the new codes do handle these problems, however, it is still necessary to establish procedures that facilitate their enforcement. Although the basic intentions of the participants are good, they cannot be carried out unless the rules and procedures are framed so as to discourage partiality. In recent years governments have tended to regard complaints as hostile diplomatic acts and have exerted strong pressures on other governments not to activate the dispute settlement mechanism. Moreover, once panels have been established, pressures have been brought on their members—usually representatives of the different governments in GATT—for favorable findings or for settlement of the dispute prior to making such findings. In all of this the "big" trading powers have a considerable advantage over the developing nations and the smaller industrial countries. Consequently, as Hudec points out, "the pressures for compliance tend to vary according to the relative power of the governments involved, creating an inequitable situation in which the rules bind the weak but not the strong."[7]

Two steps to help prevent this outcome would be to enable the GATT secretariat itself to request the establishment of panels and to ensure that nongovernmental individuals are well represented on such panels. Unfortunately, the secretariat will not be allowed to activate the panel mechanism under the new codes or Article XXIII, and government officials will still be given preference as panel members. One cannot, therefore, help but wonder whether the same unsatisfactory procedures will continue by which many potential disputes never surface because of heavy-handed political and economic pressures or are smoothed over once they do surface rather than being settled on the basis of consistently applied rules. On the other hand, the creation of so many separate committees that can establish panels would seem to indicate that the GATT members at least expect many more disputes and panel decisions than in the recent past.

One part of the enforcement mechanism that is not likely to be very effective is that enabling the various committees to authorize retaliation or other appropriate action when their recommendations are not followed. Only once in its history has the GATT membership authorized retaliation.[8] Rather than trying to enforce panel decisions, the GATT membership has tended to accept a panel's decision and then to rely upon the resulting international pressures to secure compliance. Usually, the parties to the dispute have accepted the panel findings, although in a famous 1976 decision on tax practices relating to export subsidies neither the United States nor the other party to the dispute, the European Community, implemented the panel's decision. The fact of the matter is that governments are far from willing to yield the kind of authority that would make retaliation sanctioned by other GATT members an effective compliance measure. If retaliation is used too frequently, it is likely to push members into using pressures to block the formation of panels or into withdrawing from the various codes. Nonetheless, the dispute settlement procedure can be effective without this last step, provided the procedure is regularly utilized and the decisions are realistic yet impartial and well reasoned.

OECD Steel Committee

An agreement reached outside the GATT framework but with important implications for the trade negotiations is the creation of a new International Steel Committee within the Organization of Economic Cooperation and Development (OECD). The committee's mandate states that governments need to work together not only to "ensure that trade in steel will remain as unrestricted and free of distortion as possible" and to "encourage reduction of barriers to trade" but "enable governments to act promptly to cope with crisis situations in close consultations with interested trading partners," to "facilitate needed structural adaptations . . . and promote rational allocation of productive resources," to "avoid encouraging economically unjustified investments," and to "facilitate multilateral cooperation consistent with the need to maintain competition, to anticipate and, to the extent possible, prevent problems." Among the committee's functions are following world supply and demand conditions in steel and developing "common perspectives" as well as establishing "where appropriate, multilateral objectives or guidelines for governmental policies."

The U.S. steel industry is reportedly pleased with the creation of this international committee. However, one must be somewhat concerned that the committee might turn into a cartel-like arrangement blocking needed adjustment in the industry and reducing its long-run efficiency.

Aircraft Agreement

Early in the Tokyo Round there was considerable hope for a series of sector negotiations in which the various tariffs and nontariff measures affecting a particular product line would be discussed within one group rather than among different groups organized on the basis of types of nontariff trade barriers. The only manufacturing area where such negotiations have been successful is the aircraft industry. Led by the United States, the participants have reached an agreement that frees trade on all civil aircraft and engines and on most parts and that commits the signatories to limit trade-restricting actions with regard to standards, government purchasing policies, quantitative restrictions, financing, and inducements. A committee on trade in civil aircraft is established for surveillance, consultation, and dispute settlement purposes. In view of the fact that U.S. dominance of the aircraft market is threatened by the announced intentions of the European Community, Canada, and Japan to build national aerospace industries of their own, this agreement should be widely appreciated in this country.

Agriculture

Agricultural trade barriers have long been among the most difficult to remove, for fairly obvious political reasons. The current negotiations have proved to be no exception to this general experience. Reportedly tariff and nontariff concessions affecting almost $4 billion worth of U.S. agricultural exports (out of total agricultural exports of about $27 billion) were made by other countries. These cover meat, grain products, tobacco, fruit, vegetables, wine, nuts, and oilseed.

Agreements have also been reached on dairy products and bovine meat. These agreements establish councils for exchanging information about production and marketing conditions and for consultations among member representatives concerning world conditions and policies in these product areas. In addition, the dairy arrangement establishes minimum prices for milk powders, butter, milk fat, and cheese below which commercial trade is prohibited. An effort has also been made under the auspices of the United Nations Conference on Trade and Development (UNCTAD) to formulate a new wheat trade convention to replace the one expiring in June 1979. So far this has not succeeded. There are still disagreements over the size of the wheat reserves to be held as well as the prices at which to add and subtract from these reserves.

THE TARIFF-CUTTING FORMULA

In the Kennedy Round negotiations the tariff-reducing rule finally agreed upon was a cut of 50 percent across the board, subject to a "bare minimum" of exceptions. (Of course, the fact that the average cut in manufactures came to 35 percent meant there was considerable slippage in the "bare minimum" notion.) The European Community pressed vigorously for a so-called harmonization formula whereby the higher the duty on an item, the greater the percentage cut in the duty. The United States opposed this approach for several reasons. The major one was the belief that, since all the harmonization formulas proposed by the EC resulted in a very modest average duty reduction, the EC was using this argument as a means of opposing a significant tariff reduction. Moreover, while there are good consumer-welfare reasons for reducing high duties a greater percentage, it seemed unfair to subject producers in high-duty industries to considerably greater pressures from import competition than producers in low-duty industries. The high-duty industries are often precisely the ones where the difficulties of adjustment for labor and capital are the greatest. Congress recognized this fact by allowing cuts of up to 100 percent for tariffs of 5 percent or below but of only 50 percent for duty rates above 5 percent. Furthermore, a constant percentage cut already puts high-duty industries under somewhat greater import pressure than low-duty industries. Suppose, for example, that the international prices of two products are fixed at $100 each, and the import duty on one is 50 percent while on the other 10 percent. When the first good is imported, it will sell for $150 in the domestic market (ignoring transport and other costs), whereas the other good will sell domestically for $110 when imported. Cutting the duty 50 percent on each will reduce the selling price on the first product to $125, or by 16.7 percent, and on the second to $105, or by only 4.5 percent.

In the Tokyo Round negotiations the United States proposed a tariff-cutting formula of 60 percent across the board. (This was the maximum cutting authority permitted under the 1974 Trade Act, although again duties of 5 percent or less could be completely eliminated.) The European Community countered with a harmonization formula. Specifically, the percentage cut in each duty would be the level of the duty itself. Moreover, the process would be repeated four successive times to reach the final rate. For example, a 40 percent duty would be cut by 40 percent to 24 percent. This would then be cut 24 percent to 18.2 percent; the 18.2 percent figure would be reduced by 18.2 percent to 14.9 percent. This would finally be cut by 14.9 percent to 12.7 percent. While for high duties the cut under this formula would be greater than the 60 percent proposal of the United States, the average cut on all dutiable items would amount to only about 30 percent.

In various simulations the United States discovered that with likely exceptions the employment and trade effects from a given average percentage cut achieved through harmonization formulas were actually somewhat more favorable for this country than those resulting from a uniform cut. In view of the strong position taken by the EC on the issue and the absence of real enthusiasm in this country for a significant cut such as 60 percent, the United States tentatively agreed to the harmonization approach provided the average cut was considerably greater than the EC's formula yielded. The final formula agreed upon was proposed by the Swiss. The rate at which a duty is cut is the rate of duty itself divided by the duty rate plus 0.14. Thus, the rate at which a 30 percent duty would be cut is 0.30/(0.30 + 0.14) = 0.68 or 68 percent. There is no economic rationale for the particular formula. It was selected from among others because it gave an average cut of about 40 percent (before exceptions) and most governments found the degree of harmonization acceptable. The United States is constrained somewhat in following the formula in that it cannot reduce any tariff above 5 percent by more than 60 percent. However, it can—and did—reduce duties 5 percent or below by more than this percentage in order to raise its average cut after exceptions to a level comparable to that of the other major participants. The average percentage cut on dutiable manufactures that will be made by the United States is 31 percent.

As one who was involved in the harmonization hassle in the Kennedy Round, I can only express admiration at the ability of the Tokyo Round technicians to sell to their more practical-minded superiors and to private business and labor groups an esoteric formula like $t/(t + 0.14)$ (where t is the tariff rate) as the tariff-reducing rule for the Multilateral Trade Negotiations. Moreover, one wonders why industries that must, for example, accept a 59 percent cut in their protective tariff because the level of this duty is 20 percent do not object to the undue burden when they observe a duty cut of only 52 percent in industries protected by a 10 percent tariff. Perhaps such factors as the fairly low levels of most duties, the eight-to-ten-year stretchout period for the duty reductions, and recent fluctuations in exchange rates that dwarf these tariff cuts have greatly diminished the concerns of various economic groups over the exact nature of the tariff reductions affecting them.

There is understandable concern by legislators over the possible adverse employment effects of the tariff reductions. However, detailed studies of these effects indicate not only that the overall employment impact is likely to be extremely small but that instances of adverse regional or industry effects can generally be easily absorbed through normal labor turnover and market growth in the region or industry as well as by staging the cuts over eight to ten years. My own simulation of a 50 percent reduction (with certain product exceptions) yields a net impact on total employment of only −15,000 jobs or about $2/100$ of 1 percent of the labor force.[9] Studies by Deardorff and Stern and by Cline and others estimate the aggregate employment impact of a 50 percent cut at −24,000 and +24,000 jobs, respectively.[10]

Regional and occupational effects are also quite small. For example, the labor impact in New England—the region which incurs the largest net loss, according to my calculations—is only −3,000 jobs. When one considers that this number is based on a 50 percent rather than a 30 percent reduction, that a major import-sensitive New England industry (footwear) included in the 50 percent calculations is in fact being excluded from any duty reductions, and finally that the cuts will be staged over at least eight years, the conclusion can only be that this (or any other) region should not be concerned about adverse employment effects from the Tokyo Round tariff reductions.

Since there is much evidence that the U.S. comparative advantage position in international trade is based on a relatively abundant supply of human capital and an ability to create new technology, it is not surprising that the demand for highly skilled workers tends to increase whereas that for comparatively unskilled workers tends to decline as a result of multilateral tariff reduction. These effects are, however, again very small. My estimates are that a 50 percent cut would tend to increase employment of those involved in research and development by 14⁄100 of 1 percent and of other professional and technical workers by 8⁄100 of 1 percent. On the other hand, the initial impact on semiskilled and unskilled production workers is an employment decline of 14⁄100 of 1 percent and 8⁄100 of 1 percent, respectively, in the number employed in these skill groups. However, the estimates do show that certain industries in which recent market growth has been low or negative could be faced with a considerable adjustment problem when faced with a 50 percent duty reduction. These include certain textile products not subject to quotas, nonrubber footwear, electronic tubes, glass products, ceramic tiles, pottery products, and primary lead and zinc.

The response to these occupation and industry figures should not be to demand that no duty cuts producing these results be made but rather to try to ensure that adjustment takes place in a noninjurious manner. Reciprocal duty reductions afford the country one of its few opportunities of moving to a higher living standard in a predictable and controllable manner. (Just the static net welfare gain to the nation of a 50 percent reciprocal cut is estimated at over $1 billion.)[11] By combining active adjustment assistance policies with less-than-formula cuts and longer staging periods, affected workers can be shifted either to higher earning positions, or, if necessary, be protected until they voluntarily leave or retire. The preferred approach is to use adjustment assistance policies, but unfortunately our programs in this field are still quite primitive and lack political support from labor. Consequently, the administration has used the technique of either excluding from duty cuts most of the above industries or reducing tariffs in these sectors only modestly. While this is a second-best approach, it should at least eliminate any credible charges that the actual duty reductions will cause appreciable injury to any industry or occupational group. . . .

NEW AREAS FOR NEGOTIATION

The prospects for preventing either the intensification of protectionism or the rapid growth of government-managed international trade depend

. . . upon the development of new or better rules in areas of recent protectionist activity that were not covered in any significant detail in the Tokyo Round negotiations. New international rules are most needed in the trade with respect to: state-owned or state-controlled enterprises that compete with trading firms subject to the constraints of the private-enterprise system; restrictive trading practices by business; and trade in services. While they will not be discussed further here, efforts are also needed within the GATT framework to contain the use of multiple legal approaches to harass importers;[12] and to ensure that trading blocs do not act as permanent obstacles to trade liberalisation on a multilateral basis. Moreover, in addition to these traditional areas of trading relationships, there are an increasing number of "grey" areas in which trade matters and policies traditionally excluded from consideration within the framework of commercial policy are becoming more interdependent and which, therefore, require greater efforts as policy coordination. These include the interrelationships between trade and policies affecting the balance-of-payments, aid and debt servicing, international investment, technology transfers and commodity agreements. Most of these subjects are best dealt with in forums other than the GATT, but this organisation should become more deeply involved in coordinating policies in these various fields.

State Enterprise Trade

. . . Governments in market-oriented economies are to an increasing extent taking over trading and producing activities traditionally undertaken by private enterprise. Private firms competing internationally with such state-owned enterprises frequently claim they must contend with dumping and subsidisation practices by these state firms that are impossible to detect and thus broach through the standard GATT articles relating to these matters. Nor has Article XVII on state-trading enterprises proved to be effective in dealing with this type of trade. If, as some think, East-West trade will grow significantly in the near future, the issue of minimising trade distortions in a trading world where state-owned and private firms compete and resolving the international conflicts resulting from this competition will become even more important within a few years.

Attempting to determine whether state-owned enterprises are engaged in dumping or export subsidisation is likely to be an exercise in futility. There is, however, a simple and feasible alternative for dealing with this type of trade. First, it should be recognised that from the overall welfare viewpoint of the importing country, dumping and export subsidisation are not in themselves economic "bads." These activities tend to increase real income in the importing country at the expense of the exporting country. What is really objectionable about them is if they result in such large-scale and sudden import-competing pressures that domestic workers and capital-owners suffer serious injury. The GATT "serious injury" test for imposing temporary import controls can be interpreted as determining when equity considerations for the affected factors dominate the total welfare-increasing effects of a great import supply. Extending this thought to state-trading leads to the conclusion that on the import side the "safeguard" rules of the GATT can be used to deal with this type of trade. Import restraints would be imposed only if it were determined that the increased imports from state-trading firms caused or threatened to cause serious injury to a domestic industry. What would differ, however, from the usual use of this article is that, if import restraints were deemed to be appropriate, there would not have to be a link between these actions and domestic measures of adjustment.

The export side is more difficult to deal with. Under some circumstances, state enterprises are established to carry out some fundamental goals relating to growth or equity considerations, for which the government is willing to sacrifice short-run efficiency considerations. Provided governments compensate for the withdrawal of the import "concessions," or accept an equivalent withdrawal of "concessions" by exporters, there is little that can be done about such actions. Others may not approve of them but sovereignty over internal affairs must be a recognised fact of international life. In other cases, though, government enterprises come into being and are operated at a loss because of political pressures to bail out economically weak firms. The loss of export markets to foreigners is the same as if quotas or subsidies had been employed to prop up the industry. And, just as the use of quantitative import restrictions as a safeguard measure should be tied to plans for adjusting to the realities of world resource conditions, so too should such plans be part of government take-overs of weak firms. Unless governments extend this principle to public ownership under these circumstances, this procedure will become more and more important as a loophole in the GATT rules. Of course, it is not always easy to distinguish these two sets of cases, but this is a function for GATT panels.

Restrictive Business Practices

Unlike the charter of the International Trade Organisation, which was proposed (but not accepted) shortly after World War II, the articles of the GATT do not include any rules concerning restrictive business practice. The omission of such rules seems hard to justify, especially in view of the rapid growth of multinational enterprises. The tariff-reducing provisions of the GATT are aimed in part at eliminating windfall profits that accrue to domestic producers because of government restrictions. Yet it is evident that many firms sending goods abroad also possess the market power to extract monopoly profits. Moreover, they often can engage in discriminatory pricing policies among countries—a practice condemned in the GATT if it causes "material injury."

The reasons for the omission of a code on business practices stem from the pro-government and pro-business (as opposed to pro-consumer) bias of the GATT. Consumer interests were of some concern to the founders of GATT, but import duties, for example, were regarded primarily as highly visible instruments of governments that restrict access to both output markets and supplies and thereby jeopardise international political stability. Tariff reduction, therefore, was an important matter of concern to governments. The various provisions dealing with internal taxes, health and safety standards, national security, *et cetera*, indicate other areas where the interests of governments were either protected or promoted in the GATT. The producer bias of the agreement manifests itself in such areas as dumping and subsidisation. Consumers in countries receiving dumped or subsidised goods gain from the lower prices resulting from such actions. The interests, however, of domestic producers who might suffer economic losses are given priority over consumers; and they have the right to request their governments to impose anti-dumping or countervailing duties if foreign producers sell below their domestic price. Similarly, some governments do not regard the pricing policies of exporting firms as proper concerns of governments, even though such policies may raise prices to domestic consumers.

Pressure for the establishment of a code on restrictive business practices has not come from consumers, who are poorly organised, but from the governments of developing countries and, interestingly, from some governments of developed countries as well. The developing countries complain that the absence of effective competition from domestic producers makes them prime targets for monopolistic exploitation by producers in the industrialised economies. Producers in certain developed countries, the United States for instance, where foreign monopolistic practices are generally unlawful, have become concerned about the diversionary impact of restrictionist agreements among private producers in other countries.

If the GATT is to become an effective central organisation for dealing with international trading problems that reduce world income and increase political tensions among nations, the gap in its articles of agreement on private business practices must be filled. What would be involved is simply the extension to all international trade of the kind of antimonopoly rules that currently apply to domestic trade in most industrialised countries. Agreements such as that concluded between European Community and Japanese steel producers would not be permitted. Similarly, the developing countries as well as the smaller industrial countries would be able to prevent the kind of discriminatory pricing practices among countries recently illustrated within the European Community by exports of bananas to its various members. The settlement of disputes arising under the new code would represent a major new responsibility for the GATT; and it would severely test the "panel" approach to resolving controversies, but the challenge to the organisation must be accepted.

Trade in Services

The seven rounds of multilateral trade negotiations that have been held under the GATT since World War II, including the Tokyo Round negotiations, have dealt primarily with government measures affecting international trade in physical goods. Even if the subject matter of the GATT is restricted to trade issues, not only should its scope be enlarged to include private business practices affecting trade but the scope of trade should also be broadened to include services.

The services sector has come to provide a major source of employment and income in the more industrialised countries. In the United States and Canada about 60 percent of the labour force is employed in this sector and 60 percent of the GNP originates there. For West Germany, France, Japan, and the United Kingdom, the labour force figure is between 40 and 50 percent, while the GNP percentage ranges from 40 to 60 percent.[13] While many service sectors do not engage in international transactions, the fact that trade in "invisibles" now accounts for about 25 to 30 percent of all international transactions indicates, in a crude way, the importance of service activities in international trade. Moreover, the services sector, like the industrial sector, is undergoing an increasing degree of internationalisation and inter-country penetration.[14]

Rather than attempting to delineate the proper scope for any negotiations on restrictions on international transactions in the services sector by framing a definition distinguishing "goods" from "services"—a task that is by no means a simple one—it seems most useful to deal with the services issue by concentrating on various private and public measures affecting the international activities of those industries traditionally listed as engaged in supplying services. It has been through the efforts of these industries that the subject has received greater attention in the 1970s and future negotiations will probably be framed in specific industry terms. A recent report by an inter-agency task force of the United States Administration, set up to investigate the subject, examined eighteen service industries, namely: accounting, advertising, auto-truck leasing, banking, communications, computer services, construction engineering, education services, employment services, equipment leasing, franchising, health services, hotels, motels, insurance, legal services, motion pictures, civil aviation, and shipping.[15] Of these industries, insurance, motion pictures, civil aviation, shipping and construction engineering were considered to be faced with serious international problems from an American viewpoint. These include extensive government subsidisation, government ownership, restrictive licensing arrangements, duties and quotas, standards that sometimes discriminate needlessly against foreign firms and government purchasing policies that favour domestic suppliers. Such measures also impede the trading activities of the other industries included in the above list. Though the problems are not as serious for these industries as the other five, they are likely to become more burdensome unless international action to reduce trade distortions in services is taken soon.

Not surprisingly, the task force in the United States concluded that government policies with regard to the foreign investment activities of service industries were even more constraining than those affecting trading activities in services. The services sector is a good case of where it is difficult to separate trade and investment matters, since to provide the service, foreign investment is often necessary.

American trade negotiators actually possessed the authority under the Trade Act of 1974 to negotiate on services in the Tokyo Round negotiations and most other delegates presumably could easily have obtained such authority under their parliamentary forms of government. There was general agreement though not to press for such negotiations in view of the absence of detailed knowledge about the problems involved and the complexity of the other issues to be discussed. The situation is likely to be corrected in the near future as more private and government studies of barriers to international trade in services are undertaken.

Setting aside investment and repatriation questions, there is no difference, in principle, between the distortions affecting trade in services and those affecting trade in goods. For example, a subsidy to a domestic shipping or film industry is no different from a subsidy to a domestic coal or computer industry. What distinguishes the services sector from the goods sector (and probably accounts for its exclusion thus far from GATT negotiations) is the greater extent to which services are subject to national policies that are inconsistent with a market solution to resource allocation. Nations believe they need a certain size shipping industry for national defence purposes; they want a national airline system for reasons of pride and prestige; or they wish to encourage a local film industry in order to preserve and enhance the country's cultural heritage. As stated earlier, while others may not always agree with a particular country's mix of such goals, the right of a country to make such judgments must be respected. These objectives, however, usually do not imply fixed trade positions in each area. A country may be quite willing to reduce its domestic shipping activities in return for trade concessions in other service areas or in commodity fields. In other words, negotiations of the traditional GATT variety can still be mutually productive to the participants, even in areas where "non-economic" national goals apply. This applies with even greater force to the several service fields where self-interest on the part of the industry rather than any lofty national goal is the basis of the protectionism. The various GATT codes developed for dealing with subsidies, government procurement *et cetera* also can be readily applied to the services area. A Code of Liberalisation of Current Invisible Operations has been negotiated in the Organisation for Economic Cooperation and Development but it is only partially effective and has not served to control the protectionist trend in the services sector of the world economy.

A beginning has been made on the subject with the setting up of a working party by the Trade Committee of the OECD to develop an inventory of restrictions on international transactions in the services sector.

INTEGRATING TRADE ISSUES AND RELATED POLICIES

Balance-of-Payments Policy

The increasing interdependence of national economies as well as the growing degree of state intervention in economic life is making the need for international coordination of economic policies in different fields even more urgent. One international non-trade subject that is touched on explicitly in the GATT is balance-of-payments policy. Countries are permitted to introduce quotas on a temporary basis when faced with significant balance-of-payments problems. Oddly, the use of a uniform import levy, or surcharge, in these circumstances was considered inconsistent with the GATT. One of the changes achieved in the Tokyo Round negotiations that most observers agreed was much needed was to give preference to a uniform import levy over quotas as a trade measure for meeting balance-of-payments crises.

Trade, Aid and Financial Policies

Another relationship between trade policy and balance-of-payments conditions that is becoming more important concerns the trade, aid and financial policies of the developed countries toward the developing nations. Private banks, national governments, and international institutions are providing financial assistance and advice to foster capital formation and industrialisation in developing countries. At the same time, the established industrial countries are becoming increasingly reluctant to accept exports of certain manufactures from these countries.

The only way the developing countries, though, can earn the foreign exchange needed to amortise their external debt is to increase their exports. Financial groups within the advanced industrialised countries are anxious to avoid defaults on the part of the developing countries, while other domestic economic interests exert pressures that increase the likelihood of such defaults. Obviously there is a need for better coordination of trade and financial aid policies, not just within individual countries but between the GATT, the World Bank and the aid and export credit agencies of the major industrial countries. The World Bank would seem to be the best organisation for the leadership role in this effort.

International Investment

A frequent proposal over the last several years has been to establish a GATT–like organisation that would deal with international investment issues. The rapid rise of direct investment by multinational enterprises in both smaller developed and developing countries has been especially important in leading to this proposal. These enterprises have often been accused of a long list of "unfair" practices ranging from engaging in discriminatory pricing and investment practices to using their power to promote the political influence of a foreign state. But another source of pressure for such an organisation stems from private firms which engage in international investment and object to the many government controls over investment and the repatriation of earnings that hamper their operations. The impact of these policies on trade patterns can be illustrated with reference to the services industries discussed earlier.

The previously cited OECD code on invisibles as well as another OECD code, on the Liberalisation of Capital Movements, covers some of these matters, but as noted earlier, they are not very effective. An OECD code covering the behaviour of multinational enterprises in foreign countries also exists. None of these codes provides though for any dispute-settlement procedures as does the GATT; nor do the codes have the binding force, such as it is, of agreements signed within the GATT framework.

Pressures for an agreement and organisation to control direct investment activities of multinational enterprises have weakened in recent years. In part this seems due to the greater investment activities of multinationals based in other countries besides the United States; for example, a surprising amount of investment by multinationals domiciled in the developing countries is taking place. Most developing countries and small industrial nations have also passed legislation controlling the activities of multinational enterprises and have found these to be quite effective in satisfying their national goals with respect to these private organisations. Consequently, while conceptually a GATT–type institution is needed in the investment field, the lack of a strong demand for it at this time makes it an issue of lower priority.

Technology Transfers

As industrialisation spreads among the developing countries, the concerns about the transfer of technology increase in both developing and developed countries. Countries in which industrialisation is beginning to take hold fear that firms in the advanced industrialised countries make available only obsolete and non-competitive technology and extract monopolistic profits when making available this technology. On the other hand, labour groups in the advanced industrialised economies often claim that the full social cost in the country, in particular those associated with labour displacement, are not taken into account in the transfer process. Both of these sets of concerns lead to requests for some type of control over the international transfer of technology.

If as has been suggested, the GATT is broadened to include both private business practices and trade in services, issues relating to technology transfer can be handled within this new framework. Charges concerning the unreasonable pricing of technological services, for example, could be handled in the same manner as similar charges concerning trade in physical goods. Issues relating to the national benefits and costs of technology transfers are best handled at the national level and through other GATT channels. Rapid transfers causing significant unemployment in a domestic industry, for example, can be dealt with most effectively through a country's own industrial adaptation policies and the safeguard rules of the GATT.

Commodity Agreements

The key request of the developing countries in their proposals for a New International Economic Order, namely an Integrated Commodities Program, also raises trade issues outside of the traditional GATT framework. While the ITO charter included a chapter on commodity agreements, the GATT does not bring these agreements under its jurisdiction. This has caused few problems to date because of the failure of most such agreements, but the likelihood that commodity agreements will grow in importance increases the prospects of conflicts between GATT rules and the operation of these agreements. It is quite unlikely, however, that the primary product agreements in which the developing countries are interested will ever be brought within the GATT, since many affected countries are not GATT members. Thus it is very important that the representatives from the GATT participate in the establishment of commodity agreements so as to minimise needless conflicts on rules and procedures. A permanent consultative arrangement is also essential between the GATT and the various commodity organisations.

Multiple Exchange Rates

Multiple exchange rates are still another non-trade policy measure with important implications for the structure of trade. Obviously different exchange rates for different goods have similar effects to tariffs and export subsidies on the goods. Fortunately the fact that most developed countries have adopted uniform exchange rates for commodity transactions since the late 1950s has prevented any serious conflicts between exchange-rate and trade policy from arising among the major trading nations. However, a different exchange rate for capital transactions has sometimes been used in these countries and, as concern about liberalisation in services increases, a need for greater coordination on this matter will arise. The exchange-rate practices of the developing countries pose a more serious problem. These countries often use multiple exchange rates in commodity transactions; and their gradual liberalisation *vis-à-vis* international trade as they assume greater GATT responsibilities could be negated by offsetting changes in multiple exchange rates. Such matters are theoretically covered by Article XXIII of the GATT, which deals with actions by members that impair the value of concessions granted by other members, but there should be a more detailed statement of possible objectionable measures, including multiple exchange rates, in the Article. A formal consultative arrangement between the International Monetary Fund (IMF) and the GATT is also needed to ensure that measures taken to deal with balance-of-payments crises are consistent with GATT rules.

NOTES

1. The contracting parties are the members of the GATT acting in a collective manner.
2. Robert E. Hudec, *The GATT Legal System and World Trade Diplomacy* (New York: Praeger Publishers, 1975), appendix A; and Robert E. Hudec, *Adjudication of International Trade Disputes*, Thames Essay no. 16 (London: Trade Policy Research Centre, 1978), pp. 5–6, n. 2.
3. 41 U.S.C. 10a–10d.
4. Robert E. Baldwin, *Nontariff Distortions of International Trade* (Washington, D.C.: Brookings Institution, 1970), pp. 70–78.
5. The products now covered are benzenoid chemicals, rubber-soled footwear, canned clams, and certain knit gloves.
6. Hudec, *Adjudication of International Trade Disputes*, p. 11.
7. Ibid., p. 3.
8. Ibid., p. 82.
9. Robert E. Baldwin and Wayne E. Lewis, "U.S. Tariff Effects on Trade and Employment in Detailed SIC Industries," in William G. Dewald, ed., *The Impacts of International Trade and Investment on Employment* (Washington, D.C.: U.S. Department of Labor, 1978).

10. Alan V. Deardorff and Robert M. Stern, "A Disaggregated Model of World Production and Trade," presented to a conference on Micro Modeling for International Trade Policy, University of Western Ontario, London, Ontario, February 23–24, 1979, processed; and W. Cline, N. Kawanabe, T. Kronsjo, and T. Williams, *Trade Negotiations in the Tokyo Round* (Washington, D.C.: Brookings Institution, 1978).

11. Robert E. Baldwin, John H. Mutti, and J. David Richardson, "Welfare Effects in the United States of a Significant Multilateral Tariff Reduction," *Journal of International Economies*, 10, (August 1980).

12. The development of this form of non-tariff protection is discussed, in the American context, in Malmgren, "Significance of Trade Policies in the World Economic Outlook," *The World Economy*, October, 1977.

13. High level Group on Trade and Related Problems, *Policy Perspectives for International Trade and Economic Relations*, Rey Report (Paris: OECD Secretariat, 1972).

14. An early review of restrictions on international transactions in the services sector of the world economy, on which subsequent studies have been based, is contained in Brian Griffiths, *Invisible Barriers to Invisible Trade* (London: Macmillan, for the Trade Policy Research Centre, 1975).

15. Task Force on Services and Multilateral Trade Negotiations, *US Service Industries in World Markets: Current Problems and Future Policy Development* (Washington: Department of Commerce, 1976).

6. Statement on U.S. Aims at the World Trade Ministers' Meeting: One Industry's View

THE SEMICONDUCTOR INDUSTRY ASSOCIATION

ABSTRACT

Our point of departure for trade policy is that there is no good substitute for complete openness across international borders to international trade, investment and knowledge. While most of the major advances in semiconductor technology have been wholly American, in fact the first microprocesser was put together by a group of engineers working in California for a foreign customer.

The salient point is that as in no other area of international trade and investment, in knowledge-intensive goods there is a basic synergy that makes international exchange extraordinarily beneficial. The flow of technology, trade and investment across borders benefits all nations.

To restrict trade is ultimately self-defeating. When the Japanese chose to restrict minicomputer imports in the early 1970s, they slowed progress in a thousand of their domestic industries, limited the evolution of the applications for computers in Japan, and weakened the development of the software industry in Japan. Today, Mexico and Brazil are seeking to take a great step forward, but are injuring themselves seriously in that attempt.

One would suppose that the truth of this proposition—that openness in high technology trade and investment is globally beneficial—would be a self-evident proposition. Yet increasingly, trade and investment in high technology goods are being curtailed, restricted and rechanneled.

Every time we read of an American company's joint venture abroad, and the article notes that the U.S. shareholder has taken a 49 percent equity position in the new company, that so much local content will be included in the new products, that technology transfer has been required, we can see the hand of a foreign government working against the normal operation of the free market. Every time we read of a major nationalization of a foreign high technology firm, we have to begin to wonder whether that firm will behave in the marketplace according solely to commercial interests. Every time we read about a new government program sponsoring cooperative research and development, we should enquire whether foreign-owned companies, even those resident in the country concerned, are eligible to participate.

There is abroad, for high technology trade and investment, a neomercantilism that is spreading throughout the industrialized world, including the newly industrializing countries. It is becoming apparent that the major determining factors of high technology trade in the future will be neither the average tariffs on industrial goods which in developed countries will only average 4% in 1987, nor the codes of conduct with respect to nontariff barriers. The basic assumption has been that open market conditions will prevail when barriers and distortions at the border are removed. Increasingly in the high technology area, this assumption cannot be accepted.

The U.S. Administration has suggested to our major trading partners that the problems of trade and investment in high technology must be made a matter of priority concern in the upcoming international negotiations under the auspices of the GATT. This priority is well-founded, and immediate steps are essential if extraordinary damage is to be avoided to the creation and development of those products of the future which hold the greatest promise for mankind. In this testimony, the Semiconductor Industry Association submits some proposed topics for international negotiation which deserve serious consideration at the GATT ministerial meeting in the fall of this year.

INTRODUCTION

The importance of the upcoming GATT ministerial scheduled for this fall cannot be overemphasized. It will be the single most important factor in determining which issues will receive international attention in the next decade. It is therefore imperative that the Unites States take maximum advantage of the meeting to ensure that the highest priority concerns of this nation in eliminating remaining trade barriers and expanding foreign market access are addressed at this session.

Distortions of international trade in high technology products deserve and demand a place at the very top of the U.S. list of priority issues.

Indeed, the Administration has committed itself to an immediate, aggressive response to problems of trade and investment in high technology. Administration officials have repeatedly emphasized that high technology will be one of the major trade issues of the decade, and that it will press for liberalization in this area. USTR Brock* testified last October, advocating a more than reactive policy for the United States—"A more forward-looking approach in the high technology industries—a preventive perspective both domestically and internationally." Speaking recently at Davos, Brock included the challenges facing the U.S. high technology industries on the list of U.S. high priority items to be addressed at the GATT ministerial. In his Statement on U.S. Trade Policy, he assured us that future negotiating efforts within GATT would extend international discipline to this new sector. We strongly affirm that the problems in this sector—a sector vital to the United States and to every other nation—have reached a critical level, and are already impairing wider relations among major trading nations.

Many of the problems in high technology trade and investment serve as prime examples of the broader barriers to services and investment the United States is seeking to eliminate, and effectively illustrate the danger of allowing existing trade-distorting measures to continue. High technology issues require a more specialized focus, however. These industries are of unique importance to every nation and to worldwide technological progress. Technology changes so quickly and forms of government intervention are so diverse and so pervasive that anything less than an immediate, comprehensive and direct approach to high technology issues will not succeed.

We urge adoption of a two-tiered approach. In the near term, the United States should actively seek to open foreign technology markets to U.S. trade and investment through negotiations on a bilateral level. Concurrently, it is essential that we utilize the GATT ministerial to lay

*"Statement of Ambassador Brock (USTR) Before the Ways and Means Committee Subcommittee on Trade, Oversight Hearings on Trade Policy," October 29, 1981, p. 13.

the groundwork for the future expansion of our efforts to the multilateral level in order to establish an improved framework for international trade and investment.

A SECTORAL FOCUS IS APPROPRIATE AND ESSENTIAL

We agree that a sectoral approach to most international trade problems is neither necessary nor appropriate. However, a sectoral focus is essential and is the only effective approach to current high technology trade issues.

High technology is not just another significant product sector. Defined by input rather than product, its parameters cut across other product sectors and will shift with time to encompass any product highly dependent on extensive research and development and constant innovativeness. These are the products generally in the forefront in determining any nation's industrial strength and future competitiveness. Singling out high technology trade problems for special focus is quite different from sectoral negotiations on a purely product-specific basis.

No other category of products is as uniquely important to every nation. Semiconductors are one example. Because of their defense-related uses, semiconductors are crucial to the U.S. national security. In addition, this is a core industry, feeding into all other major U.S. industries. Not only are semiconductors vital to the future growth and competitiveness of the U.S. computer, telecommunications and electronics instrumentation industries and to pioneer industries like robotics and genetic engineering, they are absolutely critical to the future health of our steel, automobile and textile industries. The importance of products such as these to every nation's industrial base, national defense and economic health, to international technological progress, and to the free international flow of information, is rivaled by no other sector. Focussing on high technology trade and investment problems must therefore be high on all nations' agendas.

There is an additional impetus for international consensus in this sector. High technology problems are affecting broader trading relations between GATT members, and raise the threat of further unilateral protectionist measures and the undermining of the GATT system if progress is not imminent.

A sectoral focus is mandated by the pervasiveness, diverse nature and difficulty of quantifying the obstacles to free trade and investment in this sector. A comprehensive approach is the only truly effective alternative.

Unlike most sectoral trade problems, we are not dealing here with the familiar situation of foreign government protection of infant or ailing industries in response to domestic economic and political pressures. Our trading partners are protecting and promoting their highly competitive high technology industries with the intention of taking advantage of the open U.S. market by expanding exports from a sector insulated from foreign competition.

Many of these problems involve issues which cannot be dealt with adequately under existing GATT law. High technology products are by definition new and constantly changing. The adverse effects of current foreign government policies will be felt in the future and are immediately neither apparent nor quantifiable. To deal effectively with government measures protecting and promoting their high technology industries, existing GATT provisions must be strengthened and expanded.

A strong precedent exists for this type of approach. Multilateral agreement on a sectoral issue has been achieved within GATT in the area of civil aircraft. The 1979 Agreement on Trade in Civil Aircraft provides an excellent model and precedent for a multilateral focus on high technology issues, due to the significant parallels between the two sectors in industry importance, types of problems, and mutuality of benefits. Like the high technology sector, the U.S. civil aircraft industry had been dominant internationally since its inception. In the late seventies, this position was seriously challenged by foreign competition stemming in large part from foreign government subsidization, restrictions on market access, and a range of unfair trade-distorting policies and practices. Like the high technology industry, the civil aircraft industry is of particular importance to the U.S. economy and trade balance, and is peculiarly dependent on access to world markets. As with high technology, international agreement would benefit the industries and economies of all nations.

GATT members were able to reach agreement establishing a framework to govern trade in the civil aircraft sector. The agreement is directed at eliminating the adverse effects of a myriad of trade-distorting measures, encouraging continual worldwide innovation, and ensuring that producers of all signatory nations are provided fair and equal competitive opportunities. The high technology sector is an even stronger candidate for international negotiation and agreement.

THE HIGH TECHNOLOGY ISSUE

Much of the progress achieved to date in expanding and liberalizing international trade and investment is being eroded by a wave of neomercantilism. Policies and measures implemented by foreign governments today echo the mercantilist policies of Western European nations three centuries ago. Motivated by the desire to build strong nation-states, and perceiving total world economic welfare as finite and any benefit to one nation therefore only achievable at the expense of another, each government pursued an aggressive, nationalistic economic policy aimed at securing a favorable balance of trade. To achieve that end, governments vigorously protected and promoted their industries and regulated trade in order to limit imports and expand exports. There are striking and disturbing parallels between the range of tariffs, subsidies, financing, anticompetitive devices and industrial policies during that time of nationalism and international animosity, and those prevalent today.

Today our trading partners are increasingly intervening in the normal flows of international trade and investment, with the similar intent of expanding exports and restricting access to their markets. Such short-sighted actions threaten to eradicate the progress achieved to date within the GATT, to deny all nations the benefits of free trade, and to return us to an era of protectionism and retaliation.

This neomercantilist movement is in no area more dramatic than in high technology. Having recognized the critical nature of high technology industries and their direct relation to each nation's international competitiveness, foreign governments have made those industries the focus of nationalist policies. Our trading partners, including many of the newly industrialized countries, are unfairly protecting and promoting their industries while restricting foreign access through a range of tariff and nontariff barriers and other trade-distorting measures such as government and joint government-industry planning and establishment of objectives, toleration of anticompetitive practices, investment performance requirements, subsidization, sponsorship of limited-access joint research projects, and preferential financial and taxation measures. In contrast, the United States market is substantially free of government intervention, and is open to foreign imports and investment.

The European Community is developing a sweeping program designed to coordinate research, design and production efforts in order to achieve a unified European market and expand its share of the world market. Microelectronics has received particularly high priority by the EC Council and Commission. A recent Commission report proposed measures to coordinate and exchange information about national initiatives in this area, a concerted effort to develop relevant knowledge and skills within the Community, and the promotion of a European production capacity in the most advanced integrated circuits. In addition, individual European governments support and protect their industries through a range of programs and policies.

In France, for example, development of technologically advanced industries and the encouragement of related research is a central element in the latest five-year plan. As part of this effort the French Government promotes its integrated circuit industry through a program involving funding of $150 million over a five-year span, sponsorship of *R&D* projects, and measures to increase production capability, and encourages the assimilation of U.S. technology through joint ventures with U.S. firms. In addition, French research and development efforts are rewarded with tax benefits such as a credit for *R&D* expenditures, high depreciation rates for research facilities, and special tax treatment for venture capital companies investing a high proportion of capital in innovation. These measures are complemented by export-enhancing and import-inhibiting policies such as mixed credit programs, industry-government cooperation in organizing and financing large projects, discriminatory public procurement policies, and conditioning foreign access on performance requirements.

Measures implemented by the German Government are even more striking, in light of Germany's market orientation and relatively open trade policy. The German Government provides an exceptionally high level of funding for research and development, even relative to other European nations. In 1978, for instance, the German Government financed 47 percent of total *R&D*. The German Government influences the development of its high technology sector through a well-developed government-industry communications network composed of research institutions which administer government *R&D* funds, and advisory committees.

Through its New Technologies Program, the German Government has targeted certain key industries such as microelectronics, telecommunications, bioengineering and optic and control engineering, in an effort to ensure the international competitiveness of German industry in all high technology-related industries. Targeted industries receive government *R&D* funding on the basis of cost sharing. As part of its promotion of the microchip industry, the amount provided annually to one electrical company alone is estimated at $40 million.

The Japanese Government has adopted a national policy of promoting its high technology industries, emphasizing in particular the development and commercial application of state-of-the-art and next generation technologies. Attention is focused on the semiconductor industry, where the government coordinates a joint government-industry effort to improve the Japanese capacity in the greatest-volume, fastest-growing sector of the market. This effort is specifically geared to overtaking the U.S. lead in that sector. The programs are aided by tax incentives, low interest rates, accelerated depreciation and debt-leveraged financing. Moreover, the government's targeting of the semiconductor industry has made this a low-risk area, greatly improving access to private capital.

Direct government support of the industry is coordinated with policies which discourage imports and restrict foreign investment. U.S. firms seeking to export to, or invest in, Japan confront nontariff barriers ranging from discriminatory government procurement policies and internal procedures, preferential access to capital, government subsidization, and loans and guarantees for Japanese firms, to difficulties in recruiting personnel.

The more advanced developing countries are exhibiting the same neomercantilist tendencies. Those nations are increasingly aware that acquisition of foreign technology and their own technology-generating capabilities are integrally related to their development process and to their ability to maintain any level of international competitiveness. The result is a pervasive use of performance requirements and other policies restricting market access, government monopolization and funding, and tax and financial incentives.

Brazil is a prime example. The Brazilian National Development Plan is aimed in part at achieving competitive strength in numerous industrial sectors through increased acquisition and use of high technology. As part of that effort market access is denied to foreign firms representing a substantial competitive threat to Brazilian enterprises, or is severely limited through import restrictions and performance requirements. Through its computer program, for example, the Brazilian Government conditions foreign investment on the introduction over time of increased levels of Brazilian content. The Mexican Government similarly relies heavily on trade and investment restrictions and export incentives to promote its electronics and telecommunications industries.

The crisis currently facing the U.S. semiconductor industry illustrates dramatically the adverse consequences of policies like these. Our semiconductor industry is seriously threatened by foreign industrial policies and that threat will only increase in severity, absent a U.S. response.

Profit and employment figures for the industry look healthy, and our industry is still dominant internationally, but those indices are deceptive. The U.S. lead is declining. Despite increases in foreign semiconductor consumption, U.S. exports have not grown substantially.

Foreign semiconductor producers are challenging U.S. dominance in those memory chip sectors which will be most important in the future. Although the U.S. industry currently has 63 percent of the overall market share in the 16K RAM (16,000 bits Random Access Memory) market, it has only 30 percent of the market for the 64K RAM, expected to be the largest-selling chip by 1985. Foreign producers are well positioned in the race to manufacture the 256K RAM. Leadership in this sector is most important, since these are the most advanced, state-of-the-art products and demand for them is expanding at three times the rate for semiconductors as a whole.

Improved access to world markets is critical to the U.S. industry for two interrelated reasons. First, due to the structure and nature of the industry, access to capital and economies of scale are increasingly crucial. Second, if foreign industries are allowed to remain within their insulated environments of protection and support, our industries will ultimately be unable to compete.

THE NEED TO RESPOND

A failure to respond to this new incidence of mercantilism—particularly prevalent in the high technology field—would adversely affect each individual nation and the international system as a whole. In our highly interdependent international economic system, maximum worldwide development of high technology is undeniably in the best interests of all. To adopt short-sighted policies focused exclusively on national achievement is to divert us from the path of maximum efficiency and progress, and can only be counterproductive.

Elimination of the barriers to free international trade and investment can be the only logical goal in this sector for any nation. The global economies of scale and the access to capital essential to any viable high technology industry can only be achieved if market restrictions are eliminated. Moreover, except through fair international competition, the level of innovativeness so vital to high technology cannot be maintained.

By definition, high technology products are in the forefront of technological progress in every sector. Identified not by product usage but by input (the amount of research and development), the high technology sector takes the most sophisticated, innovative products from many product sectors, to form the wave of the future. Maximum development of this sector, which can only be achieved through unrestricted trade and investment flows, is vitally important to every nation.

These products and industries occupy a unique position in every national economy. Because of their diverse and pervasive uses, measures which deter progress in this area by restricting international free trade and investment in high technology, ultimately deter progress in a whole range of important industries.

High technology products play a uniquely central role in the international flow of information. As recognized in the Florence Agreement, the free flow of ideas between and among nations benefits society as a whole and is in the interest of each individual nation.

To persist in restricting market access and seeking to expand exports would be an ultimately fruitless effort for any nation. Even purely national goals are not likely to be achieved in the current atmosphere. The new incidence of mercantilism threatens to return us to a new period of retaliation and protectionism. Developed and advanced developing nations alike would soon find foreign markets closed to them.

POLICY PROPOSALS

We and our major trading partners must succeed in coping with our high technology trade problems through a process of negotiation and agreement. Otherwise, unilateral implementation of protectionist and retaliatory measures is inevitable.

Immediate expansion of foreign market access can be achieved through negotiated bilateral agreements to eliminate existing barriers to high technology trade and investment. The proposed "High Technology Trade Act of 1982" would authorize the President to negotiate and enter into such agreements. It would also ensure the maintenance of the consensus achieved through mutual concessions which forms the foundation of GATT, by expanding the scope of presidential responses, allowing the president to address a wider range of unfair market barriers, and permitting him to limit where necessary the exports and investments of foreign nations which persist in pursuing neomercantilist policies.

Bilateral agreements should be the stepping stone to establishment of a comprehensive multilateral framework for dealing with high technology issues. Multilateral agreements will take time, and it is essential that GATT mechanisms be activated now to identify the issues, define the approach, and establish a timetable. We urge the Administration to utilize the GATT ministerial to seek commitments from our trading partners to negotiate and enter into agreements to achieve mutual market access in the high technology sector.

In order to result in an effective and acceptable solution, any negotiations and agreements—whether on a bilateral or multilateral level—would have to encompass commitments on certain fundamental points.

The obvious starting point is the reduction and elimination of existing tariff and nontariff barriers. To this end:

The United States, Japan, and the European Communities should pledge to reduce tariffs in key products such as semiconductors and computer products to a level of parity, and then to eliminate those tariffs.

Participants should commit themselves to eliminate particular nontariff barriers. Specifically, the United States should seek elimination of customs practices, product standards and rules of origin which restrict access to the Japanese and EC markets.

The United States, Japan and the EC should pledge to discourage the adoption of private "buy domestic" policies. Japan should recognize the less formalized but very pervasive "buy Japan" mentality, and should commit itself to opening Japan *in fact* to industrial procurement, enhancing its efforts through financial and regulatory inducements.

All participants should commit themselves to the freest possible international information flow, pledging not to interfere with the outward flow of nonstrategic technology and products.

Little progress is possible, however, without affirmative action on the part of all participants, evidencing an authentic commitment to liberalizing trade in this area:

All participant governments should pledge to adopt or maintain an open market and a liberal trade and investment policy, with no diminution of existing market access, and progressive liberalization of barriers.

The United States should seek commitments from foreign governments to review aspects of their domestic environments (including macroeconomic policies such as taxation, distribution systems, capital allocation and currency valuation) to determine their effect upon trade and investment, with a view to expanding and facilitating imports of goods, services and investment.

The United States should seek commitments from its trading partners to jointly monitor increased market access, and to improve the supply of data relevant to that monitoring.

Equally essential to significant progress are measures to achieve greater cooperation and coordination of national policies:

The United States and the European Communities should agree to coordinate their actions and policies in response to Japanese trade and investment issues, and the United States should seek a similar commitment from Japan concerning EC trade issues.

The three nations should agree upon a common approach to investment performance requirements in developing countries.

The United States, Japan and the EC should negotiate an international interconnect agreement.

All three nations should agree to conform to an improved safeguard system for the high technology sector under GATT discipline.

Obstacles to open market access are particularly prevalent in the areas of services and investment—areas not currently subject to international agreement. It is therefore imperative that:

The United States, Japan and the EC should commit themselves to taking affirmative steps to facilitate and ensure "national treatment" for foreign investment. This would include access to industry or industry/government-sponsored joint research and development projects and to capital markets on an equal basis with indigenous firms. The European Communities and Japan should pledge to extend this national treatment principle to their public procurement of telecommunications equipment. The national treatment commitment would also require participants to refrain from imposing performance requirements, such as forced technology transfers or minority equity participation requirements.

The United States, Japan and the EC should agree to mutual liberalization of trade in services, including software, data processing, information flows and data communication tariffs.

Naturally, international agreement on the issues we have outlined will be of limited success if not backed by urgently needed domestic measures. The United States must consider measures to make the domestic environment more conducive to the international competitiveness of U.S. firms, matching where possible the structural and policy advantages of foreign firms. Equally important are joint industry and government efforts to improve competitiveness through taxation measures, export financing, export controls, antitrust policy and improved management policy. Finally, the government should vigorously monitor import prices and quantities in order to target and take legal action against illegal, unfair or injurious trade practices.

CONCLUSION

The challenge facing our high technology "sector" is of critical importance both to the United States and to the international trading system. Its importance domestically derives from the crucial nature of these industries. If we lose our lead in this area, our defense capability will decline and our entire industrial system and international competitive position will suffer. The challenge is important internationally because it is a very visible manifestation of the consequences of the new type of trade distortions that are proliferating and undermining the GATT system. It is also important because if the friction within this sector is not alleviated, the likely result will be a further deterioration in relations between major trading nations, and the imposition of unilateral measures which will counteract the benefits already achieved within GATT.

7. Statement on U.S. Aims at the World Trade Ministers' Meeting: A Labor View

RUDY OSWALD

The AFL-CIO welcomes this opportunity to discuss U.S. plans for the next major meeting of the GATT trade ministers in November 1982, because these ministerial meetings have so much influence on international trade. The United States approach should be to emphasize U.S. rights for reciprocity and fair trade, as Congress has already directed by law. It is time to take stock of where we are. It is not time for new multilateral negotiations either for new codes or for new global negotiations on services.

Almost 16 million Americans now need full-time jobs—9.3 million unemployed, 1.2 million too discouraged to look for work, and 5.4 million on part-time work but wanting full-time jobs. These facts are seldom considered when assessing international trade's impact on the nation. But the AFL-CIO and its affiliates are aware that imports have been compounding the tragedy of U.S. recession and tight money. U.S. negotiators should not continue to ignore the cost of trade on this economy while ballyhooing its benefits.

The General Agreement on Tariffs and Trade (GATT) is an international agreement on general rules for conducting international trade. GATT is also the name of an international organization which administers these rules of international trade.

Since 1947, the United States government has taken part in seven rounds of tariff-cutting negotiations. The onesidedness of many GATT rules has often cost U.S. jobs and production.

The latest GATT round, the Tokyo Round, not only reduced tariffs but also clarified existing rules in at least nine codes and broadened the coverage of the GATT. Congress authorized U.S. implementation of the codes in the Trade Agreements Act of 1979.

Rudy Oswald is director of the Department of Economic Research for the American Federation of Labor and Congress of Industrial Organizations.

Certainly no more codes should be completed and brought to the Congress for approval until there is some understanding of the results of the massive agreements reached less than three years ago. It is time to weigh whether the codes have resulted in what was promised when they were adopted by the Congress. If the codes do not interpret GATT rules in a way that is fair and beneficial, more codes will only add to that inequity.

Certainly the U.S. trade patterns fail to show benefits: while the export-import balance appears only slightly worse in the past year, the composition has changed.

While imports of manufactured goods rose 13 percent in 1981, exports of manufactured goods were up only 7 percent. There has been inadequate attention to the composition of exports. The dollar value of exports does not tell the full story in terms of jobs and products. For example, the U.S. exports much raw material involving relatively little labor instead of manufactured goods and processed foods which require considerable labor input.

The AFL-CIO Convention in November 1981 stated:

> The multilateral trade codes adopted in 1979 require constant monitoring and the enforcement of U.S. rights. Only the negotiated provisions should be enforced, particularly in the area of government procurement, where many U.S. agencies, state and local governments were specifically exempted from the requirements of the codes.

But such monitoring has not taken place. Nor has there been enforcement of U.S. rights.

In each code, it seems there is a Catch 22 that apparently can protect foreign countries which interfere with U.S. trade rights, while the U.S. producer and worker group are unfairly disadvantaged.

The implementation of the subsidies code has raised major problems, some of which we have already detailed for this subcommittee. The code states that subsidies on manufactured exports are a violation of GATT. But the definition of subsidies and the implementation have not resolved the problems created by subsidized trade.

One of the major concessions during the 5 years of negotiations of the MTN was the demand by our trading partners—principally the European Communities—for an injury test in this subsidies code. The U.S. agreed to change its law that required a countervailing duty on imports which had been subsidized. The U.S. changed its law in 1979. When the steel industry sought relief in 1979 under the code, it was charged with protectionism, and the U.S. law was not carried out. Now three years later, subsidized steel products are entering the U.S. at an even greater rate and while the complex procedures are now underway, no relief has been granted.

More recently, promises to the Congress on subsidized imports from developing countries have been broken. Countries are allowed an injury test by the U.S. government even if they do not agree to abide by the code or to phase out their subsidies.

The posture of the U.S. as an inept negotiator, turning industry after industry over to foreign producers who ship subsidized exports to the U.S. has a devastating effect on American firms and workers whose production and jobs are lost as a result.

The current state of affairs has nothing to do with free trade or with sensible foreign relations. Instead, each country seeks to be exempted from any obligations because other countries have been excused. But the U.S. is held to GATT obligations as if fixed in concrete. That is a one-way street.

A similar one-way street exists for the government procurement code.

The government procurement code was heralded, for example, as the promise of $80 billion in U.S. exports. Instead, the details of the code which were carefully negotiated are virtually unknown and not enforced. Massive U.S. exports have not developed, and massive U.S. imports have been encouraged.

The code specifically does not apply to state and local governments in any country. But members of two administrations now have advised the states that it would be a violation of the "spirit of the code" to have Buy American legislation. Thus the code has been used to promote U.S. imports—not to promote U.S. exports.

A key negotiation for implementation of the code with Japan was an agreement on telecommunications. But after three years of trying to get contracts with Japan's Nippon Telephone and Telegraph Company (NTT), the only contract is one by Motorola for 500 pocket bells (*Business Week,* December 1981). A later report indicated that only 100 could be sold now. The rest had to be tested or go through some other procedure. Thus a vast telecommunications market is effectively closed to U.S. exporters, while U.S. orders for virtually every type of government purchase are still granted to foreign bidders at the expense of U.S. producers.

Full reporting on government procurement is overdue. Vague reference to the "codes" or to "international obligations" give no clear answers about what the codes mean or what the U.S. obligations actually are.

The aircraft code reduced U.S. tariffs on aircraft and many aircraft parts to zero immediately. But other nations have continued to subsidize their aircraft production and it is not clear whether their tariffs have been reduced in the same way.

The licensing code should be reviewed in detail. The MTN included a code to determine what the rules should be for licensing imports—a practice many nations follow. This is not a free trade practice. The requirement for a license in order to import amounts to a restraint on trade, however it is practiced. It restrains U.S. exports. But other countries would only agree to sign a code on certain rules about how licensing would be conducted, not on ways to abolish licensing. Unless the other nations can show that they have lived up to this code, there should be U.S. action to retaliate.

Other codes on customs valuation, dairy arrangements, and bovine meat arrangements and the Group "Framework" had all been agreed upon by April, 1979, three years ago. It is time for a review of what has happened to each in detail and what the future prospects are for developing reciprocal trade. Instead there seems to be little monitoring and no clear information about all of these agreements.

Until such reviews are satisfactorily resolved, no new codes should be completed.

The code on "safeguards," which was not finished in 1979, could be a deterrent to effective action under the GATT rule that already exists for "safeguards" to protect industries that are suffering from the assault of harmful imports during this downturn. Article XIX of the General Agreement on Tariffs and Trade allows each GATT member to take temporary action to restrain imports that are threatening to injure a domestic industry. America needs "safeguard" action now. A new code is not needed. But enforcement of existing U.S. law is needed. Instead, the interpretation of U.S. law makes proof of injury even more burdensome than Article XIX requires. The result: no help when industries need it.

No injured industry has ever achieved the relief it sought under Section 201, which is the "safeguards" section of the U.S. law. Since the 1974 Trade Act was passed, only 9 of 45 cases have received any restraint on imports. The ITC usually recommends less than industry seeks—be it quotas or tariffs or tariff quotas—and the President either ignores the International Trade Commission's recommendation altogether or grants less than it calls for.

Specialty steel, color TV, shoes, industrial fasteners—nuts, bolts and screws—are examples of the industries where relief has been phased out or phased down.

These are just a few examples of major industries that are affected. Small producers of parts essential to these industries usually get no relief at all.

U.S. basic industries, already in need of revitalization, have been severely injured by the impact of expanded imports on top of the recession. Steel has suffered import penetration of about 20–25 percent of the U.S. market since last August. Auto imports in 1981 increased their share of a falling market to 31 percent in January. Apparel imports were over 33 percent of the market. Machinery and machinery parts imports caused new concern in a weakened market. With import pressure mounting, virtually every type of manufacturing and related services felt the brunt of lost orders both at home and abroad.

Under current procedures, the cost, the data requirements and the complex legalisms are so difficult to overcome that injured industries and groups of workers cannot afford to bring actions for relief from inrushes of imports or dumping. This is not fair trade policy. This policy of inaction leads to more unfair trade. The law should be enforced, improved, and emergency procedures established to prevent the outrush of key industries, especially during this recessionary downturn.

Meanwhile, foreign nations retain their trade barriers, make temporary and permanent provisions for new barriers to trade and ignore Article XIX. The Europeans have restraint agreements on Japanese steel, autos, etc. The U.K. has announced it will act to curb flooding imports. The Japanese have raised their commodity tax on autos and protected their aluminum industry.

A vague, new code on safeguards to weaken these options would worsen already unfair conditions. America does not need a new code. It needs to act to save its industries.

The AFL-CIO supports efforts to help U.S. service industries attain access to foreign markets in specific cases and to deal with specific problems involved. But the diverse industries in services do not add up to a whole "sector" that can be discussed in an entirety in global negotiations. Neither the U.S. nor its trading partners has done enough homework to launch a global negotiation by starting "working parties," to list trade barriers in services at the next GATT Ministerial meeting in November.

Services represent a huge combination of issues too long overlooked in trade policy. For U.S. banks, shipping companies, airlines, broadcasting, advertising, insurance and many other types of firms, the policy issues seem clear: discrimination against their foreign expansion calls for action by the U.S. government. But a clear definition of the "sector" is not available anywhere.

For many years, AFL-CIO policies have also called attention to effects at home. Seven out of ten U.S. jobs are now in "services." American seamen were the first to experience the export of service jobs after World War II. The AFL-CIO does not want to see jobs in services—now the majority of jobs in the U.S.—traded away as manufacturing jobs have been.

A commitment to overall negotiations in services, therefore, should await more specific solutions through bilateral negotiations and action to solve American service problems in trade—both at home and abroad. While trade laws already provide authority to act and negotiate on services, the authority has not been used to get enough experience or solve enough real problems to give a realistic basis for overall negotiations. To make America wait for another five years for the hope of global negotiations—whatever they may mean—will assure that specific problems in specific service sectors will continue to get inadequate attention. Problems for airlines, shipping companies, credit card companies, etc., need solutions—not global negotiations.

Immigration policy is an integral element when services are discussed in distinction to when products are negotiated. But there is no recognition of this problem in the vague talk about services negotiations.

Negotiations involve concessions, but concessions that would be considered by service negotiators have been virtually ignored. Personal privacy, for example, is an issue in terms of "free trade in data transmission" abroad. Do we want to forfeit personal privacy in the U.S. to get help for data transmission from abroad? A code won't solve this. The issue of requiring that nationals perform certain jobs is a major complaint of the U.S. service industries about "barriers" they face abroad. Does the U.S. want to give up U.S. standards for lawyers, doctors, accountants, nurses, electricians, etc? Services involve human beings. They are not tradable digits.

The United States cannot afford to urge all the rest of the nations to come to the table to negotiate by proclaiming that the U.S. has a trade surplus in services. But the dollar volume of the "service" account is heralded as a surplus because the current account is in surplus from dividends on foreign investment or because the statistics report profits of U.S. industries (not necessarily returned to the U.S.) as a huge "surplus." That gives the U.S. a weak bargaining leverage and diverts attention from, and delays or prohibits action on, specific current problems.

Other deficiencies of data in the service sector also make global negotiations unrealistic. The statistical reporting of employment is different nationally and internationally. The "services" now being discussed are not necessarily "services" in U.S. employment statistics. Construction employment is considered a set of "goods production" industries in the U.S. nationally but is considered "services" internationally.

There has been no attention to the kinds of employment already lost or jobs that will be gained by expanded services internationally. Nor has there been any recognition that dollar volume of service transactions does not necessarily imply a proportionate relationship to gains in employment. It may in fact be negative. Particularly in high technology industries, the transfer of jobs to other countries may accompany "sales" of services.

The United States should, therefore, go to the ministerial meeting to examine how the GATT agreements are working and with the intention to assure the reciprocity that is implicit in the GATT and stated in U.S.

law. New codes and new issues should await specific efforts and specific actions to solve current problems.

The U.S. needs to place temporary restrictions on harmful imports during this recession. It needs to vigorously enforce the reciprocity provisions of the Trade Act. The fashioning of new remedies to assure a strong and diversified U.S. industrial structure is essential for America's well-being.

8. The GATT Ministerial: A Postmortem

JEFFREY J. SCHOTT

The General Agreement on Tariffs and Trade (GATT) will mark its 35th anniversary in 1983. Never before has its discipline over world trade been more needed, yet never before has it been in such imminent danger of collapse. Record unemployment and stagnating growth in the United States and Europe threaten to unleash a torrent of protectionist measures to safeguard domestic industries and jobs against foreign competition. The global recession has already had a dramatic impact on world trade, which has declined in terms of both value and volume in 1981 and 1982.

Under these circumstances, it is noteworthy that ministers from the world's leading trading nations survived five harrowing days and nights of negotiations in Geneva in November 1982 and produced an agreement that, at least temporarily, has slowed the global drift towards protectionism. On that basis, many ministers, including U.S. Trade Representative William Brock, hailed the ministerial results as a clear, albeit modest, step forward for free trade and the GATT.

Yet if one looks closely at what was achieved and asks whether the meeting either helped resolve any existing trade problems or will have any significant impact on the way governments respond to trade problems in the future, the results appear far more modest. Indeed, the Ministerial gave no clue as to what governments will do during the next few years to respond to the growing demands for protectionism. As will be seen in the following section, the ministerial declaration

Jeffrey J. Schott is a Senior Associate of the Carnegie Endowment for International Peace.

contains little more than a reaffirmation of the *status quo* of international trade relations, and, as such, fails to arrest the increasing erosion of confidence in the world trading system.

MINISTERIAL DECLARATION

Trade agreements and international communiques are often written in a special diplomatic code, and the declaration issued at the close of the GATT Ministerial was no exception. The following is a rough translation of the "code-words" used in the declaration to portray the commitments entered into on the key trade issues dealt with by the ministers.

1. *"Cease-fire" on protectionism.* Prior to the Ministerial, there were high hopes that countries would agree to a call for a "cease-fire" before protectionist skirmishes broke into open trade warfare. It was not to be. The language agreed to is no more than a pious recitation of national commitments to GATT principles. All the declaration commits ministers to do is "to make determined efforts"—which is one step down from a hard commitment—to avoid actions which specifically violate GATT rules or in other ways distort trade flows.

The experience since the Ministerial demonstrates that the "cease-fire" commitment has had little discernible impact on national trade policies. The proof of the pudding is in the eating:

The French ignored the ministerial declaration (and the GATT) by discouraging imports of Japanese video-tape recorders (VTRs), insisting that they enter France through a tiny and remote customs house in Poitiers. Their sin was subsequently compounded by the European Community (EC), which pressed Japan to agree "voluntarily" to restrict sales of both VTRs and color TVs throughout Europe.

The United States has cajoled the Japanese into extending their voluntary export restraints (VERs) on U.S. auto shipments for a third year.

Both the United States and the EC have tightened their already restrictive bilateral textile quotas imposed on developing country (LDC) exporters.

The declaration has failed to stop the United States and the EC from firing the first shots (via subsidized wheat flour sales to Egypt and China respectively) in a growing agricultural trade war.

Some will argue that these actions do not violate the letter and law of the GATT. Unfortunately, most trade problems today involve measures whose status under GATT and whose impact on trade is in dispute. For example, the United States argues that VERs on autos are consistent with GATT safeguard rules; the EC likewise justifies its ongoing steel and auto import restraints, and argues that its much maligned agricultural policies actually facilitate trade. None of these issues is as clear-cut as the imposing countries maintain, however. They fall into a gray area where there is no common interpretation of GATT obligations. These differences were glossed over in the text of the ministerial declaration, precisely because countries were not willing to change their policies and firmly agree *not* to impose new barriers to trade.

2. *Safeguards.* The failure of ministers to commit themselves to a cease-fire on protectionist measures implies in turn a less than full commitment to the development of new GATT rules on safeguards (which are measures permitted under GATT for the temporary protection of domestic industries seriously threatened or injured by import competition). One must question how serious countries are in negotiating the terms of a new GATT safeguards system when they are unwilling to make any changes in their existing policies towards protectionism.

In the declaration, ministers called for the negotiation in 1983 of a "comprehensive understanding" on safeguards. There is nothing new in this language that hasn't appeared in previous abortive attempts in the GATT to draw up an agreement on this subject. Indeed the negotiating charge is practically identical to the terms of reference developed at the *start* of the Tokyo Round talks in 1975.

Two major issues prevented an agreement on safeguards during the Tokyo Round: (a) the types of measures that would be covered under the pact; and (b) whether countries could apply safeguard actions selectively (that is, *not* on a most favored nation or MFN basis). Differences over these issues were sidestepped in the ministerial declaration, which called for the understanding "to be based on the principles of the General Agreement." For the Europeans, this meant that the accord would *not* apply to inter-industry agreements and voluntary export restraints; for the LDCs, however, the language implied a rejection of selectivity (which the EC has insisted on in order to restrict imports from advanced LDCs without having to hit trade from all sources, that is, on a MFN basis). These are the same positions that led to the breakdown of the Tokyo Round negotiations.

In short, the Ministerial made no progress in bridging the gap between countries in this area. Indeed, an agreement has become even less likely since the Ministerial was held, because the United States has abandoned its efforts to seek an understanding between the EC and the LDCs (through a system of "consensual selectivity") and has again sided with the LDCs against the selective application of safeguards. As one GATT purist noted, 1983 will mark the 30th anniversary of attempts to negotiate GATT rules on safeguards; 1984 will most likely mark the 31st anniversary.

3. *Trade in services.* In planning for the Ministerial, the United States placed the highest priority on initiating a work program on services in the GATT. U.S. Trade Ambassador Brock called barriers to trade in services "perhaps the most important of the emerging trade issues" for the 1980s. In spite of U.S. efforts, however, ministers gave short shrift to a U.S. proposal on services.

In essence, nothing substantive was agreed to on services except that the subject would be on the agenda of the next GATT meeting in 1984. All the text does is to "invite" countries to study their trade in services and to share such work with other GATT members. The GATT Secretariat is limited to a clearinghouse role—compiling and distributing the information received.

In the words of one Geneva delegate, the language on services is "the nearest thing possible to a vacuum." No one is committed to doing anything except coming back in 1984 and restarting the debate over whether the GATT should cover services trade. Indeed, the explicit rejection of the U.S. proposal that would have had the GATT Secretariat analyze information on services trade received from individual countries and from other international organizations (such as the Organization for Economic Cooperation and Development and the United Nations Conference on Trade and Development) really sets out a *negative mandate* that compels the GATT to avoid any formal efforts in this area.

4. *Dispute settlement.* If the decision of the ministers is fully implemented, there will be some minor, yet useful, procedural improvements in the adjudication of GATT disputes. The declaration spells out in surprising detail procedural reforms to facilitate dispute settlement procedures. Most noteworthy are calls for (a) the greater use of trade experts outside of Geneva to sit on GATT panels; (b) a greater role for the GATT Secretariat in the analysis of the facts and legal points at issue in disputes; and (c) a commitment by parties to a dispute not to block the GATT consensus needed to approve the terms of a settlement. (In the past, disputes have dragged on for years just because the "guilty" country refused to allow GATT to condemn its practice.)

However, here again the caveat "this does not prejudice the provisions. . . in the General Agreement" has been added to undercut the ministerial commitment. Clearly, GATT provisions have precedence over ministerial declarations. The fact that some delegations (read the EC) insisted on the inclusion of such references indicates that they believe the language has no real meaning and that they will have no compunction about backing away from these commitments if it suits their interests in a particular case.

5. *Agricultural subsidies.* The Ministerial achieved about all that could realistically have been expected in regard to agricultural trade problems: it commissioned a new committee on agriculture to study agricultural

trade "in light of the objectives, principles and relevant provisions of the General Agreement." This is weak tea indeed when one considers that it is the interpretation of those very principles and provisions that is at the heart of most of the agricultural trade disputes. Nonetheless, it is significant that there will be a reexamination of those rules—which in itself implies the possibility of changes in the consensual interpretation of GATT obligations relating to all aspects of national agricultural programs, including the trade effects of price support and export subsidies.

What the meeting did not do was to make any headway towards resolving the bitter trade disputes between the United States and the EC. The main cause of these disputes has been the export subsidies granted to European farmers (under the EC's common agricultural policy, or CAP) which allow them to reduce their export prices down to world market levels. Because of these subsidies, EC exports have taken a growing share of world markets in such products as wheat flour and sugar. The United States has been concerned not only about lost export markets in third countries, but also about the dampening effect these subsidized goods have had on world prices—and, in turn, on farm prices and incomes in the United States.

The Ministerial was not the place to try to resolve this thorny issue. Bilateral meetings in Brussels had already been scheduled for early December 1982 to take up agricultural trade problems. However, domestic political pressures in the United States (and the presence on the U.S. delegation of several senators and congressmen from farm states) forced the United States to put forward the unrealistic demand that the EC phase out its agricultural export subsidies within five years. All this did was to exacerbate bilateral tensions and to sour the negotiating climate for the meeting in general.

There really was no need for this. The EC will have to make changes in the CAP anyway in the next few years because of budgetary constraints resulting from the pending accession of Spain and Portugal. The strident U.S. position merely forced the EC to embrace the protectionist views of the French and to lead them to issue a post-ministerial clarification, which emphasized that the EC had *not* made any "commitment to any new negotiation or obligation in relation to agricultural products."

6. *North-South issues.* A great deal of space was devoted to the need to assist developing countries, but none of the commitments was nearly as significant for LDC trade as what was done or not done in general on the issues of safeguards and textiles. Safeguards were discussed above. On textiles, the ministers commissioned a study to seek, in effect, ways to preempt a blow-up of the multi-fiber arrangement (MFA)—such as almost occurred in December 1981—when the MFA comes up for renewal at the end of 1986. At the insistence of the LDCs, prominent

attention was given to the need eventually to apply GATT obligations to trade in textiles in place of the more restrictive terms of the MFA. The GATT Committee on Trade and Development was also asked to study ways to increase North-South trade, in particular through improvements in GSP (Generalized System of Preferences) for products exported by the least-developed countries.

THE GATT IN 1983*

The Ministerial is likely to have a negative effect on the work of the GATT in the coming year. The failure of ministers to bite the bullet and take the politically difficult steps needed to stem the protectionist tide has set an unfortunate precedent. Geneva trade delegates will find it extremely difficult to do more than what was agreed to by their ministers; as a result, the GATT will be under further strains and will find it harder and harder to deal with current trade problems.

What this all means is that 1983 will be a year of turmoil for world trade. As unemployment in the United States and Europe soars past the 30 million mark, governments will continue to bend to protectionist pressures. Without the benefit of new international trade rules and agreements to buffer governments against protectionist pressures, it is likely that new trade restrictions will proliferate in blatant disregard of GATT obligations.

Nothing done by the ministers in any way prepares the GATT for this forthcoming attack. Indeed, it would be a mistake even to regard the ministerial declaration as a guide for what will and will not be done in the GATT over the next two years. It is likely that during 1983 the GATT work program will be substantially reshaped to meet some of the key demands of the United States and the EC that were either overlooked or unfulfilled during the Ministerial.

In particular, GATT members will have to decide on (1) the specific terms of reference for the new studies commissioned by the ministers, and (2) the allocation of budgetary resources for those projects. Moreover, issues such as services and high technology trade will undoubtedly come up again in the GATT Council. So will some of the dicey agricultural subsidy issues, as a result of the reports of the expert panels ruling on the U.S.-EC trade disputes on wheat flour and pasta. In addition, preparations for UNCTAD VI in June in Belgrade will spur a reevaluation of the meager proposals endorsed by ministers to deal

* Editor's note: This section has been included even though 1983 did not turn out to be a devastatingly bad year for GATT and world trade, as Schott expected, nor did 1984 bring ominous events. In fact, the tenth annual summit meeting of major western leaders, held in London in June 1984, yielded some promising results. President Reagan and Japanese Prime Minister Nakasone pushed for a new round of multilateral trade negotiations beginning in 1986, however, the Europeans were cool to the idea.

with the complex of North-South trade problems. These developments will be the source of continued friction in the GATT, both between the United States and the EC and between developed and developing countries.

LESSONS OF THE MINISTERIAL

Are there any lessons to be learned from the Ministerial? Reviewing the damage, I humbly offer the following suggestions to trade ministers:

1. *Don't expect too much from the GATT* until you are prepared to take the necessary steps *at home* to renounce protectionism. Inflated expectations can only damage the credibility both of the GATT as an institution and of the free trade principles it represents.
2. *Don't expect too much from the EC.* While in statistical terms it is the world's largest trading bloc, it does not have an integrated trade policy and usually is forced to represent the position of its most protectionist member in global trade talks. U.S.–EC agricultural trade problems therefore need to be handled through bilateral channels.
3. *Do expect more—in fact insist on it—from the Japanese.* Japan cannot be allowed to remain a passive participant in the management of the world trading system.

Let me explain these points in a little more detail:

1. The United States had inflated expectations for both a series of new trade initiatives on services, trade-related investment, and high technology trade, and for dramatic changes in European agricultural policies. The latter were particularly damaging to the GATT. Domestic political pressures forced the United States to stress agricultural issues at the expense of more realistic and attainable objectives. Many senators and representatives from farm states actually attended the meeting to ensure that their interest would be forcefully advanced. Congressional presence on the delegation served only to polarize positions on agriculture and prevent accommodation, however. This played into the hands of the French, who were the most ardent opponents within the EC of efforts to reform the CAP.

The GATT is not the kind of vehicle that can be used to force political changes in other countries of the magnitude required to resolve U.S.–EC agricultural trade disputes. As a consequence, when the U.S. effort failed, the result was a growing skepticism—particularly in the U.S. Congress—over the efficacy of GATT rules and procedures. Such feelings could make it increasingly difficult to forestall new protectionist legislation in the 98th Congress. A U.S. local content bill for autos is the most obvious and dangerous possibility of things to come.

To his credit, Ambassador Brock readily admitted the dangers of protectionism (in fact, he called the local content bill the worst trade bill in fifty years). However, he also threatened Congressional revenge if other countries didn't support the U.S. initiatives. Unfortunately, this sent a clear signal that—as was the case with sanctions—the United States was willing to shoot itself in the foot to show its resolve in the short run. However, it was also clear that the United States would want to avoid such actions over the medium and long term—and thus they would be short-lived. The threats were hollow because other governments knew the United States still held the ultimate responsibility for the maintenance of an open world trading system.

2. The Ministerial underscored the feebleness of EC trade policy. While that policy is nominally set in Brussels by the EC Commission, the real power still rests in national capitals. The lack of harmonization of tax and other policies among the EC member states means that national policies predominate—Commission trade policy is usually a least common denominator of various national policies that paper over often significant differences in the trade perspectives of member states. Consider the problems the U.S. executive branch has with one Congress, and multiply it ten times: that provides a fair picture of how hard it is to implement trade policy in the EC. As such, EC trade policy does not have a singular focus or direction—and is often held hostage, as it was during the Ministerial, to the views of its most extreme member (in this case, the French).

3. The Japanese also deserve some share of the blame—not for what they did, but for what they did not do. The Ministerial was noteworthy for the absence of attacks against Japan. Indeed, it was the only trade meeting in recent memory where Japan was not taken to task for failing to open its domestic market to imports. As such, the Japanese were content to play possum and not stir up the waters.

The Japanese tactic was myopic and harmful to their long-term trade interests. Japan depends on trade for essential energy resources and food supplies. It needs to have access to foreign markets for its manufactured exports in order to pay for those imports. Without the GATT to buttress the global defense against protectionism, those markets are in jeopardy. Indeed, the Japanese know that they would have the most to lose if the GATT system fell into disuse or disintegrated into regional trading blocs.

Instead of asserting some leadership in support of initiatives to strengthen the GATT, however, the Japanese stayed quiet and let the meeting (and the GATT) drift aimlessly towards its denouement. This was odd. The trade problems that Japan faces with both the United States and Europe will not soon diminish. Inaction, however, will undermine efforts to resolve them through multilateral means (via the GATT) and will lead to more abrasive bilateral confrontations. As one of the world's leading trading nations, Japan will have to contribute more to the maintenance of the GATT system and take more responsibility for multilateral solutions to world trade problems, many of which are laid—rightly or wrongly—on its doorstep.

EROSION OF CONFIDENCE

Ministers left Geneva with a sense of accomplishment in the face of very trying circumstances, but those from the major trading countries also left with a strong sense of frustration and a feeling that trade problems need to be dealt with in a more pragmatic fashion and on a bilateral basis. In particular, the failure of the major trading nations to take the politically difficult steps to renounce protectionist policies was an especially telling blow to the GATT as an institution. As such, the Ministerial—for all its rhetoric about free trade principles and strengthening the GATT—dealt a heavy blow to multilateral discipline over trade, and thus contributed to the further erosion of confidence in the GATT.

9. The 1980s: Twilight of the Open Trading System?

C. MICHAEL AHO and THOMAS O. BAYARD

There will be almost unprecedented economic and political strains on the open international trading system in the 1980s.[1] If these large and growing problems are not resolved, they will eventually threaten the credibility and viability of the entire system. This prospect is certainly not historically unprecedented. The periodic crises which have beset the international trading system have frequently provoked warning of its impending collapse. In retrospect, these prophesies of doom were greatly exaggerated. The system has shown itself to be remarkably resiliant and healthy.

Why, then, is there reason to believe that the international trading system is any less stable and viable now, or in the near future, than it

C. Michael Aho and Thomas O. Bayard are on the staff of the Office of International Economic Affairs, United States Department of Labor, as Director and International Economist, respectively.

was in the past? Our diagnosis is that there are a number of long-run economic and political trends which, combined with a continuation of current economic problems and serious policy conflicts in and among the major industrialised countries, *could* lead to the gradual deterioration and ultimate collapse of the system—a process in some ways similar to the decline and fall of the system in the 1930s.[2]

Demographic changes, technological advances and increasing international competition will require significant adjustments in the product and factor markets of the major industrialised countries in this decade. In large part, these changes will be dictated by internal conditions in individual countries, but, given the linkages between national economies, pressures to adjust will be transmitted fairly quickly across countries through trade, technology and financial flows. But these necessary adjustments may prove difficult, or altogether impossible, in some countries, especially in the context of the current recession.

In many countries, especially those in Western Europe, certain social institutions and laws tend to reduce economic flexibility and adaptability. Efficient adjustment to long-run changes may require that these institutional rigidities be relaxed. The current recession, however, has increased the political pressures (and perhaps the short-run political pay-offs) for governments to attempt to protect and expand employment by tightening job-security laws, increasing income-maintenance and subsidy programmes and trade interventions.

At the same time that long-run economic trends require that rigidities be reduced and adjustment be facilitated, short-run economic conditions and political considerations may lead to the opposite policy response. Moreover, the use of distortionary short-run palliatives for current unemployment problems has delayed the adjustments required by long-run trends and, too, reinforced existing pressures to protect and insulate various social groups from internal and external economic changes. Indeed, many of the current obstacles to adjustment may be the cumulative result of the frequent use of ostensibly short-run or temporary distortionary policies. The combined impact of past interventions which delayed needed adjustments and prospective structural changes makes it likely that adjustment issues will become paramount in the 1980s.

The fundamental question is this: given the conflict between the need to adjust and demands to erect barriers to adjustment, how will governments respond? Will government policy be directed towards facilitating adjustment or will it attempt to resist the required changes? If the policy response is to attempt to postpone or avoid the frequently painful process of adjustment, the prospects are for intensified protectionism and conflict in the international trading system.

The long-run trends and the potential impact of the current worldwide recession on growth and structural adjustment are discussed in the next section. Then, these historical trends and current problems are related to current, and possible future, policy conflicts and debates within and among the industrialised countries. The discussion is speculative, at best, but in our opinion it tends to lead to the conclusion that, if left unchecked and unresolved, these problems and conflicts will place the international trading system in severe jeopardy before the end of this decade. The article concludes with policy options to avert the growing threat to the system.

SOURCES OF CONFLICT IN THE INTERNATIONAL TRADING SYSTEM

In this section we discuss how long-run trends, combined with the current recession, are likely to result in conflicts in the international trading system.

Secular Trends

There is widespread agreement that a significant structural shift occurred in the major industrialised countries in the last ten years. Although the precise timing of the shift is debated, 1973 is a reasonable break point. In the countries of the Organisation for Economic Cooperation and Development (OECD), average annual productivity growth (gross domestic product [GDP] per person employed) fell from 4 percent in the years between 1960 and 1973 to about 1.7 percent between 1973 and 1980, real GDP growth declined from 5 percent to about 2.6 percent, the rate of increase in consumer prices rose from 4 percent to over 10 percent and the unemployment rate rose from 3 percent to over 5 percent. OECD data and projections for 1981–83 indicate a continuation and possible worsening of this situation.[3]

No single factor can fully explain the shift to slower growth and higher inflation rates. It is likely that the slowdown in the 1970s was in part the culmination of various economic and social trends and government policies. In what follows, recent important trends and policies and their implications for future economic growth and adjustment are discussed. The major theme is that the conflict between the need for economic adjustment and obstacles to adjustment will continue and may, perhaps, intensify.

1. Demographic Trends. While it is difficult to summarise demographic changes in the industrialised countries without simultaneously obscuring important differences, several general trends which may cause labour-market frictions or further government interventions in these markets are apparent. The baby boom after World War II has resulted in a large increase in the number of young people in the labour force in most OECD countries. At the same time, female participation rates have increased.[4] These young and female entrants generally have lower skill levels, less employment stability and higher unemployment rates than prime-age male workers.

Although these demographic trends are not the only, or even the most important, cause of high and rising unemployment, they contribute to the problem in a number of ways. The increase in the supply of relatively unskilled labour occurs at a time when changes in the industrial composition of gross national product (GNP) have increased the demand for skilled labour. In addition, although young people are probably the most geographically mobile of all demographic groups, women, especially those who are married, are relatively immobile. Both of these factors tend to increase labour-market frictions and the need for price and quantity adjustments in labour markets, especially in a time of slow overall economic growth.

High and rising unemployment rates for young people and women pose a number of policy problems for governments, which are under pressure both to reduce unemployment rates for these groups over time and to reduce the costs of unemployment in the short run. There are trade-offs in the equity and efficiency implications of these goals.

Attempts to reduce the private costs of unemployment by increasing unemployment-insurance coverage for these groups and raising benefit levels and the maximum duration of benefits may act to increase both participation rates and the duration of unemployment. Attempts to target these groups with special employment or training subsidies may help to reduce, at least temporarily, their unemployment problems, but these gains may come at the expense of higher unemployment for non-targeted groups, particularly during periods of slow economic growth. Attempts to preserve employment through job-security laws may reduce lay-offs during downswings, but, by imposing fixed costs on firms, they also tend to reduce gains in employment during upswings as well as the average level of employment over the entire business cycle.

To varying degrees, women, young people and temporary immigrant guest workers have played a role as buffers over the business cycle. Their entry into labour markets during upswings helped to facilitate expanded production. During downswings they tended to leave the labour force, or return home in the case of immigrants, so reducing measured unemployment rates. The steady growth of labour-market interventions such as unemployment insurace and job-security laws and the somewhat slower extension of civil rights protection to temporary immigrants (especially in Western Europe), however, may have reduced the flexibility of labour markets over the business cycle. The potential problem with labour-market interventions of this sort is that, while they are desirable on equity or political grounds, they can have negative implications for the longer-run efficiency of labour-market adjustment.[5]

2. *Industrial Convergence.* There appears to have been convergence in the industrial structures and underlying resource endowments of the major industrialised countries in recent years. These changes in structure may portend slower economic growth in the foreseeable future, an increased emphasis on distributional questions and growing conflict over trade policies.

In all the industrialised countries, the shares of agriculture, mining and manufacturing in total GNP have declined, while the share of the services sector (including government services) has increased. Because it emerged from World War II with a large modern industrial base, the United States has tended to precede the other industrialised economies in this 'maturation' process. The services sector now accounts for roughly 70 percent of GNP in the United States. The proportion of GNP devoted to services is generally lower in the other OECD countries, but it is growing.

The structural shift to services may imply a long-run decline in growth rates for the mature industrialised countries.[6] Historically, productivity growth in the services sector has been slower than in manufacturing and agriculture, in part due to the labour-intensive nature of many service industries and the lesser availability of large economies of scale. In the absence of increased capital accumulation or continuous technological progress (and the so-called micro-electronic revolution may be the basis for such progress), growth in the services sector relative to the goods-producing sector will tend to reduce the underlying economy-wide rate of growth. If this hypothesis is correct, it suggests that the industrialised countries will experience difficulties in maintaining historical growth rates as their economies mature.

The shift to the services sector also has important distributional implications. If wage increases are tied to productivity growth, wages in the services sector will tend to fall relative to those in manufacturing. Attempts to maintain parity in wage increases across sectors could impose significant cost increases for services with low price and high income elasticities of demand, such as education, health and the array of government services. Combined with slow overall economic growth, declining relative wages in the services sector may increase pressures for governments to intervene in labour markets to improve distributional equity, but it is likely to be at the expense of some allocative efficiency.

The other aspect of industrial convergence is that overall factor proportions between the industrialised countries are becoming increasingly similar. Rapid capital accumulation, both physical and human, and transfer of technology between the industrialised countries have narrowed the traditional Heckscher-Ohlin basis for comparative advantage.

The share of the United States in total world capital declined from 53 percent in 1958 to 32 percent in 1975. Japan's share rose from 4 percent to 15 percent in the same period and West Germany's share rose from 6 percent to 11 percent. In 1958 the ratio of capital to labour in the United States was eight times that in Japan and three times that in West Germany. By 1975 the ratio in the United States was only slightly higher than in Japan and somewhat lower than in West Germany.[7] Differences in relative wages in manufacturing have also declined, but not as rapidly.[8]

As differences in relative factor endowments and costs have declined, so has the traditional basis for comparative advantage in trade among the industrialised countries. If industrial structures and resource endowments are converging, the unit gains from trade among developed countries will tend to decline. Correspondingly, in a multi-commodity world of generally constant returns, small changes in cost conditions can potentially cause large shifts in trade, sectoral production and employment.[9]

The convergence of industrial structures may help to explain the rapid growth in intra-industry trade (that is, trade using similar factor proportions and technology) among the industrialised countries. Some observers have argued that post-war successes in trade liberalisation have occurred precisely because intra-industry trade allowed domestic industries to internalise both the costs and liberalisation, with relatively small shifts in production, employment or income distribution across industries.[10]

As will be discussed in more detail later, industrial convergence may have important implications for both trade liberalisation in the future and for conflicts over trade policy. The gist of the argument is that growing similarity in industrial cost structures among the industrialised countries and slower overall growth will increase the need to adjust output and employment to relatively small changes in costs and prices abroad. Correspondingly, ostensibly 'domestic' economic policies which change costs and prices of internationally traded goods will fall increasingly under the heading of trade policy.[11] Finally, the growing use of non-tariff interventions will make it increasingly difficult to continue to liberalise intra-industry trade in the future.

3. Competition from Newly Industrialising Countries. All the OECD countries are experiencing increased competition in established industries from the newly industrialising countries. In 1970 only 5 percent of OECD manufactured imports came from developing countries. By 1980 the share had risen to almost 11 percent. Although much of the increase has been concentrated in certain politically sensitive industries such as textiles and footwear, this competition can be expected to increase and spread to other industries during the 1980s.

The newly industrialising countries also represent some of the fastest growing markets in the world today. In spite of initial pessimism about their ability to cope with the two oil crises, these advanced developing countries have continued to grow and their markets provide expanding opportunities for trade and investment.

The newly industrialising countries will present major challenges and opportunities in this decade. The rapid increase in manufactured imports from the newly industrialising countries will add to existing pressures to adjust output and employment in traditional labour-intensive industries.[12] The need to adjust will broaden and intensify as the newly industrialising countries of today move up the technological ladder into new products and, too, as other newly industrialising countries emerge.

Growth in the newly industrialising countries can also provide increased opportunities for OECD exports and investment. By contrast to the predominantly intra-industry nature of trade among the industrialised countries, trade between the industrialised and developing countries is largely inter-industry—the industrialised countries export capital goods and import consumer goods and intermediate inputs. A reallocation of resources in the industrialised countries away from traditional labour-intensive consumer goods and towards skill-intensive capital goods would increase productivity growth in both groups of countries.[13] In the 1970s OECD exports to the newly industrialising countries grew at roughly the same rate as intra-OECD trade and could expand even more rapidly if the newly industrialising countries assume their rights and responsibilities as fully-fledged participants in the international trading system *and* if the industrialised countries accept the necessity for structural adjustment in traditional industries.

4. Technological Change. The rate of technological change since World War II has been rapid and the benefits of new technology developed in one country have quickly diffused through trade, investment and technology flows to the other partners in the international trading system. It is almost impossible to predict the rate of technological change; and it is correspondingly difficult to assess its potential impact. Our discussion focusses on three aspects of technology. Two of these have relatively clear-cut implications for the near future: the fact that the other major trading countries are catching up with the technological levels of the United States and the growing importance of technology in international trade. The third aspect is the effects of the introduction of the new technologies on adjustment and employment.

There are a number of oblique indicators that the technological preeminance of the United States is eroding.[14] Expenditures on research and development as a share of GNP have fallen continuously since 1964, while the shares have risen in France, West Germany, and Japan. The share of scientists and engineers in the American labour force has fallen slightly since 1965, while the shares in West Germany and Japan have doubled and are approaching American levels. The number of patents granted to the United States by foreign countries reached a peak in 1969; and the patent balance of the United States with other countries has declined steadily. These trends have been reflected in a gradual erosion of the position of the United States in high-technology trade: its share of the export market has fallen and its import penetration has risen.

Imperfect as these indicators are, they suggest that the technology gap between the United States and its major industrialised trading partners has narrowed. If, as we suspect, the transitional catch-up period is ending, the prospects are for somewhat slower growth in the OECD countries in the 1980s.[15] Of course, this need not be the case. Recent advances in micro-electronics, robotics, fibre optics, and genetics could have a large impact on total factor productivity and growth. In fact, there are many indications that the major industrialised countries will devote more resources to the development of new technology and innovations in the next decade.

Technology-intensive trade is an increasingly important component of the total manufactured exports of developing countries. The share of technology-intensive exports in total OECD manufactured exports rose from 30 percent in 1962 to over 37 percent in 1977.[16] The dynamics of technology-intensive trade are likely to encourage the leading exporters of these types of goods to increase their research-and-development expenditures over time.

The notion of the product cycle suggests that countries producing technologically advanced products will enjoy short-run monopoly gains from trade, but that as the technology diffuses abroad and the production process becomes standardised, production will shift abroad to countries where production costs are lower.[17] In order to maintain or expand their share of trade in technology-intensive goods the leaders must continue to develop new technologies and new products.

The growing importance of technology-intensive trade has several important implications for long-run growth and the need for adjustment in the industrialised countries. The movement of products on the low end of the technology-intensive scale to foreign production locations requires adjustment of labour and capital and provides an incentive to develop new products to absorb these resources. If the required adjustments are permitted to occur, this reallocation of the production of certain products to less advanced countries and the reallocation of resources within the more technologically advanced countries to products on the upper end of the technological scale is a potentially important stimulus to growth in both groups of countries.

There is some danger, however, that the narrowing of the technology gap among the advanced countries, combined with the growing importance to them of trade in high-technology products, may provoke more government interventions designed either to protect existing products from foreign competition or to stimulate the development of new products which can compete in world markets. As we discuss later in the article, national efforts to resist adjustment or to subsidise exports may become a potentially important source of conflict in the future.

Finally, how will technological change affect adjustment and employment? The introduction of new technologies spawned by the revolution in micro-processing and robotics will probably accelerate the process of structural change. As learned during the debate on automation in the 1960s, these technological changes need not have adverse effects on employment as long as the economy is expanding, because growth itself is an important lubricant for easing necessary labour-market adjustments. But in the current economic environment of slow growth, rapid labour-force expansion and increased competition in traditional labour-intensive industries, rapid technological change will make it vital that labour markets function as flexibly and efficiently as possible. Failure to adjust will simply prolong unemployment and social strain and will reduce the long-run prospects for growth.

Moreover, these technical changes cannot be resisted for very long by any single country or group of countries. Those who attempt to resist the technological advance which contributes to increased productivity and real incomes will see it adopted by their foreign competitors. Trade pressures will reflect internal adjustment problems, but they may provoke a protectionist response.

In addition, the introduction of new technologies will lead to increased interdependence as firms seek to obtain components from different countries. An example of this trend is the Sinclair ZX81 computer, among the world's least expensive computers, which is produced with components form Malaysia, Japan, the Philippines, El Salvador, the United Kingdom and the United States. As another example, at a technological fair in Chicago in 1982 none of the newest products on display was developed or produced in a single country. The prospects are that this internationalisation of production will continue during the 1980s.

5. *Higher Energy Prices.* Predicting energy prices in the future is difficult. Nonetheless, even if real energy prices remain constant or fall in the next few years, the adjustments required by the oil-price rise and the consequent slowdown in growth in the industrialised economies will

probably extend into the 1980s. Our discussion focusses on the longer-run implications of the increase in energy costs.

The effect of the oil-price rise has been to require significant adjustments within the domestic economies of the oil importers, as well as for the international trading system as a whole. Governments have been faced with many painful policy dilemmas, most notably the conflict between the need to adjust to higher oil prices and demands to minimise the burden and costs of adjustment.

The rapid escalation of oil prices in the 1970s placed considerable pressures on the domestic economies of oil importers. The domestic impact of the oil-price rise was three-fold: (i) The adverse shift in the international terms of trade required a reduction in living standards (or in the rate of growth in real income). (ii) The increase in energy costs, combined with the need to reduce living standards, put upward pressure on wages and prices and increased political pressures on governments to cushion the blow by stimulating their economies and instituting a variety of programmes to protect employment in hard-hit (generally energy-intensive) industries. (iii) The increase in energy costs reduced the productivity of much of the existing capital stock and imposed pressures both to develop energy-saving production techniques and to reallocate labour and capital.

Many observers attribute a considerable part of the recent slowdown in growth and productivity and the rise in inflation to the change in energy prices.[18] The common explanation is that energy and capital are complementary inputs and together are substitutable for labour. A rise in energy prices reduces the derived demand for capital, reduces capital accumulation and increases the demand for labour over time. The decline in the ratios of captial to labour contributes to slower growth in productivity and real wages. These substitution effects are reinforced by the terms-of-trade effects of higher import prices on income. The process of adjusting to higher energy prices may involve considerable time, perhaps as much as twenty years, given the durable nature of the capital stock and the lags involved in conservation efforts.[19]

Policy responses to the oil shock were varied. Some governments, notably of the United States and perhaps of West Germany and Japan, appear to have adopted a 'hands-off' policy and have allowed real incomes and wages to fall. Other governments, including those of the United Kingdom and the Scandinavian countries, appear to have attempted to insulate various groups from the shock by stimulating their economies and instituting a variety of income-maintenance and job-security programmes.

Some observers attribute recent differences in rates of growth in employment among the OECD countries to differences in their policy responses to higher energy prices. Since 1974, labour-force growth averaged 0.6 percent for the European Community, 2.3 percent for the United States and 0.8 percent for Japan, but there has been virtually no growth in total employment in the countries of the Community, while total employment grew at an annual rate of about 2 percent in the United States and at about 1 percent in Japan.[20]

While clearly debatable, the argument is that the substitution effect of the oil-price rise should have been to stimulate demand for labour and total employment, if real wages were allowed to adjust. The implication (which has not to our knowledge been empirically verified) is that those countries with low growth in employment failed to allow real wages to fall and/or otherwise impeded labour-market adjustment. The further implication is that these countries will continue to experience slow growth in employment until they make the necessary adjustments.

The oil-price rise also had important implications for the stability of the international trading system. Initially, the oil-exporting countries' inability to spend their increased revenues put pressures on the international financial markets to recycle these funds. It is a tribute to the efficiency of the system that this recycling has been accomplished without the major disruptions feared at the time. The oil-price rise also required the oil importers to increase their exports over the longer run. Although there were certainly domestic pressures for protectionism and beggar-thy-neighbour export policies, the international trading system managed to function smoothly and, in fact, the Tokyo Round of multilateral trade negotiations, conducted under the auspices of the General Agreement on Tariffs and Trade (GATT) in 1973–79, continued the impetus towards trade liberalisation. In addition, higher oil prices imposed an enormous burden on many Third World countries. Their inability to pay for their oil imports with exports has stimulated demands for increased aid flows and a reordering of the international trade and financial system to increase the transfer of income to them.

6. Foreign Direct Investment. Foreign direct investment is an important intermediary mechanism for the international transfer of products, factors and technology. Most of the foreign direct investment is undertaken by large multinational enterprises from concentrated industries. The large increases in foreign direct investment in the 1960s came from American-based multinational enterprises, but it has now spread to firms from other countries and it constitutes a major force integrating the world economy.

The foreign investment activity of American firms increased substantially in the 1960s and has not declined in the aftermath of the collapse of the Bretton Woods system or the oil shock of 1973. In fact, compared with domestic investment, foreign investment by the United States may be more important today. The ratio of foreign investment in plant and equipment by American firms in manufacturing to the same investment in the United States exceeds 30 percent, compared with a ratio of less than 20 percent during the 1960s.[21] Even when the depreciation of the dollar is taken into account, American firms appear to be investing relatively more in plant and equipment overseas now than they did during the 1960s.

The volume of foreign direct investment by other countries has increased substantially in recent years. For example, the annual inflow of foreign direct investment in manufacturing in the United States has more than tripled since 1974. This expansion of foreign direct investment has increased the rate of diffusion of new products and processes internationally. The increased rate of diffusion in the foreign production of technology-intensive products through American-based multinational enterprises has been documented in a study for the National Science Foundation, in Washington.[22]

Many countries, particularly developing countries, have realised the potential role that foreign direct investment can play in the transfer of technology and have established incentives to attract investors. Apart from the question of whether foreign investment substitutes for home exports, these investments often distort the pattern of trade because the investment incentives are often linked to export-performance requirements. Industrialised countries have also begun to use or to consider local-content legislation as a method of protecting sensitive industries.[23] In the absence of greater international discipline the use of these trade-distorting investment practices is likely to increase.

Because most foreign direct investment is done by large firms from oligopolistic industries, foreign direct investment belongs more to the theory of industrial organisation than it does to the theory of international trade or of capital flows. Because of the increasing interdependence of world markets and in some industries increasing global concentration ratios, questions arise as to what constitutes the competitive market for anti-trust purposes and what remedies are available to contain restrictive business practices by firms from different countries operating in concert to secure sales in third markets. American firms, particularly those involved in heavy machinery, claim that they are at a disadvantage in their attempts to export, for in third markets they are in competition with consortia of firms from Western Europe and Japan.[24]

Current Recession

The major industrialised countries are currently faced with economic stagnation and most are experiencing record levels of unemployment. Among OECD countries, economic growth averaged only 1.2 percent in 1980 and 1981 and unemployment rose from 5.3 to 7.3 percent. The number of unemployed workers increased by over 50 percent in the past two years. The prospects are for continued slow growth, at least through 1983, with rates of unemployment continuing to rise. The OECD forecasts that by the end of 1982 over 30 million workers (8.5 percent) will be unemployed, almost 17 million of them being in Western Europe (10 percent). By the end of 1983, the OECD forecasts almost 32 million workers will be unemployed (9 percent), over 17 million in Western Europe (10.5 percent).

Western Europe is pervaded by a 'gloom and doom' atmosphere which some have labelled 'Euro-pessimism'. The problem is not merely cyclical because employment in Western Europe has not increased since the 1973 oil shock. This is due in part to Western Europe's price and cost (wage) structure in manufacturing which is out of line with the rest of the world.

Given increased competition from abroad, the rapid introduction of new technologies and the maturation of the 'baby boom' generations, West Europeans believe that the prospects for growth in employment are bleak. In their best growth years, employment in Western Europe expanded by only 300,000. Western Europe's labour force is now expanding by 1 million workers annually.

With record high unemployment rates for young people and prime-age males in many countries, governments throughout Western Europe are politically vulnerable. The high unemployment rates are unlikely to come down soon because of the inflexibilities in labour markets caused in part by strict job-protection laws and generous unemployment-insurance benefits.[25]

These labour and social policies are deeply imbedded in European society. Since it is politically easier to blame failings on someone else and it is easier to separate international markets than to give up or change social policies, the international trading system is jeopardised. This implies increasing pressure for protection and government intervention in the countries of Western Europe.

OECD forecasts for the United States have unemployment rising to 10.3 percent in the first half of 1983 before falling to 10 percent by the end of 1983. Official forecasts of the United States Administration are more optimistic. The Administration forecasts that growth will increase significantly later this year with unemployment peaking during the summer and declining thereafter. Although the Administration has continued to argue for less government intervention and is pushing for further trade liberalisation,[26] political pressure to intervene is building in the United States Congress, as exemplified by the spate of bills on trade 'reciprocity' and training programmes for displaced workers. If the recession is protracted this pressure will continue to build.

Japan's sustained economic growth and low unemployment rate are relatively unaffected by the deep recession in the rest of the world. The capacity of the Japanese economy to adapt and to adjust to shocks such as the oil-price rise or the evolution of the world economy is remarkable. The flexibility of Japan's labour market is one of the most important factors contributing to her continuing economic success.[27]

In sum, most OECD countries are under enormous political pressure to do something, anything, to alleviate quickly the current and the prospective problems of unemployment. The political instability in many countries makes it likely that government intervention to protect domestic markets will be adopted unless there is a strong international political commitment which reaffirms the belief in an open trading system.

International Economic Environment

Concerns about the integrity and future viability of the international trading system have been raised because of unresolved problems over existing rules, the lack of progress in implementing the codes negotiated in the Tokyo Round deliberations and the emergence of new actors and new issues. In addition, wide fluctuations of exchange rates in recent years have increased the concern and attention given to exchange rates as a determinant of competitiveness and trade patterns. Finally, the success of the Tokyo Round negotiations in reducing tariffs has led to new and less transparent forms of protection that are often carried out by executive rather than legislative bodies.

Because of the lack of progress in implementing the Tokyo Round codes on non-tariff barriers, there is growing concern, especially in the United States, that they have been over-sold. To date, for example, American producers have made very few sales to Nippon Telephone and Telegraph (NTT) of Japan under GATT Code on Government Procurement. The GATT Code on Subsidies and Countervailing Duties has been a source of concern with respect to developing countries, particularly India, and the perennial problem of agricultural subsidies has worsened in the past year.

Other continuing problems such as the lack of an adequate safeguard mechanism and dispute-settlement procedures are also undermining the credibility of the international trading system, to say nothing of the problems in specific industries such as steel and automobiles which affect all major trading partners. The European Community and the United States have both expressed grave concern over the size of their growing trade deficits with Japan. Increasingly the parties seek to solve these problems on a bilateral or discriminatory basis rather than by seeking multilateral agreement or abiding by the spirit and letter of the GATT rules.

The major policy challenge for the industrialised countries is to find ways to induce and encourage the newly industrialising countries to become full partners in the open trading system. The key problem is to assure mutual market access. Simply put, the industrialised countries have many sticks but very few carrots to bring the newly industrialising countries to the bargaining table. While the newly industrialising countries have enjoyed the benefits of rapid growth in their exports to the industrialised countries, they feel they have few positive incentives to open their own markets to imports and investment. It may be possible, however, to convince the newly industrialising countries that negotiations on market access can be mutually beneficial in preserving, but more importantly expanding, two-way opportunities for trade.[28]

The industrialised countries complain that the newly industrialising countries have erected a variety of trade barriers, both traditional (tariffs and import quotas) and highly inventive ones (for example, performance requirements and investment and foreign-exchange controls). The complaint of the newly industrialising countries against the industrialised countries is that their cascading structure of tariffs and their increasing reliance on 'voluntary' export restraints (VERs) and orderly marketing arrangements (OMAs), as well as the uncertainty caused by the use or threat of safeguards and by 'graduation', all inhibit their trading opportunities.

An agenda for mutual expansion of trade between developing and developed countries would include all these issues. For example, given the growing trend towards international sourcing of parts and components, there is common interest in both developed and developing countries in reducing trade barriers on these goods. The developing countries, by virtue of their long history of import restrictions, may be reluctant to recognise that mutual reductions really would benefit them. They should be made to recognise, however, as the developed countries have long understood, that in the absence of active multilateral attempts at liberalisation, pressures to restrict trade may prove irresistable.

The growing volume of East-West barter or counter-trade is a major departure from the free market principles underlying the open trading system.[29] Although there are many explanations for the phenomenon, there is suspicion that it is frequently used by state trading agencies to exercise monopoly power. Current high unemployment rates have intensified competition among the Western countries for Eastern export markets and Eastern monopsony power may allow them to extract concessionary prices (or export credits) from Western firms or governments.

The success of post-war tariff reductions may have helped contribute to the proliferation of non-tariff trade distortions. Although the Tokyo Round codes represent an important step towards dealing with many of these newer non-tariff interventions, new distortions are constantly emerging. Future efforts at liberalisation may face considerable difficulty in identifying, let alone quantifying, the effects of many trade-distorting practices because the policy-making process itself is often opaque. Greater transparency in policy making is required to evaluate the effects of ostensibly domestic policies, which also have the potential to affect international trade. The fact that many trade-distorting policies are conducted by administrative fiat rather than by legislative action may make it even more difficult to liberalise them.

A number of new developments have raised issues which are not covered by existing GATT rules. International trade in services is becoming more important, but many service industries, such as data processing and telecommunications, are often strictly regulated for non-economic reasons. Service industries are diverse, ranging from shipping to banking to construction and telecommunications, and a wide variety of barriers to trade exist. The question is whether a common conceptual framework can be developed to establish the basis for negotiations. The lack of a unifying theme is an obstacle to early discussion of service issues on a multilateral basis. At present the OECD is studying trade in services on a sectoral basis and at the GATT ministerial meeting last November a study plan was initiated.

The use of trade-distorting investment practices such as export-performance requirements and local-content requirements has increased in recent years. What began in developing countries such as Mexico and Brazil may now spread to industrialised countries, as Canada and the United States consider new legislation on domestic content. Unless checked by international agreement these practices will undermine the open trading system.

As a result of the industrial convergence of the industrialised countries at the high-technology end of the manufacturing spectrum, the role of the government as an innovator and purchaser of high-technology processes and products has become more of an issue. This is reinforced by active national industrial policies which seek to promote 'winners' in prestige industries such as aircraft, semi-conductors and telecommunications.[30]

Along with the need to integrate the advanced developing countries into the international trading system, services and trade-distorting investment practices are issues which urgently need to be incorporated into the GATT work programme. None of these issues has been addressed in the current framework of GATT rules. Analytical work needs to be done by the GATT Secretariat to lay the groundwork for future negotiations on these issues.

Finally, the side fluctuations in exchange rates in recent years have increased the attention given to exchange rates in trade policy discussions. The concerns raised cover both the level and fluctuations in the level of the exchange rate. There is considerable controversy over whether or how long exchange-rate disequilibria can persist.

Currently, the American dollar is said to be over-valued and the Japanese yen to be under-valued. Both rates, of course, reflect underlying macro-economic conditions in the two countries as well as in the rest of the world. The widespread belief that these are disequilibrium rates has been a major source of international conflict between the United States, Japan and the countries of Western Europe.

As we have argued above, in an increasingly integrated world economy, price changes in one country are quickly transmitted to the rest of the world. Because the exchange rate is a single piece of information it is often used as a summary indicator and is interpreted as the 'cause' of changes in an industry's competitiveness. This is not to argue that exchange-rate changes do not affect the competitiveness of a country's industrial base. Firms producing standardised products which are close substitutes for those produced in different countries are the most likely to be affected by the changes in the exchange rate. But they were also affected through changes in relative price levels by changes in the quantity of reserves under the Bretton Woods system. It was simply less noticeable then. The issue of the correct level for an exchange rate is a perennial one. To analyse it correctly requires that the micro-economic trade relationships be analysed in a macro-economic framework. To focus exclusively on exchange rates is often to ignore more fundamental causes of changing competitiveness and pressures for adjustment.[31]

IMPLICATIONS FOR THE FUTURE OF THE OPEN TRADING SYSTEM

What does all this portend for the future of the open international trading system? By contrast to many earlier prophesies of doom, our prognosis is not based on the system's inability to survive any single shock like the oil-price rise, a series of debt defaults or even the cyclical wave of the 'old' protectionism. Indeed, one of the strengths of the system is that these highly publicised and visible periodic shocks and ripples seem to impel policy makers into cooperative efforts to deal with them. Rather, our concern is based on an analysis of longer-run secular trends which simultaneously are likely to undermine long-run growth prospects, to inhibit necessary economic adjustments and to deprive the system of leadership. The process is certainly not inevitable, but if it continues, the international trading system will gradually lose its dynamism, growth in the volume of world trade will slow down, international institutions will become increasingly unable to deal with trade frictions and, at the very end, weakened, leaderless and inflexible, the system may collapse in a final orgy of protectionism.

In what follows, we attempt to weave the strands of our earlier discussion into a scenario for the future. While it is admittedly very bleak we fear the process is entirely possible. Nothing would please us more than to be wrong.

A major theme in our earlier analysis of trends is that the prospects in the foreseeable future are for continued slow growth relative to the 1960s and early 1970s in the major industrialised countries. This is in part due to underlying structural changes. Demographic shifts have increased the supply of relatively unskilled labour, while the high-growth sectors in most economies are likely to require increasingly skilled workers. Both time and resources will be necessary to accumulate human and physical capital in order to raise the productivity of these workers. The rise in energy prices and the growing importance of the services sector will also contribute to slow growth in productivity.

This slow economic growth is also related to government policy. In the 1960s and early 1970s governments responded to demands for improved social justice and concerns about the quality of life by instituting a variety of programmes and laws which traded off some allocative efficiency for equity considerations. In a period of high and rising per capita income in the industrialised countries, the social cost of these programmes appeared to be acceptable. Growth in many of these programmes continued through the 1970s, increasingly in response to demands that certain groups be protected from the distributional effects of slower growth, structural change and inflation. In the context of slow growth and high unemployment in the 1980s, these programmes increasingly are challenged as too costly, because of their negative impact on growth and the economy's ability to respond quickly and efficiently to cyclical and secular changes.

The proliferation of programmes which, however meritorious their primary objective, also impede the economy's long-run growth potential poses a serious problem for policy makers, especially when unemployment is high. Few governments can imperiously ignore current political pressures to maintain or to expand unemployment-insurance, job-security and subsidy programmes which reduce the private costs of unemployment and structural adjustment. To the extent that they succumb to these pressures, policy makers are forced into a faustian bargain in which they trade away some long-run growth and adjustment for the amelioration of current pain and suffering.

The major point in our analysis of longer-run trends is that the pressure and need for adjustment will increase in the 1980s. The proclivity to apply 'quick fixes' to long-run problems will simply perpetuate the problems. More important, the longer the delay in making the adjustments when pressures are mounting, the greater must be the proliferation of distortionary palliatives and, consequently, the more difficult and probably cataclysmic will be the eventual adjustment.

Domestic problems of slow growth and painful necessary adjustments will spill over into the international trading system and exacerbate problems in a number of ways. Although international trade is more frequently a symptom than a cause of domestic sectoral problems, both policy makers and the general public are eager to find foreign scapegoats. Much of the current criticism in Western Europe of high American interest rates and the concern about imports from Japan and the newly industrialising countries in both the United States and Western Europe is of this nature. The response can be direct protectionism—escape-clause or safeguard actions, VERs, OMAs and the like.

But at least these direct trade interventions are controllable or amenable to control within the current GATT framework. Perhaps partly for this reason, but also in part because ostensibly domestic economic policies also can have an impact on trade flows and, thence, on sectoral employment problems, governments are increasingly prone to use policies which currently are not adequately covered by international rules. Examples are trade-distorting investment practices, domestic-content and export requirements and a variety of indirect subsidies to traded-goods sectors such as agriculture and high-technology products.

With the convergence in industrial and cost structures within the industrialised countries, even relatively small changes in prices of traded goods can cause potentially significant shifts in trade and employment.[32] Governments facing domestic employment problems have obvious short-run incentives to use indirect trade distortions to shift the costs of unemployment and structural adjustment abroad, especially given the lack of GATT rules governing their use and their lack of transparency.

As serious as current trade distortions and policy conflicts are—to the extent that they are merely cyclical phenomena in response to the current recession (or to disequilibrium exchange rates)—they alone do not necessarily constitute a fundamental threat to the future of the open trading system.[33] The more important danger is that long-run economic and political trends and the severity of the recession make it increasingly likely that the 'new' protectionism will become a secular rather than a cyclical phenomenon.[34] Moreover, it is unlikely that the system itself will be institutionally capable of dealing with the problem.

The difficulty is that the policy response to growing long-run pressures for structural adjustment, reinforced by current high unemployment, is likely to be a continuation and expansion of interventions which directly and indirectly distort international trade. Attempts to shift the costs of unemployment and structural adjustment abroad are at best temporary and illusory solutions. Ironically, since these interventions both perpetuate and exacerbate old problems and often create new ones, it becomes even more likely that they will proliferate in the 1980s.

One cause of the spread of interventionist policies is that policy makers often ignore the inter-industry effects of intervention in one problem sector on the rest of the economy. Attempts to assist one industry may simply exacerbate problems in others. Some part of the American automobile industry's competitive problems may be due to attempts to protect the steel industry from foreign competition.[35]

Another reason for protectionist policies tending to proliferate within an economy is that the observed success of one industry in obtaining protection may both increase demands for assistance in other sectors and lower the resistance of policy makers to these pressures.[36] An important consequence of this process is that it creates an environment in which entrepreneurs may find that the short-run returns to lobbying for government assistance exceed the returns to investment in new capital and technology.

This diversion of resources from investment to lobbying clearly reduces the long-run growth potential of the economy, as well as contributing to static resource misallocation.[37] The 'rational' (that is, based on observation of historical government response to pleas for protection) expectation that government assistance may be forthcoming (or continued, when 'temporary' measures expire) also reduces factor mobility in industries which would otherwise have clear incentives to adjust.[38]

Intervention to bolster output and employment in one sector has no long-run effect on aggregate production and employment in a world of flexible exchange rates and high capital mobility. Although policy makers may be under the illusion that they can export their problems, interventions in one sector simply redistribute the burden of unemployment and adjustment to other domestic traded-goods sectors, as exchange rates and international capital flows respond over the long run.[39] The limited and temporary effectiveness of trade interventions may create a cycle in which governments come under pressure to increase their intervention continuously.

The potential effectiveness of policies to support import-competing industries or to promote export-oriented sectors is further reduced when the likely responses of other trading countries are considered. The immediate foreign response is likely to be direct retaliation. The conflict over export subsidies and credits and the spread of local-content requirements are examples of this process.

The longer-run effects may be even more serious. The growing suspicion that other countries are directly or indirectly affecting trade flows creates an environment in which the fundamental legitimacy of the principle of free trade is damaged. The rise of the concept of 'fair trade' as a justification for further intervention to correct real or imagined foreign distortions is a reflection of this trend.

The credibility of the international trading system's rules and institutions is also undermined (i) because many trade-distorting practices are not covered by existing rules and (ii) by the institutional slowness in resolving trade disputes. The rapid proliferation of practices not covered by the GATT contributes to the perception that the GATT system is inflexible and therefore is ineffective in dealing with these problems. The tendency is to circumvent the GATT entirely and to rely on bilateral solutions to multilateral problems.

The international trading system's ability to deal with emerging trade problems is also hampered by changes in the international distribution of economic and political power. These changes may make it increasingly difficult to achieve the international political consensus that is necessary to resist current protectionist pressures and to develop new and flexible rules to deal with trade problems.

Charles Kindleberger's analysis of the collapse of the international trading system in the 1930s suggests that the stability of the system depended in large part on the existence of a single country which, by virtue of its economic and political power, could act as a leader, both in absorbing shocks to the system and in cajoling and bullying the other members into cooperative efforts to resist protectionism. The United Kingdom played this role prior to 1920, but the inter-war period was characterised by the absence of strong leadership and cooperation.[40]

If Professor Kindleberger, of the Massachusetts Institute of Technology, is correct, the parallels between the 1930s and the 1980s are disturbing. The United States played the leading role in efforts at trade liberalisation after 1945. But the pre-eminence of its power has eroded. The European Community has a combined GNP and volume of trade comparable to the United States. Japan is also a growing force in international trade. While the Community and Japan have an abiding interest and commitment to the principle of free trade, they have not taken the lead in defending it. Moreover, many new actors, the newly industrialising countries, the members of the Organisation of Petroleum Exporting Countries (OPEC) and the Communist countries, are playing an important role in international trade, yet they have no deep-rooted commitment to free markets.

Several long-run trends will make it increasingly difficult for the United States to continue to play the leading role in defending the open trading system. In the early post-war period the United States accounted for a large share of world trade, but trade itself was a relatively unimportant component of its total output. Changes in the trade policy of the United States could have a large impact on the rest of the world, but it would have a relatively small impact on the American economy. In 1960, for example, the United States accounted for 16 percent of total world exports and 24 percent of developed-country exports, while exports of goods and services were only about 6 percent of American GNP.

In the 1970s the United States' share of trade began to decline, while its share of trade in American GNP rose. By 1980 the American share of total world exports fell to 11 percent, the American share of developed-country exports declined to 17 percent and American exports grew to 13 percent of GNP. In large part, because international trade played a relatively small role in the American economy, there was little domestic opposition to trade liberalisation. As the importance of trade has grown, it has become increasingly difficult for policy makers in the United States to achieve a strong domestic consensus in support of trade liberalisation. These trends are likely to continue in the 1980s.[41]

The picture that we paint is fairly bleak. Long-run trends which portend slower growth, but more pressures to adjust output and employment, give rise to policy interventions which directly or indirectly distort trade flows and further inhibit growth and adjustment. The tendency to view international trade as a zero-sum game, in which trade policy can be used to alleviate domestic problems temporarily, will in fact transform trade from a positive-sum to a negative-sum game as interventions spread and intensify within individual countries and provoke retaliation abroad. Erosion of credibility in the existing institutional framework will further weaken the open trading system.

Preoccupation with domestic problems and a decline in power will reduce the ability of the United States to lead and, too, the willingness of the other major industrialised countries to support the open trading system. The threat to the system posed by these trends is much more serious than the periodic shocks and crises of the past, precisely because the process is gradual, less perceptible and less amenable to a 'quick fix' or a one-shot change in the rules.

CONCLUSIONS

We do not believe that the collapse of the open trading system is inevitable. Much of our dire scenario is predicated on the continuation and possible worsening of current secular trends. Predictions about the future are notoriously inaccurate. It may well be that economic growth will accelerate and that adjustment problems and protectionist pressures will abate in the short term. We may also be too pessimistic about the flexibility and efficacy of market forces in facilitating growth and adjustment in labour markets, even in the presence of policy-induced distortions.[42] In the period between 1970 and 1980, for example, both Japan and the United States were able to generate nine jobs for every ten entrants into the labour force. By contrast, the West European economies were able to create only about four new jobs for every ten new labour-force entrants.[43] Clearly some countries have been able to make the necessary adjustments to structural changes. Nevertheless, the open trading system is in grave danger if present trends continue. In what follows, we suggest domestic and trade policy options to help avert the threats to the system.

The long litany of causes of the current situation suggests that one cannot point to any single factor as the predominant explanation.[44] Certainly, many of the factors contributing to slow growth and adjustment problems are due to long-term structural changes which are not amenable to quick fixes, although they can be affected in the longer run by government policies. In both the short run and the longer run the appropriate role of domestic economic policy is to ensure that government interventions promote rather than impede growth and adjustment. In practice, this means that governments must carefully explore the equity and efficiency implications of current and prospective economic policies and programmes.

This last statement does not imply adherence to the Marie Antoinette school of social justice which abjures equity considerations. Rather, it is to argue that in a period of slow growth, a careful evaluation of the pros and cons of factor- and product-market interventions (i) should help raise the level of public debate on equity and efficiency concerns, (ii) may help improve the policy mix and (iii) may have a valuable demonstration effect on other countries. There are hopeful signs that the OECD's "positive adjustment' exercise has helped to educate policy makers to the need to consider the broader and longer-run implications of government regulation.

The growth in both government intervention and economic interdependence makes obsolete the distinction between ostensibly domestic and international trade policies. Many of the current trade frictions are the result of the international spill-over effects, intentional or not, of 'domestic' policies. The recent OECD proposal to ensure greater transparency of domestic policy has much merit (and some problems) and should be debated and explored carefully because, at the very least, it can help rid policy makers of some myopia.[45]

Finally, we have argued that the preservation of the open trading system requires strong leadership—a country which acts as a protector and enforcer of the principles of free trade. We also argued that the United States is increasingly unwilling, or unable, to play this role. What, then, is meant by leadership?

The United States, by default, must continue to play the role of initiator of efforts at stabilisation and liberalisation, but the European Community and Japan must increasingly assume some of the burdens and responsibilities commensurate with their size and stake in international trade. In principle, this means taking a less parochial attitude towards the larger problems confronting the international trading system; and, in the current context, it means that Japan should take unilateral steps to dispel the widespread perception that Japanese markets are closed to certain imports and that the Community should refrain from holding long-run efforts at trade liberalisation hostage to the resolution of current trade disputes.

The GATT ministerial meeting was convened last November to strengthen confidence in the open trading system by reaffirming the commitment of the signatory countries to resist protectionist pressures and to move forward with efforts at further liberalisation of trade. It was hoped that the combination of a credible political statement and a realistic agenda to deal with current and prospective trade problems would help governments deflect or delay action on protectionist demands at home. A moratorium on the proliferation of trade distortions, in turn, would allow governments to pursue a longer-term strategy to reduce impediments to adjustment and establish a basis for non-inflationary growth.

In fact, what emerged from the GATT ministerial meeting was a weak political declaration, barely credible in view of the European Community's qualifying statement, and a vapid work and study programme, hardly promising given the debate surrounding issues like trade-distorting investment practices and trade in agriculture and services. The divisiveness of the ministerial meeting showed that the multilateral GATT framework is ineffectual in the face of the decline in unilateral American power and in the absence of concerted leadership by the major trading countries. Those countries in a position to act decisively in defence of the open trading system were hindered by strong political pressure from domestic interest groups, especially agricultural interests.

Although it is too early to determine the ultimate effects, failure to achieve meaningful results at the GATT ministerial meeting may have further poisoned confidence in the open trading system. The apparent inability to deal with the crucial issues in a multilateral forum may give additional impetus both to traditional protectionist measures in import-competing sectors and to more recent notions of defensive 'strategic interventions' in export-oriented sectors. A number of governments are building 'war chests' and threatening to subsidise exports unless others abandon their alleged violations of free trade principles.

The retreat from the multilateral and non-discriminatory approach to trade issues embodied in the GATT and the growing threat of unilateral actions to punish or prevent alleged abuses are clearly a great danger for the liberal trading system, but they now appear to be almost inevitable. Perhaps the best that can be expected is that the very dangers posed will themselves act as a deterrent to irresponsible actions, although the history of the 1930s does not make us sanguine about that prospect.

There is still scope for quiet diplomacy among the major trading countries to avoid provoking a trade war. In the absence of a single predominant leader, it is possible and necessary for like-minded countries to form coalitions in support of some semblance of free trade, at least among themselves—the United States and Japan and some of the other Pacific Basin countries are obvious candidates. Moreover, since most trade-related problems are fundamentally domestic problems which require policies to promote internal adjustment and growth, there is still scope for policy makers to exercise leadership at home in focussing the domestic policy debate on these issues rather than seeking foreign scapegoats. This, of course, will require considerable political courage and foresight.

The problems confronting the open trading system are very grave. Failure to deal with them is a prescription for disaster.

NOTES

1. This article is based on a paper presented at the National Bureau of Economic Research's Summer Institute in International Studies in August 1982. The views expressed are those of the authors and do not necessarily reflect those of the United States Department of Labor or the United States Administration. The authors are grateful to Richard Blackhurst, William Diebold, John Martin, Rachel McCulloch, Jan Tumlir and Ray Vernon for comments on an earlier draft. All remaining errors are solely the responsibility of the authors.
2. For a discussion of the collapse of the international trading system during the 1930s, see Charles P. Kindleberger, *The World in Depression, 1929–39* (Berkeley: University of California Press, 1973).
3. Unless otherwise stated, the statistics in this article are from: *Main Economic Indicators,* OECD Secretariat, Paris, various issues; *Economic Outlook,* OECD Secretariat, Paris, December 1981 and July 1982; and *Analytical Report,* prepared for the meeting of the Manpower and Social Affairs Committee at Ministerial Level, MAS/MIN (82) 2 (Paris: OECD Secretariat, 1982).
4. These trends in female participation rates and the growth of young entrants may have peaked in the United States, but they are expected to continue through the early 1980s in Western Europe and to decline after that. For a discussion of demographic trends in different countries and how they are expected to affect labour-force growth, see *Analytical Report* (OECD), *op. cit.*
5. For a discussion of the effects of the Trade Adjustment Assistance programme on labour-market adjustment, in particular the effects of unemployment insurance, see C. Michael Aho and Thomas O. Bayard, 'Costs and Benefits of Trade Adjustment Assistance' in Robert E. Baldwin (ed.), *The Structure and Evolution of Recent US Trade Policy* (Chicago and London: University of Chicago Press, 1983).
6. For a formal analysis of what follows, see William J. Baumol, 'Macro-economics of Unbalanced Growth,' *American Economic Review,* June 1967.
7. See E. E. Leamer, 'An Empirical Study of Changing Comparative Advantage', Office of Foreign Economic Research, United States Department of Labor, Washington, mimeograph, 1980; and H. P. Bowen, *Changes in the International Pattern of Factor Abundance and the Composition of Trade,* Economic Discussion Paper No. 8 (Washington: Office of Foreign Economic Research, United States Department of Labor, 1980).
8. See L. J. Kotlikoff, Leamer and Jeffrey Sachs, *The International Economics of Transitional Growth: the Case of the United States,* Working Paper No. 773 (Cambridge, Mass.: National Bureau of Economic Research, 1982).
9. This is less likely when products are highly differentiated.

10. See Paul Krugman, 'Technology Gaps, Technology Transfers and the Changing Character of US Trade', National Bureau of Economic Research, Cambridge, Mass., mimeograph, 1982.

11. This point is made very clearly in Richard Blackhurst, 'The Twilight of Domestic Economic Policies', *The World Economy*, December 1981.

12. Although there is considerable debate on the impact of developing-country exports on employment in the developed countries, it is probably fairly small. See Anne O. Krueger, 'Protectionist Pressures, Imports and Employment in the United States,' *Scandinavian Journal of Economics*, Vol. 82, No. 2, 1980. But these pressures are likely to intensify in the 1980s. See Helen Hughes and Jean Waelbroeck, 'Can Developing-country Exports Keep Growing in the 1980s?', *The World Economy*, June 1981.

13. See William H. Branson, 'The Productivity Slowdown of the 1970s: Effects and Policies', National Bureau of Economic Research, Cambridge, Mass., mimeograph, 1982.

14. See Aho and Howard F. Rosen, *Trends in Technology-intensive Trade*, Economic Discussion Paper No. 9 (Washington: Office of Foreign Economic Research, United States Department of Labor, 1980).

15. In W. D. Nordhaus, *Economic Policy in the Face of Declining Productivity Growth*, Conference Paper No. 141 (Cambridge, Mass.: National Bureau of Economic Research, 1981) it is hypothesised that a large part of the current OECD-wide slowdown in productivity may be due to 'depletion' of opportunities for rapid technological change, including a narrowing of the technology gap.

16. Aho and Rosen, *op. cit.* Technology-intensive goods are defined as those with a research-and-development component greater than the average for manufacturing.

17. See Raymond Vernon (ed.), *The Technology Factor in International Trade* (New York: Columbia University Press, 1970); and Krugman, 'Technology Gaps, Technology Transfers and the Changing Character of US Trade', *op. cit.*

18. It has been suggested that 40 to 60 percent of the reduction in OECD growth in the 1970s can be explained by price increases of imported intermediate inputs, including oil, other industrial raw materials and foodstuffs. See Michael Bruno and Sachs, 'Import Prices and Stagflation in the Industrial Countries: a Cross-section Analysis'. *Economic Journal*, September 1980.

19. See Nordhaus, *Economic Policy in the Face of Declining Productivity Growth, op. cit.* Dr. Nordhaus doubts, however, that the oil-price rise can account for much of the slowdown. See Nordhaus, 'Oil and Economic Performance in Industrial Countries', *Brookings Papers on Economic Activity*, No. 2, 1980.

20. *European Economy* (Brussels: Commission of the European Community, 1981); and *OECD Economic Outlook: Historical Statistics* (Paris: OECD Secretariat, 1982).

21. *Report of the President on US Competitiveness* (Washington: US Government Printing Office, for the Office of Foreign Economic Research, United States Department of Labor, 1980).

22. Vernon and W. H. Davidson, 'Foreign Production of Technology-intensive Products by US–based Multinational Enterprises', National Science Foundation, Washington, mimeograph, 1979.

23. For example, Canada, in addition to her Foreign Investment Review Act of 1973, established, in 1980, a National Energy Programme calling for more local control of energy production. As an indication of the current mood in the United States, a proposed bill calling for 90 percent local-content production in the automobile industry was co-sponsored by 195 members of the House of Representatives (out of 435). The bill passed the House in December 1982 and is likely to be reintroduced in the Congress in 1983.

24. For a discussion of collusion among producers of electrical machinery in their sales to Brazil, see R. S. Newfarmer, 'Imperfect International Markets and Monopolistic Prices to Developing Countries', *Cambridge Journal of Economics*, March 1982.

25. In general, the percentage of GDP devoted to unemployment compensation increased between 1970 and 1979 when standardised by the unemployment rate and the percentage was considerably higher in many of the West European countries than in the United States.

26. See, for example, the testimony of William E. Brock, the United States Trade Representative, before the Sub-committee on Trade, Senate Finance Committee, 24 March 1982.

27. For a comparison of labour-market adjustment policies and processes in the United States and Japan, see James Orr and Haruo Shimada, 'US-Japan Comparative Study of Employment Adjustment', Office of Foreign Economic Research, United States Department of Labor, forthcoming. They conclude that the relatively smooth employment adjustment in large Japanese firms is due to the internal organisation of these firms which promotes an ability and willingness to adapt to changing circumstances.

28. For empirical evidence supporting the superiority of 'outward-looking' trade policies over import-substitution policies as far as development is concerned, see, for example, I. M. D. Little, Tibor Scitovsky and M. FG. Scott, *Industry and Trade in Some Developing Countries: a Comparative Study* (Oxford: Oxford University Press, for the OECD, 1970); Krueger, *Foreign Trade Regimes and Economic Development: Liberalization Attempts and Consequences* (Cambridge, Mass.: Ballinger, for the National Bureau of Economic Research, 1978); Jagdish N. Bhagwati, *Foreign Trade Regimes and Economic Development: Anatomy and Consequences of Exchange Control Regimes* (Cambridge, Mass.: Ballinger for the National Bureau of Economic Research, 1978); Krueger, Hal B. Lary, Terry Monson and Narongchai Akrasanee (eds), *Trade and Employment in Developing Countries:* Volume 1, *Individual Studies* (Chicago and London: Chicago University Press, for the National Bureau of Economic Research, 1980).

29. See *East-West Trade: Recent Developments in Counter-trade* (Paris: OECD Secretariat, 1981).

30. For an extensive discussion of the trade policy issues in technologically advanced industries, see Jack Baranson and Harald B. Malmgren, 'Technology and Trade Policy: Issues and an Agenda for Action', a report prepared for the Office of Foreign Economic Research, United States Department of Labor, and the Office of the United States Trade Representative, mimeograph, 1981.

31. See, for example, Blackhurst and Jan Tumlir, *Trade Relations under Flexible Exchange Rates,* GATT Studies in International Trade No. 8 (Geneva: GATT Secretariat, 1980).

32. Our earlier caveat that industries characterised by highly differentiated products are less vulnerable to price changes applies here.

33. C. Fred Bergsten, Director of the Institute for International Economics, Washington, has argued that disequilibrium exchange rates are responsible for outbreaks of protectionism and conflict. See C. Fred Bergsten, 'The Villain is an Over-valued Dollar', *Challenge,* March-April 1982.

34. Most protectionist policies, although cast as temporary programmes designed to control the pace of adjustment, tend to become permanent obstacles to adjustment. The Multifibre Arrangement, formally called the Arrangement Regarding International Trade in Textiles, is a classic example. See Donald B. Keesing and Martin Wolf, *Textile Quotas against Developing Countries,* Thames Essay No. 23 (London: Trade Policy Research Centre, 1980); and Gerard Curzon, 'Neo-protectionism, the MFA and the European Community', *The World Economy,* September 1981.

35. This and other examples were given by Anne Krueger, of the University of Minnesota, at a conference on American trade policy sponsored by the National Bureau of Economic Research and the National Science Foundation, in Washington, on 4–5 March 1982. The case of steel is an interesting example of the problems involved in attempting to use trade policy to solve underlying structural problems. A number of domestic problems (access to capital, out-dated technology, regulation *et cetera*) in the industry were identified in Anthony Solomon, *Report to the President: a Comprehensive Program for the Steel Industry* (Washington: US Government Printing Office, for the United States Department of the Treasury, 1977). In spite of this, trade policy was the means chosen to deal with all of these problems.

36. P. A. Messerlin, 'The Political Economy of Protectionism: the Bureaucratic Case', *Weltwirtschaftliches Archiv,* Vol. 117, No. 3, 1981.

37. Stephen P. Magee and William A. Brock, 'A Model of Politics, Tariffs and Rent Seeking in General Equilibrium', mimeograph, 1981, cited in Gregory Grossman and J. David Richardson, *Issues and Options for US Trade Policy in the 1980s: Some Research Perspectives,* research progress report (Cambridge, Mass.: National Bureau of Economic Research, 1982). For a survey of the political economy of protection, see Baldwin, 'The Political Economy of Protectionism', in Bhagwati (ed.), *Import Competition and Response* (Chicago and London: Chicago University Press, 1982).

38. See Richardson, 'Opaque and Transparent Trade Policy: Some Expectational Considerations', Department of Economics, University of Wisconsin, mimeograph, 1978. Moreover, attempts to mute protectionist pressures by granting workers in adjusting industries trade adjustment assistance may also reduce labour mobility. See Aho and Bayard, *loc. cit.*

39. Even the short-run stimulus is reduced as investors build the history of government intervention into their expectations. See Barry J. Eichengreen, 'A Dynamic Model of Tariffs, Output and Employment under Flexible Exchange Rates', *Journal of International Economics,* August 1981.

40. Kindleberger, *op. cit.*

41. According to private forecasters such as Data Resources, in Lexington, Massachusetts, merchandise exports (as opposed to exports of goods and services) are expected to rise from 9 percent of GNP in 1980 to 12–14 percent by 1990.

42. The growth of the 'underground economy' may be a reflection of this. See *Analytical Report* (OECD), *op. cit.;* and Michael Piore and Charles Sabel, 'Italian Small Business: its Implications for American Industrial Policy', in Laura Tyson and John Zysman (eds), *American Industry and International Competition* (Ithaca: Cornell University Press, forthcoming).

43. Calculated from *Labour Force Statistics 1969–1980* (Paris: OECD Secretariat, 1982).

44. We differ in our emphasis on this with the analysis in the following: Melvyn Krauss, *The New Protectionism: the Welfare State and International Trade* (New York: New York University Press, 1978); Tumlir, 'International Economic Order: Can the Trend be Reversed?', *The World Economy,* March 1982; and Blackhurst, *loc. cit.*

45. For some economic implications, see Richardson, *op. cit.*

III. The United States in the World Economy: Issues of the 1980s

This section examines the position of the United States in the world economy. Its aim is to show how complex American international economic relations have become. The contributions identify the economic and political stresses that have resulted from this growing economic integration, discuss necessary adjustments, and propose policy responses. An effort has been made to present different views of these strains and adjustments. Likewise, alternative policy directions are represented in the writings.

Each year the Council of Economic Advisers issues a report summarizing the state of the economy. In recent years more and more attention has been devoted to international issues. The first reading in this section is a chapter taken from the Council's 1983 report. Is is a thoughtful analysis of trends and patterns that merits inclusion for its lasting value; more recent issues of the Council's annual reports will not surpass its analysis although they will bring events and facts up to date. This document offers excellent reviews of major topics that will occupy citizens and policymakers of the United States throughout the remainder of the century: the competitiveness of U.S. industries, the changing character of American balance of payments relationships, the role of the dollar, and the threat of overhanging international debt.

The second paper was written by the editor of this book. Although his opinions are, to a large extent, reflected in the choice of essays, this paper is included to make explicit the editor's values and assessments of current international economic issues. The editor expresses in this paper a general acceptance of the conventional economists' endorsement of free trade and, likewise, does not seriously contest the current consensus in favor of flexible exchange rates. He presents the views of institutional economists—or at least of one institutional economist—on international trade, technology, and financial affairs, and contrasts them with those more commonly held among economists.

The essay by J. M. Finger discusses in depth some of the political problems involved in developing a national consensus on trade policies. He discusses the way in which various appeals for relief from foreign import pressures have been handled under current procedures. He contrasts the objective handling of appeals under anti-dumping and countervailing-duty statutes with reliance on more politicized channels. He describes the problems less-developed countries face in adopting more liberal policies. Lastly, he suggests ways in which the American and other policymaking mechanisms can be made to work better, with more appropriate weight being given to beneficiaries of liberalization.

The American automobile and steel industries have been fundamental to the economic growth of this country in the twentieth century. With their allied supplying industries they have formed the core of the industrial base of the economy. These industries have also been in the forefront of those seeking special protection from foreign competition. "Voluntary" quotas were put into place to restrain imports of Japanese automobiles and the steel industry sought relief from foreign steel imports, including activation of anti-dumping laws.

Mordechai Kreinin examines the competitiveness of the United States automobile and steel industries. He finds that poor management decisions and high labor costs share the blame for the loss of competitive position. In the automobile industry management, workers, and stockholders must accept lower returns and their reduced compensation must be passed on to the consumer via lower car prices. In the steel industry compensation of workers must likewise be reduced. Productivity must be raised by considerable new investment, which may be difficult for the industry to fund without transitory governmental aid.

Robert Reich's paper reviews efforts by the United States and Europe to counter trade pressures on their old industries and declares them largely futile. He believes that the free trade argument is no longer a convincing rebuttal to calls for protection. Comparative advantage is not the result of passively exploiting existing technologies, labor skills, or natural resources but can be created by proper governmental guidance and a total social commitment. Reich argues that the United States should abandon government efforts to shield weak industries from foreign competition and instead should develop a trade policy based on active government leadership directed towards transforming the economy. He advocates designing a program to push technological advancement and to create human resources. In short, he believes the bias of government intervention should be in favor of emerging industries rather than senescent, declining industries.

Reich's endorsement of governmental action to identify and nurture new export industries is controversial. Many economists believe that nations' records of success in such endeavors are very poor. Some doubt that Japan's industrial policy, the archetypical illustration, has really had much impact on that country's export performance.

In his remarks that conclude this section Martin Feldstein argues with great force that governments do not do a good job of choosing winning and losing industries. He expresses doubt that a national industrial policy will raise the rate of economic growth or enhance economic welfare. He believes that the proper role for government is to remove barriers to business innovation and operation and create an environment in which private agents can make the most of technological and profit opportunities.

10. The United States in The World Economy: Strains On The System

THE COUNCIL OF ECONOMIC ADVISERS

During the 1970s the world's market economies became more integrated with each other than ever before. Exports and imports as a share of gross national product (GNP) reached record levels for most industrial countries, while international lending and direct foreign investment grew even faster than world trade. This closer linkage of economies was mutually beneficial. It allowed producers in each country to take greater advantage of their country's special resources and knowledge, and to take advantage of economies of scale. At the same time, it allowed each country to consume a wider variety of products, at lower costs, than it could produce itself.

Underlying the growth in world trade and investment was a progressive reduction of barriers to trade. The postwar period was marked by a series of agreements to liberalize trade: both multilateral, like the Kennedy Round, and bilateral, like the Canada–U.S. auto pact.

In spite of its huge benefits, however, this liberalized trading system is now in serious danger. Within the United States, demands for protection against imports and for export subsidies have grown as a combination of structural changes, sectoral problems, and short-run macroeconomic developments has led to a perception that we are becoming uncompetitive in world markets. In Europe, a growing structural unemployment problem, aggravated by the recession, has increased protectionist pressures. In the developing countries a financial crisis threatens the integration of capital markets and is pushing many countries back toward the exchange controls and import restrictions they had begun to dismantle.

These problems must not be allowed to disrupt world trade. If the system comes apart—if the world's nations allow themselves to be caught up in a spiral of retaliatory trade restrictions—a long time may pass before the pieces are put back together.

This chapter reviews the strains on the international economic system and the policies by which the United States is attempting to overcome them. It is divided into four sections. The first section discusses long-term changes in U.S. competitiveness. The correction of widespread misconceptions about the competitive position of the United States is essential if we are to get through the difficult period ahead without making major policy mistakes. The second section of the chapter is devoted to financial developments and their effects on trade, especially the appreciation of the dollar and its likely effects on the U.S. trade balance. Two final sections examine macroeconomic and financial problems in Europe and the developing countries.

LONG-RUN TRENDS IN U.S. COMPETITIVENESS: PERCEPTIONS AND REALITIES

Concern over the international competitiveness of the United States is as high as it has ever been. It is argued with increasing frequency that U.S. business has steadily lost ground in the international marketplace. This alleged poor performance is often attributed both to failures of management in the United States and to the support given to foreign businesses by their home governments. Feeding the perception of declining competitiveness is the persistent U.S. deficit in merchandise trade, especially the imbalance in trade with Japan.

Changes in U.S. trade performance must, however, be put into the context of changes in the U.S. role in the world economy. This wider approach reveals that much of the concern about long-run competitiveness is based on misperceptions. Although the recent appreciation of the dollar has created a temporary loss of competitiveness, the United States has not experienced a persistent loss of ability to sell its products on international markets; in fact, in the 1970s the United States held its own in terms of output, exports, and employment. Changes in the relationship of the United States to the world economy, however, have made the United States look less competitive by some traditional measures.

Aggregate Performance of the United States and Other Developed Countries

Discussion of U.S. competitiveness often gives the misleading impression that the United States has consistently performed poorly relative to other industrial countries. The U.S. share of world trade and world GNP did in fact decline throughout the 1950s and 1960s, reflecting the recovery of the rest of the world from World War II, together with the narrowing of the huge and unsustainable U.S. technological lead. In the 1970s, however, this long decline leveled off.

From 1973 to 1980, real gross domestic product (GDP) in the United States grew at an annual rate of 2.3 percent, compared with 2.6 percent in the other Organization for Economic Cooperation and Development (OECD) countries.

From 1973 to 1980 the U.S. share of OECD exports remained nearly constant, declining from 17.6 to 17.2 percent.

Over the same period, employment in the United States grew at 2.1 percent a year, compared with only 0.5 percent in the rest of the OECD countries.

The United States, in part as a side effect of its relatively rapid growth in employment, did do poorly by comparison in one respect, productivity growth. Output per worker grew at only 0.2 percent in the United States, compared with 2.2 percent a year in the rest of the OECD countries. Productivity is, of course, crucial to living standards; ultimately, the level of consumption per capita depends on the level of output per worker. But there is no necessary relation between productivity and competition in international markets. Slow growth in productivity only hampers a country's international competitiveness if it is not offset by correspondingly slow growth in real wages. If U.S. workers, for example, were to receive real wage increases equal to those granted in other countries while their productivity failed to increase at a comparable rate, U.S. industry would find itself increasingly uncompetitive. The fact is, however, that this did not occur, as the comparative experience of the United States and the European Economic Community illustrates. From 1973 to 1980 output per manufacturing worker in the European Economic Community rose at an annual rate of 2.7 percent, but real compensation rose at an annual rate of 4.1 percent. By contrast, output per worker in the United States rose 1.1 percent annually, while real compensation rose only 1.8 percent annually. In fact, until the recent rise in the dollar's exchange rate, it was workers in the European Economic Community, rather than those in the United States, who were probably pricing themselves out of the world market in spite of their relatively good productivity performance.

The overall performance of the United States, then, does not suggest a long-term problem of competitiveness. The shift from persistent trade surplus to persistent deficit which occurred over the last decade is, however, often misinterpreted as a sign of an inability to compete. In fact, changes in the structure of the U.S. balance of payments are more the result of changes in the U.S. saving and investment position than of slow productivity growth.

The Changing Structure of the U.S. Balance of Payments

In the 1950s and early 1960s the United States normally had a trade surplus and invested heavily in other countries. In the years after 1973, however, the United States normally had a trade deficit, and annual investment by foreigners in the United States began to approach annual U.S. investment abroad. The shift in the U.S. trade balance was closely connected with the shift in investment flows.

Taken as a whole, U.S. international transactions always balance. Any force tending to increase or decrease the balance in one category of transactions sets in motion a process leading to exactly offsetting changes in balances in other categories. For example, an increase in foreign demand for U.S. exports tends directly to improve the trade balance, but this improvement leads to a rise in the dollar's exchange rate against foreign currencies. The exchange-rate appreciation in turn leads to increases in imports, a worsened balance on services, and so on. Similarly, an increased desire by foreign residents to invest in the United States is reflected in an increase in the capital account but leads to an appreciation of the dollar and an offsetting decline in other parts of the balance of payments.

The shift in the U.S. trade balance from persistent surplus to persistent deficit was largely an offset to changes in the U.S. capital account. In the 1950s and the first half of the 1960s, rates of return on capital were lower and wage rates were higher in the United States than in other industrial countries. Since the United States suffered no war damage, its capital stock was intact, and the diffusion of U.S. technology abroad created a demand for new capital investment in the recipient countries. The result was that returns to investment were higher abroad than in the United States, and the United States was a heavy net foreign investor. The counterpart to this foreign investment was a persistent surplus on current transactions, including merchandise trade.

By the 1970s the other industrial countries had narrowed or eliminated these differences in capital and labor costs. The result was that the demand for new capital abroad was no longer a great deal larger than it was in the United States. At the same time, the supply of savings in the United States was restricted by a low national saving rate (the lowest among the major industrial countries). Thus the United States ceased to be a major net exporter of capital, and the current account of the balance of payments moved from surplus to rough balance. Meanwhile, the U.S. balance on items other than merchandise trade improved: the deficit in military transactions fell, the surplus in services rose, and, in particular, the accumulation of past foreign investments

TABLE 1. Structure of the U.S. Balance of Payments, as Percent of GNP, 1960–80

TYPE OF BALANCE	PERCENT OF GNP		CHANGE, PERCENTAGE POINTS
	1960–66	1974–80	
Merchandise trade	0.86	−0.80	−1.66
Investment income	.74	1.06	.32
Military transactions	−.41	−.03	.38
Travel and services	−.04	.12	.16
Remittances	−.44	−.30	.15
Current account	.70	.06	−.64

Source: Department of Commerce, Bureau of Economic Analysis.

began to yield increasing income. This meant that a balanced current account was associated with a deficit in merchandise trade.

Table 1 and Figure 1 show how the structure of the U.S. current account has changed, measuring its components as percentages of GNP.

Figure 1. Structural Changes in the Current Account Balance

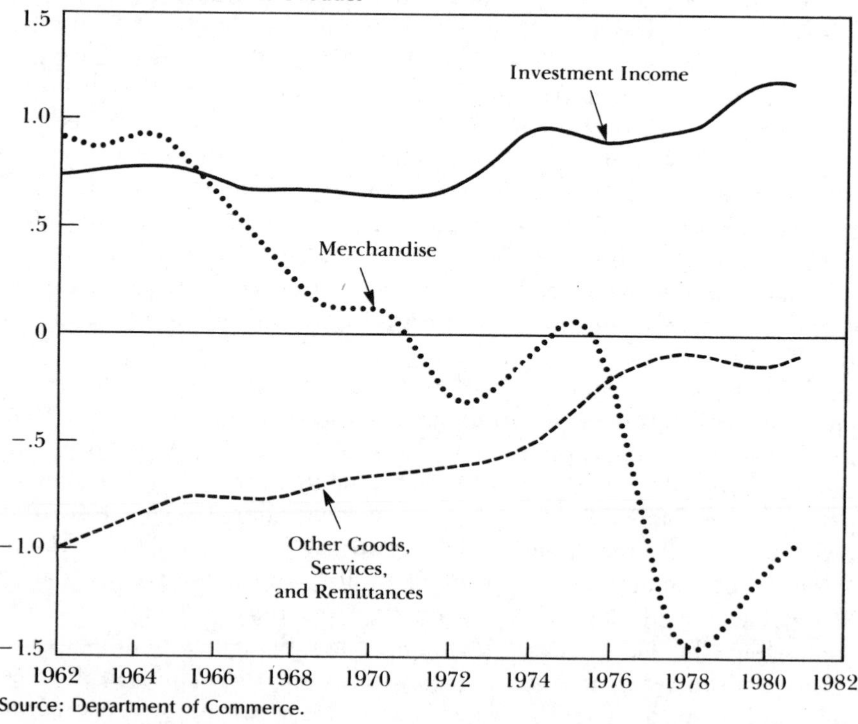

Source: Department of Commerce.

Note: Data are 16–quarter weighted centered moving averages.

TABLE 2. Trade Balances by Commodity Group as Percent of GDP, United States, Japan, and the European Economic Community, 1980
[Percent of GDP]

COMMODITY GROUP	UNITED STATES	JAPAN	EUROPEAN ECONOMIC COMMUNITY
Total	−1.45	−0.99	−2.23
Primary products	−1.93	−10.11	−5.41
Food, beverages, and tobacco	.40	−1.26	−.41
Crude materials excluding petroleum	.54	−2.15	−1.23
Mineral fuels	−2.87	−6.71	−3.77
Manufactures	.48	9.12	3.18
Machinery and transport equipment	−.42	3.09	.88
Other manufactured goods	.90	6.02	2.30

Source: Organization for Economic Cooperation and Development.

The perception of diminished U.S. competitiveness stems not only from the U.S. trade deficit but from an impression that U.S. trade performance compares poorly with that of other countries, especially that of Japan. Japan runs a huge surplus in its manufactures trade, while the United States runs only a small one, and Japan also has a large surplus in its bilateral trade with the United States. These facts are often attributed to Japanese trade restrictions. Japan does maintain restrictions which seriously hurt U.S. businesses. Trade restrictions, however, do not in the long run improve the Japanese trade balance; as discussed more fully below, they lead to offsetting increases in other imports or declines in exports. The main explanation of Japan's surplus in manufactures trade and in trade with the United States is that Japan, with few natural resources, incurs huge deficits in its trade in primary products, especially oil, and with primary producers, especially the Organization of Petroleum Exporting Countries (OPEC). The surpluses in the rest of Japan's trade offset these deficits.

Table 2 and Figure 2 show the differences in the structure of the Japanese, European, and U.S. trade accounts. They show clearly how the huge Japanese surplus in manufactures offsets large deficits in primary products.

Corresponding to the Japanese sectoral deficit in primary products, especially oil, is a regional deficit with OPEC. Japan makes up for its deficit with OPEC by running surpluses in its trade with other regions. The extent of this regional imbalance—and its contrast with the U.S. position—is shown in Table 3. The point here is similar to that already made with respect to the overall U.S. trade balance: looking at Japanese–U.S. trade in isolation is misleading. The Japanese surplus in trade with the United States is largely a response to the rise of OPEC.

Figure 2. Composition of Trade, 1980

Percent of Gross Domestic Product

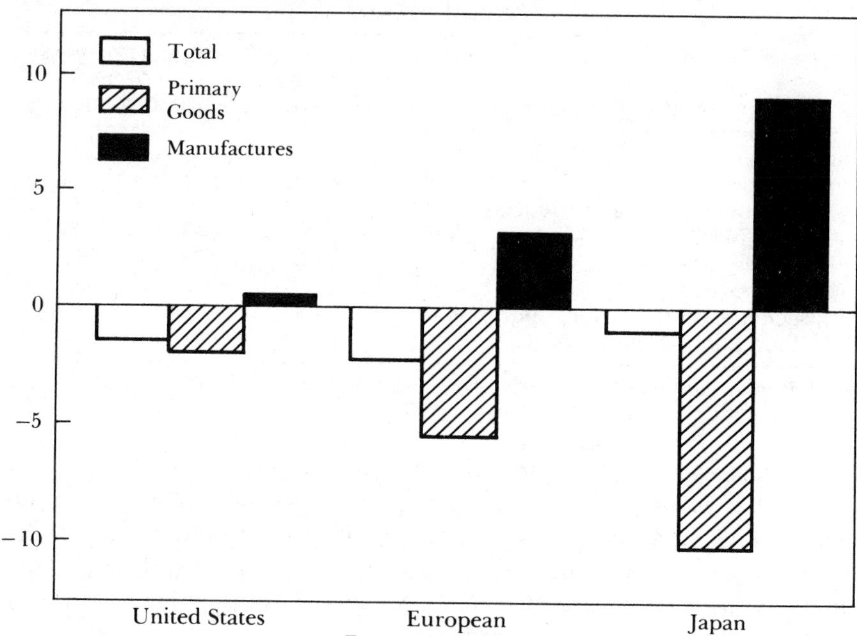

Source: Organization for Economic Cooperation and Development.

Although Japanese trade policy does not play a central role in causing the bilateral trade imbalance with the United States, Japanese import restrictions remain a major source of friction. Japan maintains a variety of nontariff barriers against imports. These include import quotas for a number of agricultural products and "red tape" barriers against manufactured goods, such as stringent inspection requirements applied against imported goods but not against Japanese products. These trade restrictions probably do not lead to a larger overall Japanese trade surplus. If they were removed, the yen would depreciate and increased

TABLE 3. Trade Balances by Region as Percent of GDP, United States and Japan, 1980
[Percent of GDP]

REGION	UNITED STATES	JAPAN
Industrial countries	0.23	1.92
Oil-exporting countries	–1.45	–3.20
Non-oil developing countries	.52	1.46

Source: International Monetary Fund.

TABLE 4. U.S. Trade Balances by Sector as Percent of GDP, 1972–79 [Percent of GDP]

ITEM	1972	1979
U.S. comparative advantage:		
Research-intensive manufactures	0.93	1.63
Resource-intensive products, other than fuels	.06	.67
Invisibles (services and investment income)	.40	1.44
U.S. comparative disadvantage:		
Nonresearch-intensive manufactures	−1.27	−1.44
Fuels	−.27	−2.41

Sources: International Monetary Fund, National Science Board, and Organization for Economic Co-operation and Development.

Japanese imports in the currently protected sectors would be offset by reduced deficits or increased surpluses elsewhere. Japanese trade restrictions do, however, distort the composition of U.S. trade with Japan, imposing serious costs on some U.S. producers. As the fastest growing and second largest market economy, Japan has a responsibility to help sustain the open trading system. A major trade liberalization by Japan would do much to relieve the political strains on that system, while the failure of Japan to make more than token concessions would intensify them.

The Problem of Uncompetitive Sectors

Analysis of the overall U.S. trade deficit and the bilateral deficit with Japan suggests that worries about U.S. competitiveness are based in part on a misunderstanding of the situation. There is no question, however, that increased foreign competition has forced some sectors of the U.S. economy to contract.

This is partly a consequence of the fact that trade has become more important to the U.S. economy. Specialization by nations is the reason for international trade. If the United States is to expand its trade, the U.S. economy must become more specialized. This means that some sectors will grow and others will shrink. During the 1970s the United States developed increasing surpluses in areas in which it already enjoyed a comparative advantage and developed increasing deficits in sectors in which it was at a disadvantage. Some illustrative numbers are given in Table 4.

Specialization of this kind is desirable both for the United States and for its trading partners. Specialization and trade raise the efficiency of the world economy as a whole by allowing each country to concentrate on doing what it does relatively well, and by allowing increased economies of scale. But greater specialization can leave those involved in the contracting sectors worse off, at least temporarily. Attempts to prevent adjustment through trade barriers or subsidies, however, impose severe costs on unprotected sectors.

Some sectoral reallocation of resources, then, is a normal consequence of the increasing U.S. integration into the world economy. This is not the whole story, however. Some sectors of the U.S. economy are confronted by a problem that is not simply the result of market forces. Broadly speaking, these sectors fall into two groups. In one group are sectors where firms or their workers, accustomed to having substantial market power, now find that they have priced themselves out of the world market. In the other group are sectors which are hurt by foreign protectionism or export subsidies.

Market Power and Competitiveness. The "problem" of diminished market power in some sectors actually derives from a desirable aspect of trade: the fact that trade increases competition. One of the major benefits of an increasingly open U.S. economy is that it reduces the problems of monopoly and market power, thus increasing efficiency and helping consumers. But the transition to more competitive markets can prove painful. When an industry accustomed to having domestic market power encounters international competition, it must accept a reduction in the premium in prices and wages it previously commanded over other sectors of the economy. Both firms and workers may be reluctant to accept this implication of increased competition, and idle capacity and unemployment may result. Prices and wages in some U.S. heavy industries are probably too high to be sustainable in an integrated world economy.

Policies of Foreign Governments. A different problem is posed when foreign governments engage in protective or export promotion measures that harm U.S. producers. U.S. trade negotiators have emphasized four particular areas of concern:

1. *Agriculture:* Japan and the European Economic Community have high protective barriers against U.S. agricultural products. Further, the European Economic Community now engages in massive subsidized export of agricultural products to dispose of the surpluses created by its price-support program. These measures depress world prices of agricultural products, imposing substantial costs on U.S. producers in a sector where the United States holds a clear comparative advantage.
2. *High technology:* In recent years, many countries have come to view the high-technology industries as vehicles for economic growth and have sought to promote them through a complex mix of policies—outright subsidies, export credit subsidies, research subsidies, preferential procurement by state-owned enterprises, and so on. The United States holds a comparative advantage in high-technology products, and the U.S. export market share has remained roughly constant since 1973. Nevertheless, there is concern

that in some specific areas, especially aircraft, foreign subsidies are threatening the position of U.S. producers.

3. *Services:* The United States has developed an increasingly strong net export position in services. Services, however, have never been recognized as being under the rules of the international trading system, and trade in services is limited by a maze of foreign government regulations.
4. *Investment:* Many countries impose "investment performance requirements" on foreign investors in exchange for the right to invest or to receive investment incentives. Many of those performance requirements are trade-related, requiring foreign companies to export more, reach a specified level of local content, or reduce imports.

Challenges to U.S. Trade Policy

The next few years are critical for the international trading system. Accumulating structural problems have combined with short-run macroeconomic stresses to produce a resurgence of protectionist pressures. The Administration's aim, nonetheless, is to preserve and extend the benefits of freer trade. To do this will require resisting protectionist pressures at home while continuing to urge foreign governments to eliminate their more objectionable trade-distorting policies.

Responding to Foreign Actions. The practices of foreign governments pose extremely difficult issues for U.S. trade policy. The United States customarily seeks to induce other nations to move in the direction of freer trade. The dilemma is how to do this without imposing costs on ourselves that exceed the benefits from changes in other countries' policies.

Trade-distorting measures, whether they take the form of protection against imports or the promotion of exports, hurt the country which adopts them as well as other countries, even when they are a response to foreign trade-distorting practices. If foreign governments limit imports from the United States and we respond in kind, the initial results will be further reductions in economic efficiency at home and higher domestic prices. If foreign governments subsidize exports, depressing world prices for U.S. products, a countersubsidy by the United States will depress prices still further. The belief that departures from free trade are automatically called for if other countries do not play by the rules is a fallacy.

Intervention in international trade by the U.S. Government, even though costly to the U.S. economy in the short run, may, however, be justified if it serves the *strategic* purpose of increasing the cost of interventionist policies by foreign governments. Thus, there is a potential role for carefully targeted measures, explicitly temporary, aimed at convincing other countries to reduce their trade distortions.

There are obvious risks in such a course of action. Instead of inducing other countries to move toward freer trade, U.S. pressure might set off a cycle of retaliation which would leave everyone worse off. There are also domestic political risks. Trade measures intended to be temporary may end up permanent and institutionalized. The need to balance the strategic objective of reducing foreign trade barriers against the harm which might be caused by U.S. retaliatory measures explains the U.S. policy of negotiating for freer trade while holding open the possibility of more direct action as a last resort.

Responding to Problem Industries. The problems of industries which have recently lost their traditional market power also pose a serious policy dilemma. There is strong pressure to give these industries at least temporary relief from imports, in the hope that lower wage and price increases and improved productivity will eventually make them competitive again. On the other hand, protection reduces the incentives for both firms and workers to make these changes. Furthermore, protectionist measures, however temporary they are supposed to be, tend to become permanent. The limitation of protection for these problem industries is a central goal of U.S. economic policy.

EXCHANGE RATES AND THE BALANCE OF PAYMENTS

During 1982 the dollar rose against other major currencies to its highest level since the beginning of floating exchange rates in 1973. The strength of the dollar provided some benefits to the U.S. economy by reducing import prices and thus accelerating progress against inflation. On the other hand, the strong dollar caused severe problems by decreasing the cost competitiveness of exported U.S. goods.

Causes of the Dollar's Strength

Exchange-rate movements are not well understood. Econometric models of exchange-rate determination proposed in the past decade have not shown any consistent ability to track past exchange-rate movements, let alone predict future changes. Nevertheless, careful analysis can narrow the range of plausible explanations of the dollar's rise.

The recent appreciation of the dollar, unlike many earlier exchange-rate movements, did not simply reflect contemporaneous changes in relative price levels. The well-known theory of purchasing power parity suggests that the rate of change in the exchange rate should equal the difference between the foreign and domestic inflation rates. Over the

Figure 3. Real Exchange Rates of Major Currencies Against The Dollar

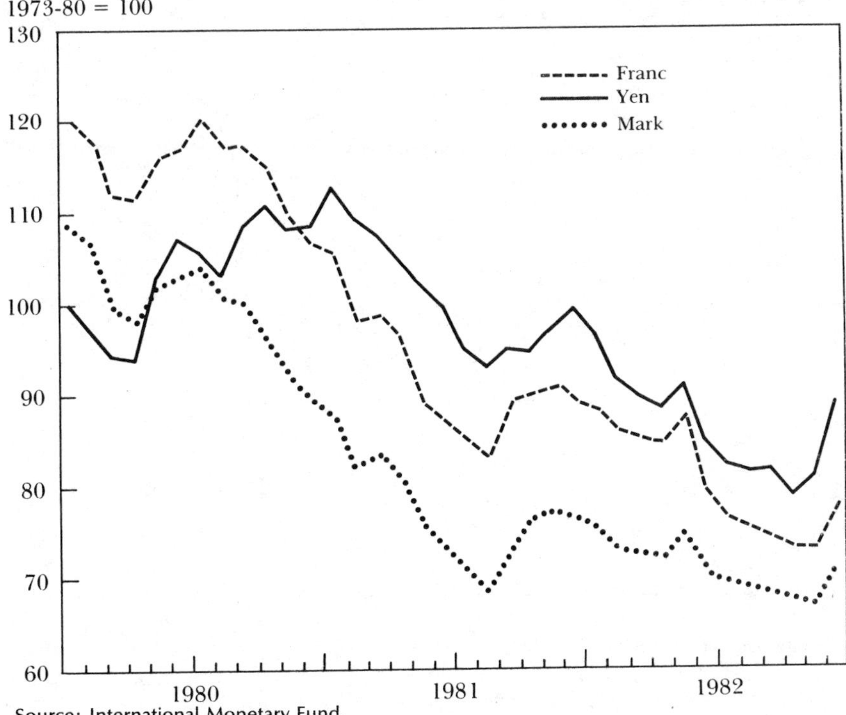

Source: International Monetary Fund.

Note: Consumer prices used as deflator.

very long run, or in situations of very large differences in inflation rates, the purchasing power parity theory has proved to be a useful guide. But the theory has little or no power to explain the recent rise of the dollar. Price increases over the past 2 years in Germany and Japan, for instance, were lower than in the United States. Yet the dollar appreciated dramatically during that period against both the mark and the yen. Stated differently, the rise of the dollar was not simply a nominal but also a real appreciation, as illustrated in Figure 3.

Large exchange-rate movements may also occur because of shifts in world demand for a country's exports or changes in a country's demand for imports. An example of such an event was Great Britain's discovery of oil in the North Sea, which has played at least some role in the high level of Great Britain's real exchange rate relative to other European currencies.

No comparable event accounts for the appreciation of the dollar, although U.S. oil imports have declined sharply. The rise of the dollar was not initially accompanied by a deterioration of the trade balance, a fact which might seem to suggest that there was an increase in demand

Figure 4. International Real Short-Term Interest Rate Differentials

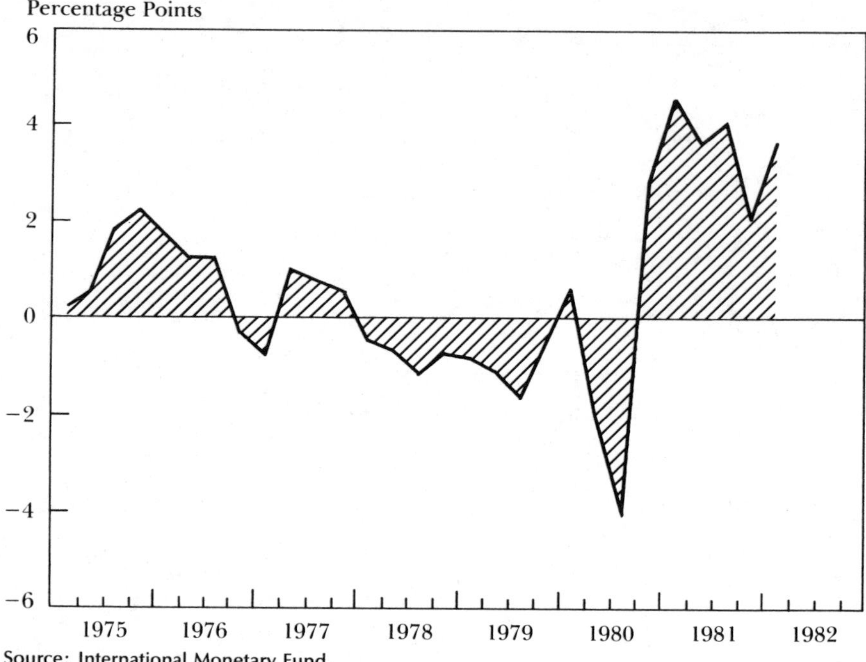

Source: International Monetary Fund.

Note: Data are U.S. rate minus average of rates for major industrial countries weighted by GNP, adjusted for differences in consumer price inflation.

for U.S. goods. The initial lack of deterioration, however, stemmed from lags in the effect of the exchange rate on the trade balance rather than from a shift in either export or import demand, and the U.S. trade deficit grew rapidly in the second half of 1982.

What the rise of the dollar seems clearly to reflect is a rise not in the demand for U.S. goods, but in the demand for U.S. assets. The reasons for the increased attractiveness of investment in the United States are somewhat controversial, but the effects are not. In order to buy U.S. assets, foreigners must first acquire dollars. The increased demand for dollars drives up the exchange rate.

One important factor in the increased demand for U.S. assets was that real interest rates in the United States were high relative to real interest rates elsewhere. Real interest rates are not directly measurable, since they equal the nominal rate minus *expected* inflation. But some rough measure is attainable by computing the nominal rate minus *actual* inflation. Figure 4 shows the differential in real interest rates computed in this way between the United States and other industrial countries. The chart suggests that the real interest rate in the United States was substantially higher than foreign rates in recent years.

But events in the fall of 1982 cast some doubt on whether real interest rates alone can explain the dollar's strength. As U.S. short-term interest rates fell sharply, the differential between short-term interest rates in the United States and other countries was greatly reduced. Yet the dollar continued to rise. The explanation for this may lie in the difference between short- and long-term rates. Most exchange-rate models suggest that long-term real rates, and not short-term ones, are what affect the real exchange rate. A notable feature of the U.S. financial scene in the fall of 1982 was that long-term rates did not fall nearly as much as short-term rates. At the same time, long-run inflation expectations may have declined, so that it is unclear how much long-term real interest rates actually fell.

Many observers believe that other factors besides real interest rates help explain the dollar's strength. In particular, the unsettled state of the world economy—particularly the problems in Europe and Latin America described later in this chapter—may have created a desire on the part of investors for a safe haven for their funds. The United States, according to this argument, is still regarded as the most politically and economically stable of the market economies and has become a financial refuge in troubled times. While the importance of this factor is hard to assess, the worldwide search for financial security may partially explain this country's rising capital account surplus and its growing current account deficit.

An Undervalued Yen?

The explanations of the strong dollar discussed so far leave out a view which has received considerable attention—that the strength of the dollar reflects deliberate undervaluation of their currencies by our competitors, especially Japan. This view is important enough in its implications for U.S. international economic policy to deserve separate treatment.

Arguments that the yen is undervalued are of two types, which are basically independent of one another. One argument is that the Japanese government has persistently kept the yen undervalued. The other is that the Japanese have only recently engineered a decline in the yen to gain competitive advantage. Neither of these views appears correct in light of the actual behavior of Japan's balance of payments and exchange rate.

If the first allegation—that the yen has been persistently undervalued—was correct, Japan would run persistent current account surpluses in excess of what seems justified. We would also expect Japan to have experienced exceptionally rapid growth in its foreign exchange reserves. Neither of these was the case:

TABLE 5. Real Appreciation of the Dollar against Major Currencies to August 1982

[Percent change from base year to August 1982[1]]

BASE YEAR	FRENCH FRANC	GERMAN MARK	JAPANESE YEN
1971	−1.0	−2.1	−25.3
1972	11.8	9.5	−13.1
1973	27.9	31.4	2.0
1974	21.4	31.0	6.4
1975	39.5	33.7	7.3
1976	29.6	28.8	10.9
1977	29.4	35.9	24.3
1978	43.0	50.1	[2]53.1
1979	50.8	53.8	36.8
1980	51.6	44.2	25.9
1981	21.1	11.3	[2]22.9

[1] Percent change in the price of the dollar in each currency, adjusted for differences in consumer price inflation.
[2] Indicates a base year relative to which the August 1982 exchange rate of the yen looks lower than that of the other currencies.

Source: Board of Governors of the Federal Reserve System.

From the beginning of floating exchange rates in 1973 through 1981, Japan had an average surplus in its current account of only 0.15 percent of GNP. This was not much more than the U.S. figure for the same period (0.11 percent), considerably less than that of Germany (0.47 percent), and much less than the U.S. surplus of the early 1960s (0.70 percent).

From the beginning of floating exchange rates in 1973 to the third quarter of 1982, Japan's reserves minus gold grew at an annual rate of 4.8 percent, far less than the 9.7 percent rate of reserve growth for all non-OPEC countries.

These facts contradict the view that the yen was persistently undervalued. There remains the possibility that the yen's weakness during much of 1982 was excessive in some sense. A natural question is whether, after adjustment for purchasing power parity, the yen fell more against the dollar than other currencies. The answer to this question depends on the base period used for comparison. For most base periods, however, the real depreciation of the yen against the dollar appears smaller than that of the French franc and the German mark. Table 5 shows an illustrative set of numbers. As the table shows, only for a few base periods does the yen appear more "undervalued" that the other two currencies.

The actual behavior of the Japanese balance of payments and exchange rate thus do not support the view that there is any special undervaluation of the yen—that is, they suggest that exchange-rate movements over the last several years stemmed from a strong dollar rather than a weak yen. An examination of Japanese policy by the U.S. Treasury supports this conclusion. This study found that Japan has attempted to isolate its domestic capital market from world capital markets, but that this has tended to limit capital outflow rather than inflow, supporting rather than weakening the yen. Japanese capital controls have been relaxed in recent years, a move which the United States supports even though the result will be a weaker yen and an increase in Japan's current account surplus. In the 1980s, Japan may well become more of a capital exporter than it was in the 1970s, and thus have larger current account surpluses. These surpluses, if they materialize, will result from Japan's high domestic saving rate, which gives Japan a natural role as an exporter of capital to the rest of the world.

To show that there is no special yen issue is not to deny that a substantial deterioration has occurred in the relative cost position of U.S. firms. This deterioration was actually larger relative to other industrial countries, but since Japan is the United States' most important competitor, the depreciation of the yen worries U.S. firms more. There is no special yen issue, but the strong dollar does pose genuine problems.

Effects of a Strong Dollar on U.S. Trade

The rise of the dollar was associated with a large rise in the production costs of U.S. firms relative to those of foreign competitors. To take one measure, unit labor costs in U.S. manufacturing rose 32 percent relative to those of a weighted average of other industrial countries from their low point in the third quarter of 1980 to the second quarter of 1982. This rise in relative costs has at least temporarily reduced the international competitiveness of U.S. industry dramatically. Other U.S. exporting and import-competing sectors, especially agriculture, have also been squeezed.

Despite this deterioration in competitive position, it was only in the third quarter of 1982 that the U.S. trade deficit began to show a significant increase. This delay was in line with previous experience of the effect of exchange rates on trade. The full effect of changes in exchange rates on the volume of exports and imports is felt only after some time has passed, because some trade takes place under contracts signed in advance and because customers do not always change suppliers immediately when relative prices change. The short-term effect of a rise in the dollar is to reduce import prices, which actually tends to *improve* the trade balance. Although the negative effects eventually dominate, some econometric estimates suggest that the full negative effect is not felt for more than 2 years.

As the effects of the strong dollar are increasingly reflected in U.S. trade, the trade deficit will widen. Economic developments elsewhere in the world will also contribute to a widening trade deficit. The recession in other industrial countries will depress the demand for U.S.

exports, and financial constraints in developing countries will lead them to import less. Both developments will have negative consequences for U.S. exports. Record trade and current account deficits in 1983 will almost surely result.

Whether the trade and current account deficits persist will largely depend on U.S. macroeconomic policies, particularly on the fiscal side. If large budget deficits are allowed to continue to depress the U.S. national saving rate, real interest rates may rise again, sustaining or even increasing the high real exchange rate of the dollar. In this case the trade deficit could remain high for several years.

A large and sustained trade deficit would result in an economic recovery which would be "lopsided" in the sense that exporting and import-competing sectors would not share in the gains. Should this occur, government, business, and labor officials must bear in mind that even though protectionist foreign trade practices distort the composition of world trade and reduce economic efficiency both in the United States and abroad, large trade deficits are not the result of unfair foreign competition. Large projected U.S. trade deficits are a result of macroeconomic forces, particularly large budget deficits. The main sources of the U.S. trade deficit are to be found not in Paris or in Tokyo, but in Washington.

Responses to The Strong Dollar

The temporary adverse effects of a strong dollar create pressure to do something for the exporting and import-competing sectors. Three kinds of policies might be used: microeconomic intervention in the form of protection or export subsidies, direct intervention in the foreign exchange market, and changes in monetary and fiscal policy.

Protection and Export Promotion. The negative effect of the strong dollar on the competitiveness of many U.S. firms has fueled pressures for an interventionist trade policy. These pressures must be resisted. Protecting import-competing industries or subsidizing exports is not just a harmful long-run policy. With a floating exchange rate, such policies would fail to improve the trade balance or create employment even in the short run.

The exchange rate always moves to clear the market. An increase in exports or a reduction in imports would lead to an increased demand for or reduced supply of dollars on the world market, raising the exchange rate. This would lead to a further loss of competitiveness in the sectors not protected or promoted. An export subsidy for agricultural products would worsen the situation of the auto industry, an import quota on steel would hurt the competitiveness of the aircraft industry, and so on. Although these indirect effects may seem of doubtful importance in the real world, they are not. That governments cannot simultaneously protect everyone is a basic principle of international trade.

Instead of creating additional employment and output, the distortion of trade through protectionist policies or export promotion would probably reduce them. Market-distorting policies reduce the efficiency of the economy. Thus, a turn to protectionism could create a "supply-side" shock that might have the same kind of stagflationary effects as an oil price increase. The effects would prove still worse if, as is likely, U.S. actions were to provoke foreign retaliation.

Although protectionism and export subsidies provide no answer to the problems caused by a strong dollar, the pressure to use them is increasing. Many of the exporting sectors, which make up the traditional constituency for freer trade, appear to have become convinced by the strength of the dollar and the resulting loss of U.S. competitiveness that a more interventionist policy is needed.

Exchange-Market Intervention. Since March 1981 the United States has abstained as much as possible from direct intervention in the foreign exchange market. This unwillingness to intervene is based on doubts about whether exchange-market intervention is effective or desirable. As long as the Federal Reserve continues to pursue a policy of targeting monetary aggregates, any U.S. intervention on the foreign exchange market must be *sterilized*—that is, offset by other transactions on domestic financial markets. These transactions are likely to wipe out most of the effect of the initial exchange-market intervention.

The process of sterilization is straightforward. If the U.S. Government attempted to drive up the price of foreign exchange and weaken the dollar by buying foreign securities, the Federal Reserve would issue dollars to pay for the foreign assets. In order to prevent these dollars from increasing the U.S. money stock, however, the Federal Reserve would then have to withdraw an equal number of dollars from the market by selling Treasury bills. The only net result would be that the world's supply of dollar-denominated assets would increase, while its supply of assets denominated in other currencies would fall.

The increase in the level of dollar-denominated assets would probably have little effect on the exchange rate because of the sheer size of world financial markets. The world market in dollar-denominated securities includes not only the dollar assets actually owned abroad—foreign deposits in U.S. banks, foreign holdings of Treasury bills, Eurodollar deposits, and the like—but also all those dollar assets which are potentially tradeable. Thus, the total pool of internationally mobile dollar assets is probably in the trillions of dollars. This makes it questionable whether even very large interventions in the exchange market can have much effect on the exchange rate.

Macroeconomic Policies. Although the government cannot significantly affect exchange rates through direct intervention, monetary and fiscal policies do indirectly affect the exchange rate. A feasible strategy for bringing the dollar down would involve looser monetary policies and tighter fiscal policies. Both of these changes would tend to lower real interest rates (at least in the short run), making capital movement into the United States less attractive and thus driving down the value of the dollar.

Despite its unfortunate effects on the U.S. balance of trade, however, monetary restraint is the prime weapon in the fight against inflation. Disinflation, as we have learned, unfortunately involves substantial costs. Under fixed exchange rates the heaviest costs of monetary contraction and disinflation fell on the interest-sensitive sectors of the economy, such as construction and consumer durables. With floating exchange rates, however, much of the burden also falls on exporting and import-competing sectors, which are injured by the rise in the value of the dollar.

A tighter fiscal policy would also lower real interest rates and lead to a lower dollar. Under fixed exchange rates, budget deficits crowded out domestic investment. With a floating exchange rate they crowd out exporting and import-competing products as well. A reduction in deficits would lead—with some lag—to an improvement in the trade balance as well as higher investment.

The strength of the dollar has put considerable strain on the resolve of the United States to remain committed to free trade. This strain is not unique to the international sector. The recession and high interest rates have also put a strain on the resolve to let other types of markets, from housing to labor markets, operate freely. If there is special reason for concern about the international side, it is because of the danger that mistakes in U.S. policy could set off a spiral of retaliation among all the major trading nations.

The competitiveness of U.S. business as a whole—as opposed to that of particular sectors—and the balance of payments are macroeconomic phenomena. Microeconomic interventions cannot cure macroeconomic problems; they can only make one sector better off by hurting other sectors even more. The most effective strategy the United States can pursue for its exporting and import-competing sectors is to get its overall economic house in order—above all, by bringing budget deficits and real interest rates under control.

MACROECONOMIC PROBLEMS IN EUROPE

More than 90 percent of the output of the industrial countries, and more than 70 percent of the output of the world's market economies,

TABLE 6. Economic Performance by Major Industrial Countries, 1973–82
[Percent]

ITEM	UNITED STATES	FOUR LARGE EUROPEAN COUNTRIES[1]	JAPAN
Growth rate in:			
Real gross domestic product (GDP), 1973–80	2.3	2.2	3.7
Real GDP per employed person, 1973–80	.2	2.2	3.0
Real GDP, 1980:I–1981:IV	–.2	.1	2.3
Level:			
Consumer price inflation, year ending 1982:II	6.8	10.2	2.4
Unemployment rate, 1981	7.6	7.4	2.3

[1] France, Germany, Italy, and United Kingdom.

Source: International Monetary Fund and Organization for Economic Cooperation and Development.

is produced by the United States, Japan, and the European Economic Community. Table 6 shows some comparative figures for the three. The most striking feature of the table is the favorable performance of Japan by all measures. The United States and the European Economic Community look rather similar in their less favorable performances. They experienced nearly the same growth rates before 1979, have suffered nearly equal decelerations of growth since then, and had roughly the same unemployment rate in 1981. The U.S. inflation rate was lower than that in Europe, but the United States also showed lower productivity growth.

Behind the similarity of U.S. and European experience, however, lies a major difference. The U.S. economy, whatever its other difficulties, has provided employment opportunities for a rapidly growing labor force. The current high unemployment rate is a cyclical problem, not the result of a persistent failure of employment to expand. In Europe, by contrast, employment was virtually stationary over the last decade, and unemployment has risen in every year since 1973. This is a worrisome aspect of the European situation.

For a given rate of unemployment, the strains on society are probably greater if employment is stagnant than if it is growing. Growing employment means that more new jobs are always opening up, offering job losers a chance for reemployment and new entrants to the labor market a chance to get their first job. If employment is stationary, workers who have lost their jobs may stay unemployed for a long time, and young people may never find jobs. The results of near-zero employment growth are painfully visible in Europe, where long-term unemployment (more than 6 months) is several times higher than in the United States, and where the share of youth unemployment in the total pool of unemployed has risen steadily since 1973.

TABLE 7. Employment and Unemployment in the European Economic Community, 1973–80
[Percent]

YEAR	INCREASE IN EMPLOYMENT	UNEMPLOYMENT RATE
1973	1.1	2.8
1974	.1	3.0
1975	−1.1	4.2
1976	−.1	4.9
1977	.4	5.2
1978	.6	5.3
1979	.8	5.3
1980	.2	5.7

Source: Organization for Economic Cooperation and Development.

How did the problem arise? The causes of structural unemployment are always controversial, but a key element in the European employment problem was probably rapid increases in real labor costs in the first half of the 1970s in the face of declining productivity growth and rising oil prices. These increases in labor costs—which stemmed at least in part from increases in social insurance payments—squeezed profitability. Firms closed their marginal plants and invested in increasingly capital-intensive techniques, which helped to sustain the rate of productivity growth but also led to employment stagnation.

The unemployment problem in Europe is not caused solely by excessive labor costs. The periods of rapid increase in European unemployment, in 1973–76 and since 1979, came during business cycle contractions (Table 7). The most recent rise in unemployment is probably mostly due to restrictive monetary and fiscal policies adopted by the European countries following the oil price shock of 1979. These policies were adopted out of concern that the rise in import prices resulting from that shock—and, later, the further rise in import prices resulting from the appreciation of the dollar—would lead to an uncontrollable inflationary spiral. Thus, recent developments in the European economy are to some extent similar in character to those in the United States, which have also resulted largely from disinflationary policies. The European situation is more serious, however, because the current recession comes on top of a steadily growing structural unemployment problem.

The United States has a major stake in the success of the European countries in dealing with their macroeconomic problems. The stake is not simply due to the fact that the major European countries are also allies of the United States, nor is it simply due to the fact that roughly one-quarter of U.S. exports go to Western Europe. More than this, Europe is a key part of the world economy, with an aggregate GNP as large as that of the United States itself. If European countries remain mired in economic stagnation and turn toward increased protectionism as a consequence, little chance will remain of saving the open trading system.

THE INTERNATIONAL DEBT PROBLEM

Different problems from those facing the United States and Europe afflict the economies of the developing nations. The problems of these economies have accumulated over the last several years and are products of both domestic policy mistakes and external developments, such as oil price increases, the recession in industrial countries, and high real interest rates. In the summer and fall of 1982 the problems came to a head in the form of a sharp reduction in international lending to the developing countries.

Debt-Financed Growth in The 1970s

Until recently, the growth of such middle income developing countries as Brazil, South Korea, and Taiwan was widely viewed as one of the great success stories of the 1970s. Particularly notable was their success in expanding exports of manufactured goods. While the growth of these exports did give rise to some adjustment problems in industrial countries, the successes of some middle income countries were undoubtedly a highly favorable development for the United States. Such success provided a dramatic demonstration to other countries of the potential of market-oriented economic policies.

An important aspect of growth in the developing world, however, was heavy borrowing from foreign sources. There is nothing inherently wrong in external borrowing to finance growth. Some of the developed countries, including the United States, relied heavily on foreign capital during earlier periods of industrialization. But some developing nations borrowed too much, investing in projects of doubtful productivity. When overly optimistic expectations about export earnings and interest rates turned out to have been wrong, these countries found themselves in serious financial difficulty.

From 1973 to 1981 the medium- and long-term external debt of non-oil developing countries rose at an annual rate of more than 20 percent. Lenders might have viewed this rate of increase as more alarming than they did, were it not for several factors which appeared to indicate that the eventual repayment of the debt would not impose a severe burden on borrowing countries. These factors included:

A rapid growth in the ability of these countries to service their debt. Exports of the non-oil developing countries grew at an annual rate of 18 percent.

Very low real interest rates. From 1973 to 1979 Eurodollar rates in London, which set the basis for most international lending, averaged 8.5 percent, while U.S. wholesale prices rose at an annual rate of 9.8 percent. Even allowing for the fact that third-world borrowers paid small spreads over the Euromarket rate, the real interest rates they paid were still negative.

Special factors which appeared to ensure rising export earnings in the future. The most important of these was oil reserves, which were essentially treated as an asset against which countries could safely borrow.

Causes of The Liquidity Problem

Excessive borrowing by some developing countries made an eventual financial problem inevitable. The proximate factor which brought the era of debt-financed growth to a halt was, however, a sharp deterioration in the world economy. The rise in oil prices in 1979 was a blow to many debtor countries, and further strains resulted from disinflation in the United States and other industrial countries. The factors which led to a loss of lender confidence in the developing countries included:

The effects of the world recession on export demand. The rapid export growth of the 1970s came to an abrupt end in the early 1980s. Exports of the non-oil developing countries actually fell by 7.5 percent from the first half of 1981 to the first half of 1982. Exporters of primary products were hit particularly hard: real commodity prices fell by 25 percent from the fourth quarter of 1980 to the second quarter of 1982.

High real interest rates. In 1981 and the first half of 1982, Euromarket interest rates averaged 16 percent, while wholesale prices in the United States rose at an annual rate of only 4.5 percent.

The appreciation of the dollar. Since most international debt is denominated in dollars, while commodity prices tend to follow a weighted average of industrial country currencies, the effect of the rise in the value of the dollar was a sudden increase in the size of developing country debt relative to prospective export earnings.

The result of these developments was that banks, which had been willing to lend large amounts to developing countries throughout the 1970s, lost confidence that the loans would be promptly repaid. The debtor countries were highly vulnerable to such a loss of confidence. Much of their debt was of short maturity, so that a large fraction of their debt required refinancing each year. Argentina, Brazil, and

Mexico, for example, must make annual payments of principal and interest which exceed their total exports of goods and services. During the 1970s these large financing needs did not pose a problem, since countries were able to roll over their debt as it came due. In the summer and fall of 1982, however, banks became reluctant to make new loans and roll over old ones, first to Mexico and then to other countries. The result was a quick exhaustion of the foreign exchange reserves of the major debtors.

Implications of The Debt Problem

The debt situation of the developing countries poses two problems for the world economy. Although quite unlikely, failure to resolve the debt situation in an orderly way could lead to major financial market disruptions. More likely—indeed, it has already happened to a considerable extent—is a situation of forced austerity in debtor countries, with adverse effects on world trade and output.

Risks to Financial Markets. The threat of a financial disruption arises from the possibility that debtor countries will be unable to live within their new financial constraints. The unwillingness of banks to lend as much as in the recent past means that debtor countries will need to cut their imports or expand their exports. In the case of the most heavily indebted countries, this will almost certainly mean achieving substantial trade surpluses in spite of depressed demand for their exports. The concern of lenders that some debtors will not be able to achieve the required adjustment is precisely what makes them reluctant to lend.

Fortunately, a serious financial disruption is unlikely. The debtor countries and the banks which are their major creditors share a strong interest in an orderly resolution of the debt problem. For the debtor countries, maintaining good financial standing is essential if they are to maintain access both to world capital markets and to their export markets. At the same time, banks realize that demanding too rapid a repayment from debtor countries could prove counterproductive, and they are probably willing to provide enough financing so that debtor countries can more easily handle the financial squeeze. Although banks find themselves in somewhat of a "prisoner's dilemma" situation, in which no one bank will want to lend if it believes that the loans will only go to repay other banks, this problem should not prove insoluble. The banking community should be able to work with the International Monetary Fund (IMF) in negotiating agreements which balance an adequate degree of new lending to the debtor countries with realistic economic adjustment plans. To aid in this process, the Administration and representatives of other industrial nations recently agreed in principle to an enlargement of the IMF's resources.

Perhaps the most important safeguard against a financial crisis is the ability of the governments and central banks of the major industrial countries to provide a safety net for the international financial system. Central banks act as lenders of last resort for commercial banks, providing effective protection against banking panics. At the same time, industrial country governments have demonstrated their willingness to help provide temporary financing for developing countries in order to bridge the interval until agreements can be reached with the IMF. (The IMF recently concluded agreements with Mexico, Argentina, and Brazil.)

Effects on World Trade. Although a serious disruption of the international financial system is unlikely, for all of the reasons cited, serious problems still exist. Even under optimistic assumptions, those developing countries with high ratios of debt to exports will be forced to improve their trade balances substantially in order to pay the interest on their debt. Much of this trade balance improvement will probably come through reductions in imports, involving painful reductions in output and real wages in the debtor countries. This will also depress demand for the products of industrial countries—particularly the United States, which has especially close trading relations with some of the major Latin American debtors. The debt problem of the developing countries may worsen the U.S. trade balance by $10 to $20 billion and reduce U.S. GNP by one-half percentage point or more from the level it would otherwise reach.

The Outlook for Debtor Nations. The problems of the developing countries are not insoluble. If growth in the world economy resumes and real interest rates fall to historical levels, the debt burden of even the most heavily indebted countries will become much more manageable. Mexico and Brazil, among the most heavily indebted countries, both have debts well below half their GNPs. At a historically typical real interest rate of 2 percent, the real burden of debt service would fall to less than 1 percent of GNP—a fully manageable level in a growing economy.

The key to recovery from the debt problem, however, lies in increased exports from the debtor countries. Import restrictions by the developing countries can only accomplish so much in improving their trade balances. Imports have already fallen considerably in high debt countries in the last year, leaving limited room for further cuts. As growth resumes among the debtor countries, they will tend to import more, and will need to export more to pay for the imports. They will not be able to do this if the industrial countries, including the United States, institute new protectionist measures. Yet as developing countries attempt to increase their exports, strong political pressures will develop in the industrial countries to stop them. Leaders in the industrial countries must realize that shutting out imports from the developing world will not only incur the usual costs of protection—higher prices to consumers and jobs lost in unprotected sectors—but also will threaten the basic stability of the world financial system.

11. American Foreign Economic Policy: Challenges of the 1980s

JOHN ADAMS

The making of U.S. foreign economic policy is never an easy task. Complex international and domestic aims and interests must be balanced. U.S. farmers want open European markets for their grain but if Europe is pushed too hard on this issue the resulting ill-will may affect European attitudes toward U.S. investment or common security measures. Damage to U.S. textile producers from Asian imports may prompt steps for quotas that in turn alienate friendly governments. Tension is often high when U.S. legislators consider key international bills and broad global and national aims are confounded by specific, well-organized interests. Recent cases in point are the acrimonious affray over the expansion of resources for the International Monetary Fund and demands for "reciprocity" in export access. In the 1980s similar skirmishes are likely to abound, and mount in scale, because of the growing and unavoidable integration of the U.S. economy with the economies of the rest of the world.

In his recent study of long-run economic growth in the world's major market economies Angus Maddison calls the period 1950–1973 the "Golden Age."[1] During this span output per person rose by 3.8 percent per year. This was 2.4 times the average rate of growth of the capitalist world since 1820. A primary source of this unprecedented prosperity was the expansion of international trade. Exports of the chief industrial economies grew at the rate of 8.6 percent per year and multiplied more than six-fold.[2] This rate was also more than twice that of the long-term historical experience. Growth in the industrial economies interacted

John Adams is Professor of Economics at the University of Maryland, College Park.

with growth in the socialist and third world countries, and many in the latter group broke out of centuries of stagnation and poverty.

The United States not only participated fully in the global expansion of trade, income, and employment after 1950, but provided primary leadership in creating many of the conditions that made that expansion possible. The post-war Bretton Woods agreement of 1944 yielded the International Monetary Fund (IMF) and the World Bank. The United States was a major mover in the creation of the European Economic Community (EEC) and in the revitalization of the Japanese economy. The General Agreement on Tariffs and Trade (GATT) became effective in 1948, with broad tariff reductions taking effect following the Kennedy Round (1962–1967) and Tokyo Round (1974–1979) discussions. To conduct these negotiations the U.S. Congress conferred wide negotiating authority on the executive branch via the Trade Expansion Act of 1962 and the Trade Reform Act of 1974. These two measures reflected a deep national consensus that trade liberalization would be broadly beneficial to consumers, workers, and businesses in the United States.

There is little doubt that the emergence of the IMF, World Bank, EEC, and GATT as working international institutions greatly enhanced global economic integration and contributed to the nurturing of an international atmosphere in which trade and investment could flourish. During the 1970s the world economy passed through a period when events moved unfavorably for continued growth and development. These international institutions came under stress and had to adapt to these changed circumstances, a process still going on. Lagging growth, low productivity gains, high inflation, high unemployment, and slumping core industries affected most advanced national economies. These changes gave renewed vigor to ancient calls for national isolation and market and job protection.

In hearings before the Senate's Subcommittee on International Trade, Senator Max Baucus of Montana summarized some of these tensions and fears when he said:

> In my view, the United States is No. 1. There is this book about Japan being No. 1. I think we are No. 1, too, not only in [economic leadership] but in another sense. It is the sense of self-preservation. We have got to worry about ourselves first before we worry about Japan or any other country.
>
> And it is true that we do not like protectionism, but I think it is more true that we are going to have to stand up for ourselves, that we are going to have to take corrective action. Whether that is retaliation or whether it is protectionism—whatever it is—something is going to happen here.
>
> The people are going to force us in Congress to be protectionist or to take retaliatory action or take protective action. . . . For too

long we have been too nice in the world and I think the American people are ahead of us.[3]

In contrast, Senator Charles Mathias of Maryland opened hearings of the Subcommittee on International Economic Policy by saying: "One thing that I think must be understood is that Americans cannot separate themselves from the difficulties of others."[4]

W. Michael Blumenthal, chairman of Burroughs Corporation and a former Secretary of the Treasury, remarked in Mathias's hearings:

> Bringing the international situation under control, it seems to me, is very much in the U.S. interest—I would even say in the 'selfish' U.S. interest—and a few simple numbers, Senator, I think indicate that.
>
> Twenty percent of our industrial production is exported today. Thus we cannot hope to prosper if the present economic difficulties of the rest of the world are not resolved.
>
> One in six workers in manufacturing owes his job to exports.
>
> One-third of U.S. corporate profits is derived from foreign activities.
>
> Two out of five farming acres in the United States are dedicated to foreign markets. . . .
>
> Roughly half of [Burroughs's] total activity is tied into exports and foreign investments. . . .
>
> Clearly we cannot prosper and we have been held back in our progress by the general problems of the international situation.[5]

It is obviously too simple to reduce the competing interests shaping American foreign economic policy to "protectionists" and "internationalists." The economics and politics of the debate are far more complex and subtle, even vague and unknown, than this. What may be useful in this policy sketch is to select some important problem areas for comment. These have been chosen by looking at the relevant content of *The New York Times* and *Wall Street Journal* for the last two years and by reading testimony from recent congressional hearings.

There are seven foreign economic policy topics currently under debate in Washington and around the country: (1) trade liberalization versus protection, (2) trade in services and world investment policy, (3) international movements of people, (4) technology and science in the world economy, (5) the value of the dollar and the world payments system, (6) the Japanese Question, and (7) North-South economic relations.

These issues will be examined from the point of view of institutional economics. It is possible here neither to do justice to the full complexities of these questions nor to capture the entire range and depth of the institutionalist perspective. Institutionalists generally accept, with some amendment, the orthodox case for freer trade. They would favor "constructive free trade," that is, a trade policy that would make allowance for labor adjustment and would be consistent with a nation's long-term national development strategy. They have written very little about international finance, so it is difficult to look to them for full guidance on policy in this area. There are important differences between the institutionalist recommendations and the conventional economic wisdom in the areas of trade and finance. These will emerge in the following discussions of the seven problem areas. A policy summary at the end will highlight the institutionalist contribution to foreign economic policy debate. . . .

TRADE LIBERALIZATION VERSUS PROTECTION

While favoring freer trade, institutionalists believe that the achievement of liberalization depends upon the balance of competing against interest groups, not upon the mere repetitious intonement of the arguments of Adam Smith and David Ricardo. They advocate, therefore, cushioning the impact on genuinely affected groups through labor retraining and relocation, thereby helping to maintain full employment. Pressures for protection arise from individuals, groups, firms, and communities threatened by foreign competition in the form of imports. To defuse these pressures it is necessary to allay the fears that give rise to them. This means that there must be a national program that can provide sufficient inducements and safeguards to affected people, firms, and regions. This does not mean that government largesse must be used to sustain inefficient production. What it does mean is that the affected individuals' basic subsistence, health, and pension benefits must be provided for when industries yield ground to imports. Since the United States lacks national health and pension programs, the feared insecurity of job loss is a prime source of pressure to restrain imports. Of course, the aim of any package of dislocation measures must be to put people back to work in productive jobs in dynamic industries and areas.

Institutionalists support a nationally directed strategy of scientific, educational, technological, and economic development that will identify future export advantages and not permit a weakening of the nation's competitive position. This technological strategy should operate in concert with the adjustment or relocation measures just discussed. Institutionalists therefore do not seek a national industrial strategy devised as a program of pro-industry steps. The development of trade advantages is seen as the product of a program of scientific and technological training and research, rather than as the outgrowth of financial incentives provided directly to private firms. Labor and consumer interests must be given equal weight in such a strategy.

The adoption of a national policy to deal with trade-caused dislocation, by mitigating concerns about workers' health, incomes, jobs, and old-age security, in conjunction with a national technological development strategy will create conditions conducive to trade expansion and rapid domestic growth, insofar as such growth is trade-related. There remains the need to coordinate national trade and development policies with other nations. Decisions about the nation's trade policy should be made in conjunction with other nations, bilaterally and in multilateral organizations, and at as great a distance as possible from the influence of special industrial and labor interests.

Recent experience suggests that these important institutionalist ideas have been neglected—that the direction of movement has been away from pro-trade policies to anti-trade policies.

If the benefits from the Kennedy and Tokyo rounds of GATT negotiations have been so great, it is fair to ask why the momentum for further tariff reductions has abated in the early 1980s. One reason is that the successes of the early rounds were based on the reduction of visible protective devices in areas where there were large gains to be had at little cost. As economic integration has grown, however, further advantages from specialization can arise only by the displacement of long-established industries that must lose market share to imports. Furthermore, governments and businesses have become more adroit at creating artificial and unfair trade advantages in such forms as subsidies and rebates. Additionally, nations ask trading partners for "voluntary" restrictions on their exports.

These new protectionist measures arise from the pressures of interest groups—workers and businessmen—in import-competing industries. Such non-tariff devices are hard to identify, weigh, and remove. When core industries are threatened, political pressures behind protectionist demands may become irresistible. In December 1982, the United Auto Workers helped push through the House a bill requiring foreign automobile exporters to utilize U.S.–produced parts or face a loss of access to the U.S. market. Lee Iacocca, president of Chrysler Corporation, called for quotas on Japanese car imports in an August 1983 newspaper statement.[6] A spokesman for the American Iron and Steel Institute likewise advocated steel import quotas in testimony before Congress in April 1983.[7] The AFL-CIO has recently sought a wide application of trade restrictions to remedy unemployment in a spectrum of industries.[8]

These pressures might not matter if they amounted to nothing more than the usual self-serving pleas of poorly managed, uncompetitive industries and grasping unions. What is possible is that their cumulative weight will be sufficient to lead to a coalition of interlocking interests, which would reverse the United States' commitment to trade liberalization. Consumers, farmers, and export-oriented firms might not be able to resist such an alliance. The election year of 1984 may be crucial. The *Wall Street Journal* noted in July 1983 that there were signs that the administration was yielding ground to many different industries seeking special treatment. Relief was granted specialty steels, fifty-six different categories of textiles emanating from Southeast Asia, and motorcycles (to protect the last U.S. producer, Harley-Davidson, and its 2,000 employees). Export subsidies for some agricultural transactions were permitted.[9]

These U.S. actions stemmed from internal pressures but also reflected the lack of foreign responsiveness to recent U.S. initiatives. As in the United States, European governments have bent before strong internal pressure and slowed or reversed movements toward liberalization. High rates of unemployment, slow rates of productivity growth, inefficient farmers, excessive wage settlements in industry, and poor management have helped generate European antipathy to new U.S. proposals. The ultimate danger is that the reversal of the commitment of the Americans, Europeans, and Japanese to trade liberalization will usher in a new era of selfish, destructive beggar-thy-neighbor policies.

The Williamsburg summit of late May 1983 reiterated the commitment of the world's major trading nations to resist protectionist forces. GATT discussions in Geneva in November 1982 had produced little progress and the Williamsburg statement, while strong, painted over underlying political difficulties. Indeed, the GATT results were so tepid and inconclusive that they weakened the proponents of liberalization in the United States and elsewhere. The United States sought action or debate on several crucial topics: a serious recommitment to new rounds of trade liberalization; defining appropriate safeguards for domestic producers threatened by imports; a product counterfeiting code; reduction of barriers to trade in services; a global investment policy; attention to trade in high-technology goods and agriculture; and discussion of the role of developing countries in world trade, including improved market access.[10] Not only was the United States unable to work toward agreements in these areas, but serious discussion of most was not even initiated.

In addition to careful identification and defusing of protectionist interests via better labor management policy and industrial foresight, institutionalists place great emphasis on the technological factor in determining a nation's trade advantages. Recent debate about U.S. productivity levels, scientific and educational policy, and the mounting excess of imports over exports in the balance of trade has reflected orthodox concerns in this area. The 1983 *Report* of the President's Council of Economic Advisers has a very lucid discussion of these topics. It points out that the trade deficit reflects changes in the U.S. service balance, investment income, and capital movements, and does not indicate a deteriorating comparative position. The report does identify the problem of lagging sectors such as autos and steel, remarking that because of monopoly power, "prices and wages in some U.S.

heavy industries are probably too high to be sustainable in an integrated world economy."[11]

Institutionalists, and others, will find this a sensible document—just as most congressional committees hear sensible comments from those experts who do not clearly represent special pleading. Where institutionalists differ is in recognizing the crucial role of special interests. They recognize that while some special interests seek protectionism for purely selfish reasons, that protectionist sentiment also arises when workers, businesses, and communities are threatened by imports in a situation where adequate unemployment benefits, health care benfits, and pension security are lacking. They would advise undercutting such sentiments by introducing appropriate federal programs. Institutionalists also believe in the dynamic nature of comparative advantage and thus call for a guided national trade and development strategy that would ensure full employment and provide a matrix for scientific, educational, and technological progress. When these matters are taken care of they believe that the balance of trade, balance of payments, and value of the dollar will adjust appropriately and not constitute problems for policy makers.

TRADE IN SERVICES AND WORLD INVESTMENT POLICY

As the U.S. and European economies have experienced a shift in employment and economic activity toward services and away from industry, services have assumed a more important role in international commerce. Services in the balance of payments include banking services, transportation, insurance, tourism, investment income, and royalties on technology. The United States sought, at the GATT meeting in Geneva in 1982, to engage in discussions about easing restrictions on services trade and about a global investment policy. Most nations have extensive restrictions on such activities as shipping and banking. Similarly, foreign investors are exposed to special requirements, such as limitations on their portion of ownership. Furthermore, non-domestic firms may be required to follow ordained "performance requirements," such as to export a proportion of their output, hire a certain fraction of domestic workers, or provide packages of employee benefits.

Institutionalists, like orthodox economists, have not generally treated these relatively new matters in any depth. There is agreement in favoring freedom of action and nondiscrimination between foreign and domestic activities. Nonetheless, in smaller and less-developed countries that do not yet have mature financial institutions or that cannot cope effectively with large multinational firms, institutionalists worry that unbridled access opened to large U.S. banks, shippers, and corporate investors could be damaging in the absence of local oversight. They thus favor cooperative negotiations between host governments and alien businesses so that the relationships involved in the provision of services, capital, and technology are mutually advantageous. While they endorse a world investment code, its content, oversight mechanisms, and enforcement provisions would thus differ strongly from that likely to be advocated by orthodox economists and U.S. negotiators. They would favor international consultancy under the auspices of international agencies to mediate investment arrangements between companies and countries.

INTERNATIONAL MOVEMENTS OF PEOPLE

In the modern world, nation states zealously preserve their autonomy. One power of this autonomy is that of differentiating sharply between citizens and foreigners. Apart from social reasons for doing this, the prime motive is to preserve local labor from external competition. Yet, sometimes it is in the national interest to import labor to do jobs that local people will not or cannot do or to provide cheap labor for agricultural or industrial businesses. Various countries in the Middle East and Europe imported much labor in the 1960s and 1970s. The United States has attempted selectively to admit skilled aliens on a permanent basis while permitting unskilled, cheap labor to enter only for temporary agricultural work. In fact, permanent labor has flooded in illegally from Mexico, the Caribbean, and other parts of Latin America. U.S. and world labor movements thus reflect complex motives and restrictions—some selfish and some humanitarian, as in the case of political refugees.

Orthodox economists do not study movements of people in any depth for two reasons. First, such movements are thought to be largely social and political. Secondly, the comparative advantage trade model assumes that labor is not mobile internationally. If labor did move freely, there would be less trade because workers would gravitate to high wage countries until worker incomes around the world were equal (with allowance for skills). Since labor costs are a major source of trade advantages, the reduction of labor cost differences would contract the scope for exchange. Orthodox economists also assume the nation state is an immutable institution and will not usually challenge the national right to retain control over labor immigration.

The institutionalist view is contrasting. Institutionalists welcome the freer movement of people internationally, even at the cost of some social conflict and domestic economic losses. They support a gradual transformation to a world in which the power of nation states is reduced and people are freer to move toward working and living conditions of their own choice. The United States endorses such freedom for residents of the Soviet Union and, in general, has in practice a convoluted but relatively open position on immigration. There is de facto tolerance of the influx of Hispanic labor. Institutionalists recommend a national labor policy that is more open and more coherent so that such problems as social and linguistic integration, educational access, and the impact on domestic unskilled workers may be squarely addressed.

An international issue affecting the less-developed countries is the "brain-drain" of doctors, engineers, and other highly trained persons toward the United States and richer countries. Often such movements stem from poor educational and research facilities overseas or from repressive or decaying political situations. Institutionalists favor such movements, in the interest of individual liberty, despite their negative impact on less-developed societies. The answer is to be found in improving conditions in the home countries, not in restrictions. Orthodox calls, such as that of Jagdish Bhagwati's, for a tax on migrant incomes to effect income transfers to home governments are anathema.[12]

TECHNOLOGY AND SCIENCE IN THE WORLD ECONOMY

The transfer of ideas—as technology embodied in capital or trained workers or as disembodied pure ideas and knowledge—is crucial to the integration of world societies. The developed states hold much technological and scientific knowledge and most advances take place there. Exchanges of knowledge occur along several transmission channels. These include scientific exchanges, transnational education, and the dissemination of scientific literature. Most technologies that have commercial value are protected by proprietarial patents. Borrowers must then either pay fees under licensing agreements or welcome foreign firms under various arrangements.

Orthodox economists generally accept the view that scientific and technological advance is stimulated by the patent system and that the multinational corporation is the best vehicle for most technology transfer. Institutionalists reject both of these propositions. They believe that social and intellectual conditions are more important than property rights in determining the pace of scientific advance. University research and free inquiry, often governmentally sponsored, are seen as the major factors. Property rights, they think, actually retard the dissemination of knowledge since they confer monopoly rents.

Institutionalists advocate public international agencies to support a global approach to science. Research on space and the oceans should be a collective human endeavor. Disease control should likewise be a universal concern, not a source of private profits; this would lead to more resources devoted, for example, to tropical diseases rather than to the self-inflicted health problems associated with smoking, obesity, and lack of exercise in the rich lands.

The institutionalist position is that international cadres of engineers, scientists, and educators should establish mechanisms for the quick dissemination of knowledge worldwide. To the extent that multinational corporations are involved, such activities—and proprietarial payments such as royalties and licensing fees—should be internationally arbitrated.

THE VALUE OF THE DOLLAR AND THE WORLD PAYMENTS SYSTEM

The most regrettable thing about international finance to institutionalists is that it distracts attention from some of the fundamental economic issues discussed above and below. Both in economics and in business, obsession with monetary matters obscures and deflects intellectual and applied energies from real matters of production, distribution, and technological and scientific progress.

There is much debate as to whether the dollar is currently overvalued or whether, a few years ago, it was undervalued.[13] There is similar concern about the value of the yen.[14] Institutionalists largely agree with sensible, mainstream analysis of the balance of payments and the value of exchanges. Again, the 1983 *Report* of the Council of Economic Advisers is levelheaded about these matters.[15] Testimony to Congress on the dollar-yen rate and its relation to the United States and Japanese balances of trade and payments is likewise sensible.[16] The broad-brush consensus is that there is little to worry about. Since David Hume, economists have taken the view that governments can do little to affect their economy's trade and payments balances short of marshalling a legion of direct controls, which may have only transient effects.

Institutionalists do know that Milton Friedman and the monetarist advocates of free exchange rates were wrong about one vital matter. An early argument for freer rates, when the IMF accord still enforced relatively fixed rates, was that the domestic economy would be largely if not wholly isolated from external forces, such as macroeconomic fluctuations and policies in other nations. Domestic fiscal and monetary policy authorities could then concentrate on using these instruments to remedy domestic unemployment and inflation. It has turned out that significant interdependencies—financial and real—remain, and may have even expanded considerably, following the move to fluctuating rates.

As the linchpin of the international system, the dollar remains a peculiar currency, since it is both domestic and international in use.

The role of the United States as a high-interest, secure haven for foreign wealth has led to influxes of funds to purchase U.S. financial and real assets, thus inflating the value of the dollar and probably depressing U.S. exports. These subjects are well-grasped in conventional discussion. Institutionalists and most orthodox economists share the view that there are very complex interactions among the exchange rate and balance of payments and domestic prices, interest rates, and income.

Institutionalists argue that money is an evolving complex of ideas, symbols, and substances.[17] They do not believe the U.S. dollar should be asked to serve as both a domestic and international currency. They thus recommend moves toward the use of a global money or monies. They would welcome a strengthened IMF with strong power to regulate the amount of international liquidity and with the authority to direct public and private capital flows as needed to facilitate real economic activity. Such an agency should, in particular, pay special heed to the trade and credit problems of the developing nations.

Institutional economists endorse the idea that relatively free exchange markets in which rates are set by supply and demand forces are a workable, desirable thing. The idea of "relatively free exchange rates" is closely akin to the idea of "constructively free trade" in that governmental and international agency oversight is necessary to make sure that the market system works properly. For practical purposes the commitment to "relatively free rates" implies that a government should maintain an interest in what the national rate is and be willing to intervene on a transient basis when speculation or short-run capital movements threaten to move the exchange rate too far away from what is judged a proper level.

THE JAPANESE QUESTION

Institutionalists suspect that much of the hostility to the Japanese is generated by the fact that they are non-European and that Americans have difficulty in understanding, relating to, and operating in a foreign culture. Specific issues such as the value of the yen, the legitimacy of the Japanese government's measures to aid Japanese businesses and exporters, and perceived Japanese resistance to U.S. imports stem from this incomprehension. At the same time, people in the United States have failed to understand how hard, and probably how unwise, it would be to mimic Japanese management-labor and business-governmental relations. What is needed is much better grounding among Americans in Japanese language, culture, and history (and possibly in U.S. language, culture, and history). Given these things, there is nothing in the often exaggerated Japanese–U.S. differences over trade access and business practices that cannot be bridged. The two nations have too much at common stake not to work out reasoned accords. Orthodox analysis of specific trade and financial relations between the two economies is generally of high order and can be counted on to give direction to such discussions.[18]

The irritant in Japanese–U.S. trade is that the United States has a huge trade deficit with Japan. This spawns a number of concerns: that the yen is (possibly deliberately) undervalued; that the Japanese government unfairly subsidizes research costs and exports; that the Japanese have somehow repealed the law of comparative advantage. Actually, the trade deficit with the Japanese means nothing in isolation from the remainder of Japan's and the United States' trade relations. The fact of the matter is that Japan is resource-poor and thus runs an almost equally enormous trade deficit with suppliers of fuels and raw materials. On the other side, the United States has a giant trade surplus with the EEC and to some degree with the less-developed nations that supply Japan with energy and resource inputs.

Many U.S. businesspeople complain that it is hard to do business in Japan. A good deal of this friction arises because U.S. businesspeople do not know how to do business in Japan. They do not speak the language or understand Japanese business and social customs. It is a safe prediction that if Americans learned as much about Japan and the Japanese as the Japanese now know about the U.S. and Americans that many of their complaints would die away. U.S. businesses would do better to send their executives to a nearby university for training in Japanese studies rather than to Washington to lobby for either barring Japanese products "until they see reason" or for aid in "cracking the tough Japanese market."

NORTH-SOUTH ECONOMIC RELATIONS

The institutionalist position on foreign aid and development is covered in Wendell Gordon's contribution to this set of policy statements.[19] Orthodox economists stress the increasing importance of the third world as a market for U.S. goods and as a repository for U.S. investment. More U.S. imports of raw materials and manufactures are coming from the developing economies. Institutionalists do not disagree with these blatantly self-interested arguments, but put more weight on humanitarian and equity objectives.

Institutionalists have long been concerned with the history of rich-poor or north-south relations. They differ sharply from orthodox economists in doubting that trade and investment in the nineteenth and early twentieth centuries worked to spread incomes and employment from the rich to the poor countries. The brute fact of a widening income gap between rich and poor during the colonial period is sufficient to cast considerable doubt on the inherent beneficence of purely market-guided trade and investment. Even without recourse to the more malevolent mechanisms posited by theories of imperialism or the laughable "world systems" analysis, institutionalists assert that markets and private agents, in conjunction with colonial governments, did a poor job of inducing world development.

Believing that markets and private businesses are insufficient in and of themselves to guarantee equitable global development, institutionalists endorse multilateral aid agencies and international mechanisms for the diffusion of technology and ideas. They support international supervision of corporate activities, including monopolization, technological research and diffusion, and location of production. Many institutionalists advocate some system of global taxation aimed at income redistribution toward the poor of the world, if such transfers are aimed at raising productivity levels. They would support vigorous population control measures, famine relief coupled to long-term agricultural development aid, and meeting basic needs for water, food, shelter, and good health.

POLICY SUMMARY

The review of seven major topics in international affairs has highlighted important distinctions between institutionalist and orthodox analysis and policy recommendations. It is useful to reiterate and summarize the latter to conclude this policy statement.

First, institutionalists advocate a constructive free trade position. Recognizing the danger of capitulation to special protectionist interests, institutionalists recommend that liberalization negotiations and mechanisms be isolated from them as much as possible. At the same time opposition to liberalization should be defused by attention to the readjustment problems of affected labor and capital. Guidance of long-run national development should take the form of programmed scientific, engineering, and production strategies determining the proper roles of labor, business, government, and the universities.

Second, institutionalists recommend the adoption of global agreements on trade in services and investment policy. The content of such agreements, however, is likely to be substantially different than that currently endorsed by orthodox economists and U.S. negotiators.

Third, the freer movement of people and the reduction of barriers to migration imposed by nation states are strongly espoused by institutionalists.

Fourth, recognizing that science and technology are collective human enterprises, institutionalists support the creation of global organizations for the guidance, support, and spread of knowledge-creating activities. Institutionalists oppose selfish proprietary exploitation of knowledge.

Fifth, institutionalists deplore excessive concern with such financial matters as the value of the dollar or gold, and recommend that more attention be devoted to non-financial topics. The growth of stronger international financial institutions with broad functions, and of international money, is endorsed.

Sixth, The Japanese Question is not considered of great significance, except insofar as it embodies a certain crosscultural hostility. Recommended are stronger educational efforts on this side of the Pacific to make Americans more knowledgeable about Japan.

Seventh, institutionalists believe that world development requires constant attention, especially in those areas of the globe where basic health, food, and security needs are not being met. Multilateral agencies, focusing on raising productivity through the transfer of knowledge, should be given the chief role.

Most of the above steps would require weakening the sway of the two institutions that currently dominate movements of goods, people, and ideas in the world: the nation state and the multinational corporation. Institutionalists visualize traffic in goods, movements of people, and exchanges of knowledge taking place under international covenants. They encourage the strengthening of current international institutions—for example by investing them with more authority and providing them with some intrinsic revenue–raising powers—and the creation of new agencies where required. Such developments would move hand in hand with the evolution of a system for popular representation and democratic expression at the global level. . . .

NOTES

1. Angus Maddison, *Phases of Capital Development* (Oxford and New York: Oxford University Press, 1982), p. 92.
2. Maddison, *Phases*, pp. 44, 60.
3. *U.S. Approach to 1982 Meeting of World Trade Ministers on the GATT*, Hearing before the Subcommittee on International Trade of the Committee on Finance, United States Senate, 97th Congress, Second Session (Washington, D.C.: U.S. Government Printing Office, 1982), p. 24.
4. *Global Economic Outlook*, Hearings before the Subcommittee on International Economic Policy and the Committee on Foreign Relations, United States Senate, 98th Congress, First Session (Washington, D.C.: U.S. Government Printing Office, 1983), p. 1.
5. *Global Economic Outlook*, p. 28.
6. Lee Iacocca, "World Trade: What U.S. Firms are Up Against," *The Washington Post*, August 2, 1983, p. 417.
7. *Global Economic Outlook*, pp. 501ff.
8. *U.S. Approach*, pp. 101ff.
9. Art Pine, "Reagan Alters His Free-Trade Stand," *The Wall Street Journal*, July 25, 1983, p. 15.

10. See *U.S. Approach, passim*; also, Jeffrey J. Schott, "The GATT Ministerial: A Postmortem," *Challenge* (May–June 1983): 40–45.
11. "The United States in the World Economy: Strains on the System," *Report of the President's Council of Economic Advisers, 1982* (Washington, D.C.: U.S. Government Printing Office, 1983), p. 59.
12. Jagdish Bhagwati, "Taxing the Brain Drain," *Challenge* (July–August 1976): 34–38.
13. David Hale, "Learning to Love an Overvalued Dollar," *The Wall Street Journal*, August 8, 1983, p. 16.
14. Yoshiro Araki, "On Balance, the Weak Yen Hurts Japan," *The Wall Street Journal*, August 8, 1983, p. 17.
15. *Report of the President's Council*, Chap. 3, 1983.
16. *U.S. Economic Relations with Japan*, Hearing before the Committee on Foreign Relations, United States Senate, 98th Congress, First Session, on the Impact of the Yen-Dollar Exchange Rate (Washington, D.C.: U.S. Government Printing Office, 1983).
17. Walter C. Neale, *Monies in Societies* (San Francisco: Chandler & Sharp, 1976).
18. See, for example, the testimony of C. Fred Bergsten in *U.S. Economic Relations*, pp. 23ff.
19. Wendell Gordon, "The Implementation of International Development," *Journal of Economic Issues* 18 (March 1984): 295–314.

12. Incorporating The Gains From Trade Into Policy

J. MICHAEL FINGER

Those who are convinced of the economic and political importance of maintaining an open international trading system face two challenges, namely to find a way to arrest the slippage towards protection which is occurring in the policies of industrial countries and to bring these countries and the developing countries, which are becoming significant elements in the world economy, to dismantle the restrictions on imports which they maintain. To an economic theorist, these would appear to be similar tasks, for trade liberalisation and protection are, in economic logic, opposite directions on the same scale.

But to a political theorist the differences are more evident than the similarities. Trade liberalisation and protection are, in government, completely different processes. Trade is liberalised through highly visible multilateral negotiations conducted under the auspices of the General Agreement on Tariffs and Trade (GATT), while trade restrictions are imposed through much less visible administrative mechanisms, such as anti-dumping and countervailing-duty procedures and safe-

J. Michael Finger is a senior economist on the World Bank's Development Policy Staff.

guards or escape-clause mechanisms. These institutions have been much less extensively studied than the GATT negotiations, even though, as G. C. Hufbauer, a well-informed analyst and former trade official in the United States Treasury Department has observed, 'administered protection has been the leading edge of trade policy at least since 1975'.[1]

Indeed, a major initiative of the United States in the Tokyo Round negotiations of 1973–79 was aimed at these administrative procedures. Codes were negotiated which specified in detail the way a country would undertake a countervailing-duty or anti-dumping investigation, grant import licences, assign values for customs purposes *et cetera.* It was hoped that making national procedures consistent with these codes would reduce the degree by which they favour domestic sources over foreign ones; that is, reduce the degree of protection implicit in them. In like manner, systematic procedures for the settlement of disputes between countries were laid out and it was hoped that as cases passed through the dispute-settlement process a body of case law and precedent would be established which all countries would come to respect.

In effect the process of import regulation would be 'Americanised'. Each national government would codify its administrative procedures for deciding whether or not to approve petitions from its industries for protection from import competition. Procedures would be standardised and both importers and the complaining domestic industry would be assured access to the information on which the government would base its decision. As precedent built up, the government would have a painless means for handling pressures for protection. And if the effects of these decisions ever appeared to compromise the likewise codified interests of another country, a similarly constructed and therefore similarly painless international mechanism would resolve the dispute. This is a seductive idea, but not one likely to work. Not even Americans do things that way.

RULES AND TRANSPARENCY

The United States Administration's procedures for managing domestic pressures for protection include two different 'tracks', the technical and the political.

The anti-dumping and countervailing-duty mechanisms are technical procedures. Their determinations are defined by hundreds of lines of legislation and thousands of lines of administrative regulation. Furthermore, the decision whether or not to impose anti-dumping and countervailing duties is directly tied to those technical determinations. In order to assure that the rules are followed, a party to a case may appeal against the Administration's determination in the federal courts.

Examination of the record of such cases confirms that they are, indeed, technical not political determinations. John Odell, an American political scientist then at Harvard University, examined the outcomes of about two dozen such cases which involved Latin American countries.[2] He found that the proportion of cases 'won' by the Latin American countries was not affected by application of political pressure—either through the American Secretary of State or directly to the Treasury Department, the agency which administered such cases over the period studied by Professor Odell.

Two colleagues and I recently studied the entire record of cases decided between 1975 and 1979, more than 200 cases.[3] We tested statistically for the influence of a number of non-technical or political factors, from the importance to American foreign policy of the country against which the case was filed to the threat that because the administering agency (then the Treasury Department) was not finding affirmatively often enough, responsibility for such cases should be shifted elsewhere. None of these political factors turned out to have any influence. Furthermore, a list of technical variables—the kind of economic and accounting factors one finds in rules and regulations—did have very significant explanatory power.

Escape-clause cases are a different matter. They involve an open political process, one in which the interested parties can effectively argue about the relevant criteria and not just about whether the predetermined criteria are satisfied. Each escape-clause case includes an injury investigation, which is conducted by the US International Trade Commission (ITC). If the ITC determines that import competition has brought injury to the complaining domestic producers they send the President their recommendation for the appropriate remedy.

But escape-clause cases differ from anti-dumping and countervailing duty-cases in two important ways: (i) the meaning of injury is much less precisely defined by law and regulation and (ii) the President's decision is not tied to the outcome of the injury investigation. He may refuse to restrict imports or grant other forms of relief even though the ITC found injury and, moreover, in the face of a 'no injury' determination, he may negotiate an agreement to limit imports, as was done in the recent motor car case. This is not a unique example. Robert E. Baldwin, of the University of Wisconsin, found insignificant association between the outcome of the ITC's injury determination and the decision which the President eventually made in the case.[4]

Here the record shows no tendency towards systematisation. Indeed, while the more technical or bureaucratic track tends towards regularity, the higher-level politically-accountable track tends towards singularity. Robert Walters, a political scientist at the University of Pittsburgh, analysing a series of recent trade cases, comes closest to this conclusion: 'It has proven almost impossible for the US political system to approach the steel crisis, Chrysler's collapse, the automobile crisis, and the difficulties of other industries as different manifestations of the same genre of challenge.' Although the United States Administration eventually reached decisions in each of these cases, Dr Walters described the decision process as a 'consensus of avoidance'.

The usefulness of the American proposal that more detailed rules be written can be boiled down to two questions:

(a) Would elaboration of the rules make for more effective management of pressures for protection; that is, would it increase the number of cases resolved (at either the domestic or the international level) 'by the rules' and reduce the number of petitions for protection which become open and political issues, requiring significant attention by politically-accountable officials?

(b) Would more detailed rules increase the likelihood of negative responses to pressures for protection and/or reduce the frequency of such petitions?

Experience in the United States suggests that the answer to both questions is 'No'. In the recent motor car case the ITC followed the relevant rules and determined that the American industry was not eligible for import relief. Threats soon followed that the Congress would, by direct vote, limit imports of motor cars. A more subtle, and perhaps more important, threat was that unless the President took action, car-industry supporters in Congress would hold hostage his tax-cut bill, the centerpiece of the Reagan Administration's supply-side economic programme.

The lesson from this example is that whether or not pressure for protection leads to a rules-track case or becomes an open and political issue is not determined by the existence of rules applicable to that case; it is determined by the political significance (closely proxied by the economic size) of the case.

This generalisation is strongly supported by the record of cases decided under the Trade Act of 1974. The average technical track (anti-dumping or countervailing-duty) case involved less than one tenth of the value of imports of the average escape-clause case; and the 40 escape-clause cases covered almost three times the value of imports of the 177 anti-dumping and countervailing-duty cases. Furthermore, the escape-clause cases which ended up as orderly marketing arrangements or 'voluntary' export-restraint agreements were four times as large as those resolved in accordance with the ITC's interpretation of the relevant rules.[5]

Why do all the non-trivial cases evade the rules track and become open, political issues? Perhaps it is because governments of the signatory countries to the GATT have taken on the responsibility to maintain the openness of their economies and yet they have outfitted themselves with the means and procedures to manage domestic pressures for protection which capture the discomforts of international competition, but not its benefits.

The ITC, for instance, in injury determinations, is required to investigate injury to domestic producers of products which compete with imports. The law, which is completely consistent with the GATT, allows no such investigation of gains to users of imports—either to other producers who use the imported good as an input or to consumers of a finished good. These interests may express their opinion as to whether or not the petitioners for protection have demonstrated injury to themselves from import competition, but the rules do not allow a demonstration of the gain, or saving, to the users of the imports. The pricing tests in anti-dumping and countervailing-duty procedures are similarly, although not so obviously, biased. In the United States, where the rules for these procedures are available for examination, they have been found to proscribe for foreign sellers a number of trade practices which parallel anti-trust law does not take away from domestic sellers. How this is done is explained in an article in the *Journal of World Trade Law* by William Dickey, who was formerly in charge of enforcing the American anti-dumping and countervailing-duty laws at the Treasury Department.[6]

Furthermore, only the *precision of the rules*, not their *economic subject matter*, changes as one moves from the technical to the more political decision mechanisms. The legal objective of the anti-dumping and countervailing-duty mechanism is to police the fairness of trade practices and it pursues that objective by restricting imports; in design, from unfair exporters only. It is therefore an economic instrument with the power to restrict imports and the simple idea of greed suggests that it will attract those with an interest in imports being restricted—not only firms and industries beset by unfair competition but also, more generally, those least favourably situated *vis-à-vis* their foreign competitors' costs. They will, the logic of economic anthropology suggests, attempt to make their needs fit its scope and its scope fit their needs. As this suggests, the details of American law and administrative regulations have been changed over time so that even the *pricing* investigation in such cases has come to turn on the same matters as does an escape-clause case. My colleagues and I have pointed out relevant specifics in our 1982 study. In corroboration, we found that among the technical factors examined those which related to comparative costs were the most powerful predictors of the outcome of anti-dumping countervailing-duty cases.[7]

To meet its commitment to maintain openness, the government of a signatory country must rally interests to whom the rules track gives no voice. Likewise, interests that are harmed by the petitioned-for trade restrictions which come forward on their own must apply pressure directly on politicians. They are *excluded* from the rules track *by the rules*.

In minor cases a one-sided decision mechanism might work well. To quantify only one dimension of protection can be relatively inexpensive and if the rules and regulations for doing so are sufficiently complex, they might prevent the more widely dispersed consumer interests from being aware of their losses.

West Europeans, I am told, seem generally less aware than Americans that protection has a cost to consumers and are also more respectful of the government's authority. Hence it is in the tradition of governments in Western Europe to operate relatively closed administrative mechanisms; that is, mechanisms for which the decision criteria are not specified and the information to be fed into a decision is not made public. In this view, elaborate procedures are the United States Administration's way to evade an accountability which West Europeans simply do not ask of their governments.

While the obfuscation provided by elaborate procedures can prevent a small case from becoming a public issue, it cannot transform an important case into an obscure one. So long as procedures do not provide channels for all the interests at play, transparency in decisions on industrial policy in the United States brings impotence and a search for a more obscure way, not unquestioning public acceptance to the decision. As the American public's awareness of the escape-clause mechanism grew, the United States Administration shifted towards using the anti-dumping and countervailing-duty procedures. (This shift has been noted by Rodney de C. Grey, a long-time Canadian trade official.[8])

In turn, attempting to use the anti-dumping or countervailing-duty provisions to manage the highly publicised pressures of the steel and motor car industries stripped them of much of their obscurity. The United States Administration has thus shifted to a different source of authority, namely the provisions on unfair trade practices in the Trade Agreements Act of 1979. These provisions, not the more familiar but exhausted parts of American trade law, provide the basis for 1980s-style 'reciprocity'.

Transparency is, to the present system, the antithesis. A responsive government cannot *openly* disenfranchise major interest groups and survive. That is why transparency does not make the management of trade policy easy for the United States and why West Europeans simply do not bother with it.

The problem is not that openness in decision making is bad. Rather the problem is that the philosophy behind the current set of decision-making rules is one-sided. Openness allows an importer to challenge a domestic industry's demonstration that imports are doing it harm. But it does not allow the importer to demonstrate that the *gains* to the importer and to his customers are at least as large. Rather than fixing this bias, openness makes it more obvious and hence *reduces* the likelihood that the question as to whether to protect an industry will be resolved within the rules-defined decision mechanism.

BRINGING IN THE DEVELOPING COUNTRIES

International reciprocity has been the motive force in the series of GATT negotiations held in the post–World War II period, through which most industrial-country tariffs have been reduced to minimal levels. Although economic theory, supported by a long list of estimates of the costs of protection, demonstrates rather plainly that the user or consumer gains from unilateral removal of a trade restriction almost always exceed the costs to those displaced by import competition, the mercantilist tendency, to view imports as the cost of trade and exports as the gain, is strong. Countries have always excluded some products from their tariff reductions not necessarily because the costs (to competing domestic producers) would exceed the gains (to consumers); they have done so for fear that some displaced producers might make sufficient political trouble to block the negotiations. This has limited the exchange of concessions to products on which cost differences among the industrial countries were small and the result has been growth in intra-industry trade—a country's exports expanding in the same sectors as its imports. Such small cost differences, however, were observed over a wide range of products and, in consequence, the tariff reductions negotiated covered most of the industrial sector.

But the most labour-intensive industries, where cost differences between countries were large, experienced minimal tariff cuts. In spite of faster growth in the 1950s and early 1960s and fuller employment, reciprocity from Japan, then *the* major supplier, was not sufficient for the United States Administration and governments in Western Europe to overcome resistance from the producer interests that would lose in order to achieve the larger consumer gains.

Trade liberalisation by developing countries in the period since World War II has been primarily a matter of domestic evaluation of the domestic pluses and minuses, not of international negotiations. Even among the older industrial countries, the GATT negotiating process has not been effective where cost differences were large. Between developed and developing countries, the cost differences (one way or the other) are large in nearly all sectors and therefore not much can be expected from the old system of reciprocal concessions qualified by the understanding that no significant (or material) costs will be imposed on a domestic interest, no matter how large the accompanying savings to other domestic interests. Trade liberalisation by developing countries will continue to depend on a country's coming to realise that its *domestic* benefits exceed its *domestic* costs.

What can the present GATT system contribute to that realisation? The answer is very little. It institutionalises the idea that any move towards openness which meets with domestic resistance is to be avoided. What is needed is guidance as to how the domestic interests which would gain from that liberalisation might be organised and how their needs might be brought to bear on the relevant policy decisions.

Common sense and a very brief inquiry suggest that developing countries have regular procedures for responding to domestic pressures for protection. A preliminary investigation in one country, Indonesia, revealed a strong functional similarity with the procedures of the United States.[9] In Indonesia, a petition for a higher tariff or an import quota is addressed to a cabinet minister, usually the Minister of Industry. It is then referred to a trade policy team composed of staff from the trade, finance and industry ministries. This team then attempts to determine (i) Indonesian capacity and unit costs, (ii) Indonesian demand at a price which covers domestic costs and (iii) the tariff rate which would bring the world price up to the level of Indonesian costs or the equivalent import quota. As with an escape-clause case in the United States, the technical formality or precision which these steps suggest is more apparent than real. When Indonesian officials were asked if they always aimed protection at the observed level of the domestic industry's costs they replied that they do not. On the other hand, they were aware that a commitment to aim at the level of costs of exporters (from developed or developing countries) would usually not provide protection. Hence the practice in Indonesia preserves considerable discretion for officials to assess how deserving the petitioning industry may be and how likely the industry would be to become competitive on world terms if granted protection.

The formalised part of such a case deals only with the idling of domestic capacity and the policy response which would negate this injury—as would emergency protection applied under Article XIX of the GATT. Following the letter of the GATT might require that minutes be taken when the Indonesian team discusses with importers or domestic producers the information it has collected and perhaps that tables be prepared for a few additional variables, But their procedure captures the same spirit as do currently sanctioned procedures taken by industrial countries. Suggesting that import relief be provided only when there is a 'material' or 'substantial' amount of injury or idle domestic capacity would make Indonesian procedures more complex, but it would not change the economic sense of them.

The Indonesian Government is seriously considering tariff reform (liberalisation) and realises full well that before it can implement such reform it must make the case *in Indonesia* that the economic benefits *to*

Indonesia will exceed the costs. It would be hard to advise them that strict adherence to the GATT can help them or even that the GATT demonstrates how the countries which promote it have realised and institutionalised the gains from international trade.

CONCLUSIONS AND RECOMMENDATIONS

The approach to trade embodied in the principles and rules of the GATT is based on a belief by the participating countries that the benefits of an open system of international trade would exceed the costs. But the GATT system does not bring participating countries to weigh all the benefits they derive from international trade against the costs. The record of the tariff negotiations and the administrative parts of the General Agreement certainly illustrate this.

It is not likely, then, that passing the same plough over the field again will till the soil any deeper. If progress is to be made towards controlling the administrative procedures through which trade restrictions come into being or towards dispelling the resistance of both industrial and developing countries to further liberalisation, some additional weight must be added to the plough. This weight should be the *gains* from international trade—the interest of those who *save* because of access to foreign products and markets and who bear the costs of government restrictions on that access. The aim should be to move beyond the mercantilist concept of the gains from international trade now built into national and international institutions which manage these matters and to move towards a more balanced concept which includes the beneficial side of imports, not just the harmful side.

I offer three suggestions for achieving this aim. They would probably rank 1-2-3 in terms of acceptability, but 3-2-1 in terms of usefulness. The third suggestion is critical to making the second effective; and the execution of those two would be the strongest expression of the first.

The first task for the leadership of the trade policy community is to recognise the instinct of policy makers to seek foreign scapegoats for the effects of domestic indecision or wrong decisions. Efforts should be made to publicise the simple truth of classical economics, namely that trade restrictions by one country, no matter what any other country does, has for that country larger costs than benefits.

Disputes over international trade almost always overlie *national* decisions with larger *domestic* costs than benefits. Dispute-settlement procedures that build on the same concepts as lead to the wrong domestic choice should not be expected to set things right, no matter how detailed they might be made. Good relations among countries cannot be based on an attempt to choose through international bargaining among options whose *domestic* effects make a *domestic* decision onerous.

One of the major accomplishments of the international monetary conferences held in the mid-1970s was that there emerged from them an international consensus that domestic stabilisation was necessary before international stabilisation could be achieved. A parallel consensus on trade matters is sorely needed.

A way must be found to build the gains from international trade into national decisions on trade matters. Under present national rules, sanctioned by the GATT, the national commissions and bureaus which evaluate trade matters take into account only the costs to domestic producers from import competition. Savings to other industries which use imported inputs, or to consumers, are not taken into account.

The economic sense of this change is obvious and the political sense is compelling. Now, those who bear the costs of trade interference by their government have no choice but to go over the heads of the formalised decision processes and apply pressure on politicians. If these pressures had a technical outlet, trade matters might escalate less quickly into political disputes.

The third task is to begin a process to create a greater public awareness of the domestic costs of protection, a process to educate the groups which bear the costs of their own government's protectionist policies, and thereby to help bring into the public mind a non-mercantilist sense of the gains from international trade.

It would be relatively easy to verify that procedures to measure the gains from international trade and to identify the gainers had been added in those countries which employ formal and open administrative mechanisms. But in the European Community, for example, two thirds of anti-dumping and countervailing-duty petitions result in 'undertakings' or 'arrangements' on which a minimal amount of information is released—either about the nature of the arrangement that the Community has reached with the exporter or about the way in which the Community calculated the domestic benefits and costs which that course of action would entail.[10]

It might therefore be necessary to harness again the mercantilist instinct for exports and allow trading partners to calculate and publicise the costs to a country of that country's trade policies. The Argentines would buy television time in Japan to show an Argentine family enjoying a big roast beef and to show Japanese families how much of that roast beef they would have after the Government of Japan took its slice. The United States would buy space in French newspapers to publicise how much the French Government spends to subsidise exports, perhaps under the headline 'Your government gave more money last year to international corporations than to the "x" poorest countries in the world'! In 1978 the South Koreans might have sponsored a television spot as follows:

> As the first innings of the World Test Series ends, the television picture flicks to a scene of happy children dancing their way down the street to the shoe shop singing, 'New shoes for school, new shoes for school!' They gambol one by one into the shop, but as the twelfth one comes to the door, Uncle Sam, in striped trousers and white beard, steps forward and throws the child out, saying, 'No shoes for you this year, kid.'
>
> The voice-over then explains: 'The US, Korean and Taiwanese governments have just concluded an agreement which will reduce the number of children's shoes available for sale in the US by one twelfth. That means somebody doesn't get any.' Then back to the ballgame.

This is perhaps inaccurate or one-sided. But for once let the other side calculate the welfare triangles and explain how domestic supply is perfectly elastic at a level really no higher than costs in exporting countries.

'Or, if it is not now it will be sometime in the future if the following investment schedule . . .' 'Can we have the chart, please? Charlie, you've got it upside down, Charlie. Thanks, Charlie.' 'Anyway, you see on the chart . . .'

This is the same exchange of information we usually get on such matters. But the modes of expression that the two sides usually employ have been switched.

Without domestic appreciation of their domestic benefits, 'standstill' arrangements on trade restrictions are soon outflanked by new forms of protection which escape the letter of the agreement. We should agree to harness the interests of the exporters to detect these flanking movements and to identify their costs. Eternal vigilance is the price of free trade and the profit motive is the most vigilant force afield.

NOTES

1. G. C. Hufbauer, 'Analyzing the Effects of US Trade Policy Instruments', National Science Foundation, Washington, mimeograph, October 1981.
2. John S. Odell, 'Latin American Trade Negotiations with the United States', *International Organization*, Spring 1980.
3. J. M. Finger, H. Keith Hall and Douglas R. Nelson, 'The Political Economy of Administered Protection', *American Economic Review*, June 1982.
4. Robert E. Baldwin, 'The Political Economy of US Import Policy', draft manuscript, July 1981, ch. 4.
5. Finger, Hall and Nesson, *loc. cit.*
6. William L. Dickey, 'The Pricing of Imports into the United States', *Journal of World Trade Law*, May–June 1979.
7. Finger, Hall and Nelson, *loc. cit.*
8. Rodney de C. Grey, 'A Note on United States Trade Practices', paper prepared for a conference on Trade Policy in the Eighties, sponsored by the Institute for International Economics, held in Washington on 23–25 June 1982.

9. Finger, 'Administered Protection in the United States and Indonesia', World Bank, Washington, mimeograph, March 1982.

10. For details, see Nelson, *The Political Structure of the New Protectionism*, World Bank Staff Working Paper No. 471 (Washington: World Bank, 1981).

13. Wage Competitiveness In the U.S. Auto and Steel Industries

MORDECHAI KREININ

This paper explores reasons for the deterioration of the U.S. International competitive position in the motor vehicle and iron and steel industries between the early 1960s and the early 1980s. It does so by inquiring into the behavior of labor production cost (which in turn consists of labor compensation and productivity) in each of the two industries relative to that in all manufacturing within the U.S., Japan, and Germany, over the period under review. The results suggest an erosion in the U.S. comparative advantage in the two industries. No such erosion occurred in Japan. The important European countries are also studied. Beyond the question of "change over time," the paper examines the level of costs at a point in time (in 1980, with a partial update to 1982). Using the same approach, it estimates the degree to which U.S. wage rates in the two industries would have to decline to make their products competitive, first with Japan and second with Germany. Policy conclusions are drawn in the final section.

1. TRADE PERFORMANCE

In recent years, public and professional attention has been focused on structural changes in the U.S. economy. The most often mentioned losers in this transformation are the so-called "traditional industries," automobiles and steel. Indeed, the U.S. competitive position in these two industries deteriorated markedly in the last two decades while that of Japan improved.

Mordechai Kreinin is Professor of Economics at Michigan State University.

TABLE 1. Foreign Trade in Motor Vehicles and Steel: The U.S. and Japan (in billions of current dollars)

	ALL MANUFACTURES			ROAD MOTOR VEHICLES*			IRON AND STEEL		
YEAR	*X*	*M*	*Balance*	*X*	*M*	*Balance*	*X*	*M*	*Balance*
				(A) United States					
1963	13.3	6.9	6.4	1.3	0.6	0.7	0.5	0.7	–0.2
1981	151.9	143.0	8.9	15.8	29.0	–13.2	2.9	12.2	–9.3
				(B) Japan					
1963	4.9	1.5	3.4	0.2	0.0	0.2	0.7	0.1	0.6
1981	145.3	27.1	118.2	32.4	0.5	31.9	16.7	1.1	15.6

Source: GATT, *International Trade,* Various Issues, Appendix Tables.

* Note: These figures include U.S. trade with Canada, which is regulated by the bilateral agreement covering automobiles and parts. In 1981, exports to Canada were $8.4 billion while imports from Canada stood at $9.0 billion.

Table 1 highlights developments that took place between 1963 and 1981. While no significant U.S. trade imbalance existed in the two industries in the early 1960s, they both moved into sizeable deficit positions in the early 1980s—in contrast to a large surplus for all manufacturing. (And this has occurred despite U.S. restrictions on steel imports.) In other words, while the U.S. net trade position in all manufactured products improved during the 1970s, the country's positions in the two industries under review deteriorated consistently. Likewise, the U.S. share in total manufacturing exports of the industrial countries increased slightly at the end of the past decade. But its share in the export of autos and steel declined markedly. No such differential performance is observable in the case of Japan. On the contrary, in terms of the trade balance as well as its share in world trade, the two industries under review forged ahead of total manufacturing.

Under a strand of the literature known as "revealed comparative advantage," it has become customary to glean comparative advantage from trade performance. This paper *departs* from that tradition. It inquires into changes in the *domestic cost structure that may have accounted for the deterioration in the U.S. competitive position in the two industries between the early 1960s and the early 1980s.*[1] Beyond the question of "changes over time" the paper also examines the *level of cost at a given point in time (in 1980)* to derive additional policy conclusions.

In both its aspects—the changes over time and the level in the early 1980s—the study focuses on labor production costs. In turn, these are made up of two components: labor compensation (wages, salaries and benefits) and labor productivity. In some sense this approach places the paper in the tradition originated by D. G. A. Macdougall (1951 and 1952) and developed into a strand of empirical literature relating comparative advantage to labor costs. (Still, there are important differences between them.) The focus on labor costs is not to suggest that labor is solely responsible for the loss in competitive standing in these two industries. Indeed, it is not intended here to assess blame for the current plight of the industries. The role of management decisions is highlighted in the next section. And certainly material costs, which are not included here, are important.

II. THE ROLE OF MANAGEMENT DECISIONS

A. *Steel.* Although many steel executives cite high labor costs as the main reason why the steel industry is in trouble, "poor management decisions, particularly in capital spending, bear as much responsibility for the mill's current plight as do high wages and benefits," (O'Boyle, 1983). While the U.S. industry far outpaced its Japanese counterpart in capital spending during 1950–1980, and 3/4 of the U.S. steelmaking capacity is fairly "modern," the *type* of investments appears to account for a large technological gap. In particular, U.S. steelmakers are blamed for failing to introduce early enough, and invest in, two technological breakthroughs: the basic oxygen furnace and continuous casting.[2]

To overcome the resulting cost disadvantage, some steel companies contemplate the importation of basic steel for fabrication into steel products in the U.S. Also, it appears that the 60 or so mini-mills in the U.S. which are using more efficient equipment and are unencumbered by high labor cost compete effectively in the market place.

B. *Autos.* Until the mid–1970s the automobile market was viewed as consisting of two distinct segments: large and small cars, with a rather low substitution elasticity between them. The U.S. manufacturers catered to the first segment, while foreign producers concentrated on the second. Substitution between the two was limited, so that a "reasonable" price differential between large and small cars was sustainable.

But that situation changed dramatically with the sharp rise in the price of gasoline, first in 1974 and again in 1979–80. American consumers became highly conscious of fuel efficiency, and a massive switch towards smaller cars was in the making. American producers were slow to make the change to smaller cars. Thus, wrong management decisions with respect to the product mix were largely responsible for the initial massive penetration of the U.S. market by Japanese cars. But that was rectified by the early 1980s. By now the U.S. companies are able to accommodate this change in consumer demand, and new generations of smaller, fuel-efficient cars are coming off the U.S. assembly lines. This conversion process requires tens of billions in investment dollars.

As a result of this process, the distinction between U.S. and foreign-built cars has grown increasingly blurred. And consequently, cost-price factors have become of ever rising importance in determining market share. Price has long been the basis for competition *within segments* of the automobile market; but as the product became more homogeneous it is becoming a very important factor in the *entire* market. Although quality considerations are exceedingly important in consumer purchase decisions, cost-price factors are dominant. It makes sense to analyze trends in production costs in the industry.

While the present study concentrates on labor cost, there is no denying that other costs also enter price calculations. Material and management costs, as well as the "just-in-time" inventory control techniques and the clustering of related plants, are often cited as examples of Japanese cost advantages. Additionally, U.S. protection of the steel industry, through voluntary export restraints (VERs) and the trigger- and surge-price mechanisms, has raised the price of this input to auto production to about 15 percent above the world market level. Finally, the high exchange value of the U.S. dollar in 1982–83 certainly undermined the competitive position of these, as well as other industries, on world markets.

III. THE IMPORTANCE OF LABOR COSTS

Yet, it is important to examine labor production costs for several reasons. First, they are the most important component of production costs. In the case of motor vehicles they are estimated at 46 percent of all costs. It is sometimes pointed out that each one dollar per hour in wage rate translates into one billion dollars cost to the industry. Second, at least some, if not most, of the effects of the poor management decisions influence productive efficiency and are captured in the labor productivity figures. And thirdly, the U.S. automobile companies are truly multinational; they can shift production of components, parts, or final assembly around the globe so as to minimize production costs. Labor costs thus become a main determinant of plant location. Hence, comparative U.S.–foreign labor costs are of prime importance to future production and employment in the U.S.

Indeed, many studies (Abernathy et al, 1981; U.S. Department of Transportation, 1980) have been devoted to international comparisons of labor costs in a particular industry, such as motor vehicles or steel. For example, the study by Abernathy et al makes such a comparison between the U.S. and Japan. It estimates that Japan enjoys a cost advantage over the U.S. in cars landed in this country of anywhere between $1,000 and $1,700 per unit. The main factors responsible for this cost differential are: (1) lower Japanese wage rates (Mid–1980 U.S.

hourly compensation in the automotive industry was $15—more than double its Japanese counterpart of $7, converted from the yen at the then existing exchange rate.); (2) fewer man-hours required per vehicle, or higher productivity, in Japan; (3) differential costs in management of inventories, materials and components. These advantages are partly offset by freight cost and the 2.9 percent U.S. import duty.

IV. APPROACH

Practically all studies comparing production costs between countries, including those for motor vehicles and earlier ones pertaining to steel, do so at a given point in time (i.e., a recent year) and limit themselves to one industry. The international cost comparison involves at least two elements: (1) labor productivity; and (2) labor compensation, either per hour or per employee. Productivity can be measured in some absolute units (such as the number of hours required to build a vehicle of a certain type and with comparable characteristics in each country), roughly comparable across countries. In contrast, labor compensation is estimated in different currencies, and must be converted from one currency to another by the use of the prevailing exchange rate, such as the dollar-yen rate.

Exchange rates of the main industrial countries fluctuate, or float, in response to market conditions. But in many cases, including Japan, the float is "managed" by the central bank, and sometimes it is heavily managed. In the case of the deutsche mark, Germany is a member of the European Monetary System, so that the mark is pegged to six other currencies, and its rate relative to the dollar is affected by conditions in other European countries as well as in Germany. For this and other reasons, the prevailing exchange rate may deviate from the long-run equilibrium rate, rendering the comparison of labor compensation inaccurate.

Another way of making the same point is to emphasize the partial-equilibrium nature of the usual approach. In the case of autos, it may show a Japanese labor-cost advantage of, say, 25 percent over the U.S. But suppose Japan had a similar cost advantage in all or most industries. Then all we are saying is that the Japanese yen is undervalued. Raising its market value relative to the dollar (or equivalently lowering the value of the dollar relative to the yen) to its equilibrium level would eliminate or reduce the cost advantage in auto production.

While international cost comparisons of a single industry are interesting, they do not address the crux of the issue. They must be embedded in the total economy. In particular, what is necessary is to *rank* all industries *within each* country by order of their production cost: from the lowest- to the highest-cost industries. This is equivalent to ranking them by comparative advantage. The exchange rate then determines the cut-off points between three types of industries: the export industries (those with lowest cost); the nontraded goods industries; and the import-competing industries (Kreinin, 1983, chapter 11). A variant of this approach is employed in the present study, first for the U.S. and then for Japan (and to some extent for the main European countries). *Within each country, the behavior of labor costs in (a) motor vehicles and (b) iron and steel is considered relative to their counterparts in the entire manufacturing sector.*

Two variants of this approach are used. First, an index-number formulation shows the changes in labor cost relative to alternative base periods in the late 1950s as well as early and mid-1960s. This could explain the deterioration of the U.S. competitive position in the two industries from the early 1960s to the early 1980s. Should the data reveal a rise in the labor cost in one of the industries (or both) far in excess of the national manufacturing average, it can be inferred that the industry moved down in the ranking by comparative advantage (if one assumes no similar change in the structure of costs abroad).

The second variant examines the level of labor production costs at a given point in time: 1980 (the latest year for which all the needed data are available), with partial updates to 1982. Again the international comparison is that of domestic *ratios* between the cost in a particular industry and that of manufacturing as a whole. As such it is free of any exchange-rate bias. This comparison addresses the following question: Given labor productivities and Japanese wage rates, what level of labor compensation in the U.S. makes the two U.S. industries internationally competitive under a long-run equilibrium exchange rate (one that conforms to purchasing-power parity)?

Aside from data problems mentioned later, two caveats need to be indicated at the outset. First, in computing the cost ratio between each of the two industries and total manufacturing, the industry under question is itself included in all manufacturing (the denominator). Second, the ideal cost comparison is between labor cost in the particular industry and labor cost in the economy as a whole, or in the entire tradeable sector rather than the manufacturing sector. (The denominator is not comprehensive enough.) This is particularly important for the cost comparison at a point in time (Part VI) because of the different structures of the U.S. and the Japanese and German economies, the U.S. being a major exporter of farm products. These two biases lead to an *understatement* of the U.S. cost disadvantage in the two industries under review. But they cannot be remedied with the available data.

V. TRENDS IN LABOR COSTS SINCE THE EARLY 1960s

Two earlier papers (Anderson and Kreinin, 1981; Kreinin, 1982) examined the trends of labor production costs in the motor-vehicle and

TABLE 2. Indices of Labor Compensation, Productivity, and Unit Labor Cost in Iron and Steel and All Manufacturing for 1980 (1964 = 100) in Five Countries

	HOURLY COMPENSATION		OUTPUT PER HOUR		UNIT LABOR COST	
Country	*Iron and Steel*	*All Mfg.*	*Iron and Steel*	*All Mfg.*	*Iron and Steel*	*All Mfg.*
United States	382	316	119	141	321	224
Japan	725	807	352	394	206	205
Germany	448	461	227	217	197	212
United Kingdom	827	898	119	167	689	538
France	754	632	221	233	341	271

Sources: "International Comparisons of Productivity and Labor Costs, in the Steel Industry: United States, Japan, France, Germany, United Kingdom; 1964 and 1972–80." Prepared by the U.S. Department of Labor, Bureau of Labor Statistics (BLS), Office of Productivity and Technology, September 1981 (unpublished data); and BLS, International Comparisons of Manufacturing Productivity and Labor Cost Trends," Washington, D.C., May 20, 1983.

the iron and steel industries (separately) relative to all manufacturing. The first study is confined to the United States and shows trends between 1957 and 1977; while the second study includes both the U.S. and Japan (plus the main European countries in the case of iron and steel) and covers the period 1964–1980.[3]

A. *Iron and Steel.* The first of the two aforementioned studies pieced together data from the Census and Surveys of Manufacturers, the Handbook of Labor Statistics, and other sources, to determine the behavior of U.S. labor cost in steel over a 20-year period beginning in 1957. The following conclusions emerge: Between the years 1957 and 1977, hourly compensation in iron and steel increased at a rate well above that in all U.S. manufacturing, while labor productivity increased at a rate below the national manufacturing average. This combination shows that unit labor cost in the U.S. steel industry increased at a rate well above the national average. Clearly the steel industry declined in the ranking of U.S. industries by comparative advantage. The decline started in the early 1960s and intensified in subsequent years.

A new iron and steel data set which became available in 1980 made possible the second study (Kreinin, 1982). Compiled by the Bureau of Labor Statistics (BLS), it shows changes in productivity, labor compensation, and unit labor cost between 1964 (= 100) and the 1972–80 years, for the five major industrial countries. These data can be collated with comparable BLS statistics pertaining to all manufacturing in 11 countries (including the above five) for 1950–82. The indices for 1980 are shown in Table 2. (The intervening years, 1972–79, are deleted in the interest of conserving space, but are available in the original study.)

Throughout the period 1964–80 the growth rate in unit labor cost in the U.S. iron and steel industry increased at a faster rate than that of all U.S. manufacturing. What is more, the difference between the two has widened over time for two reasons: Labor compensation in steel grew much faster, and labor productivity slower than in all manufacturing. Table 2 shows that between 1964 and 1980, unit labor cost in iron and steel grew by 221 percent compared to only 124 percent growth in the case of all manufacturing. Clearly iron and steel declined in the ranking of U.S. industries over this period, continuing a trend begun during the late 1950s. Regardless of the base year, the U.S. is shown to have lost its comparative advantage in steel. The erosion was a consistent trend, spanning a period of over 20 years.

By contrast, in Japan, the unit labor-cost index in iron and steel (1964 = 100) was considerably below that of all manufacturing in 1972–74; somewhat below in 1975–76; and somewhat above in 1977–78. By the end year, unit labor cost in iron and steel was in line with its counterpart in the entire Japanese manufacturing sector. Both the index of labor productivity and of labor compensation in iron and steel stood below that of their respective counterparts for all manufacturing by the same proportion.

In Germany, iron and steel improved its position as the rise in labor compensation in that industry lagged somewhat behind the national manufacturing average, while productivity forged slightly ahead. In France, unit labor cost in iron and steel rose faster than in all manufacturing because compensation grew faster while productivity rose more slowly in steel. Finally, the erosion in the British iron and steel industry position occurred because the productivity lag behind that of all manufacturing was far in excess of the compensation lag. Not available are corresponding statistics for the semi-industrial countries, such as South Korea or Brazil, that are gradually acquiring competitive advantage in steel production.

The U.S. iron and steel industry slipped in the ranking of industries by comparative advantage, a slippage which began over two decades ago. Hourly compensation in steel nearly quadrupled between 1964 and 1980, relative to a three-fold increase in all manufactures. Over the same period, advances in labor productivity in steel failed to keep pace with that in all manufactures. These two factors combined to push the unit labor cost index in iron and steel well above that of all manufacturing. In contrast, the Japanese and German iron and steel industry maintained its rank order among all manufacturing industries in the respective countries. Whatever happened in the international market place was due to gradual and prolonged slippage of the industry position in the United States and not to any unusual (exemplary or otherwise) performance in Japan or Germany.

B. *Motor Vehicles.* The first of the two aforementioned studies concluded that the position of the U.S. motor-vehicle industry did not deteriorate relative to all industries during the 1957–67 decade. Table

TABLE 3. Indices of Hourly Labor Compensation, Output per Employee-Hour and Unit Labor Cost in Motor Vehicles and All Manufactures for 1980 (1967 = 100)

	LABOR COMPENSATION		OUTPUT PER HOUR		UNIT LABOR COST	
Country	*Motor Vehicles*	*All Mfg.*	*Motor Vehicles*	*All Mfg.*	*Motor Vehicles*	*All Mfg.*
United States	314	297	139	135	227	207
Japan	660	609	322	297	205	205

Source: Table 6.7 and 6.8 in M. Kreinin, "U.S. Comparative Advantage in Motor Vehicles and Steel", *op. cit.*

3 provides the data necessary to assess developments between 1967 and 1980. (The intervening years are deleted in the interest of conserving space. Figures for these years are given in the original study.)

In 1967–72, unit labor cost in the U.S. motor-vehicles industry moved roughly in line with that of the manufacturing sector in general. Between 1972 and 1977, unit labor cost in auto production advanced *somewhat* faster than its couterpart in all manufactures. While productivity in the automobile industry first kept pace with, and then advanced ahead of that in all manufactures, the differential was more than offset by an even greater differential in workers' compensation (wages and fringe benefits).

Finally, in the last three years, the difference in unit labor cost between motor vehicles and all manufactures grew wider. Part of the decline in labor productivity in 1979–80 was undoubtedly cyclical, reflecting the deep depression in the industry and its well-known correlation with labor productivity. But for the most part, the widening gap in unit labor cost was a result of a rapidly increasing differential in labor compensation between the auto industry and all manufacturing.

To some extent, this may have resulted from the cost-of-living escalator in the United Auto Workers (UAW) contract, coupled with the high rate of inflation in the late 1970s. The Department of Labor estimates that only about nine million workers are covered by some cost-of-living clause (COLA). A common COLA provides for a one-cent-per-hour increase for every 0.3-point rise in the Consumer Price Index. But for part of the three-year contract negotiated in 1979, the auto workers won an especially lucrative arrangement: a one-cent-per-hour wage increase for every 0.26-point rise in the Consumer Price Index.

Clearly, the United States appears to be in the process of losing comparative advantage in motor vehicles. But unlike steel, the process has begun in recent years.

It may be asked whether the Japanese car industry gained comparative advantage by moving upward along the Japanese ranking of industries. Although during 1965–80 there were periodic deviations in either direction, unit labor cost in the motor vehicles industry moved roughly in line with that for all manufacturing. The recent erosion in the U.S. competitive position in motor vehicles is due to unfavorable developments in this country rather than to unusually favorable developments in Japan.

Unfortunately, the author is not in possession of such consistent series for the German auto industry. But an index of labor productivity does exist for 1962–78. Productivity in the motor-vehicles industry advanced roughly in line with that in all manufacturing in 1962–66, somewhat more slowly during 1967–73, and increasingly more slowly in the 1974–78 years.[4] In contrast, labor compensation in the automobile industry advanced precisely in tandem with that of all manufacturing in 1975–82.[5] It would appear that Germany was losing its comparative advantage in automobile production in the second half of the 1970s.

In sum, the trends in labor production costs provide an explanation of the deterioration of the U.S. performance on world markets in the iron and steel and motor vehicles industries. There has been a deep erosion, of at least 20-years' standing, in the U.S. comparative advantage in iron and steel. There has been some erosion, of a more recent vintage, in the U.S. comparative advantage in motor vehicles.

VI. THE LEVEL OF LABOR PRODUCTION COSTS

This section employs the same approach to compare the *level* of labor production costs at a point in time between the U.S. and Japan for 1980, and between the U.S. and Germany for 1979. In each industry, as well as in all manufacturing, value added per employee is used as a proxy for labor productivity. In conjunction with labor compensation, this yields labor production costs. Inter-country comparisons are made strictly of cost *ratios* between the industry and all manufacturing.

A. *The U.S. and Japan.* Two problems of data comparability limit somewhat the usefulness of this exercise. First, the compensation figures available in the official BLS tabulations refer to production workers only. Second, in the case of motor vehicles, the Japanese statistics encompass transportation equipment as one category and do not offer any further breakdown. With these reservations in mind, Table 4 compares the relevant ratios in the two countries for 1980, the latest year for which a complete data set is available. Only 1980 compensation and not productivity figures are available for the European countries. In the case of both industries, their ratios are well below those pertaining

TABLE 4. Ratios of Labor Productivity and Compensations within the U.S. and Japan, 1980

	LABOR COMPENSATION			VALUE ADDED PER EMPLOYEE	
INDUSTRY RATIO	*U.S.*	*Japan*	*Germany, France, U.K.*	*U.S.*	*Japan*
Iron and Steel/All Manufactures	176%	174%	111–112%	122%	186%
Motor Vehicles/All Manufactures	162%	123%	108–124%	114%	114%

Sources: Value added per employee: U.S. Bureau of the Census: 1980 Annual Survey of Manufactures; Bank of Japan; *Economic Statistics Annual,* 1982; *Labor Compensation*; BLS Unpublished tabulations, *op. cit.,* 1975–1982.

to the U.S. The following discussion is limited to the U.S. and Japanese comparison.

In the case of iron and steel the ratio of labor compensation in the industry to that in all manufacturing is the same in the two countries. On the other hand, the comparable productivity ratio is 122 percent for the U.S. and 186 percent for Japan. Given the productivity ratios and the Japanese compensation ratio, the U.S. labor-compensation ratio (iron and steel relative to all manufactures) would have to be 114 percent instead of its current level of 176 percent. In other words, average labor compensation would have to decline by 35 percent (but still remain 14 percent above the U.S. manufacturing average), in order for the U.S. to be competitive with Japan in iron and steel. Preliminary figures for 1982 show a labor-compensation ratio of 189 percent for the U.S. and 175 percent for Japan. If one assumes no change from 1980 in the productivity *ratios*, average U.S. compensation in iron and steel would have to drop by 40 percent from 1982 levels to make the industry competitive with Japan.

A reverse situation obtains in the case of motor vehicles. There, the productivity ratio is identical in the two countries. But the compensation ratio in the U.S. is 162 percent, while in Japan it is only 123 percent. To be competitive with Japan in that industry (given 1980 productivity ratios and Japanese compensation ratios), U.S. labor compensation would have to decline by 24 percent (but it would still remain above the U.S. manufacturing average by 23 percent).[6] Preliminary compensation figures for 1982 show a ratio of 165 percent for the U.S. and 125 percent for Japan, yielding the same result.

B. *The U.S. and Germany*. With data from various sources, it is possible to piece together the comparison between the United States and Germany in 1979 shown in Table 5.

In both industries, the U.S. productivity ratio (to all manufacturing) exceeds that of Germany; but the compensation ratio in the U.S. exceeds that of Germany by an even greater amount.

TABLE 5. Ratios of Labor Productivity and Compensation within the U.S. and Germany, 1979.

INDUSTRY RATIO	LABOR COMPENSATION		VALUE ADDED PER EMPLOYEE	
	U.S.	*Germany*	*U.S.*	*Germany*
Iron and Steel/All Manufactures	167%	112%	126%	109%
Motor Vehicles/All Manufactures	151%	123%	113%	104%

Sources: BLS, unpublished tabulations, *op. cit.*, and German *Statistical Yearbook for 1982*. Labor compensation refers to production workers only.

Given the productivity ratios and the German compensation ratio, the U.S. compensation ratio in iron and steel cannot exceed 129 percent in order for the U.S. to be competitive with Germany in that industry. U.S. compensation in iron and steel would have to decline by 23 percent to meet this goal. Provisional estimates for 1982 show a labor-compensation ratio of 189 percent in the United States and 113 percent in Germany. If one assumes no change from 1979 in the productivity *ratios*, average U.S. compensation would have to decline by 31 percent from 1982 levels to make the industry competitive with Germany.

In the case of motor vehicles, given the productivity ratios and the German compensation ratio, U.S. compensation in the industry cannot exceed 137 percent of its counterpart for all manufacturing. In other words, labor compensation in the motor-vehicle industry would have to decline by 9 percent in order for the U.S. to be competitive with Germany. Provisional estimates for 1982 show a labor-compensation ratio of 165 percent in the U.S. and 125 percent in Germany. If one assumes no change from 1979 in the productivity *ratios*, average U.S. compensation would have to decline by 18 percent from 1982 levels to make the industry competitive with Germany.

C. *Summary*. In sum, average labor compensation in the iron and steel industry would have to decline by 31–40 percent and in the motor-vehicle industry by 18–24 percent from their 1982 levels in order to make these industries competitive with Germany and Japan, respectively. For the reasons outlined at the end of Section IV, these estimates of the necessary reductions are probably lowerbound. However, in both cases, compensation would still remain above its counterpart in all U.S. manufacturing. An implied comparison between Germany and Japan can be made using the above results.

VII. POLICY IMPLICATIONS

Although both industries under review find it difficult to compete with foreign producers, there are important differences between the two.

The problems of the steel industry go far deeper and are of much longer standing than those of the automobile industry. The U.S. motor vehicle industry is financially stronger than steel, and its problem is of recent vintage. Additionally, steel is a critical input to many industries. For example, it has been estimated that over 15 percent of value added in automobiles consist of steel (entering directly into car production or indirectly through components). Any protective measures that increase the domestic price of steel (VERs, trigger price mechanisms, quotas or whatever) constitute a tax on the steel-using industries. Thus, if the domestic steel price is raised by 15 percent above world market level, the cost of car production rises by 2–3 percent.

No public policy measures are called for in the case of the U.S. motor vehicle industry. The product mix has already been brought into line with consumer demand. What is needed is further improvement in quality, increased productivity through automation and plant modernization, and meaningful wage concessions. The low U.S. inflation rate will slow the upward COLA adjustment on its own. But beyond that, the UAW membership needs to recognize that there is a trade-off between the level of compensation and the level of employment in the industry; and that in terms of the compensation *ratio* shown in table 4 the U.S. is way out of line with the rest of the industrial world. Clearly, in asking labor to make concessions, equal or even greater sacrifices need to be offered by top management, stockowners, and other elements of the industry. It is also important to insure that most of the savings be passed on to consumers in the form of lower prices. The situation does not call for further import controls as requested by the UAW. In fact, there is evidence that the VER agreement with Japan served mainly to shift import to European sources, to raise Japanese export prices, and to cause product upgrading by the Japanese industry with further price increases. Any employment effects are at best minimal and at worst negative.

Steel is a more serious case. A feature of the industry that is important for policy deliberations is the great dispersion of plant efficiency around the industry average (to which the figures in this study pertain). If left to market forces, the industry, which had a capacity of 145 million tons of basic steel in 1977, may decline to around 80 million tons. There would also be a move towards specialty steel products made by both the large companies and the mini-mills, partly out of imported basic steel. And this, despite the assortment of trade restrictions that are being used to limit imports. All the restrictions accomplish is to prolong the agony, perpetuate inefficiency, and raise the U.S. price of steel, which in turn increase production costs of the steel-using industries. Efforts by the industry and the USW to further restrict imports should be resisted.

A combination of two steps is needed to revitalize part of the industry. (It is perhaps too late to restore the entire industry to its original glory.) (a) Very substantial wage and benefits cuts must be made (a mere slowdown in compensation increases will not suffice).[7] It must be realized that the compensation *ratio* is way out of line with that prevailing in Europe (Table 4). (b) There is a need to modernize some plants, to bring their productivity up to international standards. If it is determined that a huge shrinkage in the nation's basic steel-making capacity is injurious to national defense, then part of the modernization process can be financed by long-term loans out of the defense budget. But these should be made only in conjunction with wage, benefits, and dividends concessions, as well as large industry commitment of funds for the same purpose. Direct assistance is preferable to a transitory tariff (See Hufbauer, 1982, chapter 3.) with proceeds devoted to modernization, first because it does not directly violate our obligations under the General Agreement on Tariffs and Trade, and second, because unlike import restrictions, it would not raise the domestic price of steel and thus would not impair the competitive position of steel-using industries.

NOTES

1. Note that not the entire depression in the two industries can be attributed in import penetration. But international competitiveness is the focus of this paper.
2. It is estimated that in 1980, 60 percent of U.S. steel capacity was of the basic oxygen variety, compared to 76 percent in Japan and 78 percent in Germany. Only 20 percent of the U.S. capacity employed continuous casting, compared to 60 percent in Japan and 46 percent in Germany.
3. Footnote 9 in the second article outlines other differences between the two papers.
4. Data compiled from the German *Statistical Year Book.*
5. BLS, *Hourly Compensation in Motor Vehicles and Equipment Manufacturing 1975–82,* December 1982, and *Hourly Compensation in Manufacturing 1975–82,* December 1982, unpublished tabulations.
6. The author has experimented with some unpublished statistics to adjust for the two problems of data comparability mentioned at the beginning of this section. The estimates for iron and steel remain intact. In the case of motor vehicles, U.S. labor compensation would have to be 11 percent above that for all manufacturing for the U.S. to be competitive with Japan. This would require a reduction of 31 percent in labor compensation in the auto industry.
7. Unfortunately, this will not be easy in either of the two industries. In an article cited in the *Wall Street Journal* (June 13, 1983, p. 1), Gregg Easterbrook suggests that given the choice between competitive pay levels or joblessness, many union members opt for the latter. "Reasons range from union rules that eventually disenfranchise laid-off members to unemployment benefits close to working pay."

REFERENCES

Abernathy, William J., James J. Harbor, and Jay M. Menn, *Productivity and Comparative Cost Advantages: Some Estimates for Major Automotive Producers,* a mimeographed report to the Department of Transportation, Feburary 1981.

Anderson, R. G., and M. E. Kreinin, "Labor Cost and U.S. Comparative Advantage in Steel and Motor Vehicles," *The World Economy*, June 1981, *4*, 199–208.

Hufbauer, Gary, ed., *U.S. International Economic Policy 1981*, Georgetown University International Law Institute, April 1982, Chapter 3.

Kreinin, M. E., *United States' Comparative Advantage in Motor Vehicles and Steel*, included as Chapter 6 in Brazer and Laren, eds., *Michigan's Fiscal and Economic Structure*, University of Michigan Press, 1982.

Kreinin, M. E., *International Economics: A Policy Approach*, Harcourt Brace Jovanovich, 4th edition, 1983, Chapter 11.

Macdougall, D. G. A., "British and American Exports: A Study Suggested by the Theory of Comparative Costs," *Economic Journal*, December 1951, *61*, 697–724 (Part I), and September 1952, *62*, 487–521 (Part II).

O'Boyle, Thomas F., "Steel Management Has Itself to Blame," *Wall Street Journal*, May 17, 1983, *201*, p. 34. CCI p. 34.

U.S. Department of Transportation. *The U.S. Automobile Industry, 1980*, Washington, January 1981, p. 87.

14. Beyond Free Trade

ROBERT B. REICH

The United States is now engaged in a divisive debate over international trade. On one side are disciples of the principle of free trade—the touchstone of American trade policy in the postwar era. Free traders argue that the interests of the United States, and of the world, continue to lie in reducing barriers, subsidies and other government interventions which distort the natural pattern of specialization and trade among countries. On the other side are those calling for policies to protect American industry from foreign competition. Protectionists argue that imports are causing massive unemployment and eroding the nation's industrial base.

The two camps have recently found common ground in the view that the United States must "get tough" with trading partners which protect

Robert B. Reich teaches business and public policy at the John F. Kennedy School of Government, Harvard University.

or subsidize their own industries. By threatening to close American markets or subsidize American traders if other nations fail to abandon their own interventions, free traders and protectionists can both serve their concerns. More than 30 bills were introduced in the 97th Congress urging government action to enforce reciprocity by retaliating against foreign trade barriers and subsidies. Last December the Senate adopted a resolution sought by a Florida-based machine-tool manufacturer; the measure endorsed the manufacturer's request for President Reagan to deny investment tax credits to U.S. companies that purchase Japanese computerized machine tools, on the grounds that Japanese industrial policies give Japan's machine-tool manufacturers an unfair competitive advantage. The Reagan Administration is now warning the Japanese that the United States will commence formal countervailing duty proceedings unless the Japanese cease their practice of favoring certain industries with low-interest loans and special immunities from antitrust constraints.

The Administration also has asked Congress for a $2.66-billion standby fund to match export financing by foreign governments. Already the Administration is providing generous subsidies on the sale of $150-million worth of wheat flour to Egypt, in retaliation against state-assisted flour exports by France. Even the Council of Economic Advisors—long a bastion of free trade purism—has embraced the strategy of retaliation. In its 1983 report to Congress the Council asserted that "even though costly to the U.S. economy in the short run, [retaliation] may . . . be justified if it serves the *strategic* purpose of increasing the cost of [trade interventions] by foreign governments."[1]

It is an ideal political solution. By framing the issue as the proper American *reaction* to foreign transgressions we need not directly face the painful choice between free trade and protection. We can avoid articulating the national goals underlying our trade policy. Protection can be the sword of the free traders in their assault upon foreign trade practices while it simultaneously serves as a shield for those anxious to preserve American jobs. Everyone seems to win.

But no one wins. Import barriers that merely preserve established businesses impose heavy costs on American consumers who must now pay more for the goods they purchase. Barriers and domestic subsidies reduce producers' incentives to innovate and to invest in new products and processes by relieving the pressure of foreign competition. They reduce workers' incentives to seek retraining and to relocate for new jobs. At the same time, interventions aimed at preservation retard the development of other nations' economies; in particular, they block the less-developed nations from "inheriting" the industries for which they are becoming better suited by virtue of their cheaper labor or favored access to markets and raw materials. Finally, they tempt other nations to retaliate in kind, and risk triggering a trade war of import barriers and export subsidies spiraling devastatingly higher, as they did in the 1930s. There is nothing new about any of these arguments. They have been used for years by the free traders themselves. They are no less valid against free traders who now endorse tactical protectionism as a bargaining chip against our trading partners.

The problem is that the classic principle of free trade no longer offers any practical or politically compelling alternative to protectionism. The recent collapse of free-trade ideology into retaliatory protectionism attests to the bankruptcy of that ideal in the present international economy. The sources of this breakdown lie deeper than the current worldwide recession and an over-valued dollar, both of which obviously imperil political assent to an open trading system. The free-trade ideal has been eroding—both within the United States and among America's trading partners—for over a decade. The erosion originates in the profound structural changes that have been reshaping the world's economy.

Since the late 1960s the economies of the United States and every other industrialized nation have been rocked by the emergence of Japan as a powerful exporter of steel, automobiles, and advanced consumer electronics products; by the emergence of South Korea, Taiwan, Hong Kong, the Philippines, Mexico, and Brazil as efficient producers of synthetic textiles, footwear, automobile components, and simpler consumer products, and the rapid movement of some of these nations into steel production and shipbuilding; by improvements in the technology of transportation, communications, and international financial and engineering services, all of which have permitted manufacturing processes to be fragmented and parcelled out across the globe to wherever specific tasks can be performed most efficiently; by the progressive saturation of the American and some West European markets with standard consumer products like automobiles and appliances, and the sudden growth of Asian and Latin American markets for these goods; and by the emergence of certain new technologies (optic fibers, semiconductors, lasers, recombinant DNA) whose commercialization—although critical to the continued competitiveness of a wide range of businesses—entails large investments and greater risks than most firms are accustomed to accepting.

These changes have put governments in industrialized nations under pressure to maintain employment in steel, autos, textiles, consumer electronics, and shipbuilding; to help upgrade plants and equipment in these and other industries; to encourage scrapping of excess capacity; to organize marketing or purchasing cartels; to provide retraining and relocation assistance for workers laid off in distressed industries; to sponsor new industries in hard-hit regions; to underwrite energy costs; to help convert capital equipment to lower-cost energy sources; to sponsor research and development; to nurture new technologies and underwrite the costs and risks of bringing them to market.

Policies inspired by new foreign competition operate either by raising the barriers to entry or by altering the cost structures of selected industries. Entry barriers have been raised through changes in antitrust laws, rules governing patents, trademarks and licensing health and safety regulations, and government procurement restrictions, and by orderly marketing agreements and voluntary export restraints, as well as by straightforward tariffs and quotas. Costs have been reduced through government-subsidized loans, loan guarantees, tax credits, accelerated depreciation allowances, employment and training subsidies, research grants, and favorable credit or tax treatment for purchasers. Most of these interventions have been targeted selectively—on specific industries rather than across the board—because the sharp disruptions of the last 15 years have imposed disparate burdens and created different opportunities across industries.

Reviewing the widely varying forms and effects of intervention reveals that current American trade policy harbors an inherent contradiction: *Our* government must not intervene, since intervention by assumption distorts production and saps our competitive strength. At the same time, we must not permit *other* governments to intervene, since intervention gives our industrialized rivals unfair competitive advantage. Recognizing the contradiction illuminates the reality that free-trade ideology obscures.

Some interventions, rooted in incoherent economic goals or political pressure to spare powerful minorities the pain of adjustment, impose net costs on a country. Some interventions shift adjustment costs onto other countries, benefitting the nation undertaking them but burdening the rest of the world. And some interventions are strictly positive-sum, accelerating economic progress and adding to the world's wealth. To dismiss all these interventions as lamentable "distortions" is neither economically illuminating nor politically compelling. Refusing to discriminate among the different types of interventions prevents us from rejecting the first, resisting the second, and encouraging the third.

Many interventions respond to important side effects of market decisions—the large social costs and social benefits that surge through national economies under stress. To fail to intervene—even if inaction were politically possible—would be to allow severe dislocations to occur by default. We may take issue with specific interventions, specifically those which do not accommodate changes in the global economy, but merely prop up the status quo. But to object to all interventions on the ground that barriers and subsidies are at odds with the ideal of free trade sets principle above ultimate purpose. Free trade is not an end in itself, but a means to a higher living standard for the world's people.

Government interventions that make economic transitions smoother, more equitable, and more efficient can serve precisely this purpose.

What is the proper end of U.S. trade policy? The issue no longer can be weighed on the familiar scales of free trade versus protection. Our failure to craft a national strategy for responding to the structural changes occurring in the world's economy confines us to a confused and contradictory trade policy. Our trading partners do not know what we want because we have failed to articulate it, or even to acknowledge the choices we face. By default, we are adopting a trade policy that preserves our old industrial base, and freezes structural change and progress in the United States and around the globe.

The postwar American ideal of free trade assumed a steady expansion of capital-intensive, standardized production within all industrialized nations. Comparative advantage among them was perceived to depend upon differences in the relative abundance of capital and labor, which in turn depended on national differences both in citizens' willingness to defer consumption and accumulate capital, and in the historic inheritance of capital stock. Comparative advantage was assumed to change over time; even the "backward" nations would eventually progress sufficiently to support capital-intensive industries. But development would be evolutionary, and shifts would be slow, regular, and predictable. It stood to reason that the best policy for ensuring both steady expansion and steady change would be a gradual reduction in trade barriers. That way, each nation could exploit large economies of scale in the type of production in which it currently enjoyed a comparative advantage, while incremental changes in investment and capital accumulation slowly altered the terms of trade.

Neoclassical trade theory was built upon a much older intellectual foundation. Adam Smith and David Ricardo had based their potent arguments for free trade principally on geographic differences in natural endowments, implying a quite static distribution of advantages. A nation had no choice but to realistically accept the economic station its land and climate had assigned it. As machine-based industry developed and spread, later theorists refined the model to accommodate the importance of physical capital. This "factor-proportions" model turned on the observation that some peoples were better than others at making and using machines, for reasons that had little to do with natural resources. Comparative advantage became less a matter of given endowments, more a matter of chosen investments.

Yet because it grew out of an era when technologies changed gradually, and when colonialism and devastating world wars stifled or distorted international economic adjustment, neoclassical trade theory never fully acknowledged the profound difference between comparative advantage as a fact of natural endowments and comparative advantage as an ever-changing product of social organization and choice. Until very recently, observing that the United States was rich in capital while Korea was rich in unskilled labor seemed as comfortably solid a comparison as observing that Portugal was sunny and suited for grapes while Ireland was verdant and suited for sheep. This was the theoretical basis of the free-trade principle that informs American trade policy today.

Just as the Ricardian model had viewed world trade largely in terms of the textile industry which Britain then dominated, so was the U.S. postwar trade policy shaped by attention to America's dominant industries: steel, chemicals, automobiles, rubber, and electrical machinery. Stability and predictability, to ensure that fixed costs could be recovered, were the only principles of public policy necessary to encourage investment. Potential efficiencies in world-scale production promised to preserve American dominance in these industries.

The postwar free-trade ideal was appropriate to its time, an era of unprecedented mass consumption of standardized goods. A new, relatively homogeneous generation of consumers was exercising pent-up demands for homes, cars, and all sorts of steel and plastic gadgets. Throughout the 1950s and 1960s the American economy grew less by innovating than be expanding the scale of its basic production processes and thus reducing unit costs. Western Europe followed that lead. There were relatively few breakthroughs in new products or processes, and very little real competition. But demand seemed insatiable and prosperity reigned. Free trade both enabled the rest of the world to share in this expansion and permitted the United States to preserve its preeminence.

The ideal was codified in the General Agreement on Tariffs and Trade (GATT), signed in 1947, and articulated in more detail in the subsequent Dillon (1960–1961) and Kennedy (1963–1967) rounds of tariff negotiations. It was expressed in the principles of nondiscrimination, reduced government intervention and the formal negotiation of trade disputes. The GATT structure succeeded reasonably well because all parties (except the less-developed nations) had a stake in making the system work so they could share in American-led prosperity; and because the United States possessed sufficient economic and political power to enforce its vision. The volume of world trade increased dramatically, exceeding annual growth in world production. Between 1913 and 1948, world trade had risen two and a half percent per year on average; world production, only two percent; between 1948 and 1973, trade increased by seven percent per year, and world production by five percent.

The principal departures from the ideal were agricultural commodities and textiles, the two areas where potential foreign competition threatened American producers from the start. U.S. representatives to GATT insisted on an exception for primary commodities. The United

States already had restricted imports of dairy products, wheat, and peanuts. Sugar quotas went into effect in 1948. Later came "voluntary" agreements with Taiwan on mushrooms, with Australia and New Zealand on beef, and with Mexico on strawberries and tomatoes. Farm subsidies were similarly exempt: in 1955, when the contracting parties to GATT adopted provisions limiting the use of export subsidies, they effectively excluded primary commodities from coverage. By 1982, the United States was spending over $18 billion a year on purchasing and storing wheat, dairy products, and corn, and on providing low-interest loans to farmers; the government spent over $2 billion merely to raise milk prices (a sum that just about equalled the year's net new lending by the Export-Import Bank to promote overseas sales by American manufacturers).

Policies to preserve the textile industry followed a related logic of escalating preservationism. In 1957 Japan agreed to limit its textile exports to the United States. This was followed five years later by a multilateral agreement (the Long Term Arrangement) designed to protect North America and Europe against cotton textiles from Japan and [other] developing nations; it was extended in 1967 and again in 1970. In 1971 the United States initiated agreements with Hong Kong, Taiwan, and Japan, restricting their exports of wool and man-made fibers. Then in 1974 came the first Multi-Fiber Agreement, which restricted synthetic textiles as well. The latest Multi-Fiber Agreement allows importing nations to negotiate bilateral quotas with exporters. About 80 percent of U.S. textile imports are now covered by individual country restrictions. The United States recently has imposed new restrictions on textile exports from Hong Kong, South Korea, and Taiwan, limiting them to an annual increase of just 1.5 percent per year. In mid-January 1983, the Reagon Administration reduced quotas on some textiles and clothing from China (not a signatory of the Multi-Fiber Agreement) and froze other Chinese textile and clothing exports at or near existing levels.

These two exceptions to the postwar ideal of free trade contained the seeds of its disintegration. Agriculture and textiles were the only significant sectors where free trade would impose major adjustment costs on American producers. The world market for farm goods was limited. Competitors in Canada and Australia had not been crippled by war. And American agricultural interests expected that once the worst of the devastation was repaired, West European nations would soon become largely self-sufficient in food, and even exporters. Thus American farmers saw little to gain and much to lose from free trade, and simply rejected the principle. (In fact the potential world market and the American competitive edge have both proved greater than expected, and for decades the United States has tried to recant its own exception and bring agriculture under the banner of free trade.)

In textiles the causes were different but the effect was the same: some American interests foresaw sizable immediate losses from free trade, and U.S. negotiators obtained exemptions from the rules. The world market for textiles, unlike the market for food, was expected to grow, but early in the postwar era it was clear that low-wage countries were better suited for much textile manufacturing.

In nearly every other industry, free trade promised nothing but expanding American exports. Accepting the principle was painless, and its limits unexamined. But in both cases where free trade would have called for substantial immediate adjustment on the part of significant economic groups in the United States, the principle was unceremoniously abandoned. There were no public policies to guide adjustments of this magnitude.

The free-trade principle—and the codes and institutions that were growing up around it—made no reference to the problem of structural adjustment. These early departures from the ideal foreshadowed its widespread breakdown today.

Even when the adjustment problems of the United States and Western Europe loomed larger in the 1970s, America continued to view the issues narrowly in terms of the free-trade ideal. During the Tokyo Round of negotiations, the United States continued to seek international agreements to limit government interventions that "distort" international trade. Several of the codes that emerged—governing public procurement practices and non-tariff barriers—were informed by the free-trade ideal. But the subsidies code reflected no consensus on what sorts of subsidies were out of bounds; the code did little more than establish processes to ensure that retaliation was not disproportionate to the offense.

During the 1970s trade accords became progressively less coherent or conclusive because the premises on which the postwar free-trade ideal had been founded were no longer applicable to large segments of industrialized economies. Comparative advantage was no longer an almost static phenomenon based on slowly evolving capital endowments. The hourly output of workers in certain less developed nations like South Korea and Taiwan was quickly catching up to the output of workers in the United States and other industrialized nations because they were starting to use many of the same machines, purchased from international engineering and capital-equipment firms with money borrowed from international banks.

The pace of structural change was dramatic. In the mid-1960s, Taiwan, Hong Kong, Korea, Brazil, and Spain specialized in simple products that required large amounts of unskilled labor but little capital investment or technology—clothing, footwear, toys, basic electronic assemblies. Japan's response was to shift out of these products and into processing industries like steel and synthetic fibers, which called for substantial capital and raw materials, but still used mostly unskilled and semi-skilled labor and incorporated relatively mature technologies not subject to major innovations. Ten years later, the newly industrialized countries had followed Japan into basic capital-intensive processing industries. Japan, meanwhile, had become an exporter of steel technology instead of basic steels, and moved its industrial base into products like automobiles, color televisions, small appliances, consumer electronics, and ships—businesses requiring technological sophistication as well as considerable investment in plant and equipment.

By 1980, Taiwan and the other rapid industrializers had themselves become major producers of complex products like automobiles, color televisions, tape recorders, CB transceivers, microwave ovens, small computers, and ships. Korea already has the world's largest single shipyard; the Pohang steel mill is one of the most modern plants in operation. Almost all the world's production of small appliances is now centered in Hong Kong, Korea, and Singapore. Meanwhile, poorer countries like Malaysia, Thailand, the Philippines, Sri Lanka, and India are inheriting the production of clothing, footwear, toys, and simple electronic assemblies.

Far from halting this migration of high-volume, standardized production, automation actually has accelerated it. Sophisticated machines are readily transported to low-wage countries. Robots and computerized machines are substituting for semi-skilled workers. Automated inspection machines are reducing the costs of screening out poor-quality components, thereby encouraging firms in industrialized nations to farm out production of standardized parts to developing nations.

In the face of this rapid movement into high-volume, standardized production, Japan—and to a lesser extent West Germany and France—have sought to shift their industrial bases to products and processes that require skilled workers—precision castings, specialty steel, special chemicals, and sensor devices, as well as the design and manufacture of fiber-optic cable, fine ceramics, lasers, large-scale integrated circuits, and advanced aircraft engines. Skilled labor has become the only dimension of production where advanced industrialized nations can create and retain an advantage. Technological innovations can be bought or imitated by anyone. Production facilities can be established anywhere. Financial capital now flows around the globe at the speed of an electronic impulse. But production processes that depend on skilled labor must stay where the skilled labor is.

Some skill-intensive products or processes require precision engineering, complex testing, and sophisticated maintenance. Others are tailored to the special needs of customers. The remainder involve technologies that are changing rapidly. All three categories are relatively secure against low-wage competition. All depend largely on experience and know-how—often developed within teams of employees who blend traditionally separate business functions of design, engineering, purchasing, manufacturing, distribution, marketing, and sales. Just as the main source of comparative advantage changed over a century ago from static natural endowments to slowly accumulated capital stocks, so now the new importance of skill-intensive production makes comparative advantage a matter of developing and deploying human capital. This second change is more dramatic than the first. In a very real and immediate way, a nation *chooses* its comparative advantage. The flexibility of its institutions and the adaptability of its work force govern the scope of choice. Decisions on human-capital development define a nation's competitive strategy.

Most discussions of Japan's competitive success focus, either admiringly or accusingly, on its tactics, while neglecting the fact that these tactics are effective largely because they are rooted in a coherent strategy for progressively adopting higher-skilled, higher-valued economic activities.

As Japan has reduced its commitent to basic steel, basic petrochemicals, small appliances, ships, and simple fibers, it has dramatically expanded its capacity in the higher-valued, more specialized segments of these industries. Japan's production of high quality polyester-filament fabrics, requiring complex technologies and skilled labor, now accounts for 40 percent of its textile exports. Japan's steel production has shifted to custom-cast steels with new additives and different levels of purification: high-tensile-strength steel, light enough to be used in fuel-efficient cars; steel mixed with silicon, designed to improve the efficiency of power transmissions and electric motors; corrosion-resistant steel. While it upgrades its steel production processes, Japan is moving rapidly into wholly new industries. Already Japan has more than half of the world market in 64K memory chips. It has led in the introduction of the next generation—256K chips. It is on the verge of outpacing the United States in super computers. It is gaining significant shares of the world market in industrial ceramics and composite materials. It is substantially ahead in photovoltaics and the application of robotics.

West Germany and France are having more difficulty adapting their economies, but each country is making progress. Although the recent recession has slowed industrial adjustment in both nations, West Germany continues to shift into specialty steel, precision machinery, specialty chemicals, and biotechnologies; France, into aircraft, nuclear-powered generators, satellite technology, and electronic switching equipment.

These nations' governments are working with their businesses and labor unions to accomplish the shift. They are ensuring that managers obtain long-term capital and that workers obtain retraining. They are selectively raising entry barriers and reducing costs in an effort to alter the pattern of national investment, and thereby to accelerate structural change in their economies. They have undeniably made mistakes. On occasion they also bow to the demands of older industries to maintain the status quo. Often, they find it difficult to achieve consensus about the best strategy for adjustment. They are having problems coping with the current recession while trying to maintain flexibility. But these nations understand the inevitability and urgency of structural change, and the central importance of easing and accelerating the transition.

As the free-trade ideal has become hopelessly inadequate to guide these shifts, international economic agencies and formal trade processes sponsored by the United States have been gradually bypassed and enfeebled. Only the easiest of disputes are settled within the GATT system; most major issues of global economic change are dealt with outside it. Bilateral, voluntary export agreements are the rule. Japan now voluntarily limits its exports to Western Europe of automobiles, machine tools, television tubes, and video tape recorders; and its exports to the United States of automobiles, semiconductors, and many other items. The European Community limits its sales of steel to the United States.

Quotas, tariffs, and other barriers are being imposed on a wide range of products. The European Community maintains a tariff of 17 percent on integrated circuits. Australia, South Africa, Spain, Mexico, and 26 other nations require fixed percentages of domestic content in automobiles assembled within their borders. France is restricting imports of video tape recorders by subjecting them to detailed inspections and deliberate delays.

Some government subsidies are being devoted to older industries. Over the last five years the European Community has invested more than $30 billion in steel. Other subsidies are being directed at emerging businesses. In 1982, Japan unveiled two programs that together devote $750 million to pursuing world leadership in developing and producing the next generation of computers. Japan's $200-million project to develop very-large-scale integrated circuits already has enabled that nation to take the lead in that field. France is spending $20 billion on electronics over the next five years; Germany and France together are investing heavily in satellite technology.

The GATT, which condones or condemns trade practices exclusively by reference to market standards, has little to say about the growing fraction of trade conducted largely outside market channels, such as transfers of raw materials and intermediate goods within multinational firms and issues concerning wholly or partly public enterprises. Several governments are increasing their ownership interests in industry. West European governments already have equity holdings in petrochemicals, steel, railways, coal, gas, oil, shipbuilding, telecommunications, airlines, aerospace, and automobiles. Of Western Europe's 50 largest industrial companies, governments have an ownership stake in 19. In France alone, public corporations now account for almost 30 percent of French sales, 22 percent of the nation's workforce, and almost 52 percent of all industrial investment. These state-owned companies typically subsidize other companies by selling certain goods and services at prices below cost. France has long subsidized the sale of state-supplied coal. State-owned or state-managed banks in many West European nations and in Japan provide special supports to exporting companies. State-owned companies also typically purchase what they need from domestic suppliers. Most national railways, telecommunications, and power-generating entities are excluded from the GATT procurement code.

The free-trade ideal has also been crumbling within the United States. In many respects its erosion here has been more dramatic than elsewhere, and has set a precedent for other nations. Since the late 1960s, the pattern has become well established: American industries suddenly faced with foreign competition have threatened to file complaints with the government alleging foreign "dumping" in the United States of goods priced lower than production costs, or foreign subsidies which render the imports unfairly cheap. Anxious to avoid protracted litigation and the trade and diplomatic frictions accompanying it, the United States often has responded by negotiating a voluntary agreement with the exporting nation, setting a limit to the volume of exports shipped to the United States. As structural changes continue and the exporter adapts by becoming more efficient, the drama repeats itself, with the resulting restrictions becoming even tighter than before.

In 1969, U.S. steel producers pressured the government to obtain voluntary limits on the tonnage of steel that could be exported to the United States from Western Europe and Japan. When these failed to stem the tide, the industry filed anti-dumping petitions. In 1978, the Carter Administration agreed to impose a "trigger-price" mechanism, which effectively barred imported steel from entering the country at any price below the computed cost of production by Japan's most efficient producer plus transport charges, overhead, and a stipulated profit margin. After the steel industry filed new anti-dumping petitions in 1980, the trigger price was increased by 12 percent. After the steel industry again filed countervailing duty cases in 1982, alleging that steel exporting nations were unfairly subsidizing their industries, the Reagan Administration negotiated a formal quota on steel exports from Western Europe, limiting sales to 5.44 percent of the U.S. market. Other steel exporting nations now are seeking similar quota shares of the U.S. market.

In 1977, the U.S. government negotiated a marketing agreement with Japan, limiting Japanese exports of assembled color televisions to just under 1.6 million units annually. Similar agreements subsequently were negotiated with Taiwan and South Korea. In 1978, the government substantially increased tariffs on CB radio transceivers. In 1981, the

Reagan Administration forced Japan to limit its automobile exports to the United States to 1.68 million vehicles; this has predictably encouraged other importing nations to demand similar assurances from the Japanese. At about the same time the Administration allowed duties to be reimposed on $3.8-billion worth of imports from Hong Kong, South Korea, Taiwan, Brazil, and Mexico, substantially increasing the protection accorded American manufacturers of car parts, electrical goods, fertilizers, and chemicals. Meanwhile, officials pressured Japanese electronic equipment manufacturers to limit their exports to the United States and to provide assurances about minimum prices. Congress has also been busy devising new barriers: there is now a 25-percent tariff on trucks manufactured abroad, and 80 percent of the parts of federally funded mass-transit vehicles must be fabricated in the United States.

All told, by 1982, the U.S. product sectors protected overtly by non-tariff barriers—when weighted by each sector's share of total consumption in manufacturing—covered 34 percent of the market for American manufacturers. In Japan the comparable figure was 7 percent; in Canada, 10 percent; in West Germany, 20 percent; in France, 32 percent.[2]

American industries threatened by foreign competition also have been propped up by a wide assortment of government subsidies, special tax provisions, and subsidized loans and loan guarantees. These forms of assistance have mushroomed since the late 1960s, as global competitive pressures have increased. In 1981, for example, the overall rate of U.S. tax subsidies to business as a percent of manufacturing fixed investment (the difference between the actual tax reduction resulting from the purchase of plant or machinery and what that tax reduction would have been under a neutral formula based on estimates of the asset's useful life) was 12.8 percent. In France, the rate was 4.4 percent; in Japan and West Germany the rate was actually negative.[3] By 1982, tax expenditures benefiting American business—in the form of targeted tax credits, special depreciation allowances, and accelerated depreciation—totalled $222 billion. That same year U.S. government-subsidized loans to business totalled over $7 billion in direct outlays; an additional $8.7 billion was allocated in the form of new commitments for loan guarantees. None of the tax expenditures, and only a portion of the loans, appeared as direct outlays in the federal budget.

Finally, the United States continues to grant substantial subsidies and impose severe trade barriers under the pretext of national security. Approximately 55 percent of all research and development in the United States is funded by the government (a much higher percentage than in any other industrialized nation), and the bulk of this support is linked to national defense: government outlays for defense research and development have increased by about $9 billion since 1981, while non-defense research and development has increased by only $600 million. Some of these expenditures, more or less by chance, yield spin-offs of new commercial products. Most are narrowly designed for military hardware.

Some connections to national defense are even more attenuated. Merchant shipping is assumed to be a "strategic" industry; as a result, foreign merchant ships are barred from U.S. coastal trade, while the American government spends approximately $500 million per year subsidizing the shipbuilding industry. The United States is now quietly negotiating bilateral cargo-shipping deals with the Philippines, Indonesia, and South Korea—in effect cartelizing several Pacific shipping lines. Crude oil from Alaska's North Slope may not be shipped to Japan, for fear that such trade will compromise America's hoped-for energy independence. Recently, the U.S. government pressured American Telephone and Telegraph (AT&T) to award a large fiber-optics contract to a U.S. company rather than to Fujitsu, the lowest bidder, out of fear that the United States might otherwise grow too dependent on Japan for this strategically important product. (Protection of the U.S. watch industry was once defended on the ground that only watchmakers had the skills necessary for designing bomb sights, and recent demands for barriers against Chinese textiles warn of the danger of inadequate domestic capacity for making military uniforms.)

Demands for relief to U.S. industries in competitive trouble are growing louder. This is understandable. In 1980—before the current recession got underway—58 percent of the U.S. labor force was employed in an industry which had experienced an overall decline in employment since 1973. In addition, four of the industries with slow employment growth (tobacco, automobiles, primary metals, textiles) were among the five industries with the largest average plant size.[4] Adjustments are particularly difficult for these groups. Private risk capital is generally unavailable for restructuring these industries toward higher value-added and more competitive production. Workers have no ready alternative employment in the geographic area; and they are reluctant to leave for fear of losing seniority rights and pension credits at work, selling their homes at depressed prices and buying new homes in regions where homes cost much more, and sacrificing whatever employment security their spouse might have in a local job.

The free-trade ideal is not necessarily incompatible with these mounting worldwide demands for import barriers and subsidies. The United States could continue to view all these measures—both abroad and at home—as exceptions and stop-gaps, and seek to contain them. Or we could continue to ignore their variety, ubiquity, and magnitude, and concentrate instead on the shrinking arena in which the ideal of free trade still applies. Or we could redefine "free trade" in such a way that many of these measures fall within a margin of permissible departures from the ideal. Or we could simply match other nations' barriers and subsidies (and expect them to match our own) in an attempt to create a "level playing field" for free trade.

The United States could embark upon any one of these strategies, or all of them. But any such attempt would be futile, because the traditional choice between free trade and protection has become almost irrelevant to the dynamic of structural change in the world economy. Free trade is almost a sideshow. The central issues of international trade policy now concern the relative speed at which national economies are evolving to higher value-added production.

The practical policy choices facing the United States and every other industrialized nation are whether (and to what extent) to preserve existing jobs and industries, and whether (and how) to help move capital and labor to higher value-added and more competitive production. Both choices imply an active role for government. But the first is politically and administratively easier to accomplish than the second, at least in the short run. Most people are afraid of change, particularly when they suspect that its burdens and benefits will fall randomly and disproportionately. By the same token, many policies to preserve the status quo—like barriers against foreign competition and special tax benefits propping up deteriorating balance sheets—do not entail active and visible government intervention. No bureaucrats intrude on corporate discretion. Congress votes no budgets. The costs do not appear on any national accounts, and those who bear them are seldom aware of the source or extent of the burdens.

On the other hand, policies designed to ease and accelerate an economy's transition to higher value-added and more competitive production often require that govenments work closely with business and labor to ensure that the sharp changes required do not impose disproportionate costs on some or windfalls for others; that workers have adequate income security and opportunities for retraining; that emerging industries have sufficient capital to cope with the high costs and risks of starting up when these costs and risks are beyond what private investors are willing to endure; and that industries in difficulty have sufficient resources to reduce capacity in their least competitive parts and restructure their most competitive. All of these activities entail an active and explicit government role.

The most attractive option is obvious. Preservationism, here or abroad, imperils our future prosperity and that of the rest of the world. The international economy can be compared to a mill wheel driving the process of structural change in each national economy, pushing each into higher-valued production, and generating, ultimately, an ever-richer world. The current that propels the wheel is the flow of goods and services from country to country. Any attempt to dam up the current—say, to maintain jobs in the U.S. steel industry by blocking exports of Brazilian steel—reduces the current's force and slows down the wheel. Brazil has smaller earnings with which to repay its international loans and its growth is stalled. It thus imports fewer U.S. products, and America's growth is slowed. Once the mill wheel begins to decelerate, it is difficult to restore the momentum short of unblocking all the dams and letting the current surge. But the sort of convulsive economic adjustments required to get the world economy moving again under these circumstances are far more difficult to arrange. In the present period of slow growth and high unemployment, a progressively larger proportion of firms and workers become hostage to protectionist policies.

The alternative to preservationism—rapid movement to higher value-added production—is not without its own strains and disruptions. For 15 years American and West European industry has been buffeted by Japan's speedy shift into steel, automobiles, and consumer electronics; the movement of South Korea, Taiwan, and Brazil into these same product areas is now causing further strains. Meanwhile, Japan's forays into advanced microelectronics and composite materials seriously threaten America's future industrial base—as does West Germany's shift into biotechnologies and France's rapid development of telecommunications technology. In addition, competition among nations for leadership in the same emerging businesses creates what might appear to be its own zero-sum game.

But these sorts of tensions and disruptions are the necessary price of a dynamic world economy. Transformations to higher value-added production enlarge the world's wealth. They speed the current under the mill wheel. They generate cheaper and higher-quality products for consumers worldwide. Japan's automobile successes have hurt the American automobile industry, but the fact is that Americans now have access to better automobiles at lower costs; so, too, with steel from Brazil and new drugs from West Germany.

The apparent zero-sum standoff in international competition for leadership in the same emerging businesses is illusory. Competition to develop new products and serve new markets fuels innovation and change. Emerging products and processes can take an infinite variety of forms, incorporating different features and serving different product "niches." Moreover, the race to improve on products and processes already in the market—leapfrogging over competitors' current offerings—makes the current flow even faster. Such shifts are a positive-sum game.

The American interest lies in promoting the rapid transformation of all nations' industrial bases toward higher-value production, while discouraging zero-sum efforts to preserve the status quo. But this strategy requires that the United States abandon its condemnation of all government interventions as illegitimate departures from the free trade ideal.

U.S. trade policies have had just the opposite effect, discouraging positive adjustments at home and abroad. Part of the problem is that America's failure to discriminate between desirable government interventions and undesirable ones—treating them all as somehow illegitimate and thereby forcing them outside the channels of international scrutiny and negotiation—has ceded much of the initiative to political coalitions bent on preserving the status quo. Informal voluntary export agreements of the sort now covering substantial portions of the world market for steel, automobiles, textiles, and consumer electronics are almost certain to be undertaken as last-ditch efforts to save jobs.

America's formal trade policies also have signaled to our trading partners that we deny the legitimacy of active adjustment. For example, when the U.S. Commerce Department determined last June that Britain was unfairly subsidizing British Steel—but failed to consider that the subsidies were being used by British Steel to reduce capacity and retrain redundant workers—the United State appeared to reject this adjustment strategy outright. Yet capacity reductions and retraining programs organized by affected industries with government help are among the most effective ways of easing the shift of capital and labor out of declining sectors. Indeed, the U.S. steel industry stands to gain substantially from such reductions in the world steel-making capacity. This is not to suggest that all subsidies to distressed industries are positive. Subsidies distort the world economy, and injure the United States, when they serve simply to maintain existing production facilities and jobs at the expense of other nations.

Similarly, when the U.S. Commerce Department preliminarily determined earlier this year that Matsushita was "dumping" radio pagers in the United States at a price that did not permit Matsushita to recover its costs—but failed to consider that Matsushita actually was pricing in anticipation of significant gains in experience and scale efficiencies as it expanded—the United States appeared to deny legitimacy to the aggressive marketing necessary to rapidly commercialize new technologies. Anticipatory pricing to gain high market share in an emerging industry is one of the most effective investments that growing businesses can make—with or without the aid of their governments. Consumers of radio pagers the world over stand to gain from the rapid emergence of such a low-cost product. But we should not turn a blind eye to all instances of foreign pricing below production costs. Such pricing policies in declining businesses merely serve to retard structural change, and may export unemployment during down-turns in a business cycle.

Or consider our formal stand on high technology trade. When the United States argued at last November's GATT Ministerial Meeting that developing nations should remove all import barriers against products incorporating advanced technologies, and industrialized nations should stop subsidizing the commercialization of these technologies, the United States merely seemed bent on maintaining its own lead. Yet the right kinds of government interventions can validly help these nations gain the know-how and production scale that will let them become highly efficient producers in some of these new areas. Other import barriers and domestic subsidies can also of course simply shield obsolete domestic technologies from superior foreign ones and retard global economic progress.

Perhaps the saddest irony is that our formal machinery for responding to the allegedly unfair practices of our trading partners has tended perversely to block industrial change at home. In recent years, America's primary interventions in trade policy have arisen from anti-dumping and countervailing duty cases, the results of which can only shield domestic producers from foreign rivals. As international competition has intensified, many U.S. firms have used these mechanisms to shield their domestic market and avoid the pressure to adapt.

The United States has had a countervailing duty law since 1897. Yet duties were only imposed 41 times in the law's first six decades. None were imposed between 1959 and 1967. But as foreign competition heated up between 1967 and 1974, the government imposed duties 17 times. In 1976, the United States entered 15 countervailing duty orders; in 1978, 12. In recent years duties have been used less to offset subsidies on exports from our industrialized trading partners, and more to block incursions by developing countries using aggressive pricing to break into new markets. Of the 38 cases since 1979 where the government found that foreign export promotion measures warranted duties, 22 concerned imports from seven newly industrialized nations.[5]

Prior to 1973, the United States had never countervailed against a domestic subsidy (as opposed to direct export subsidies); since then it has done so more and more often. Once the Commerce Department finds dumping or subsidization, and the International Trade Commission determines that U.S. companies have been injured (even if the foreign practice was not the major cause of the injury), customs officials have no choice but to levy duties on the imports. Even a preliminary finding of "reasonable indication" of unfair practice and domestic injury triggers a requirement that the importer post bond for the estimated duty. Together, these provisions give domestic industries enormous leverage in their battles to ward off foreign competitors.

The current spate of bills in Congress calling for "reciprocity" against foreign trade barriers and subsidies—and the Reagan Administration's new "get tough" policies threatening retaliation against these practices—suffer from the same perversity. Even if a foreign trade barrier or subsidy is patently a zero-sum attempt to preserve the status quo, it makes no sense for the United States to express its opposition in a way that retards industrial adjustment in this country as well.

In short, the United States has no coherent trade strategy. It has no principles for determining which practices of foreign nations and firms should be opposed, and which practices should be encouraged or even emulated. Posing the issue as free trade versus protection is no longer valid in a world economy undergoing rapid structural change where all governments are active participants, either orchestrating or retarding adjustment. That outmoded choice offers no guidance to political leaders in all industrialized nations who must respond to the needs of thousands of workers displaced by imports. Because the United States has no realistic policy, and because the old choice offers no practical alternative, the real choice—between preservation and adjustment—is being made implicitly by the United States in favor of preservation.

What sorts of principles might guide a new trade policy to encourage positive adjustment at home and among our trading partners? I can only suggest a rudimentary framework—no more than a set of guidelines for further debate and discussion. The details would need careful examination and elaboration by policy-makers and negotiators.

First, however, two notes of caution: the United States still accounts for over one-fifth of global production and nearly one-fourth of the total national product of all non-communist nations; in dollar value, our exports of goods comprise almost 11 percent of the world's total. The dollar remains a medium of exchange for 80 percent of non-communist trade, and constitutes 75 percent of central bank reserves. Thus the size and influence of the American economy places limits on what actions the United States can take toward our trading partners without shifting the dynamics of the world economy. We cannot merely imitate the successful strategies of another nation, like Japan, which has learned to play well a particular kind of game; our actions inevitably alter the rules of the game itself.

The second point to bear in mind is that "industries" are, strictly speaking, just convenient fictions. They are in fact shifting groups of competitors, clustered around particular products and processes. Rarely are two firms engaged in precisely the same effort. The clustering is thicker for some products and processes than for others, and the pattern is always changing. At any given time some clusters will be doing quite well; others, poorly. Thus it is misleading to speak about the decline of "steel" or "textiles" as a whole, or the emergence of "semiconductors." Some businesses associated with steel—certain specialty steels or steel minimills, for example—remain highly competitive within advanced nations; some textile businesses will continue to perform successfully. On the other hand, some activities entailed in making semiconductors (like stuffing circuit boards), and the manufacture of some lines of standardized semiconductors (like 16K RAMS) probably can be undertaken more efficiently in a developing nation. Thus in seeking to accelerate adjustment we should not aim to abandon broad categories of activities like steel, nor to embrace broad categories like semiconductors. Instead, we should aim to shift all of these clusters of businesses to higher value-added segments and more competitive outputs.

A new trade policy that assumes and accommodates structural change in the world economy would distinguish among three distinct categories of trade friction, each linked to a different type of business: (1) low-skilled, standardized businesses; (2) cyclical businesses; and (3) high-skilled, emerging businesses. A strategic trade policy would be designed to facilitate adjustment within each category.

Low-skilled, standardized businesses can be found in basic steel, cotton and simple synthetic textiles, metal-working, most shipbuilding, and basic chemicals. These businesses are characterized by long runs (or large batches) of fairly simple commodities, technologies that are evolving slowly, a relatively low level of skills demanded in the production process, and often intensive use of energy. Notwithstanding that capital costs may be high in some of these businesses, it is relatively easy for newly industrialized nations like South Korea, Taiwan, Hong Kong, Singapore, Brazil, and Mexico to pursue them and become strong competitors. Their labor costs are low, they often have access to cheap raw materials, and their markets for such standardized products often are growing rapidly.

The task for the United States and other advanced industrial nations is to ease the adjustment of their firms and workers out of these businesses as quickly as possible. The least competitive firms should be induced to close, thereby giving the more competitive time in which to consolidate operations and shift to higher value-added production. Underutilized plant and equipment should be scrapped or put to other uses. Workers should be retrained. New businesses should be encouraged to move into affected communities. All this typically requires an infusion of external resources, since distressed businesses and their communities are unlikely to possess the wherewithal to do it themselves.

Thus government subsidies linked directly to these adjustments should be encouraged, both within the United States and in other advanced industrial nations. A similar case can be made for some protection from lower-cost imports for a limited time during the transition, *if* it is specifically linked to a plan for capacity reductions and retraining. Domestic consumers will pay higher prices for these goods in the interim, but the higher prices may be viewed as a justifiable tax to help finance the transition. In fact, one import relief law (the so-called "escape clause") explicitly provides for protection in order to facilitate "orderly adjustment," although this proviso is generally ignored in practice. An escape clause with enforceable adjustment requirements might serve as a vehicle for useful negotiations between industry and government on the pace and direction of adjustment.

For example, Japan's recent efforts at redeploying people and capital out of low-skilled, standardized businesses have been relatively successful. Since 1978 the government has helped businesses organize adjustment cartels to scrap excess capacity and find alternative employment for their workers. Between 1979 and 1981, public and private agreements concerning 14 businesses led to an average capacity cut of 23 percent, accompanied by a rise in capacity utilization from 69 percent to 79 percent and an increase in the ratio of imports to domestic production from 15 percent to 24 percent. Shipbuilders have cut back production by 37 percent; aluminum smelting, by 62 percent; urea production, 42 percent; ammonium, 26 percent; nylon and polyester fiber, 12 percent; wet phosphoric acid, 18 percent. Of course not all such efforts have met with success. Electric-furnace steel manufacturers have used the cartel's protection to increase capacity by 14 percent. And other Japanese steel-makers, faced with competition from cheap South Korean steel, are pressing the government to impose antidumping levies. But the officially sanctioned machinery for scrapping and retraining has in general eased adjustment.

Other advanced nations are installing such adjustment mechanisms with varying degrees of success. If the United States is to have any workable alternative to protection, it must create similar instruments for easing the transition. At a minimum, the United States should refrain from countervailing against foreign subsidies, or retaliating against foreign trade barriers, when these practices are directly tied to capacity reductions and retraining programs.

On the other hand, the United States can legitimately object to certain of our trading partners' practices—like subsidizing exports and setting prices below production costs—which merely retard the shift of capital and labor out of these businesses. Such preservationist policies complicate adjustment and concentrate its costs. They can make it harder to design and implement national transition strategies. Even more objectionable, in terms of the ultimate goal of worldwide economic advance, these policies often end up slowing growth within developing nations (which otherwise would shift into these low-skilled, standardized businesses), and thus constrain the expansion of export markets for more complex goods produced in advanced nations.

But it makes no sense for the United States to retaliate against these zero-sum policies by imposing countervailing duties or antidumping levies on imported products that have benefitted from them, or by providing American manufacturers in the same businesses with export subsidies of their own. These steps merely retard economic change in the United States while at the same time imposing even greater hardships on developing nations. Instead—for a whole range of low-skilled, standardized businesses—the United States should seek international agreements with other advanced industrial nations, establishing targets and timetables for capacity reductions, the scrapping or conversion of existing plant and equipment, and retraining of workers. The United States might seize the initiative by proposing an international adjustment fund to help finance these transitions. Payments into the fund would be proportional to a nation's current employment in designated low-skilled, standardized businesses; drawing rights would be proportional to a nation's reductions in capacity and employment.

The European Community already has undertaken a few tentative steps in this direction, but these initiatives have been hampered in part by contrary U.S. policies. In December 1979, for example, member governments agreed to a Commission proposal to extend aid to the European textile industry for capacity reductions and conversion of plant and equipment. But it was particularly difficult for the Community to implement this policy due to the continuous flow into Western Europe of cheap U.S. synthetic fibers whose manufacturers had access to petroleum feedstocks at regulated prices below world market levels. During the past five years the Commission also has recommended targets for capacity reductions in steel, and has provided funds for conversions. But these steps too have been only partially successful. Although the Commission has the power to require that member states' steel subsidies be used for capacity reductions and retraining, certain nations—like Italy—actually have increased capacity during the interim. Moreover, the recent flow of tax benefits and government-subsidized loans from the United States to its own steel industry, coupled with mounting efforts to protect American steel from foreign competition, has emboldened some European steel-makers to demand similar preservationist policies there.

Agreements among advanced industrial nations concerning targets and timetables for phasing out low-skilled, standardized businesses would need to be complemented by trade policies accommodating developing nations' adoption of these same businesses. For example, while no legitimate function is served in advanced nations by granting these businesses export subsidies or in pricing these products below production costs, trade practices like these can in some cases help developing nations achieve the production scale necessary to become profitable. For developing nations shifting into standardized businesses, export subsidies and below-cost pricing policies are often best viewed as investments to gain economies of scale. At the least, therefore, a trade policy geared to adjustment would not indiscriminately counter developing nations' export promotion measures with countervailing duties or antidumping levies.

Cyclical businesses typically entail high fixed costs in plant, equipment, and labor. They also are quite sensitive to even small declines in aggregate demand, since prospective buyers often will delay purchases until markets recover. Taken together, these two features—high fixed costs and business-cycle sensitivity—guarantee trouble for these businesses during recessions. Large numbers of employees are laid off; investments in new equipment are postponed. When the economy picks up again, it is often difficult for firms in these businesses to regain their competitive footing, particularly if firms in other nations have been cushioned during the trough. In the meantime, the social costs of unemployment often are substantial.

In all advanced industrial nations there is an understandable temptation to grant these cyclical businesses special treatment during recessions—to subsidize them, to help them price below production costs, and to block imports—thereby maintaining employment and capacity rather than bearing the social costs of unemployment and the high unit costs of reduced capacity. But this strategy quickly can turn into a zero-sum game. With every advanced nation seeking in effect to export its unemployment and excess capacity problems, no costs are avoided; they are merely shifted to the least nimble international player.

For the United States in particular this is a losing game. Some other nations may be small enough and their trade sufficiently inconspicuous to impose temporary costs on other nations without running the risk of retaliation. For obvious reasons, the United States is not in this enviable position. We cannot keep our cyclical businesses afloat at the expense of the rest of the world because other nations facing similar problems surely will respond in kind.

Our trade position is made doubly difficult because GATT mechanisms can seldom effectively counter such foreign practices. The formal machinery of anti-dumping, countervailing duties, and escape-clause proceedings is generally too cumbersome; informal negotiations leading to voluntary export agreements are too slow. By the time imports have claimed a noticeable market share, it is often too late for U.S. businesses to recoup. They will have already laid off workers and delayed investments.

Nevertheless, we should view these foreign trade practices in perspective. Periods of worldwide unemployment and underutilized capacity are caused by declining demand, not by predatory trade practices. Zero-sum trade practices can reallocate and concentrate these costs, but they do not create them. The long-term competitiveness of America's cyclical businesses has been jeopardized more by their short-sighted investment and employment practices than by unfair foreign trade measures.

For example, not until 1975 did the Japanese begin to make substantial headway in semiconductors. And they could do so in large part because American chip-makers were standing still. As the U.S. economy was staggering under the impact of the oil-price rise, commercial purchasers of semiconductors in the United States reduced their demand sharply. The government's defense and aerospace budgets were contracting at the same time. As a result, U.S. chip-makers cut their capital equipment purchases by half and laid off thousands of skilled workers. By contrast, the Japanese chip-makers—with their tax privileges, government loans and subsidies still in place—could afford to maintain capacity and improve their technology in anticipation of the next economic upturn. When the market began to rebound, American chip-makers had difficulty attracting back skilled workers and regaining technological momentum. Still smarting from the recession, American executives were reluctant to add new capacity. When the market took off again in 1978, they were caught short. Just to keep its own customers supplied, Intel was forced to buy chips from Hitachi at the rate of 200,000 a month; International Business Machines (IBM) had to purchase 10 million Japanese chips for its small computers. By the end of 1978 the Japanese chip-makers had captured 40 percent of the world market for 16K RAMS. History has been replayed for both semiconductors and machine tools in the current recession.

Thus a "tough" U.S. trade policy for cyclical businesses is less relevant to their competitive strength than industrial and macroeconomic policies designed to reduce their vulnerability to recessions. In many of these businesses we have failed to maintain competitiveness because our capital markets do not provide adequate long-term financing, because our workers lack durable ties to their firms, and because we have chosen to control inflation by periodically cooling the U.S. economy to a near freeze. Other advanced industrial nations have adopted quite different policies. For example, our trade conflicts with Japan over cyclical businesses have been most intense during periods when the yen was undervalued (1970–71, 1976–77, and 1981–82). In the most recent period, that disparity has been directly related to America's tight money and loose fiscal policies, and Japan's loose monetary and tight fiscal policies.

Thus, the U.S. trade strategy for cyclical businesses should be twofold: first, we should continue to discourage foreign export subsidies and below-cost pricing. But more important, we should seek to coordinate our macroeconomic policies with those of our trading partners, so that currency values do not fall too far out of line with underlying trade demand. And we should create counter-cyclical industrial policies which would help maintain employment and capacity in our key cyclical businesses during troughs in the business cycle. These policies might take the form of development banks to provide long-term financing, and government-subsidized retraining vouchers to allow employees to use recessions as occasions to upgrade their skills.

Emerging businesses in advanced industrial nations are characterized by rapid technological change. All depend largely on skilled labor. Examples include the design and fabrication of optical-fiber cable, large-scale integrated circuits, advanced aircraft engines, complex polymer materials, and products derived from recombinant DNA. Many of these businesses are found in the higher-valued more specialized segments of older industries—for example, automobile transaxles, aramid (high-strength synthetic) fibers, and corrosive-resistant steel. And in many of these businesses, such as office communications and computer-aided manufacturing, the traditional line between goods and services is becoming blurred.

Every industrialized nation is racing to gain scale and experience in these businesses; national strategy, not natural endowment, is the key to competitive advantage. Every nation—including the United States, through the back door of the National Aeronautics and Space Administration (NASA) and the Department of Defense—is subsidizing research, development, and commercialization. Some nations also are erecting import barriers on the theory that these businesses represent "infant industries" which must be temporarily sheltered. Finally, in anticipation of burgeoning markets, some firms are setting prices substantially below current production costs. Which of these practices should the United States oppose? Which should it emulate?

Subsidies to accelerate development should be welcomed. New, higher-valued products and new processes for generating them add to the world's wealth. Even if every nation aims for leadership in the same field, this will not become a zero-sum game, since an infinite range of variations and improvements can be achieved, and intense competition will spur even greater progress.

For emerging businesses featuring rapid technical change and continuously evolving products, even below-cost pricing should be welcomed as a positive-sum strategy. Such a pricing strategy signals the anticipation of a substantial drop in costs and prices as producers gain greater scale and experience. The producer gambles that there will be sufficient demand to generate a healthy return if and when the firm gains a substantial market position; the gamble is made more risky by the possibility that a competitor will bring out a new product generation in the meantime. Because this form of competition keeps prices low, all consumers benefit. Moreover, given the dynamic nature of the market, below-cost pricing under these circumstances is not predatory—any competitor can leapfrog to a new and better product. Below-cost pricing is just one means of investing in (and betting on) a particular production generation.

The United States has two handicaps in this race. The first is the share of resources devoted to defense-related research and development, which leads only occasionally and by accident to commercially competitive products or processes. This problem is best addressed by boosting support for non-defense research and development, and by creating a new mechanism (perhaps a White House Industrial Development Board) capable of assessing the effects of major defense projects on U.S. commercial competitiveness and identifying alternative plans for achieving defense objectives in ways that offer richer benefits for the rest of the economy.

The second handicap takes the form of antitrust policies which discourage joint research ventures among domestic firms in international competition. This can be remedied by altering the antitrust laws explicitly to permit such joint ventures when the world market share of the relevant U.S. firms is under, say, 25 percent.

But there is no reason why the United States should erect trade barriers against foreign emerging businesses which enjoy targeted subsidies or set prices below production costs. Barriers only reduce domestic competition. They allow American producers to opt out of the international race for the next cheaper or better generation. So long as markets are growing and changing rapidly, the financial health of domestic firms in these businesses depends not on heavy investment in existing production capacity or on a stable pool of customers, but on rapid adaptation and quick exploitation of new opportunities—a set of organizational skills that can be honed best in a highly competitive global market.

Nor does the "infant industry" argument provide a sound rationale for protecting emerging businesses. Such protection rarely will help a domestic firm catch up to a foreign competitor enjoying a head start in scale and experience. Since technologies are changing rapidly, a better strategy is to encourage domestic firms in their efforts to leapfrog to the next product generation and establish a leading position there. Domestic producers intent on making such a leap may benefit from government subsidies (particularly in cases where the prospect of delayed and contingent returns makes venture capital markets balk), but not from protection against imports of the product they aim to surpass.

Import barriers may also jeopardize the international competitive positions of domestic industrial purchasers who would have to pay more for their supplies, or settle for components of poorer quality. U.S. pressure on Japan to reduce exports of 64K RAMS surely places American computer manufacturers at a competitive disadvantage relative to Japanese computer manufacturers who have ready access to better and cheaper chips. Similarly, were the President to disallow investment tax credits for the purchase of numerically controlled machine tools manufactured in Japan, as some machine-tool makers have urged, American producers of automobiles and construction equipment would no longer have access to superior Japanese machine tools at a low cost.

The United States *should* oppose foreign trade barriers which block U.S. exports of high-technology products. But because such tactics are apt to hurt these other nations at least as much as they do U.S.

producers, the United States has an opportunity through international negotiations to convince its trading partners that the route to competitive success in emerging businesses lies more in the right kind of subsidies than in import barriers.

A final facet of the American strategy for emerging businesses concerns the investments in the education, training, and group learning which now define advanced nations' comparative advantage and determine their capacity to adopt new high-value businesses. Financial capital formation is becoming a less important determinant of a nation's well-being than human capital formation. Financial capital is highly mobile; international savings are flowing around the globe to wherever they can be put to use. Nor is basic invention any longer the key to competitive leadership. Technological innovations can be bought or imitated by anyone: Britain has continued to lead the world in major technological breakthroughs while its economy declines. But a nation's store of human capital—the skills and knowledge embedded within the work force—is relatively immobile internationally, and directly determines the speed and efficiency with which new products can be developed and brought to market.

The quality of public education will continue to be critically important. But since many of the most relevant skills can best be learned on the job, it is becoming increasingly important to develop and attract emerging businesses that will invest aggressively in the training and development of their employees.

Some 70 percent of the value added in American manufacturing currently derives from firms that have branches, subsidiaries, or joint ventures outside the United States; a similar percentage of manufacturing income in Japan, West Germany, Sweden, and Britain is earned by multinational enterprises. Thus the internal decisions of these firms help shape the pattern of international employment. But the important issue is not how these multinationals allocate jobs. It is how they allocate their investment in people.

Japanese multinationals, for example, are now actively engaged in worldwide investment programs. But their underlying strategies are geared to increasing the real wages of Japanese workers over the long term. Japanese companies are establishing facilities in America and Western Europe for assembling automobiles, trucks, and appliances. Because these assembly facilities require relatively low-skilled labor, they do not threaten the interests of progressively more skilled Japanese workers. So long as the highest-value portion of the production process remains behind in Japan, foreign-based assembly facilities contribute to the standard of living of Japan's citizens by increasing the demand for the sophisticated components they produce.

Meanwhile, Japanese companies are entering joint ventures with American companies in the emerging fields of biotechnology, "fifth generation" computers, fiber optics, and advanced integrated circuits. By the terms of these agreements, most advanced research and engineering are to be done in Japan. The U.S. firms thereby gain access to the Japanese market, but Japan reaps the more durable benefit of investments in its human capital. Japanese firms also are producing aircraft under licensing agreements with McDonnell Douglas and Lockheed, rather than buying the aircraft outright; this arrangement enables Japanese workers to learn about up-to-date aircraft manufacturing systems and technologies. In the short run these joint ventures and licensing agreements are more expensive than direct purchases would be, but in the long run they will increase the store of skills and knowledge embedded in the Japanese work force and thereby permit Japan to be more competitive in these industries in the future. The extra cost simply represents sound investments in human capital.

At the same time many Japanese producers are supplying American manufacturers with high value-added products and components. Xerox already is producing many of its small copiers in Japan. Motorola operates an integrated-circuit design center and a test center there. AT&T soon will be selling in the United States cellular mobile-telephone equipment produced in Japan. Of the 16 U.S. firms that built manufacturing facilities in Japan during the first half of 1982, ten were in the business of making advanced semiconductors, and four in biotechnology and fine chemicals. Beginning in 1984, both General Motors and Ford will be importing subcompacts, diesel engines, and transaxles from Japan. All these arrangements also serve to develop Japanese know-how, rather than the long-term skills of the American work force.

Governments in many other nations are beginning to distinguish between direct investments in their nations which merely create new jobs and those which also increase the quality of their labor force. They therefore are bargaining with multinationals for more human capital investment: Italtel, Italy's state-owned telecommunications equipment manufacturer, recently entered into an agreement with General Telephone and Electronics (GTE) to develop an electronic telephone-switching system for the Italian market on condition that the manufacturing facilities be in Italy. GTE gets an inside track on future business in Italy, but Italtel gets the know-how. France has invited Motorola to establish a semiconductor division there and has offered investment incentives on condition that Motorola set up a research and development department in France to help train French engineers. Various governments' conditional offers of market access have led IBM to establish nine research laboratories in Europe and Asia. Ireland is offering incentives for multinationals to establish full-scale manufacturing, research and development, and European-wide administrative facilities in that country.

The United States must understand that government expenditures in the form of subsidies, loan guarantees, and tax benefits designed to keep or lure high value-added emerging businesses within the United States are no less legitimate investments in the education of America's labor force than are investments in the public schools. Properly conceived, these are not zero-sum efforts to increase employment at home at the expense of employment elsewhere; they are positive-sum policies to enhance the skills and know-how of American workers while increasing the wealth-creating potential of the world. In the long run they may constitute our most important strategy for emerging businesses.

These guidelines for active trade strategies that distinguish among declining, cyclical, and emerging businesses are no panacea for trade conflicts. Frictions will remain. Indeed, policies based on the principles outlined here would surely inspire heated debates about which businesses fit within each category, and whether trade practices in fact are being used to shift to higher value-added production or merely to preserve the present industrial base.

The point is not so much to reduce or eliminate frictions, but to change the nature of the debate and the focus of attention. Rather than preoccupy ourselves (and our trading partners) with endless and empty disputes over whether a particular practice constitutes an unwarranted subsidy, a particular firm is engaged in dumping, a certain domestic industry has suffered an injury, or certain nontariff barriers are disruptive to free trade, these new trade strategies would focus the debate squarely on the central question of whether the practices in question serve to accelerate adjustment or maintain the status quo.

The international economy is changing too rapidly to expect that we can discover any immutable principles to guide it automatically on its way. Structural changes are painful, and the vagaries of politics inevitably will play a larger role in setting trade policy in the United States and in every other nation in the years ahead. Thus we need a set of strategic concepts which are consistently applied and which clearly alert our trading partner to what we conceive to be our interest. For the same reason, a formal court-like apparatus for fact-finding and disposition of trade disputes will prove to be less useful than an ongoing process of political debate and negotiation, in which all sides are permanently engaged.

The choice is clear. The forces of preservation will continue to gain ground without U.S. leadership in the opposite direction. Already steel, autos, textiles, and video tape recorders have succumbed to fixed world quotas on their way to becoming cartel arrangements. The United States should approach our trading partners with a lively awareness that adjustment is inherently difficult, that active government intervention is inevitable and sometimes desirable, and that—through explicit strategies and an ongoing process of negotiation and compromise—we can change zero-sum international conflict into a positive-sum enterprise for world growth.

NOTES

1. Economic Report of the President, February 1983, Washington: GPO, 1983, p. 61.
2. Estimate from William Cline, "Exports of Manufactures from Developing Countries: Performance and Prospects for Market Access," Washington: Brookings Institution, 1982. This estimate does not reflect the severity of the protection accorded the products in question.
3. See Bulletin for International Fiscal Documentation, Organization for Economic Cooperation and Development, July 1981.
4. See R. Lawrence, "Deindustrialization and U.S. Competitiveness: Domestic and International Forces in U.S. Industrial Performance 1970–1980," Washington: Brookings Institution, October 19, 1982.
5. Mexico, Uruguay, Argentina, Spain, Brazil, Republic of Korea and Taiwan. Trade Action Monitoring System, Office of the U.S. Trade Representative.

15. Is Industrial Policy The Answer?

MARTIN FELDSTEIN

Thank you. I am very pleased to be with all of you and to participate in this distinguished forum.

In the year ahead, many Americans are likely to be asking themselves the question: "Is industrial policy the answer to America's economic problems?" Industrial policy has become the fashionable slogan among Democratic politicians and some of their new intellectual advisers. But just what does industrial policy mean? What are the economic problems that it is intended to solve? And is an industrial policy really the answer to those problems? These are the questions that I will discuss in my remarks today.

Let's look first at just what "industrial policy" means. Although millions of words have been written about industrial policy, there is no clear general statement of what its advocates propose. But the essential feature of all industrial policy proposals is the notion that the government should be given a bigger role in the economy. The underlying

Martin Feldstein is Professor of Economics at Harvard University.

assumption is that the government knows best and that the American economy would function better if the forces of the market were replaced by the votes of politicians and the decisions of government bureaucrats.

The enlarged role for the government takes three separate forms in most industrial policy schemes: government planning, government subsidies, and government protectionism. Government planning would decide which industries and firms would expand and which would contract and die. Government subsidies would try to ensure that the firms picked out for success would flourish even if they made losses instead of profits. Protectionism would impose barriers to imports from abroad, forcing American businesses and consumers to buy products made here even if their price is higher and their quality lower.

I am convinced that each of these forms of interference with the market economy is a mistake that would weaken the American economy and hurt American consumers. But before I discuss the reasons that have led me to this conclusion, I want to comment briefly on the problems that the proponents of industrial policy say that it will solve.

The primary goal of industrial policy is improving the U.S. international trade balance by increasing U.S. exports to the rest of the world and especially by reducing imports to the United States from other countries. Without the rise in the imports of autos, steel, and consumer electronics in recent years, and the strong deterioration of our trade balance, I very much doubt that we would now be hearing about industrial policy. The second proposed purpose of industrial policy is to raise the rate of real economic growth. The slow pace of economic growth in the 1970s and the pair of back-to-back recessions that began in 1980 contributed to a climate in which many people concluded that "something" had to be done to foster a higher rate of growth.

Each of these goals is clearly important and should be among the central concerns of American economic policy. But why should anyone believe that an industrial policy holds the key to achieving these goals? Perhaps the most persuasive argument to many people is that Japan has had an industrial policy and has enjoyed a very strong balance of trade in manufactured goods, and a high rate of growth during the past two decades.

But despite the worthwhile nature of the goals on which the advocates of industrial policy focus and the success of the Japanese economy, I am convinced that the introduction of more government planning, of government subsidies and of trade barriers would be counterproductive. The advocacy of industrial policy is based on a misdiagnosis of our international competitiveness, an incorrect assessment of Japan's success with industrial policy, and a naive faith in the benign effect of government intervention. Today I want to address each of these three errors on which the support of industrial policy rests. Then I will look at what should be done to improve international competitiveness and increase economic growth.

INTERNATIONAL COMPETITIVENESS

I'll begin with the misdiagnosis of our international trade problem. It is of course true that we will have a record trade deficit this year in which our imports of goods from the rest of the world exceed our exports by some $70 billion. Moreover, next year's trade deficit is likely to exceed $100 billion. Although these trade deficits are a serious problem for the American economy, they are not a permanent or long-term problem that calls for new institutions, for increased government planning or for protectionist barriers.

The unusually large trade deficits at the present time are temporary and reflect three special conditions. First, the economic recovery in the United States is currently more advanced and more powerful than the recoveries in the other industrial countries. As a result, our imports have increased more rapidly than the imports of our major trading partners. Second, the debtor countries of the developing world have recently been forced by a shortage of credit to reduce their imports sharply. Their period of reducing imports has now generally come to an end and many of the debtor countries can now begin increasing their imports.

The third, and I believe most important, reason for the current trade deficit is the temporarily high exchange value of the dollar relative to the values of the currencies of other major industrial countries. During the past three years, the dollar's value has increased about 50 percent relative to the values of those other currencies. Since that is equivalent to a 50 percent increase in the prices of American-made goods relative to the prices of goods made elsewhere, it is not at all surprising that American firms have had a difficult time selling their products in world markets while foreign firms have found it increasingly easy to sell their products in the United States.

The high value of the dollar and the resulting large current account deficits cannot persist indefinitely. The dollar's value must fall sometime in the years ahead, reducing the substantial trade imbalance. The primary reason for the dollar's unusual recent strength has been the high real interest rate in the United States. Therefore an increase in private savings or a decrease in government budget deficits will help to bring the dollar back to a competitive level more rapidly.

A further word on this subject may be helpful. The combination of a low private saving rate in the United States and a substantial increase in government deficits leaves the American economy with insufficient domestic savings to finance the domestic investment that businesses and households want to do at the existing level of real interest rates. Between 1979 and 1982, the net savings available for private investment in businesses and in housing fell from 6.9 percent of GNP to only 1.5 percent of GNP. The resulting domestic capital vacuum has sucked in capital from the rest of the world, using high real interest rates as the lure. But this increased capital inflow is only possible if there is an equal increase in the net flow of goods and services from the rest of the world. Thus the real cause of our recent trade imbalance has been the decline of domestically available savings. As private saving increases and the government's budget deficit shrinks, the trade deficit will also be reduced.

Of course, not all of the problems of international competitiveness that are being felt by American businesses and their employees are due to the temporary influences of business cycle conditions, the contraction of debtor country imports, or the unusually strong dollar. Some industries are also experiencing the natural evolution of the shifting patterns of production around the world. Labor intensive industries and other industries with many low skill jobs continue to move to countries where wages are very much lower than in the United States. Since much of the employment in the so-called high technology industries has become the routine assembly of components, these activities are also moving abroad. This shifting location of production is part of the natural evolution of world markets in response to the changing patterns of comparative advantage, an evolution that has been raising the standard of living of consumers and producers around the world for centuries.

There are, in addition, special problems in a few of the U.S. heavy industries in which wages are very much higher than the wage levels elsewhere in our economy for workers with similar skills and education. During the years in which other countries of the world were not able to produce competitive products, these American industries had a monopoly on our domestic market and could afford to pay abnormally high wages. But as new countries have developed the ability to produce competitive products and changes in shipping technology have given them access to American markets, the American industry has lost its monopoly on our domestic market. Foreign competition can bring down the costs of these products to American buyers. American firms cannot compete effectively if they pay wages that are very much out of line with the general level of American wages (unless similar differentials exist overseas). Protectionist measures enacted under the label of industrial policy can permit these out-of-line wages to persist, but only by raising prices to American buyers. When the buyers are American consumers, those higher prices mean a lower standard of living. When the buyers are American businesses, the higher prices for basic inputs make the products that they produce more expensive to American consumers and less competitive with imports from abroad. In this way, protectionism simply begets more protectionism and brings our system of world trade into jeopardy.

In summary, then, neither the temporary problems that have caused the recent surge in our trade deficit, nor the natural evolution of world production patterns, nor the unsustainable wage levels in a few industries is a justification for an increased role for government in the economy under the label of industrial policy.

JAPAN'S INDUSTRIAL POLICY

Let me turn next to the notion that we should imitate Japan's industrial policy in order to enjoy Japanese economic performance. There is no denying the success of the Japanese economy, which has had a 4.7 percent real rate of economic growth since 1970, which now has an unemployment rate of 2.5 percent and which anticipates a merchandise trade surplus this year of about $30 billion. There is also no denying that Japan has had an industrial policy that has combined some guidance of industrial development by the Ministry of International Trade and Industry with trade protection for selected industries and financial protections for some ventures against the risk of bankruptcy.

But the causal connections between Japan's economic performance and its industrial policy is much more doubtful. Many careful analyses of the Japanese economy have concluded that the sources of Japan's success are to be found elsewhere and that industrial policy has had little or no effect, and perhaps an adverse effect, on Japan's economic performance. Moreover, virtually all experts of Japan agree that, even if Japan's industrial policy has helped the Japanese economy, it cannot be successfully transferred to the United States because of political and cultural differences that reflect Japan's development as an isolated island nation which differs from the West in everything from religion and social structure to population density and ethnic homogeneity.

The most obvious indication that Japanese-style industrial policy cannot be successfully transplanted abroad and may not be an explanation of Japan's own economic success is the poor performances of the European countries that have adopted industrial policies. The British government in the late 1960s and 1970s adopted extensive industrial planning and government subsidies, only to see its economy suffer. The British have now rejected this approach and are trying to reduce government interference in their economy. For over a decade, the Italian government has increased controls over the private economy and subsidies to industries of all kinds. Now Italian industry languishes, the Italian budget deficit grows, and experts within Italy and outside agree that major changes are needed to reduce the government's adverse effect in the economy. More generally, there is a widespread understanding in Europe that government planning and barriers to change during the past decade have made the European economies less competitive in world markets, have slowed Europe's economic growth, and have contributed to the dramatic rise in European unemployment since 1970. Although American employment has had its ups and downs over the past decade, total employment in the United States has increased since 1970 by 26 percent or more than 20 million jobs. During the same period, employment in Europe has shown no increase and the unemployment rate has increased more than 3-fold.

Moreover, in sharp contrast to the European economies, the industrial countries of southeast Asia that have practiced free trade and avoided industrial policy type government interference have had spectacularly high rates of real economic growth. Since 1970, real GNP has grown at a 9.2 percent annual rate in Singapore, at 8.6 percent in Taiwan, and at 9.1 percent in Hong Kong.

Today is not the time for me to discuss the question of whether industrial policy has helped or hurt the Japanese economy. I merely want to establish that most countries with industrial policies have not enjoyed economic success while other countries with relatively little government interference have enjoyed high rates of real economic growth. There is certainly no basis in this world-wide experience for believing that a U.S. imitation of Japanese industrial policy would help our economy.

I believe that the primary reason for Japan's own impressive economic performance are to be found elsewhere. Let me just mention three interrelated reasons. First, Japan has been catching up with the real income level of other industrial countries. Japan's per capita real income rose from 14 percent of the U.S. level in 1952 to 61 percent in 1975 and is still below the U.S. level. Such rapid economic growth is not uncommon when a country begins from such a low base and was easier for Japan because it was still recovering from the Second World War.

Second, Japan has had a remarkably high rate of savings and capital accumulation. While net private saving has averaged about 7.4 percent of GNP in the United States for the past three decades, the corresponding saving rate in Japan has been 24 percent or more than three times as high. Japan's higher rate of capital accumulation has meant a faster rate of economic growth, a lower cost of capital, more rapid introduction of new technology and a more competitive exchange rate.

Finally, Japan's school system appears to produce an adult population that is better trained in basic mathematics and science and that is much more likely than their American counterparts to seek out education in engineering and technology.

The combination of a low starting level, a remarkably high rate of saving, and a very strong educational system can explain Japan's high rate of economic growth without invoking any special role for industrial policy. The strength of Japan's trade balance in manufactured goods deserves one more word of explanation. The primary reason for Japan's success as an exporter of manufactured goods is that it has to be in order to pay for the food, raw materials and oil that it cannot produce at home. In 1980, for example, Japan's exports of manufactured goods exceeded its imports of manufactured goods by an amount equal to 9 percent of Japan's GNP; by contrast, the United States imported nearly as much in manufactured goods as it exported. But in the same year, Japan had to spend more than 10 percent of its GNP on net imports of food, petroleum and other crude materials, leaving its total trade balance in deficit. The value of the yen adjusts to make manufactured goods competitive enough to pay for Japan's needed imports.

None of this excuses Japan's continued use of trade barriers to close the Japanese market to sales of some American products. But it does show that Japan's perennial trade surplus in manufactured goods is the result of Japanese necessity rather than successful industrial policy.

FAITH IN GOVERNMENT INTERVENTION

It is not surprising that Americans have become concerned about our low rate of growth in the past decade or about the sharp increase in the trade deficit since 1980. It is also not surprising that there has been substantial interest in the success of the Japanese and perhaps some wishful thinking that, by emulating their style of economic organization, we might achieve faster growth without the personal sacrifices required by a more rigorous education or a higher saving rate. But what is surprising to me is the notion that Americans might be convinced to put more faith in government planning and subsidies. We Americans have long been properly skeptical about any calls for increased government power. In recent years, American voters and their elected representatives have shown that as a nation we want less government regulation and a reduction in government spending and taxes. Let's look therefore at the three ingredients of industrial policy: government planning, government subsidies, and protectionism.

The central idea in industrial policy is that the government should be picking the winners and losers among American industries, or, to use the fashionable jargon, the "emerging industries" and "decaying industries". But who would in fact do the choosing? The politicians and bureaucrats who make these critical choices would have neither the incentives nor the ability to pick winners as well as the private market place now does. Their decisions would be subject to short-term political scrutiny but would not be subject to the long-term market accountability of private investments.

There is no shortage now of private finance for innovative ideas in the new high technology businesses and in other fields, that, although risky, promise a high rate of return. It is far better to let private investors sort out these competing opportunities and risks than to leave such investment decisions to government bureaucrats.

At the other end of the economic spectrum are the declining firms and industries. Some of these, like the horse carriage makers of the past, cannot expect to have a permanent place in the American economy. Others are potentially viable and should be rescued by new infusions of capital, by management changes, or by changes in work rules and wage rates. The private market, with an eye on long-run profitability, can make those decisions and force those changes in current practice. But if the government were given a mandate to save decaying industries, there would be irresistable political pressures to use government largesse to prevent the changes that should be made. The inefficient producer, the industry with excess capacity, and the firm that pays exorbitant wages might all be propped up. Without the market discipline imposed by the requirement of long-term financial viability, well-intentioned bureaucrats and carefully calculating politicians alike would inevitably be led to waste our nation's resources on investments that, however apparently deserving or palpably vote-producing, actually lack intrinsic economic merit.

The provision of subsidies involves problems that go beyond the limits of bureaucratic ability and the incentives for political distortion. Subsidies require real resources that must be taken away from other uses. It is not enough to ask whether it would in some abstract sense be good to subsidize this or that new venture or declining firm. It is necessary to ask whether using resources in these activities is better than using those resources elsewhere in the economy. When private firms buy capital and labor in the marketplace, they are automatically putting their own projects to the test of whether they can earn enough from their output to bid the needed inputs away from their best alternative uses. When the government pays for subsidies through taxation or deficit finance, there is no test of whether the resources would have been better employed elsewhere.

Perhaps the gravest danger of starting a program of government subsidies for individual industries is that it would be irreversible. As new and apparently worthy cases for government largesse were identified around the country, Congress would appropriate more and more money. If there is anything that we have learned about government programs, it is that once started, no matter how temporary they are intended to be, they are extremely difficult to stop or to shrink.

The third facet of industrial policy is protectionism. Indeed, there are some advocates of an industrial policy who do not want increased government planning and direct subsidies but who believe that the label of industrial policy provides a convenient veneer of respectability for the blatantly protectionist policies that they do favor.

I have already commented on the harmful effects on American consumers and business buyers of tariffs and quotas that limit imports from abroad. Any such barrier to imports is a subsidy to the American producers that are protected from foreign competition. The subsidy may add to profits, may finance above market wages, or may just permit inefficient production. But in any case it hurts American consumers and those businesses that are forced to pay more for their inputs.

When foreign governments use explicit subsidies to capture American markets, our government has a legal obligation to impose anti-dumping penalties and countervailing duties. But the fact that foreign countries use tariffs and other barriers to prevent American products from competing in their markets is not a reason for us to hurt ourselves by erecting barriers to their products here. It is a reason for strenuous negotiations and economic pressures aimed at opening those markets.

Protectionism is a dangerous habit. It saps the competitive spirit of those who use it and impedes the natural adjustment of economic markets. And, like other social diseases, it is inherently contagious. Protectionism here would induce retaliatory protectionism abroad. In the end, we would all suffer from the shrinking of world markets and from the restriction of each nation's ability to produce those products for which it is best suited.

WHAT SHOULD BE DONE?

In short, I believe that industrial policy—the government planning, the subsidies and the protectionism—is not only useless but harmful. It would inevitably misdirect resources to serve political purposes rather than to enhance economic growth. It would inevitably squander public funds, increasing the burden on today's taxpayers and on those taxpayers who must finance a growing national debt. And it would inevitably promote trade barriers that would hurt American consumers and weaken the world economy.

What then should the government be doing to foster the aims of economic growth, high employment and improved international competitiveness? The primary focus of government policy should be to strengthen the natural forces of the private economy by reducing the burdens and disincentives that are imposed by existing government laws.

The most important aim of such government policy should be to increase the rate of capital formation. A higher rate of capital formation fosters growth directly and permits a more rapid introduction of new technologies. The lower cost of capital and the faster technological advance also enhance the competitiveness of American industrial products in world markets.

To increase the rate of capital formation, the tax laws were reformed in 1981 in ways that reduced the burden of taxation on personal saving and on business investment in plant and equipment. The sharp decline in the rate of inflation since 1980 has also raised real after-tax rates of return and thereby increased the incentives to save and invest. As we look to the future, it is important to raise the nation's rate of saving by reducing the government budget deficits and to seek new ways in which the tax laws could be revised to reduce the disincentives that still restrict the rate of capital formation.

A second way in which government policy can enhance growth and the international competitiveness of American products is by fostering research and development. Since the benefits of research accrue not only to the firms that do the research but also to other firms as well, the market place may not do enough research and development activity. To remedy this, the Reagan Administration has followed a three part strategy. First, the National Science Foundation funds for basic research have been increased substantially. Second, a special tax credit for research and development outlays by private firms now rewards higher levels of research activity. And, finally, the Administration has recently introduced legislation that would eliminate the antitrust barriers that currently prevent collaborative research activities among private firms.

My purpose now is not to review an extensive list of policies that the Reagan Administration has adopted or that might usefully be pursued in the future. Rather I want to leave you with this final thought: The strength of the American economy rests upon its millions of individual employees, entrepreneurs and managers. The proper role of the government is to provide an economic environment within which their natural vitality can contribute most to economic success. Our market economy and its system of rewards for superior performance have made the American economy the most productive and innovative in the world. An industrial policy that increases government planning, government subsidies and international protectionism would only be a burden on our economic life and a threat to our long-term economic prosperity.

IV. The International Monetary System: Operation and Management

From the end of the Second World War through 1971 the major countries of the world were committed to a relatively fixed exchange rate system. In 1973, following a last effort to save this system, a number of important countries permitted their rates to float. In a pure floating or flexible rate system the values of national currencies are determined exclusively by supply and demand.

In practice, few countries have permitted their exchange rates to vary totally at the mercy of market forces. The major European states have adopted a joint float in which exchange values between any two of their currencies are more or less fixed within a narrow range. Even currencies that have been permitted to float do so under the watchful eye of the domestic monetary authority, which sometimes intervenes to prevent excessively wide swings in exchange rates. Since there is some degree of management involved, this type of exchange rate policy is called a "dirty float" or "managed float." Many smaller and Third World nations have found it best to peg their currencies to the dollar, the SDR (an International Monetary Fund accounting unit), or a basket of important currencies, thus following essentially fixed rate policies. The combination of these various practices is a global mechanism that can best be called a relatively flexible rate system.

The world now has over a decade of experience with the new relatively flexible rate system. It is an appropriate time to evaluate the performance of this mechanism. There are three questions to consider: 1) Has the system permitted rapid, orderly growth of world trade and capital movements? 2) Have shocks to the system, such as that associated with changes in the price of oil, been absorbed by appropriate rate adjustments? 3) Have national governments been able adequately and independently to control internal prices, interest rates, and other aggregate economic variables by application of monetary and fiscal policies?

When the flexible rate system was adopted the expectation was that a clear "yes" could be answered to each of these questions. It was believed that a flexible system would facilitate trade and capital movements, absorb shocks, and permit great freedom for internal policy action. In contrast, the fixed rate system was judged to have become incapable of serving these functions.

The case for the flexible system is now well articulated in most textbooks. Certainly the system has performed well, given the immensity of the strains on the international economy since 1973. Nonetheless, constructive evaluation and criticism of the operation of the mechanism are appropriate and necessary.

This section opens with an essay by Donald Kemp, who delineates the role that balance of payments measures played in the fixed rate regime. He examines the complicated relationships between a nation's balance of payments and the domestic economy. The balance of payments accounts are a record, in monetary terms, of a nation's international transactions for a fixed period, usually one year. Under a fixed exchange rate system, the net movements of goods and funds revealed by the accounts were of considerable interest. When inward and outward movements were not equal in value the consequence was an increase or decrease in a country's holdings of reserves: gold and other reserve assets. Changes in a country's asset position could induce or require changes in the national money supply with implications for the behavior of national income, employment, prices, and interest rates. An eroding asset balance could forewarn of a decision to devalue the national currency, creating a potential for immense windfall speculative gains. Small wonder then that balance of payments statistics were closely watched and that the calculation of various component balances—of merchandise, trade, of the whole current account, and of others—was a crucial ritual.

With the move to flexible rates, goods and money movements had an immediate impact on the exchange rate itself. Eyes shifted from monitoring the balance of payments towards observing the behavior of the rate. The balance of payments accounts have not been abandoned as a focus of interest, however, because the various items and derivative balances still provide information about many international economic activities.

Kemp argues that balance of payments measures are of little or no use in a flexible rate system, although various items in the accounts may have some interest. Unfortunately, the wisdom of this position has not prevailed, and newspapers and newscasters persist in reporting the monthly balance of merchandise trade and other balances as if they carried grave importance for us all. Nor has the virtual elimination of gold as a significant international reserve asset done much to reduce press concern with its daily price gyrations. What has not abated either is the implicit view that a strong dollar—that is, one with a historically high value in comparison to other currencies—is a good thing and a symbol of national pride. With flexible rates, a given rate is a good thing only insofar as it reflects the current interplay of international currency transactions, without regard for its level or direction of movement.

The next four essays in this part of the collection assess the experience with flexible rates and reconsider the merits of relatively fixed rates.

The paper by Artus and Young reviews the ideas and hopes that led to the development of an ultimately convincing case for the adoption of flexible rates. Permitting the exchange rate to vary was supposed to permit more freedom of action for governments to manage the internal economy and, simultaneously, to achieve speedy equilibration of surplus or deficit trade balances. They point out that these hopes have been only partially realized. Exchange rates have been less stable than advocates of flexibility expected, and imbalances on the trade account have not fully and quickly eradicated themselves.

In the third contribution, Rachel McCulloch focuses on the question of whether floating rates have performed well in accommodating trade and investment flows. She points out that, although flexible rates have been unstable, traders and investors have been able to function despite the introduction of greater risk into their activities. It was believed that less rigid rates would stimulate reduction in the use of protective devices, since movements in exchange rates would make the use of such instruments more or less futile. As it has turned out, however, protectionism has grown, in part because of the instability of exchange rates. Even under flexible rates a nation's currency may remain overvalued and intensify calls for protective relief. In general, she says, economists have not clearly thought through connections between movements of the exchange rate and internal economic adjustments; nor have they grasped fully links between rates that are perceived to be "too high" or "too low" and therefore engender successful industry calls for protective relief.

The next two papers are by John Williamson. He goes beyond the ambivalent assessments of Artus and Young and McCulloch to argue the case for openly managed rates and discuss techniques of exchange rate supervision. Williamson says the key problem under flexible rates is that misalignments of currency values are common and persistent. This leads to a variety of costs and undesirable effects on internal economic stability and growth. A solution is to specify a desired target rate or narrow band of rates for the national currency. Such a rate or band might be constantly adjusted after considering such variables as the internal rate of inflation. Williamson believes that the appropriate instrument for managing the exchange rate is monetary policy, although monetary policy managers may also have other objectives in mind.

The special drawing right (SDR) is a type of international reserve asset. The origins and development of the SDR are discussed by William J. Byrne. SDRs were originally created in 1970 to supplement gold and dollars as a means of providing countries with reserves that could be employed when needed in the pre-1973 fixed exchange rate system. Originally given a fixed gold and dollar value, the SDR has more recently been valued with reference to a basket of major currencies, following the adoption of floating rates. The function of the SDR has also changed under the new regime. While it continues to serve as a reserve asset and can be employed when countries wish to influence the values of their currencies, it is now used widely as an accounting unit to denominate international transactions.

John Williamson discusses next the experience of countries which have had difficulty in meeting international obligations and then appealed to the International Monetary Fund for added liquid reserves. The Fund has been criticized, often by those it is trying to assist, for imposing stringent terms or "conditionality" on its extension of resources to countries trying to cope with payments problems. Generally, as conditions for receiving credits, countries have been expected to devalue their currencies, tighten monetary policy, and reduce governmental deficits. They may be required to liberalize imports and create conditions favorable to export expansion.

Such actions are suitable when a country has a fundamental payments or "solvency" problem but are not necessarily needed if the deficit is transitory and the country is moving through a period of "illiquidity." National sovereignty and pride are involved and newly-independent countries do not welcome what is regarded as IMF intervention in their domestic affairs. Indeed, fragile governments may be toppled if they devalue their currencies and try to rein in expansionary monetary and fiscal policies. Even large countries (the U.K., Brazil) have wondered whether the costs of using IMF facilities may not have been too high.

A concern is that if the IMF does not serve as an international watchdog then nations may lack discipline and find it easy to overcommit themselves to imports, borrow excessively, and let domestic inflation rage out of control. All of these actions pose some threats to the stability of the international financial system. Williamson does not reject the basic necessity for IMF conditionality but does argue for refinement of its application.

A special problem of the international monetary system since the early 1970s has been the rapid expansion of international debt, particularly of funds owed to private banks by Eastern European and Third World countries. There is the fear that countries will not be able to make timely payments of interest and principal to lenders and that American and world banks could face collapse, an event that would create disastrous disarray in world financial markets.

The last article, by James Barth and Joseph Pelzman, outlines the dimensions of the international debt problem and discusses the role of the International Monetary Fund (IMF) in assisting borrowing and lending nations. The rapid increase in international lending, particularly from private banks in the United States and Europe, stemmed from several factors. First, the immense revenues that accrued to oil-exporting countries entered the international banking system. At the same time, faced with the prospect of paying unexpectedly large oil bills, non-oil producing countries sought credits. The relatively rapid growth of exports from oil and non-oil countries gave banks grounds for optimism about the capacity of nations to service higher debt obligations in the future. Financial deregulation in the United States and the competitive expansion of American banks overseas, an arena where many had little experience, may have created an environment in which the extension of credit was not subjected to careful scrutiny.

During the 1980s interest rates rose sharply as the United States and other major countries attempted to restrain inflation. Restrictive monetary policies were implemented at a time when the world economy passed into a period of recession. Borrowing countries, including oil exporters such as Nigeria and Mexico, which had entered aggressively into international credit markets found themselves experiencing lower than expected export growth, as rich country expansion slowed down, and paying increasingly high interest rates. The result was a classic credit squeeze in which export earnings were insufficient to meet current import obligations and service payments on existing debt. Possible solutions were to seek even more short-term credit, if that could be arranged, or to negotiate for an extension of existing obligations through debt renegotiation. The IMF found itself increasingly drawn into the payment problems of debtor nations as they sought use and expansion of IMF resources to manage their external payment burdens.

16 Balance-of-Payments Concepts—What Do They Really Mean?

DONALD S. KEMP

The Advisory Committee on Balance-of-Payments Statistics Presentation of the Office of Management and Budget is currently holding meetings on the usefulness of current balance-of-payments concepts. The Committee is interested in hearing suggestions regarding ways in which international data may be presented in a more useful format. These hearings reflect a growing concern in government, academia, and the business community over the meaning of balance-of-payments data as currently reported.

While the subject of balance-of-payments reporting techniques has been debated since the inception of the practice, the debates have intensified lately as a result of a number of factors. On the one hand, there has been a surge of interest in what has been called the monetary approach to the balance of payments.[1] This approach to payments theory views international transactions within a framework that differs significantly from the current conventional wisdom.[2] If one views international transactions within this monetary framework, the currently employed balance-of-payments concepts have little meaning. On the other hand, the problems of interpreting current balance-of-payments concepts have further intensified as a result of the evolution of a system of floating exchange rates among the world's major trading countries and the rapid accumulation of international reserves by the members of the Organization of Petroleum Exporting Countries (OPEC).

This article discusses the general concept of the balance of payments as well as the appropriateness of various measures of this concept. Its aim is to foster a better understanding of the balance of payments and the meaning of the various measures of this concept that are currently used. In light of the issues raised in this discussion, some proposals for the reform of the method of presenting data relating to international

Donald S. Kemp is currently a vice-president of Chase Manhattan Capital Markets Corporation.

transactions will be made. The discussion will allude to the following propositions:

1. There is a widespread misunderstanding of the forces that give rise to, and the impact of, balance-of-payments deficits and surpluses and exchange rate movements.
2. This misunderstanding has led to undue concern on the part of policymakers, inducing costly recommendations for trade restrictions, controls on capital movements, and export promotion in order to solve balance-of-payments and exchange rate "problems" which simply do not exist.
3. The way balance-of-payments statistics are currently reported serves to exacerbate these misunderstandings.
4. The above propositions apply under both fixed and floating exchange rates. However, the problems alluded to are particularly acute now that we have switched from one exchange rate regime to another. This is because the implications of the switch are confusing in themselves and because many of the ways in which balance-of-payments statistics are reported have been made completely obsolete as a result of the switch.

FUNDAMENTAL MISUNDERSTANDING

The fundamental misunderstanding alluded to in the first proposition stems from the fact that most balance-of-payments analyses focus on either the current or the capital account separately. In order to place the balance of payments in its proper perspective, it is necessary that all accounts be considered simultaneously. In addition, one must recognize that the transactions recorded in balance-of-payments statistics bear the same relationship to foreign and domestic monetary policies as do purely domestic transactions to domestic monetary policy.

Viewed within a monetary framework, balance-of-payments surpluses and deficits and movements in exchange rates are the result of a disparity between the demand for and supply of money. The exact process by which the disparity is corrected is a technical issue and subject to alternative interpretations.[3] Basically, however, when such a disparity exists, spending units attempt to draw down (build up) their money balances through the purchase (sale) of real and/or financial assets. In so doing they increase (decrease) the demand for all assets. Under alternative situations the exact pattern by which spending units adjust their money balances in this fashion will be different. The pattern will depend on, at a minimum, the cause of the change in the quantity of money supplied relative to the quantity demanded, the initial conditions under which the change occurred, and the impact of other exogenous events on spending units. However, this point is that an excess supply of or demand for money will be cleared through the markets for goods, services, and securities. Furthermore, and what is crucial for an understanding of the balance of payments, in an open economy (one in which there are international trade and capital transactions) the markets through which money balances are adjusted extend beyond national boundaries.[4]

Suppose, for example, that the domestic monetary authorities increase the money supply in country j, which leads to an increase in the demand for goods, services, and securities in that country. Any such increase in domestic demand will result in a tendency for prices of domestic real and financial assets in country j to rise, in the short run, relative to those in foreign markets. As a result, spending units in country j will simultaneously reduce their purchases of domestic real and financial assets in favor of foreign assets while domestic suppliers of these assets will seek to sell more at home and less abroad. At the same time, foreign spending units will decrease their purchases of the assets of country j and foreign suppliers will attempt to sell more of their own assets in country j. All of these factors work in favor of an increase in the demand for imports and a decrease in the demand for exports in country j.[5]

Adjustment Under a System of Fixed Exchange Rates

Under a system of fixed exchange rates, the adjustments described above will result in an accumulation of money balances by foreigners in return for the real and financial assets they sell to spending units in country j. This exchange of money balances for real and financial assets will be captured in the balance-of-payments statistics as an overall deficit in the trade and capital accounts.[6] The foreign recipients of these money balances have the option of converting them into their own currencies at their respective central banks. These foreign central banks will then present the balances they accumulate through such conversions to the central bank in country j in return for primary reserve assets. Since these primary reserve assets are one of the components of a country's monetary base (and thus a determinant of its money supply), the effect of this transaction will be a decrease in the money supply of country j back towards its initial level and an increase in the money supplies of its surplus trading partners.

Under a system of fixed exchange rates, the primary channel by which international trade and capital transactions can have an impact on aggregate economic activity is via the international reserve flows described above and their subsequent impact on the money supply (both foreign and domestic).[7] However, one is unable to gauge the magnitude of this impact by looking at either the trade or the capital accounts separately. For example, the effects on aggregate economic activity of a deficit in the merchandise trade account *alone* could be partially or fully neutralized by a surplus in one of the capital accounts. If such a situation arose, the negative aggregate demand effects resulting from an increase in imports of goods would be partially or fully offset by an inflow of capital and a resulting increase in investment demand. If the two effects fully offset each other, there would be no gain or loss of international reserves and the money supply would not be affected by the international trade and capital transactions.

In light of the above considerations, the crucial balance-of-payments concept is that which captures all transactions reflecting the adjustment of the supply of money to the level demanded. That is, the balance-of-payments concept which is most useful as a measure of the impact of international transactions on the domestic economy is one in which the only transactions considered "below the line" are those which have an influence on domestic and foreign money supplies.[8] Henceforth, we will refer to this balance as the *money account*. For the United States this account would be composed of a composite of changes in U.S. primary reserve assets (gold and holdings of foreign currency balances) and changes in foreign deposits at Federal Reserve Banks.[9]

Adjustment Under a System of Freely Floating Exchange Rates

Under a system of freely floating exchange rates the balance of payments (on a money account basis) is always in equilibrium (total imports equal total exports) and there are no money supply changes associated with foreign transactions. In this case the adjustment to the disparity between the supply of and demand for money is accomplished by changes in domestic prices and exchange rates (which change concomitantly with, and accommodate, the required movement in domestic price levels).

In order to analyze the process by which the required adjustment takes place under free floating exchange rates, it is necessary to begin with an analysis of the market for foreign exchange. The demand for imports determines the demand for foreign exchange and the demand for exports determines the supply of foreign exchange. The exchange rate will always seek the level at which the quantities of foreign exchange supplied and demanded are equal, and thus also the level at which the value of import demand equals the value of export demand. Thus, in value terms, imports will always equal exports and there is never either a surplus or a deficit in the balance of payments (on a money account basis).

Let us now return to the previous example in which there is an increase in the quantity of money supplied relative to the quantity demanded. As in our previous example, there will be an increase in the demand for imports (the demand for foreign exchange) and a decrease in the demand for exports (the supply of foreign exchange).

Under freely floating exchange rates, the inevitable consequence will be a rise in the exchange rate (the price of foreign currencies in terms of the domestic currency).[10] As such a rise in the exchange rate is the natural consequence of the existing money stock exceeding the quantity of money demanded.

The upshot of the foregoing analysis is that under fixed exchange rates the crucial balance-of-payments concept for gauging the impact of international trade and capital transactions on the domestic economy is the balance in the money account. Furthermore, exchange rate movements and money account deficits and surpluses are merely part of the adjustment mechanism by which a disparity between the existing supply of and demand for money is being corrected. They are symptoms of a problem, but they themselves are not the problem. The fact is that equality between the supply of and demand for money must and will be restored, and the money account deficits and surpluses and exchange rate movements are merely a mechanism by which the required adjustment is accommodated.

Most furor over balance-of-payments statistics and exchange rate movements stems from the failure to recognize the above proposition. For example, the belief is widespread that deficits in the trade account are "bad" because they represent a net drain on demand for the output produced in the deficit country. In reality, however, one is unable to gauge the impact of international transactions on domestic demand by focusing on the trade account alone. Even if a trade account deficit is not offset by a surplus in the capital account, the resultant deficit in the money account merely reflects the fact that the stock of money exceeds the quantity of money demanded. Somehow this disparity must be and is corrected. In a regime of fixed exchange rates, the money stock will be decreased automatically through the outflow of international reserves which is associated with the money account deficit.

In a similar fashion, most concern over the depreciation of a currency in a regime of floating exchange rates is also misdirected. It is curious that the belief is widely held that the depreciation of a nation's currency is a cause of domestic inflation. To the contrary, depreciations are not the source, but are the result of inflationary pressures. The depreciation occurs for the same reason that money account deficits occur with fixed exchange rates—that is, because there exists a disparity between the supply of and demand for money which must be corrected.

When such a disparity exists under floating exchange rates, the excess supply of money itself will result in an increase in the demand for domestically supplied real and financial assets as well as for foreign exchange (the demand for foreign supplies of real and financial assets). Consequently, all prices (the price of foreign exchange included) will rise. As with all increases in the price level, the result will be an increase in the demand for money as spending units attempt to maintain the real value of that proportion of their wealth that they elect to hold in the form of money balances. In short, the original disparity between the demand for and supply of money will be corrected via a rise in domestic prices and a depreciation in the foreign value of the domestic currency (a rise in the price of foreign exchange).

In view of the foregoing analysis, balance-of-payments deficits and surpluses and exchange rate movements should *not* be viewed as evils that are to be avoided at all costs. They are not problems in themselves, but are one of the means by which other problems are corrected. In fact, in light of the nature of the forces which give rise to them, they are, in a sense, desirable.

BALANCE-OF-PAYMENTS CONCEPTS

Since they are summaries, balance-of-payments data are presented in categories composed of similar types of international transactions (for example, merchandise trade, long-term capital, etc.). The transactions grouped together in any particular category are similar in that, given the existing institutional framework within which they occur, the forces giving rise to, and the impact of, them is supposed to be similar.[11] To the extent that any set of groupings ever was appropriate or informationally useful, this usefulness can be greatly diminished if there are changes in the forces which give rise to, or the impact of, that particular set of transactions, or if there are changes in the institutional framework within which these transactions occur. Thus, given the changes which have occurred in the field of international trade and finance in the last few years, it would not be at all surprising to find that some previously meaningful balance-of-payments groupings had become almost meaningless.

Foremost among these changes has been the movement of the world's major trading nations from a fixed to a floating exchange rate regime and the surge in the accumulation of official reserves by OPEC members. In this section the current methods of presenting balance-of-payments statistics will be analyzed in light of these changes. Each individual account will be discussed in terms of its relevance prior to these changes and, where appropriate, in light of the movement to floating exchange rates and the rapid growth of OPEC reserves.

Current Account

The current account measures the extent to which the United States is a net borrower from, or net lender to, foreign countries as a group. With the exception of unilateral transfers (gifts and similar payments by American governmental units and private citizens to foreign resi-

EXHIBIT 1. Summary Explanation of U.S. Balance of Payments

(To be used in conjunction with Table 1)

The U.S. balance of payments is a summary record of all international transactions by the Government, business, and private U.S. residents occurring during a specified period of time.

As a series of accounts and as a measure of economic behavior, balance of payments transactions are grouped into seven categories: merchandise trade, services, transfer payments, long-term capital, short-term private capital, miscellaneous, and liquid private capital. We successively add the net balance of the above categories in order to obtain:

Merchandise Trade Balance
Goods and Services Balance
Current Account Balance
Basic Balance
Net Liquidity Balance
Official Settlements Balance

Below the dashed line there are two additional categories, U.S. liabilities to foreign official holders and U.S. reserve assets. These serve to finance the transactions recorded above the dashed line.

There are interrelationships between these accounts. For example, the credit entry associated with an export of goods could result from the debt entry of a private bank loan, a Government grant, a private grant, or an increase in U.S. holdings of foreign currency or gold.

Merchandise Trade: Exports and imports are a measure of physical goods which cross U.S. boundaries. The receipt of dollars for exports is recorded as a plus and the payments for imports are recorded as a minus in this account.

Services: Included in this account are the receipt of earnings on U.S. investments abroad and the payments of earnings on foreign investments in the U.S. Sales of military equipment to foreigners and purchases from foreigners for both military equipment and for U.S. military stations abroad are also included in this category.

---

dents), all of the transactions recorded above the line in this account represent the transfer of real assets (goods and services) between the United States and its trading partners.[12] The transactions recorded below the line in this account represent the means by which the United States is able to finance the purchase of net imports from other countries or, in the case of a surplus, how net exports have been financed by our trading partners. For example, the United States had a $4 billion deficit on current account in 1974. This means that, on balance, the United States received $4 billion more in goods and services (imports) than it gave up (exports) in return. The United States was able to do this by borrowing $4 billion from foreigners. The borrowing was financed through a net of all of the transactions which appear below the line in the current account. Thus, for the purpose of balance-of-payments analysis, the value of the current account balance lies in its usefulness as a measure of the net transfer of real resources between the United

(*continued*)

Transfer Payments: Private transfers represent gifts and similar payments by Americans to foreign residents. Government transfers represent payments associated with foreign assistance programs and may be utilized by foreign governments to finance trade with the United States.

Long-Term Capital: Long-term private capital records all changes in U.S. private assets and liabilities to foreigners, both real and financial. Private U.S. purchases of foreign assets are recorded as payments of dollars to foreigners, and private foreign purchases of U.S. assets are recorded as receipts of dollars from foreigners. Government capital transactions represent long-term loans of the U.S. Government to foreign governments.

Short-Term Private Capital: Nonliquid liabilities refers to capital inflows, such as loans by foreign banks to U.S. corporations, and nonliquid claims refers to capital outflows, such as U.S. bank loans to foreigners. These items represent trade financing and cash items in the process of collection which have maturities of less than three months. The distinction between short-term private capital and liquid private capital is that the transactions recorded in the former account are considered not readily transferable.

Miscellaneous: Allocations of special drawing rights (SDRs) represent the receipt of the U.S. share of supplemental reserve assets issued by the International Monetary Fund. SDRs are recorded here when they are initially received by the United States. The category errors and omissions is the statistical discrepancy between all specifically identifiable receipts and payments. It is believed to be largely unrecorded short-term private capital movements.

Liquid Private Capital: This account records changes in U.S. short-term liabilities to foreigners, and changes in U.S. short-term claims reported by U.S. banks on foreigners.

NOTE: For analytical purposes the dashed line below the official settlements balance could be moved. For example, if this line were placed under one of the balances above, then all transactions below that line would serve as financing, or offsetting, items for the balance above.

States and the rest of the world. Another way of viewing this balance is that it measures the change in our net foreign investment. In other words, in 1974 foreigners invested (made loans amounting to) $4 billion in the United States.

This balance carries additional significance in that it is a component of the nations's GNP accounts. It is included in the GNP accounts because it is *supposed* to capture the contribution of foreigners to domestic aggregate demand. However, it alone tells us very little about the impact of international transactions on domestic economic activity. It only measures the magnitude of foreign demand for current output (goods and services) and completely ignores the impact of foreign investment decisions on U.S. economic activity. As mentioned previously, transactions in the capital account could offset completely the impact of current account transactions on the U.S. money supply. As such, implications drawn from the current account regarding the domestic impact of foreign transactions can be highly misleading.

EXHIBIT 2. International Transactions, 1974p

	MILLIONS OF DOLLARS
Merchandise exports	$100,047
Merchandise imports	108,027
Service exports	42,600
Service imports	31,431
Unilateral transfers (net)	9,005
Direct investment abroad	6,801
Direct investment in U.S.	2,308
Portfolio investment abroad	1,951
Portfolio investment in U.S.	1,199
Deposits abroad (demands, time, at Central Bank)	1,129
Deposits in U.S. (demand, time, at Central Bank)	20,746
Money account balance	46

Sources: *Survey of Current Business,* Board of Governors of the Federal Reserve System *Bulletin, Treasury Bulletin.*

These same objections are equally appropriate, if not more so, to the two more narrowly defined balance-of-payments concepts—the merchandise trade balance and the goods and services balance. While these balances are among those which receive the greatest amount of attention, their implications for the domestic economy are greatly overstated.

Basic Balance

The basic balance isolates long-term capital transactions above the line along with all of the transactions included in the current account. All capital flows involving assets whose original maturity exceeds one year are defined as long term, and therefore "basic" transactions. The original theoretical justification for the basic balance seems to be that it catches the *persistent* forces at work in the balance of payments and thus could be a leading indicator of long-run trends.

However, this is clearly not the case. Both portfolio investments and long-term private loans are included in long-term capital, and both are now highly sensitive to short-run changes in interest rates and changes in expectations about relative inflation rates, monetary policies, and growth. The meaningfulness of the long-term capital concept might have some appeal on a theoretical basis, but data problems make its empirical counterpart extremely difficult to construct and, therefore, it is not very useful.

Net Liquidity Balance

The net liquidity balance may be thought of as a measure of the total of U.S. dollars which accrue to foreigners, during an accounting period,

TABLE 1. U.S. Balance of Payments, 1974p

(BILLIONS OF DOLLARS)

		NET BALANCE	CUMULATIVE NET BALANCE
Merchandise trade			
Exports	+97.1		
Imports	−103.0		
MERCHANDISE TRADE BALANCE		−5.9	−5.9
Services			
Military receipts	+3.0		
Military payments	−5.1		
Income on U.S. investments abroad	+29.9		
Payments for foreign investments in U.S.	−16.7		
Receipts from travel and transportation	+10.2		
Payments for travel and transportation	−12.7		
Other services (net)	+0.3		
Balance on services		+9.1	
GOODS AND SERVICES BALANCE			+3.2
Transfer payments			
Private	−1.1		
Government	−6.1		
Balance on transfer payments		−7.2	
CURRENT ACCOUNT BALANCE			−4.0
Long-term capital			
Direct investment receipts	+2.3		
Direct investment payments	−6.8		
Portfolio investment receipts	+1.2		
Portfolio investment payments	−2.0		
Government loans (net)	+1.0		
Other long-term (net)	−2.4		
Balance on long-term capital		−6.7	
BASIC BALANCE			−10.6
Short-term private capital			
Nonliquid liabilities	+1.7		
Nonliquid claims	−14.7		
Balance on short-term private capital		−13.0	
Miscellaneous			
Allocation of special drawing rights (SDR)*			
Errors and omissions	+5.2		

TABLE 1. *(Continued)*

(BILLIONS OF DOLLARS)			
		NET BALANCE	CUMULATIVE NET BALANCE
Balance on miscellaneous items		+5.2	
NET LIQUIDITY BALANCE			−18.3
Liquid private capital			
Liabilities to foreigners	+15.7		
Claims on foreigners	−5.5		
Balance on liquid private capital		+10.3	
OFFICIAL SETTLEMENTS BALANCE			−8.1
The official settlements balance is financed by changes in U.S. liabilities to foreign official holders			
Liquid liabilities	+8.3		
Readily marketable liabilities	+0.6		
Special liabilities	+0.7		
Balance on liabilities to foreign official holders		+9.5	
U.S. reserve assets			
Gold	0.0		
Special drawing rights	−0.2		
Convertible currencies	0.0		
IMF gold tranche	−1.3		
Balance on reserve assets		−1.4	
TOTAL FINANCING OF OFFICIAL SETTLEMENTS BALANCE			+8.1

* There was no SDR allocation for 1974. P—Preliminary

NOTE: Figures may not add because of rounding.

as a result of all of the transactions recorded above the line—that is, imports and exports of goods and services, unilateral transfers, inflows and outflows of long-term capital, and nonliquid short-term capital. Below the line it combines the changes in our reserve assets and the changes in our liquid liabilities to both private and official foreigners. The original intent of this balance was to measure the change in *potential* pressure on our reserve assets. The thinking was that official institutions could use their dollar assets to buy our reserve assets; private holdings of dollars were a potential threat if private foreigners sold their dollars to central banks, who could in turn use them to buy our reserve assets.

There are a number of problems with this measure which make its relevance and usefulness highly questionable. These problems are both theoretical and empirical and are greatly magnified by the recent institutional changes which have occurred in international finance.

The main empirical problem with this measure is that it attempts to distinguish between liquid and nonliquid liabilities. Every U.S. liability to foreigners has a combination of attributes, some of which qualify them for classification as liquid and some of which qualify them for classification as nonliquid. As a result, the classification of many assets as liquid or nonliquid must be somewhat arbitrary. For example, foreign portfolio investments in the United States are classified as nonliquid liabilities. However, these liabilities of the United States are readily convertible into liquid form—that is, they may be sold at any moment in time for cash or a demand deposit. Thus, the exchange market implications of the growth of foreign portfolio investments in the United States are not much different from those of a growth in foreign-held bank deposits (which are classified as liquid).

Suppose, however, that all liabilities to foreigners could be meaningfully subdivided into liquid and nonliquid categories. It would still be inaccurate to declare that all liquid liabilities to foreigners represent potential pressure on our reserve assets. There are many reasons why foreigners wish to hold liquid claims against the United States, not the least of which is for transactions purposes. The U.S. dollar is indeed an international currency which may be used in transactions throughout the world. Only those foreign-held claims which are in excess of those desired for transactions purposes can be rightfully considered as a potential source of pressure on our reserve assets.

While it is surely impossible, for empirical as well as theoretical reasons, to determine what proportion of total U.S. liabilities are being held for transactions purposes, the proportion is probably large. In order to determine accurately potential pressures on our reserve assets, it would be necessary to further subdivide U.S. liquid liabilities to foreigners into those held for transactions purposes and those held for speculative (or other) purposes. Indeed, it is only this latter category of liquid claims that represents potential pressures on our reserve assets.

The above problems have become decidedly more acute in the wake of the quadrupling of petroleum prices and the surge in the dollar holdings of OPEC members. Since the transacting currency of OPEC members is the U.S. dollar, the role of the dollar as an international medium of exchange, and thus its transactions demand, has been greatly enhanced. At the same time, many OPEC members have been accumulating extensive dollar denominated liquid claims. While this may be only a short-run phenomenon, the fact is that these liquid U.S. liabilities do not represent a potential threat to our reserve assets. Rather, these liabilities represent only a short-term depository for OPEC receipts while they decide how they wish to extend the maturity distribution of their claims into long-term (and therefore nonliquid in balance-of-payments parlance) investments.

To the extent that there ever did exist a conceptual basis for trying to measure the net liquidity balance, that basis no longer exists as a result of the shift from a system of fixed to one of floating exchange rates. With floating exchange rates there is no potential pressure on our primary reserve assets because the dollar is no longer convertible into them.[13]

Official Settlements Balance

The official settlements balance is intended to measure the change in dollar balances which accrue to foreign official institutions only. In this balance-of-payments concept all private transactions are counted above the line, whereas in the net liquidity balance some private transactions (liquid private capital flows) are counted below the line. The original intent of this balance was to measure *directly* the net exchange pressure on the dollar and on U.S. reserve assets.[14] Since only those dollar denominated U.S. liabilities which are held by foreign official institutions could be exchanged for reserve assets, this balance focuses on only those transactions which give rise to changes in these liabilities.

The usefulness of this balance has always rested on the questionable distinction between private and official transactions. The idea is that all transactions listed above the line are the result of market-determined private (autonomous) actions and all transactions below the line are the result of official (accommodating) actions undertaken in support of fixed exchange rates. The thinking was that all official transactions could be considered as accommodating and all private transactions as autonomous. This probably never was the case and certainly is not the case now, given recent institutional changes in international finance.

The rapid accumulation of reserves by official agencies of OPEC members are included below the line in this balance, but they are clearly not the result of official action aimed at stabilizing exchange rates. These OPEC reserves largely represent investment decisions by OPEC members which are based on considerations of income, liquidity, and risk. In other words, many official transactions are clearly autonomous and not accommodating, and should therefore be included with other autonomous transactions above the line.

While the above discussion relates to the blurred distinction between autonomous and accommodating transactions, there are other problems which blur the distinction between private and official transactions. For example, many foreign official institutions invest their dollar balances in the Eurodollar market. The result of such transactions on the balance-of-payments accounts is to increase private (Eurodollar bank) claims on the United States and reduce official claims. However, in reality, since the foreign official institution still maintains ownership and control of a claim against the United States, there has been no reduction in official claims against it.

To the extent that the official settlements balance ever did measure what it was supposed to measure, the relevance of this concept has disappeared as a result of the shift to floating exchange rates. As a result of this shift, exchange rates authorities are no longer *obligated* to present movements in exchange rates through official intervention in the foreign exchange market. The net exchange pressure on the dollar is no longer captured by changes in reserve asset holdings.

PROPOSALS FOR REFORM

In view of the considerations aired in the foregoing discussion, it is often the case that the present method of presenting balance-of-payments data is more misleading than useful. In some instances the balances currently reported have absolutely no economic meaning and often do not give an accurate measure of the impact of international trade and capital transactions on aggregate economic activity. This is because none of the currently reported balances capture the effects of international transactions on the money supply, and it is primarily through their effects on the money supply that these transactions have any appreciable impact on aggregate economic activity.

Under fixed exchange rates there is only one really meaningful balance—the balance in the money account. This account is the only one that captures the effect of international transactions on the money supply. However, at present this balance is not reported. Under freely floating exchange rates there are no meaningful balance-of-payments concepts, because in this case international transactions have no impact on the money supply. In this case the money account is always in balance, and therefore of no significance.

Thus, there is little, if any, reason why the publication of balance-of-payments data in the currently employed format should be continued. Not only is this format virtually without economic meaning, but it is often quite misleading. While there are many theoretical and empirical problems associated with any kind of aggregation of data pertaining to international transactions, the problems are unnecessarily exacerbated by the present practice of drawing balances on the various subaccounts (that is, the merchandise trade balance, the goods and services balance, the current account balance, etc.). These problems could be significantly reduced if the data were just presented and no balances were drawn.

In a world of freely floating exchange rates, changing pressures on the dollar are captured by movements in the exchange rate and not by some theoretically and empirically meaningless balances. For this reason, it would be helpful if international trade data were to include changes in the effective exchange rate.[15] However, we recognize that the current exchange rate arrangement cannot be realistically considered as an experiment with freely floating exchange rates. It is rather an experiment with a "managed float."[16] Whether recent official intervention activities have had any effect on the exchange rate or not, the fact is that they, as will any official exchange rate intervention activities, have had an impact on the U.S. monetary base. Thus, as it turns out, given the current "managed float," both the money account balance and changes in the effective exchange rate each convey some useful information.

Thus, any proposals for reform of the methods of presenting balance-of-payments data should include, at a minimum, a recommendation that the currently employed balances not be drawn and that the words "deficit" and "surplus" be dropped from any reference to international data. This would not prevent individuals from computing balances if they wished; it would only remove the implied government sanction of these concepts as economically meaningful.

In addition, any proposed reforms should address themselves to the obviously arbitrary classification of certain transactions as relating to liquid, illiquid, short-term, or long-term capital flows. They should also recognize that under a managed float changing pressures on the dollar are captured by movements in the exchange rate and the money account balance. With these goals in mind, a classification scheme similar to that presented in Exhibit 2 is suggested (see page 240).

The advantages of this type of approach to the classification of international data are as follows:

1. No balances are computed or reported.
2. It allows individuals to make their own judgments regarding whether or not a particular transaction is related to liquid, illiquid, short-term, or long-term capital flows and to draw their own conclusions regarding the significance of changes in these flows.
3. It recognizes that pressures on the dollar are reflected in changes in exchange rates and in the money account balance and not by changes in the volume of a particular subset of transactions.

CONCLUSION

The current method of presenting data relating to international commerce attempts to group transactions so that the net of the transactions included in any category (the balance in that account) is significant for some reason in sign and amount. The transactions grouped together in any particular category are *supposed* to be similar in that, given the existing institutional framework within which they occur, the forces

FIGURE 1. Nominal and Effective Dollar Devaluation

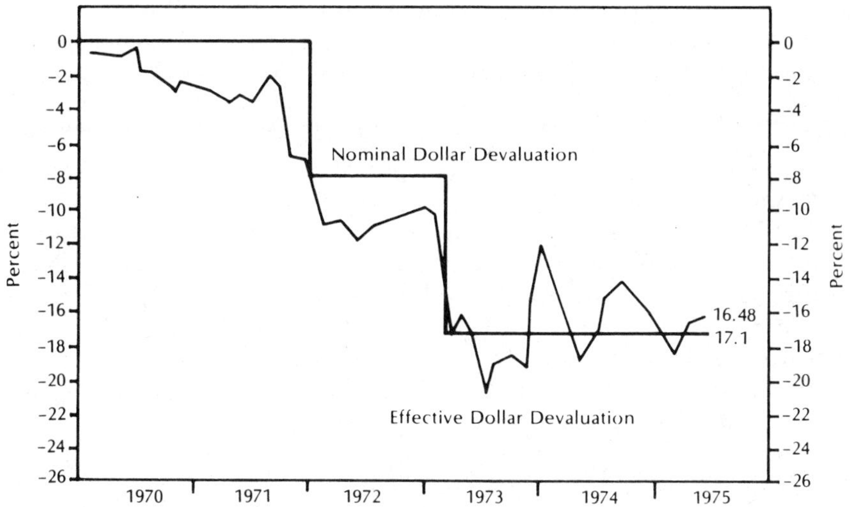

Sources: IMF and the Federal Reserve Bank of New York.

Note: Nominal devaluation is measured by the change in the dollar price of gold. Effective devaluation is measured by the appreciation of eleven major currencies relative to the par values which prevailed as of May 1970. The appreciation is then weighted by separate export and import shares with the United States based on 1972 trade data.

Latest data plotted: May.

giving rise to, and the impact of, them is *supposed* to be similar. The idea is that the balance in that account should serve as a guide to policymakers as they attempt to gauge the impact of international transactions on domestic economic activity.

A particular balance is an appropriate guide to policy or is informationally useful only to the extent that it is based upon a correct perception of the forces which give rise to, and the impact of, the transactions included therein. The thrust of this article is that the balances highlighted in current balance-of-payments statistics are based on an incorrect perception of such forces and impacts. As such, these balances have very little economic meaning and are, therefore, often a misleading guide to policymakers. As an alternative, it is suggested that international trade and capital transactions be viewed within the framework presented in the first sections of this article.

Therefore, the conclusion of this article is that the present methods of presenting data concerning international transactions should be reformed so that it more closely reflects the underlying economic realities of international commerce. At a minimum, any such reform should include a discontinuation of the practice of calculating the balances which are currently presented. While this would not prevent individuals who wish to do so from calculating such balances, it would remove the implied governmental sanction of these balances as having some special economic or policy implications.

In addition, the above reform would also result in a discontinuation of the constant references to "deficits" and "surpluses" in the balance of payments. The words "deficits" and "surpluses" in this regard convey meanings that are not at all appropriate to the realities of the impact of international commerce on domestic economic activity. For example, every month we hear that the merchandise trade account was either in "deficit" or "surplus." A deficit in this account merely means that the United States imported more merchandise than it exported during that month. In other words, the United States receives more goods during that month than it was forced to give up, and it was able to do so by borrowing from foreigners. Despite the stigma associated with the word "deficit", the information tells us virtually nothing about the overall impact of international commerce on domestic economic activity.

NOTES

1. For a discussion of this approach, see Donald S. Kemp, "A Monetary View of the Balance of Payments," *Federal Reserve Bank of St. Louis Review* (April 1975), pp. 14–22.

2. The monetary approach is concerned with the impact of the *balance of payments* on the domestic economy via its impact on the money supply. In contrast, the current conventional wisdom in payments theory (the elasticities and absorption approaches) is concerned primarily with the *balance of trade* alone and assumes that either there are no monetary consequences associated with international transactions or, to the extent the potential for such consequences exists, they can be and are neutralized by domestic monetary authorities.

3. For a thorough discussion of the process by which such a disparity is corrected, see Roger W. Spencer, "Channels of Monetary Influence: A Survey," *Federal Reserve Bank of St. Louis Review* (November 1974), pp. 8–26.

4. The existence of free international markets for goods, services, and securities is a fundamental assertion of the monetary approach to the balance of payments. See Kemp, "A Monetary View of the Balance of Payments," p. 16.

5. The terms "imports" and "exports" refer to more than just imports and exports of goods and services. It includes all transactions which involve the purchase or sale of domestic assets (real and financial) in foreign markets. For example, the purchase of a foreign security by a U.S. citizen would be considered an import.

6. A deficit in the trade account reflects an exchange of money balances for real assets (goods and services). A deficit in the capital account reflects the exchange of money balances for financial assets. In order to determine the total accumulation of money balances by foreigners, it is necessary to combine all of the trade and capital accounts.

7. Within the monetary approach framework there are other channels through which international transactions can have an impact on aggregate economic activity. For example, some changes in the terms of trade and in the volume of trade and capital flows can affect the productive capacity of a given economy. However, it should be noted that both of these channels relate to the concept of the gains from trade, which is distinctly different from the concept of the balance of payments. The only other channel through which international transactions can have an impact on aggregate economic activity is through their impact on the ownership of the total money stock. For example, the size of the total U.S. money stock (as currently measured) is not affected by changes in foreign-owned deposits at U.S. commercial banks. However, the distribution of the total U.S. money stock between U.S. and foreign ownership is affected by such changes. This source of

international influence on the U.S. economy would be significant only if the volume of foreign-owned deposits was large and if the behavior pattern of foreign dollar owners differed significantly from that of domestic dollar owners. The evidence relating to this issue is, as yet, highly tentative. However, the consensus seems to be that the influence of foreign-owned deposits on the U.S. economy is minimal. For a discussion of the concept of a domestically owned money stock, see Albert E. Burger and Anatol Balbach, "Measurement of the Domestic Money Stock," *Federal Reserve Bank of St. Louis Review* (May 1972), pp. 10–23.

8. Balance-of-payments accounting is based on the principle of double entry bookkeeping. Total debits must equal total credits, and therefore it is impossible for the entire balance of payments to show either a deficit or a surplus. The only way we can observe a difference between credits and debits is to select certain items out of the balance of payments and compare credits and debits for the given subset of items. A particular subset is usually chosen because the net of the transactions included therein is significant, for some reason, in sign and amount. According to current usage, an imaginary line is drawn through the balance of payments so that the items selected for a subset appear "above the line" and the remaining items are said to be "below the line." For a more thorough discussion of standard balance-of-payments statistics presentation, see John Pipenger, "Balance-of-Payments Deficits: Measurement and Interpretation," *Federal Reserve Bank of St. Louis Review* (November 1973), pp. 6–14.

9. The *money account* captures the net impact of all international transactions on the U.S. money supply. Of all international transactions, the only ones that affect the money supply are those that affect some component of the monetary base. Since U.S. holdings of gold and foreign currency balances (primary reserve assets) and foreign deposits at Federal Reserve Banks are the only components of the monetary base that are affected by international transactions, the entire impact of these transactions on the money supply can be captured by observing the changes in these items. As such, the *money account* includes changes in only these items below the line.

10. That is, the domestic currency will depreciate in value relative to other currencies. Other currencies will now be worth more units of domestic currency than before.

11. See Exhibit 1 and Table 1 for an outline of the groupings currently employed in balance-of-payments data presentation. These illustrations will be useful references for the remainder of this article.

12. The current account excludes earnings on direct investments which are both earned and reinvested abroad. However, these reinvested earnings are no different than other sources of U.S. income from abroad in the sense that they represent a transfer of command over real resources. In recent years these reinvested earnings have been quite large. For example, in 1971 they amounted to $3.2 billion, while in 1972 and 1973 they amounted to $4.7 billion and $8.1 billion, respectively.

13. Under fixed exchange rates the United States stood ready to buy and sell foreign currencies in order to support the value of the dollar at a specific price in terms of other currencies. Primary reserve assets (international reserves) are stocks of gold and foreign currencies held by the U.S. Government in the event that such market intervention became necessary. For example, a decrease in the demand for dollars vis-à-vis gold or foreign currencies was accommodated by the purchase of dollars in return for foreign currencies or gold from the stocks of reserve assets. Thus, the dollar was said to be readily convertible into our reserve assets. However, with floating exchange rates the U.S. Government is no longer *obligated* to intervene in the market for foreign currencies and changes in the demand for the dollar are accommodated by movements in the dollar exchange rate. In other words, with floating exchange rates the U.S. Government no longer *guarantees* the convertibility of the dollar into its reserve assets.

14. The official settlements balance was originally supposed to reflect the effects of past measures taken in support of the fixed dollar exchange rate, while the net liquidity balance was supposed to reflect the potential need for such measures in the future. This is because the net liquidity balance includes liquid *private* capital, a potential source of future pressure on fixed exchange rates, below the line. On the other hand, in the official settlements balance the only transactions carried below the line are those which reflect past *official* measures.

15. The change in the effective exchange rate is a trade weighted average of changes in the exchange rate between the dollar and the currencies of the United States' trading partners.

16. In other words, exchange rates are currently neither fixed at an officially specified level nor are they allowed to move completely free of official foreign exchange market intervention.

17. Fixed and Flexible Exchange Rates: A Renewal Of The Debate*

JACQUES R. ARTUS and JOHN H. YOUNG

For some time the view has been developing that the flexible exchange rate system has not accomplished as much as many of its supporters had hoped. More recently, in the discussions associated with the adoption of the European Monetary System, there has been a renewal of interest in the advantages and disadvantages of adopting some form of pegging. It may be time, therefore, to review the extent to which a decade of analysis and experience has altered the thinking on the choice of an exchange rate system. As in the earlier debate, the discussion of fixed and flexible rates in recent years has been almost exclusively directed to the choice of exchange rate systems for developed countries, and the scope of this paper is similarly limited.

The case for a flexible exchange rate system was generally based on hopes of what would result, and the case against on fears of what might happen. Section I of this paper provides a critical analysis of some of the views widely held by adherents of flexible rates. It is pointed out that few today would defend flexible rates on the grounds that they permit governments to take advantage of a long-term trade-off between employment and wage increases, and thus make it possible for countries to have permanently higher rates of economic activity at the expense of higher inflation. Also, it is argued that many adherents of flexible

* Charts have been omitted.

Jacques R. Artus is Assistant Director of the Research Department holds degrees from the Faculty of Law and Economics in Paris and from the University of California at Berkeley.

John H. Young was Deputy Director of the Research Department of the IMF when the paper was written and later became Deputy Director of the African Department.

rates gave inadequate weight to the slow speed of adjustment to relative price changes in the goods markets. They thus exaggerated the contribution that exchange rate changes would make in the short run to external adjustment, and similarly overestimated the extent to which flexible rates would insulate countries from external influences and leave them free to pursue domestic objectives through the use of domestic economic policies.

Section II takes a similarly critical approach to some of the fears raised by opponents of flexible rates. Some of the concerns are found to have had some basis, particularly the fear that flexible rates would tend to be fluctuating rates, and it is suggested that exchange rates might continue to show considerable instability even under relatively stable underlying economic and financial conditions. There is less empirical evidence to justify other concerns, namely, that flexible rates would have adverse effects on trade and capital flows, but some of the most marked exchange rate instability has been too recent to show much effect as yet. Finally, a brief analysis is given of the complex and mixed relationship between flexible rates and inflation.

Section III draws together the main conclusions and discusses the search for greater exchange rate stability. It is pointed out that, notwithstanding the drawbacks of flexible rates, the conditions likely to exist in a number of member countries over the next few years will give rise to a continuing need for a measure of exchange rate flexibility, and some analysis is given of the problems of achieving the requisite amount of flexibility under pegged rates. The section concludes with a brief discussion of the relationship between monetary policy and exchange rate stability. It is pointed out that keeping a close eye on external conditions in determining monetary policy can help in setting limits to short-run exchange rate instability, and that some national monetary authorities are already giving greater weight than in the past to existing or potential exchange market developments.

I. THE CASE FOR FLEXIBLE EXCHANGE RATES

Much of the earlier support for flexible rates was based on the weakness of the pegged rate system, and Milton Friedman's classic article published in 1953 promised only modest benefits from the adoption of flexible rates. In the main, flexible rates were expected to isolate a country from monetary disturbances originating abroad and to help reconcile countries' divergent rates of monetary growth. It was also expected that flexible rates would lead to a smooth working of the external adjustment process without excess crises or the need for controls on trade and capital flows. Many of those who supported flexible rates in the 1960s, however, expected much more from them.

They believed, in particular, that there was a long-term trade-off between employment and inflation, and saw exchange rate flexibility as an opportunity for individual countries to adopt price-employment objectives of their own choosing. It was also widely held that flexible rates would help to achieve stable growth, in particular by providing a significant measure of insulation from external shocks, real as well as monetary. In the event, the flexible exchange rate system has not accomplished all that its supporters had hoped, and we consider each of the areas in which developments have turned out somewhat differently than expected.

Flexible Rates and the Trade-Off

The case for exchange rate flexibility was initially built on a belief that various countries cannot for long maintain the same inflation rate because of the undesirable but unavoidable tendency for governments to mismanage their currencies to various degrees. This was clearly the view advanced by Friedman (1953, pp. 179–80):

> Governments of "advanced" nations are no longer willing to submit themselves to the harsh discipline of the gold standard or any other standard involving rigid exchange rates. They will evade its discipline by direct controls over trade if that will suffice and will change exchange rates before they will surrender control over domestic monetary policy. Perhaps a few modern inflations will establish a climate in which such behavior does not qualify as "advanced"; in the meantime we had best recognize the necessity of allowing exchange rates to adjust to internal policies rather than the reverse.

Differential rates of inflation must inevitably lead to exchange rate adjustments, and flexible exchange rates were seen to provide the least inconvenient form of adjustment. Flexible rates were not viewed as the first-best system, but only as a second-best system that had to be used because political realities made the fixed rate system unworkable.

This argument based on political realism was soon, however, to be accompanied by the view that it would be desirable for countries to be left free to choose their own inflation rates because there is a long-term trade-off between inflation and unemployment. The choice of the inflation rate came to be seen as an important prerogative of a government, and flexible exchange rates were going to make it possible for each country to maintain its optimal inflation rate. This view was apparent, for example, in Johnson (1969, p. 18):

> On the one hand, there exists a great rift between nations like the United Kingdom and the United States, which are anxious to maintain high levels of employment and are prepared to pay a price for it in terms of domestic inflation, and other nations, notably Western Germany, which are strongly adverse to inflation. Under the present

> fixed exchange rate system, these nations are pitched against each other in a battle over the rate of inflation that is to prevail in the world economy. . . . Flexible rates would allow each country to pursue the mixture of unemployment and price trend objectives it prefers, consistent with international equilibrium, equilibrium being secured by appreciation of the currencies of "price stability" countries relative to the currencies of "full employment" countries.

The notion that countries were faced with a trade-off between inflation and unemployment enjoyed considerable vogue during the 1960s, following Phillip's article in 1958. A case can be made that the notion that there was any significant long-run trade-off between inflation and unemployment was never consistent with well-established generalizations about economic behavior. This is indicated by the low-key way in which the original basic criticism of the trade-off was made. Milton Friedman's initial critique of the long-term trade-off was made as part of a comment on a paper by Robert Solow. As Friedman (1966, pp. 58–60) put it in a very matter-of-fact fashion:

> The basic fallacy is to suppose that there is a trade-off between inflation and employment; that is, to suppose that by inflating more over any long period of time, you can have on the average a lower level of unemployment. . . . By speeding up the rate of monetary expansion and aggregate demand, you can unquestionably increase output and employment temporarily . . . only until people adjust their anticipations . . . from a logical point of view, the true trade-off is between unemployment today and unemployment at a later date. It is not between unemployment and inflation. There is no long-run, stable trade-off between inflation and unemployment.

Similarly, when Phelps (1972) looked back at his critical analysis of the long-run trade-off argument, he drew attention in a footnote to the fact that Professors Fellner and Wallich had put forward similar views at Yale University prior to the discovery of the Phillips curve, and such reasoning could be found in the writings of Von Mises in the 1920s and between the lines of the work of the classical economists.

It is, nevertheless, easy to see how the trade-off concept caught on among economists and policymakers. In the first place, it was really a codification of experience rather than a new idea. In the past, it had generally been true that periods of recession or depression had been characterized by reduced wage and price increases, and in the extreme case by absolute declines. Similarly, periods of prosperity had usually been associated with higher than average wage and price increases. It was not surprising, therefore, that plotting wage increases on the vertical axis and unemployment on the horizontal axis led to a cluster of points that suggested a curve that was downward sloping to the right. Second, there appeared to be ample evidence that economies react in this way in the short run, with the rate of wage increase declining when unemployment was relatively high and tending to rise during periods of relatively low unemployment. From this, it was only one step to the view that a stable Phillips curve could be combined with a preference function for a particular society to derive an optimum choice of unemployment and inflation for an economy. Since it was assumed that each economy had its unique Phillips curve and its unique set of preferences for inflation and unemployment, it was not to be expected that countries would choose the same level of wage and price increases.

As indicated above, the final step in which the Phillips curve was used to choose a particular combination of unemployment and inflation over the long run was the one which might have given pause; and it was certainly true that few were prepared to take this step without qualifications. Some, for example, recognized that after a time wage earners would start building expected future price increases into their wage bargains and that any particular trade-off would not be stable. It was argued, however, that it would take time for wage earners to adjust to rising prices, and that employment gains could be made today at the expense of higher inflation and unemployment at some later stage. This kind of *apres nous le déluge* thinking served temporarily to maintain a rear-guard action, but with the surge of inflation in the late 1960s it became impossible to ignore the not-so-long-run inflationary effects of trying to raise employment permanently by using expansionary monetary or fiscal policies. There would thus be few today who would argue for flexible exchange rates on the grounds that they give countries a significant amount of freedom over the long run to choose a higher level of employment at the expense of more rapid price increases. The case for flexible rates as a first-best system on these grounds can be dismissed. As will be argued later in this paper, the more prosaic case based on political realities cannot be dismissed as easily.

Flexible Rates and External Adjustment

Flexible rates were also expected to facilitate greatly the working of the international adjustment process, particularly among industrial countries. In the longer run, flexible rates would ensure that, at any given level of economic activity, the supply of and demand for foreign exchange originating from current account transactions would be consistent with the foreign investment flows that reflect longer-run differences in propensities to save and in investment opportunities among countries. In the short run, they would ensure that financing flows would be available to offset any short-run excess demand for, or supply of, foreign exchange originating from current account transactions and longer-run foreign investment flows without unduly large variations in the exchange rate. Demand-management policies would thus be free from external constraints.

Many of the advocates of flexible rates were, of course, careful to point out that flexible rates were not an instant cure for all external adjustment problems. They recognized that, in particular, protracted imbalances inherited from the fixed rate period could not be eliminated overnight. More generally, they realized that trade flows would adjust to exchange rate changes only after a certain lag. It was also appreciated that, where underlying economic conditions were unstable, private capital flows might be insufficient to prevent some exchange rate overshooting while adjustments in the goods market were taking place. On the whole, however, flexible rates were expected to prevent the recurrence of the protracted external maladjustments experienced in the 1960s and early 1970s, and to eliminate gradually the imbalances inherited from the past at little cost in terms of exchange rate stability.

To a large extent, these expectations have not been realized. To begin with, the adjustment process in the goods market has not worked well. The Federal Republic of Germany, Japan, and Switzerland have maintained very strong current account positions despite the appreciation of their currencies both before and after the establishment of flexible rates. The total current account surplus of these three countries increased from about $8 billion in 1972 to $31 billion in 1978. On the other side, the United States has continued to experience recurring current account deficits despite the marked effective depreciation of the U.S. dollar that took place during that period. There is, of course, no reason to expect all industrial countries to have the same balance of payments structure, since there may be long-run differences among countries in propensities to save and in opportunities for investment. What is required for payments equilibrium, however, is that capital flows should also adjust to differing savings and investment propensities. It has been noted that existing financial conditions in the major surplus countries, the Federal Republic of Germany and Japan, are not well suited for channeling savings abroad on a regular basis. (See Kindleberger, 1976 for the Federal Republic of Germany and McKinnon, 1978 for Japan.) In the present case, the fact that this pattern of current account balances is not an equilibrium one is apparent from the pressures on exchange markets that it generates.[1]

The difficulties with the adjustment process in the goods markets are also apparent from the resurgence of trade restrictions (see International Monetary Fund, 1978). The argument that flexible rates would remove the balance of payments motive for restrictions on international trade has clearly not been validated. Countries do not seem to be prepared to accept Friedman's (1969, p. 118) view that "if you have a flexible rate and you reduce tariffs, movements in the exchange rate will automatically protect you against having any adverse balance of payments effects, and therefore you are not exporting or importing unemployment." Instead, there has been a tendency toward protectionism on current transactions.

The persistence of the same pattern of current account imbalances eight years after the currency realignment of 1971 and six years after the widespread adoption of flexible rates cannot be blamed on any failure of exchange rates to move. Over a number of years, rates have changed in the right direction and by large amounts. It is, of course, easy to point out that either the current balances of the private capital flows would have had to adjust if the authorities had not intervened in the foreign exchange markets. This, however, is begging the question. The authorities intervened because current account imbalances were putting excessive strains on exchange markets. It is these strains that must be explained.

Economic developments in the 1970s had the unfortunate effect of increasing existing current account imbalances (see Artus, 1979). A marked reduction of the long-run rates of growth in the three surplus countries, the Federal Republic of Germany, Japan, and Switzerland, was accompanied by a fall in domestic investment relative to saving.[2] At the same time, the main deficit country, the United States, was faced with a gradual fall in its production of natural gas and crude petroleum, which led to a sharp increase in its dependence on imports of energy. The position of U.S. manufacturers in their domestic markets was also eroded by the continuous growth of Japanese exports and the emergence of such countries as the Republic of China, the Republic of Korea, and Singapore and Hong Kong as major exporters.

These developments, however, do not explain fully the failure of the adjustment process to work more effectively over the past few years. Another reason seems to be that not enough consideration was given to the requirements for a successful adjustment through exchange rate changes. It has been known since the development of the absorption approach in the late 1940s,[3] and the rediscovery of the monetary approach by Polak (1957), Johnson (1958), and others, that current balances can be changed only if domestic absorption is changed relative to output, and that changes in exchange rates are not likely to have much lasting effect on this ratio via the effects of relative prices or otherwise if the monetary authorities are willing to validate any incipient price changes brought about by exchange rate changes. In particular, if a country is running a large deficit on its current account and wishes to alter this situation, it will have to cut its absorption through the use of a more restrictive monetary and fiscal policy unless it has spare capacity available.

A restrictive policy alone, however, may contribute only to an extended period of unemployment and an extremely slow adjustment in the relative prices between domestic goods and foreign goods[4] because of the downward inflexibility of goods and factor prices that may prevail in the short and medium run. The advantage of an accompanying exchange rate devaluation is that it changes relative prices directly. If the changes in relative prices are sustained and the foreign trade price elasticities are significant, the decrease in the real domestic demand for goods in general may be offset by a switch in foreign and domestic demands toward domestic goods, so that there is no fall in the level of output.

In brief, flexibile rates can play a useful role only if three interdependent conditions are met: (1) there is a supporting demand-management policy, (2) changes in the relative prices between domestic goods and foreign goods are sustained, and (3) a shift in relative prices leads to a switch in domestic and foreign demand between foreign goods and domestic goods.

The first condition for effective adjustment through flexible exchange rates was not often present during the past five years. Flexible rates did not work better because, in part, demand-management policies were not usually directed toward adjustment of current account imbalances.[5] Cutting the inflation rate, even at the cost of sluggish domestic aggregate demand, was the major policy target in the surplus countries, while the United States placed a higher priority on reducing unemployment in the short run. After maintaining restrictive policies through 1974, the United States reversed course in 1975–76 and allowed a sustained expansion of domestic demand to develop, accompanied by a rising inflation rate. The Federal Republic of Germany, Japan, and Switzerland, by contrast, relaxed their restrictive policies more gradually. The shift toward a policy stance that was more consistent with the longer-run need for external adjustment took place only in the course of 1978, when the surplus countries rapidly expanded their money supplies and the United States moved to a more restrictive monetary policy.[6]

To some extent, domestic absorption may in fact have been left in certain cases to respond perversely, via the investment effect, to the change in the exchange rate. McKinnon (1978) has focused attention on this aspect of the exchange rate mechanism. Countries with a depreciating currency tend to experience an increase in the profitability of producing internationally tradable goods, at least initially, because prices in local currency increase more rapidly than the money wage rate. This leads to an increase in investment, in domestic absorption, and in imports. Opposite effects occur in countries with an appreciating currency. These effects should subside in the long run if the money stock remains unchanged, but, in the meantime, they delay the adjustment process. These effects can, however, easily be exaggerated. There is no doubt that in the surplus countries in the past few years the main causal nexus was, with lags at each step, from restrictive domestic policies to sluggish levels of economic activity, to large current account surpluses, and to exchange rate appreciations, rather than in the opposite direction.

The lack of supporting demand-management policies was not the only problem. A persistent change in the price ratio between domestic goods and foreign goods implies a sustained change in the real wage rate. In the period of high inflation that has prevailed since the early 1970s, money illusion and wage adjustment lags have been reduced and, with explicit and implicit wage indexation clauses widespread in labor contracts, an adjustment of real wages is difficult to bring about. Johnson (1969) and others argued that, under a flexible exchange rate system, exchange rate adjustments would occur gradually, and their impact on the cost of living might remain unnoticed.[7] The integration of the world economy has now proceeded so far, however, that the residents of few, if any, countries have the illusion that the local currency price of imported goods is not a major determinant of the cost of living. In fact, they may be particularly sensitive to exchange rate induced domestic price changes. Exchange rate changes may thus fail to have a lasting effect on the real wage rate, even if the initial impact is to move it back to its equilibrium level. Labor resistance, at least in the case of a depreciation, may gradually move it back to its initial disequilibrium position.

This vicious circle mechanism has been heavily focused on by the critics of flexible rates; see, for example, Economistes Belges de Langue Française (1977). This effect should not, however, be exaggerated. First, the lags involved in the adjustment of the money wage rate to the consumer price index have not been eliminated. Second, and more important, the adjustment of the money wage rates to the consumer price index is not beyond the power of the authorities to alter. This will be discussed in Section II. What is striking, in fact, is the size and persistence of the efficient changes in relative labor costs and goods prices brought about by the exchange rate changes, at least for the major industrial countries.[8]

A further disappointment as far as flexible rates and the adjustment process are concerned has been the slow speed of adjustment to changes in relative costs and prices in the goods markets. The extreme case is provided by Switzerland, where exports were still rising in 1978 *in volume terms* despite the 30 to 50 percent loss in cost and price competitiveness experienced during the previous five years. Swiss exporters are highly specialized and do not have in many cases the possibility of shifting their production to the domestic market.[9] Instead, they have shifted the composition of their export sales toward highly technical products and luxury goods with low price elasticities. The adjustment is certainly easier in larger and more diversified economies, but even in such cases it remains a lengthy process. It is very common to point out that, in order to become established or to expand in a new market, it is important to develop a distribution network, parts and service suppliers, and a reputation for reliability and quality. During the 1960s German, Japanese, and Swiss manufacturers supplied high-quality goods at very competitive prices, and developed entrenched market positions in a number of products. In the process, these countries became strongly export oriented. Such a process cannot be reversed rapidly.

This is not to say that foreign trade flows do not respond in time to variations in relative prices. General economic reasoning and the historical evidence is convincing on this point, and the bulk of the econometric results point in the same direction.[10] Stern, Francis, and Schumacher (1976), after reviewing more than 130 studies on price elasticities in international trade, conclude that "typical" long-run demand elasticities vary between –0.50 and –1.50 for total imports and between –0.50 and –2.00 for total exports. The studies reviewed are based on data for the 1950s and 1960s. The estimates may be somewhat too high for the 1970s if, as McKinnon (1978) argues, a floating rate regime increases exchange rate uncertainties and weakens the incentives of traders to respond to cost and price differentials among countries. Estimates based on more recent studies tend to show, however, that while the long-run price elasticities may be smaller now they remain substantial. Estimates from the International Monetary Fund's world trade model (see Deppler and Ripley, 1978 for a description of the model) that are derived from data that cover the period through 1977, for example, suggest a range of –0.50 to –1.00 for total imports and of –0.50 to –1.50 for total exports (Table 1).

Econometric estimates of the time lags involved in price effects range widely in the literature from no lag to a mean lag of three or four years. The most persuasive studies tend to find a mean lag of about two years; see, for example, Beenstock and Minford (1976). Over the first few quarters, the volume effects of an unanticipated change in the exchange rate is bound to be small, if only because of the long lags between orders and deliveries. In the Fund's world trade model, for example, the sum of the elasticities of demand for imports and exports is smaller than unity for 9 of the 14 industrial countries over the first year and a half (see Table 1). With the perverse effects of an exchange rate change on the terms of trade that prevail over that period (Spitäller, 1979), the result is the well-known J-curve effect. Initially, the trade balance worsens with an exchange rate depreciation and improves with an appreciation. This kind of lag no doubt explains why countries are often tempted to use more direct tools, such as trade controls, despite their welfare costs.

TABLE 1. Point Estimates of Foreign Trade Price Elasticities of Demand in the Fund's World Trade Model[1]

	Imports		Exports		Sum	
Country	*Short-run*	*Long-run*	*Short-run*	*Long-run*	*Short-run*	*Long-run*
Canada	−0.69	−0.69	—	—	−069	−0.69
United States	−0.03	−1.07	−0.20	−1.05	−0.23	−2.12
Japan	−0.25	−0.37	−1.68	−1.68	−1.93	−2.05
France	−0.49	−0.49	−1.23	−1.53	−1.72	−2.02
Germany, Fed. Rep.	−0.28	−0.58	−0.03	−0.60	−0.31	−1.18
Italy	−0.09	−0.09	—	—	−0.09	−0.09
United Kingdom	−0.25	−0.25	−0.10	−0.45	−0.35	−0.70
Belgium	−0.43	−0.43	−1.15	−2.45	−1.58	−2.88
Denmark	−0.16	−1.10	−0.47	−0.53	−0.63	−1.63
Netherlands	−0.04	−0.04	−0.08	−1.03	−0.12	−1.07
Austria	−0.03	−0.03	−0.66	−0.89	−0.69	−0.92
Norway	−0.75	−2.45	−0.95	−1.85	−1.70	−4.30
Sweden	−1.60	−1.60	−1.49	−1.50	−3.09	−3.10
Switzerland	−0.02	−0.02	−0.96	−1.48	−0.98	−1.50
Average	−0.37	−0.66	−0.64	−1.07	−1.10	−1.73

Source: Deppler and Ripley (1978). The results presented here were obtained by aggregating the estimate for foodstuffs (SITC0 + 1), raw materials (SITC2 + 4), fuels (SITC3), and manufactures (SITC5–8) on the basis of 1977 trade flows.

[1] The short-run response elasticity is the coefficient of the average of the relative price term over the preceding two half years; the long-run response elasticity is based on the cumulated response over four years.

Flexible Rates and Stable Growth

Another major argument for flexible rates was that they would make it possible for national authorities to achieve more stable rates of economic growth. The argument was based on three propositions: (1) flexible rates insulate a country's level of economic activity from foreign expansion and contraction; (2) flexible rates increase the degree of control of the authorities over the money supply and allow them to use both monetary and fiscal policy to influence the level of economic activity without constraint from the external balance; and (3) the efficacy of monetary policy is greatly enhanced by flexible rates, that is, the effects of a given change in the money supply on the level of economic activity is larger under flexible rates.

The events of recent years suggest that all three of these propositions are questionable. The degree of economic interdependence seems to have been, if anything, greater since 1973 than before, particularly among European countries, whether in the "snake" arrangement or not. Similarly, there has been no sign either of greater economic stability brought about by an increase in the control of the authorities over the money supply or of much evidence of an increase in the efficacy of such policies.

The conclusion of greater insulation from variations in economic activity abroad under flexible rates is based on two assumptions: (1) a real external disturbance leads to an exchange rate change and (2) the exchange rate change prevents the external disturbance from having an effect on the domestic economy.[11] The effect of a fall in foreign demand, for example, is seen to lead to a depreciation of the exchange rate rather than to a deterioration of the trade balance, which would have a deflationary effect on the domestic economy. These two assumptions, however, seem to be valid only to a limited extent.

Whether an external disturbance leads to an exchange rate change will depend in part on whether the disturbance is viewed as being temporary. In the case of a temporary disturbance, capital flows may have a stabilizing influence on the exchange rate as market participants maintain their views on the longer-term equilibrium value of the exchange rate. When the background is stable and there is a belief in a "normal" exchange rate, as during much of the period in which the Canadian dollar floated in the 1950s, offsetting effects of this kind have been found. Indeed, it is possible to envisage capital flows playing an even more active role. If the fall in foreign demand results from a recession abroad, accompanied by a decrease in the rate of return on investment, capital may tend to move to the home country, where the level of economic activity is sustained and the interest rates are higher. Modigliani and Askari (1973) argue that this factor may more than offset the effect of the worsening of the trade balance, so that the exchange rate appreciates rather than depreciates.[12] In this case, flexible rates would increase the impact of foreign disturbances on domestic economic activity.

In the above discussion of the external adjustment process, however, it was noted that capital flows had not offset completely the effects of demand induced disturbances on the current account in recent years. As pointed out in that discussion, the key factor in the failure of the exchange rate to provide insulation is the lag in the response of trade flows to changes in relative prices.

All the major econometric models of world trade—including the LINK model presented in Ball (1973) and the Fund's world trade model described in Deppler and Ripley (1978)—show conclusively that year-to-year changes in the volume of imports and exports are dominated by variations in real aggregate demand. During the first one or two years, offsetting effects that may result from exchange rate induced variations in relative prices are generally only a small fraction of the effects of demand changes. Even over a longer period (for example three years) the effect of demand changes remains large relative to the offsetting effects of exchange rate changes. Some calculations of the magnitudes of the fall in exchange rates necessary to offset increases in demand for 14 industrial countries based on the Fund's world trade model were included in the Fund's *Annual Report, 1978*. The results indicate that an increase of 1 percent in manufacturing output maintained for three years has a strong negative effect on the trade balance in all 14 countries, ranging from 1½ to 3⅓ percent of 1977 imports. It was estimated, by comparison, that in most cases exchange rate declines of 5 to 15 percent would be necessary to produce the same trade balance effects.

There are, thus, strong grounds for concluding that a flexible rate does not provide an automatic mechanism that will insulate a country's level of economic activity from foreign expansion and contraction.[13] If a flexible rate contributes to a more stable rate of growth, it would be because it frees the authorities from any balance of payments constraint and allows them to direct demand-management policies toward the achievement of domestic stability, or because it increases the degree of control of the authorities over the money supply and enhances the efficacy of demand-management policies.[14]

Until recently, it was thought that flexible rates would allow the authorities to control the money supply (or, more precisely, the monetary base); and, indeed, that is true if the flexible rate regime is one where the monetary authorities never worry about exchange rate developments in forming their monetary policy. It has become obvious in recent years, however, that such a policy of benign neglect may lead in many cases to exchange rate instability. Artus (1976) and Dornbusch (1977), among others, have focused attention on the high elasticity of the exchange rate with respect to (unanticipated) changes in the money supply. While there is some difficulty in explaining this high elasticity (a further discussion of this issue is given later), the evidence is clear that uncoordinated monetary policy changes among countries often tend to lead to large changes in exchange rates. Even if the money supply is kept stable in the various countries, exchange rate instability may be a problem because of the short-run instability of the demand for money.

These considerations do not, of course, detract from the fact that flexible rates allow the authorities to maintain, in the longer run, a monetary growth that is consistent with their ability to keep a low inflation rate. They do, however, indicate the consequences that can follow from attempts to use monetary policy to affect the level of economic activity over the short run without regard to the effects on the exchange rate.

The argument that flexible rates enhance the efficacy of demand-management policies, particularly monetary policies, has also turned out to be somewhat deceptive. The argument is similar to the one presented for insulation. It was derived from the observation that the change in money supply is likely to be accompanied by a variation in the exchange rate that would reinforce the effect of the money supply change. As discussed above, however, the response of the volume of the foreign trade flows to a change in the exchange rate is likely to be so small in the short run that the additional expansionary effect would not be noticeable. A further weakness in the efficacy argument is that price increases caused by the exchange rate depreciation may sharply reduce the expansionary effect of the increase in the money supply. Monetary policies affect the level of economic activity only if prices in the goods markets adjust slowly to a monetary change. By speeding up the price adjustment, flexible rates reduce the efficacy of monetary policies.[15]

The efficacy argument is also to some extent misleading. The magnitude of the effect of a given policy change is important, but it is even more important that the effect of that policy change be foreseeable. There is not, unhappily, much reason to believe that flexible rates increase the extent to which the authorities can reliably estimate the quantitative effect of a certain discretionary change in monetary policies. This effect will depend to a large extent on the behavior of the exchange rate and the magnitude and timing of the effects of exchange rate changes on prices and on the level of economic activity in the short run. In this area, it is particularly difficult to make reasonably accurate forecasts.

II. THE CASE AGAINST FLEXIBLE EXCHANGE RATES

If the advantages of flexible rates have fallen short of the expectations of their advocates, it must also be recognized that their drawbacks have been less damaging than was anticipated by their detractors. The word drawback may not even be appropriate to characterize the disasters that some suggested would occur if flexible rates were adopted. It was argued—for example, by Roosa (1967, p. 52)—that, as a practical matter, a system of flexible rates was not workable. As he put it:

> . . . I have never met anyone who has attained the competence of a seasoned trader who would be prepared to continue in the business if, by some sleight of hand, all parities were to be abandoned and the central banks were barred from entering the markets in their own currencies. Many, and I include myself, would probably want to withdraw from trading activities even under the sort of flexible-rate system in which the central banks were allowed a role, so long as there were no parity guidelines to get us into the right ball park.

These fears were rapidly discarded as experience was gained with the new system. Three other traditional arguments against flexible rates have, however, shown more staying power, but only in a milder form than initially advanced. The first is that flexible rates are inherently unstable; the second, that exchange rate uncertainties disrupt domestic and international economic relations; and the third, that flexible rates promote faster inflation.

Exchange Rate Instability

Advocates of flexible rates had suggested that exchange rates would reflect "underlying economic conditions"; as long as these conditions were stable, exchange rates would also be stable. The underlying economic conditions in question were not precisely defined, but the impression was left that exchange rates would move only to the extent necessary to offset differential rates of inflation and to compensate for changes in real factors, such as tastes and production techniques, that usually take place only gradually. These views, however, never seemed to prevail completely over the argument that flexible rates would be unstable and would disrupt domestic and international economic relations.

After six years of flexible rates, a good deal of evidence has been accumulated that indicates that flexible rates tend to be unstable in the commonsense meaning of moving up and down a lot from day to day, month to month, and year to year. . . .

Much of the exchange rate instability . . . reflects the marked domestic and international instability of recent years, including the breakup of the par value system, the oil price increase of 1973, high and divergent inflation rates, and the worldwide recession followed by recoveries at varying rates among industrial countries. However, there are also a number of developments that suggest that exchange markets with flexible rates may be characterized by the kind of instability generally found in other markets that are strongly influenced by expectations. The "cycles" in the U.S. dollar/deutsche mark rate in 1973–76 are the first development that attracted attention in that context. Then came (1) the sudden and extremely rapid depreciations of the Italian lira, French franc, and pound sterling in 1976, followed in 1977–78 by the recovery of these currencies, in particular the pound sterling; (2) the appreciation and then sharp fall in the Canadian dollar in 1976–78; and (3) the rapid depreciation of the U.S. dollar against the deutsche mark, Swiss franc, and Japanese yen in 1977–78, culminating in the October 1978 crisis. In all these cases, there seems to be the same lack of parallelism in the short run between the exchange rate change and the broad movements in the major monetary aggregates and price indicators.[16] Exchange rates were sticky for a certain period, then changed suddenly, overshot, and finally moved back to some extent, a pattern that is alien to the gradual adjustment expected by advocates of flexible rates.

In part, the stickiness of exchange rates reflected governmental intervention. This is clear for the Italian lira, French franc, and pound sterling, where the authorities intervened in the foreign exchange market on a significant scale during 1974–75. More generally, the authorities concerned, with the exception of the U. S. authorities in 1977, did not encourage exchange rate adjustments during periods in which the nominal exchange rate tended to be stable while the underlying economic and financial conditions were changing. They tended, rather, to reinforce the inertia of private market participants. In addition, however, reasons for the instability must be found in the nature of the exchange rate determination process. Nordhaus (1978, p. 250) has argued that volatility is to be expected in an "auction market" such as the exchange market under floating rates simply because there are incessant surprises. As he puts it:

> In those pure auction markets where prices are the main shock-absorber, considerable price volatility is the result. These conditions generally prevail in raw foods and commodities markets, in markets for many financial instruments such as common stocks, or when a regime of pure floating exchange rates exists. Such volatility is an intrinsic feature of real-world auction markets—markets in which there are incessant surprises due to weather, changes in taste, inventions, political upheaval, inflation, recession, and boom, etc.[17]

This auction market characteristic is important, but it certainly does not account fully for the magnitude of the observed short-run exchange rate movements. To understand why a large measure of instability may be an inherent characteristic of flexible rates, it is useful to review recent developments in the analysis of exchange rate determination. The basis of this analysis is that exchange rates among currencies are the relative prices of these currencies and therefore sensitive to any change in the supply of, or demand for, financial assets denominated in these currencies. Indeed, at every point in time the exchange rate must be at such a level that the amount of financial assets denominated in a particular currency matches the amount that market participants desire to hold. This is not to say that relative prices in the goods markets do not influence exchange rates, but the adjustment process in the goods markets works so much more slowly than in the financial asset markets that they play a somewhat secondary role in the short run.[18] The important contribution of this approach is that, by treating exchange rates as financial asset prices, it focuses attention on the strong influence of expectations. Thus, it is not only the amount of assets available today that influences asset prices but also the amount expected to be available tomorrow. It is the instability of these expectations that appears to be a major factor in short-run exchange rate instability.[19]

It is easy to explain why the expectations of market participants tend to be unstable. Forecasting the future course of monetary and other management policies in different countries relative to each other is normally, at best, a matter of guesswork. Mussa (1976), among others, has pointed out how tenuous the information that forms the base for such forecasts usually is, and how any new piece of information, even if somewhat unreliable, may lead to a substantial revision of exchange rate expectations and a sharp movement in the spot rate.[20] The instability of expectations is increased further if market participants have reason to believe that domestic price changes related to exchange rate variations may lead to accommodating changes in the money supply. Furthermore, the money supply is not the only element that affects the exchange rate, so that, even if the authorities gradually stabilize expectations with respect to monetary policies by respecting preannounced monetary policy targets, exchange rate expectations would not necessarily be stable.

All these elements are, of course, not new to the debate. The new element, however, is the realization that, once the authorities refuse to be limited to policies that will keep the exchange rate along a predetermined time path or at a certain parity, market participants will normally be quite uncertain as to the future path of the exchange rate even when underlying economic conditions are not markedly unstable. Thus, there seems every likelihood that flexible rates will continue to show some short-term instability in response to the inherent instability of market participants' expectations. Of course, the more unstable the underlying economic conditions are, the more unstable expectations will be.

The instability of expectations is not the only factor leading to exchange rate instability. Various institutional rigidities have also been focused on in the context of the asset market approach to explain exchange rate instability. McKinnon (1976) has pointed out that there might be an inadequate supply of private capital available for taking net positions in either the forward or spot markets on the basis of long-term exchange rate expectations.[21] Thus, cyclical variations in the demand for foreign exchange originating from trade or financial activities that may be sustained for a number of years may lead to large exchange rate movements because of a lack of investors with both the funds and the willingness to take a longer-run open position. Branson (1977), Dornbusch (1976), and Kouri (1976) have, rather, focused on the slow speed of adjustment in the goods markets in cases of unexpected monetary policy changes to explain exchange rate instability. Although their models differ, they all embody the hypothesis that asset markets are continuously in equilibrium, while the goods markets adjust only gradually. They show that under such conditions the immediate response of the exchange rate to a monetary policy change overshoots the new longer-run equilibrium rate.[22]

This "monetarist" explanation of exchange rate movements should not obscure the fact that the inadequate current balance adjustment discussed in Section I is also one of the causes of exchange rate instability.[23] The first reason is that a current account surplus leads to an accumulation of net foreign assets. This in turn may lead to an appreciating exchange rate to the extent that a fall in the relative price of foreign assets is needed as an incentive for domestic agents to increase the share of these assets in their portfolios.[24] Probably more important, however, is the impact of current balance developments on exchange rate expectations. The emergence of a current account surplus that is not related to temporary disturbances may, at times, be rightly interpreted as an indication that a rise in the real exchange rate is required if a lasting adjustment is to take place.[25] How much of a change in the nominal rate will be necessary to bring about the needed adjustment is, however, the type of question that cannot be answered with any degree of certainty. Market participants will, therefore, continually reassess their views of the needed exchange rate change on the basis of actual current balance developments without always being able to discount properly the effects of temporary divergences in economic cycles, J-curve effects of exchange rate changes, and so forth.

A further possible source of instability in the present system is related to the fact that several currencies are held by central banks as part of their international reserves. Any major action to change the composition of these reserves could lead to sharp exchange rate movements and disorderly market conditions. Because holders of large reserves are conscious of the possible harmful effects of their actions on the value of their portfolios and on the system as a whole, they tend to avoid major portfolio shifts. As a result, they may maintain larger stocks of certain reserve currencies than they would choose to have, and the possibility that some of these balances might come on the market creates uncertainty in the minds of both private and official holders. The overhang of official sterling balances seems to have played a destabilizing role through 1976.[26] More recently, there have been signs that actual or potential diversification out of U.S. dollar reserve balances was a factor in the weak behavior of the U.S. dollar in 1978.

The inherent instability of expectations, limitations on the role of stabilizing capital movements, the slow speed of adjustment in the goods markets, the persistence of current account imbalances, and the existence of a multiple reserve currency system account for much of the volatility in exchange market behavior in recent years.[27] There are, moreover, cases in which extrapolative expectations or bandwagon behavior on the part of market participants appears to have played a role. Dooley and Shaffer (1976) have found some tentative evidence indicating that such effects may occur, and it is hard to explain exchange market developments in October 1978 without reference to extrapolative expectations or bandwagon effects. Out of 22 market days in October, the U.S. dollar depreciated against the deutsche mark on 19 days, with the other 3 days characterized by relatively flat movements.

The Costs of Instability

While the evidence is building up to suggest that a floating rate system is characterized by a good deal of what is commonly regarded as exchange rate instability, it is not clear how important any detrimental effects of this instability have been or will prove to be. With forward rates of exchange seeming to contain little information on actual movements of spot rates in the future (see Cornell, 1977), this instability is probably accompanied by an increase in uncertainty. It is difficult, however, to assess the detrimental effects that may follow from the increase in uncertainty. These detrimental effects[28] could include (1) a reduction in foreign trade, (2) a decline in foreign investment, and (3) the adverse effects resulting from changes in the value of reserve currencies.

The risks of a dislocation of international economic relations was a major theme of the critics of a flexible rate system in the 1950s and 1960s. It was argued that exchange rate flexibility, by increasing the uncertainty associated with international transactions, would discourage both foreign trade and international investment.[29] The additional uncertainty associated with foreign trade could be related to the risk of exchange rate changes during the period between contract and settlement, or to the risk of changes in the relative cost and price competitiveness of countries because of exchange rate changes. Supporters of flexible rates argued that forward markets could be used to take care of the first type of risk, and that over the long run exchange rate changes would reflect changes in price and cost competitiveness.

The experience of the past few years has indicated that some of the difficulties likely to be encountered by those engaging in international transactions were treated rather casually in the earlier debate. It might appear that a businessman has eliminated exchange risk if he covers his position with a forward transaction, but, if his competitor does not and is thereby able to offer goods at a lower price, the forward transaction does not eliminate all the consequences of a change in the spot rate. Further, little was said about the difficulties firms would encounter in avoiding major fluctuations in their profit figures, and the problems that would be posed by their own internal accounting arrangements or externally applied accounting standards.

While life may have become more complicated for those engaged in international transactions, this does not necessarily mean that there has been a significant effect on foreign trade or investment. Indeed, to date, the statistical evidence tends to be negative. Hooper and Kohlhagen

(1978) introduced various proxies for exchange rate uncertainty (variability) in import and export volume equations for the United States and the Federal Republic of Germany for 1965–75, and found they did not play any significant role. Various tests making use of the Fund's world trade model have also failed to detect any systematic effects of exchange rate uncertainty on disaggregated trade flows for individual industrial countries through 1977.

The evolution of the trade pattern of the snake countries is also interesting in this context. While the proportion of intra-snake manufacturing trade to non-snake trade expanded in the late 1960s and early 1970s, it contracted slightly between 1972 and 1977 despite the increased stability of intra-snake exchange rates relative to exchange rates with non-snake countries during that period.[30] Such tests are not precise enough to reject the hypothesis that exchange rate instability has had harmful effects on foreign trade flows. But even taking into account the limitations of the data and the fact that there are likely to be long lags in the response of trade to exchange rate instability, these tests do raise doubts that *major* effects have been present.

Exchange rate instability did not have more of an effect on international trade in part because facilities for hedging have normally remained adequate. It is only in a few instances, such as the case of the Italian lira in early 1976, that forward markets have dried up because of excessive uncertainty.[31] The costs of hedging in such markets as measured by the bid-ask spreads have increased with the move to flexible rates, but they still represent only a minute fraction (usually about 1/10 of 1 percent or less) of the value of a currency. Forward contracts for as long as a year are not unusual, and, at a price, a trader can always cover by borrowing in one market and lending in the other. In many cases, multinational corporations can hedge internally by matching the timing of their future receipts and disbursements in particular currencies. It remains difficult, however, to hedge against the risk that exchange rate movements that are sustained for, say, two to three years may temporarily change relative costs and prices in the goods markets.

It is even more difficult to assess the effects of exchange rate instability on long-term investment flows, which cannot be easily covered in forward markets or through other hedging mechanisms. So far, little evidence has accumulated that financial and nonfinancial enterprises have significantly curtailed international capital movements in response to exchange rate fluctuations. To the extent that it is expected that changes in relative price levels and shifts in exchange rates will tend to be offsetting, some built-in safeguards are present, and the other major determinants of investment flows then tend to dominate decisions. These include, in foreign direct investment, positive advantages in terms of direct access to material inputs, skilled labor, markets, and so forth. It is worth emphasizing, however, that even if exchange rates adjust to relative price and cost levels over the long run, instability in exchange rates and relative prices in the short run can have detrimental effects, because in planning their investment strategy firms must put a high weight on expected rates of return in the early years of a project. These rates of return are uncertain in situations of exchange rate instability.

Exchange rate instability involving a major reserve currency raises particular problems. For example, developments with respect to the U.S. dollar in 1978 had major repercussions throughout the system, as virtually every country found some of its important bilateral rates changing significantly. Moreover, with the bulk of official reserves held in U.S. dollars, this meant major changes in the value of international reserves, and put pressure on reserve holders to consider diversifying their portfolios. The precipitous decline in the U.S. dollar relative to the deutsche mark and the Japanese yen generated a pronounced reaction against the floating system. It may turn out, retrospectively, that this was a structural change that needed to take place and would have been difficult in the extreme to bring about without the contribution made by the free play of market forces. The immediate effect, however, was to add to the disillusionment with the floating rate system.

These brief comments on the costs of exchange rate instability have touched upon the conventional quantifiable costs. While there are clearly some grounds for the kind of irritation that seems to have developed about the operation of the flexible rate system, the extent of the reaction is somewhat surprising.[32] Why is it that it is rare these days to hear vigorous criticism of fluctuations in other financial markets, such as the equity or bond markets, and such strong feelings about exchange rate fluctuations? Complacency about stock market fluctuations was not always the general rule. Keynes's comments in his *General Theory* (p. 159) are well known:

> Speculators may do no harm as bubbles on a steady stream of enterprise. But the position is serious when enterprise becomes the bubble on a whirlpool of speculation. When the capital development of a country becomes a by-product of the activities of a casino, the job is likely to be ill-done. The measure of success attained by Wall Street, regarded as an institution of which the proper social purpose is to direct new investment into the most profitable channels in terms of future yield, cannot be claimed as one of the outstanding triumphs of *laissez-faire* capitalism—which is not surprising, if I am right in thinking that the best brains of Wall Street have been in fact directed towards a different object.[33]

There is little echo of this view in current discussions of equity markets, but clearly there is a good deal of this kind of sentiment in discussions of exchange markets. There are, no doubt, many reasons for this, the most obvious being that any "cure" for equity market instability may be either impossible to find or worse than the disease. Decades of experience under the gold standard and under par values do not, however, suggest that stability in exchange rates is either impossible or necessarily hazardous to the effective operation of economies. Moreover, the ordinary public can escape direct involvement in equity markets, even if some of their resources are committed to these markets by their pension funds or insurance companies. The exchange rate, however, has very broad effects on all who produce or consume goods and services that are traded internationally. Thus, the statement that no government can be indifferent to the exchange rate is as much a political as an economic observation.

Flexible Rates and Inflation

Few characteristics of modern society have failed to be identified as a cause of inflation, and flexible rates are no exception. The fact that the present inflation originated and developed under pegged rates at least limits the extent to which flexible rates can be identified as a possible culprit. Even among those who have no doubt that persistent increases in prices in terms of any particular currency cannot occur unless the authorities responsible for that currency follow accommodating policies, there are some who argue that there are inflationary risks associated with flexible rates. These arguments are all variants of the notion that it is harder to maintain the discipline of prudent monetary and fiscal policies under flexible rates than under fixed rates.

It has often been suggested, for example, that changes in exchange rates can exercise asymmetrical effects. It is argued that nominal prices in goods markets are inflexible downward, so that initially the increase in the domestic prices of goods tends to be larger in depreciating countries than the decrease in these prices in appreciating countries.[34] Whether this is so is arguable,[35] but in any case a permanent effect on the overall price levels in the two countries is not to be expected as long as no change is made in their demand-management policies. Thus, the argument has to be pushed one step further.

The second level of the argument is that the money wage rate is inflexible downward.[36] Thus, a fall in the domestic prices of traded goods leads to a fall in profit margins and in the level of economic activity in the appreciating country, while in the depreciating country a rise in wages in response to the depreciation reduces any increase in profit margins or in the level of economic activity. There is, thus, a fall in the aggregate level of economic activity for the two countries taken together. Under such conditions, the monetary and fiscal authorities may take expansionary action, and exchange rate variations could thus lead to more expansionary policies and thus to a higher rate of inflation for the world as a whole.

A criticism of this line of argument has been raised by Crockett and Goldstein (1976). This criticism is that the exchange rate instability under discussion is to a large extent short run. Given the slowness of the effects of exchange rate changes on activity levels and resource allocation in the goods markets, it is unlikely that short-run exchange rate movements have any noticeable effects on these variables and unemployment. There is, therefore, no reason to suppose that the authorities will adopt more expansionary policies in response to week-to-week or month-to-month fluctuations. This general point is valid, but there are also cases of longer-run exchange rate instability.

It has also been argued that undue reliance on the exchange rate to correct certain external and domestic imbalances can push a country into a vicious circle of depreciation and inflation. Typical cases are those where labor unions succeed in obtaining an increase in the money wage rate that exceeds the increase in the marginal value product of labor, or where an exogenous shock, such as the oil price increase of 1973, leads to a deterioration in the terms of trade. If real wage rates are inflexible downward and demand-management policies are accommodating, then currency depreciation can lead to price increases, owing to the presence of imported goods in the price index, and this in turn leads to higher increases in wages that lead to higher prices, more depreciation, and a further feedback to prices, wages, and the exchange rate.

Asymmetrical price and wage effects and vicious circles would have very limited effects on inflation if the authorities did not accommodate incipient domestic costs and price increases by following expansionary monetary policies. Thus, it is demand-management policies rather than flexible rates that are the fundamental factor, and the case for a positive association of flexible rates and inflation rests on the view that there may be occasions in which the authorities feel constrained to accommodate incipient domestic cost and price increases rather than accept temporary unemployment. Against this must be counterbalanced the greater freedom stable countries have had to pursue prudent policies, and thereby to enjoy a virtuous circle of currency appreciation and falling rates of price increase. It should also be noted that depreciating rates have not freed governments from pressures to take strong action to check adverse developments. Indeed, rapid depreciation is widely regarded as clear evidence of imprudent policies, and the fact that an underlying disequilibrium is not masked by a fixed rate and restrictions on the flow of goods and capital has in a number of cases played a positive role in bringing about adjustment.

III. THE SEARCH FOR GREATER EXCHANGE RATE STABILITY

While it is too early to draw any final conclusions, there is no doubt that there has been disillusionment with the floating rate system. It is true that floating rates have cleared exchange markets without traditional balance of payments "crises" and that flexibility has made it easier for rates of inflation to differ from country to country. These are, however, mixed blessings if the rates at which exchange markets clear fluctuate widely and if, as is increasingly recognized, the freedom to inflate is a form of license which, if exercised, brings more costs than benefits. A country can avoid importing inflation, but even then the system is not without its dangers if the exchange rate appreciation goes to the point, as in the case of Switzerland in 1978, of threatening to have industrial effects that might prove to be excessive over the long run. Finally, given the lags in the response of goods markets to exchange rate changes and other factors, external adjustment problems have persisted, and the ability of national authorities to stabilize growth rates has turned out to be about as limited under flexible rates as it was under the par value system.

It is true that the more extreme fears on which the case against flexible rates was built have not proved to be justified. Foreign exchange markets have adapted to the flexible rate environment, and so far there is little evidence that flows of foreign trade or international capital movements have been significantly curtailed in response to exchange rate fluctuations. The marked short-run variability of rates has, nevertheless, generated hostility toward the flexible rate system.

This hostility might have been contained if the exchange rate instability had been limited to the first two or three years of floating and if, as seemed possible in 1975 and 1976, the system had tended to settle down. The events of 1977–78, however, have rekindled the fears that instability may be an inherent characteristic of the floating system. Thus, as a result of both experience and analysis, it is less clear now than it appeared a few years ago that, if the major industrial countries were to succeed in achieving orderly economic growth with reasonable price stability, this would automatically bring exchange rate stability. In short, it now appears that national stability is a necessary, but probably not a sufficient, condition for exchange rate stability. This has contributed to skepticism among policymakers on the benefits of a floating rate system and encouraged support for greater fixity. The renewed attempt to develop a European Monetary System is one example of this search for stability.

THE CONTINUING NEED FOR EXCHANGE RATE FLEXIBILITY

While there is a strong and widespread desire for greater stability of exchange rates, there is no escaping the fact that this implies a substantial measure of domestic economic stability, and such stability is not going to be easy to achieve over a wide range of countries. It might be thought that the widespread view that there is no significant trade-off between inflation and unemployment over the long run would make it easy to muster support for policies that could bring economies down from a high rate of inflation to a significantly lower one. But just as the knowledge that freer trade increases welfare does not eliminate the short-run adverse effects arising from the reduction of trade barriers, and therefore does not remove opposition to tariff cutting, so the fact that there are serious transitional difficulties in bringing down rates of wage and price increases has been a major inhibiting factor in achieving national stability.

Part of the difficulty arises from the nature of labor markets where, even in the absence of formal union contracts, there is a long-term contractual relationship between employers and employees.[37] Without a strong anti-inflation consensus, it is difficult to convince employers and their employees that an announced intention to curb expenditure and reduce inflation really means that the economic climate has changed, and that major adjustments in price expectations and wage demands should be made. If those setting wages and salaries are not convinced, wage settlements, whether made with unions or not, will not decline rapidly enough to prevent a sharp rise in unemployment. The rise in unemployment pressures governments to reverse their restrictive policies, and if this happens it becomes increasingly difficult to mount a convincing anti-inflation program later.

A number of countries have drifted into this kind of vicious circle and found it difficult in the extreme to extricate themselves. Other countries have been fortunate in having or developing public attitudes on inflation that have led to much more decisive results. In countries where it is generally agreed that inflation is a serious threat, then, if the government announces restraining action, the public is ready to believe that in fact money expenditure will be controlled and that it would be foolish not to adjust. The adjustment of employers and employees which then follows helps to prevent unemployment from rising to politically dangerous levels. There is, therefore, little pressure for a reversal of policy, and this reinforces the anti-inflation program. The same countries that have benefited from public hostility to inflation have also had other advantages in achieving reasonable price stability with limited effects in terms of unemployment for their own nationals.

Both the Federal Republic of Germany and Switzerland adjusted to a lower level of economic activity, in part by decreasing the number of foreign workers employed in their economies. In Japan, the employment policies of firms are such that the number of firings have been limited. Thus, those that have the ability to control inflation have also been able to pass along some of the social costs to others, or have had social arrangements that limited the political risks of economic slack.

It is not to be expected that differences in rates of inflation among countries will be eliminated in the near future. The more stable countries will understandably be reluctant to follow policies that will lead to a return to significant rates of price increase. At the same time, a number of inflating countries have great difficulty in persevering with policies that would reduce their rates of inflation substantially over the next few years. Some believe that pegged rates in and of themselves will lead to the necessary conversion to a belief in reasonable price stability in the latter countries. While there are some feedbacks from exchange rates to domestic decisions on inflation, in a world which is as far away as this one from belief in the verities of the gold standard or the sanctity of a particular exchange rate, it is unlikely that there will be a strong response to such a simple appeal. Thus, the need for a considerable measure of exchange rate flexibility is likely to remain for some years to come.

Problems of Pegged Rate Systems

The justification for some form of pegging, or its approximation in the form of heavily managed floating, that would allow for the needed exchange rate flexibility while avoiding any undue variability is clear in principle. Given existing domestic and foreign circumstances and policies, there are adjustment paths for exchange rates that would minimize the adjustment costs to economies. Market forces may lead to different, more erratic adjustment paths. If the authorities had the objective of minimizing adjustment costs, and if they could discount temporary disturbances better than private market participants, they could steer rates more directly to their longer-run equilibrium levels. However, what if, as it appears likely, neither market participants nor the authorities have any precise view of what the longer-term equilibrium exchange rates are? Given that uncertainty, the authorities' stabilizing role does not derive from knowledge that is denied to market participants, but rather from the fact that the amount of resources available to them enables them to set the price, if that price is a reasonable one.

As long as the rates set by the authorities are within the band constituted by what private market participants view as realistic exchange rates, then setting rates is simply a way of getting short-run expectations to coalesce on specific, if somewhat arbitrary, values. Smoothing out adjustment paths may, therefore, have little to do with having deeper insight than that of private market participants; it may simply call for a commitment on the part of the authorities to set and maintain reasonable exchange rates.

That a pegged rate system can be successful in terms of reducing short-run exchange rate instability has been demonstrated by the relative success of the snake arrangement for those that remained within it. There are, however, major risks in any governmental policy to control the exchange rate. The main risk arises from the tendency of the authorities to maintain excessive rate rigidity. It is not that the authorities will necessarily be unaware of the need for a rate change, although this is a problem, but rather that they often cannot resist the temptation to maintain an overvalued rate as a form of price control, or an undervalued rate as a form of production incentive. They may resist depreciation because such an event is viewed by the public, often rightly, as a sign that the authorities have followed inflationary policies. They may also resist an appreciation because it would be unpopular with those in export or import-competing industries. A formal pegged system, as opposed to a heavily managed float, seems particularly subject to this danger of excessive rate rigidity, since changes in pegged rates are more noticeable, and more politically difficult to make, than a gradual change in the intervention points under a managed float.

Successful resistance to exchange rate change on one occasion encourages further resistance later, and the exchange system soon becomes increasingly fixed. If, however, the conditions for fixity are not met, the ultimate result is an exchange rate crisis followed by a major exchange rate movement. Private market participants soon lose any confidence they may have had in the ability of the authorities to set a rate that is realistic, and there may even be a presumption that, if a rate is set by the authorities, it is probably wrong.

It is this natural tendency of the authorities to resist market pressures, even when they reflect changes in the underlying economic and financial conditions that led to the breakup of the Bretton Woods system in the early 1970s, and, as Oort (1974), the former Dutch Treasurer-General, and others have noted, there is no indication so far that this tendency has disappeared. In fact, as noted in previous sections, while it is certainly true that floating rates have tended to be unstable, part of the instability experienced in exchange markets in recent years can be directly attributed to vain attempts by the authorities to maintain exchange rate rigidity in the face of changing underlying economic and financial conditions.

Even if this inherent bias toward fixity could be avoided, a pegged system remains difficult to manage. If there are disparities in policies and performance, changes in pegged rates have to be quite frequent. Those operating in exchange markets are therefore likely to be confronted every year, if not every few months, with situations in which rates are likely to change, and there is little doubt as to the direction such changes will take. This leads to protective steps by those with foreign exchange exposure, and they may be joined by others looking for a speculative gain. This problem can be avoided only by making more frequent changes in the pegged rate, which can, therefore, be so small that they are not worth anticipating. Under these circumstances, a pegged rate system tends to be transformed either into a gliding rate system or back into a floating rate system.

A number of countries, of course, do at present peg their currencies to a single currency or a basket of currencies, and do so with underlying conditions that lead to periodic devaluations. These are generally countries, however, with relatively undeveloped financial markets. It is not clear that pegged rates among major industrial countries could be subject to frequent variations by significant amounts without leading to exchange markets that would be more nervous and volatile than they are under managed floating. This may set limits to what might be called premature pegging.

It might appear that a gliding rate system would be the solution, because it would reduce the risks of inappropriate rates by taking into account automatically some of the changes in underlying economic and financial conditions. The differences with a pegged rate system, however, are more a matter of degree than of kind. The difficulty in a gliding peg system lies in the choice of the formula. Since there are no simple objective indicators that can be relied upon to reflect the changing underlying conditions, exchange market disequilibria can build up under a gliding rate system nearly as fast as under a pegged system. For example, an attempt to fix the rate between the Japanese yen and the U.S. dollar since the early 1970s on the basis of some indicators of relative domestic prices of manufactures or relative unit labor costs in manufacturing would have been disastrous. Domestic prices and unit labor costs tended to rise faster in Japan than in the United States during that period, so that the value of the yen in terms of U.S. dollars would have been gliding downward on the basis of such indicators. More sophisticated indicators can be designed (see Artus, 1978 and Kenen, 1975), but ultimately there is always the same need for discrete changes in the rate at not infrequent intervals.

Flexibility is not the only condition required for the achievement of greater exchange rate stability. As pointed out in Section II, monetary and financial factors play an important role in the short-run determination of the exchange rate, and if greater exchange rate stability is to be achieved, careful attention must be given by the authorities to exchange market developments in reaching decisions on monetary policy.

Over the years, monetary authorities have adopted various indicators as a guide for their actions. Under the international gold standard, the maintenance of that standard was the prime policy objective, and the international position was crucial in determining the discretionary actions of central banks. Under looser international arrangements, central banks felt that they had greater, though limited, freedom to focus on the credit conditions, or more narrowly on the interest rates, that would contribute to domestic objectives. These indicators had their weaknesses and were particularly open to misinterpretation during periods of inflation. More recently the emphasis has been on monetary quantities, with a number of major industrial countries establishing targets for various monetary magnitudes. While adherence to monetary targets has proved to be difficult, an approach of this kind has seemed helpful in moving in the direction of greater stability. Experience and analysis suggest, however, that if greater stability of exchange rates is to be achieved, whether under managed floating or some form of pegging, the authorities will need to pay closer attention to international considerations in making short-run decisions on demand-management policies. Indeed, the exchange rate may often perform as a better indicator for monetary policy than interest rates or monetary aggregates, particularly in periods where the demand for money is unstable and the monetary aggregates subject to statistical problems. There is some evidence that recently national authorities have moved in that direction and have been giving greater thought to exchange market developments in determining monetary policy.

NOTES

1. Artus (1979) contains a detailed discussion of this issue.
2. The current account surplus is by definition equal to domestic output minus domestic absorption, or to domestic saving minus domestic investment.
3. For a review of the development of the absorption approach, see Rhomberg and Heller (1977).
4. The argument presented here in terms of domestic goods and foreign goods needs to be modified when the elasticity of substitution between internationally tradable goods produced by the various countries is extremely high. In such a case, the argument must be developed to some extent in terms of internationally tradable goods versus nontradable goods.
5. For a detailed analysis of the policy choices made by the Federal Republic of Germany, France, the United Kingdom, the United States, and Sweden during 1972–75, see Black (1977).
6. It is worth noting that in the case of the three countries that shifted to supporting demand-management policies in 1976, the external adjustment worked relatively well during 1977–78. In France and Italy, however, the imbalances were not really deep rooted, and in the United Kingdom, North Sea oil played a major role.
7. As Kindleberger (1969, p. 95) humorously put it, it is only "banana republics" that get excepted by Johnson from flexible rates on the ground that "they do not have the illusion that the price of bananas in local money is a major determinant of the cost of living, as contrasted with the price of imported goods."

8. See Chart 1 in original article. Both the text and the following note can be read with profit without the chart. Not surprisingly, Chart 1 shows also that changes in relative export prices tend to be smaller than changes in relative deflators of value added, which are themselves smaller than changes in relative unit labor costs. Part of the lack of change in relative export prices is a purely mechanical reflection of common cost elements (e.g., internationally traded raw material inputs) in relative export prices, but it is certain that the evidence also indicates that part of the exchange rate effect works through changes in profit margins and supply incentives. Aggregate indices could be misleading, but careful studies on specific types of manufactured goods by Kravis and Lipsey (1977) and Kravis, Lipsey, and Kalter (1977) confirm these findings.

The deflator of the gross domestic product originating in manufacturing is used as a proxy for wholesale prices for manufactures in Chart 1 because of the poor quality of a number of national indices for wholesale prices of manufactures (e.g., the Belgian, French, and Italian indices), which put an unduly low weight on finished products.

9. The weakness of aggregate demand in the Swiss market has also prevented any major shift from export markets to the domestic market.

10. It should not be necessary for the economics profession to repeat the unfortunate experience of the early postwar period, when the notion of a dollar shortage was developed despite the difficulty of reconciling such a result with economic theory and economic history. "Prices don't matter" is a proposition on about the same plane as "money doesn't matter."

11. The insulation issue is discussed here to a large extent from a single-country rather than a global point of view. Taking into account the likelihood that disturbances of various kinds may tend to affect the various countries at the same time leads to extremely complicated theoretical models that do not add much to the understanding of the basic issues involved, since there is no reason to assume stable patterns of covariances among these disturbances.

12. This point had been raised earlier by Fleming (1962). Some empirical evidence confirming that hypothesis for the specific case of Canada during the 1950s can be found in Rhomberg (1964).

13. It similarly follows that real disturbances originating at home will tend to be transmitted abroad in large measure under flexible rates, and thus their effects on the domestic economy will be diffused.

This conclusion is also verified by empirical studies (e.g., Ripley, 1978), which seem to suggest that the international transmission of fluctuations in economic activity is no less powerful under flexible rates than under fixed rates.

14. In recent years the insulation argument has been seen to depend more and more on the ability of the authorities to use policy instruments for reaching domestic targets without being constrained by the external balance rather than as a purely automatic mechanism. See, for example, Tower and Willett (1976).

15. It is mainly on the basis of this argument that many authors, such as Argy (1975), have concluded that monetary policy will tend to have stronger price and weaker employment effects in the short run under flexible rates.

16. [See Charts 2, 3, and 4 in original article. The text and this note may be read with profit without the charts.] The 26 percent and 34 percent depreciations of the U.S. dollar against the deutsche mark and Japanese yen, respectively, from end-June 1977 to end-October 1978 in particular, were out of proportion with underlying developments, at least in terms of either rates of monetary growth or inflation rate differentials. Rates of change in Ml and the gross national product (GNP) deflators are indicated below. A comparison based on other monetary and price indicators can be found in the Fund's *Annual Report, 1979* (Table 11, p. 38).

	Money (MI) *(Percentage change based on period averages)*				GNP Deflator *(Percentage change)*			
	1975	*1976*	*1977*	*1978*	*1975*	*1976*	*1977*	*1978*
Germany, Fed. Rep.	14.1	10.2	8.3	13.8	6.7	3.3	3.6	3.5
Japan	10.3	14.2	7.0	10.8	12.8	5.5	5.4	3.7
United States	4.5	5.1	7.2	8.3	9.6	5.2	5.9	7.2

17. Nordhaus also points out that the day-to-day variability of the Dow-Jones industrial average in the recent period had been almost 0.5 percent a day, compared with 0.1 and 0.2 percent for the nominal value of the U.S. dollar as measured by a trade-weighted index.

18. Several variants of this "asset market" approach are presented in the papers included in *Scandinavian Journal of Economics*, Vol. 78 (No. 2, 1976), and discussed in Bilson (1979), Dornbusch and Krugman (1976), Shadler (1977), and Isard (1978).

19. Here also the word unstable is used in its commonsense meaning of moving up and down frequently, rather than in the sense of moving continuously away from equilibrium once disturbed.

20. Countries may have monetary targets, but in practice such targets are not often respected for long and thus do not necessarily stabilize the expectations of market participants with respect to the future time paths of money supplies.

21. As Isard (1978) notes, the unwillingness of banks and multinational corporations to take open positions on the basis of longer-run exchange rate expectations is to some extent related to the imprecision of these expectations.

22. For a review of these various models, see Bilson (1979), Schadler (1977), and Isard (1978).

23. It is somewhat astonishing in this context that most of the recent economic literature on exchange rate determination completely discarded this factor up to about 1978, at which time Dornbusch (1978, p. 90) noted that "the current account has just made it back as a determinant of exchange rates."

24. Some empirical evidence for this effect has been found by Artus (1976), Branson, Halttunen, and Masson (1977), and Porter (1977).

25. At other times, the surplus on current account may be the result of factors that provide their own offset to the current account surplus in the form of capital flows.

26. In February 1977, a medium-term stand-by credit facility of the equivalent of $3 billion was extended to the Bank of England by a group of European central banks and the central banks of Canada, Japan, and the United States. This facility could only be drawn on if U. K. official reserves were less than the equivalent of $6,750 million, and it has not been used in the succeeding two years.

27. Other factors of volatility have also been mentioned. Girton and Roper (1976) have focused on the substitution between the noninterest-bearing portions of different countries' money stocks that may occur when the expected rate of inflation, and therefore the expected rate of return on fiat money, differs among countries. Such portfolio shifts do not necessarily take place gradually over time and may be the cause of sudden exchange rate movements. Kareken and Wallace (1978) have even advanced the view that the choice between different fiat moneys is "of the all-or-nothing variety," so that in a floating rate system without stringent capital controls there is simply no equilibrium value for the exchange rate. There is little if any empirical support for the view when put in this extreme form. As Haberler notes, the uncertainty about future inflation rates and, of greater importance, the legal provisions, the extra cost of transactions of using different money, and the sheer inertia of the public, ensure the local dominance of national money, except under conditions of hyperinflation. Even in Germany in 1920–23 the substitution was slow. Under more normal circumstances, the substitution is quite limited, as demonstrated by all available historical evidence. (See Brillembourg and Schadler (1979) for an attempt to use econometric techniques to estimate the substitution elasticities among major currencies.) It is perhaps worth adding that if a country wishes to discourage a flight from its noninterest-bearing money, it is possible to arrange to pay interest, even on currency.

28. For a previous discussion of a number of these detrimental effects, see Artus and Crockett (1978).

29. In his *Treatise on Money*, Keynes (pp. 333–34) differentiated between the effects of exchange rate fluctuations on foreign trade and foreign investment. On the first, he commented: "So far as foreign trade is concerned, I think that the advantage of fixing the maximum fluctuations of the foreign exchanges within quite narrow limits is usually much over-estimated. It is, indeed, little more than a convenience." On international investment his view was different: "When we come to Foreign Lending, however, the advantages of a fixed exchange rate must . . . be estimated much higher. In this case the

contracts between borrower and lender may cover a far longer period than would be contemplated by any practicable dealings in forward exchange."

30. The snake countries considered here are Belgium-Luxembourg, Denmark, the Federal Republic of Germany, the Netherlands, and Norway.

31. Forward markets do not exist for the currencies of a number of developing countries. Normally, however, these currencies are pegged to a major currency, and the forward market for that currency can be used for hedging purposes. Those currencies that are pegged to a basket can achieve partial hedging by operating in the forward market of a major currency.

32. Surveys of U.S. entrepreneurs are reviewed in Burtle and Mooney (1976). For a survey of U. K. entrepreneurs, see Oppenheimer (1978). U. K. businessmen seem to react more negatively than their U.S. counterparts to exchange rate instability.

33. It is interesting that one of Keynes's proposals for dealing with this problem, namely, a "substantial Government transfer tax on all transactions" to discourage the "predominance of speculation over enterprise" in the stock market, has recently been repeated by Tobin (1978) for exchange market transactions.

34. A recent version of this position is attributed to Laffer and Mundell by Wanniski (1974).

35. For a discussion of the empirical evidence on this point, see Crockett and Goldstein (1976).

36. It has been pointed out that, given prevailing inflationary conditions, the inflexibility problem is not relevant since there is sufficient room for rates of change of prices and money wages to be reduced because of exchange rate movements without ever becoming negative (see, for example, Claasen (1976)). This point is not crucial, however, since the downward inflexibility may apply to some extent to the rate of change of the money wage rate as well as to its level.

37. Hicks (1932) drew attention to the special nature of labor markets in his early work on wage theory. Gordon (1974) provided a neoclassical explanation of the tendency of short-run adjustments to a fall in demand to come in the form of employment declines rather than wage changes and a more rudimentary presentation of the argument can be found in the 1972 report of the Canadian Prices and Incomes Commission (for which Gordon was a consultant). A number of others, including Baily (1974), Azariadis (1976), Barro (1977), and Fischer (1977) have discussed the consequences that follow from the contractual nature of transactions in labor markets.

REFERENCES

Argy, Victor, "The Dynamics of Monetary Policy under Flexible Exchange Rates: An Exploratory Analysis," in *Papers in Monetary Economics* (Reserve Bank of Australia, 1975), pp. 1–42.

Artus, Jacques R. (1976). "Exchange Rate Stability and Managed Floating: The Experience of the Federal Republic of Germany," *Staff Papers,* Vol. 23 (July 1976), pp. 312–33.

——— (1978), "Methods of Assessing the Long-Run Equilibrium Value of an Exchange Rate," *Journal of International Economics,* Vol. 8 (May 1978), pp. 277–99.

——— (1979), "Persistent Surpluses and Deficits on Current Accounts Among Major Industrial Countries" (unpublished, International Monetary Fund, May 24, 1979).

———, and Andrew D. Crockett, *Floating Exchange Rates and the Need for Surveillance*, Essays in International Finance, No. 127, International Finance Section, Princeton University (May 1978).

Azariadis, Costas, "On the Incidence of Unemployment," *Review of Economic Studies,* Vol. 43 (February 1976), pp. 115–25.

Baily, Martin N., "Wages and Employment Under Uncertain Demand," *Review of Economic Studies,* Vol. 41 (January 1974), pp. 37–50.

Ball, Robert J., ed., *The International Linkage of National Economic Models* (Amsterdam, 1973).

Barro, R. J., "Long-Term Contracting, Sticky Prices, and Monetary Policy," *Journal of Monetary Economics,* Vol. 3 (July 1977), pp. 305–16.

Beenstock, M. C., and A. P. L. Minford, "A Quarterly Economic Model of Trade and Prices 1955–1972," in *Inflation in Open Economies,* ed. by J. M. Parkin and G. Zis (University of Manchester, 1976).

Bilson, John F. O., "Recent Developments in Monetary Models of Exchange Rate Determination," *Staff Papers,* Vol. 26 (June 1979), pp. 201–23.

Black, Stanley W., *Floating Exchange Rates and National Economic Policy* (Yale University Press, 1977).

Branson, William H., "Asset Markets and Relative Prices in Exchange Rate Determination," *Sozialwissenschaftlich Annalen,* Vol. 1 (1977).

———, Hannu Halttunen, and Paul Masson, "Exchange Rates in the Short Run: The Dollar-Deutschemark Rate," *European Economic Review,* Vol. 10 (December 1977), pp. 303–24.

Brillembourg, Arturo, and Susan M. Schadler, "A Model of Currency Substitution in Exchange Rate Determination, 1973–78," *Staff Papers,* Vol. 26 (September 1979), pp. 513–42.

Burtle, James, and Sean Mooney, "International Trade and Investment under Floating Rates: The Reaction of Business to the Floating Rate System," in *Exchange Rate Flexibility,* Proceedings of a Conference on Exchange Rate Flexibility and the International Monetary System, Sponsored by the American Enterprise Institute for Public Policy Research and the U.S. Department of the Treasury, ed. by Jacob S. Dreyer, Gottfried Haberler, and Thomas D. Willett (Washington, 1976).

Canada, Prices and Incomes Commission, *Inflation, Unemployment and Incomes Policy* (Ottawa, 1972).

Claasen, Emil-Maria, "World Inflation Under Flexible Exchange Rates," *Scandinavian Journal of Economics,* Vol. 78 (No. 2, 1976), pp. 346–65.

Cornell, Bradford, "Spot Rates, Forward Rates and Exchange Market Efficiency," *Journal of Financial Economics,* Vol. 5 (August 1977), pp. 55–65.

Crockett, Andrew D., and Morris Goldstein, "Inflation Under Fixed and Flexible Exchange Rates," *Staff Papers,* Vol. 23 (November 1976), pp. 509–44.

Deppler, Michael C., and Duncan Ripley, "The World Trade Model: Merchandise Flows," *Staff Papers,* Vol. 25 (March 1978), pp. 147–206.

Dooley, Michael P., and Jeffrey R. Shafer, "Analysis of Short-Run Exchange Rate Behavior, March 1973 to September 1975," International Finance Discussion Paper, No. 76, Board of Governors of the Federal Reserve System (Washington, February 1976).

Dornbusch, Rudiger (1976), "Expectations and Exchange Rate Dynamics," *Journal of Political Economy,* Vol. 84 (December 1976), pp. 1161–76.

——— (1977), "What Have We Learned from the Float?" (unpublished, Massachusetts Institute of Technology, February 24, 1977).

——— (1978), "Monetary Policy under Exchange Rate Flexibility," Federal Reserve Bank of Boston, Conference Series, No. 20, *Managed Exchange-Rate Flexibility: The Recent Experience* (October 1978).

———, and Paul Krugman, "Flexible Exchange Rates in the Short Run." *Brookings Papers on Economic Activity: 3* (1976), pp. 537–75.

Economistes Belges de Langue Française. 2e congrès, 5/6 Novembre 1976: *Economies ouvertes face aux mutations internationales: rapport préparatoire (Centre Interuniversitaire de Formation Permanente).*

Fischer, Stanley, "Long-Term Contracting, Sticky Prices, and Monetary Policy: A Comment," *Journal of Monetary Economics,* Vol. 3 (July 1977), pp. 317–23.

Fleming, J. Marcus, "Domestic Financial Policies Under Fixed and Under Floating Exchange Rates," *Staff Papers,* Vol. 9 (November 1962), pp. 369–80.

Friedman, Milton (1953), "The Case for Flexible Exchange Rates," in his *Essays in Positive Economics* (University of Chicago Press, 1953), pp. 157–203.

——— (1966), "Comments," in *Guidelines, Informal Controls, and the Market Place: Policy Choices in a Full Employment Economy,* ed. by George P. Schultz and Robert Z. Aliber (University of Chicago Press, 1966), pp. 55–61.

——— (1969), "Discussion," in *The International Adjustment Mechanism,* Federal Reserve Bank of Boston, Conference Series, No. 2 (October 1969), pp. 109–19.

Girton, Lance, and Don Roper, "Theory and Implications of Currency Substitution," International Finance Discussion paper, No. 86, Board of Governors of the Federal Reserve System (Washington, August 1976).

Gordon, Donald F., "A Neo-Classical Theory of Keynesian Unemployment," *Economic Inquiry,* Vol. 12 (December 1974), pp. 431–59.

Haberler, Gottfried, "Flexible Exchange Rates: Theories and Controversies Once Again" (unpublished, American Enterprise Institute for Public Policy Research, Washington, February 1979). This is scheduled to be published in a memorial volume for Egon Sohmen.

Hicks, John R., *The Theory of Wages* (London, 1932).

Hooper, Peter, and S. W. Kohlhagen, "The Effect of Exchange Rate Uncertainty on the Prices and Volume of International Trade," *Journal of International Economics,* Vol. 8 (November 1978), pp. 483–511.

International Monetary Fund (1978), *The Rise in Protectionism,* IMF Pamphlet Series, No. 24 (Washington, 1978).

———, *Annual Report of the Executive Board for the Financial Year Ended April 30, 1978 and 1979* (Washington, 1978 and 1979).

Isard, Peter, *Exchange-Rate Determination: A Survey of Popular Views and Recent Models,* Princeton Studies in International Finance, No. 42, International Finance Section, Princeton University (May 1978).

Johnson, Harry G. (1958), "Towards a General Theory of the Balance of Payments: Studies in Pure Theory," in his *International Trade and Economic Growth* (London, 1958).

——— (1969), "The Case for Flexible Exchange Rates, 1969," Federal Reserve Bank of St. Louis, *Review,* Vol. 51 (No. 6, June 1979), pp. 12–24.

Kareken, John, and Neil Wallace, "International Monetary Reform: The Feasible Alternatives," Federal Reserve Bank of Minneapolis, *Quarterly Review* (Summer 1978), pp. 2–7.

Kenen, Peter B., "Floats, Glides and Indicators: A Comparison of Methods for Changing Exchange Rates," *Journal of International Economics,* Vol. 5 (May 1975), pp. 107–51.

Keynes, John Maynard (1930), *The Treatise on Money,* Vol. 2 (London, 1930).

——— (1936), *The General Theory of Employment, Interest, and Money* (New York, 1936).

Kindleberger, Charles P. (1969), "The Case for Fixed Exchange Rates, 1969," in *The International Adjustment Mechanism,* Federal Reserve Bank of Boston, Conference Series, No. 2 (October 1969), pp. 93–108.

——— (1976), "Germany's Persistent Balance-of-Payments Disequilibrium Revisited," Banca Nazionale del Lavoro, Quarterly Review, Vol. 29 (June 1976), pp. 135–64.

Kouri, Pentti J. K., "The Exchange Rate and the Balance of Payments in the Short Run and the Long Run: A Monetary Approach," *Scandinavian Journal of Economics,* Vol. 78 (No. 2, 1976), pp. 280–304.

Kravis, Irving B., and Robert E. Lipsey, "Export and Domestic Prices Under Inflation and Exchange Rate Movements," Working Paper No. 176, National Bureau of Economic Research (New York, 1977).

———, and Eliot Kalter, "Export Prices and Exchange Rates," Working Paper No. 182, National Bureau of Economic Research (New York, 1977).

McKinnon, Ronald I. (1976), "Floating Foreign Exchange Rates 1973–74: The Emperor's New Clothes," in *Institutional Arrangements and the Inflation Problem,* ed. by Karl Brunner and Allan H. Meltzer, Carnegie-Rochester Conference on Public Policy, Vol. 3 (Amsterdam, 1976), pp. 79–114.

———, (1978) "Exchange-Rate Instability, Trade Balances, and Monetary Policies in Japan and the United States" (mimeographed, Stanford University).

——— (1979), *Money in International Exchange: The Convertible Currency System* (Oxford University Press, 1979).

Modigliani, Franco, and Hossein Askari, "The International Transfer of Capital and the Propagation of Domestic Disturbances Under Alternative Payments Systems," Banca Nazionale del Lavoro, *Quarterly Review,* Vol. 26 (December 1973), pp. 295–310.

Mussa, Michael, "The Exchange Rate, the Balance of Payments and Monetary and Fiscal Policy Under a Regime of Controlled Floating," *Scandinavian Journal of Economics,* Vol. 78 (No. 2, 1976), pp. 229–48.

Nordhaus, William D., "Statement," in *The Decline of the Dollar,* Hearings Before the Subcommittee on Foreign Economic Policy (95th Congress, 2nd Session, Washington, June 22, 1978), pp. 249–53.

Oort, Conrad J., *Steps to International Monetary Order,* Proceedings of the Per Jacobsson Foundation (Tokyo, 1974), pp. 7–52.

Oppenheimer, Peter, *et al, Business Views on Exchange Rate Policy: An Independent Study by a Group of Leading Economists,* commissioned by Confederation of British Industry (London, July 1978).

Phelps, Edmund S., *Inflation Policy and Unemployment Theory: The Cost-Benefit Approach to Monetary Planning* (New York, 1972).

Phillips, A. W., "The Relation Between Unemployment and the Rate of Change of Money Wage Rates in the United Kingdom, 1867–1957," *Economica,* Vol. 25 (November 1958), pp. 283–99.

Polak, J. J., "Monetary Analysis of Income Formation and Payments Problems," *Staff Papers,* Vol. 6 (November 1957), pp. 1–50; reprinted in *The Monetary Approach to the Balance of Payments* (International Monetary Fund, Washington, 1977), pp. 15–64.

Porter, Michael, "The Exchange Rate and Portfolio Equilibrium" (mimeographed, Monash University, 1977).

Rhomberg, Rudolf R., "A Model of the Canadian Economy Under Fixed and Fluctuating Exchange Rates," *Journal of Political Economy*, Vol. 72 (February 1964), pp. 1–31.

———, and H. Robert Heller, "Introductory Survey," in *The Monetary Approach to the Balance of Payments* (International Monetary Fund, Washington, 1977), pp. 1–14.

Ripley, Duncan M., "The Transmission of Fluctuations in Economic Activity: Some Recent Evidence," in *Managed Exchange-Rate Flexibility: The Recent Experience*, Federal Reserve Bank of Boston, Conference Series, No. 20 (October 1978), pp. 1–21.

Roosa, Robert V., "Second Lecture," in Milton Friedman and Robert V. Roosa, *The Balance of Payments: Free Versus Fixed Exchange Rates*, American Enterprise Institute for Public Policy Research, Rational Debate Seminars, No. 4 (Washington, 1967), pp. 25–67.

Shadler, Susan, "Sources of Exchange Rate Variability: Theory and Empirical Evidence," *Staff Papers*, Vol. 24 (July 1977), pp. 253–96.

Spitäller, Erich, "Short-Run Effects of Exchange Rate Changes on the Terms of Trade and the Trade Balance" (unpublished, International Monetary Fund, October 31, 1979).

Stern, Robert M., Jonathan Francis, and Bruce Schumacher, *Price Elasticities in International Trade: An Annotated Bibliography* (London, 1967).

Tobin, James, "A Proposal for International Monetary Reform," Cowles Foundation for Research in Economics, Discussion Paper No. 506 (Yale University, October 1978). This is scheduled for publication in the *Eastern Economic Journal*.

Tower, Edward and Thomas D. Willett, "The Theory of Optimum Currency Areas and Exchange-Rate Flexibility," Special Papers in International Economics, No. 11, International Finance Section, Princeton University (1976).

Wanniski, Jude, "The Case for Fixed Exchange Rates," *Wall Street Journal* (June 14, 1974), p. 10.

18. Unexpected Real Consequences of Floating Exchange Rates

RACHEL MCCULLOCH

After a decade of floating exchange rates, international monetary reform is again in the air, and it is thus timely to ask how well (or badly) the current system is functioning.* But compared to what? Because the current monetary arrangements came into effect following years of vigorous debate on the merits of exchange-rate flexibility, some observers appear to forget that these arrangements were not in reality "designed" or even "adopted" by the International Monetary Fund. Rather, the present regime was initiated by the collapse of the Bretton Woods system, following prolonged and heroic salvage efforts. As late as 1972, a report on international monetary reform by the Executive Directors of the IMF failed even to mention flexible exchange rates as a viable long-term option (IMF, 1972), while an earlier report explicitly concerned with the role of exchange rates in the adjustment process had devoted only one of seventy-eight pages to floating rates (IMF, 1970). The markedly after-the-fact Second Amendment of the IMF Articles of Agreement to legalize the status quo merely reflected recognition of member governments' inability to agree on an alternative—any system imposing even minimal restraints on national policies—rather than an affirmation of the benefits of floating.

The central and still unresolved issue in the fruitless debate over international financial arrangements was the desire to preserve national autonomy in the face of growing economic and political interdependence. Since the present time seems no more propitious than the

Rachel McCulloch is Professor of Economics at the University of Wisconsin.

* This paper is adapted from one prepared for the Wingspread Conference on the Evolving Multiple Reserve Asset System, July 28–30, 1982. I am grateful to J. David Richardson for extensive and stimulating discussions of the subject. I am indebted also to Robert E. Baldwin, Charles P. Kindleberger, Michael Rothschild, André Sapir, Janet Yellen, and conference participants at Wingspread and the 1982 National Bureau of Economic Research Summer Institute for helpful suggestions, and to the University of Wisconsin Graduate School for financial support.

early 1970s for the willing sacrifice of national sovereignty by IMF members, any argument for system reform must be solidly grounded in the accumulated experience with floating, not by reference to the dogmas of the Bretton Woods era. This Essay is an eclectic assessment of that experience, with particular reference to the ways in which events have confounded both advocates and critics of floating. Although there is some discussion of the consequences of the floating-rate regime for worldwide macroeconomic performance, the main focus is on microeconomic issues—specifically, the role of floating rates in facilitating or retarding the growth of world trade and investment.

INTERNATIONAL MONEY AND THE GOALS OF BRETTON WOODS

National money, in its time-honored functions as medium of (indirect) exchange, unit of account, standard of deferred payment, and store of value, is supposed to facilitate the efficient allocation of resources in production and consumption. Although the precise nature and magnitude of the efficiency gains have never been spelled out fully in economic analyses, monetary history gives clear evidence of significant real resource costs and unanticipated redistributions of wealth when money fails to perform its traditional functions. At the same time, control of a nation's money supply also constitutes a potent tool of macroeconomic management and an alternative to taxation as a means of financing government expenditure. Thus, conflicting objectives confront those who conduct monetary policy, and there are both microeconomic and macroeconomic bases on which to judge their performance.

Analogously, the international monetary system is supposed to facilitate an efficient allocation of resources worldwide, presumably through trade guided by comparative advantage, but it also has important consequences for global macroeconomic conditions. This twofold function was explicitly recognized in the Articles of Agreement of the International Monetary Fund approved at Bretton Woods in 1944, which listed among the purposes of the Fund:

> To facilitate the expansion and balanced growth of international trade, and to contribute thereby to the promotion and maintenance of high levels of employment and real income and to the development of the productive resources of all members as primary objectives of economic policy (Articles of Agreement, Article I, ii).

As inadequacies in the Bretton Woods system became apparent during the 1960s, criticisms and proposals for reform likewise fell into two distinct categories.

Macroeconomic Performance

The Bretton Woods system was held to impart a deflationary bias to the world economy on account of the asymmetrical positions of surplus and deficit countries—at least in the rules, if not in the actual behavior, of member nations. At a time when the prospects for "fine tuning" of national macroeconomic performance seemed bright, the obligations of member nations under the Bretton Woods rules appeared to limit the ability of elected governments to deliver the combination of inflation and unemployment desired by their constituents. Although theory suggested that control of two instruments—monetary policy and fiscal policy—should allow enlightened policymakers to achieve both "internal balance" and "external balance," thoughtful analysts stressed that other objectives, notably adequate long-run growth, could be jeopardized by this textbook solution.

Because the Bretton Woods rules appeared to constrain national governments, advocates of reform and especially of increased exchange-rate flexibility appealed to the need for greater macroeconomic independence. Most reform proposals, however, called for modification rather than scrapping of the Bretton Woods rules. Two popular evolutionary plans were the crawling peg and the widening of exchange-rate margins, the latter actually adopted in 1971 as part of the short-lived Smithsonian Agreement. Interestingly, Cooper had seen wider bands as a feasible means of increasing independence but noted a disadvantage "from the viewpoint of fostering international cooperation . . . of *not* affording an occasion for close international consultation" (1968, p. 263).

Subsequent events suggest that advocates of increased flexibility failed to distinguish adequately between institutional and economic constraints on the actions of national policymakers. The collapse of the Bretton Woods system clearly increased the national sovereignty of IMF members with regard to the conduct of macroeconomic policy but had at most a minor effect on the ability of member nations to achieve desired outcomes. Countries acquired the technical capacity to pursue autonomous monetary policies because they were no longer required to peg their exchange rates, but they were severely constrained in exercising this autonomy on account of the undesirable effects of large exchange-rate movements on their domestic economies. Furthermore, the system of flexible exchange rates could not suppress structural interdependence; the system proved to offer ample channels for the continued international transmission of macroeconomic disturbances.

Even so, the chief flaws in the standard macroeconomic arguments for flexibility had less to do with their predictions about independence than with the now-evident defects in the macroeconomic paradigms, both Keynesian and monetarist, on which they were based. That national economies failed to respond according to the predictions of ingenious 1960s models can be blamed on many aspects of human behavior that are usually assumed away for analytic convenience. Perhaps most important and surely most striking is the demonstrated capacity of market participants for profitable innovation—a description more optimistic than the pejorative "structural instability" sometimes conjured up to explain the failure of econometric models to predict human behavior in times of rapid economic and social changes.[1]

Controlling Inflation

A related issue in the pre-1973 debate concerned the implications of the exchange-rate regime for the propensity of national officials to engage in inflationary policies. According to one standard argument, "the need to defend a fixed rate or a par value induces monetary and fiscal authorities to take greater care to prevent inflation; if floating rates were adopted, discipline would be weakened and countries would be more likely to pursue inflationary policies" (Solomon, 1977, p. 287). Indeed, the case for flexibility as a means of increasing macroeconomic independence implies precisely that some nations will opt for higher inflation rates when freed from the "external constraint" of a fixed parity. A similar but distinct argument is that a democratic government (or even one that is not so democratic) may find defense of a par value a politically acceptable reason to resist the competing claims of various domestic groups for increased shares of a relatively fixed national income (Caves and Jones, 1973, p. 444). As Caves and Jones note, however, a government might just as well point to "disgraceful" depreciation of a flexible rate. In the post-1973 period some have done exactly that.

The standard arguments sometimes acknowledged the inflationary potential of exchange-rate changes themselves, whether rates are flexible or adjustable, but only after 1973 did attention shift to this line of causation and thus away from the "nail-the-flag-to-the-masthead" argument for fixed rates. Although the inflationary pressures attending any devaluation or depreciation had long been emphasized by experts on less-developed countries, analyses for the industrialized nations tended to ignore the possibility, perhaps because of their Keynesian underpinnings. For example, the "absorption" literature stressed the importance of aggregate excess capacity in determining the degree to which the effects of a devaluation would be quickly offset by induced inflation.

The post-1973 inflationary experience was too dramatic to be ignored. Much subsequent debate has therefore centered on whether flexibility provides an independent source of inflationary pressure via a "ratchet" mechanism that pushes up domestic prices when a currency's value declines but fails to push them down at times of currency appreciation. Despite its intuitive appeal, however, empirical evidence for the ratchet effect appears to be weak (Goldstein, 1980). One important competing explanation for the failure to anticipate fully the inflationary impact of devaluation or depreciation was the tendency to underestimate the true openness of industrial economies, or, more precisely, the strength of the linkage between international prices of traded goods and domestic prices of nontraded goods (on this linkage, see Chipman, 1981, and McKinnon, 1981).

Living with Exchange Risk

Pre-1973 microeconomic arguments for floating exchange rates stressed their role in encouraging "unrestricted multilateral trade" (Friedman, 1953, p. 137). While rigidly fixed exchange rates like those of the classical gold standard were conceded to provide many of the benefits of a single world money, the Bretton Woods system of adjustable pegs had major shortcomings. Balance-of-payments disequilibria were frequently met by direct controls on trade and capital flows rather than the domestic macroeconomic policy responses prescribed by the "gold-standard rules of the game." Advocates of exchange-rate flexibility argued that it would produce appropriate exchange-rate movements, ensure prompt balance-of-payments adjustment, and thus obviate the need for direct controls that distort global resource allocation. But although proponents of flexible rates were virtually unanimous on this point, some critics foresaw incentives for protectionism (see, e.g., Wallich's comments in Haberler *et al.*, 1969, p. 362).

Of course, even pegged rates could and did change. Therefore, the appropriate comparison was not between floating and fixed rates but between rates changing by small amounts on a day-to-day basis and those changing by substantial percentages at longer intervals and usually only after macroeconomic policy debacles, welfare-reducing direct controls, and repeated foreign-exchange-market crises. Some critics warned, however, that the day-to-day movements of floating rates would not be small. Skeptics envisioned low price elasticities, long lags, exchange-rate overshooting, and destabilizing speculation that would result in wide fluctuations in market-determined rates—a specter of the 1930s that (along with competitive devaluation) the IMF Articles of Agreement specifically pledged to exorcise. Large fluctuations in rates, it was said, would increase the uncertainty facing international traders and investors. Although forward markets and a variety of other, more complicated mechanisms could provide transactors with insurance against rate changes, some warned that the additional cost would push world trade back toward barter (Kindleberger, 1970, p. 224).

Subsequent events have provided ample reason for extreme modesty on the part of prognosticators in both camps. Market-determined exchange rates have exhibited instability beyond the fondest nightmares of fixed-rates fanatics, yet trade and investment flows seem relatively unaffected by these changes. Blackhurst and Tumlir (1980, pp. 13–16) have noted that the volume of world trade continued to grow more rapidly than production throughout the 1970s, consistent with their hypothesis that the major determinant of changes in the level of trade is underlying GNP growth. Examining the effects of exchange-rate uncertainty on the multilateral and bilateral trade flows of the United States, Germany, and several other industrial countries for the period 1965–75, Hooper and Kohlhagen (1978, p. 505) "found absolutely no significant effect on the volume of trade (at the 0.95 level) despite considerable effort and experimentation. . . ." They did find a significant impact on prices, suggesting that the absence of any impact on volume might reflect relatively inelastic short-run supplies of exports or, alternatively, substantial hedging by importers and exporters.

These apparently contradictory phenomena may also be reconciled by the observation that the only alternatives to risky international transactions are risky domestic transactions. Of the many large risks of all types that any commercial endeavor now entails, exchange-rate uncertainty may be relatively minor compared with the benefits of foreign trade and investment. The risk is appreciable but the profitability even more so. As foreign-exchange risk is highly diversifiable, international operations provide an important means of diluting risks associated with domestic transactions rather than an independent addition to risk.

MARKET-DETERMINED EXCHANGE RATES

The central message of recent experience is that the foreign-exchange market is an asset market and that the economic laws governing exchange rates are fundamentally similar to those governing other asset prices—with stock and bond markets providing obvious domestic analogies. In fact, while exchange rates have indeed been volatile, their volatility has been less than that of stock prices (Frenkel and Mussa, 1980). Some recent literature has attempted to judge whether the volatility of observed asset prices is "excessive," i.e., unjustified by movements in their fundamental determinants. Shiller (1981) found evidence that the volatility of stock prices is excessive in relation to underlying uncertainty about future dividends, at least if risk neutrality is assumed. Although his statistical methodology has been questioned by subsequent researchers, any similar test of exchange-rate behavior rests on still shakier ground. As Meese and Singleton (1982) have pointed out, a test of whether exchange-rate volatility is excessive must be predicated on the validity of a particular structural model, and there are several active contenders. Furthermore, as Frenkel and Mussa note, even a determination of excessive volatility has no obvious policy implications.

Related to these findings is the discovery that the celebrated "law of one price" is not strictly enforced by real-world markets and that purchasing power parity, which perhaps ought not to have held in any case, has evidently collapsed (Frenkel, 1981).[2] As a consequence, the once-prevalent notion that an exchange rate behaves like the ratio of two national price indices must be scrapped and the role of exchange-rate movements in equilibrating international transactions reevaluated.

Controls on Trade and Capital Flows

A market-determined exchange rate necessarily equates day-to-day supply and demand for a nation's currency, whether or not supplemented by official reserve transactions. Thus, the need for direct controls motivated by overall balance-of-payments considerations is indeed eliminated by floating rates. The result has been, as predicted, an important reduction in the use of capital controls for balance-of-payments purposes. But asset preferences can and do produce significant prolonged divergences between the market price of a currency and its apparent "real" worth as determined by purchasing power parity. There is therefore no reason to expect a floating-rate system to eliminate incentives for direct controls motivated by current-account considerations.

While current-account balances have exhibited surprising (though lagged) responsiveness to rate movements, the reverse effect of current-account imbalances on exchange-rate movements is evidently much weaker. Indeed, floating rates react only to the extent that current-account imbalances constitute one type of "news" affecting asset preferences. Accordingly, macroeconomic incentives for protection, to increase domestic aggregate demand as well as to achieve sector-specific goals, are largely unaffected by floating rates.

The actual post-1973 experience has been characterized by the persistence and even extension of sectoral protection in the major industrialized countries, mainly for industries that are losing their competitiveness in relation to counterparts in Japan and especially the newly industrializing countries. Although there has been no apparent trend toward the increased use of protection (or competitive devaluation) as a means of macroeconomic stimulus, an assumed net gain in aggregate employment is customarily used—as in the Bretton Woods era—to bolster the case for proposed sectoral interventions, especially when large industries such as apparel and automobiles are involved.

The Cambridge Economic Policy Group has promulgated a macroeconomic case for across-the-board protection of British industry, but with no noticeable effect thus far on the policies of the Thatcher government. Japan is sometimes accused of engaging in policies to prevent appreciation of the yen, especially through restrictions on inward foreign investment. But the main evidence presented in support of this hypothesis is unbalanced bilateral trade with the United States, a condition that also accompanied an allegedly overvalued yen in previous years.

Further aspects of the relationship between protection and exchange-rate movements are considered in subsequent sections.

Implications for Foreign Direct Investment

The "overvalued" dollar of the 1960s was singled out as an important reason, even *the* important reason, for the large volume of U.S. direct investment abroad, particularly in Europe. Through acquisitions of existing national enterprises and the construction of new plant and equipment, U.S.-based multinationals achieved a major presence in the protected markets of the newly created European Economic Community—investments all the more attractive at prevailing exchange rates. This role of disequilibrium exchange rates in foreign-investment decisions was initially confirmed by events of the 1970s. As the dollar plummeted in relative value through two devaluations and subsequent market depreciation, foreign direct investment in the United States grew with unprecedented rapidity—enough to make the United States the world's leading *host* country (in absolute but not relative terms) by the end of the decade. Yet the strengthening of the dollar since 1978 has not stemmed the flow of new foreign direct investment, and exchange-rate volatility has had no noticeable impact on its volume.

Why have foreign investors been undeterred by exchange-rate turbulence? There are several plausible lines of explanation, not mutually exclusive, that invoke the *relative* advantages of multinational firms over national enterprises. Thus, the finding that foreign direct investment continued to increase after 1973 does not rule out real costs associated with increased exchange-rate uncertainty.

As already noted, one anticipated benefit of floating that has actually materialized is a marked reduction in the use of direct capital controls. This trend facilitates new or expanded investments, while at the same time increasing their attractiveness by improving prospects for the unimpeded repatriation of profits and royalties. Moreover, direct investment decisions are based on long-term plans, for periods during which even a pegged rate might well be expected to change. Over the life of an investment, the effects of volatility on profits largely cancel out, whereas cumulative movements in exchange rates, whether pegged or floating, mainly compensate for differential rates of domestic inflation or productivity growth across countries. A floating-rate system might even stimulate investment by easing such compensating exchange-rate adjustments and thereby reducing the likelihood of new direct controls on capital or trade flows during the investment period.

Foreign direct investment is also influenced by many considerations apart from exchange risk or the lack of it. If, as past studies suggest, protection is an important motive for direct investment, the recent protectionist swing in the United States—both actual and threatened—may have elicited investments intended to protect large expenditures already incurred in the development of the lucrative U.S. market. Recent Japanese investments in the United States may fall into this category. Furthermore, the accumulation of wealth by OPEC surplus nations has increased demands for assets of all kinds, and the post-1973 "internationalization" of the supply of saving probably favors U.S. assets because of the relative size and stability of the American economy. However, official statistics are uninformative on this point, since many OPEC investments are held anonymously through third-country intermediaries.

Finally, as suggested above and exactly contrary to pre-1973 conventional wisdom, floating may provide an important independent incentive for foreign direct investment. Input-price uncertainty is a recognized motive for vertical integration; a regime of floating rates accordingly provides incentives for vertical multinational integration. Together with centralized management, vertical integration allows a substantial reduction in the variability of profits due to exchange-rate movements between input-source countries and the downstream user.[3] This explanation fits the Canadian floating-rate period, which was marked by continued expansion of U.S. direct investments in Canadian extractive industries. Likewise, the reduction of input-price uncertainty may be a second motive (in addition to increased actual and threatened protection) for recent Japanese investments in the United States. Horizontal global expansion may similarly be favored by floating rates. For production operations in which minimum efficient scale is relatively low or scale economies unimportant, global diversification of production facilities allows firms some opportunity to optimize with respect to medium-term movements in real exchange rates as well as enhanced leverage in dealings with national labor unions.[4]

The vertical and horizontal expansions motivated by exchange-rate variability help to explain the rapid growth of intra-industry and intra-firm trade during the 1970s. They have opposite implications, however, for the responsiveness of trade flows to movements in exchange rates. While vertical integration allows a firm to ignore changes in the rate, horizontal integration offers opportunities to profit from them through adjustments in trade flows.

EXCHANGE RATES, RELATIVE PRICES, AND COMPETITIVENESS

A major surprise of the 1970s was the discovery that the United States is not a closed economy. The old and erroneous characterization (see, e.g., comments by Wallich in Haberler *et al.*, 1969, pp. 360–361) rested in part on a confusion of *traded* with *tradable* goods; for a large country like the United States, openness is consistent with low ratios of exports and imports to total domestic shipments.[5] Closely linked was the failure to anticipate the importance of exchange-rate changes for domestic prices. Early and crude estimates of the inflationary impact of dollar devaluation assumed that the prices of imported goods would be the only ones affected.

Elasticities and the Law of One Price

Analysts had been misled in part by the traditional elasticities approach to exchange-rate changes. The elasticities approach entailed a basically Keynesian view of price movements. Domestic-currency prices (or supply curves) for exports and import substitutes were assumed to be independent of the exchange rate. A related assumption, crucial but always implicit, was that domestic and foreign goods are not highly substitutable, so that domestic producers of tradables face appreciably downward-sloping demand curves for their outputs even in the long run. Given these assumptions, the primary effect of a devaluation would be to alter the relative prices of domestic goods and their foreign counterparts, shifting domestic and foreign demands toward domestic goods. A devaluing nation with some excess capacity could therefore expect a durable improvement in the international price competitiveness of its export and import-competing industries and a resulting durable improvement in its trade balance. The same logic was carried over to open-economy versions of Keynesian macroeconomic models, in which the exchange rate served as a policy instrument for switching aggregate expenditure between foreign and domestic markets.

The unexpectedly large impact of exchange-rate changes on domestic prices in the United States, along with the many cases in which devaluation failed to produce a durable improvement in the trade balance, led analysts to discard the elasticities approach and its underlying assumptions. With considerable fanfare, the era of the monetary approach was ushered in. Central to the elasticities approach is the implicit assumption that the law of one price is not applicable; domestic-currency prices of domestically produced tradables can move independently of the domestic-currency prices of their foreign counterparts. Exponents of the monetary approach chose an opposite but equally extreme assumption, making the law of one price the centerpiece of their models. Domestically produced exports and import-competing goods were now taken to be perfect substitutes for their foreign counterparts; accordingly, their domestic-currency prices were necessarily identical at all times.

Under these new assumptions, a devaluation must increase the prices of domestically produced tradables to restore equality with the prices of their foreign substitutes. For a small country, the domestic prices of all tradables would rise by exactly the amount of the devaluation. Accordingly, an exchange-rate change affects primarily the prices of tradables relative to those of nontradables, rather than the prices of domestic goods relative to those of foreign goods. While the higher relative prices of tradables implies an increase in their domestic supply, domestic demand is shifted *away* from all tradables toward nontradables, eventually raising the prices of the latter and restoring the initial allocation of resources in domestic production. A key implication of such models is that devaluation cannot improve the internal price competitiveness of domestic suppliers.

But again events confounded theories, and again the problem centered on the law of one price—unduly disregarded in the elasticities approach but exalted beyond empirical justification by advocates of the monetary approach. As producers of almost any tradable good will be happy to affirm, exchange-rate movements *are* important for the overall international competitiveness of domestic industries; for some nonnegligible period, exchange-rate movements can and do alter the prices of domestic goods relative to those of foreign goods.

While the law of one price (for any one "good") assumes a high degree of substitutability in consumption or production between domestic tradables and their foreign counterparts, as well as markets that are highly competitive, empirical investigation reveals that these conditions do not hold for most tradable goods, at least over the relatively short periods with which macroeconomic policy is concerned. Rather, for reasons having to do with product differentiation, trade barriers, delivery lags, distribution, and servicing, tradables are heterogeneous in their adherence to the law of one price, or, more precisely, in their adherence to its preconditions. "Substantial changes in exchange rates typically have substantial and persistent effects on the relative common currency prices of closely matched manufactures produced in different countries" (Isard, 1977, p. 948).

Recognizing that tradable goods are heterogeneous brings the analysis almost full circle to a framework in which elasticities again play a key role. An important implication is that the price effects of devaluation are not typically uniform across industries producing tradable goods.

Sectoral Consequences of Changes in Exchange Rates

Sector-specific consequences within the aggregate of "tradables" attracted the attention of econometric modelers first (see, e.g., Hooper and Lowrey, 1979). More recently, theorists have also begun to explore the crucial role of "structural" characteristics such as supply elasticities and wage rigidities of wage indexation in open-economy macroeconomic analysis, thereby sacrificing some of the simplicity and elegance of highly aggregated models but shedding new light on sectoral effects (see Branson, 1982, and references cited there).

Where substitutability and therefore cross-price elasticities are high and markets competitive, there will be strong forces equating the domestic-currency prices of foreign-produced goods with those of domestically produced versions. A devaluation will therefore cause domestic prices to rise—by the full amount of a devaluation in the case of a small country that has no appreciable effect on international prices. Domestic supply, employment, and profits will rise; domestic consumption will fall.

For an industry in which domestic and foreign versions are highly imperfect substitutes, devaluation has much weaker short-run consequences for the domestic price. The increased domestic-currency price of the imperfect foreign substitute results in an outward shift in the domestic industry's downward-sloping demand curve. The effects on equilibrium price thus depend crucially on conditions of domestic supply. Domestic output, employment, and profits will rise; domestic and foreign consumption of the industry's output will rise on account of the favorable movement in its relative price. Moreover, with goods or services that are highly differentiated, each *producer* faces a distinctly downward-sloping demand curve, so that markets may be characterized by price discrimination. In such markets, an exchange-rate change may actually have a "perverse" effect on output and price, although not on profits.

Exchange-rate changes also affect industry supply curves through their consequences for the domestic-currency prices of tradable inputs. As noted above, the size of price changes depends critically upon the extent to which foreign and domestic versions are highly substitutable; the speed with which these price changes are reflected in higher production costs depends on the extent to which suppliers are bound by long-term commitments. One measure of the total impact of devaluation on a given industry through both output and input markets is the *net* effect on industry value added. As in the analysis of the "effective protection" that a nation's tariff schedule provides to a particular industry, i.e., the percentage by which industry value added per unit of output can exceed its free-trade level, a calculation can in principle be made of the *net* effect of "exchange-rate protection" on an industry's value added. A devaluation will raise domestic-currency value added by exactly the percentage of the devaluation only for an industry in which domestic and foreign goods are highly substitutable on both the output and input sides *and* effects on world prices of the industry's output sales and input purchases are negligible. Otherwise, either a smaller or larger increment is possible.

A last dimension of the sectoral consequences of devaluation concerns the division of increased industry value added between industry-specific and mobile factors. If the supply of mobile factors ("labor") is available at a fixed nominal reward, as in the case of a binding minimum wage, industry profits will increase by the full increment in value added. But because devaluation raises the cost of living and also tends to increase the demand for variable factors of production, there may be some upward adjustment in wages, whether determined by a competitive market, union contract negotiation, or legislation of a real minimum wage. On the other hand, devaluation—as opposed to depreciation of a floating rate—is often accompanied by an "incomes policy" intended to hold down wage adjustments, thus reducing the real wage and raising the proportion of increased industry value added accruing as profits.

Adjustments to Real Shocks

Although real shocks were hardly new in the 1970s, their interaction with a floating-rate system provided beleaguered policy analysts with considerable food for thought. As predicted, floating rates prevented the recurring exchange-market crises that no doubt would otherwise have accompanied the OPEC price shocks and ill-advised policy responses to them. And, although floating rates themselves did little to ease the adjustment of less-developed oil importers, most of which still peg their rates in any case, a largely private recycling process solved the immediate problem of inadequate balance-of-payments financing. Indeed, even critics of floating rates are usually quick to acknowledge that no alternative system could have survived the stormy 1970s. On the other hand, the actual adjustment process was quite different from that anticipated by most analysts, principally because of the unexpected ways in which OPEC surplus nations spent their vastly increased earnings.

According to the standard pre-1973 debate, flexible rates were supposed to insulate a country from external shocks, while fixed rates would allow the burden of internal shocks to be shared with trading partners. As already noted, the increased macroeconomic independence offered by flexible rates proved to be largely illusory. Moreover, the standard fixed vs. flexible arguments, based on conclusions from one-sector macroeconomic models, necessarily ignored the sector-specific impact of many shocks and thus obscured the sector-specific aspects of the resulting adjustment process. In response to this latter discovery, enterprising theorists have recently come forward with models of such hitherto uncelebrated maladies as "Dutch disease" (see, e.g., Corden, 1981, and Neary, 1982).

As in the analysis of exchange-rate changes, the crucial missing insight was that "the" tradables sector is in fact a set of heterogeneous industries. Furthermore, each has at any time a collection of industry-specific factors that can be shifted elsewhere only at considerable cost. Therefore, in a floating-rate system, the good fortune of one tradable-goods industry, whether technological progress, a mineral discovery, or a favorable price movement in the world market, can become bad news for other tradable-goods industries through two mechanisms: exchange-rate appreciation and the bidding up of rewards to factors mobile between sectors. The result is "Dutch disease" or "de-industrialization" or the problem of "lagging sectors," i.e., ones in which output falls and the rewards to industry-specific factors decline. Moreover, "the decline in the relative size of non-booming sectors is a necessary component of the economy's adjustment toward a higher level of income" (Heary, 1982, p. 20). Thus, a conflict arises between efficient resource allocation and certain other national objectives, such as developing and maintaining an industrial sector of a certain size or maintaining the incomes of sector-specific factors.

All this assumes, of course, that the exchange rate moves in the direction suggested by the effect on the current-account balance, an effect that may be weak in practice. Furthermore, a national government wishing to avoid the consequences of appreciation can intervene in the foreign-exchange market, directly or indirectly, thus protecting other tradables sectors from injury. Corden (1981) has suggested that this is a primary motive for "exchange-rate protection." In such a case, or with a pegged rate that is not revised upward, the good news means reserve accumulation and attendant inflationary pressure rather than appreciation. Thus, the problem of adjustment can at least be postponed—for better or worse. It would be for better if the good news were temporary or reversible, because a stable rate could eliminate the unpleasant and perhaps undesirable squeeze on other tradables, although probably at the cost of some inflation.

While a sensible comparison of effects under the two regimes requires some specification of the way in which private and official agents form expectations, the outcomes may be quite similar in the long run. The reason is that a macroeconomic policy cannot eradicate the "supercompetitiveness" of one tradable-goods sector over the rest. Through internal mechanisms such as competition for inputs, the less-competitive sectors will still be squeezed. For example, it is noteworthy that the balance (in current dollars) of U.S. trade in "high-technology" goods has grown almost exponentially since 1960, while the trade balance in all other manufactures is roughly its mirror image. There is no apparent discontinuity in this pattern between the 1960s and 1970s, except for a higher variability in the 1970s that probably reflects underlying macroeconomic fluctuations and large jumps in real exchange rates. But for a government determined to slow the movement of resources out of uncompetitive tradables industries, there is still an obvious solution in the form of sectoral intervention or "industrial policy."

CAUSES AND CONSEQUENCES OF PROTECTION

Freer trade was one widely anticipated advantage of flexible exchange rates that failed to materialize. The conventional wisdom predicted that exchange-rate flexibility would facilitate trade liberalization (e.g., Baldwin, 1970, pp. 20–21, and Bergsten, 1972, pp. 8–9). Yet the post-1973 period has in fact been marked by the proliferation of new and subtle trade-distorting measures. Furthermore, Bergsten and Williamson (1982) offer evidence that exchange-rate volatility has actually intensified the ever-present clamor for more and better protection from foreign competition.

According to the usual pre-1973 argument, exchange-rate flexibility would eliminate the perceived need for protection and in any case neutralize its benefits. This argument rested on errors concerning both the motives for protection and its consequences in a flexible-rate system. A floating rate obviates the perceived need for direct controls on foreign transactions only to the extent that protection is motivated by overall balance-of-payments considerations; it does not eliminate incentives for protection as a tool of macroeconomic stabilization or to achieve sector-specific goals. The implicit assumption that balance-of-payments considerations dominated trade-policy choices before 1973 may have stemmed from a confusion of the underlying motives for protection with the public rhetoric used to justify it.[6] Since overall balance-of-payments considerations were in most instances merely a secondary motive for protection, the elimination of this motive has had only minor consequences for its use.

Sectoral Consequences of Protection

Gains achieved by protected domestic industries would be completely off-set by resulting exchange-rate movements only under highly implausible circumstances. The notion that it is somehow irrational for industries to seek protection because it will be offset by currency appreciation (Friedman, 1981) is another example of the misleading conclusions that are drawn from macroeconomic models with insufficient "structure." In both industrialized and developing countries, real-world protection is a microeconomic, industry-specific phenomenon. Although broad coalitions may form to support or oppose major changes in national trade legislation, the level and type of actual protection are almost always determined on an industry-by-industry basis. Even the "across-the-board" tariff cuts achieved in the Kennedy Round of multilateral trade negotiations singled out numerous specific industries for exemptions from cuts. Too many recent macroeconomic analyses of protection are based on models in which only one good is produced domestically (e.g., Eichengreen, 1981). These models provide useful insights concerning asset-market channels through which protection can have unanticipated and complex general-equilibrium consequences. But, because they necessarily omit the important sector-specific effects that are at the very heart of trade policy, they can provide only partial, and sometimes misleading, information concerning the real-world policies that presumably motivate their construction.

As soon as its industry-specific nature is recognized, the analysis of protection becomes identical to that of the industry-specific shocks discussed in the previous section. Protection of some tradables is likely to worsen the economic prospects of other, less-favored tradables. As before, whether the protection of some industries transforms others into lagging sectors depends in part on whether the exchange rate actually appreciates. In the case of protection, however, the outcome has an additional element of ambiguity, since some protective devices, such as "voluntary" export restraints, can cause a deterioration rather than an improvement in the trade balance and hence a depreciation rather than an appreciation (to the extent that the trade balance does influence the exchange rate); see Meade's classic analysis (1951, Chap. XXI) and Richardson's (1982) treatment of "modern" commercial policy. Adequate analysis of industry-specific effects requires a model with at least two sectors producing tradable outputs.

Identification of sectoral consequences also helps to clarify the underlying rational motives for apparently irrational policies. One particularly interesting example is the prevalence of overvalued exchange rates among developing countries, along with extensive trade and credit controls. Taken together as a coherent policy package, this adds up to a hefty subsidy to a preferred sector, typically import-competing industrial production. While trade barriers protect domestic markets, an overvalued exchange rate allows required capital equipment and intermediate inputs to be purchased at bargain prices, and capital-export prohibitions facilitate access to low-cost credit. The resulting disadvantage to producers of other tradables is one important reason for the much-remarked failure of third-world agriculture to achieve the production levels suggested by its obvious comparative advantage. Like all generalizations regarding developing countries, this one clearly disregards many important national differences. However, the pattern seems to fit a large number of countries.

Volatility and Protectionism

The volatility of the dollar since 1973 has resulted in prolonged departures from purchasing power parity and large exogenous swings in the international competitiveness of U.S. producers of tradable goods. The unexpected increase in protectionism over the same period raises the question whether the current system has actually been an important *cause* of increased protectionism.

Bergsten and Williamson (1982) have recently suggested that there is a "ratchet" effect of exchange-rate fluctuations on the average level of protection.[7] While prolonged overvaluation of the dollar gives rise to new arguments for all manner of sectoral protection, as in 1981 and 1982, any new protection is likely to persist long after the overvaluation has disappeared. Moreover, they argue, even undervaluation might add to protectionist pressures by attracting resources into industries with secularly declining international competitiveness, or at least slowing their exit. When the inappropriately low currency value finally moves upward again, protection will be demanded.

While this hypothesis is intuitively appealing and seems consistent with the recent protectionist fever in the U.S. Congress, there is again a problem of distinguishing appropriately between the underlying motives for protection and its public justification. The quest for favorable government intervention (in all forms, including, but certainly not limited to, trade policies) is a fact of economic life. As long as governments are responsive to demands for sectoral intervention, efforts to obtain, retain, and increase such benefits represent a capital investment comparable to research and development, advertising, and other intangibles that have a favorable impact on profits. (The analogy is imperfect, however, because investment in obtaining favorable government intervention is usually undertaken by a trade association or labor union and therefore has a "free rider" aspect that does not occur with most advertising or R & D.) However, managers, union officials, and the public do tend to view asymmetrically profits vs. losses and overtime vs. layoffs. Therefore, both the industry "demand" for government intervention and its politically determined "supply" may be expected to increase when national unemployment is high, as in 1981–82. Furthermore, while protection is only one possible type of favorable legislative or administrative action among many (including government procurement regulatory or tax relief, technical assistance, and subsidized credit), the political cost of intervention in this particular form is probably less when the exchange rate is widely acknowledged to be overvalued, as in 1981–82. For these political-economic reasons, it is plausible to expect industry–specific intervention to increase when national unemployment is high and to take the specific form of new trade barriers when the dollar is overvalued.

Yet the actual cases cited to support this link between protection and overvaluation (e.g., textiles, steel, sugar, shoes) are ones with chronic competitiveness problems, not fundamentally healthy industries put temporarily into the red by an overvalued dollar. For some, protection from imports is a national vice extending back into the 1950s. This suggests that exchange-rate overvaluation can provide the politically expedient occasion for new protection of declining industries, interacting with other determinants of increased protectionism, without being the fundamental cause. It must also be noted that the empirical evidence for the persistence of sectoral intervention seems to be weak. Because of strong domestic lobbies against, as well as in favor of, protection, import relief provides only a brief respite for many industries from the consequences of shifting comparative advantage.

CONCLUDING REMARKS

Much of the pre-1973 debate on international monetary reform proved to be irrelevant, for two reasons. First, international political realities precluded the "choice" or "design" of a new system. Perhaps Bretton Woods was a unique phenomenon, at least for modern times. But, more important, the post-1973 system of flexible exchange rates has functioned in ways that are markedly different from the predictions of most analysts on either side of the debate.

In many regards, the academic arguments in favor of increased flexibility never improved on Friedman's pioneering (1953) case. Yet Friedman, as well as most others, erred in their most fundamental prediction, that flexible rates would be stable if national monetary policies were stable. We live in times of too much daily economic "news" from other sources to avoid large fluctuations in market-determined exchange rates. As Mussa aptly remarked, "The smoothly adjusting exchange rate is, like the unicorn, a mythical beast" (1979, p. 9). Moreover, while these fluctuations probably do imply significant real costs to those engaged in international commerce, their effects on trade and investment flows are very different than anticipated. In particular, day-to-day movements in currency values offer an independent motive for international transactions, as a means of diversifying exchange risk.

If there is a single salient lesson to be learned by scrutinizing academic research on exchange rates in the light of post-1973 events in the international monetary system, it is the great mischief that can come from paying insufficient attention to economic structure in macroeconomic analysis. While theorists necessarily strip reality down to a bare minimum of basic relationships, the same basics are not appropriate for all questions. For the large number of policy issues arising from the interactions of individual industries within a single economy, macroeconomic models with only one aggregate tradable can provide at best a partial understanding and sometimes a seriously flawed account.

NOTES

1. Meese and Rogoff (1983) found that a random walk performed as well out of sample as any estimated structural model of exchange-rate determination. In an earlier version of the same paper (Meese and Rogoff, 1981), the authors attributed the poor out-of-sample performance of these models to "structural instability." But the authors noted in the revised version that it is more accurate to describe the problem as one of omitted variables or other misspecifications of the underlying structural relationships. In other words, simple models cannot predict complex responses.

2. Although there is a rich literature spanning at least four decades on the reasons why purchasing power parity need not hold over short or even long time periods (see, e.g., Chipman, 1981), the notion persists that its absence somehow violates fundamental precepts of rational economic behavior.

3. Centralized management also facilitates optimization of foreign-exchange exposure, reducing the need for forward-market cover. Aliber (1983) has suggested that the lower cost of internal cover provides an advantage to multinational firms over domestic ones.

4. Expanded international operations in the 1970s may also reflect efforts to minimize the impact of exchange-rate movements on reported profits. Despite all the good reasons adduced by economic theorists to show that rational managers should be indifferent to the variability of accounting profits, managers persist in their concern about period-to-period fluctuations in reported earnings. F.A.S.B. Statement Number 8, the Financial Accounting Standards Board's first attempt to develop standardized accounting principles for a world of day-to-day movements in exchange rates, resulted in large and probably meaningless fluctuations in reported earnings (Hekman, 1981). The resulting storm of protests produced F.A.S.B. Statement Number 52, which broadens the definition of exposure and calls for an adjustment to net worth rather than to earnings.

5. Openness also increased in the 1970s, but authors of textbooks on macroeconomics nonetheless continue to relegate any consideration of openness to the final chapters.

6. Two indirect pieces of evidence for the dominance of other motives are levels of protection that vary markedly across industries and the use of quantitative restrictions with ambiguous balance-of-payments consequences. However, any positive balance-of-payments consequences can be viewed as reducing the political cost of providing protection to favored sectors.

7. Bergsten and Williamson call for policies to ensure that the value of the dollar does not stray too far from its "fundamental equilibrium rate," defined by analogy to the Bretton Woods criterion of fundamental disequilibrium for a parity change and distinguished from day-to-day market equilibrium. But while uncontroversial arguments in favor of greater stability constitute much of the paper, there is no indication of how the authors' proposed solution (which amounts to a wide-band peg and would thus appear to share many of the flaws that led to the end of the Bretton Woods system) could be successfully implemented.

REFERENCES

Aliber, Robert Z., "Money, Multinationals, and Sovereigns," in Charles P. Kindleberger and David B. Audretsch, eds., *The Multinational Corporation in the 1980s*, Cambridge, Mass., MIT Press, 1983.

Baldwin, Robert, *Non-Tariff Distortions of International Trade*, Washington, D.C., The Brookings Institution, 1970.

Bergsten, C. Fred, *The Cost of Import Restrictions to American Consumers*, New York, American Importers Association, 1972.

Bergsten, C. Fred, and John Williamson, "Exchange Rates and Trade Policy," paper prepared for the Institute for International Economics Conference on Trade Policy in the Eighties, Washington, D.C., June 23–25, 1982.

Blackhurst, Richard, and Jan Tumlir, *Trade Relations under Flexible Exchange Rates*, Geneva, General Agreement on Tariffs and Trade, September 1980.

Branson, William H., "Economic Structure and Policy for External Balance," paper prepared for the NBER/IMF Conference on Policy Interdependence, Washington, D.C., Aug. 31, 1982.

Caves, Richard E., and Ronald W. Jones, *World Trade and Payments*, Boston, Little, Brown, 1973.

Chipman, John, "Internal-External Price Relationships in the West German Economy, 1958–79," *Zeitschrift für die gesamte Staatswissenschaft*, 137 (September 1981), pp. 612–637.

Cooper, Richard N., *The Economics of Interdependence*, New York, McGraw-Hill for the Council on Foreign Relations, 1968.

Corden, W. M., "Exchange Rate Protection," in R. N. Cooper *et al.*, eds., *The International Monetary System under Flexible Exchange Rates: Global, Regional, and National*, Cambridge, Mass., Ballinger, 1981.

Eichengreen, Barry, "A Dynamic Model of Tariffs, Output and Employment under Flexible Exchange Rates," *Journal of International Economics*, 11 (August 1981), pp. 341–359.

Frenkel, Jacob A., "The Collapse of Purchasing Power Parities during the 1970s," *European Economic Review*, 16 (May 1981), pp. 145–165.

Frenkel, Jacob A., and Michael L. Mussa, "The Efficiency of Foreign Exchange Markets and Measures of Turbulence," *American Economic Review*, 70 (May 1980), pp. 374–381.

Friedman, Milton, "The Case for Flexible Exchange Rates," in *Essays in Positive Economics*, Chicago, University of Chicago Press, 1953.

———, "Do Imports Cost Jobs?" *Newsweek* (Feb. 9, 1981), p. 77.

Goldstein, Morris, *Have Flexible Exchange Rates Handicapped Macroeconomic Policy?* Special Papers in International Economics No. 14, Princeton, N.J., Princeton University, International Finance Section, 1980.

Haberler, Gottfried, Henry C. Wallich, Peter B. Kenen, and Fritz Machlup, "Round Table on Exchange Rate Policy," *American Economic Review*, 59 (May 1969), pp. 357–369.

Hekman, Christine R., "Foreign Exchange Risk: Relevance and Management," *Managerial and Decision Economics*, 2 (1981), pp. 256–262.

Hooper, Peter, and Steven W. Kohlhagen, "The Effect of Exchange Rate Uncertainty on the Prices and Volume of International Trade," *Journal of International Economics*, 8 (November 1978), pp. 483–511.

Hooper, Peter, and Barbara Lowrey, "Impact of the Dollar Depreciation on the U.S. Price Level: An Analytical Survey of Empirical Estimates," International Finance Discussion Paper No. 128, Washington, D.C., Board of Governors of the Federal Reserve System, January 1979.

International Monetary Fund, *The Role of Exchange Rates in the Adjustment of International Payments*, Washington, D.C., 1970.

———, *Reform of the International Monetary System*, Washington, D.C., 1972.

Isard, Peter, "How Far Can We Push the 'Law of One Price'?" *American Economic Review*, 67 (December 1977), pp. 942–948.

Kindleberger, Charles P., *Power and Money*, New York, Basic Books, 1970.

McKinnon, Ronald I., "The Exchange Rate and Macroeconomic Policy: Changing Postwar Perceptions," *Journal of Economic Literature*, 19 (June 1981), pp. 531–557.

Meade, James E., *The Balance of Payments*, London, *Oxford University Press* 1951.

Meese, Richard, and Kenneth, Rogoff, "Empirical Exchange Rate Models of the Seventies: Are Any Fit to Survive?" International Finance Discussion Paper No. 184, Washington, D.C., Board of Governors of the Federal Reserve System, June 1981.

———, "Empirical Exchange Rate Models of the Seventies: Do They Fit out of Sample?" *Journal of International Economics*, 14 (February 1983), pp. 3–24.

Meese, Richard A., and Kenneth J. Singleton, "Rational Expectations and the Volatility of Floating Exchange Rates," unpublished paper, 1982.

Mussa, Michael, "Empirical Regularities in the Behavior of Exchange Rates and Theories of the Foreign Exchange Market," *Carnegie-Rochester Conference Series on Public Policy,* 11 (1979), pp. 9–55.

Neary, J. Peter, "Real and Monetary Aspects of the 'Dutch Disease'," paper prepared for the International Economic Association Conference on Structural Adjustment in Trade-Dependent Advanced Economies, Yxtaholm, Sweden, Aug. 2–6, 1982.

Richardson, J. David, "Four Observations on Modern International Commercial Policy under Floating Exchange Rates," *Carnegie-Rochester Conference Series on Public Policy,* 16 (Spring 1982), pp. 187–220.

Shiller, Robert J., "Do Stock Prices Move Too Much to Be Justified by Subsequent Changes in Dividends?" *American Economic Review,* 71 (June 1981), pp. 421–436.

Solomon, Robert, *The International Monetary System, 1945–1976*, New York, Harper & Row, 1977.

19. The Case for Managed Exchange Rates

JOHN WILLIAMSON

The case for managing the exchange rate rests on the costs imposed by volatility and misalignments: the measures developed in the previous section show that both have been large and, if anything, increasing under floating. This section therefore proceeds to examine the nature of the costs involved. Having concluded that the major problems are those posed by misalignments, it goes on to enquire into possible causes of misalignments and subsequently to ask what would be sacrificed in using monetary policy to limit misalignments. The case for a managed rather than free-floating exchange rate rests on the judgment that the costs of misalignments exceed the benefits of treating the exchange rate as a residual in policy determination.

COSTS OF VOLATILITY

It has traditionally been argued that an increase in price uncertainty resulting from more volatile exchange rates would lead to a reduction in trade and other international transactions. There is no doubt that a great deal of intraday volatility leads to wider buy-sell spreads, and those higher exchange transaction costs presumably do something to curtail trade, but spreads are still so low that the effect is minimal. What is much more important is the possibility that uncertainty regarding the domestic currency value of receipts from foreign transactions may lead to a bias against foreign trade, perhaps accompanied by a bias toward increased direct foreign investment as a way of servicing foreign markets less exposed to the vagaries of volatile exchange rates. Economists have for some time been searching for such effects. Until recently no evidence had been presented that trade among the industrial countries had been hampered by exchange rate volatility (see Clark and Haulk, 1972; Makin, 1976; and Hooper and Kohlhagen, 1978), although

John Williamson has taught economics in Great Britain, Brazil, and the United States. He is currently a Senior Fellow at the Institute for International Economics in Washington, D.C.

there was some evidence that exchange rate uncertainty has inhibited the trade of developing countries (see Coes, 1981, on Brazil, and Diaz-Alejandro, 1976, pp. 66–69, on Columbia).[1] However, new work by Cushman (forthcoming) reports a significant negative effect of volatility of the real exchange rate on the trade level of several industrial countries.

That it proved easier to find evidence of the negative effect of exchange rate volatility on the trade of developing countries than it did in the case of the developed countries should not occasion surprise. Where adequate forward markets exist, traders can cover forward and so limit the impact of exchange rate volatility when they find this troubling. (It is not true that exchange risk can be *eliminated* by the use of forward markets, since there are virtually always lags between the decision to sign a contract and the ability to cover forward, as well as uncertainties about the precise time when payment will be received; but the impact of volatility can certainly be *reduced* by forward covering.) By and large, there exist reasonable forward markets, at least for short maturities, among the currencies of the industrial countries, but not for the currencies of the developing countries.

It has been suggested that short-run volatility of exchange rates may do something to contribute to longer run misalignments (Shafer and Loopesko, 1983). It is also true that volatility between the currencies of the industrial countries complicates the task of economic management in the developing countries, since it confronts these countries with the need to choose between stabilizing their effective exchange rates (which minimizes macroeconomic shocks) and stabilizing their bilateral rate against a major trading currency (which minimizes the risk of traders, who need to invoice in a specific currency).[2] Furthermore, exchange rate volatility diverts considerable managerial talent to the commercially necessary but socially unproductive activity of covering not only trade risk but also balance-sheet positions (even on a quarterly basis). But for all that, exchange rate volatility is a nuisance rather than a major source of concern: if this were the *principal* drawback in present arrangements, it is doubtful whether it would be worth contemplating major changes.

COSTS OF MISALIGNMENTS

The costs of misalignments have received surprisingly little analysis in the economics literature up to now, presumably because misalignments—as opposed to volatility—have not traditionally been recognized as a likely consequence of floating. Indeed, Shafer and Loopesko (1983) list as the first of four principal claims advanced by advocates of floating a decade ago that:

> Price-adjusted or real exchange rates would be maintained relatively constant by stabilizing speculation, and would change mainly in response to shifts or trends in the equilibrium terms of trade between economies.

In fact misalignments were not eliminated by floating; indeed, the measures of the previous section suggest that misalignments have been about as large under floating as they were in the breakdown stage of the Bretton Woods system, when the approach adopted above suggests they reached some 20 percent to 30 percent for both the dollar and yen.

Such efforts as have been made to identify the costs of misalignments have generally pointed to the costs to a particular country at a specific time: to the unemployment caused by overvaluation or the inflation resulting from undervaluation. (See, for example, the cover story in *Business Week*, 27 June 1983.) There is, however, something unsatisfactory in this approach, inasmuch as the unemployment in country A has two (at least partial) offsets—less unemployment in its trading partners, and less inflation for itself.[3] When the position of the country is reversed, as it presumably is sooner or later, the country will benefit from lower unemployment (though suffer from increased inflationary pressure). It is only insofar as this sequence leads to less satisfactory long-run performance than would be attainable with the exchange rate maintained at its fundamental equilibrium level that one is entitled to attribute the cost to misaligned exchange rates.

There would seem to be six distinguishable costs imposed by misaligned exchange rates. These need not all apply simultaneously: indeed, by their nature several of them are *alternatives*.

Consumption Variations

This cost was first analyzed by Hause (1966) and subsequently elaborated by Johnson (1966). Suppose, it was argued, a country maintains a pegged exchange rate at an overvalued level for a time. Then, to preserve full employment when confronted with the fall in export demand and the rise in imports consequential on overvaluation, it will have to expand demand for nontradable goods by enough to absorb the resources released from the tradable goods industries. But expanding demand for nontradables (especially when the substitution effect is pushing consumers to buy relatively more tradables) involves increasing consumption above the long-run sustainable level.

The policy also involves an unsustainable trade deficit, so in due course a devaluation occurs adequate to generate a current account surplus to recoup the reserve loss that resulted from the preceding overvaluation. To release resources for the balance of payments, consumption has to be cut back (even *below* the long-run sustainable level). But there is much evidence that most people feel worse off if they are obliged to vary their consumption sharply from one period to the next, even if their *average* level of consumption is no lower. Indeed, the notion forms the basis for the "permanent income hypothesis" and "life-cycle hypothesis," both of which postulate that people save primarily to even out their consumption stream to match their long-run, rather than current, income, and which are generally accepted as containing an important element of truth. Thus the dissatisfaction resulting from alternation of splurge and austerity constitutes the welfare cost of living with misaligned exchange rates.

Harry Johnson actually termed this "the welfare cost of exchange rate stabilization," on the implicit premise that significant misalignments would occur only when governments pegged exchange rates at levels that become misaligned, e.g., through differential inflation. It is obvious, however, that the analysis applies to misalignments *per se*, no matter what their source. It applies as much to the cutback in consumption that Americans must expect some time in the future to compensate for the looming trade deficit (the counterpart to present budgetary profligacy) as it does to the austerity that Mexicans are currently suffering as a consequence of having pursued similar policies in the period 1978–82; the difference in exchange regimes is immaterial. But the previous section suggests that misalignments have probably been as large since the advent of floating as they were in the worse phase of Bretton Woods. Johnson's label for this cost is a graphic illustration of the fact that economists failed to foresee that floating rates might lead to the large misalignments that have occurred.

Adjustment Costs

The cost discussed above presumes that resources can be shifted costlessly between industries producing tradable goods and those producing nontradables. In reality this is far from true. The labor and capital released from employment in the auto and steel industries in the United States as a result *inter alia* of dollar overvaluation cannot be redeployed costlessly into producing the missiles and running the video arcades that are the counterpart to the U.S. budget deficit.

Such adjustments can undoubtedly occur in the long run (however much noneconomists are prone to doubt it). But the process of adjustment requires the retraining of labor and the construction of new capital equipment, both of which absorb real resources. One of the reasons that the concept of the equilibrium real exchange rate is defined in long-run terms, as the rate that would be expected to secure an appropriate current account balance over the cycle as a whole, is precisely because it makes no sense to incur the costs that would be involved in shuttling resources back and forth so as to maintain continuous payments balance.

In a recent paper, J. David Richardson (1982) describes as "divergence mistakes" the errors that firms make when resource-allocation decisions are based on misleading price signals, such as misaligned exchange rates. He argues:

> Divergence mistakes are costly not only because of human aversion to risk, but also because temporary competitive imbalances can generate empty shelves and storage lots in one location, excessive inventories in another, and resource-diverting arbitrage that transfer goods from the latter location to the former. The three respective resource allocational costs associated with divergence mistakes are waste from rationing, waste from excessive stockpiles, and waste from unnecessary transportation and redistribution.

Adjustment costs have received a certain amount of attention in the trade literature, in the context of the dislocation costs involved in liberalizing trade. The general conclusion (e.g., Magee, 1972) seems to be that such costs are significant, though well worth incurring in order to effect a permanent improvement in the allocation of resources. Obviously the cost-benefit comparison would look very different if the costs were accepted not in order to achieve an allocational improvement, but rather in response to temporary (and thus misleading) price signals.

Unemployment

The discussion up to now has supposed that full employment is maintained when an overvaluation develops. But in fact a major reason that adjustment is costly is that it does not start instantaneously. In the first instance, the labor and capital released from US tradable-goods industries as a result of dollar overvaluation simply remain unemployed, running to waste. The process of retraining typically starts only after months and years of unemployment, while capital redeployment is usually possible only as capital depreciates. Indeed, because of the costs of redeploying resources between sectors, it makes sense to undertake such adjustment only if there is an expectation that the shift in demand will be long-lasting.

Where it is expected that an overvaluation will prove temporary, unemployment in the tradable goods industries is a rational response to misalignment. Whether it is also socially optimal depends on how temporary the misalignment turns out to be. One of the problems of unstructured floating is that it leaves every agent to make his own inexpert judgment as to whether a change in the exchange rate represents a signal that should influence resource allocation or a temporary blip that should be ignored. In consequence it may well be that a change in the real exchange rate that is needed to effect adjustment is initially largely ignored, leading to larger unemployment costs than are necessary.

Productive Capacity

In an uncertain world, firms cannot be sure when an overvaluation is sufficiently temporary to merit adjustment rather than a decision to ride out the period of slack demand. An overvalued exchange rate may therefore induce a firm to scrap capacity that could be productively employed at equilibrium prices. Similarly, multinationals may shift new investment overseas and come to rely on foreign sources of supply. Even if a firm is convinced that it is worth maintaining its capacity until the misalignment is corrected, its creditors may not be so convinced. Firms that would be viable on the basis of equilibrium relative prices may be forced into bankruptcy, and capacity may again be destroyed inappropriately in the process. Recent experience in both the United States and Britain suggests that these dangers of an erosion of the industrial base, or "deindustrialization," are all too real.

Analogous effects in overstimulating investment in the tradable goods sector may occur during a prolonged period of undervaluation, as arguably occurred in Germany and Japan in the 1960s. When the misalignment is corrected, the excessive investment will prove to have been unjustified and will have to be abandoned (or subsidized). If repeated misalignments give rise to great uncertainty about the equilibrium level of competitiveness, one might expect investment to be discouraged even though the exchange rate was not on average either overvalued or undervalued.

Ratchet Effects on Inflation

It has often been hypothesized that a sequence of overvaluations and undervaluations tends to ratchet up the price level more than would occur with the maintenance of a similar pressure of demand and a constant real exchange rate. It is observed that depreciation produces strong inflationary pressures; as prices of imported inputs and consumer goods rise in consequence of depreciation, the prices of domestically produced goods are pulled up too, and trade unions seek (and are in a strong position to obtain) wage rises needed to prevent an erosion of living standards. Appreciation, it is argued, does not induce equivalent pressures to cut domestic prices and wages.

This is not to argue that a combination of weak demand and overvaluation does not contribute to restraint in wage demands (witness the recent United Auto Workers "givebacks"), but merely that the restraint is weaker than the pressure for wage increases in the opposite situation. Consequently a depreciation followed by an appreciation will leave the price level higher than it would otherwise have been. A recent paper (Kuran, 1983) provides new theoretical support for the notion that firms may react asymmetrically to pressures for price rises and falls, with similar incentives generating a larger rise than fall.

There have been several empirical attempts to detect such a ratchet effect. Goldstein (1980, pp. 13–17) provided a careful survey of this literature. He found conclusive evidence that important prices decline in appreciating currencies and no evidence of an asymmetry with the rise in depreciating currencies. He also concluded that the econometric evidence is not favorable to the hypothesis that increases in costs have a significantly different effect on prices than decreases. He therefore concluded that the hypothesis is without empirical support. This is perhaps convincing if one is assessing the effects of short-run *volatility* of the exchange rate, where induced price changes might not have time to affect wage claims. But the finding is certainly not decisive so far as *misalignments* are concerned, inasmuch as all it shows is that no ratchet effect exists on *prices* for a given path of wages. Yet surely at least 80 percent of the concern about "downward price inflexibility" has always been about downward *wage* inflexibility, and specifically that a depreciation may encounter real wage resistance. Goldstein himself adds in a footnote:

> If wage-rate indexation formulas are asymmetrical or if real-wage resistance in general is asymmetrical, depreciations will raise labor costs by more than equivalent appreciations will lower them, thus imparting an upward bias to the inflation rate. In such circumstances, however, it is not clear why exchange rates rather than the wage-setting rules themselves should be regarded as inflationary, since any factor that moves the price level up and down will add to inflation in such an environment.

If one were assigning blame among various social institutions, one might well place more odium on the relevant wage-setting practices than on the exchange rate regime. But if one wants to know whether large and persistent exchange rate swings have unfortunate effects in the world in which we live, the stylized facts of downward wage inflexibility and real wage resistance imply that the answer is "yes."[4] Weak empirical support for this presumption was presented by Kenen and Pack (1980, p. 20, table 1).

Protectionism

It can be persuasively argued on both theoretical and empirical grounds that overvaluations tend to generate strong protectionist pressures. The theoretical argument observes that protection is demanded by industries that can plausibly blame a decline in demand on foreign competition. Demand does of course vary in response to the business cycle as well as foreign competition, and it is widely believed that recession is the principal source of protectionist pressures. But the 20 percent decline in demand in a typical industry as a result of a severe recession can easily be dwarfed by the effect of a 20 percent fall in the price of imports. Moreover, in the latter case the imports *are* the source of the domestic industry's troubles. Furthermore, the protectionist coalition is likely to be far broader when it is not just the industrial cripples that find themselves unable to match import competition.

It may be asked whether there is not likely to be an offsetting pressure in favor of trade liberalization that comes into play when a currency is undervalued. Such an effect is possible, although one may doubt whether it will be as strong as the protectionist pressures that arise in times of overvaluation. But, in addition, resources may be induced to enter export- and import-competing industries because of the artificially favorable competitive position generated by undervaluation. When the undervaluation subsequently disappears, those industries may then have to seek import restrictions or subsidies to avoid sharp cutbacks in their scale of operation. Thus over time a sequence of overvaluation and undervaluation is likely to ratchet up the level of protection.

On the empirical level, Bergsten (1982) observes that the three major postwar episodes of tension in US–Japanese trade relations in 1970–71, 1977–78, and since 1981 all originated in periods of an overvalued dollar (especially in terms of the yen). The first of these episodes produced widespread congressional support for the protectionist Mills bill and Burke-Hartke bill, despite the fact that unemployment was low when those efforts began. Protectionist pressures remain severe at the present time in the United States, reflecting the overvalued dollar, and despite the recovery.

MISALIGNMENTS MATTER

In contrast to exchange rate volatility, which is a troublesome nuisance rather than a major source of concern, exchange rate misalignments undermine economic performance in several central dimensions: they may generate austerity, adjustment costs, recession, deindustrialization, inflation, and protectionism. The strange fact is that misalignments have rarely even been considered by economists as a possible consequence of floating. There seem to be two reasons for this. One is that the professional view of floating was largely molded by the experience of the Canadian dollar in the 1950s, when no major misalignment emerged.[5] It was indeed often taken as axiomatic that floating would serve to *avoid* misalignments. The other is that major misalignments are typically most easily explained by some inept piece of macroeconomic policy making (e.g., the US creation of a structural budget deficit, precipitate Japanese abolition of capital export controls, UK monetary and fiscal tightening when oil price increases were causing an attempt to shift into sterling) rather than as the result of any intrinsic dynamics of floating exchange rates, such as "bandwagon effects" or responsiveness of exchange rates to current accounts which in turn respond with a long lag to exchange rates.

But is it really true that floating would be vindicated by a finding that misalignments emerge only because countries adopt foolish policies? Not necessarily. If one starts with a presupposition that countries should choose their fiscal and monetary policies without regard to what is happening abroad, then one can hardly avoid endorsing floating rates, for this is indeed the only regime capable of reconciling uncoordinated policies. But the question is whether countries *ought* to select their policies in this way. Not only does the fact that we live in an interdependent world, where the policies adopted in one country have profound impacts on the course of events elsewhere, imply that countries have a responsibility to consider the interests of their partners, but the attempt to pursue policies that will not be acceptable to others is likely to lead to actions that are against the country's own long-run interests. It is a failing of the floating regime that the pressures to coordinate policies are so weak that countries have had the leeway to adopt policies so internationally inconsistent as to generate severe misalignments. Attempts to manage exchange rates would focus attention on causes of international inconsistency, like the structural fiscal deficit in the United States, and make it that much harder for such policy aberrations to be tolerated.

Since the major problem posed by floating rates is the emergence of misalignments, the major emphasis of policy should be on limiting the size of misalignments. This is not to say that reduced volatility would not also be desirable: in fact lower volatility and lesser misalignments are likely to prove complementary, since not only would smaller volatility reduce the noise in the exchange rate that helps generate and sustain misalignments, but greater confidence that future misalignments will be avoided would help pin down the rate in the short run. But the basic focus of exchange rate management should be on estimating an appropriate value for the exchange rate and seeking to limit deviations from that value beyond a reasonable range. It will be assumed in what follows that management is indeed directed to that end.

CAUSES OF MISALIGNMENTS

If management is to be directed to limiting misalignments, it is important to consider the possible causes of misalignments. Since a misalignment has been defined as a deviation of the market rate from fundamental equilibrium, it can arise for any of three reasons (or from some combination of the three):

- a deviation of the market rate from the market equilibrium, which would occur as a result of what might be termed *misguided intervention*
- a deviation of market equilibrium from current equilibrium, which occurs as a result of what is customarily termed *market inefficiency*
- a deviation of current equilibrium from fundamental equilibrium, as a result of the stance of *macroeconomic policy*.

Misguided Intervention

Clearly one cannot rule out the possibility that intervention (or other policies directed at influencing the exchange rate) might *create* rather than limit a misalignment. Indeed, charges have sometimes been made that central banks systematically lose money in intervening and, by implication, that these policies tend to destabilize exchange rates (e.g., Taylor, 1982).

The Jurgensen Report (1983) considered these criticisms, but rejected them for two reasons. First, it challenged the conclusion that intervention has typically lost money (para. 76). It pointed out that, in calculating the profitability of intervention, Taylor had valued the dollars acquired in intervention at their value at the end of the period he studied, at which time the dollar happened to be undervalued. If one extrapolates Taylor's calculations forward into the period of a strong dollar, one gets contrary results. But that result too is misleading: a correct assessment requires that one calculate the profitability of intervention over a period when intervention has balanced out, so that terminal stocks are the same as initial stocks, thus sidestepping the problem of valuing the terminal (and initial) stocks of foreign exchange. The Jurgensen Report stated that such studies have been made in official circles and affirmed that most such calculations have shown intervention to have been profitable. A published example of these studies is Mayer and Taguchi (1983).

The second reason the Jurgensen Report rejected the charge that official intervention has been a costly failure is that it accepted the contention of Mayer and Taguchi that intervention could be unprofitable but nonetheless stabilizing. A simple way of seeing the basic point is to consider the case where the authorities succeed in stabilizing the rate perfectly, in which case they would make zero profits. But if they marginally "overstabilized" they would make a loss, no matter how great the instability that would have occurred in the absence of intervention.

Despite that qualification, the evidence that intervention has in general been profitable does suggest that it has not usually been "misguided," in the sense of amplifying misalignments. Nevertheless, there have been instances of the latter. One way in which such instances can arise is through countries' pursuing intervention policies of the "leaning-against-the-wind" variety when a misalignment is being *corrected* (rather than created), as happened *inter alia* with Japan in 1976. This demonstrates the inappropriateness of leaning against the wind as a strategic guide to intervention policy, given that the major object of policy should be to limit misalignments. For that purpose the authorities cannot escape taking a view of the appropriate rate (or range of rates).

Most instances of misguided intervention could probably have been avoided had the authorities given explicit consideration to the choice of an appropriate real exchange rate target. But there is at least one case where the authorities had sought to estimate such a target and nevertheless intervened in a way that was obviously (in retrospect) misguided; namely, the British attempt to cap the rise in sterling in 1977. . . .The rate the authorities attempted to defend in mid-1977 was below the FEER. This suggests two morals. The first is the danger of allowing recent experience—in that case, the experience of the speculative crisis of 1976—an excessive weight in influencing judgments of the long-run concept of fundamental equilibrium. The second is the desirability of allowing a wide range around the preferred FEER to accommodate reasonable doubts about its true value. Had those precepts been respected, Britain would have avoided the misfortune of buying up large quantities of dollars at a very high (sterling) price, in the process subjecting itself to unwanted monetary pressures as well as losing money on the operation.

Market Inefficiency

Popular and political discussion of exchange rates frequently blames "speculators" for "selling currencies short," creating "bandwagon effects," and causing "overshooting."[6] Professional economists have typically gone to the other extreme, arguing that speculators play a socially beneficial role in ensuring that the latest information is incorporated in exchange rates, that foreign exchange markets are efficient, that expectations are rational,[7] and that, if bandwagon effects really existed, they would present unexploited profit opportunities to speculators.

There have been a series of attempts to test the hypothesis that the foreign exchange market is efficient since the advent of floating a decade ago. The most recent and most authoritative of these were commissioned by the Working Group on Exchange Market Intervention. The relevant paragraphs of the resulting report (Jurgensen Report, 1983, paras. 61–66) are worth quoting in full:

> The value of intervention in stabilising exchange rates depends to a critical extent on the working of the exchange market and its role in the process of exchange rate determination. For this reason, the

Working Group examined in detail the extent to which exchange markets are "efficient" in the sense that they take account of all information which is relevant for the determination of exchange rates. If exchange markets rapidly and fully assimilated such information and translated it into appropriate spot and forward rate levels, there would be one less reason for monetary authorities to intervene directly in the markets. Efficient exchange markets would not, for example, allow repetitive bandwagon-type exchange rate movements to emerge.

Empirical tests of exchange-market efficiency are based on the propositions that : (a) transaction costs are minimal; (b) all relevant information is utilised by exchange market participants; and (c) assets denominated in different currencies are perfectly substitutable in private portfolios. If all three propositions are satisfied, then the forward exchange rate should constitute the best available predictor of the future spot rate. On these assumptions, the use of any other variables such as inflation and interest rate differentials should not produce better forecasting results than the forward rate nor should the consistent application of simple exchange trading rules using these variables yield positive returns. Both suppositions were tested empirically.

The tests provided clear evidence that consideration of readily accessible information on inflation and interest rate differentials yielded a better prediction of the future spot rate than that implied by the forward rate. Moreover, the repeated application of certain foreign exchange trading rules indicated a high probability of making some profit. However, some members thought that the results for some currencies may have been affected by the existence of capital controls, although the results were similar for the six bilateral US dollar rates tested. Other time series studies performed by the Group confirmed the existence of better predictors of the future spot rate than the forward one.

This evidence can have three different explanations, which are not necessarily mutually exclusive. As transaction costs are usually neither very large nor particularly variable, it is generally thought that they do not explain the observed results. Consequently, the test suggests that markets are inefficient and/or that investors require time-varying risk premia because assets in different currencies are not perfect substitutes for one another. Views differed among the members of the Working Group as to how to interpret this outcome. Those members who were inclined to attribute the existence of systematic and exploitable prediction errors primarily to variable exchange risk premia considered it highly implausible that exchange market participants should systematically ignore low-cost information that is relevant to the determination of the exchange rate. Other members tended to interpret the result of the empirical tests as evidence of exchange market inefficiency. Their view was based on the general failure of empirical studies conducted to date to produce evidence that would explain potential risk premia entirely in terms of their theoretical determinants. Moreover, relevant information might be ignored by market participants as a result of the high cost of properly processing it. Thus, expectations might be rational in the everyday sense of the word although not conforming to the technical concept of efficiency.

Doubts about the efficiency of exchange markets have also been expressed in most case studies of exchange rate developments—at least to the extent that bandwagon effects can be regarded as a sign of exchange market inefficiency. All countries had identified bandwagon movements at particular times, and some countries intervened to forestall the emergence of bandwagon effects. For example, Canada had seen the risk in July and August 1981 that the decline in the Canadian dollar might feed on itself, and the UK authorities had been concerned to prevent any fall in the pound sterling from becoming self-sustaining in June to October 1981. Japan stated that there had been several periods in which bandwagon effects had been very much in evidence. In particular, between January and October 1978 the yen was said to have risen continuously on several occasions without any significant new information having been supplied to the market, and the upward movement in the exchange rate on one day appeared to have been the determinant of the yen's appreciation on the following day. Italy interpreted erratic exchange rate movements at the end of February 1976 as raising a suspicion that bandwagon effects were at work.

The Working Group noted that the test results indicated that intervention may have had a significant impact on exchange rates—irrespective of whether markets are inefficient or whether variable exchange risk premia exist. If markets are inefficient in the sense that they fail to assign appropriate weight to information on macroeconomic variables in determining exchange rates, action to influence the exchange rate including intervention could be an effective component of macroeconomic policies. In this case intervention would have an impact through its influence on expectations—for example, its demonstration effect—about future underlying economic conditions or policies. Alternatively, if exchange markets are efficient and unexploited profits are indicative of time-varying risk premia, intervention could still be an effective policy tool. This would be so because official operations in the exchange market, by changing the currency composition of private portfolios, would alter risk exposures in the various currencies and thus have a lasting effect on exchange rates.

In other words, there is serious reason to doubt whether exchange markets are efficient. One cannot legitimately take it for granted that the market rate will always approximate current equilibrium.[8] Some intriguing explanations as to why exchange markets may at times generate exchange rates bearing no systematic relationship to current equilibrium are starting to emerge. Rudiger Dornbusch (1983, pp. 18–20) has perhaps the most comprehensive succinct discussion of such explanations to date:

The first is familiar from the recent literature on financial markets and concerns the possibility that exchange rates, in part, are determined by irrelevant information. Market participants may have the wrong model of fundamentals, and their expectations, based on the wrong model, will affect the actual exchange rate. If there is sufficiently high serial correlation in the irrelevant variables, it may be impossible to discern the systematic forecast errors using conventional efficiency tests. But the exchange rate will be significantly more volatile than is warranted by the true model.

This point is important because market participants may be impressed by a plausible fundamental variable, attribute explanatory power to it, and, consequently, make their expectations actually come true. Then, when some other variable moves, attention may shift to a different "main factor," which, in turn, comes to dominate the exchange rate for a while.

Exchange rates carried by irrelevant beliefs are troublesome, not only because of the excess variance but also because shifting from one irrelevant factor to another will precipitate major exchange rate collapses. The possibility that exchange rates are sometimes far out of line with the fundamentals cannot be discounted. It is important to recognize this, because in the past economists may have given excessive weight to the notion that the market knows "the model" and, at the same time, is rational. It is quite conceivable that a number of fashionable factors, such as fiscal discipline, basic monetary control, long-run strength in manufacturing, *Angebotsfreundliche Gesellschafts-politik* (supply side policy) play a role, one at a time.

The second source of disequilibrium exchange rates is expectations about the possibility of regime changes and has been called the "peso problem." In this perspective exchange rates are influenced not only by current fundamentals but also by agents' expectations that there are given probabilities that fundamentals may change in specific directions. If market participants have sufficiently strong beliefs that a given course of policy will not be followed, they may, in fact, make it impossible for the authorities to follow that course. Under flexible exchange rates, this problem may become acute because the exchange rate is so flexible a price and so much governed by expectations. It may well be argued, as was done in the discussion of the French stabilization experience under Poincaré, that speculators are the true judges of fundamentals and that a collapse of the exchange rate brought about by adverse capital flows is irrevocable evidence of a program of stabilization that was out of touch with fundamentals. But such an argument must be viewed as simplistic by anyone who recognizes that stabilization policy has a wide range of indeterminacy.

The third source of disequilibrium exchange rates can be explained using the analogy of bubbles. A bubble exists when holders of an asset realize that the asset is overpriced but are nevertheless willing to hold it, since they believe there is only a limited risk of a price collapse during a given holding period; therefore, asset holders expect to be able to sell eventually at a price that will provide them with sufficient capital gains to compensate them for running the risk of a collapse. An analogous situation occurs when a currency has appreciated more than can be considered justified by fundamentals and overvaluation is widely thought to prevail, but appreciation is expected to continue until some disturbance causes the crash. There are no models of such a crash as yet, but it should be clear that an essential ingredient is the arrival of new information that diverts a sufficient number of speculators from keeping the bubble growing.

There is also quite a widespread feeling among those in contact with the foreign exchange markets that the behavior of the current account plays a larger role in determining exchange rates than is allowed by the currently dominant strand of economic theorizing. It is maintained that, rather than peering into the distant future to make well-informed forecasts of how the current account will respond to the exchange rate, the market takes its cue from the actual contemporaneous behavior of the current account, even when this is distorted by the *J*-curve or other temporary phenomena. It is easy to see that such behavior can generate self-perpetuating cycles in the exchange rate. A depreciated rate eventually creates a surplus, which causes the rate to appreciate. Since this initially enlarges the surplus (because of the *J*-curve), the rate "overshoots" (in a general sense of the term, rather than in Dornbusch's technical sense), which ultimately causes a deficit, which leads to an excessive depreciation, and so on.

An imaginative recent paper by Schulmeister (1983) tries to integrate this type of idea with those of interest arbitrage and "bandwagon effects." For a time the market may be willing to finance a current account deficit (for example) because of a higher interest rate offered by the deficit country, but the longer this persists, the more uneasy will the market become. Eventually the exchange rate starts to slip, and as it does so more and more speculators jump on the bandwagon. The rate stabilizes again only when it has so overshot the equilibrium level as to raise worries that it may start to rebound.

Such theories as these have not yet been fully articulated and appraised, nor have they been absorbed into the mainstream of economic thought—let alone subjected to rigorous empirical testing. But Nurkse's (1944) warning about the characteristics of speculative conduct in foreign exchange markets now looks a lot less far-fetched than it was generally rated a decade ago. As Keynes (1936, p. 156) argued with his analogy to a beauty contest in which the winner is whoever comes closest to guessing the popular order, conduct that is quite rational for individual participants may in a speculative market add up to social behavior that appears wildly irrational. All of this suggests that exchange markets may experience severe misalignments as a result of market equilibrium deviating from current equilibrium.

Macroeconomic Policy

But there is yet another way in which misalignments can arise: from macroeconomic policy's pushing current equilibrium away from fundamental equilibrium. For example, a country may embark on a program of determined monetary restraint as a means of ridding itself of inflation. Unless accompanied by complementary fiscal and incomes policies, such a program will entail a rise in real interest rates and hence a real appreciation (as has been seen in recent years in both Britain and the United States). Conversely, an attempt to stimulate demand by unbalanced monetary expansion will lead to a real depreciation.

How great the misalignment caused by such a policy proves to be depends on the degree of asset substitutability. In the case of perfect substitutability beloved by economic theorists, an expectation that real interest rates were going to remain 4 percent above those abroad during a three-year period of disinflation would cause the current equilibrium exchange rate to appreciate by 12 percent.

The movements of real effective exchange rates shown in the appendix figures suggest that changes have at times of severe disinflation been much larger than this. One interesting question is whether this could be explained by imperfect substitutability. This possibility seems to have been largely disregarded by many economists, apparently on the rather casual ground that the speculative capital flows prior to an expected change in a pegged exchange rate can be enormous. What this overlooks is that the *incentive* to shift funds out of a currency about to be devalued is astronomical too. Someone who shifted funds from the French franc to the DM for the weekend of their recent 8 percent realignment earned 3½ percent in two days, annualized yield of 45,643 percent! It is no wonder that a lot of money moves when faced with such an incentive,[9] but this tells us nothing useful about asset substitutability.

It has to be said that it is not clear that imperfect asset substitutability is capable of explaining why exchange rates change so much in response to interest differentials. The usual view would be that a 1 percent rise in the dollar interest differential would have *less* effect if assets are worse substitutes, since it would motivate a smaller attempt to shift into dollars. Paul S. Armington (1981) has argued, however, that investors value the interest component of the yield of an asset more highly than the capital gain component because of the high degree of uncertainty that attaches to the latter. Although this argument seems intuitively plausible, it has not yet been given a respectable theoretical base. Until this matter is clarified, it would be wrong to attach excessive weight to the apparent fact that exchange rates over-react to changes in interest differentials. But it would also be wrong to ignore the possibility that a reform of the exchange rate mechanism that served to reduce the uncertainty attaching to longer-run exchange rate movements could drastically cut the misalignments that result from a given interest rate differential.

COSTS OF LIMITING MISALIGNMENTS

If misalignments are caused primarily by misguided intervention, their elimination would be costless: all that would be necessary would be for the authorities to abstain from such intervention. The evidence does not, however, suggest that such a free ride is available. To the extent that misalignments are caused by market inefficiency or macroeconomic policy, any limitation of misalignments might require a deliberate willingness to sacrifice other policy objectives. The sacrifice actually involved might prove to be minimal where misalignments arise because of inefficiency, or if exaggerated misalignments result from modest interest differentials because of low asset substitutability. The "sacrifice" may also turn out to be a blessing in disguise to the extent that the management of exchange rates forces an international coordination of economic policy that is needed for everyone's long-run good but would not otherwise occur. But even in that case policymakers will want to know what freedom they would need to give up in order to manage the exchange rate to limit misalignments.

The case for a managed exchange rate is distinct from the case for either a fixed or a floating exchange rate, either of which can generate misalignments. Unlike a fixed exchange rate, a managed rate can be so managed as to neutralize inflation differentials (thus preventing misalignments emerging from differential inflation) or to change the real exchange rate, when that would be helpful either to promote adjustment to a long-lasting change in real circumstances or to react to an abnormal temporary (e.g., cyclical) situation. Unlike a freely floating exchange rate, a managed rate allows the possibility of absorbing variations in the desire to hold different currencies in changes in the supplies of the various currencies, rather than in their prices (exchange rates). Management can therefore prevent such shifts in portfolio preferences from generating misalignments.

The costs of managing exchange rates to limit misalignments depend upon both the technique adopted for that purpose and the regime with which managed rates are compared. It is argued in the next section that, while other techniques, like sterilized intervention, may be able to give limited assistance, a serious commitment to exchange rate management leaves no realistic alternative to a willingness to direct monetary policy at least in part toward an exchange rate target. The nature of the sacrifices involved in adopting such a strategy may best be understood by comparison with the two textbook regimes of fixed and freely floating exchange rates.

Managed versus Fixed Rates

Fixed exchange rates are more effective than managed rates in reducing short-run volatility and in producing certainty in long-run *nominal* comparisons. Managed rates produce more certainty in *real* comparisons. If the earlier argument regarding the relative significance of misalignments and volatility is accepted, this difference indicates an advantage for managed rates.

About the only traditional argument in favor of fixed rates that continues to apply against managed rates is that a fixed rate serves to anchor the national price level. If a small country pegs its exchange rate to the currency of a large trading partner and then pursues those policies—notably monetary policy—needed to maintain the peg constant, there is no doubt that the inflation rate of the small country will tend to follow that of its large partner, at least in the long run. For suppose that inflation were too high: then arbitrage pressures from abroad would start to discipline domestic prices directly, the country would lose reserves and the money supply would fall, and unemployment would rise (on account of both the unfavorable trade balance resulting from uncompetitive exports and the cut in spending resulting from monetary stringency) and discipline wage increases. Provided that the country stuck to its fixed exchange rate—which may mean allowing the money supply to fall, and create a recession—inflation would eventually be brought back into line.

A country that manages its exchange rate with a view to preserving price competitiveness cuts itself off from this discipline. If its inflation starts off being higher than abroad, it depreciates its currency to neutralize that excess inflation and creates enough additional money to ensure that the depreciation actually occurs. Thus all the stabilizing forces that drag inflation back down under a fixed exchange rate are ruptured. Worse still, if a country did not start off with excess inflation but decided to hold its exchange rate at a more undervalued level than was consistent with equilibrium of the real economy, a policy of rigidly managing the exchange rate to preserve competitiveness would lead to an explosive inflation.

Any country that plans to manage its real exchange rate therefore needs to be certain that it has an adequate alternative to an exchange rate peg as a means of controlling inflation. That alternative must include a willingness to take domestic measures—including a willingness to adopt restrictive fiscal measures to a point where, if all else fails, unemployment rises—in response to a rise in inflation. It must also include a willingness to adjust the target for the real exchange rate if there is evidence that the target has been set at a level inconsistent with equilibrium of the real economy.

The strategy of using domestic demand–management policy rather than a pegged exchange rate to control inflation will seem more natural to large and relatively closed economies than to the small open economy. But even in the latter case there is much to be said for it. The "global monetarist" claim that inflation could be controlled on the cheap by pegging the exchange rate and relying on arbitrage—the "Law of One Price"—has been decisively discredited by the experiences of Argentina and Chile (Ardito-Barletta, 1983). It is now abundantly clear (as it always should have been) that controlling inflation by pegging the exchange rate involves the same painful process of allowing unemployment to rise as is involved in the domestic route to inflation control. The difference is that inflation control through foreign competition concentrates the recession on the internationally competitive sector, which undermines medium-term prospects and offends conventional canons of equality of sacrifice. A country that has enough discipline to stick to an exchange rate peg when inflationary pressures develop can just as well take the domestic measures needed to restore price stability.

Managed versus Free-floating Rates

The fact remains that a country abandoning the external inflation anchor does need a domestic replacement. If fiscal and incomes policies are ruled out for ideological reasons as being too "Keynesian," the only alternative is a monetary growth rule. That is, of course, the solution favored by many advocates of free floating. Many of the arguments traditionally deployed in favor of floating rather than fixed rates are irrelevant in the present context—in particular, managed rates are just as capable of neutralizing differential inflation and of contributing to the adjustment process as are floating rates. But the assignment of monetary policy to domestic or exchange rate objectives remains at the heart of the issue.

Harry G. Johnson (1969) was one of those who used to claim that the central advantage of floating was the liberation of monetary policy to pursue "domestic objectives." Keynesian floaters regard the pursuit of domestic objectives as the choice of an interest rate appropriate to securing the right level and composition (between consumption and investment) of demand.[10] Monetarist floaters interpret pursuing domestic objectives as securing a fixed rate of growth of the money supply. Both regard the need to defend an exchange rate as diverting monetary policy from its primary task.

Obviously one can accept the contention that monetary policy has important domestic objectives without abandoning the conviction that it should also be influenced by considerations of external competitiveness. The position advocated in this study is not that monetary policy should be directed solely to managing the exchange rate, but rather that it should seek to strike a balance between the need to manage the domestic economy and the need to limit misalignments.

Opposition to this view seems to come from two distinct, both extreme, parts of the monetarist spectrum. On the one side are those global monetarists with a misplaced confidence that, because of the "Law of One Price," everything that can be accomplished by monetary policy is achieved by pegging the exchange rate. On the other hand are those free floaters who argue that allowing considerations of external competitiveness to influence monetary policy has to be justified by special claims to superior knowledge on the part of the authorities. Thus Steven W. Kohlhagen (1982, p. 24) recently wrote:

> For official intervention to make sense, central banks must either have more information than the market (and be willing to act correctly on it in a way that affects market prices) or have a more socially optimal taste for risk than the market collectively. How many central banks have a good sense of society's optimal risk preference or the market's actual taste for risk and know how to intervene to correct for any deviation between the two at a given time? If central banks have information that the market does not have, how do or should they use it? Why not release it? Only if that is impossible does it make sense perhaps to intervene and push the rate in the inevitable direction. But if the information never becomes public, or the central bank was wrong about its effect, or new information or new economic conditions negate or swamp the old information, such intervention can be destabilizing rather than stabilizing.
>
> Why do central bankers feel that they know whether or not the market rate is correct? In point of fact, there is no right rate at any specific time. The correct exchange rate is the one that will bring about external equilibrium in the desired time period, given current information and risk aversion. The market's notion of the "desired time period" may not be the social optimum, but is the central bank's? Who should determine it? Should the soon-to-be-evident US deficit be corrected in two quarters, one year, or two years? As there is no "right rate," what target should a central bank adopt for intervention?

It is certainly possible to visualize circumstances where Kohlhagen would be correct. In a country that conducted its monetary policy according to a rigid monetarist rule of predetermining a constant growth rate of the money supply, the central bank could hope to improve on the judgment of the market only if it has access to superior knowledge or if the private market suffers from some pathological state such as socially excessive risk aversion or time discounting, or a propensity to engage in speculative runs. And if one believes that the best monetary policy is a fixed rate of monetary growth irrespective of circumstances, for example because one believes that only unanticipated monetary policy can influence output and that it does that by cheating the public, then one can logically advocate free floating on the grounds that Kohlhagen does.

But suppose instead that one believes that good monetary management can help to stabilize output by offsetting shocks emanating from the private sector. Then the authorities have to decide what set of policies will best further that objective. The market will of course set the exchange rate in the light of the policies chosen, and its expectations of future policies. Suppose that the central bank and the market have identical information and that both know the correct model, in the now-traditional rational expectations scenario (see footnote 7). Then if the authorities decide to set monetary policy solely with a view to best achieving the internal balance objective, that is what they will tend to achieve, since by hypothesis they will build in the correct private sector reactions to their policy. But given that there is in general a conflict between internal needs and external competitiveness, that is not the optimum policy, which involves striking a balance between both. Specifically, it involves taking account of where the exchange rate should be in order to generate an appropriate long-term level of competitiveness. The key point is that the authorities, unlike the private market, have macroeconomic objectives, and need to concern themselves with *all* the implications of the policies they adopt. The exchange rate is too important to be treated as the residual.

This is a position that seems quite congenial to a number of economists who would consider themselves monetarists (as well as to many who would not identify with that label). For example, the influential British financial journalist Samuel Brittan has repeatedly urged that pursuit of a target rate of monetary growth should be overriden where necessary to keep the exchange rate within reasonable bounds. The distinctly monetarist Swiss National Bank, and to a lesser extent the Bundesbank, actually applied such an override when the Swiss franc and DM appreciated to a damaging degree in late 1978. One of the leading monetarists at Chicago, Michael Mussa (1981, p. 16), has argued that the authorities can be presumed to have an informational advantage in that "the central bank possesses a certainty of knowledge about its future monetary policy and its relationship to the behavior of exchange rates that is not available to private market participants." Alexandre Lamfalussy (1981) has similarly argued that "intervention means that the authorities are putting their money where their mouth is."

Kohlhagen is correct in arguing that the case for the authorities seeking to manage the exchange rate rests on their being able to "know whether or not the market rate is correct." But he is quite wrong in suggesting that this demands superior knowledge on their part, for what they need to ask themselves is not whether the rate approximates *current* equilibrium but how it stands in relation to *fundamental* equilibrium. The market simply does not ask itself what rate can be expected to clear the flow market for foreign exchange over any specific time period, optimal or otherwise, as Kohlhagen seems to imagine. Rather, the market sets a rate which equates the desire to hold different currencies with the current supplies, where those desires are influenced *inter alia* by market expectations of what is going to happen in future, including expectations of how attractive policy is going to make it to hold different currencies at various dates in the future. If one wishes the foreign exchange market to bring about external equilibrium over some even remotely optimal time period, one has no alternative but to figure out what that period is and what set of macroeconomic policies will induce the market to choose a rate consistent with achieving equilibrium over that period. In other words, one needs to estimate the FEER and manage the rate to approximate it!

There is something of a mystery as to how the market is supposed to be capable of pinning down the exchange rate to a value consistent with fundamental equilibrium in the long run, as supposed in much of the technical economic literature, if governments are unable to assess the approximate level of fundamental equilibrium. Note that there is a basic difference between a fish market and the foreign exchange market as regards the information sets available to the market on the one hand and the authorities on the other. In a fish market, market participants collectively know all there is to know about demand and supply; the government does not, and hence one can safely predict that a government attempt to fix prices will end in a mess. In the foreign exchange market, both market participants and governments have to resort to essentially similar speculation about the level of fundamental equilibrium. One reason for wanting governments to focus on the issue is that in doing so they would not be distracted by all the other considerations that inevitably concern market participants, like forecasting future government policy or the possibility of riding a speculative bandwagon.

Another reason for wanting governments to focus on the question of identifying FEERs and limiting deviations from them is the belief that this would lead to a better balance in policy formation. It is true that, as Gottfried Haberler (1983) has recently argued, the emergence of an exchange rate misalignment *may* stimulate a government to take needed policy actions—e.g., the role of the weak dollar in motivating a shift to anti-inflationary policies in the United States in 1978–79. But it would surely be better if governments were forced to act by the *need to prevent misalignments from emerging* rather than to try to correct the damage done once a misalignment has emerged. Not only would this lead to a prompter acceptance of needed policy changes, but it should contribute to a better policy mix. The present excessive level of real interest rates could hardly have arisen had governments not been able to treat the exchange rate as a residual and thus relax their concern to maintain a proper balance between fiscal and monetary policy.

BENEFITS AND COSTS OF EXCHANGE RATE MANAGEMENT

It has been argued in this section that the major costs of floating exchange rates stem from the misalignments that they have allowed to emerge, rather than from the annoyance of high volatility. Those costs were identified as an alternation of splurge and austerity, adjustment costs, unemployment in the tradable goods industries, deindustrialization, a ratchet effect on inflation, and protectionist pressures. Although there has been little systematic work directed to measuring thoses costs, the presumption is that they are large, and provide a significant part of the explanation for the weak economic performance of the world in the decade since floating was adopted.

The costs of attempting to curb the costs of free floating depend on why misalignments arise. There is no practical way of decomposing the responsibility for misalignments among the three possible causes identified, namely, misguided intervention, market inefficiency, and macroeconomic policy, although there seems reason to believe that both of the last two factors have been important. To the extent that market efficiency is the source of the problem, exchange rate management need not involve any systematic sacrifice of internal policy objectives, although it will require a willingness to direct policy toward exchange rate management rather than to let the exchange rate be the residual. But where macroeconomic policy is responsible, governments may face a real choice between the monetary policy that is appropriate for internal versus external objectives. If they decide to give some weight to external objectives, they need to wield a sufficiently comprehensive set of policy instruments to ensure that the main internal objectives can still be attained, most specifically to ensure the control of inflation. There is, however, a converse side to this argument: namely, that the attempt to achieve domestic and external objectives simultaneously will create pressures for a balanced policy mix, which is likely to be beneficial both to a country's partners and, in the long run, to itself.

NOTES

1. The main source of exchange rate uncertainty in the case of the developing countries in question was the erratic pegging practices of their governments rather than the erratic market movements of a floating rate, but the impact on the private sector is similar.
2. See Williamson (1982).

3. Haberler reminds us forcibly of this offsetting benefit of an overvalued exchange rate.

4. Indeed, with real wage resistance, a period of overvaluation may build in real wage aspirations that are not consistent with a subsequent return to full equilibrium, but instead would generate inflationary pressure at full employment and the former equilibrium real exchange rate. Suppose, for example, that a 30 percent real appreciation raises real wages by 10 percent. It might be that a subsequent depreciation would be allowed to cut real wages by 5 percent before encountering wage resistance, but that would still make a return to full macroeconomic equilibrium unattainable. This suggests that the tight money/overvalued exchange rate strategy of inflation control adopted *inter alia* by Margaret Thatcher and Martinez de Hoz may actually make it more difficult to return to noninflationary full employment.

5. There was some concern in Canada at the appreciation of the Canadian dollar in the mid-1950s but this was mild indeed compared to experience since 1973.

6. "Overshooting" has often been used as synonymous with what is here described as a "misalignment." Some of us regret this deviation from Dornbusch's (1976) original usage, where the term described a situation where the market and current equilibrium (which were identical in his model, due to the assumption of perfect foresight) temporarily moved more than the fundamental (nominal) equilibrium (following a shock that altered the latter) for the quite specific purpose of maintaining interest parity in the presence of sticky prices.

7. Expectations are said to be "rational" when those involved have a correct perception of how the world works ("know the structure of the model") and make the best possible use of all available information to forecast the future. The attraction of the concept is that, if everyone has such expectations and acts on them, the expectations will prove self-fulfilling. Rational expectations are the stochastic analogue of perfect foresight. See Begg (1982) for an excellent introduction and survey of the now-abundant literature.

8. Note that "time-varying risk premia"—or low asset substitutability, in language that is still more familiar to some—influences the deviation of current equilibrium from fundamental equilibrium rather than that of market equilibrium from current equilibrium. That is, with imperfect asset substitutability a change in interest rates will lead to a different change in current equilibrium to that which would occur with perfect asset substitutability. Comment on the potential role of low asset substitutability in contributing to deviation of the market rate from fundamental equilibrium is therefore reserved till the next subsection.

9. It is also reported that short-term interest rates rose so high in France that someone who got the timing wrong and borrowed francs to shift funds to the DM two weeks before the realignment occurred would have lost money on the operation. This does not alter the basic point that the incentives involved are an order of magnitude larger than those encountered in routine financial management (nor does it reassure one that such circumstances can be anything but disruptive).

10. Keynes himself certainly believed this freedom to use interest rates for domestic demand management to be of crucial importance: see Keynes (1936, p. 349).

20. Techniques of Exchange Rate Management

JOHN WILLIAMSON

The preceding [selection] identified two crucial conditions that must be satisfied if a country is to manage its exchange rate with a view to limiting misalignments. First, it must make sure that it has an adequate "anchor" to prevent inflation from taking off. Abandonment of both the traditional anchors, a fixed nominal exchange rate peg and a fixed monetary growth rule, can only be undertaken safely provided there is a firm commitment to a balanced use of domestic demand policy to control inflation.

For example, so long as the United States is unwilling to use fiscal policy to ensure that inflation does not revive, that burden will have to be carried by monetary policy, which will curtail the extent to which monetary policy can be directed toward the exchange rate. The case for nevertheless seeking a move toward greater exchange rate management in the United States at the present time rests on the twin hopes that this would increase the pressure for a more responsible fiscal policy and that the mere delineation of objectives might make some contribution toward modifying the overvaluation of the dollar.

The second precondition for a policy of exchange rate management to make sense is that the authorities possess a reasonable ability to identify the fundamental equilibrium exchange rate. This is an exercise that used to be undertaken routinely in the days of the Bretton Woods system, whenever a par value change was considered. It is an exercise that many countries continue to perform regularly, and in which the IMF takes a keen interest and claims considerable expertise when it comes to dealing with small deficit countries with pegged exchange rates. It is an exercise that on one occasion, prior to the Smithsonian Agreement of December 1971, formed the basis of a major and ultimately successful diplomatic negotiation.[1] And it is an exercise that could be performed again on a multilateral basis if the will were there. . . . It may not prove possible to diagnose FEERs with any great

John Williamson has taught economics in Great Britain, Brazil, and the United States. He is currently a Senior Fellow at the Institute for International Economics in Washington, D.C.

degree of accuracy, but approximate figures would suffice to support a great improvement in performance.

Not only must the authorities possess the *ability* to diagnose FEERs to a useful degree of approximation, but they must be prepared to exercise that ability and abandon the silly pretense that the exchange rate is none of their business. Any strategy intended to limit misalignments requires the authorities to develop a view of where the exchange rate would need to be to achieve a level of competitiveness that would be sustainable and appropriate in the long run. This view may be expressed as a real rate—in which case it will have to be translated into the nominal rate implied by prevailing price levels before the policy implications are apparent. Or it may be expressed as a nominal rate—in which case it will have to be adjusted regularly in response to differential inflation. It may be published, in the form of a central target or a band or range. Or it may be treated as confidential. But in some form or other the authorities must have, and recognize at least to themselves that they have, what one may naturally term a "target" for the level of the exchange rate. That is the basic minimum condition for any attempt to manage the exchange rate to limit misalignments. (A policy of "leaning against the wind" designed simply to slow down any exchange rate change does not require the authorities to develop any view as to the correct level, but neither can it be expected to limit misalignments in any systematic way.)

Having persuaded themselves that the exchange rate is a topic on which they owe it to the public to take a view, the authorities would have to make a series of further decisions:

- whether to commit themselves to a peg with formal margins, or to float with a "target zone" with "soft margins"
- how wide any band or target zone should be
- how the target rate should be changed
- whether to publish their target rate
- what policy instruments should be used to limit deviations of the exchange rate from its target.

PEGGING VERSUS FLOATING

An exchange rate is said to be "pegged" if the authorities accept an obligation to prevent the market rate from deviating by more than a specified amount (called the "margin") from the peg. Twice the margins gives the band, the maximum range within which the exchange rate is allowed to move without a change in the peg (or central rate).

An exchange rate is said to "float" if the authorities do not accept an obligation to limit the range of the market rate. It floats "freely" or "cleanly" if the authorities do not take any actions designed to influence the behavior of the exchange rate. It is said to be "managed" if the authorities attempt to influence the behavior of the rate without committing themselves to hold it within a specified range.

"Target zones" seem to mean different things to different people. To some they mean a wide band. To others they mean an unpublished band. To others the word "zone" is used with the deliberate purpose of providing a *contrast* to the word "band," to indicate a range beyond which the authorities are unhappy to see the rate move, despite *not* being prepared to precommit themselves to prevent such movements. Since the first two concepts have straightforward alternative titles while the third is an important concept that lacks an alternative simple description, the term will be used in that latter sense here. It is important to understand that, in this sense, a system of target zones is a *form of floating*, rather than a form of pegging. Target zones have "soft margins" which the authorities are *not* committed to defending.

If one is thinking of providing a framework for a worldwide return to a structured exchange rate system, it seems clear that the greatest degree of commitment that it would be realistic to contemplate—at least in the first instance—is a system of target zones with soft margins. The United States, in particular, could not be expected to make a greater commitment of monetary policy to external objectives—and would be right in refusing any greater commitment, at least until fiscal policy is brought under control. This is not to exclude closer arrangements among some groups of countries, e.g., the EMS, nor the possibility of further moves at a later date.

BAND OR ZONE WIDTH

The considerations that are relevant in choosing the width of a formal band are rather different from those relevant to choosing the width of a target zone. A country that commits itself to defending specified margins needs to make sure that those margins are wide enough to allow it to adjust its central rate without provoking an exchange crisis, and wide enough to allow it to absorb an appropriate part of the temporary shocks it encounters in movements of the exchange rate.

The first point may be graphically illustrated by the differing experiences of France and Denmark in the last (March 1983) EMS realignment. France devalued by 8 percent relative to the Deutschemark, the dominant currency in the EMS. As shown in Figure 1, this meant that any speculator who bought DM from the Banque de France before the realignment, when the franc was at its weak margin at point C, and sold them afterwards when the franc was at its new strong margin at D, made a profit of 3½ percent. In contrast the Danish krone was devalued only by 3 percent. Hence the speculator who sold Danish

FIGURE 1. The EMS realignment of March 1983

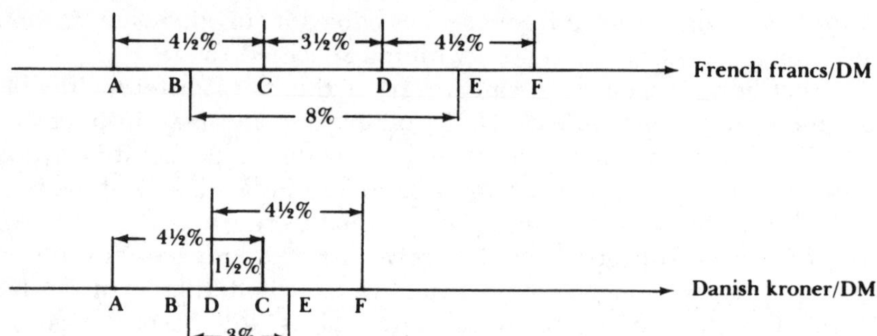

kroner at point C (in the bottom part of the diagram) had to buy them back at point D and *lost* 1½ percent in the transaction. The moral is that, as long as the band width is greater than the change in the central rate, it is possible to adjust central rates without generating speculative crises. Since there is no minimum necessary size of changes in central rates, however, this does not really pose much of a constraint on the choice of band width, except in countries that have hangups about the frequency of changes in central rates.

A more important constraint arises from the desirability of being able to absorb certain shocks in the exchange rate without having to adjust the central rate. Suppose, for example, that there is a cyclical rise in the foreign interest rate which the domestic country does not wish to follow since it does not consider itself subject to inflationary pressure. Then it would wish to allow its currency to depreciate, to the point where the market considered the prospect of a subsequent appreciation sufficient compensation for continuing to hold the same stock of low-interest domestic assets. It is preferable to accommodate such temporary shocks by movements within the margins rather than by changes in central rates for several reasons: so as not to give misleading signals for resource allocation, so as not to lessen confidence in the probability of a subsequent rebound of the rate, and so as to allow the initial adjustment to a shock to be made instantaneously. How wide the margins needed for this purpose depends on how large the interest rate differentials likely to be needed to provide autonomy of domestic action. With perfect asset substitutability, an ability to hold a 3 percent interest differential for two years would require margins of 6 percent.

Although less critical in determining the width of a target zone, inasmuch as the rate can be allowed to float outside the soft margins when that appears expedient, both these considerations remain relevant. But the most important criterion relates to the accuracy with which FEERs can be diagnosed. . . .It was suggested that they should be treated as having a margin of error of up to 10 percent. It would be misleading to identify a target zone narrower than the range of rates one is not prepared to label "clearly wrong," which suggests that target zones might initially be set at ± 10 percent. If the technical resources at the disposal of official institutions were brought to bear on making estimates of FEERs, it should be possible to improve on the exercises reported above and in consequence move to narrower zones. Another factor that might work in the same direction is any success that a more orderly exchange rate system has in curbing exchange rate swings: given the long lags in the adjustment of trade flows to exchange rates, a major uncertainty now facing balance of payments' econometricians is that of knowing what level of competitiveness should be credited with generating the observed current account outcomes.

CHANGING THE TARGET ZONE

Where the object of exchange rate management is to limit misalignments, target zones or central rates[2] will have to be changed to reflect differential inflation and changes in real exchange rates needed to promote adjustment. The only question is whether these changes should be made continuously in the light of accruing information or discontinuously as under the Bretton Woods system.

The latter alternative has nothing to commend it but nostalgia. Especially in a system of relatively narrow bands such as the EMS, the use of this antiquated practice virtually guarantees repeated exchange crises, of the character recently suffered by France, so long as significant differences in inflation rates persist. In its first two years (as in the final years of the snake) EMS realignments were small enough to be almost contained within the band, but they have recently been reaching levels of 8 percent or even 10 percent, with the predictable consequence of reviving exchange crises. There is no reason why differential inflation should not be neutralized by regular small changes in central rates (at, say, weekly intervals), according to a formula agreed six months or even a year in advance.

This amendment of EMS practice would in no way threaten the notable success that the EMS has enjoyed in forestalling intra-EMS misalignments of the type that have plagued the independently floating currencies. It would, admittedly, reduce the pressure that the EMS is supposed to create for a convergence in inflation rates, but it is not obvious that is a disadvantage, since the main reason for wanting inflation to be convergent—rather than low—is to enable the EMS to survive without exchange crises. Once that need were satisfied by the alternative route of adopting crawling central rates, each country would be freed to concentrate on reducing inflation to the lowest possible rate consistent with satisfactory performance of the real economy.

The need for crawling changes in the zone is less compelling in a target zone system. Nonetheless, it seems highly desirable to modify the target zone continuously in the light of the latest available information. That will require the use of "crawling zones."

PUBLICATION OF TARGET ZONES

Many officials still seem to take the view that, unless their country is to commit itself to a peg with formal margins, it is a matter of great importance that any exchange rate target they may have should be treated as a state secret. They remember the battles against speculators in the dying years of the Bretton Woods system, and witness with horror the continued struggle of the French authorities to keep the French franc in the EMS, and conclude that the way to avoid humiliation is to try to suppress any market knowledge of what they would like to see happen. They fear that any published target would become a "target to shoot at," and that if the rate moved outside the target zone it would serve to undermine their credibility.

There is a deep gulf on this issue between official and academic thinking. Thus the justification for official intervention offered by Michael Mussa (1981) is that it is a way for the authorities to guarantee their own honesty. Academic proponents of exchange rate targeting within a floating system—e.g., Ethier and Bloomfield (1975), with their reference rate proposal—have generally taken it for granted that a principal purpose of such a step would be to provide a focus for stabilizing speculation, which is possible only if the target is published. The problem that France has created for itself in the EMS arises not because it publishes the parity of the franc, but because it insists on the necessary changes in that parity being undertaken at lengthy intervals rather than in frequent small steps. Publication in itself encourages honesty and improves the information available to the market, which will be beneficial so long as policy is sensibly conducted. Indeed, one might judge whether policy is so conducted in part by its ability to withstand full disclosure and public debate.

It is surely true that many of the past examples of cases where the authorities have lost credibility as a result of their failure to achieve published targets have arisen through their becoming committed to inappropriate targets. In particular, any fixed nominal exchange rate eventually becomes an inappropriate target in the presence of differential inflation. Such situations would not arise under the type of system discussed above. But it is nonetheless possible that rates would at times stray outside target zones. The idea of "soft margins" is that the authorities should be prepared to accept such developments if they judge that to be wise. There can be no certainty that in particular instances that might not induce counterproductive psychological reactions in the markets. The best antidote is not, however, the defensive one of secrecy, but rather an honest attempt to explain what policy is and why it was adopted. The market may not always be immediately convinced, but, to the extent that the authorities have a coherent strategy that deserves to convince, one must surely believe that honesty will prove the best policy in the long run. A full target zone system should therefore provide for publication of the zones.

POLICY INSTRUMENTS

It has already been indicated that monetary policy should provide the main instrument to manage the exchange rate (which is *not* to argue that the exchange rate should be the exclusive, or even main, focus of monetary policy). There is not the slightest doubt that monetary policy provides a potent instrument for influencing the exchange rate: that is the valid central theorem of the "monetary approach to the balance of payments." It is more important to ask to what extent it is *desirable* to devote monetary policy to managing the exchange rate rather than to internal objectives, and whether there are other policy instruments that should also be directed in part to the task of exchange rate management.

Three observations may be made on the first issue. A first is that there is no point in trying to fine tune the exchange rate to a greater accuracy than one can hope to identify a misalignment. If the target zone is 20 percent wide because one lacks confidence in one's ability to identify the FEER to any greater degree of accuracy, it makes no sense to distort the monetary policy that would be preferred from a domestic standpoint in order to keep the exchange rate within some narrower range.

A second observation is that one's willingness to use policy—and that means essentially monetary policy, given what is argued about other instruments below—to manage the exchange rate should be the critical determinant of the choice between pegging the exchange rate within a formal band and floating with a target zone surrounded by soft margins. A band commits the authorities at a certain point to give primacy to the exchange rate commitment, whereas a target zone, as that term is being used here, means that a country's authorities retain the right to allow their internal objectives to override their exchange rate targets even in the event of a large misalignment. It is because it seems most unlikely that the major countries, most especially the United States, would be willing to give primacy to exchange rate management over domestic monetary targeting in the foreseeable future that target zones constitute the strongest form of management that can be contemplated for the international monetary system at a global level.

A third observation is that willingness to direct monetary policy to achieving a target exchange rate will, and certainly should, depend upon the confidence that monetary policy elsewhere will be conducted responsibly. If its partner countries are in the habit of lurching from the use of monetary policy to "go for growth" to episodes of single-minded (and single-policy) anti-inflationism, a country will have a hard choice between following their lead and allowing exchange rate misalignments to emerge. Ideally, therefore, the establishment of target zones should be complemented by an agreement to coordinate monetary policies.[3]

Are there other policy instruments that could usefully complement monetary policy in keeping the exchange rate on track? One possibility is *sterilized intervention*,[4] which in principle—when assets are imperfect substitutes—gives a measure of freedom to influence the exchange rate independently of interest rates. However, the Jurgensen Report (1983) has now provided an authoritative endorsement of the view that has commanded increasing academic support in recent years: namely, that sterilized intervention is a useful tool for smoothing out short-run exchange rate volatility but virtually impotent to remedy persistent misalignments. Given that the major problem of floating rates is the size and persistence of misalignments rather than short-run volatility, one should not rely on much of a contribution from sterilized intervention.

While sterilized intervention by a single country may be a weak tool, it might have a role to play in the context of *coordinated intervention*. The markets may be impressed by a display that both parties agree that their bilateral rate is misaligned and are prepared to do something about it, even if one country (or even both countries) involved is reluctant to allow intervention to influence its domestic monetary policy. In general, however, it is desirable that intervention be allowed to have some impact on the money supply: intervention that is less than fully sterilized is after all a way of systematically allowing the pursuit of an exchange rate target to have some influence on domestic monetary policy.

Another possible instrument is provided by *capital controls*. The attraction of capital controls is the same as that of sterilized intervention: that, if they can be made to work, they provide a degree of freedom to influence the exchange rate independently of interest rates. The use of capital controls has, however, been questioned both on the grounds of their doubtful effectiveness and their interference with an efficient allocation of capital. The question of effectiveness seems to vary a great deal between countries and over time. There *are* countries, of which the most notable example is Japan, that have had effective capital controls for lengthy periods. But there are also cases of countries (like the United States in the 1960s) that have employed capital controls that covered only certain types of transactions, which proved notably ineffective—not surprisingly, given that "money is fungible." Concerns about the inefficiencies of capital controls are sometimes rather exaggerated: it is, after all, perfectly possible to obtain major welfare gains by drawing on the international capital market to supplement domestic savings while controlling capital movements. Nevertheless, once a country has become well integrated into the world capital market, it would need pervasive controls to isolate it again. Such controls should not necessarily be ruled out under all circumstances, but they are not an attractive option to be deliberately embraced as a normal part of international monetary arrangements.

Another policy instrument that might be directed to influencing the exchange rate is *fiscal policy*. As the earlier discussion of the Feldstein doctrine illustrated, it is essential that fiscal policy be consistent with exchange rate policy. Nevertheless, fiscal policy is not well suited to be an instrument of exchange rate management, partly because it is too inflexible, and partly for the reason elaborated by Robert Mundell (1962)—namely, that fiscal policy has a "comparative advantage" in influencing domestic demand rather than the balance of payments, in comparison with monetary policy. Of course, both fiscal and monetary policy should in principle be determined simultaneously by a general equilibrium approach rather than by the "assignment" of each instrument to a single target, but it is helpful to think of the "structural" budget surplus reflecting various calls on savings and investment at a normal level of employment, while the actual budget surplus (or deficit) is allowed to vary over the cycle in the interests of stabilizing output.

A SUMMARY: THE CHARACTERISTICS OF TARGET ZONES

While there has been scattered support in recent years for the notion of "target zones," it has not been accompanied by any detailed exposition of what would be involved in such an approach. As one unfortunate result, target zones have been criticized as too rigid by some writers who were clearly interpreting the idea in a far more rigid sense than that in which it has been used here. It is hoped that the present attempt to give content to the phrase will lead to future debate being directed at substance rather than semantics.

As used here, the term "target zones" would involve:

- soft margins, rather than a commitment to prevent the rate from straying outside the target zone
- a zone perhaps 20 percent wide, outside of which rates would be considered "clearly wrong"
- a crawling zone, with the crawl reflecting both differential inflation and any need for balance of payments adjustment

- publication of the target zone
- the partial direction of monetary policy (perhaps in the form of intervention that is not fully sterilized) to discourage the exchange rate from straying outside its target zone.

NOTES

1. At least, the negotiation was successful in achieving agreement, though that agreement lasted little over a year. . . . There was good reason for the Smithsonian Agreement to break down: the dollar and the yen remained misaligned by over 10 percent and the DM by almost 10 percent.
2. Whether one names a central rate to a target zone, or simply the soft margins of such a zone, is a cosmetic question.
3. A forthcoming Institute study by Ronald I. McKinnon will address this issue.
4. Intervention in the exchange market is said to be "sterilized" when it is not allowed to affect the domestic money supply. This requires that the potential reduction in the monetary base as a result of the central bank selling foreign currency in exchange for domestic currency is prevented by a central bank purchase of domestic nonmonetary assets.

21. Evolution Of The SDR, 1974–1981

WILLIAM J. BYRNE

Special drawing rights (SDRs) are reserve assets allocated by the Fund to its members. They were introduced in 1970 as a supplement to existing reserve assets, as it was expected at that time that the growth of the volume of international reserves would otherwise be inadequate to meet the growing demand for them. SDRs were to be held by countries as part of their reserves and converted into currencies when countries were in balance of payments (BOP) difficulties, as was also the practice with gold. Since then the characteristics and nature of the asset have changed considerably, as has the system of which they are a part.

The year 1974 was particularly important in the evolution of the SDR. It had previously been valued by reference to a fixed quantity of gold, via the par value of the U.S. dollar. After 1973 par values were no longer observed and the dollar, as well as other major currencies,

William J. Byrne is in the Special Drawing Rights Division of the International Monetary Fund's Treasurer's Department.

was allowed to float. In this new regime of managed floating it was desired to give the SDR stability in exchange value that was lacking for individual currencies. To achieve this, the SDR was valued from 1974 by reference to a basket of the currencies most widely used in international trade and transactions. Countries holding SDRs in their reserves would therefore be less likely than would countries holding only one or two currencies to find the value of their reserves changing sharply in relation to the value of their imports on account of exchange rate changes.

Also in 1974 the Committee on the Reform of the International Monetary System (the Committee of Twenty) proposed that the SDR should become the principal reserve asset of the international monetary system, an objective that was incorporated in 1978 into the Fund's Articles of Agreement. Since the SDR is an international asset that is issued by the international community acting through the Fund, under agreed procedures to achieve agreed objectives, making it into the principal reserve asset means that these objectives (notably that provision of adequate global liquidity) can be better served. However, it was recognized that, if it were to become so important, the SDR could not remain an asset merely to be held for use in BOP difficulties; it would have to become as versatile in its range of uses as other reserve assets, particularly the reserve currencies. Its interest rate, which had previously been 1½ percent per annum, would also have to increase to a level closer to that earned on reserve currencies.

ALLOCATIONS

Currently all Fund members are participants in the SDR scheme and are, therefore, eligible to receive allocations of SDRs. When there is judged to be a long-term global need to supplement existing reserve assets, the Fund allocates SDRs to participants in proportion to their quotas. The Fund created SDR 9.5 billion over the three years 1970–72, allocating them to 112 member countries. In 1978 the Fund's Board of Governors concurred in a proposal by the Managing Director that noted that countries wanted to increase their reserves as the level of their international transactions rose and that such increases could be expected to continue. Accordingly, SDR 4 billion was allocated in each of the years 1979, 1980, and 1981, bringing the total number of SDRs in existence to SDR 21 billion. At the end of December 1981, SDR 16 billion were held by participants and SDR 5 billion by the Fund's General Resources Account. The resumption of allocations reversed a decline in the ratio of SDR holdings to total reserve holdings. As a proportion of total reserves, SDR holdings fell from 5.9 percent at the end of 1972 to 2.9 percent at the end of 1978, rising to 4.4 percent at the end of 1981.

The Managing Director reported to the Board of Governors in June 1981 that he was not in a position to make a proposal for further SDR allocations that would command broad support among members of the Fund and that as soon as there was such support, he would submit a proposal. At its meeting in May 1982 the Interim Committee asked the Executive Board to continue its efforts to obtain a convergence of views so that the Managing Director could frame a proposal on SDR allocations in the current period.

THE VALUATION BASKET

Between 1974 and 1978, a basket of 16 currencies was used to determine the value of the SDR in order to dampen the effects of the often erratic fluctuations in individual exchange rates that were occurring. After 1978, however, moves were made to make the SDR more usable as a private unit of account outside the Fund. In 1981, the composition of the basket was simplified by replacing the 16 currencies with those of the 5 major trading nations. (Care was taken, both when the basket method was first introduced and when its composition was altered, to ensure continuity in the value of the SDR during and after the changeover.)

Under the basket technique, the SDR is valued as the sum of fixed amounts of several currencies. To ensure maximum stability for the exchange value of the SDR, the criterion used for the selection of the currencies in the basket in 1974, and again when the basket was reviewed in 1978, was that they should be those most widely used in international trade and payments. The weight each currency was given in the basket was intended to reflect its importance in trade as well as its importance in financial markets. The basket method of valuation is illustrated in Table 1.

To reflect the changing importance of different currencies in world trade, periodic reviews and changes in the currency composition of the basket were necessary as the importance of different currencies in world trade also changed. Thus, from 1974 to 1978, the basket contained the 16 currencies whose issuing countries had a share in world exports of more than 1 percent over the period 1968–72. Between 1972 and 1976, the exports of some 18 countries exceeded 1 percent of total world exports. In 1978 it was decided, however, to maintain the size of the basket at 16. The currencies of Saudi Arabia and Iran were included in the basket for the first time and those of Denmark and South Africa were dropped.

TABLE 1. SDR Valuation Basket, 1974–81

	JULY 1, 1974–JUNE 30, 1978		JULY 1, 1978–DECEMBER 31, 1980		JANUARY 1, 1981 TO DATE		SAMPLE VALUATION, NOVEMBER 6, 1981	
CURRENCY (1)	INITIAL PERCENTAGE WEIGHT (2)	CURRENCY AMOUNTS[1] (3)	INITIAL PERCENTAGE WEIGHT (4)	CURRENCY AMOUNTS[2] (5)	INITIAL PERCENTAGE WEIGHT (6)	CURRENCY AMOUNTS[3] (7)	EXCHANGE RATE[4] (8)	U.S. DOLLAR EQUIVALENT[5] (9)
U.S. dollar	33.0	0.40	33.0	0.40	42.0	0.54	1.0000	0.540000
Deutsche mark	12.5	0.38	12.5	0.32	19.0	0.46	2.2225	0.206974
Pound sterling	9.0	0.045	7.5	0.05	13.0	0.071	1.8725	0.132948
French franc	7.5	0.44	7.5	0.42	13.0	0.74	5.6150	0.131790
Japanese yen	7.5	26.0	7.5	21.0	13.0	34.0	228.82	0.148588
Canadian dollar	6.0	0.071	5.0	0.070		U.S. dollar value of SDR 1 =		1.160300
Italian lira	6.0	47.0	5.0	52.0		SDR value of US$1 =		0.861846
Netherlands guilder	4.5	0.14	5.0	0.14				
Belgian franc	3.5	1.6	4.0	1.6				
Swedish krona	2.5	0.13	2.0	0.11				
Australian dollar	1.5	0.012	1.5	0.017				
Spanish peseta	1.5	1.1	1.5	1.5				
Norwegian krone	1.5	0.099	1.5	0.10				
Danish krone	1.5	0.11	—	—				
Austrian schilling	1.0	0.22	1.5	0.28				
South African rand	1.0	0.0082	—	—				
Saudi Arabian riyal	—	—	3.0	0.13				
Iranian rial	—	—	2.0	1.7				

Source: IMF, Treasurer's Department.
—Indicates currency not included in SDR basket.

[1] Derived from the initial percentage weights in column 2 using average exchange rates over the three months ending June 28, 1974, so that on that date the SDR's value was the same under the former valuation procedure and under the basket procedure.
[2] Derived from the initial percentage weights in column 4 using average exchange rates over the three months ending June 30, 1978, so that on that date the SDR's value was the same under the former valuation basket (in column 3) and the revised basket (in column 5).
[3] Derived from the initial percentage weights in column 6 using average exchange rates over the three months ending December 31, 1980, so that on that date the SDR's value was the same under the former valuation basket (in column 5) and the revised basket (in column 7).
[4] Middle rate between buying and selling rates at noon in the London exchange market as determined by the Bank of England, expressed in currency units per U.S. dollar except for the pound sterling, which is expressed in U.S. dollars per pound sterling.
[5] The U.S. dollar equivalents of the currency amounts in column 7 at the exchange rates in column 8—that is, column 7 divided by column 8 except for the pound sterling, for which the amounts in the two columns are multiplied.

After 1978, as the SDR began to be more widely used as a unit of account in transactions outside the Fund, the prospect of such frequent changes in the currencies included in the basket was viewed as a possible handicap to its wider role. Since a large and persistent gap existed between the value of the exports of the five leading exporters and those of the others—a gap which could reasonably be expected to continue for the foreseeable future—the number of currencies in the basket was reduced to five in 1981.

A desire for uniformity between the basket used for the valuation of the SDR and that used to establish its interest rate was another important consideration in the change to a five-currency basket. The interest rate had been determined since 1974 by reference to interest rates in the capital markets of the same five countries selected for the basket in 1981.

The relative importance of each currency in the basket is based on a somewhat broader interpretation of representativeness than that used to select the currencies. Since the United States' share in world exports of goods and services did not adequately reflect the importance of the U.S. dollar in international financial transactions, it was given a greater weight in the basket than the United States' trade share alone would warrant. In 1981, equal importance was attached to exports of goods and services in 1975–79 and of balances of each component currency held in the reserves of other members. As a result, the initial weight assigned to the U.S. dollar was 42 percent; this compared with the United States' 32 percent share in total exports of the five countries whose currencies were included in the basket.

The currency composition and weighting pattern of the SDR will be revised every five years beginning January 1, 1986, unless the Fund's Executive Board decides otherwise, so as to include the currencies of the five member countries of the Fund with the largest exports of goods and services during the latest five-year period for which full data are available. (Thus, the revision effective January 1, 1986 will include the most important currencies for 1980–84.) However, a currency will not replace another currency on the list unless the value of the exports of the country issuing the former currency over the relevant five-year period exceeds that of the country issuing the later currency by at least 1 percent. The amounts of the currencies in the revised valuation basket for the SDR will reflect both the values of the exports of goods and services by the issuing countries and the balances of these currencies held by other members. This procedure of announcing well in advance the timing of future revisions and the principles on which they will be made enables the Fund to maintain over time the representativeness of the SDR basket without the need for unexpected changes in the currency composition or weighting pattern of the basket, thereby improving the usability of the SDR as a private unit of account.

The use of the SDR as a unit of account outside the Fund has grown in importance during the period under review. A growing number of international organizations use the SDR as a unit of account. In a number of international conventions the SDR has replaced the Poincaré or Germinal francs, which are defined by reference to a fixed quantity of gold. Some 15 countries peg their currency to the SDR. It has also gained acceptance as a unit of account in international financial markets, largely because of the automatic element of portfolio diversification entailed by its basket valuation. The reduction in the number of currencies in the valuation basket from 16 to 5 gave impetus to this use, particularly because it made it easier for banks to handle SDR-denominated deposits. Time deposits denominated in SDRs are most important in terms of volume, but there is a wide range of other instruments, ranging from current accounts, through certificates of deposit and floating rate notes, to ten-year syndicated credits. However, a clearing system for private SDR payments has not yet developed. Such a system would facilitate further growth in the volume and type of SDR-denominated financial instruments and might also encourage the use of the SDR as a unit for invoicing commercial transactions. Current use of the SDR for this purpose is minimal.

THE RATE OF INTEREST

Measures affecting the rate of interest on the SDR have also been implemented in order to enhance its attractiveness as a reserve asset. The chart shows that from an initial level of 5 percent per annum in 1974, the rate has risen to the full level of the combined market rate of the basket of currencies on which it is based.

The Fund pays interest on holdings of SDRs and levies charges at the same rate on allocations. Accordingly, participants whose holdings exceed their allocations earn net interest, while those whose holdings are below allocations pay net charges, at the going rate. Since 1974 the interest rate on the SDR has been established by reference to domestic interest rates in five countries—the United States, the Federal Republic of Germany, Japan, France, and the United Kingdom. Member countries hold most of their reserves in these currencies, and the financial markets in these countries possess a range of assets of sufficient quality, with appropriate maturities and readily available daily quotations. (The assets currently included in the interest rate basket are market yields for three-month U.S. Treasury bills, the three-month interbank deposit rate in the Federal Republic of Germany, the three-month interbank money rate against private paper in France, the discount rate on two-month (private) bills in Japan, and market yields for three-month U.K. Treasury bills.)

FIGURE 1. Combined market interest rate and SDR interest rate
(July 1974–December 1981)

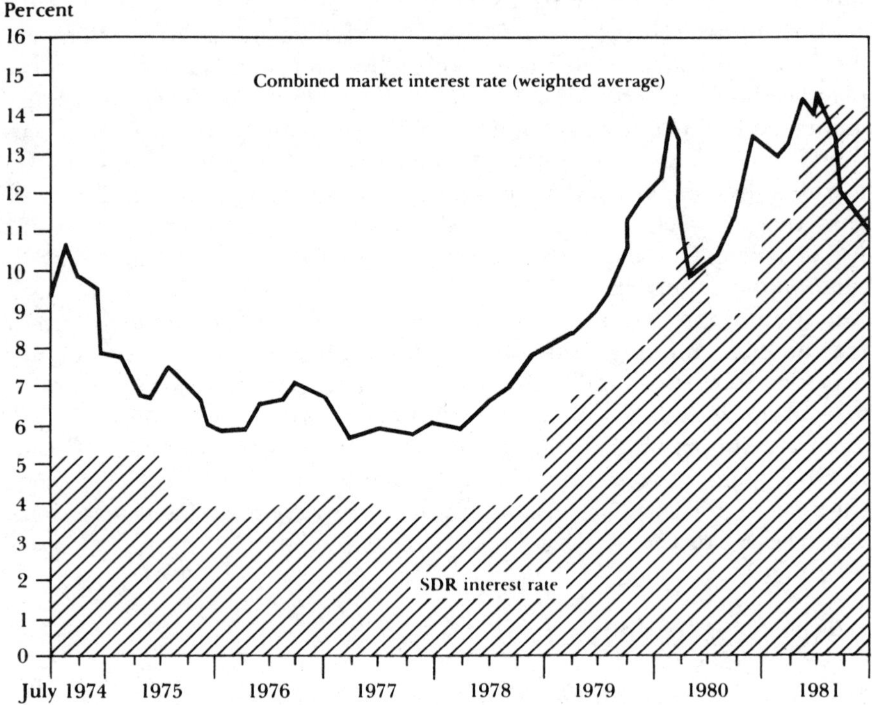

Source: IMF, Treasurer's Department.

Each interest rate is weighted by the percentage contribution of the corresponding currency to the value of the SDR. The weighted average of the five interest rates is called the combined market interest rate. During the period under review, important changes have occurred in the way in which the actual interest rate on the SDR is derived from the combined market interest rate and in the frequency with which the SDR interest rate is altered. The interest rate on the SDR was set at 5 percent per annum on July 1, 1974, about half the combined market rate at the time. It was adjusted, according to a formula, every six months. Experience showed that the SDR rate, which the workings of the formula kept at about half the combined market rate, was too low, impairing the quality of the SDR as a reserve asset. Consequently, between July 1976 and May 1981 the SDR interest rate was raised in steps to the full combined market rate. Since July 1976 it has been set quarterly rather than half-yearly to make it more responsive to variations in the combined market rate.

A MORE USABLE SDR

An important feature of the period under review has been the relaxation of different restrictions on the use of SDRs. These restrictions were generally introduced as safeguards in 1970 when the SDR scheme began. However, as the SDR and the international monetary system evolved, the emphasis changed to increasing the versatility and usability of the SDR. These restrictions therefore had less of a role to play, and they were gradually dropped.

The reconstitution requirement, which was a feature of the SDR scheme from its inception, initially required each participant to maintain a minimum average holding of SDRs of 30 percent of its average net cumulative allocation over successive five-year periods. The requirement was introduced to discourage the use of SDRs for longer-term financing and the disproportionate use of SDRs by participants because of any preference they may have had to retain other reserve assets.

However, the requirement weakened the SDR's status as a reserve asset, as there is no similar obligation to maintain minimum average balances of other types of reserve asset. With the increases in the rate of interest on the SDR, and with other improvements in its quality and usability, the Fund by the late 1970s considered the SDR a sufficiently strong reserve asset to do without the compulsory holding requirements. The required average holding was reduced from 30 to 15 percent of net cumulative allocations on January 1, 1979, and was abrogated completely, effective April 30, 1981. Participants, however, are still expected to pay due regard to the desirability of pursuing over time a balanced relationship between their holdings of SDRs and their other reserves.

When the SDR was created, only three uses were envisaged for it. The first was in transactions with designation, where the Fund designates a participant in a strong BOP and gross reserve position to provide currency in exchange for SDRs to a country wishing to convert its SDRs. Participants are obliged to accept SDRs in this way as long as their holdings are less than three times their total allocations. The second was the use of SDRs in transactions with the Fund, and the third was in sales of SDRs for currency by agreement with another participant. However, transactions by agreement were permitted only if the user of SDRs was redeeming balances of its own currency held by the other participant or if the Fund authorized the particular transaction or had made a general authorization of that particular type of transaction. With a few exceptions, the country selling SDRs was subject to the requirement of a BOP need, which also applies to the use of SDRs in transactions with designation. These limitations on the use of SDRs in transactions by agreement were established to increase the likelihood that participants in a strong BOP position would not have acquired SDRs voluntarily thereby reducing the amount they could be obliged to receive in a designated transaction.

The limitations on the free use of SDRs in transactions by agreement were eliminated between 1976 and 1978 to make SDRs more usable. In 1976 the Fund's Executive Board prescribed that participants could engage in transactions by agreement that brought the holdings of both participants closer to their net cumulative allocations. It exempted both these transactions and transactions by agreement between participants to promote reconstitution (which it had authorized earlier) from the requirement of a BOP need. After this liberalization the number and value of transactions by agreement rose sharply. In 1977 SDR 699 million were transferred in 39 transactions by agreement, compared with SDR 40 million in 6 such transactions in 1975.

The Second Amendment to the Fund's Articles of Agreement, which came into effect on April 1, 1978, further liberalized transactions by agreement. Under the amended Articles, participants may enter into transactions by agreement with all other participants, without any requirement of Fund approval of the particular transaction or the type of transaction and without any BOP need. Thus the SDR became freely usable between participants in transactions by agreement. There was a sharp increase in the value of transactions by agreement in 1981, with more participants selling SDRs in these transactions than in past years. Despite the liberalization of transactions by agreement, transactions with designation have remained quantitatively important. The Fund has also made increasing use of the SDR in its own operations, notably in payment of quota increases, for charges on the use of Fund resources, in purchases, and for interest on and repayment of Fund burrowing (see Table 2).

In order to widen the range of possible uses of SDRs, the Second Amendment also empowered the Fund to prescribe uses of SDRs that are not otherwise explicitly authorized. Between December 1978 and March 1980 the Fund adopted a series of decisions to permit the following additional uses of SDRs: (1) in swap arrangements, (2) in forward operations, (3) in loans, (4) in the settlement of financial obligations, (5) as security for the performance of financial obligations, and (6) in donations. The first uses of SDRs in loans and in settlement of financial obligations occurred in 1981.

Since the inception of the SDR scheme, the Fund has had the power to prescribe certain institutions as "other holders" of SDRs. The Bank for International Settlements was so prescribed in 1973. In the Second Amendment the Fund's power to prescribe institutions as other holders was extended to the broad category of official entities. Between 1978 and April 1982, 11 more organizations have been prescribed as other

TABLE 2. Uses of SDRs, 1974–81

(in millions of SDRs)

	1974	1975	1976	1977	1978	1979	1980	1981
Transfer by participants and other holders	**907**	**564**	**1,670**	**2,634**	**4,033**	**2,766**	**8,628**	**4,758**
To participants and other holders								
In designation	449	189	220	267	852	1,311	1,316	1,748
By agreement	379	40	353	699	1,827	319	347	927
To the Fund								
Repurchases	18	37	446	837	347	492	1,275	830
Charges	53	275	629	807	747	584	519	718
Quota payments	—	—	—	—	220	1	5,088	268
Other[1]	9	22	22	24	41	59	83	267
Transfers by the Fund	**130**	**241**	**989**	**1,145**	**1,332**	**1,472**	**2,262**	**2,636**
Purchases	4	35	430	428	1,025	1,266	1,556	1,962
To promote reconstitution	120	190	531	583	120	—	6	19
Other[2]	6	15	28	134	186	206	700	655
Total transfers	**1,037**	**804**	**2,659**	**3,779**	**5,365**	**4,238**	**10,890**	**7,394**
SDR holdings (*end of period*)								
Participants	8,858	8,764	8,655	8,133	8,110	12,479	11,803	16,411
Other holders	—	—	—	—	—	—	6	3
Fund's General Resources Account	457	551	659	1,182	1,205	869	5,572	5,019
Total holdings	**9,315**	**9,315**	**9,315**	**9,315**	**9,315**	**13,348**	**17,381**	**21,433**

Source: IMF, Treasurer's Department.

Note: Details may not add to totals due to rounding.
—Indicates zero.
[1] Primarily interest received on the Fund's holdings.
[2] Principally remuneration on creditor positions in the Fund and interest on and repayment of borrowing by the Fund.

holders, under conditions that enable them to acquire and use SDRs in transactions and operations by agreement under the same terms and conditions outlined above for participants.

Thus, in 1974–81 the Fund took a number of measures to strengthen the SDR in its role as a reserve asset. These improvements are viewed as necessary steps if the SDR is to become the principal reserve asset of the international monetary system, as called for in the Fund's Articles of Agreement.

This article has, in the main, dealt with past developments regarding the SDR. It is important to bear in mind, however, that all the issues regarding the SDR have not been closed, and that the role and the nature of the SDR continue to evolve. For example, one feature of the SDR that has been extensively discussed in the past—and continues to be debated—is the greater use of the SDR as a unit of account, including in private transactions and in financial markets. Evolution of the SDR along these lines will determine the extent to which it will become a truly international reserve asset.

RELATED READING

Robert Dunn and Robert Ley, "Special drawing rights: a review of reconstitution, 1972–76." *Finance and Development* (March 1977).

Joseph Gold, *SDRs, Currencies, and Gold: Fifth Survey of New Legal Developments*, IMF Pamphlet No. 36 (Washington, DC, International Monetary Fund, 1981).

Walter O. Habermeier, "The SDR as an international unit of account," *Finance and Development* (March 1979).

J. J. Polak, "The SDR as a Basket of Currencies," *IMF Staff Papers* (December 1979).

———, *Valuation and Rate of Interest of the SDR*, IMF Pamphlet No. 18, (Washington, DC, International Monetary Fund, 1974).

Dorothy Meadow Sobol, "The SDR in Private International Finance," *Federal Reserve Bank of New York Quarterly Review* (Winter 1981–82).

22. On Seeking To Improve IMF Conditionality

JOHN WILLIAMSON

What is the social function served by having the International Monetary Fund (IMF) lend to its member countries? At a somewhat abstract level, I would suggest that it could be defined as that of easing the external constraint on its member countries to the extent that such an easing can be expected to be advantageous to the world community as a whole. It follows immediately that the easing has to be of the external constraint provided by *liquidity* rather than *solvency*, since at best, an easing of the solvency constraint involves a resource transfer that will leave the donors worse off, while at worst, a belief in endogeneity of the solvency constraint creates moral hazard problems that undermine the incentive for economic efficiency. Hence, my conception of the principle that should be guiding the Fund's lending policies is that they ease the external liquidity constraint to the degree that is generally advantageous while preserving the intertemporal external budget constraint dictated by solvency considerations.

I. THE RATIONALE FOR CONDITIONALITY

This principle can rationalize the parallel existence of low- and high-conditionality facilities in the Fund. There is general advantage in each country having liquidity adequate to finance temporary deficits rather than being forced to adjust to them, and in having the option of making adjustments that are needed to safeguard external solvency at a measured pace while financing the interim deficit. If liquidity adequate to fulfill those legitimate needs is provided unconditionally, there is a danger that countries with myopic governments will spend more than they should, and in the process get themselves into unsustainable deficit and the world into inflation. Low-conditionality finance could safely be provided on a more generous scale than unconditional liquidity, pro-

John Williamson has taught economics in Great Britain, Brazil, and the United States. He is currently a Senior Fellow at the Institute for International Economics in Washington, D.C.

vided that it were tied to the existence of objective exogenous circumstances which produce a temporary deficit. But where a deficit cannot be presumed to be temporary, then the provision of liquidity has to be conditional on adoption of a set of measures judged adequate to secure adjustment and thus ensure that the deficit will after all be temporary. That is the basic logic of high-conditionality finance.

The preceding argument suggests that low-conditionality liquidity should be provided on a rather generous scale relative to unconditional liquidity. This is not the case at the moment: on a world scale, drawing rights under the first credit tranche and the compensatory financing facility are derisory relative to reserves (even if one excludes gold and potential bank borrowing from one's concept of reserves). To change that balance by limiting unconditional liquidity would need asset settlement and international controls on bank lending, not to mention the definitive demonetization of gold—which does not sound like a promising basis for an Action Program. To change the balance by expanding low-conditionality liquidity would be redundant so far as countries with access to the international capital market are concerned. Where it could be important is in regard to the large group of low-income countries without significant access to the international capital market. For these countries an expansion and rationalization of the compensatory financing facility as urged by Sidney Dell and Roger Lawrence (1980), so as to entitle a country to borrow whenever exogenous events result in a deficit that can be presumed to be temporary, would be a very worthwhile development. It would also be logical to restructure the repayment obligations under such a facility, so that repayment fell due as the exogenous shocks went into reverse rather than on a fixed schedule. (But the low conditionality of the first credit tranche is an anachronism that cannot be justified by the rationale developed above, nor by any other of which I am aware.)

Where circumstances are such that there is no presumption that a deficit will be reversed without policy changes, the principles suggested above imply that the provision of liquidity has to be conditional on appropriate modification in policies. There may be some scope for trusting countries to introduce such policy changes of their own volition without supervision from "grandmother" Fund. For example, I have argued elsewhere (1982, p. 16) that countries faced with an exogenous but presumptively permanent payments deterioration might be allowed low-conditionality finance for a *tapering* proportion of the deficit resulting from the adverse shock. That would provide them with time to implement adjustment policies of their own choosing. But if adjustment failed to occur reasonably promptly, they would in due course be forced back into seeking high-conditionality loans—as would a country whose deficit arose from its own policy errors as soon as its unconditional liquidity was exhausted. Under such circumstances, the basic notion that the Fund should insist on adoption of a set of policy measures that can be presumed adequate to secure adjustment as a condition for granting credit is surely correct. Yet far too many of the "radical" attacks on the Fund seem to me to deny this premise, and to amount instead to demands that the Fund relax the solvency constraint on governments that the observer judges ethically meritorious.

II. THE IMPLEMENTATION OF HIGH CONDITIONALITY

Designation of the Fund as an "adjustment institution" whose duty may involve its withholding credit until it is satisfied that a program adequate to induce adjustment is in place requires the Fund to take a view on what constitutes an adequate adjustment program. Given the fact of national sovereignty, it would in principle be improper for the Fund to dictate the form of such a program, as opposed to satisfying itself that a country's chosen program is (with reasonable probability) adequate to the task. There are undoubtedly occasions when the Fund has been insensitive in the way in which it has seemed to attempt to dictate a program.

But I am not persuaded that this is an issue which demands substantive changes in Fund policy, as opposed to a bit more tact by certain members of the IMF staff. If the Fund is not satisfied that the policy program initially laid before it by a country wishing to borrow will be adequate to secure adjustment, then it has to discuss how to make it adequate. In giving policy advice, it would be irresponsible of the Fund to advise only measures that would be certain to secure a payments turnaround and to ignore the costs to the country's domestic objectives (absorption, growth, the control of inflation, income distribution, etc.). It has to be concerned to devise a package that will respect the full range of objectives that countries consider important as well as achieving a payments recovery.

The more important question in my view is therefore that of identifying the type of macroeconomic strategy that will combine payments adjustment with satisfactory domestic performance. While this will vary depending on both the circumstances and the priorities of individual countries, and the Fund needs to be sensitive to variations in both of those dimensions, there is no getting away from the fact that the requirements of payments adjustment while respecting the interests of other countries imply that measures will ordinarily be drawn from a rather narrow set. Of course, any imaginative economic theorist can invent paradoxical cases in which the balance of payments would benefit by revaluation (low elasticities of demand and high elasticities of supply), credit expansion (output of exportables constrained by credit-financed imported inputs), increased government spending (on debottlenecking the tradable goods sector), or whatever; but one needs some pretty strong empirical evidence that such circumstances actually exist before one can prudently embrace the paradoxical option in a specific case. In general, Fund programs are bound to involve devaluation, credit restriction, and fiscal retrenchment.

One therefore cannot test whether the Fund exhibits proper flexibility as opposed to rigid monetarism by examining the frequency with which its programs involve devaluation or credit ceilings or cuts in public expenditure. A relevant test of whether Fund programs respond to the objective circumstances of countries is whether the recommended mix between expenditure-reducing and expenditure-switching policies is varied so as to avoid pushing a borrowing country significantly below internal balance. It is quite clear that the Fund is at times sensitive to this issue: see Hans Schmitt (1981) for an account of why the Fund urged a significant devaluation as a part of the Portuguese program of 1977. Discussion at the Institute for International Economics' conference on IMF Conditionality (the proceedings of which will appear in my 1983 volume) indicated that this was not an isolated instance. And the case studies placed before that conference yielded rather little evidence of the Fund having urged deflationary overkill, at least in the period 1976–81; in cases where that accusation was made, the interruption to growth was either slight (U.K.) or in retrospect it is clear that policy was on a completely unsustainable course (Jamaica, Turkey) or both (Peru). It is not clear, however, that examination of an earlier period would have found equally little evidence of Fund demands for overkill, nor is it clear that the tightening of conditionality in the course of 1981 has not jeopardized the enlightened attitude on that issue that had come to rule in the Fund during the period studied by the Institute's conference.

Two litmus tests of whether the Fund accepts national preferences are whether it accepts national decisions on the priority to be attached to combating inflation and whether (in the typical case where wages are above the market-clearing level in the tradable sector) the Fund offers countries the option of a higher level of real output in exchange for a cut in the real wage. On the first issue, the Fund has come a long way since 1967, when it opposed the expansionist policies that initiated the Brazilian "miracle" on the ground that reducing inflation should remain the top priority. All the evidence is that in its relations with small borrowing countries (as opposed to the rhetoric it directs at its major members), the Fund now accepts national views on the priority to be attached to combating inflation. On the second issue, there is not much evidence that the Fund has yet faced up to the tradeoff any more realistically than its major members.

Other policies which the Fund customarily urges on member countries include maintenance of an outward orientation; it regularly requires that borrowing members undertake not to increase restrictions on trade or current-account payments. This is in part intended to protect the general international interest in a liberal order, and in part reflects an intellectual conviction that outwardly oriented policies are in the best interests of the countries that adopt them. Aside from some concern that the speed of import liberalization urged may in some cases have been precipitate (Jamaica, Peru, Turkey), the Fund's position seems to me entirely reasonable.

III. IMPROVEMENTS IN CONDITIONALITY

I have argued up to now that there is a logic in both the broad structure of IMF conditionality and the types of measures that feature in Fund programs. In the process I have already mentioned certain improvements that seem to me to be called for: extension and rationalization of access to low-conditionality finance where payments deficits arise as a result of exogenous shocks (at least so far as low-income countries are concerned); the restructuring of repayment obligations to tie reimbursements to objective, exogenous determinants of ability to pay; and more caution in the speed at which imports are liberalized. Several other suggestions were advanced in my study that drew on the Institute's conference (1982).

1. I argued that in addition to the traditional categories of temporary, excess demand, and fundamental deficits, it is desirable to recognize the concept of a "structural deficit." This is defined as a deficit caused by a presumably permanent adverse exogenous shock which cannot be adjusted without abandoning internal balance other than by structural change. (The term is *not* being used to denote a deficit that is permanent or inevitable.) Structural deficits so defined were widespread in oil-importing developing countries following the two oil shocks—and if slow northern growth and high real interest rates are to be permanent phenomena, are now virtually universal in those countries. A structural deficit has a particularly strong claim to be financed with the aid of the international community while adjustment is effected. Given that the necessary adjustment program needs to combine a prudent demand management policy (and thus draw on the Fund's expertise) with structural adjustment (and thus draw on the World Bank's expertise), it seems logical that structural deficits be financed by parallel extended facility loans from the Fund and structural adjustment loans from the Bank. Complementary demand-side conditions would be negotiated by the Fund and supply-side conditions by the Bank.

2. The Fund has often been criticized for the distributional impact of austerity programs adopted under its guidance. It has tended to reply that it has no business interesting itself in the distributional

consequences of members' programs, and (somewhat inconsistently) that in any event, the improvement in the rural-urban terms of trade that usually results from a more outward orientation and price liberalization is distributionally progressive rather than regressive. The second proposition is probably generally true, although there are countries where the major benefits of higher agricultural prices go to landlords rather than peasants and there are other aspects of Fund programs whose impact is typically regressive, so giving little reason to believe that Fund programs are typically progressive overall. The first proposition seems to me to rest on a confusion. No one is calling for the Fund to impose its views on income distribution on its members or to adopt the Gini coefficient as a new performance criterion. What is being suggested is that the Fund should build up, and subsequently offer to those members that wish to avail themselves of it, expertise in designing and implementing equity-oriented stabilization/adjustment programs. One is happy to note that the World Bank does not suffer from the Fund's qualms on this issue (A. W. Clausen, 1982, p. 10).

3. The heart of the Fund's monitoring of the programs agreed with borrowing countries is through the performance criteria, any breach of which triggers a suspension of further disbursements. Performance criteria are normally framed in terms of domestic credit ceilings, as well as limits on credit to the public sector, limits on public sector deficits, and/or limits on public sector foreign borrowing. There are good reasons for the emphasis placed on such variables: they are policy variables, they can be objectively measured, the data to assess compliance are available promptly, a wide range of theories indicate that control of these variables is important to the payments outcome, and—in the case of the domestic credit ceiling—continued compliance with the ceiling when faced with an exogenous shock provides a stabilizing negative feedback to the balance of payments. Nevertheless, these appropriately conceived criteria appear to be applied by the Fund in an inappropriately rigid way. There are a wide range of unexpected events whose occurrence may make it appropriate to modify a target; for example, successful inflation stabilization will increase the demand for money and so justify a higher credit ceiling (especially in countries with low capital mobility). An even clearer example is provided by a country which obtains a large proportion of its tax revenue from export taxes and has accepted a ceiling to the public sector deficit as a performance criterion. An unexpected fall in export prices would then require the country to take further deflationary fiscal action to meet the target, which would in general be inappropriate; rather, the performance criterion should in that case be automatically modified. In general, the Fund should make a great effort, which it does not at the moment, to frame performance criteria as contingent conditions

which will vary with the state of the world, rather than as fixed requirements.

4. Credit ceilings are a good technical way of checking compliance with overall fulfillment of commitments to limit expenditure. The effectiveness of Fund monitoring would be increased if there were a similar assurance that the broad thrust of expenditure-switching policies would also be maintained through the program. This could be accomplished by adopting the real exchange rate as an additional performance criterion.

5. There have been marked variations in the toughness of IMF conditionality in recent years. As documented in my 1982 study, conditionality was eased in mid-1979 and tightened again in mid-1981. These variations in conditionality appear to have affected all its major dimensions: the length of programs, the severity of the retrenchment in expenditure that was required, and the prerequisite of a devaluation adequate to restore competitiveness. It is important to consider the merits of both the *timing* and the *content* of these variations in conditionality.

On the issue of timing, one can make a good case for the relaxation of mid-1979, since this coincided with the onset of the exogenously induced deficits created by the second oil shock and a new world recession, but no case whatsoever for the subsequent tightening of mid-1981, which occurred in the midst of deepening world recession. This judgment rests on the view that the Fund should seek to ameliorate the impact of world cyclical developments on its weaker members and in the process make a modest contribution to a global anticyclical policy—a view which appears to be regarded as heretical in the Fund. It is, however, a view which springs straight from the discussion of the rationale for Fund lending at the beginning of this paper, inasmuch as there is a lower world cost in easing external liquidity constraints at a time of world recession than at a time of boom.

On the question of content, the move to multiyear programs and the willingness to approve programs that did not involve the expectation of a short-run output loss were to be welcomed, and the retreat from those positions in 1981 is to be deplored. In contrast, the weakening of the requirement for adequate expenditure-switching policies (in the form of the restoration of realistic exchange rates) in the period of easy conditionality was undesirable. The whole logic of Fund programs involves borrowing countries adopting measures that will suffice to restore a viable payments position in the medium term. There can be scope for legitimate differences of view about the state that the world economy should be assumed to reach in the medium term, but there can be no excuse for failing to insist on measures that give a reasonable prospect of adjustment being achieved even if the world economy is moderately prosperous. On the other hand, and of greater immediate relevance, the Fund will lose the ability to play any cyclical stabilization role if it takes too gloomy a view of the medium-term state of the world economy whenever the world develops a recession.

I conclude that there is no case for abandoning the basic structure of IMF conditionality, but ample scope for improving its application.

REFERENCES

Clausen, A. W., "Address" to the Board of Governors, Washington: World Bank, 1982.

Dell, Sidney and Lawrence, Roger, *The Balance of Payments Adjustment Process in Developing Countries*, New York: Pergamon Press, 1980.

Schmitt, Hans O., *Economic Stabilization and Growth in Portugal*, IMF Occasional Paper No. 2, Washington, 1981.

Williamson, John, *The Lending Policies of the International Monetary Fund*, Washington: Institute for International Economics, 1982.

———, *IMF Conditionality*, Washington: Institute for International Economics, 1983.

23. International Debt: Conflict and Resolution

JAMES R. BARTH and JOSEPH PELZMAN

I. INTRODUCTION

The current interest in international debt dates from late 1981 when Poland rescheduled some of its debt and became the first East European country to do so. Roughly eight months later Mexico experienced a financial crisis that led to a three-month postponement in its debt repayments to foreign banks. Since then, other less developed countries (LDCs) and Eastern bloc nations have had similar difficulties.

James R. Barth is Professor of Economics at George Washington University. Joseph Pelzman is Associate Professor of Economics at George Washington University.

* The authors gratefully acknowledge the very helpful discussions with Michele Fratianni and Robert Keleher and are heavily indebted to the earlier research on this issue conducted by Robert Weintraub.

The concern is that some of these countries will declare a moratorium on their debt repayments if not formally default, and the amounts involved are far from trivial.[1] The total outstanding external debt of non-oil developing countries was estimated to be $664 billion in 1983 and $61 billion in 1982 for Eastern Europe. Approximately half of this debt is owed to private creditors, including international banking organizations. There are two major fears associated with a debt moratorium: First, since a large portion of the debt is owed to commercial banks, any widespread moratorium or default could lead to a collapse of the international banking system. Second, a debt moratorium could dramatically curtail international trade as credit became increasingly restricted.

The conflict over how best to resolve the debt problem centers on the extent to which the worst fears of a default will be realized. Some argue that the fears are real enough to merit immediate action, primarily in the form of increased International Monetary Fund (IMF) quotas.[2] The IMF would then have the resources necessary to help debtor countries correct their problems.[3] Underlying this view is the belief that the debtor countries are essentially solvent but are confronted with a liquidity problem. Others argue that the likelihood of the worst fears being realized is extremely low and that increased IMF quotas are not necessary to avert a collapse in international banking and trade. It is argued that permanent quota increases are incompatible with the notion that the debtor countries are temporarily not liquid. Instead of increasing IMF quotas, the IMF should borrow in the private capital markets, sell off some of its gold holdings, or both. There is the assumption that permanently larger quotas may simply increase international liquidity without providing sufficient incentives for countries to implement the fiscal and monentary policies needed to sustain long-run economic growth. Moreover, such quota increases may lump together illiquid and insolvent debtor countries and treat both in the same way. As a result, a temporary postponement of defaults may mistakenly be viewed as a long-run solution.

The conflict over international debt is seen, therefore, to be a disagreement over the extent to which there is a sizable risk of collapse in international banking and trade. Those who perceive such a risk tend to favor a permanent increase in IMF quotas to provide greater liquidity, whereas those who believe that adequate safeguards are already in place tend to favor a more temporary measure by the IMF, such as borrowing in the capital markets or selling gold. The resolution of the debt problem, thus, does not depend on whether or not the IMF has a role to play in the current situation or on whether its role is filled by dispensing resources that are currently available to it or by dispensing those resources that are made available from larger quotas. The resolution lies in whether permanently increasing IMF quotas without adequately separating illiquid from insolvent countries will generate perverse incentives by both creditors and debtors and only postpone the day of reckoning, making that day even more unpleasant.

Other issues are inexplicably linked to how the IMF responds to the international debt situation. For example, is the IMF "bailing out" large international commercial banks by providing financial assistance to debtor countries? Is the "conditionality" imposed on countries when they borrow from the IMF appropriate? Are the debtor countries insolvent rather than illiquid? How does one handle "moral hazard" in responding to the situation? And how can one prevent the debt situation from recurring?

This monograph will attempt to answer these and other questions. We will focus mainly on the implications of the international debt situation for the U.S. banking system and U.S. trade. Chapter II provides an overview of some of the basic issues underlying the international debt problem. Chapter III then examines the role of U.S. banks and the responsibilities of the FDIC and the Federal Reserve System in dealing with the problem. Chapter IV discusses the implications of the debt problem for U.S. trade. The short- and long-run proposals for reform are then compared and contrasted in Chapter V. The last chapter contains the summary and conclusions.

II. AN OVERVIEW OF THE INTERNATIONAL DEBT PROBLEM

The Economic Rationale for Debt

Despite the current debt problem, there is widespread agreement that the extension of international credit per se is not the villain. In relatively unrestricted capital markets both creditors and debtors will agree on terms that presumably benefit all parties. Debtors gain because they obtain funds that would not otherwise be available. These funds may then be used to increase current consumption, increase the capital stock for greater future consumption, or both. The mix is important, because without adequate investment (in productive plant and equipment) and sufficient infrastructure (roads and highways, educational services, and power generating facilities) output growth will be impaired, jeopardizing not only future consumption but also the ability of debtor nations to service the debt. If there is not enough longrun output growth for a country to repay its external debts, the country is essentially insolvent.

Creditors gain from the extension of credit because they prefer the compensation received when they forego the use of their funds for an agreed upon period of time to using the funds now. Whether the funds loaned are used for current consumption or investment purposes interests creditors only to the extent that they perceive the riskiness of the loan to be affected. If so, the terms of the loan will be adjusted accordingly.[4]

Therefore, international debt, like domestic debt, arises quite naturally when there are relatively unrestricted money and capital markets. Creditors and debtors alike receive benefits that are not available from domestically generated and circulated funds. Debtors can finance investment projects that would otherwise go unfunded or be funded only at the expense of foregoing more sizable amounts of current consumption, while creditors receive greater compensation or a higher return on their funds (taking into account the perceived riskiness of the loans) than would otherwise be available.

There are also differences between international and domestic debt. Although risk is always present, the types of risk differ. With foreign debts there are the added risks of exchange rate fluctuations and changes in political factors. An even more fundamental difference is collateral. All loans are based on the presumption that either the loan will be repaid or that it has sufficient collateral to secure it. For example, people do not expect the U.S. government to default on its domestic interest-bearing debts, especially given its powers to tax and to print money. Collateral, therefore, is relatively unimportant. In the event of a default for other kinds of domestic loans, however, creditors usually take possession of those real assets that serve as collateral for the loan or use such "creditor remedies" as wage assignment and garnishment to obtain a part of the debtor's future income.

With foreign loans, however, the situation is quite different. Using creditor remedies and taking possession of real assets in the event of default is a far more cumbersome and complicated process. It is no doubt for this reason that the vast majority of bank loans abroad are guaranteed by foreign governments, with the usual presumption that such loans (or sovereign debt) will not be repudiated. The international debt problem, however, has many people questioning whether this presumption is accurate. Unlike domestic debt, the powers to tax and to print money cannot be used directly to resolve the problem insofar as the debt is denominated in foreign currencies, mainly U.S. dollars.

The Evolution of the Debt Problem

When oil prices exploded in the early 1970s, oil producing countries found themselves accumulating sizable amounts of "petrodollars," many of which were recycled by international banks to non-oil developing countries (including Mexico) to help finance their imports of both oil and non-oil products. Not since the 1930s had commercial banks played so important a role in providing credit to developing as well as the Eastern bloc nations. Throughout the 1970s the debt extended to these countries was considered to be manageable, particularly since "real" interest rates were quite low or negative during this period. The 1981–82 recession dramatically changed this situation. Real interest rates rose to relatively high levels, and the value of the U.S. dollar increased substantially relative to the currencies of debtor countries. Since much of the debt is denominated in U.S. dollars and carries a floating interest rate, these developments sharply increased the debt burden. Lower commodity prices and a decline in exports of developing countries only compounded the problem by reducing foreign exchange earnings. All this resulted in the current international debt problem.

A few years ago, the Federal Reserve System decided to bring down inflation by instigating a relatively unsteady but nonetheless significant reduction in money growth. The result was largely predictable: high real interest rates and sluggish output growth. Largely because of the high rates and an increased concern for safety, the dollar's value soared in foreign exchange markets. Although the U.S. economy began recovering from the recession in early 1983, real rates of interest have remained at relatively high levels when compared to similar stages of previous postwar recoveries. Many believe that this is in large part due to Congress's failure to deal adequately with the sizable projected out-year deficits. Thus, both U.S. fiscal and monetary policies have indirectly contributed to a worsening of the international debt problem. The benefits of reducing inflation are obtained only at some cost.

The debtor nations' fiscal and monetary policies also affect the debt situation. To the extent that these policies have not been coordinated to stabilize prices and minimize budget deficits at a level of governmental spending aimed at achieving longer term real growth, borrowing from abroad was a way to avoid making some hard budgetary decisions. The recession has only accelerated the decision-making process for many countries that are having trouble repaying their debts. The concern now, of course, is whether these countries have already over-extended themselves or whether an adjustment in fiscal and monetary policies together with a worldwide recovery is sufficient to make the debt burden manageable. If countries are over-extended or insolvent, then additional lending will not solve their problems. If countries can manage their debt by adjusting fiscal and monetary policies and by participating more fully in a worldwide recovery, however, then they are temporarily illiquid and additional lending may help. Even if the latter is the case, it is not clear that the additional lending should come from or be based on increased IMF quotas.

The Size of the Problem

The total external debt of non-oil developing countries amounted to $664 billion in 1983 (see Table 1), more than a five-fold increase over

TABLE 1. Non-Oil Developing Countries, External Debt
(Billions of dollars, 1973–83)

	1973	1974	1975	1976	1977	1978	1979	1980	1981	1982	1983
Total outstanding debt	130.1	160.8	190.8	228.0	278.5	336.3	396.9	474.0	555.0	612.4	664.3
Short-term debt	18.4	22.7	27.3	33.2	42.5	49.7	58.8	85.5	102.2	112.7	92.4
Long-term debt	111.8	138.1	163.5	194.9	235.9	286.6	338.1	388.5	452.8	499.6	571.6
By type of creditor											
Official creditors	51.0	60.1	70.3	82.4	98.7	117.5	133.0	152.9	172.4	193.2	218.7
Governments	37.3	43.4	50.3	57.9	67.6	79.1	87.2	98.7	108.6	120.4	135.3
International institutions	13.7	16.6	20.3	24.8	31.0	38.4	45.8	54.2	63.8	72.8	83.3
Private creditors	60.8	77.9	95.1	114.8	137.3	169.1	205.1	235.6	280.4	306.4	353.0
Unguaranteed debt	29.3	36.0	40.8	45.9	51.4	56.4	67.3	77.5	96.7	103.9	113.7
Guaranteed debt	31.5	42.0	52.4	66.6	85.9	112.7	137.8	158.1	183.7	202.2	239.3
Financial institutions	17.3	25.6	36.7	49.0	59.1	79.5	102.9	121.6	144.5	159.5	193.8
Other private creditors	14.2	16.3	17.6	19.8	26.8	33.2	34.9	36.5	39.2	42.7	45.5
Value of debt service payments	17.9	22.1	25.1	27.8	34.7	50.3	65.0	76.2	94.7	107.1	93.2
Interest payment	6.9	9.3	10.5	10.9	13.6	19.4	28.0	40.4	55.1	59.2	55.1
Amortization[1]	11.1	12.8	14.6	16.8	21.1	30.9	36.9	35.8	39.7	47.9	38.1
Debt service ratio[2]	15.9	14.4	16.1	15.3	15.4	19.0	19.0	17.6	20.4	23.9	19.3
Interest payments ratio	6.1	6.1	6.7	6.0	6.0	7.3	8.2	9.3	11.9	13.2	11.4
Amortization ratio[1]	9.8	8.3	9.4	9.3	9.4	11.7	10.8	8.3	8.6	10.7	7.9
Ratio of external debt to exports of goods and services[2]	115.4	104.6	122.4	125.5	126.4	130.2	119.2	112.9	124.9	143.3	144.4
Ratio of external debt to GDP[3]	22.4	21.8	23.8	25.7	27.4	28.5	27.5	27.6	31.0	34.7	34.7

Source: World Economic Outlook, 1983. Tables 32, 33, and 35, pp. 200–204.

[1] On long-term debt only. Estimates for the period up to 1981 reflect actual amortization payments. The estimates for 1982 and 1983 reflect scheduled payments, but are modified to take account of the rescheduling agreements of 1982 and early 1983.

[2] Payments (interest, amortization, or both) as percentages of exports of goods and services.

[3] Ratio of year-end debt to exports or GDP for year indicated.

the past decade. When compared to gross domestic product (GDP), debt rose to nearly 35 percent of GDP in 1983 from slightly over 22 percent in 1973. The real problem, however, is reflected in the recent trend in and composition of the service payments on the debt. Since 1980 interest payments have consistently exceeded amortization, and by 1983 the interest payment alone amounted to $55 billion.

Since exports are a source of foreign exchange, it is useful to express the debt service payments as a share of the value of the exports of goods and services. The calculations in Table 1 indicate that the interest payments ratio was relatively flat during the 1973–77 period, after which it started climbing until 1981–82 when it was roughtly double its 1973 level (12 percent versus 6 percent). In other words, in recent years roughly 12 percent of all export earnings was necessary to match the interest payments on all external debt. This sharp upturn in interest payments is generating most of the current concern, especially when one considers to whom the debt is owed.

Private creditors account for $353 billion of this debt in 1983, and roughly $219 billion is owed by official creditors. Even though $239 billion of this debt is guaranteed, recent developments have led many to question the value of the guarantee. Coupled with the fact that most of this kind of debt is held by commercial banks, this explains much of the concern over the stability of the international financial system.

One weakness in interpreting the figures in Table 1 is that they are based on data for 115 countries and, therefore, mask potentially wide differences among countries. For example, ten of the 115 countries account for 53 percent of the group's external debt and 68 percent of the debt owed to private creditors, but only 39 percent of GDP and 33 percent of exports (see *World Economic Outlook*, International Monetary Fund, May 1983, p. 9).

A more detailed description of the debt position of the ten major borrowers is presented in Table 2. Over the 1973–83 period the total outstanding debt of these borrowers increased at an annual average rate of 13.5 percent, compared to a 12.2 percent increase for all non-oil developing countries. Unlike all borrowers, however, the top ten borrowers have experienced a decline in their debt service payments. In 1973 the debt service payments for these countries was $5.6 billion, or approximately 12 percent of the total outstanding debt. In 1982 this figure stood at $24.9 billion, or 10.5 percent of the total. Despite this relative decline in the debt service payments, the burden of these payments when measured in terms of both GDP and exports has substantially increased. Measured in terms of the debt service payments as a percent of GDP, payments made by the top ten have more than doubled over the 1973–82 period, rising from 1.6 percent to 3.4 percent. Even more revealing, the share of debt service payments to exports roughly doubled, rising from 11.1 percent to 22.5 percent. The

TABLE 2. Top Ten Non-Oil Developing Countries, External Debt[1]
(Billions of dollars, 1973–82)

	1973	1974	1975	1976	1977	1978	1979	1980	1981	1982
Total outstanding debt	46.3	73.6	86.5	101.6	108.3	153.6	200.4	202.4	215.3	238.1
By type of creditor										
Official creditors	26.6	32.5	34.4	38.7	42.8	49.8	53.6	52.0	52.1	52.4
Governments	19.7	21.6	24.1	28.6	30.8	34.6	60.7	39.9	36.4	39.8
International institutions	6.9	10.9	10.3	10.1	12.0	15.2	12.9	12.1	15.7	12.6
Private creditors[2]	26.6	35.7	46.8	61.7	82.4	107.2	126.7	152.1	167.0	176.3
Unguaranteed debt[2]	8.0	11.5	13.6	16.0	21.2	27.5	31.8	34.6	40.1	33.5
Guaranteed debt	18.6	24.2	33.2	45.7	61.2	79.7	94.9	117.5	126.9	142.8
Financial institutions	13.1	18.2	26.8	37.7	52.5	69.6	80.1	98.1	110.8	126.7
Other private creditors	5.5	6.0	6.4	8.0	8.7	10.1	14.8	19.4	16.1	16.1
Value of debt service payments[3]	5.6	6.5	8.1	9.2	13.6	21.7	28.7	30.8	31.7	24.9
Interest payment	1.9	2.3	3.4	3.8	5.4	7.1	10.3	15.2	16.7	10.0
Amortization	3.7	4.2	4.7	5.4	8.2	14.6	18.4	15.6	15.0	14.9
Debt service ratio as a percent of GDP		1.6	2.1	1.9	2.6	3.0	2.4	3.1	3.2	3.4
Debt service ratio as a percent of exports		11.1	12.8	11.9	14.0	17.8	18.4	19.2	20.3	22.5

Source: The World Bank, *World Debt Tables*.

[1] Totals do not include Spain for the years 1974, 1981 and 1982. The top ten borrowers include: Argentina, Brazil, India, Indonesia, Israel, South Korea, Mexico, Spain, Venezuela and Yugoslavia.

[2] Information on private non-guaranteed debt is available for Brazil, Korea, India and Yugoslavia for 1973–81 and for Argentina only for 1978–81. Data for 1982 is only for Brazil and Yugoslavia.

[3] Only on guaranteed loans.

implication is that by 1982 an average of 22.5 percent of these exports of these countries was needed to pay for interest and amortization payments on their outstanding debt, most of it in interest.

The situation is even more dramatic for individual countries.[5] In Mexico the debt service ratio as a percent of exports increased from 22.2 percent in 1973 to over 30 percent in 1982. In Argentina and Brazil, the ratio rose from 17.7 percent and 13 percent to 24.6 percent and 32 percent. For major borrowers such as Korea and Yugoslavia, however, the debt service ratio either rose modestly or declined.

An examination of the sources of this credit reveals that the role of private creditors, particularly guaranteed private creditors, has increased dramatically. In 1973 private and official creditors provided $26.6 billion in loans each; by 1982 official credits increased to $52.4 billion and credits from private creditors increased to $176.3 billion, an increase of over 600 percent. This represents almost 50 percent of the total private credit available to 115 developing countries. The exposure of the ten largest borrowers in the private credit market largely explains the concern over the stability of the international financial system, especially the private banking system.

III. WILL THE U.S. BANKING SYSTEM COLLAPSE?

One of the main fears is that a substantial portion of the foreign debt is owed to U.S. commercial banks; and if developing countries fail to repay this debt, a number of banks may become insolvent.[6] Not all of the nearly 15,000 commercial banks in the U.S. are involved in the current debt problem, but those that are constitute the largest and the most viable. As a result, any problems they experience may send shock waves throughout the entire system. Depositors might become concerned about the safety of their funds if there were a default and may start a "run" on the banking system. If such runs go unchecked, then otherwise economically healthy banks may be forced into insolvency. Whether the current international debt problem could trigger such an event is the subject of this chapter. Before dealing directly with this issue, however, it is useful to determine to what extent U.S. banks are involved in the debt problem.

U.S. Banks' Involvement in International Debt

Total debt owed to U.S. and non-U.S. banks increased rather sharply during the 1975–83 period, from $63 billion in 1975 to slightly over $268 billion in 1982 (see Table 3). U.S. banks certainly participated in this growth, but at a somewhat slower rate so that their share of the total declined from nearly 55 percent in 1975 to roughly 37 percent in

TABLE 3. Bank Claims on Non-Oil Developing Countries
(Billions of dollars, end of period)

	CLAIMS ON ALL COUNTRIES				CLAIMS ON ARGENTINA, BRAZIL, AND MEXICO			
Year	*Total*	*U.S. Banks*	*Non-U.S. Banks*	*U.S. Share of Total (%)*	*Total*	*U.S. Banks*	*Non-U.S. Banks*	*U.S. Share of Total (%)*
1975	62.7	34.3	28.5	54.5	31.5	18.7	12.8	59.4
1976	80.9	43.1	37.8	53.3	42.5	24.7	17.8	58.1
1977	94.3	46.9	47.4	49.7	50.2	25.8	24.4	51.3
1978	131.3	52.2	79.1	39.8	63.2	26.8	36.4	42.4
1979	171.0	61.8	109.2	36.1	83.0	29.9	53.1	36.0
1980	210.2	75.4	134.8	35.9	108.1	37.0	71.1	34.2
1981	253.5	92.8	160.7	36.6	134.5	46.7	87.8	34.7
1982 (June)	268.3	98.6	169.7	36.7	145.0	52.4	92.6	36.1

Source: Statement by Paul A. Volcker, Chairman, Board of Governors of the Federal Reserve System, before the Committee on Banking, Finance and Urban Affairs, House of Representatives, February 2, 1983, Table II.

TABLE 4. U.S. and Non-U.S. Bank Claims on Major Borrowers
(Billions of dollars, June 1982)

COUNTRY	TOTAL	U.S.	NON-U.S.	U.S. SHARE (%)
1. Mexico	64.4	24.3	40.1	37.7
2. Brazil	55.3	20.7	34.6	37.4
3. Venezuela	27.2	11.1	16.1	40.8
4. South Korea	20.0	8.7	11.3	43.5
5. Argentina	25.3	8.6	16.7	34.0
6. Chile	11.8	6.3	5.5	53.4
7. Spain	23.7	5.7	18.0	24.1
8. Philippines	11.4	4.8	6.6	42.1
9. Taiwan	6.4	4.4	2.0	68.8
10. Columbia	5.5	2.7	2.8	49.1
11. Greece	9.7	2.7	7.0	27.8
12. Yugoslavia	10.0	2.5	7.5	25.0

Source: Statement by Paul A. Volcker, Chairman, Board of Governors of the Federal Reserve System, before the Committee on Banking, Finance and Urban Affairs, House of Representatives, February 2, 1983, Table III.

1982. Only three countries (Argentina, Brazil, and Mexico) account for approximately half or more of this debt. Once again, although U.S. banks' claims have risen significantly over the 1975–83 period, their share of the total for these three countries has declined.

Heading the list of countries in terms of total indebtedness to banks is Mexico, with Brazil a close second (Table 4). These two countries account for nearly $120 billion of total bank claims. Three other South American countries are included in the top six borrowers, which explains the frequent references to the "Latin American" debt problem. This is even more appropriate when one takes into account the countries that have recently engaged in major rescheduling efforts.

As can be seen from Table 5, public borrowers owe a substantial portion of the total debt. Moreover, approximately 60 percent of the debt has a maturity of one year or less, and, a relatively small portion has a maturity of over five years. This means that the service payments (interest and principal) are higher than if the maturity distribution were the reverse. In this kind of situation, meeting the scheduled payments or rolling over the debt becomes much more dependent on short-run factors and, thus, requires more careful long-run planning.

Further, a large part of the debt problem is concentrated among a few banks. Non-oil developing countries owed about $103 billion to all reporting banks (171 U.S. banking organizations) at the end of 1982, slightly over half of which was owed by Argentina, Brazil, and Mexico. However, the 24 largest banks account for approximately 82 percent, or $84 billion. Moreover, the nine largest banks are owed more than three times as much as the next fifteen largest banks ($64.1 billion vs.

TABLE 5. Amounts Owed to U.S. Banks by Foreign Borrowers
(Billions of dollars, December 1982)

	PORTION OF TOTAL OWED BY				*MATURITY OF DISTRIBUTION OF AMOUNTS OWED*		
	Total Amount Owed	*Banks*	*Public Borrowers*	*Private Nonbank Borrowers*	*One Year and Under*	*Over One to 5 Years*	*Over 5 Years*
To nine largest banks							
Non-Oil Developing Countries	64.1	18.0	26.2	19.9	36.4	17.9	9.8
Argentina	5.1	1.0	2.2	1.9	3.8	1.0	0.3
Brazil	13.3	4.2	5.8	3.4	5.4	5.0	2.9
Mexico	12.9	1.7	6.3	4.9	6.5	3.6	2.7
To next fifteen largest banks							
Non-Oil Developing Countries	20.2	9.1	4.9	6.2	12.2	4.2	3.8
Argentina	1.8	0.7	0.5	0.6	1.4	0.3	0.1
Brazil	3.9	2.3	0.9	0.7	1.8	0.8	1.3
Mexico	5.1	0.9	1.4	2.8	2.8	1.2	1.0
To all reporting banks							
Non-Oil Developing Countries	103.2	35.8	36.0	21.4	60.1	27.2	15.9
Argentina	8.2	2.2	3.1	2.9	6.0	1.7	0.6
Brazil	20.4	8.7	7.3	4.5	8.8	6.9	4.8
Mexico	24.4	4.0	9.7	10.7	13.4	6.5	4.4

Source: Country Exposure Lending Survey, December 1982, Federal Financial Institution Examination Council.

$20.3 billion). Thus, the nine largest banks account for about 62 percent of the total amount owed to all reporting banks.

Because capital is the amount by which assets exceed liabilities, it is particularly important to assess the relationship of total debt to the banks' capital. If some of the debt is defaulted, then assets will decline in value, and if they drop below liabilities, then the bank becomes insolvent. By comparing debt to capital, therefore, one can determine what effect a default would have on a bank's solvency condition. For 1977 through 1982, both for all reporting banks and the nine largest banks, capital has not increased as rapidly as have loans extended to developing countries (see Table 6). Specifically, claims as a percent of capital for all reporting banks increased from 115 in 1977 to 146 in 1982 for all non-oil developing countries. If all 115 countries defaulted and their debt was immediately reduced in value to zero, then all 171 reporting banks would become insolvent. To prevent this from happening, the banks would have to increase their capital by 46 percent, or $32.6 billion. Even though the banks would still have assets, a drop in total assets by $103.2 billion (from $1,261.0 to $1,157.8 billion) would exceed their total capital of $70.6 billion, thereby forcing the banks into insolvency. For the nine largest banks, the situation is much more severe, since their claims as a percent of capital increased from 163 in 1977 to 221 in 1982 for all non-oil developing countries. Again, if the 115 countries simultaneously defaulted the nine banks would become insolvent, and they would have to increase their capital by 121 percent to prevent such a possibility.

The international debt problem, however, should not be viewed in terms of all 115 countries defaulting at once. Some of the loans, both public and private, are considered to be quite secure; and there is substantial variation in the riskiness of the loans made. If we separate three of the major debtors from the 115 countries, the extent of the problem becomes substantially modified. If, for example, Argentina, Brazil, and Mexico had defaulted on their debts in 1982, all reporting banks would have remained solvent and still have had a cushion of nearly $18 billion. The capital of the nine largest banks was sufficient to cover defaults by these three countries from 1977 through 1980. During 1981 and 1982, however, their capital fell short by $2.3 billion, or roughly 5 to 8 percent of their total capital. If Mexico were not to default, the capital would have been more than adequate to cover defaults by Argentina and Brazil.[7]

Table 7 presents more detailed information on loans to selected Latin American countries as a percent of the capital of major U.S. banks. As is evident, the degree of exposure varies greatly by both bank and country. In terms of capital the banks are most heavily exposed in large countries such as Brazil and Mexico, and least heavily exposed in smaller countries, such as Chile. As a whole, the data can put into clearer

TABLE 6. U.S. Bank Claims on Selected and All Non-Oil Developing Countries
(Data cover 171 U.S. banking organizations for 1982)

ALL REPORTING BANKS

End of Period	Claims (billions of dollars)					Claims as Percent of Capital				
	Argentina	Brazil	Mexico	Total 3 Countries	All Non-Oil Developing Countries	Argentina	Brazil	Mexico	Total 3 Countries	All Non-Oil Developing Countries
1977	2.6	12.0	11.2	25.8	46.9	6.4	29.3	27.4	63.1	115.
1978	2.8	13.4	10.7	26.9	52.2	6.1	29.4	23.5	59.0	116.
1979	4.8	13.6	11.5	29.9	61.8	9.6	27.3	23.1	60.0	124.
1980	6.9	14.5	15.7	37.1	75.4	12.1	25.4	27.5	65.1	132.
1981	8.4	16.8	21.5	46.7	92.8	14.0	28.0	35.9	78.0	148.
1982	8.2	20.4	24.4	53.0	103.2	11.6	28.9	34.6	75.1	146.

NINE LARGEST BANKS

End of Period	Claims (billions of dollars)					Claims as Percent of Capital				
	Argentina	Brazil	Mexico	Total 3 Countries	All Non-Oil Developing Countries	Argentina	Brazil	Mexico	Total 3 Countries	All Non-Oil Developing Countries
1977	1.8	7.7	6.1	15.6	30.0	9.8	41.8	33.2	84.8	163.
1978	1.8	8.5	6.1	16.4	33.4	9.0	42.5	30.5	82.0	176.
1979	2.9	8.8	6.5	18.2	39.9	13.2	40.2	29.7	83.1	182.
1980	4.2	9.4	9.1	22.7	47.9	17.5	39.2	37.9	94.6	199.
1981	5.2	10.6	11.6	27.4	57.6	19.9	40.6	44.4	105.0	220.
1982	5.1	13.3	12.9	31.3	64.1	17.6	45.9	44.5	107.9	221.

Source: Statement by Paul A. Volcker, Chairman, Board of Governors of the Federal Reserve System, before the Committee on Banking, Finance and Urban Affairs, House of Representatives, February 2, 1983, Table V, and Country Exposure Lending Survey, December 1982, Federal Financial Institutions Examination Council.

TABLE 7. Loans by Major Banks to Selected Latin American Countries as a Percent of Bank's Capital
(as of end of 1982)

Bank	COUNTRIES						Capital* (million dollars)
	Argentina	*Brazil*	*Mexico*	*Venezuela*	*Chile*	*Total*	
Citibank	18.2	73.5	54.6	18.2	10.0	174.5	5,989
Bank of America	10.2	47.9	52.1	41.7	6.3	158.2	4,799
Chase Manhattan	21.3	56.9	40.0	24.0	11.8	154.0	4,221
Morgan Guaranty	24.4	54.3	34.8	17.5	9.7	140.7	3,107
Manufacturers Hanover	47.5	77.7	66.7	42.4	28.4	262.8	2,592
Chemical	14.9	52.0	60.0	28.0	14.8	169.7	2,499
Continental Illinois	17.8	22.9	32.4	21.6	12.8	107.5	2,143
Bankers Trust	13.2	46.2	46.2	25.1	10.6	141.2	1,895
First National Chicago	14.5	40.6	50.1	17.4	11.6	134.2	1,725
Security Pacific	10.4	29.1	31.2	4.5	7.4	82.5	1,684
Wells Fargo	8.3	40.7	51.0	20.4	6.2	126.6	1,201
Crocker National	38.1	57.3	51.2	22.8	26.5	196.0	1,151
First Interstate	6.9	43.9	63.0	18.5	3.7	136.0	1,080
Marine Midland	n.a.	47.8	28.3	29.2	n.a.	n.a.	1,074
Mellon	n.a.	35.3	41.1	17.6	n.a.	n.a.	1,024
Irving Trust	21.6	38.7	34.1	50.2	n.a.	n.a.	966
First National Boston	n.a.	23.1	28.1	n.a.	n.a.	n.a.	800
Interfirst Dallas	5.1	10.2	30.1	1.3	2.5	49.2	787

Source: William R. Cline, *International Debt and the Stability of the World Economy*, No. 4, September 1983, Institute for International Economics, Table 6, p. 34.

* Bank capital includes shareholders' equity, subordinated notes, and reserves against possible loan losses.

perspective such statements as the "stock prices of the biggest banks have plunged recently, as worries over international loans have mounted" (see Tom Petruno, "Stock Plunge: Bank Backers Fret Over Debt," *USA Today*, November 4, 1983, p. 38).

The Worth of Foreign Debt

It is important to realize that not all foreign debt is worthless. For some countries, the debt is worth the value that appears in the banks' books, while for others the market value is currently below its book value. In other words, some countries are likely to fulfill the contractual terms of their loans, while others have already failed to do so and may fail to fulfill even more. The precise market value of the debt owed by various countries is currently uncertain, since it does not trade in a well-established secondary market.

Rather than comparing just the book value of the debt to bank capital, it is useful to compare the difference between the book and market values to capital. Unfortunately, however, the market value of the debt could only be accurately known if banks were to sell significant amounts of the loans to others, including possible debtor countries themselves.[8] Loans to the most heavily indebted countries that are currently experiencing difficulties would then be bought by those who believe that these countries will not completely repudiate their debts. The debtor countries may still declare moratorium or pay off the debt at less than full value, but this simply means that the market value of the debt will be less than its value on the banks' books. It does not mean that its value will be zero. Debtor countries have an incentive to refrain from completely repudiating their debt because of the cost of not being able to borrow future funds for imports.[9] As long as this cost is perceived to be high enough, debtor countries will avoid outright repudiation, which is why they might be induced to purchase their own debt at a market price below the contractual price.[10]

Some rough calculations can be made to gauge what might happen to U.S. banks if their debt was sold off at market prices that are below the book price. For all reporting banks, their total loans to all non-oil developing countries could be sold off (or written down) by 70 percent of book value with the banks remaining solvent. For the nine largest banks, the corresponding percentage is 45 percent. If the calculations are restricted to Argentina, Brazil, and Mexico, then all reporting banks could simply write off the debt and still remain solvent. The nine largest banks could sell off the debt at about 93 percent of its book value and still remain solvent. These calculations suggest that the international debt problem is far less severe as long as the market value of the debt remains substantially above zero. And this will be the case as long as the most financially pressed countries remain committed to avoiding repudiation of their debt. Even a partial default resulting in the repayment of part of the debt puts the problem in a more favorable light.

It should also be noted that by permitting banks to write off any defaulted debt over a number of years rather than immediately if the market value were reduced to zero might also enable banks to avoid insolvency. This, too, is a reason for not placing undue emphasis on simply comparing total bank claims to capital.

The Role of the FDIC and the Federal Reserve System

Some argue that without an increase in IMF quotas the international debt problem may become unmanageable, or more bluntly, the "debt bomb may explode," there will be massive bank failures, and the entire U.S. banking system will collapse. Given the frequency with which this view is expressed, it is important to explain the roles of the Federal Deposit Insurance Corporation (FDIC) and the Federal Reserve System in dealing with commercial banking problems.

The FDIC insures deposits (up to a $100,000 limit) at almost all commercial banks in the United States, ensuring the protection of depositors if the banks fail. Any defaults by debtor nations, therefore, will first affect the owners of the banks, not the depositors. If the bank does not have enough capital to absorb defaults, it becomes insolvent, and the FDIC either pays the claims of the insured depositors or arranges a merger of the failed bank with a healthy one. To satisfy claims, the FDIC maintains a deposit insurance fund, which contained $13.8 billion at the end of 1982. Based on this fund, the FDIC could handle the claims of all depositors of the nine largest banks if Argentina, Brazil, Chile, Mexico, and Yugoslavia all repudiated their debts. To handle larger defaults, the FDIC would have to borrow in the capital markets, which it is currently authorized to do up to $3 billion.

Not all deposits are covered by this insurance. Indeed, "commercial banks have many deposit accounts that are not insured in full, with uninsured deposits accounting for about 33 percent of total bank deposits. Further, commercial banks have a sizable amount of nondeposit liabilities that are not insured" (see Federal Home Loan Bank Board, *Agenda for Reform*, Washington, D.C., March 1983, p. 92). This means that the FDIC insurance fund is large enough to handle even more defaults than indicated above, although some depositors could incur losses in the event of defaults on the foreign debt owed to commercial banks. This is especially important since the current mood seems to indicate a movement toward exposing larger depositors to more of this risk. As William M. Isaac, Chairman of the FDIC, recently stated:

> For discipline to exist, there must be risk of loss. Although insurance coverage is limited to $100,000, in practice we have for years been providing implicit 100 percent protection for depositors and other creditors at most banks, particularly the larger ones. This resulted from our preference for handling bank failures through mergers. This approach is usually less expensive and less disruptive than paying the claims of insured depositors; however, the side effect has been to erode marketplace discipline and provide larger banks a substantial competitive advantage. Discipline can be restored by exposing the largest creditors to some risk of loss (see FDIC, *1982 Annual Report*, p. ix).

Given this recent development, depositors at U.S. banks may become more concerned about the safety of their deposits. It is conceivable, then, that a series of defaults or a large-scale postponement in debt repayments might set off a bank run as depositors in large banks with uninsured deposits might rush to withdraw their funds. The most serious consequence would be that otherwise healthy banks could be forced into insolvency. As all banks tried to sell off their securities and called in loans to meet deposit withdrawals, the price of these relatively illiquid assets would be depressed. As a result, the banks' assets could fall below their liabilities, forcing them into insolvency.

This need not happen if the Federal Reserve System fulfills its responsibility as lender-of-last-resort. The role of the FDIC is to protect depositors (up to a $100,000 limit) in the event of bank failures. The role of the Federal Reserve, on the other hand, is to protect illiquid banks from insolvency or failure. FDIC insurance is likely to deter runs on banks and prevent a liquidity crisis; but if it does not, the Federal Reserve is supposed to contain any crisis and keep illiquid but otherwise solvent banks from failing. If the Federal Reserve fulfills its responsibilities, it will necessarily reduce the role played by the FDIC.

If the Federal Reserve fulfills its responsibilities the international debt problem should pose no risk to the stability of the U.S. banking system. This does not mean, however, that some large banks will not incur sizable losses if some debtor nations default on their loans. What it does mean is that the failure of some banks should pose no threat to other banks. If a run were to begin, the Federal Reserve could simply open the discount window and make loans to those solvent banks that are experiencing heavy deposit withdrawals. The stability of the U.S. banking system would be preserved and the majority of the depositors of any failed banks (which held bad rather than illiquid loans) would be protected. The major losers would be the stockholders and uninsured depositors of the failed banks as net wealth transferred from them to defaulting nations.

The Concern About Foreign Branches and Subsidiaries

There is some fear that in the event of major defaults foreign branches and subsidiaries of U.S. Banks would be inadequately serviced by central banks or lenders-of-last-resort.[11] While it is true that foreign branches are not insured, when the Franklin National Bank failed in 1975 "the U.S. Federal Reserve permitted discount window borrowings to support the bank's branch in London from the time problems were announced until the bank was merged, effectively accepting responsibility for its foreign branches" (G. G. Johnson and Richard K. Abrams, "Aspects of the International Banking Safety Net," Occasional Paper 17, International Monetary Fund, March 1983, p. 35). Whether subsidiaries will be similarly treated remains to be seen. In the case of other countries, there are already examples in which similar action by central banks was not taken to assist a foreign branch or subsidiary.

In commenting on this situation, William R. Cline states:

> More generally, it could indeed happen that loopholes exist in lender-of-last-resort coverage. However, experience to date suggests that the international financial system has less to fear from a series of bank failures attributable to such loopholes than from straightforward exposure risk of banks whose LLR coverage is not in doubt but whose country loans are. Moreover, the events of 1982–83 illustrate a willingness of central banks to work together in crisis suggesting that if necessary they could agree on the division of LLR responsibility for currently ambiguous cases (see "International Debt and the Stability of the World Economy," Institute for International Economics, Policy Analyses in International Economics, No. 4, September 1983, p. 105).

A Recapitulation

All fears to the contrary, the U.S. banking system should not collapse if the debtor countries default on their debts. If the Federal Reserve System fulfills its responsibilities as lender-of-last-resort, any liquidity crisis that banks might experience would be prevented from leading to widespread insolvencies and failures. Some banks might fail due to too many foreign loans turning bad, but this is inevitable in a world of risk and uncertainty. It is possible that uninsured depositors and shareholders in these banks would suffer losses, but this too is the result of risk and uncertainty. Governmental actions aimed solely at preventing these consequences may properly be termed "bailouts." It should also be noted that the FDIC fully protects insured depositors in the event of defaults. The general concern of bank depositors, therefore, cannot be used to justify increased IMF quotas.

IV. U.S. TRADE AND DEFAULTS ON FOREIGN DEBT

Even though the U.S. banking system may not collapse, there is concern that any default on debts would result in a decline in U.S. exports to the third world. This would reduce income and employment, thereby threatening the economic recovery in the U.S. Whether or not the international debt problem could trigger substantial reduction in U.S. exports and export related jobs depends on the debtor country's reduction in imports given their increased insolvency. An ameliorating factor, however, is the role of the U.S. export-import bank, which attempts to facilitate U.S. exports by assisting importing countries at subsidized rates.

U.S. Trade with Non-Oil Developing Countries

The relative importance of non-oil developing countries in U.S. trade is only recently being appreciated. In 1970, 24 percent of U.S. exports went to non-oil developing countries; by 1980, these exports represented 29 percent of total U.S. merchandise trade, or $63.3 billion (see Table 8). U.S. imports from non-oil developing countries have also grown, comprising 14 percent of total U.S. imports in 1970 with an increase to 24 percent, or $61.6 billion, by 1980. Since then, however, U.S. exports to non-oil developing countries have decreased significantly.

One can get an even more vivid picture of this decline by focusing on the top ten borrowers. In 1980, U.S. exports to the top ten borrowers was $38.8 billion. By 1982, this figure had dropped to $34.9 billion. Examining the eight-month performances of U.S. exports to these countries in 1982 and 1983 reveals how sensitive sales are to increased liquidity concerns. U.S. exports to the top ten in January–August 1982 equalled $25 billion, compared to $19.2 billion for the same period in 1983.

Clearly, some of the decline in exports is a function of the general decline in world economic activity, especially in the U.S. If we compare the decline of the largest world debtors to the total for both non-oil developing countries and the world, the effect of the debt burden is very country specific. For example, in Argentina the decline in U.S. exports was 21.2 percent over the 1980–82 period, compared to the general decline for the top ten debtor nations of 0.5 percent per year and the decline for the world of 0.8 percent. Clearly, some of the decline in U.S. exports to Argentina is related to their debt problem. The case is very similar for Brazil, India, Mexico, and Yugoslavia. Yet, for Indonesia Israel, South Korea, and Venezuela the debt problem has not affected U.S. exports.

TABLE 8. U.S. Trade with Non-Oil Developing Countries
(Millions of dollars)

	U.S. EXPORTS						U.S. IMPORTS					
	1980	1981	1982	Jan–Aug 1982	Jan–Aug 1983	Annual Percentage Change 1980–1982	1980	1981	1982	Jan–Aug 1982	Jan–Aug 1983	Annual Percentage Change 1980–82
Argentina	2,449.3	2,127.9	1,267.8	903.1	633.5	−21.2	739.4	1,123.3	1,065.7	721.1	604.0	+12.1
Brazil	4,299.7	3,742.0	3,369.3	2,426.2	1,694.0	−8.1	3,686.0	4,332.6	4,171.4	2,586.4	3,093.9	+4.1
India	1,672.9	1,733.0	1,559.8	914.4	1,302.4	−2.3	1,099.4	1,200.0	1,396.8	899.3	1,419.2	+7.9
Indonesia	1,391.9	1,260.5	1,935.6	1,340.5	998.7	+10.9	5,134.1	5,746.9	4,086.8	2,802.7	3,063.5	−7.6
Israel	1,392.6	1,500.6	1,528.8	1,042.8	1,099.7	+3.1	941.0	1,234.9	1,162.1	823.5	871.8	+7.0
South Korea	4,403.5	4,992.7	5,318.1	3,490.5	3,790.5	+6.3	4,205.5	5,179.6	5,631.4	3,776.1	4,608.9	+9.7
Mexico	14,881.4	17,353.0	11,025.8	8,693.7	5,833.1	−9.9	12,497.6	13,703.6	15,488.0	10,134.4	10,929.3	+7.1
Spain	3,105.6	3,258.9	3,339.0	2,391.5	1,714.5	+2.4	1,203.0	1,506.0	1,475.2	1,035.9	948.9	+6.8
Venezuela	4,508.0	5,346.8	5,061.0	3,473.4	1,728.9	+3.9	5,300.6	5,575.3	4,757.3	2,971.2	3,214.0	+3.6
Yugoslavia	751.9	645.6	489.9	355.4	415.2	−5.7	448.9	445.5	355.9	238.5	237.5	−7.7
Total top 10	38,856.8	41,961.0	34,895.1	25,031.5	19,210.5	−3.6	32,255.5	40,047.7	39,590.6	25,989.1	28,991.0	+3.9
Total Non-Oil LDCs	63,304.0	67,669.0	62,296.3			−0.5	61,643.0	65,011.0	60,724.1			−0.5
Total World	216,445.0	229,433.0	211,217.0			−0.8	249,781.0	265,086.0	247,606.0			−0.3

Source: U.S. Department of Commerce

TABLE 9. Estimated External Debt Service Payments as a Percentage of Exports of Goods and Services for 1982

Argentina	44	Korea	11
Mexico	37	Thailand	10
Ecuador	30	Egypt	7
Brazil	45	Yugoslavia	14
Chile	40	Algeria	12
Venezuela	14	Indonesia	8
Columbia	25	Taiwan	5
Philippines	18	Nigeria	7
Peru	21	Malaysia	5
Turkey	13		

Source: "World Financial Markets," Morgan Guaranty Trust Co. of New York, October 1982.

Corresponding to the decline in U.S. exports to non-oil developing countries, U.S. imports from these countries have increased (see Table 8). Some argue that this increase was designed to ease their increasing debt burden. While total U.S. imports declined over the 1980–82 period from $249.7 to $247.6 billion, U.S. imports from the top ten borrowers increased over the same period from $35.2 to $39.6 billion. Over the eight-month period, January–August 1982, U.S. imports from the top ten borrowers were $25.9 billion; by 1983 this figure increased to $28.9 billion.

This phenomenon is particularly evident at the country level. For example, Argentina showed an increase in exports of 12.1 percent per year over the 1980–82 period as compared to a general decrease of 0.3 per year for total world exports to the U.S. The story is similar for Brazil, India, Israel, South Korea, and Mexico, where the annual average percentage increase in exports was 4.1, 7.9, 7.0, 9.7, and 7.1. In general, the top ten debtor countries expanded their exports to the U.S. at an annual average rate of 3.9 percent, compared to a general world decline of 0.3 percent. Clearly, these exports help ease their increasing debt problem.

It is not surprising that given the increased debt burden, one should observe a reduction in U.S. exports and an increase in U.S. imports from the major debtors. An examination of service payments as a percent of exports for a number of major borrowers in 1982 reveals immediately that in such cases as Mexico, Brazil, Argentina, and Chile, where this ratio is well above 35 percent, a reduction in imports is imminent (see Table 9). Likewise each country will simultaneously endeavor to expand export sales. Even without IMF pressure, given the relative importance of non-oil developing country trade for the U.S., such moves would cause a substantial decrease in U.S. exports to these countries and simultaneously lead to an increase in U.S. imports from them. The increased imports would be generated both by the improved exchange rate and by the necessity the U.S. feels to assist these countries.

The Costs of Reduced Trade with Non-Oil Developing Countries

To fully appreciate the potential impact on the economy of a major reduction in non-oil developing country imports from the U.S., one need only note that in 1980 each billion dollars of merchandise exports supported 23,700 U.S. jobs. In the manufacturing sector, each billion dollars of exports was related to 24,000 jobs. In 1980, over five million U.S. jobs were export related.[12]

U.S. exports are vulnerable to any long-term reduction in LDC imports. For example, during the past eight months there has been a major reduction in Argentinian purchases of airplanes, coal, and prefabricated buildings; the cutback in Brazil's imports has affected U.S. sales of wheat, drilling equipment, and electronic parts; and the decline in Mexican imports affected motor vehicle parts, gasoline, and light fuels. In all of these cases, the manufacturing sector is most severely affected, since a substantial percentage of the jobs are export related. Clearly, the U.S. has a stake in assuring that these countries do not drastically reduce U.S. imports by becoming protectionists.

While a reduction in U.S. exports to these countries would affect U.S. export related jobs, one should not forget that increased LDC exports to the U.S. would also adversely affect U.S. employment. In efforts to keep these countries solvent, by increasing imports from these countries, the U.S. may adversely affect employment in its import competing sectors.

The primary items imported by the U.S. from these countries include sugar, textiles and apparel, coffee, footwear, steel, and crude petroleum. The only item accounting for increased exports to the U.S. from Argentina was heavy fuel oils. For Brazil it was coffee, orange juice concentrate, and petroleum. For India it was shale oil. For Mexico it was crude oil, shrimp, auto parts, and coffee. Apart from textiles and apparel and footwear, the number of jobs affected by the increased exports is minimal, however. One may conclude, therefore, that an adverse impact of increased LDC debt is some reduction in U.S. exports and in export related jobs.

V. RESOLVING THE INTERNATIONAL DEBT PROBLEM

The conflict over how best to deal with the international debt problem is clearly generating widespread attention—a natural response given the size of the problem and the number and importance of the countries involved. But it also means that the resolution of the controversy becomes all the more important, since a signal will be sent to all current and prospective creditors and debtors on the way in which future problems are likely to be handled. As a result, one should be careful not to overlook the incentive effects that are associated with the proposals made to resolve the problem. Although they are difficult to quantify, incentive effects may actually be more important than the more quantifiable effects.

Consider the relatively straightforward, traditional approaches used to calculate declines in exports and jobs that may result from defaults by less developed or Eastern bloc nations. These calculations may be useful, but they do not tell the whole story. This particular cost must be weighed against the longer-run cost that may arise if these countries do not default today because of the additional funding they receive from such agencies as the IMF, but rather sometime in the future when the real extent of their debt problem may mean that it can no longer be contained with additional lending. Only then would it be realized that credit had been allocated to relatively less productive activities and away from relatively more productive activities. During the interim, however, the behavior of those who engage in international finance will have been affected. Borrowing countries may have an incentive to borrow more and may be less careful if they know they will receive assistance if they get into trouble. At the same time, private lenders may have fewer incentives to be cautious in their lending, since they are confident that the IMF or another agency will support them. Borrowing and lending that might not otherwise have occurred may occur when the IMF and other official agencies continually step in to reduce the risks of defaults.

In assessing ways to respond to the international debt problem, therefore, one must take into account incentive effects. The rules of the game condition the behavior of the participants, and when calculating the costs and benefits of various proposals any effects of changes in those rules should be considered. Specifically, one should calculate what will happen to economic activity for all future time periods based on all the proposals to resolve the problem. It is not enough to simply focus on what happens today if there are defaults and then argue that these are the total costs that an increase in IMF quotas can eliminate. One must also take into account costs that may result from putting incentives in place that might make problems more frequent and widespread and that may result in credit being allocated to other than the most productive areas.

Illiquidity Versus Insolvency

Much of the disagreement over what should be done about the debt problem revolves around the difference between "illiquid" and "insolvent" countries. If a country is illiquid it is considered to have an external debt whose service payments cannot temporarily be met on existing terms but which nonetheless are sustainable on a longer-term basis. If a country is insolvent, on the other hand, it is considered to have an external debt whose service payments not only cannot be met in the short run but cannot be sustained in the long run. It is argued that illiquid countries should be given sufficient financial assistance to keep them from becoming insolvent. If private banks are reluctant to provide such assistance, then the IMF should do so with its own funds and by enticing banks to do the same. To do otherwise, it is argued, would lead to involuntary defaults and bank failures, trade cutbacks, lost jobs, and increased protectionism.

It is not easy to determine whether a country is insolvent rather than simply illiquid, mainly because of the difficulty in distinguishing between a country's unwillingness and its inability to repay its debts. The ability to meet debt payments essentially means that in the long run the growth of a country's external debt cannot exceed the interest rate on that debt or the growth rate in the country's income. This is why so many people say that the debt problem will disappear as soon as interest rates come down and the current U.S. recovery spreads to developing countries. Viewed from this perspective, the debt problem is one of illiquidity, not insolvency, and the debts being carried on the banks' books are still basically sound.

But, will interest rates come down far enough and soon enough and will income grow fast enough and soon enough for insolvency to be ruled out? The answer depends in part on the willingness of debtor countries to implement appropriate fiscal and monetary policies to help bring about an adequate and sustainable rate of growth. In some cases, past behavior provides little hope that this will happen. Further, political factors may temper any major switch in policies or result in any near-term "correction" being reversed within a few short years. One must also be aware of the aggregation problems. That is, one country may pursue policies that would be beneficial if other countries were not pursuing similar policies. One country may successfully reduce its imports relative to its exports, but if all countries tried to do so, the result may be disastrous. IMF "conditionality" will have this effect when authorities do not adequately take into account such inter-relationships.[13]

What happens to interest rates and income growth also depends on U.S. fiscal and monetary policies. Some argue that reductions in budget deficits and faster money growth can lower interest rates, with beneficial effects on economic activity in debtor countries, including easing interest payments on their debt. However, the cost of reducing inflation in the U.S. has been substantial, even if only temporary, and one runs the risk of wasting this cost if money growth accelerates again. This seems to be why the Federal Reserve has been unwilling to let money growth revert to its former high rates for any sustained period of time. In addition, Congress has made little progress in closing the prospective budgetary gap, which has important implications for interest rates and income growth. Until this information is known, there will be substantial uncertainty about future fiscal policy (and even monetary policy due to the budget constraint) and, thus, economic activity.

Based on these considerations, there is ample reason to question whether the international debt problem reached the crisis stage for some countries solely because of the recent recession and will shortly revert to the safety zone now that a U.S. recovery is underway. Even when the recovery sets in for the big debtor countries, it is not clear that it will sustain the existing external debt to banks without some write downs or other concessions. This is especially the case when one realizes that most of the bank debt is short term, which means that the debt service payments are higher than they would be based on the same amount amortized over a longer period and that any shocks to debtor countries could jeopardize their ability to roll over the debt. Unfortunately, debtor countries appear to be unable to issue longer term bonds in exchange for the funds they owe banks (valued at market prices).

What if Debtor Countries are Illiquid?

If debtor countries are illiquid, then the current problem is temporary, and the loans are basically sound rather than simply bad. Mainly because of the recent recession and relatively high interest rates, some argue that even though countries are temporarily having trouble servicing their debts, within a few years these troubles should disappear. In the interim, however, these countries will need "bridge loans" from the IMF and banks and other assistance from such organizations as the World Bank and the Export-Import Bank. In short, external loans will require substantial and perhaps multiple reschedulings during this adjustment period. Of course, the countries will have to implement changes in their fiscal and monetary policies to put the necessary preconditions for sustainable investment and growth in place. In addition, the IMF will have to impose "conditions" on its loans rather than simply providing them with no strings attached.

Why don't the banks solve the illiquidity problem for the countries on their own? Why is it necessary for the IMF or other governmental organizations to intervene in the international borrowing and lending markets? One answer is that there are imperfections in these markets and that they periodically fail to work properly. A bank may decide it should cut back on its lending to big debtor countries for fear that if it does not other banks will do so to reduce their exposure.[14] But then the bank would be confronted with an increased exposure relative to other banks. The bank may then move quickly in order to reduce its exposure by a relatively greater degree. If *all* banks move simultaneously, however, the debtor countries may be unable to handle the cutback in lending. This may turn a liquidity problem into a crisis, which, if not checked, could turn into an insolvency problem.[15] When there is a "country run," therefore, intervention by governments and such international organizations as the IMF may be appropriate, especially when they have access to better and more timely proprietary information than does the private sector.[16]

The Role of the IMF in Liquidity Crises

If the current international debt problem is one of illiquidity, there may be justification for IMF involvement. Certainly, at present, the IMF is a focal point for the collection and the dissemination of much of the information needed to assess the credit-worthiness of developing countries. It is also in a position to provide funds to those countries most urgently facing severe liquidity problems, something private banks may not be currently doing in sufficient amounts. However, there is still the issue over what form any increase in the liabilities of the IMF should take. Should the liabilities be increased by borrowing in private capital markets or by increasing the quotas of the 146 member nations? If the current debt problem is temporary, then one would think that the increase should also be temporary. As Professor Michele Fratianni of Indiana University states, "the basic objection to a quota increase is that member governments are asked to provide a *permanent* increase in IMF resources to solve a temporary problem" (see "International Debt Crisis: Causes and Policy Prescriptions," statement by Michele Fratianni before the Subcommittee on International Trade, Investment and Monetary Policy, April 1983). This reasoning would favor an increase in borrowing on the part of the IMF, since the borrowing would be repaid as the liquidity problem disappears. The IMF would thus be right back where it started in terms of liabilities outstanding.

An increase in quotas, on the other hand, represents a permanent increase in liabilities, which would essentially provide the IMF with more discretion in its future lending to countries. In such a situation, there is the risk that the IMF would attempt to be more fully committed at all times to justify still further quota increases. Moreover, the member countries, knowing that the funds are relatively readily available, would have a greater incentive to put more pressure on the IMF to extend loans as well as not to turn to private capital markets for funds.[17] There is also the risk that countries will postpone corrective internal actions when the pool of funds upon which they may draw is enlarged. For all these reasons the case for quota increases is much weaker than an increase in IMF borrowing in the private capital markets.[18]

Regardless of what action is taken, the role of the IMF is changing from the one it played before 1971, when the IMF provided short-term loans to member countries encountering balance of payments problems. Some argue that since 1971 the IMF has been searching for something to do now that the fixed-exchange rate system has been replaced by a flexible-exchange rate (not without intervention, however). According to this view, the IMF is using the debt problem to justify a new and larger role for itself.[19] This is considered to be particularly troublesome because it takes in funds at one rate and loans them out at another rate that is typically lower,[20] becoming in this sense more like the World Bank.[21] If so, Congressional scrutiny of such an expanded function would be in order, especially if quotas are permanently increased over time.

Despite talk to the contrary, the IMF is not an international lender-of-last-resort. To serve as one, the IMF would need to be able to create money (or foreign currencies) that would be acceptable for payment of both public and private debt, something it cannot currently do. Furthermore, lenders-of-last-resort typically lend at *penalty* rates, not subsidized ones, to avoid the problem of moral hazard.

What If Debtor Countries Are Insolvent?

Based on prospective economic developments few are likely to argue that there are no countries that should be or are close to being classified as insolvent.[22] For this reason, there are those who argue that some of the loans should be written down. According to this view, it makes no sense to carry these loans on the books of the banks at full value.[23] Sheer honesty would dictate no less than full disclosure of the market value of these loans,[24] for how else are investors and depositors to evaluate the worth of various outlets for their funds? Furthermore, such information might reveal how overextended (in a structural rather than cyclical sense) some countries already are.

Of course, simply writing down some loans creates a moral hazard, since other countries may engage in behavior that is more likely to place them in a similar situation. To reduce this possibility, there should be a claim on the future income of these countries. That is, the banks would write down a portion of their foreign loans in exchange for equity instruments. This would be similar to how loan defaults are handled in the U.S. The creditor has a claim on the debtor's assets and has the opportunity to have a portion of the debtor's income garnished. The potential problem is that the debtor countries may refuse such an arrangement.[25] Nevertheless, this approach merits further consideration.

The major point is that if some countries are insolvent then it is a mistake to treat them as if they are suffering from a liquidity problem.

Providing additional loans will only postpone, not resolve, their debt problems. Such action may, moreover, distort incentives so as to only make matters worse than they would otherwise be when the day of reckoning does arrive.[26]

A Recapitulation

The conflict over what to do centers mainly on whether the debtor countries are illiquid or insolvent. For those countries that are illiquid, IMF assistance may be appropriate. However, there is still the issue of whether the IMF should intervene through increased quotas or borrowing in private capital markets. If countries are insolvent, there is the issue of how to reduce the moral hazard problem that accompanies writing down their loans.

Whatever is done will establish a precedent for similar situations in the future. For this reason, one should view how the current situation is handled as establishing the "rules" of the international borrowing and lending "game." Such rules will generate incentive effects that will influence the behavior of the participants for years to come. Serious attempts should be made not to reward imprudent borrowing and lending behavior, for to do so will only penalize those participants in the credit market who based their behavior on the belief that there would be no bailouts.

VI. SUMMARY AND CONCLUSIONS

As is now well known, international banks became heavily involved in foreign debt by recycling funds from oil producing countries to non-oil developing countries and the Eastern bloc nations. Historically, this was not a new role for banks nor one that is necessarily bad. It is, however, a role that understandably involves risk and uncertainty. It is no surprise, therefore, that once the debtor countries began having difficulties servicing their external debts attention would be focused on commercial banks. This is especially the case when one realizes that developing countries have relied almost entirely on debt rather than equity financing, with a large portion of the borrowing being short-term and coming from banks. Unlike dividends, interest payments are to be paid in bad times as well as good and unlike long-term debt, short-term debt must be periodically rolled over.

Despite the seriousness of the problem, many of the fears that have been expressed may be based on misleading data. Although the total external outstanding debt of the non-oil developing countries and Eastern European countries is gigantic, most of the debt is concentrated among a relatively few countries. As a result, we agree with Robert E.

Weintraub's statement that "there is no *aggregate* developing-world debt problem" ("How Threatening Is the World Debt? *Wall Street Journal*, May 16, 1983, emphasis added). Furthermore, not all of this debt is as worthless as some imply. The solvency position of U.S. commercial banks is nowhere near as desperate as the standard comparisons of bank debt-to-bank equity ratios indicate. It has also been emphasized that the U.S. banking system need not collapse in the event of defaults. If the Federal Reserve System fulfills its responsibilities as lender-of-last-resort, the banking system will remain intact. Of course, individual banks might fail, but that occasionally happens in a competitive economy under conditions of risk and uncertainty. Even so, however, only shareholders and uninsured depositors will incur losses, and those depositors with deposits of less than $100,000 per account are fully protected by the FDIC.

This particular view is not shared by everyone. *The New York Times*, for example, recently reported that "senior IMF officials" warned that "if new financial assistance is not made available, debtor countries could default, setting off a banking crisis" (Leonard Silk, "Monetary Fund Chief Is Firm on Actions to Curb Inflation," *The New York Times*, October 16, 1983, p. 1). But as Weintraub has stated, "under analysis, the threat of widespread bank failures and the collapse of our banking system, is found to be imaginary" (*International Debt: Crisis and Challenge*, Department of Economics, George Mason University, April 1983, p. 25).

Although the U.S. banking system may not collapse in the event of defaults, U.S. exports would surely suffer; but, this cost must not be exaggerated. Furthermore, the IMF imposed conditions on debtor countries when providing financial assistance, which may exacerbate the adverse effects on U.S. exports.

There may be imperfections in capital markets that justify some intervention by the IMF. Even if this is the case, however, the involvement need not take the form of quota increases. If the problem is only temporary, it would be more appropriate for the IMF to borrow funds in the private capital markets for a specified period of time or to sell off some of its gold holdings. Temporary problems do not require permanent increases in financial resources. The incentives for abuse, unfortunately, are too great when funds are made available permanently.

There is, moreover, a need to be sure that insolvent debtors are not lumped together with illiquid debtors. If so, the day of reckoning is only postponed, not eliminated. At the same time, there will be more calls for further strengthening the international agencies. One again, statements like the following will be made:

> If the world is to avoid another debacle such as the one that took place in the 1930's, when the monetary system broke down, it is

> essential that a strong monetary fund be the center of the system (Jacques de Larosiere, managing director of the IMF, as reported in *The New York Times*, October 16, 1983, p. 16).

> The economic distress of the poorest nations is a time bomb ticking away. (A. W. Clausen, president of the World Bank, as reported in the *Washington Post*, September 28, 1983, p. 8. It is then reported that he called on wealthier nations for immediate boosts in foreign aid and contributions to international development institutions).

Unfortunately, the international debt problem is unlikely to go away soon. Whether or not IMF quotas are increased, the problem will be around for several years, so one has to view the problem in terms of its long-run implications. Once this is done, one quickly realizes that incentives are very important. The way one problem is handled today establishes the rules of the game for future international borrowing and lending. If institutions and countries receive signals that imprudent behavior will be rewarded, then we can expect more of the same. For this reason every attempt should be made not to subsidize irresponsibility.

Finally, whenever greater intervention by the government or an international agency is advocated, it is all too often done during a so-called crisis. When immediacy drives all actions, the risks of doing the wrong things are usually too great, especially when one realizes that exaggeration is all too common during these periods. Furthermore, the burden of proof is not on those who support greater intervention. For these reasons incentives are frequently distorted by policies implemented on the basis of short-run concerns. In the words of Robert E. Weintraub,

> Judicious use of regulations and market forces is required to assure that the risks in country lending are adequately recognized by banks without chilling their international lending activities and that adequate provisions are made against mistakes and unexpected events. (*International Lending By U.S. Banks: Practices, Problems, and Policies*, Department of Economics, George Mason University, August 1983, p. 9).

VII. POSTSCRIPT

Shortly after the completion of this study the U.S. Congress approved an increase of $8.4 billion in American support for the International Monetary Fund. As a result, an agreement of February 1983 to increase the resources of the IMF by more than $40 billion was virtually assured. Unfortunately, this does not mean that the debt problem has been resolved. Instead, it is likely to be around for many years to come.

Given the uncertainty that will prevail during this period and the likelihood of further actions being taken, this study remains relevant and timely. The worse thing that could happen now is for people to believe that there is no longer a problem. As our study clearly indicates, there are extremely important issues that remain to be addressed despite any increased resources of the IMF.

NOTES

1. According to Celso Furtado, Brazil's most famous economist and a former finance minister, "Whatever happens, we can never pay all our foreign debt. The best solution is a moratorium" (see Alan Robinson, "The IMF vs. The People," *Euromoney*, October 1983, p. 93). In a recent special report, moreover, it is stated that "Latin America is struggling with severe debt problems, so much so that Brazil and Argentina appear close to default" (see World Economic Outlook," *Business Week* November 21, 1983, p. 152).

2. As of April 1983, the quotas amounted to 61 billion of SDRs, of which the U.S. accounted for 20.6 percent.

3. According to Leonard Silk, an increase in IMF quotas and an increase in the General Agreements to Borrow ". . . are urgently needed if a wave of defaults is to be avoided" (see Leonard Silk, "Economic Scene," *New York Times*, October 19, 1983). In a *Washington Post* editorial it was stated that unless the IMF was provided with additional resources, "There would be an imminent threat of the whole financial network's coming unraveled . . ." (see "Mr. Reagan and the IMF," *Washington Post*, September 28, 1983, p. 22).

4. Ultimately, of course, what matters is the marginal productivity of capital. Thus, relatively little investment spending and/or relatively unproductive investment spending over time should adversely affect the amount of credit which is eventually extended. This means that the mix of domestic spending is as important as the level of domestic spending in assessing the longer-run likelihood of default.

5. Data on the debt situation of each of the top ten countries is available from the authors upon request. Data for Eastern Bloc nations is not readily available. Therefore, these countries are not treated in detail here.

6. For a related discussion of this issue, see James R. Barth and Robert E. Keleher, "Financial Crises and the Role of the Lender of Last Resort," *Economic Review*, Federal Reserve Bank of Atlanta, January 1984.

7. It might be noted that "Argentina's widely cited total of $40 billion in foreign debts might be overstated by $10.8 billion because of back-door loan repayments by some companies trying to sneak around the country's complex exchange controls." If so, "It would apparently mean that, should push come to shove, fewer bankers than previously thought would come into court trying to force loan repayments" (see Everett G. Martin, "At Least $10.8 Billion of Argentina's Debt Called 'Unexplainable' by 2 Investigators," *Wall Street Journal*, October 7, 1983, p. 3).

8. It has recently been reported that "A secondary market in foreign bank loans has been quietly operating for some time in London . . . It has now grown to the point where the need for a Reuters screen displaying prices is being seriously debated, a sure sign of a market both maturing and coming out of the closet. Latin American loans now trade at 75% to 87% of face value" (see Peter Brimelow, "Why the U.S. Shouldn't Fill the IMF's Till," *Fortune*, December 14, 1983, pp. 59–60).

9. In this regard, M. S. Mendelsohn reports that "the danger of outright default is dismissed by most bankers and supervisors who participated in this study. They do not believe that countries will risk their trade by defaulting outright . . . In fact, the only significant defaults which have occurred in the 20th century have been on the part of two countries which chose to withdraw or felt themselves excluded from the world community for protracted periods after 1917 in one case, and after 1949 in the other." See "Commercial Banks and the Restructuring of Cross-Border Debt," Group of Thirty, New York, 1983, p. 9.

10. It might be interesting to point out what happened during the 1930s when Latin American countries experienced severe debt problems. According to H. C. Wallich, "For many years, a number of countries have been repurchasing their partially or wholly unserviced bonds. Some are doing it as part of an officially proclaimed policy, others more or less disguisedly," He goes on to say that ". . . I believe that repurchase under present conditions is not only defensible, but that for the time being it constitutes the best method of dealing with the defaulted bonds, not merely from the viewpoint of the debtor but to some extent even from that of the bondholder." See "The Future of Latin American Dollar Bonds," *American Economic Review*, June 1943, p. 332.

11. Foreign branches do not have separate legal status and thus are integral parts of the parent bank, while foreign subsidiaries are legally independent entities but wholly owned by the bank.

12. Data on employment and exports was obtained from U.S. Department of Commerce, *Employment Related to Merchandise Exports*, August 1981.

13. See Ad Hoc Committee on International Debt and U.S. Financial Policies, "The International Debt Problem, Insolvency, and Illiquidity: A Policy Proposal," in *International Lending and the IMF*, edited by Allan H. Meltzer, The Heritage Lectures, 21, 1983, pp. 33–41.

14. It is also conceivable that the largest banks made the loans with the confidence that the government would not let them fail. Recent developments, however, may have weakened this confidence so that they are now attempting to reduce their exposure to a level more consistent with their modified perception of risk. In this case, the behavior of the banks may be due to a changed perception of the role the government will play, which thereby may ironically enough induce the government to act to correct what it perceives to be a market failure.

15. This means that worthwhile investment projects that would provide the inputs necessary for expanded economic growth would go unfunded. Insolvency, in other words, refers to the unwillingness to put available resources to productive use rather than the unavailability of any human and natural resources.

16. It is reported that in the second quarter of 1983 there was no quarter-to-quarter growth in new lending to developing countries by international banks for the first time in 20 years. By contrast, new loans in the first half of 1982 grew at a $50 billion annual rate.

17. In this regard, it should be noted that 92 members had outstanding drawings at the end of 1982 as compared to 28 members at the end of 1973. Furthermore, it was stated only a few years ago that "It is often not expected that the Fund resources will actually be used, but rather that the principal benefit results from the certification of economic performance on the part of the country experiencing balance-of-payments problems." (See Irving S. Friedman and G. A. Cestango, *The Emerging Role of Private Banks in the Developing World*, Citicorp, 1977, p. 52). Actually, however, borrowings from the IMF have increased from about $9 billion in 1980 to more than $25 billion rate as of September 1983.

18. The IMF, of course, could also sell some of its gold holdings to obtain funds. Such an action, however, might be disruptive and cause the price of gold to fall by a sizeable amount. The gold may therefore be better used as collateral for IMF borrowing. Furthermore, the sale of gold would require approval of 85 percent of the weighted membership, something which is currently considered by most to be unlikely. In contrast, the IMF currently has the authority to borrow in private capital markets, requiring only a simple majority of its board of directors. See Richard A. Stuckey, *Gold in the International Monetary System*, International Gold Corporation Ltd., September 1983, p. 16.

19. In the words of Milton Friedman, "The debt crisis is a heavensent opportunity, creating the possibility that the IMF can become a world central bank." He argues, however, that "The IMF should be abolished, not expanded" (see Milton Friedman, "'No' to More Money for the IMF," *Newsweek*, November 14, 1983, p. 96).

20. It is the subsidized lending that leads some to refer to the IMF as the lender of *first* resort. It should be noted, moreover, that all countries receiving financial assistance from the IMF are charged the same interest rate.

21. Indeed, "according to Stern (echoed by Irving Friedman, both 1982), the critical distinction now relates to the respective staffs' spheres of competence rather than to the content of their respective programs" (see John Williamson, *The Lending Policies of the*

International Monetary Fund, Institute for International Economics, August 1982, pp. 22–23).

22. According to a recent report, "Brazil, let's face it, is bankrupt-insolvent" (see "The Latin American Crisis: Brazil, Mexico and Peru," *International Currency Review,* September 1983, p. 68).

23. In a recent speech Fritz Lentwiler, president of the Bank for International Settlements, stated that "there is no way the major banks can get out of this situation without writing down some of the debt" (see *New York Times,* October 2, 1983, p. F9).

24. See the comments of Sir Alan Walters, currently a scholar at the American Enterprise Institute, as reported in Hobart Rowen's piece appearing in the *Washington Post,* October 18, 1983, p. E1.

25. In this regard, the debt problem would be far less important if direct foreign investment rather than foreign borrowing had been emphasized in financing current account deficits. However, as William R. Cline points out, "Latin America, and Brazil more particularly, had celebrated a festival of nationalism in which extravagant foreign borrowing has replaced what should have been, to a much larger extent, equity financing" (see William R. Cline, "Discussion," in *Prospects for Adjustment,* ed. by John Williamson, Institute for International Economics, June 1983, p. 50).

26. See Roland Vaubel, "The Moral Hazard of IMF Lending," in *International Lending and the IMF,* edited by Allan H. Meltzer, The Heritage Lecturers, 21, 1983, pp. 65–79.

V. The Multinational Corporation in the International Economy

Multinational corporations (MNCs) are primary actors on the world scene. A single MNC's annual sales will usually exceed in value the gross national product of a small nation in which it operates. An MNC's command of managerial and technical personnel is many times that of, say, a small African or Caribbean government. MNCs produce and export goods; they exploit and import natural resources and transfer intermediate goods and partially assembled components. Some of this trade takes place within subsidiaries or divisions of the parent corporation, giving rise to the phenomenon of intrafirm trade. Corporations borrow in many capital markets and keep their financial assets in many banking systems. They speculate in exchange and commodity markets.

Multinational corporations view the world, not any given nation, as the arena for their actions. They make decisions about plant location on a global basis, assessing the investment climate and potential rate of profit in different nations, evaluating risks, costs, and other locational advantages and disadvantages. These decisions thus profoundly alter the world pattern of production, including the site and mix of employment. Most of these operations and decisions take place without any international oversight since no single nation has full regulatory powers over or knowledge of the MNCs' productive, distributive, and financial operations and plans.

Large and small, rich and poor nations welcome positive and productive actions by multinational corporations operating within their territories. They are concerned, however, that the character of their economies may be shaped by these same corporations in undesirable ways. The United States worries that jobs may move offshore when production is relocated in cheap-labor foreign countries. The countries that host such investments may want MNCs to export sufficient goods to earn the foreign exchange needed to cover repatriation of profits. Governments seek to insure that they are adequately compensated in taxes and royalties for exhaustion of natural resources. These and many other areas of tension and dispute are involved in country-company relationships.

A small selection of readings cannot cover all aspects of multinational corporate behavior in the international economy. This is an indication of how important and complicated these massive economic organizations have become and of the large role they play in every kind of international economic activity. In this section particular emphasis is placed on one facet of multinational corporate activities: the technology factor, as one of the contributors calls it. The first and last selections do, however, provide broader coverage of issues.

The first paper, by Jane Sneddon Little, examines American interests in multinational corporate activity. Major American multinationals have played a growing role overseas since 1945. At first, there seemed to be little conflict between American and host country aims and this expansion. Later, many countries in the Third World and even Europe began to react with growing alarm to the expansion of the American corporate presence. Now the United States is more apt to wonder what the conversion of companies bearing familiar household names into multinational enterprises means for its own prosperity and world economic leadership. Also, the United States has followed an open-door policy toward foreign investment and foreign companies have responded by dramatically expanding their activities in the American economy. Little provides a level-headed review of important aspects of American involvement in multinational operations, both as source and host country. Her primary conclusion is that the urgent need is not to amend our own policy but to ensure that other countries maintain openness to foreign investment from whatever source and not discriminate between local and foreign investors.

Raymond Vernon has long emphasized the connection between corporate technological innovation and trade advantages. His "product cycle" has become a staple of international trade theory. He emphasizes that technological changes are usually generated and introduced in the headquarters country of the MNC, largely because they arise from meeting specific demands in the large home market. Comparative advantage and exports then grow out of this home base operation. Later, other countries imitate or borrow the technology and establish their own production; later still, they may become exporters and even capture the original home market with low-cost supplies. By that time the MNC will have developed a new product or process so that the product cycle begins again.

Vernon notes that many products designed for the factor proportions and high income markets of the big rich countries are inappropriate for the less developed countries. He points out, however, that the best technology for low-cost production in the rich countries is often the best technology for production in the poor countries. He also believes that neglect of development of suitable technologies and products for the developing nations has diminished.

His first essay recasts the product cycle theory in light of recent developments in the international economy. As explained above, the original formulation of the product cycle stressed that innovation created a medium-term export advantage for a firm and country. Vernon finds that the spread of multinational corporate networks has been so extensive that innovations are now more quickly moved overseas to serve as the basis for production. As incomes per capita in Europe and Japan have risen to U.S. levels, American corporations no longer need initiate new products in the home market before moving production and sales overseas. He finds that the homogeneity of the world market may encourage development of uniform products, such as a "world car." Production of components may take place in different sites. These and other changes mean that the product cycle theory has continuing, but diminished, explanatory power.

Vernon's second contribution continues the reassessment of his earlier writing in light of the evolution of the international economy. He recalls his stress on the oligopolistic character of the modern MNC. Large corporations enjoy semimonopolies based on patented technologies or sheer market dominance. He discusses "threats to multinationals," noting that there have been a number of nationalizations in the past two decades. The displacement of the oil companies' hegemony with OPEC-led oil nation dominance of the world petroleum market is the most apparent manifestation of this phenomenon. Countries and their public enterprises have also become more comfortable in working out joint arrangements with MNCs, and vice versa.

In the next selection, Stephen Magee examines the property interest that MNCs have in new technologies. How can an MNC devise a strategy to maximize profits over the lifetime of an innovation? An MNC will try to maintain control over its new technologies and products as long as it can by investing resources in patent and other protection. An MNC will favor elaborate technologies over simple ones because appropriability is easier to maintain. It will prove strategic to price somewhat below the pure monopoly price to discourage emulation and then to lower prices as competition grows. Magee recognizes that there may be conflicts between the desire of an MNC to benefit from the appropriability of innovations and the needs of countries, and the world generally, to apply and use new ideas and products as widely and rapidly as possible. An obvious case would be a new miracle drug which could reduce disease and suffering. Should firm profits be given precedence over human lives? Yet, without the lure of profit would the firm continue to innovate?

Peter Drucker's article, which concludes this section, is a thoughtful review of relations between MNCs and developing nations. He examines several assumptions commonly held about these relations. He notes, first, that developing countries do not figure large in most MNC operations or plans, with most investment moving into natural resource extraction. It is neglect not "exploitation" that is most obvious. While this observation remains correct it is true that in the mid–1980s MNC activity in developing nations is increasingly moving into manufacturing.

Drucker's second point is that capital and other resources from abroad rarely matter very much in the development of a country. This is well-taken: development is largely a matter of internal policy and mobilization of internal resources. There is scope, however, for carefully considered reliance on external resources, technology, and management. Here an invitation to MNC involvement in the local economy can be catalytic. Drucker says that developing nation governments should seek to use MNCs as sources of productive resources and as channels into world export markets. He also emphasizes that joint ventures can take many forms and are a flexible way of protecting host country, domestic company, and MNC interests, and gaining mutual advantage.

24. Multinational Corporations and Foreign Investment: Current Trends and Issues

JANE SNEDDON LITTLE

ABSTRACT

Surely multinational corporations (MNCs) symobilize the internationalization of America for the U.S. public. The United States is the world's leading home and host country for these global firms. However, while our MNCs have considerable weight in some foreign countries, by most measures, foreign-owned businesses do not loom very large in the U.S. economy. Although the free flow of foreign direct investment promotes economic efficiency and world welfare, from a national viewpoint MNCs appear threatening. In particular, the U.S. public is concerned that our MNCs export U.S. jobs and that foreign MNCs can use U.S. resources to undercut our national goals. These fears are largely unfounded. On the whole, the traditional U.S. "open door" to foreign investment has served this country well. Nevertheless, many foreign governments are now trying to channel foreign investment flows to maximize their own national advantage. To protect our interests, the U.S. government is being urged to adopt similar regulations. The United States has no need for such measures; however, U.S. and world interests would be well served by an international agreement limiting efforts to distort foreign investment decisions. Because U.S. investment flows are huge by world standards but have a relatively small impact on our own economy, the United States has a unique ability to help form an international consensus on acceptable foreign investment policies.

Nothing can dramatize the internationalization of the American economy more vividly than the appearance of a Volkswagen plant in Pennsylvania or the production of the "world car" by U.S. automakers

Jane Sneddon Little is an economist with the Federal Reserve Bank of Boston.

abroad. Although foreign direct investment (FDI) often substitutes for international trade, the global spread of giant multinational corporations (MNCs) seems more obtrusive and troublesome than the customary growth of our imports and exports.

Proponents of unfettered FDI correctly suggest that it promotes economic efficiency and world welfare. From a national point of view, however, MNCs seem menacing—to prosperity at home and to sovereignty in the recipient nation. Indeed, the well-known book *Sovereignty at Bay*[1] has linked MNCs with the likely demise of the nation-state. Recently, however, it has become apparent that host governments are in fact using MNCs to tilt the benefits of FDI in their own national interest.[2]

U.S. policy in this area has generally supported freedom of investment flows worldwide. But because the distribution of the rather uncertain costs and benefits of FDI can and have been manipulated by government policy, attacks on the traditional U.S. "open-door" policy are strengthening. How should the United States react to these challenges? Its response must be developed with care, since the United States, as the world's leading home and host country for new investment flows, has a unique ability to help mold an international consensus on acceptable FDI policies.

FDI: WHAT AND WHY

FDI is an entrepreneurial capital movement that usually transfers technical knowledge or managerial skills from one country to another. Direct—as opposed to portfolio—investment implies a managerial role, although it need not confer control.

Why does FDI occur? A firm will choose foreign rather than domestic production when three conditions are met.[3] First, it must have some unique advantage that permits it to compete in a distant and unfamiliar milieu with foreign firms serving their own market. These assets, which might include technology, marketing skills, size, or favored access to inputs, must belong exclusively to the MNC—at least temporarily. Second, the MNC must also prefer to exploit these advantages itself rather than to sell or lease them to foreigners. This preference occurs because licensing tends to spoil the information monopoly the MNC developed at private cost. In addition, setting a market price for technology or marketing skills is hard. A firm may be able to achieve a satisfactory return on its research and development (R&D) outlay only by producing the final good or service itself.[4] Finally, producing abroad must also be more profitable than exporting. Access to resources, transportation costs, or tariff barriers could influence this decision.

Naturally, firm and location advantages do not remain constant. Firms tend to export very new products because production facilities should be close to the R&D staff in the early stages.[5] Inevitably, however, the knowledge behind the new product spreads, and foreign firms begin to copy it. Seeking to keep its market position by cutting costs, the originating firm may then resort to FDI.[6] Later, when guarding a dwindling monopoly advantage may not be worth the cost of operating abroad, the firm may choose to license. Finally, once the product is highly standardized, national comparative advantage determines the production site. FDI thus follows a cyclical pattern touching different industries at different times.

TRENDS IN FDI

At the end of World War II, the United States accounted for almost three-quarters of all new FDI. As other national economies grew in size and technological strength, however, European, Japanese, and even some less-developed-country firms began to invest abroad. Accordingly, the U.S. share of world FDI outflows fell to 50 percent in 1979. In addition, the United States now attracts more FDI than any other nation—about one-third of all FDI inflows.

U.S. Investment Abroad

The net value of U.S. investors' assets in their foreign affiliates—the foreign "position"—totaled $213.5 billion at the end of 1980. During the 1970s the U.S. foreign position grew 11 percent a year on average, largely financed by reinvested earnings. In 1980, for instance, the U.S. position rose 14 percent, financed by outflows from this country of $1.5 billion and by reinvested earnings of $17 billion.

A handful of statistics on the impact of U.S. FDI in Canada and Britain, the countries with the largest U.S. position, puts these numbers in perspective. In 1979, for example, capital expenditures of U.S. foreign affiliates accounted for about 15 percent of Canadian and 10 percent of British gross fixed capital formation. These same affiliates also generated one-half of Canadian and one-fourth of British exports in 1976. From the U.S. side, in turn, the FDI outflow represented a mere .5 percent of 1980 U.S. business plant and equipment expenditures, while foreign affiliate earnings in 1979 equaled about 20 percent of U.S. corporate profits. Finally, U.S. foreign affiliates accounted for an amazing three-quarters of all foreign sales made by U.S. businesses in 1976.

A shift in the geography of U.S. FDI has occurred since 1950. Neighboring Latin America and Canada then accounted for over two-thirds of the U.S. position. By 1980, however, almost half of the U.S. position was in Europe. Accordingly, Germany and Switzerland followed Canada and the United Kingdom as the nations with the largest U.S. FDI positions in 1980.

The industrial focus of the U.S. FDI has also changed in the last 30 years, with manufacturing gaining and petroleum losing emphasis. Manufacturing now accounts for over 40 percent of the U.S. position. Within manufacturing, chemicals loomed most important in 1980, followed by nonelectrical machinery, transportation, food, and electrical machinery.

FDI in the United States

The net value of foreigners' assets in their U.S. affiliates jumped 20 percent in 1980 to reach $65.5 billion at year's end. Although this value equals about one-third of the U.S. foreign position, FDI in the United States is growing almost twice as fast as U.S. investment abroad. Moreover, for the last three years the investment inflow from foreign parents to their U.S. affiliates actually outweighed the outflow from U.S. parents to their affiliates abroad.

FDI in the United States has surged during the 1970s in part because of the depreciation of the dollar on the foreign exchange markets. That development made it harder for foreigners to export to the United States, while it also reduced the foreign cost of investing in this country. Growing economic and technical strength plus social and political tensions abroad, the depressed state of the U.S. stock market, and U.S. protectionist sentiments have also contributed.

Last year almost 40 percent of the foreign position was devoted to manufacturing, while trade and petroleum each accounted for about 20 percent. Within manufacturing, chemicals predominated followed by food, machinery, and metals. Real estate investments represented only four percent of the total. Despite frequently voiced concerns about foreigners buying whole cities and much of America's farmland, in 1980 foreigners owned less than .5 percent of privately held U.S. agricultural land.

Indeed, by most measures foreign-owned businesses do not loom very large in the U.S. economy. Employment and sales of foreign manufacturing affiliates amounted to about 4.5 percent of U.S. manufacturing employment and shipments in 1979. Among manufacturing industries, the deepest penetration was in chemicals, where foreign-owned firms accounted for 14 percent of total sales. Foreign affiliate plant and equipment expenditures also represented about four percent of new U.S. business plant and equipment expenditures in 1979. Surprisingly, by contrast, foreign affiliate exports equaled almost one-quarter of U.S. merchandise exports in that year.

As for national representation, the Netherlands had the largest investment position in this country in 1980, followed by the United Kingdom, Canada, and Germany. The 13 Organization of Petroleum Exporting Countries (OPEC) members accounted for less than 1 percent of the total.

Foreign acquisitions of U.S. businesses provoke much concern. In 1979 acquisitions accounted for 90 percent of the dollar value of foreign investment projects. By comparison, 60 percent of U.S. FDI in 1979 was spent on acquisitions.

EXPORTING PROSPERITY: U.S. CONCERNS ABOUT FDI ABROAD

Public debate about the costs of FDI now centers on foreign investment in this country rather than on U.S. activity abroad. Many of the old complaints about U.S. FDI—that it exports jobs, technology, and tax revenues; hurts the balance of payments; and aggravates antitrust problems—seem less compelling than before. The export of U.S. jobs, however, remains just as lively an issue as ever—especially since more and more governments are using incentives to lure FDI to their shores.

FDI and U.S. Labor

When U.S. manufacturers assemble televisions in Mexico or produce auto parts in Canada, are they exporting U.S. jobs? The answer depends on whether sales of U.S. foreign affiliates replace exports from this country or sales by foreign firms. The actual outcome is probably a mixture of both possibilities.

The cyclical theory of FDI suggests that MNCs go abroad as their monopolistic hold on new knowledge weakens, and foreign firms begin to compete with them. Indeed, it is probably inevitable that U.S. or competing foreign firms will eventually move production to an area with a comparative advantage, such as low-cost labor. Even so, U.S. firms may speed export displacement[7] by choosing to move as soon as foreign operations become more profitable than domestic production.

On the other hand, when U.S. MNCs go abroad to avoid tariffs, discriminatory government procurement policies, and so on, their foreign sales probably replace few U.S. exports. The alternative to such FDI may be no U.S. sales at all. Moreover, U.S. natural resource ventures—in copper or bauxite, for example—clearly do not displace U.S. exports either.[8] Finally, some FDI is devoted to servicing, distribution, and so on—activities that may actually promote U.S. exports.[9]

Measuring the final outcome is very difficult. One study of FDI's impact on chosen industry exports suggests that at low levels FDI stimulates foreign sales. Overall, however, FDI has no strong impact on a given industry's export performance.[10] In other words, the evidence does not suggest that FDI exports U.S. jobs. Incentive programs are more common now than at the time of the study, however.

Another charge leveled against FDI is that it reduces labor's share of national income. Capital outflows from this country could leave U.S. labor working with less capital equipment than before. As a result, productivity and wages or employment could be lower than otherwise.

This outcome need not occur, however. First, only a small part of U.S. FDI is financed by a capital outflow from the United States. Moreover, U.S. FDI spurs economic growth in host countries. For instance, a study of FDI in Canada showed that $1.00 of FDI generated about $2.00 of Canadian capital formation.[11] This host country investment will lead to economic growth and, in turn, to increased demand for U.S. exports. Finally, a U.S. MNC's foreign operations are likely to promote its capital accumulation and R&D outlays—to the long-run benefit of U.S. labor.[12]

In actual fact, labor's share of U.S. national income rose between 1945 and 1980; thus, the evidence does not support the charge that U.S. FDI has reduced labor's share of the national pie. Nevertheless, some investments clearly hurt specific U.S. workers. Expanding U.S. trade adjustment assistance to cover these individuals would cut the social cost of such investments.

Barriers, Performance Requirements, and Incentives. Like free trade, unrestricted investment flows tend to maximize world welfare, thus benefiting host and home country. Restrictions on or incentives for FDI produce uneconomic investments and reduce world welfare.

At one time, barriers to investment were the main concern. For years, Japan limited foreigners to a few industries such as cotton spinning and ice manufacturing. Currently, Canada's national energy program offers Canadian-owned firms incentives for gas and oil exploration that are not available to foreign companies. This discrimination should help enforce its goal of reducing foreign ownership of Canadian energy firms to 50 percent by 1990.

By contrast, most countries now try to lure FDI into their economies—but on terms maximizing the gains to the nation. To this end, they compete in offering tax and credit incentives, training programs, and so on. They also set minimum performance requirements for job creation, exports, and local value-added. Of course, a requirement that 80–100 percent of a product represent domestic value-added acts like an import quota. Such quotas are illegal under the General Agreement on Tariffs and Trade (GATT), but no such rules yet govern investment flows.

Because MNCs are held hostage by their existing investments or very much want access to particular markets, perhaps because of the incentives offered, they tend to ally themselves with the host governments without much protest—generally to the detriment of their home country. Indeed, the only "empty chair"[13] at current FDI negotiations is that of the home country.

How should the United States respond to host country efforts to manipulate MNCs to their national advantage? One suggestion is that we should adopt similar schemes to maximize the benefits derived from the large volume of FDI in the United States.

THE SHOE ON THE OTHER FOOT: U.S. CONCERNS ABOUT INBOUND FDI

After years of preaching the benefits of FDI, many Americans are now reciting all the arguments about its dangers, which other host countries once made. This ironic chorus reflects the increased visibility of FDI in this country.

American Resources versus American Interests

A primary fear argues that foreign investors might use U.S. resources in opposition to the national interest. For example, Elf Acquitaine's purchase of Texasgulf, producer of 15 percent of U.S. sulphur output, helped provoke the recent outcry about FDI in U.S. raw materials.[14] Such investments seem particularly threatening when government ownership is involved. Critics fear that foreign firms will divert scarce raw materials abroad. A Texas state representative suggested, for instance, that "farmers in this country will be at the mercy" of French farmers who need the fertilizer ingredients made by Texasgulf.[15] These critics also argue that national security is involved since foreigners may be insensitive or antagonistic to U.S. interests.

These fears are largely groundless, however. First, increased exports are more often considered a gain than a loss. The Reagan administration has welcomed the recent growth in U.S. steam coal exports and has worked, like other administrations, to facilitate exports of fruit to Japan and grain to the Soviet Union.

In addition, although the United States does not subject foreign investments to registration or review, FDI in this country is not unregulated. Like most other countries, the United States limits FDI in areas related to the national interest, such as broadcasting and nuclear and hydroelectric power. Furthermore, foreign firms in this country are also subject to the same tax, securities, antitrust, and labor legislation as any U.S. firm.

In an emergency, moreover, the U.S. government has the power to impose export controls or to seize foreign assets. The president can also require any firm to accept and to give priority to defense contracts. Indeed, the experience of foreign investors abroad makes it quite clear that once an investment is made, an MNC becomes a hostage of the host government. Accordingly, MNCs have had to cooperate time and again when host governments have unilaterally changed the rules about production, taxes, repatriation, and even ownership of an affiliate.[16]

As for restricting "government" ownership, that concept is hard to define and may be irrelevant since in many countries the relationship between government and private industry is much closer than in the United States. Undesirable consequences of government ownership might be uneconomic behavior, such as investment or export subsidies. Clearly, however, the use of subsidies is not limited to government-owned firms.

Whose "National Interest"? Competition for Resources

Another set of arguments against FDI in this country amounts to complaints by Americans facing increased competition from foreigners. These individuals easily equate the national interest with their own and seek restrictions on FDI that would discriminate against other U.S. citizens.

Foreign purchases of U.S. land provoke very emotional reactions. Foreign land purchases are held to push up land values and property taxes and to prevent young Americans from going into farming. Since foreigners owned less than .5 percent of all privately held agricultural land in 1980, their impact on rapidly rising land prices must surely have been minimal. In addition, rising land values clearly help current farmers and their heirs, while restrictions on foreign land purchases would reduce demand for their assets.

Similarly, managers of U.S. firms suggest that FDI keeps them from expanding into areas where foreigners have entered. Since most industries attracting foreign investment are oligopolistic, it is not clear that U.S. companies would increase production in the absence of FDI. On the other hand, it is clear that foreign MNCs provide a most important source of fresh competition for the U.S. economy today—in part because they have some advantages, such as economies of scale, over U.S. firms trying to build from nothing.

Foreign "takeovers" of U.S. companies touch a particularly tender nerve. Observers note that low U.S. stock prices and the low foreign exchange value of the dollar in 1978–79 encouraged foreign purchases of U.S. firms. Opponents contend that acquisitions do not provide as many benefits—jobs, for instance— as greenfield investments. Accordingly, they recommend that foreign takeovers be singled out for regulation.

Opponents of foreign acquisitions are usually managers rather than stockholders of U.S. firms. Indeed, stockholders clearly benefit from foreign acquisitions. Furthermore, foreigners tend to buy companies of less than average financial health. Not only these firms, but the overall U.S. economy profits from the infusions of management skills, technology, and capital that usually accompany FDI.[17] Foreign acquisitions also provide the U.S. sellers with investable funds that could, after all, be used for greenfield projects. All in all, foreign acquisitions do not seem particularly objectionable unless, of course, the foreign MNC receives special incentives from its home government.

THE POLICY CHALLENGE

The foregoing suggests that unfettered flows of FDI promote U.S. and world welfare. How, then, should the United States deal with growing efforts of foreign governments to bend FDI to suit their own national goals? Because these efforts cause both retaliation and uneconomic investments, the outcome of this game is not just "zero-sum," but decidedly negative.

An international treaty on the use of FDI incentives, barriers, and performance requirements, a "GATT for FDI," is the obvious solution.[18] The United States has pursued this goal for several years, but progress has been limited. Members of the U.S. Congress, stung by Canadian discrimination and highly publicized takeovers of U.S. raw materials firms, are growing impatient. What are the options?

Registration of Foreign Investors

While foreigners buying U.S. agricultural land or making any investment above a certain size must file government forms, this country does not require universal registration. Opponents say registration would push the U.S. open door partially shut and deter some desirable investments. In general, however, registration seems unobjectionable. Most nations require it as do we, in effect, for some categories of investment. Universal application would fill a few data gaps—in real estate, for instance—and help hold xenophobia at bay.

Screening FDI

Since 1975 the Committee on Foreign Investment in the United States (CFIUS) has reviewed foreign investments that might have a "major" impact on the national interest. This committee has never found an investment harmful, but should it do so, it has no power to halt the project. A toothless CFIUS is clearly in an awkward position, as was pointed out by Elf Acquitaine's refusal to delay its tender-offer for Texasgulf while the CFIUS studied the case. Should the CFIUS ever find a foreign takeover contrary to U.S. interests after the fact, the damage could not be reversed without declaring an "emergency" and creating an international brouhaha.

Should the CFIUS thus be given the power to prohibit foreign investments? No, because such a change is a step in the wrong direction. It could lead foreign governments to retaliate and would hand a weapon to domestic groups pursuing their own advantages in the name of the national interest. Such powers would also prevent most foreign tender-offers for U.S. firms, since once a tender-offer is announced, the buyer must be able to move quickly. Eliminating foreign tender-offers would not promote the national interest, since foreign acquisitions can be an important source of competition in our concentrated industries. Should a purely advisory CFIUS be eliminated then? No again, for a watchdog agency ready to warn Congress of disturbing trends serves a useful function.

Tit for Tat: U.S. Incentives and Performance Requirements. The United States could try to defend its national interests by setting its own performance requirements for inbound FDI, for instance, or by establishing an "escape clause"[19] to halt any outbound FDI judged harmful. Some proponents believe these measures would yield benefits in their own right. Others see them as tools to force foreign governments into serious negotiations on a GATT for investment.[20] The dangers inherent in such measures are similar to those attached to giving CFIUS authority to stop investments—only more so.

Moreover, the United States already appears to have the weapons it needs to defend itself and prod other governments toward an investment treaty. For instance, the Special Trade Representative's Office is considering using import restrictions sanctioned by the 1974 Trade Act to retaliate against foreign performance requirements that "unjustifiably" burden U.S. commerce. The GATT subsidy code might also be used to counter FDI incentives that amount to foreign export subsidies. In addition, the Minerals Leasing Act of 1920 gives foreigners access to mineral leases on federal lands only if their country reciprocates. Accordingly, the Interior Department could strip some countries of their reciprocal status. Imaginative use of existing legislation seems less provocative and more promising than creating a new web of regulations counter to the long-run national interest.

It is hardly surprising that some governments have seized upon foreign MNCs as new tools for their economic arsenals; however, the internationalization of America has not proceeded so far that the United States need adopt other nations' policies on FDI. On the other hand, the process has gone far enough that a GATT for FDI deserves high priority.

NOTES

1. Raymond Vernon, *Sovereignty at Bay: The Multinational Spread of U.S. Enterprises* (London: Longman, 1971).
2. C. Fred Bergsten, "Coming Investment Wars?" *Foreign Affairs*, 53:136–39 (Oct. 1974).
3. John H. Dunning, "Explaining Changing Patterns of International Production: In Defence of the Eclectic Theory," *Oxford Bulletin of Economics and Statistics*, 41:275 (Nov. 1979).
4. Alan M. Rugman, *Multinationals in Canada: Theory, Performance and Economic Impact* (Boston: Martinus Nijhoff, 1980), pp. 34–38.
5. Stephen P. Magee, "Multinational Corporations, the Industry Technology Cycle and Development," *Journal of World Trade Law*, 11:304–7 (July/Aug. 1977).
6. Vernon, *Sovereignty at Bay*, pp. 66–77.
7. Ibid., p. 166.
8. G. C. Hufbauer, "The Multinational Corporation and Direct Investment," in *International Trade and Finance*, ed. Peter B. Kenen (Cambridge: Cambridge University Press, 1975), p. 288.
9. C. Fred Bergsten, Thomas Horst, and Theodore H. Moran, *American Multinationals and American Interests* (Washington, DC: Brookings Institution, 1978), pp. 71–72.
10. Ibid., pp. 82–96.
11. Richard E. Caves and Grant L. Reuber, *Capital Transfers and Economic Policy* (Cambridge, MA: Harvard University Press, 1971), p. 194.
12. Tetsunori Koizumi and Kenneth J. Kopecky, "Foreign Direct Investment, Technology Transfer and Domestic Employment Effects," *Journal of International Economics*, 10:1–20 (Feb. 1980).
13. C. Fred Bergsten, "International Investment: The Need for a New U.S. Policy," mimeographed (Statement before the Subcommittee on International Economic Policy, Committee on Foreign Relations, United States Senate, July 30, 1981).
14. Maria Shao, "Some U.S. Mining Firms Try to Turn Back Sudden Wave of Foreign Takeover Offers," *Wall Street Journal*, 19 Aug. 1981, p. 50.
15. Ibid.
16. Vernon, *Sovereignty at Bay*, pp. 44–59.
17. Jane Sneddon Little, "The Financial Health of U.S. Manufacturing Firms Acquired by Foreigners," *New England Economic Review* (July/Aug. 1981), p. 17.
18. Bergsten, "Coming Investment Wars?" p. 152; idem, "International Investment," p. 10; Hufbauer, "The Multinational Corporation," p. 305.
19. Bergsten, Horst, and Moran, *American Multinationals*, pp. 467–472.
20. Bergsten, "International Investment," pp. 10, 14–15.

25. The Product Cycle Hypothesis in A New International Environment

RAYMOND VERNON

The last decade has produced a flowering of hypotheses that purport to explain the international trade and direct investment activities of firms in terms of the so-called product cycle. My purpose in this paper is to suggest that the power of such hypotheses has been changing. Two reasons account for that change: one, an increase in the geographical reach of many of the enterprises that are involved in the introduction of new products, a consequence of their having established many overseas subsidiaries; the other, a change in the national markets of the advanced industrialized countries, which has reduced some of the differences that had previously existed between such markets.

A WORD ON THEORY

The fact that new products constantly appear, then mature, and eventually die has always fitted awkwardly into the mainstream theories of international trade and international investment. Hume, Ricardo, Marshall, Ohlin, Williams, and others have observed the phenomenon in passing, without attempting any rigorous formulation of its implications for international trade and investment theory. In the past decade or two, however, numerous efforts have been made to fill the gap. Some have dealt mainly with the trade aspects of the phenomenon.[1] But some have pushed beyond the immediate trade effects, tracing out a pattern that eventually culminated in foreign direct investments on the part of the innovating firm.[2]

According to the product cycle hypothesis, firms that set up foreign producing facilities characteristically do so in reliance on some real or imagined monopolistic advantage. In the absence of such a perceived

Raymond Vernon is Clarence Dillan Professor Emeritus of Harvard University. He is presently associated with the Kennedy School of Government.

advantage, firms are loath to take on the special costs and uncertainties of operating a subsidiary in a foreign environment.[3] One such special strength is an innovational lead.

The product cycle hypothesis begins with the assumption that the stimulus to innovation is typically provided by some threat or promise in the market.[4] But according to the hypothesis, firms are acutely myopic; their managers tend to be stimulated by the needs and opportunities of the market closest at hand, the home market.

The home market in fact plays a dual role in the hypothesis. Not only is it the source of stimulus for the innovating firm; it is also the preferred location for the actual development of the innovation. The first factor that has pushed innovating firms to do their development work in the home market has been simply the need for engineers and scientists with the requisite skills. That requirement, when gauged through the eyes of the typical innovating firm, has tended to rule out sites in most developing countries and has narrowed the choice to some site in the advanced industrialized world. As between such advanced country sites, the home market has generally prevailed.[5] Locating in the home market, engineers and scientists can interact easily with the prospective customers whose needs they hope to satisfy, and can check constantly with (or be checked by) the specialists at headquarters who are concerned with financial and production planning.

The propensity to cluster in the home market is fortified by the fact that there are some well-recognized economies to be captured by an innovating team that is brought together at a common location.[6] These include the usual advantages that go with subdividing any task among a number of specialists, and the added advantages of maintaining efficiency of communication among the research specialists.[7]

The upshot is that the innovations of firms headquartered in some given market tend to reflect the characteristics of that market. Historically, therefore, US firms have developed and produced products that were labour-saving or responded to high-income wants; continental European firms, products and processes that were material-saving and capital-saving; and Japanese firms, products that conserved not only material and capital but also space.[8]

If innovating firms tend to scan their home markets with special intensity, the chances are greatly increased that their first production facilities will also be located in the home market. In many cases, the transitions from development work to pilot plant operation to first commercial production take place in imperceptible steps. But other factors also figure in the choice. One is the fact that if the firm perceives its principal market as being at home, it may prefer a home location to minimize transport costs. The second factor is that the specifications for new products and the optimal methods for manufacturing such products are typically in flux for some time; hence, fixing the optimal location of the first production site is bound to be an exercise based on guesswork. A final factor that may explain the tendency to produce at home is the characteristic inelasticity in the demand of the earliest users of many new products. That inelasticity is thought to make the innovator relatively indifferent to questions of production cost at the time of introduction of a new product.

Once the innovator has set up its first production unit in the home market, any demand that may develop in a foreign market would ordinarily be served from the existing production unit. Eventually, however, the firm may consider other alternatives, such as that of licensing a foreign producer or of setting up its own producing subsidiary abroad. For new products, the licensing alternative may prove an inferior choice because of inefficiencies in the international market for technology.[9] If licensing is not the preferred choice, then the firm makes the usual familiar comparison between the delivered cost of exports and the cost of overseas production. That is, the marginal costs of producing for export in the home unit plus international transport costs and duties are compared with the full cost of producing the required amount in a foreign subsidiary.

Although not essential to the product cycle hypothesis, it is commonly assumed that a triggering event is likely to be required before the producer will seriously make the calculations that could lead to the creation of a foreign producing facility. The triggering event ordinarily occurs when the innovator is threatened with losing its monopoly position. In the usual case, rival producers appear, prepared to manufacture the product from locations that could undersell the original innovator.

The obvious question is why the original innovator was not already aware that the costs of production might be lower abroad. Part of the answer may lie in the indeterminateness of the threat before it has actually materialized: the difficulty of deciding what is at stake in failing to find the least-cost location, what alternative sites need to be investigated, and what the costs of investigation are likely to be.

These conditions change, however, as the threat begins to crystallize. Eventually, it may be clear that the innovator is threatened with the loss of its business in a given foreign market. At that point, the areas to be investigated as possible production sites have been narrowed while the size of the risk has been more explicitly defined. Accordingly, the decision whether to invest in added information is more readily made. Once having felt compelled to focus on the issue, the innovator will decide in some cases to set up a local producing unit in order to prolong some of the advantages that were created by its original monopoly.

TABLE 1. Networks of Foreign Manufacturing Subsidiaries of 315 Multinational Companies
1950 and 1970s

NUMBER OF ENTERPRISES WITH NETWORKS INCLUDING	180 US-BASED MNCs		135 MNCs BASED IN UK AND EUROPE	
	1950	*1975*	*1950*	*1970*
Fewer than 6 countries	138	9	116	31
6 to 20 countries	43	128	16	75
More than 20 countries	0	44	3	29

Source: Harvard Multinational Enterprise Project.

TWO CRITICAL CHANGES

The Networks' Spread

For the past three decades or so, the process of innovation, export, and investment has been progressing full tilt. One result has been a transformation in the industries in which innovations tend to be especially prominent, such as chemicals, electronics, machinery, and transportation equipment. In industries such as these, innovating firms that are limited to their own home markets no longer are very common. Instead, enterprises with highly developed multinational networks of producing units typically account for more than half the global output in their respective product lines.

In spreading their networks of subsidiaries around the world, multinational companies have followed some reasonably well-defined patterns. These patterns offer some strong clues regarding the changing perceptions of the enterprises and their likely lines of future behaviour.

First, a word on the extent of the spread itself. Table 1 compares the scope of the overseas subsidiary networks of a group of the world's largest firms in 1950 with the networks of those same firms in the 1970s. The dramatic increase in the overseas networks of such firms is apparent.

Detailed data have been developed for the 180 US firms in the group, indicating more exactly how the overseas spread took place.[10] According to these data, the overseas spread of the firms in our sample was consistent and stable throughout the three decades following World War II. Firms typically set up their subsidiaries, product lines, and new products in a sequence that began with the geographical areas with which they were most familiar, such as Canada and the United Kingdom, and eventually spread to those that had originally been least familiar, such as Asia and Africa. As time went on, however, the unfamiliar became less so, and the disposition to move first into the traditional

TABLE 2. Spread of Production of 954 New Products by 57 US–Based MNCs to their Foreign Manufacturing Subsidiaries, Classified by Period When Initially Introduced in the United States

PERIOD WHEN INTRODUCED IN US	NUMBER OF PRODUCTS	PERCENTAGE TRANSFERRED ABROAD, BY NUMBER OF YEARS BETWEEN US INTRODUCTION AND INITIAL TRANSFER	
		within 1 year after	*within 2–3 years after*
		%	%
1945	56	10.7	8.9
1946–1950	149	8.1	10.1
1951–1955	147	7.5	10.2
1956–1960	180	13.3	17.8
1961–1965	165	22.4	17.0
1966–1970	158	29.7	15.8
1971–1975	99	35.4	16.2
Total	954	18.0	14.0

Source: Vernon and Davidson, cited in text.

areas visibly declined. To illustrate: For product lines introduced abroad by the 180 firms before 1946, the probability that a Canadian location would come earlier than an Asian location was 79 percent; but for product lines that were introduced abroad after 1960, the probability that Canada would take precedence over Asia had dropped to only 59 percent.

The consequences of this steady shift in preferences could be seen in a corresponding shift in the geographical distribution of the foreign subsidiaries of the 180 firms. Before 1946, about 23 percent of the subsidiaries had been located in Canada; but by 1975, the proportion was about 13 percent, with the offsetting gains being recorded principally in Asia, Africa, and the Middle East.[11]

With numerous indications that US firms were feeling at ease over a wider portion of the earth's surface, it comes as no surprise that the interval of time between the introduction of any new product in the United States and its first production in a foreign location has been rapidly shrinking. Table 2 portrays the time lapse between the introduction of 954 products in the United States and their first overseas production via the manufacturing subsidiaries of the introducing firm.

The data also suggest in various ways that the trends just discussed have been strongly self-reinforcing. For instance, firms that had experienced a considerable number of prior transfers to their foreign producing subsidiaries were quite consistently quicker off the mark with any new product than were firms with fewer prior transfers. Besides, as firms introduced one product after another into a given country, the lapse of time between the introduction of successive products in that country steadily declined.

All told, therefore, the picture is one of an organic change in the overseas networks of large US-based firms. The rate of spread of these networks, whether measured by subsidiaries or by product lines, is slightly lower in the first half of the 1970's than in the latter half of the 1960's; but the spread persists at rates that are rapid by historical standards. Besides, the changes in the rate of spread, according to various econometric tests, seem quite impervious to changes in exchange rates or in price-adjusted exchange rates;[12] so it seems reasonable to assume that we confront a basic change in the institutional structure of the MNCs concerned.[13]

The Environmental Changes

In the period after World War II, the descriptive power of the product cycle hypothesis, at least as it applied to US-based enterprises, had been enhanced by some special factors. In the early part of the post-war period, the US economy was the repository of a storehouse of innovations not yet exploited abroad, innovations that responded to the labour-scarce high-income conditions of the US market. As the years went on, other countries eventually achieved the income levels and acquired the relative labour costs that had prevailed earlier in the United States. As these countries tracked the terrain already traversed by the US economy, they developed an increasing demand for the products that had previously been generated in response to US needs. That circumstance provided the consequences characteristically associated with the product cycle sequence: exports from the United States in mounting volume, followed eventually by the establishment of foreign producing subsidiaries on the part of the erstwhile US exporters.

But many of the advanced industrialized countries that were tracking over the US terrain were doing something more: They were closing in on the United States, narrowing or obliterating the income gap that had existed in the immediate postwar period. In 1949, for instance, the per capita income of Germany and of France was less than one-third that of the United States; but by the latter 1970's, the per capita income of all three countries was practically equal. In the same interval, Japan increased its per capita income from 6 percent of the US level to nearly 70 percent of that level. That shrinkage, of course, weakened a critical assumption of the product cycle hypothesis, namely, that the entrepreneurs of large enterprises confronted markedly different conditions in their respective home markets. As European and Japanese incomes approached those of the United States, these differences were reduced. And as the United States came to rely increasingly on imported raw materials, the differences in the factor costs of the various markets declined further still.

Not only have the differences in income levels among these major markets been shrinking; the differences in their overall dimensions also have declined. This has been due partly to the convergence of such income levels, but partly also to the development of the European Economic Community. As a result, entrepreneurs with their home base in these different markets confront conditions that are much more similar than they had been in the past.

Some of the starting assumptions of the product cycle hypothesis therefore are clearly in question. It is no longer easy to assume that innovating firms are uninformed about conditions in foreign markets, whether in other advanced countries or in the developing world. Nor can it be assumed that US firms are exposed to a very different home environment from European and Japanese firms; although the gap between most of the developing countries and the advanced industrialized countries palpably remains, the differences among the advanced industrialized countries are reduced to trivial dimensions. With some key assumptions of the product cycle hypothesis in doubt, what organizing concepts are still available by which one can observe and assess the role of innovation in the operations of the multinational enterprises of different countries?

THE GLOBAL NETWORK IN OPERATION

To try to answer the question, I have classified multinational companies crudely into three ideal types, and have sought to explore their likely behaviour.

The first type is purely hypothetical, a result of armchair speculation. Picture an MNC with an innovating capability that has developed a powerful capacity for global scanning. Communication is virtually costless between any two points of the globe; information, once received, is digested and interpreted at little or no cost. Ignorance or uncertainty, therefore, is no longer a function of distance; markets, wherever located, have an equal opportunity to stimulate the firm to innovation and production; and factory sites, wherever located, have an equal chance to be weighed for their costs and risks. But some significant economies of scale continue to exist in the development activities as well as in the production activities of the firm.

An enterprise of this sort, we can presume, will from time to time develop an innovation in response to the promise or threat of one of the many markets to which it was exposed. The firm might launch the innovative process in the market that had produced the stimulus; or, if economies of scale were important and an appropriate facility existed elsewhere in the system, in a location well removed from the prospective market. In either case, once the innovation was developed, the global scanner would be in a position to serve any market in which it was aware that demand existed; and would be in a position to detect and serve new demands in other markets as they subsequently arose. Presumably such demands would grow in other countries as they attained the income levels or the factor cost configurations of the country whose needs had first stimulated the invention. For some products, such as consumer goods, the demand in different national markets could be expected to appear in a predictable pecking order, based largely on income levels and labour costs.

The global scanner, therefore, would be in an advantageous position as compared with those firms without such a scanning capability. Firms that were confined to a country which was down the ladder in the pecking order, including most firms headquartered in the developing countries, would be at a disadvantage in relation to the global scanner. As the incomes of their home countries grew, the nonglobal producers might well perceive the opportunity to fill a growing demand; but they would be handicapped by comparison with the enterprises that were already producing in the higher income countries, including the global scanners.

In a world composed of such firms, the product cycle hypothesis would play only a very little role. Although innovating firms might prefer locations in one of the advanced industrialized countries due to the supply of engineers and scientists, the preference for a location in the home market would be weaker. The exports generated by the innovations might come from the country in which the product had initially been introduced; but then again they might not. Whatever the original source of the exports might be, the hold of the exporting country would be tenuous, as the global scanner continuously recalculated the parameters that determined the optimal production location.

The hypothetical global scanner, of course, is not to be found in the real world. The acquisition of information is seldom altogether costless; and the digestion and interpretation of information always entails cost. The typical patterns of behaviour that one observes in the real world reflect that fact.

One typical pattern, which provides the basis for a second model, consists of firms that develop and produce a line of standardized products which they think responds to a homogeneous world demand rather than to the distinctive needs of individual markets. Some firms have been able to take this approach from the very first, because of the nature of their products; the oil, chemical, and crude metals industries, for instance, were always in a position to develop and purvey a standardized line of products to world markets. But the trend has been moving beyond such products to well-elaborated manufactures: to aircraft, computers, pharmaceuticals, and automobiles, for instance.

The trends of the automobile industry in that direction are particularly striking.[14]

By standardizing their product on a world basis, firms can hope for two kinds of benefit: they can reduce or avoid the costs of processing and interpreting the information that bears on the distinctive needs of individual markets; and they can capture the scale economies of production and marketing on a global scale. Whether those advantages outweigh the disadvantages of being unresponsive to the needs of individual markets is an empirical question the answer to which may well vary by product lines and other factors; those firms that decide in the affirmative for some or all of their product lines cannot be said to be engaged in an irrational response.

Firms in this category, innovating for a global market, are obliged to play their innovational gambles for relatively heavy stakes. Accordingly, they can be expected to maintain the central core of their innovational activities close to headquarters, where complex face-to-face consultation among key personnel will be possible; in this respect, such firms are likely to perform consistently with the product cycle pattern. To be sure, with increased ease of communication and transportation, various routine aspects of the development work, not involving the most critical choices in the development process, can be spun off to more distant locations. To reduce their development costs and to respond to the pressures of various governments in whose territories they hope to do business, firms in this category are commonly prepared to establish some carefully selected development activities at distant points; but integration at the centre is still needed.[15]

Firms in this category also have a strong need to integrate their global production facilities. Seeking to exploit scale economies, they are likely to establish various component plants in both advanced industrialized countries and developing countries, and to crosshaul between plants for the assembly of final products. That pattern will be at variance with product cycle expectations.

It need not be anticipated, however, that all firms with a capacity for global scanning will commit themselves unequivocally to the development of standard global products such as the IBM 370, the Boeing 757, or the GM world car. General Motors, after all, continues to respond to certain distinctive national characteristics in some of its product lines, in spite of its commitment to a world sourcing strategy. Other automobile firms, including Renault and Chrysler, seem prepared to respond to national factors for even a larger proportion of their output, foregoing the advantages of a world product and long production runs. In computers, a number of IBM's rivals survive by their willingness and ability to adapt to the requirements of local markets, including the requirements of national governments, to a degree that would be incompatible with the standardization of their products and the global rationalization of their facilities.[16] Many European and Japanese firms still find it useful to treat the US market as a distinctive entity, justifying distinctive products and strategies.[17]

Accordingly, we can picture firms that make different decisions on the benefits of global optimization, according to the characteristics of each product line. And we can picture markets in which different firms have settled on somewhat different strategies for closely competing products. If past history is any guide, such differences can persist in a given product market over extended periods of time.[18]

A third type of innovating MNC that merits some speculative consideration is the firm whose choices of innovations and production sites remain myopically oriented to the home market while leaving all analysis of foreign markets to its individual foreign producing subsidiaries. Firms in this category simply put out their home-based innovations for production by their foreign subsidiaries; or, perhaps even more commonly, such firms allow the initiative for such decisions to come from the subsidiaries themselves.[19] Drawing from a shopping list of products generated by the headquarters unit, subsidiaries choose those that seem appropriate for intensive exploitation in their local markets. As long as the proposed production in the subsidiary seems to have no considerable impact on the facilities of the firm located in other countries, the managers at headquarters are disposed to give the local managers their head.

Firms that pursue a policy of this sort can justify their approach readily enough: One possibility is that the firm perceives the cost of interpreting the information needed for pursuing a more centralized policy in production and marketing as exceeding the likely benefits. Another possibility is that the firm has found it impossible to fashion an organization that has the capability for absorbing and being influenced by signals that originate in the subsidiaries.[20]

Where this pattern of operation exists, the hypothesized behavior of the product cycle may still be visible. But the phase of the product cycle in which the parent is responsible for serving foreign markets will be foreshortened and the oligopolistic strength of the innovating firm will be relatively weak, given the existence of firms in other markets that face similar demands and factor cost conditions.

Cases in this category will of course deviate from the pattern that a global scanner would generate. First, as long as the subsidiary is the initiator, the geographical spread of products will be affected by the risk-taking propensities and drives of individual subsidiary managers and by the resource slack of individual subsidiaries rather than by a consistent set of decision rules and allocations from the centre.[21] Second, in cases in which the initiative for transfer comes from the subsidiary rather than the parent, the possibility of producing in some third country where neither the parent nor the subsidiary is located is unlikely to be considered.

All this leads to a simple conclusion. As we search for a hypothesis that would replace the product cycle concept as an explicator of the trading and investing behaviour of the innovating multinational company, a simple variant such as that of the global scanner will not take us very far. Global scanning is not costless, even when a network of foreign subsidiaries is already in place; costs of collecting and interpreting the information, as the firm perceives those costs, may not be commensurate with its expected benefits. In assessing the benefits, flexibility may be a problem: either the flexibility that firms have lost from decisions in the past, or the flexibility they are fearful of losing in an uncertain future.

So the day of the global scanner as I defined it a few pages back is not yet here. Nevertheless, even if the global scanner is not yet the dominant model, nor perhaps ever will be, the power of the product cycle hypothesis is certainly weakened.

THE PRODUCT CYCLE RECONSIDERED

The evidence is fairly persuasive that the product cycle hypothesis had strong predictive power in the first two or three decades after World War II, especially in explaining the composition of US trade and in projecting the likely patterns of foreign direct investment by US firms. But certain conditions of that period are gone. For one thing, the leading MNCs have now developed global networks of subsidiaries; for another, the US market is no longer unique among national markets either in size or factor cost configuration. It seems plausible to assume that the product cycle will be less useful in explaining the relationship of the US economy to other advanced industrialized countries, and will lose some of its power in explaining the relationship of advanced industrialized countries to developing countries. But strong traces of the sequence are likely to remain.[22]

One such trace is likely to be provided by the innovating activities of smaller firms, firms that have not yet acquired a capacity for global scanning through a network of foreign manufacturing subsidiaries already in place. The assumptions of the product cycle hypothesis may still apply to such firms, as they move from home-based innovation to the possibility of exports and ultimately of overseas investment.

Moreover, even firms with a well-developed scanning capability and a willingness to use it may be found behaving according to the expectations of the product cycle hypothesis. As noted earlier, the specifications of new products are usually in such a state of flux that it is infeasible for a time to fix on a least-cost location. Some firms therefore are unlikely to make intensive use of their scanning capability when siting their production facility. To be sure, such innovators cannot expect to retain their innovational lead for very long, in view of the fact that the innovators of many countries now confront such similar home conditions. But a shadow of the hypothesized behaviour may well remain.

Moreover, the product cycle may gain some support as a predictive device from other developments.

One such development is the improved position of European and Japanese firms as innovators. As noted earlier, the innovations of these firms, when compared with those of US firms, have tended to place greater emphasis on material-saving and capital-saving objectives, while placing lesser relative emphasis on labour-saving measures and on new mass consumer wants. The costs of materials and capital have risen rapidly over the past few years, both in relative and absolute terms. Accordingly, it may be that the long-time emphasis of the Europeans and Japanese firms will generate an increasing demand for their innovations. The world's increased use of European and Japanese small-car technology and of Japanese steel technology are cases in point, fitting nicely within the structure of the product cycle hypothesis.

However, the product cycle hypothesis would also predict that the European-Japanese advantage on this front will only be temporary. As US firms confront factor-cost conditions in their home market that are similar to those of Europe and Japan, one would expect a stream of innovations from the Americans similar to those of their overseas competitors; General Motors, for instance, is now seen as a potential threat to European and Japanese car makers for the 1980's.

A less equivocal case for the continued usefulness of the product cycle concept is found in analysing the situation of the less-developed countries. Although income, market size, and factor cost patterns have converged among the more advanced industrialized countries, a wide gap still separates such countries from many developing areas. Accordingly, despite the fact that so many MNCs have created producing networks all over the globe, the subsidiaries of such firms located in the developing countries have yet to acquire all of the products that their parents and affiliates produce in richer and larger markets. Most of the developing countries, therefore, are still in process of absorbing the innovations of other countries introduced earlier, according to patterns that remain reasonably consistent with product cycle expectations.

The performance of firms in some developing countries, moreover, follows the expectations of the product cycle in a very different sense. Firms operating in the more rapidly industrializing group—in countries such as Mexico, Brazil, India, and Korea—are demonstrating a considerable capability for producing innovations that respond to the special conditions of their own economies.[23] Once having responded to those special conditions with a new product or process or with a significant adaptation of an existing product or process, firms of that sort are in a position to initiate their own cycle of exportation and eventual direct investment; their target, according to the hypothesis, would be the markets of the other developing countries that were lagging a bit behind them in the industrialized pecking order.

Indications that some such process was going on in a limited way in the developing countries were already being reported in the 1960's in occasional illustrations and anecdotal materials; but those early cases for the most part involved the subsidiaries of multinational enterprises, which were making modest adaptations of products and processes originally received from the foreign parents.[24] Innovations such as these sometimes gave the subsidiaries a basis for exporting more effectively to neighbouring countries that were lower on the development scale.

In the 1970's, however, the anecdotal materials began to involve firms that were headquartered in developing countries.[25] Firms were reported developing products and processes of special importance to other developing countries, to be followed eventually by the creation of producing subsidiaries in those countries.[26] Of course, the direct investments of the firms of developing countries in other developing countries have not all been of the product cycle variety. The foreign subsidiaries of firms headquartered in developing countries often maintain their position through oligopolistic strengths other than a technological lead.[27]

Accordingly, the product cycle concept continues to explain and predict a certain category of foreign direct investments. Although it no longer can be relied on to provide as powerful an explanation of the behaviour of US firms as in decades past, it is likely to continue to provide a guide to the motivations and response of some enterprises in all countries of the world.

NOTES

1. For instance, M. V. Posner, 'International Trade and Technical Change', *Oxford Economic Papers*, October 1961, pp. 323–341; Gary Hufbauer, *Synthetic Materials and the Theory of International Trade* (Cambridge: Harvard University Press, 1966); Seev Hirsch, 'The Product Cycle Model of International Trade—A Multi-Country Cross Section Analysis', *Oxford Bulletin of Economics and Statistics*, November 1975, vol. 37, no. 4, pp. 305–317; W. B. Walker, 'Industrial Innovation and International Trading Performance', mimeo. Science Policy Research Unit, Sussex University, October 30, 1975; and M. P. Claudon, *International Trade and Technology: Models of Dynamic Comparative Advantages* (Washington, D.C.: University Press of America, 1977).
2. S. H. Hymer, *The International Operations of National Firms* (Cambridge: MIT Press, 1976) based on the author's 1960 Ph.D. thesis; Raymond Vernon, 'International Investment and International Trade in the Product Cycle', *Quarterly Journal of Economics*, May

1966, pp. 190–207; W. H. Gruber and others, 'The *R&D* Factor in International Investment of US Industries', *Journal of Political Economy*, February 1967, pp. 20–37; Thomas Horst, 'The Firm and Industry Determinants of the Decision to Invest Abroad: An Empirical Study', *Review of Economics and Statistics*, vol. 54, August 1972, pp. 258–66; S. P. Magee, 'Multinational Corporations, The Industry Technology Cycle and Development', *Journal of World Trade Law*, vol. 11, no. 4, July–August 1977, pp. 297–321; P. J. Buckley and Mark Casson, *The Future of the Multinational Enterprise* (New York: Holmes and Meier, 1976); Paul Krugman, 'A Model of Innovation, Technology Transfer, and The World Distribution of Income', *Journal of Political Economy*, April 1979, pp. 253–266.

3. That is a central proposition of the S. H. Hymer work, cited earlier. See also my 'The Location of Economic Activity', in J. H. Dunning, *Economic Analysis and the Multinational Enterprise* (London: George Allen and Unwin, 1970), pp. 83–114.

4. Various empirical studies demonstrate that innovations which do not arise out of a market stimulus—innovations, for instance, that are dreamed up by the laboratory as a clever application of some new scientific capability—have a relatively low chance of industrial success. See for instance Sumner Myers and Donald Marquis, *Successful Industrial Innovations*, National Science Foundation Report No. 69–17, G.P.O., Washington, 1969, p. 31.

5. For econometric evidence of the tie between the choice of a production location, skills and innovation, see Sanjaya Lall, 'Monopolistic Advantages and Foreign Involvement by U.S. Manufacturing Industry', *Oxford Economic Papers*, forthcoming, March 1980.

6. For evidence of such clustering, see D. B. Creamer, *Overseas Research and Development by United States Multinationals, 1966–1975* (New York: The Conference Board, 1976); Robert Ronstadt, *Research and Development Abroad by U.S. Multinationals* (New York: Praeger Publishers, 1977); and Vernon, *Storm Over the Multinationals*, pp. 43–45.

7. See especially T. J. Allen, *Managing the Flow of Technology* (Cambridge: MIT Press, 1978). An important exception is pharmaceuticals, a case in which US regulation has driven the innovation process abroad. See e.g. H. G. Grabowski and J. M. Vernon, 'Innovation and Invention: Consumer Protection Regulation in Ethical Drugs', *American Economic Review*, vol. 67, no. 1, 1977, pp. 359–364.

8. For evidence, see W. H. Davidson, 'Patterns of Factor-Saving Innovation in the Industrialized World', *European Economic Review*, No. 8, 1976, pp. 207–217.

9. See Buckley and Casson, pp. 36–45, 68–69. Their observations are strengthened by data presented in Raymond Vernon and W. H. Davidson, 'Foreign Production of Technology-Intensive Products by U.S.–Based Multinational Enterprises', Working Paper 79–5, Harvard Business School, 1979, xeroxed, p. 66. These data show that in establishing a source of foreign production for 221 innovations, 32 large US-based multinational enterprises elected the subsidiary route far more frequently than licensing, but the degree of preference declined as the innovation aged. For similar conclusions relating to petrochemicals, see R. B. Stobaugh, 'The Product Life Cycle, U.S. Exports, and International Investment', unpublished D.B.A. thesis, Harvard Business School, 1968.

10. The data on which the next few paragraphs are based are presented in detail in Raymond Vernon and W. H. Davidson, 'Foreign Production of Technology-Intensive Products by U.S.-Based Multinational Enterprises', cited earlier.

11. Some measures employed in the Vernon-Davidson study—counts based on 954 individual products rather than on subsidiaries or product lines—show Latin America also increasing its relative share. See Table 17, p. 52 of the report.

12. Vernon and Davidson, pp. 19–20.

13. Although the data for testing the assumption are not at hand, I have assumed that parallel changes are occurring in European and Japanese firms.

14. See A. J. Harman, 'Innovations, Technology, and the Pure Theory of International Trade', unpublished Ph.D. thesis, MIT, September 1968, pp. 131–134; J. M. Callahan, 'GM Adopting Worldwide Purchasing Coordination', *Chilton's Automotive Industries*, July 1978, pp. 47–49; 'Ford's Fiesta Makes a Big Splash', *Business Week*, August 22, 1977, pp. 38–39; and 'SKF Reintegrates Internationally', *Multinational Business*, The Economist Intelligence Unit, No. 4, 1976, pp. 1–7.

15. Compare the observations of Sanjaya Lall, 'The International Allocation of Research Activity by U.S. Multinationals', in this issue.

16. This point is being developed in detail by Yves Doz at the Harvard Business School.

17. For evidence on Japanese firms in this category, see Terutomo Ozawa, *Japan's Technological Challenge to the West, 1950–1974* (Cambridge: MIT Press, 1974), pp. 97–98.

18. This proposition is of course consistent with the theory of strategic groups; see R. E. Caves and M. E. Porter, 'From Entry Barriers to Mobility Barriers: Conjectural Decisions and Contrived Deterrence to New Competition', *Quarterly Journal of Economics*, vol. XCI, no. 2, 1977, pp. 241–261. It is consistent also with the long established observation that different geographical locations offer different combinations of benefits and costs such that widely separated locations applying different production techniques may be competitive for sustained periods. See Max Hall, *Made in New York* (Cambridge: Harvard University Press, 1959).

19. For illustrations, see 'IBM World Trade Corporation' and 'YKK (Yoshida Kogyo KK)', both in Stanley M. Davis, *Managing and Organizing Multinational Corporations* (New York: Pergamon Press, 1979). Also, from Intercollegiate Case Clearing House, see *Corning Glass Works (A), (B), and (C)* (numbers 9–477–024, 9–477–073, and 9–477–074); *International Calculators (Australia) Pty. Limited* (9–572–641); *Veedol France* (ICH 10 M 31); *The International Harvester Company (B)* (9–512–009); *Princess Housewares Gmb H (A)* (ICH 13 M 117); *General Foods Corporation—International Division (D2)* (ICH 13 G 214); *AB Thorsten (A)* (9–414–035); and *Sanpix Industries* (9–278–673).

20. For indications of the formidable difficulties associated with developing such an organizational capability, see Allen, *Managing the Flow of Technology, op.cit.*

21. This, of course, is a familiar phenomenon, long observed by business historians and organizational behaviourists. More recently the concept has been elevated to the status of theory in Harvey Leibenstein's formulation of his X-inefficiency concept; see his *Beyond Economic Man: A New Foundation for Microeconomics* (Cambridge: Harvard University Press, 1976).

22. But see I. H. Giddy, 'The Demise of the Product Cycle Model in International Business Theory', *Columbia Journal of World Business*, vol. xiii, no. 1, Spring 1978, pp. 90–97.

23. See, for example, Julio Fidel, et al., 'The Argentine Cigarette Industry: Technological Profile and Behavior', IDB/ECLA Research Programme in Science and Technology, Buenos Aires, September 1978, pp. 92–94; C. J. Dahlman, 'From Technological Dependence to Technological Development: The Case of the USIMINAS Steel Plant in Brazil', IDB/ECLA Research Programme in Science and Technology, Buenos Aires, October 1978; and Jorge Katz *et al.*, 'Productivity, Technology and Domestic Efforts in Research and Development', IDB/ECLA Research Programme in Science and Technology, Buenos Aires, July 1978. For evidence of the increasing capacity of some developing countries to sell plants and engineering services, see Sanjaya Lall, 'Developing Countries as Exporters of Industrial Technology', *Research Policy*, forthcoming, vol. 9, no. 1, January 1980.

24. W. A. Yeoman, 'Selection of Production Processes for the Manufacturing Subsidiaries of U.S.-Based Multinational Corporations', D.B.A. thesis, Harvard University, April 1968, chap. 5; Jorge Katz and Eduardo Ablin, 'Technology and Industrial Exports: A Micro-Economic Analysis of Argentina's Recent Experience,' IDB/ECLA Research Programme in Science and Technology, Buenos Aires, August 1978; and by the same authors, 'From Infant Industry to Technology Exports: The Argentine Experience in the International Sale of Industrial Plants and Engineering Works', IDB/ECLA Research programme in Science and Technology, Buenos Aires, October 1978.

25. See for instance L. T. Wells, Jr., 'The Internationalization of Firms from Developing Countries', in Tamir Agmon and C. P. Kindleberger, *Multinationals from Small Countries* (Cambridge: MIT Press, 1977), pp. 133–166; by the same author, 'Foreign Investment from the Third World: The Experience of Chinese Firms from Hong Kong', *Columbia Journal of World Business*, Spring 1978, pp. 39–49; and A. J. Prasad, 'Export of Technology from India', unpublished Ph.D. thesis, Columbia University, 1978, pp. 123–156.

26. Extensive data on this tendency are being developed by L. T. Wells, Jr., for eventual publication.

27. Such firms also have been known, for instance, to develop special skills in the maintenance and repair of second hand machinery, and a supply of scarce spare parts for such machinery. See Wells, 'Hong Kong', and Prasad, 'India', p. 147.

26. Sovereignty At Bay, Ten Years After

RAYMOND VERNON

The author of *Sovereignty at Bay*, musing in public about his opus after ten long years, faces one very special difficulty. Practically every reader remembers the title of the book; but scarcely anyone will accurately recall its contents. For after its publication, like Aspirin and Frigidaire, the label (but not the contents) became generic. Robert Gilpin identified a "Sovereignty at Bay model," subscribed to by visionaries devoted to the proposition that the nation-state was done for, finished off by the multinational enterprise.[1] Seymour J. Rubin lustily attacked the visionaries; Lincoln Gordon ably provided supporting fire; C. Fred Bergsten was only a step behind. Even Walter B. Wriston turned briefly from his labors at building one of the world's biggest banks to cast a few stones in the same general direction.

Meanwhile, the themes of *Sovereignty at Bay*, if they were ever learned, were half-forgotten in the heady pursuit of more vulnerable quarry. Only the author and a few of his more attentive students would remember the argument of his final chapter, which concluded somewhat lugubriously:

> The basic asymmetry between multinational enterprises and national governments [that is, the capacity of the enterprises to shift some of their activities from one location to another, as compared with the commitment of the government to a fixed piece of national turf] may be tolerable up to a point, but beyond that point there is a need to reestablish balance. . . . If this does not happen, some of the apocalyptic projections of the future of multinational enterprise will grow more plausible.

ROOTS OF THE MULTINATIONALS

Because *Sovereignty at Bay* was one of the earlier works in a stream that would soon become a torrent, much of the book was devoted to

Raymond Vernon is Clarence Dillan Professor Emeritus of Harvard University. He is presently associated with the Kennedy School of Government.

chronicling and describing the phenomenal growth and spread of multinational enterprises. Interwoven in the history and the description, however, were inevitably some hypotheses about causes. Some of these, although still bearing a touch of novelty in 1971, seem hackneyed today—suggestive, I suppose, of their validity and durability. The increased efficiencies of communication and transportation, which had been reducing the costs of learning and the costs of control, were given appropriate credit as expeditors of the multinationalizing process. Oligopoly was recognized as a near-necessary condition for breeding multinational enterprises, a conclusion that simply reaffirmed a point made ten years earlier by Stephen Hymer.[2]

Two kinds of oligopoly that seemed particularly relevant in explaining the spectacular growth of U.S.-based multinational enterprises in the postwar period were explored with special attention. (The subtitle of the book, after all, was "The Multinational Spread of *U.S.* Enterprise"). One was the oligopoly based upon the special technological capabilities of the participating firms, while the other was the oligopoly based on the sheer size and geographical spread of the operating firms concerned, as in the oil and metals industries. In that context, a number of hypotheses were elaborated, which later would be tested and retested in various contexts. The most widely known of these, particularly applicable to the technology-based oligopolies, came to be called the product-cycle hypothesis. I shall have more to say about that concept in a moment. But there were other propositions, which also were exposed to considerable testing in subsequent years, such as the follow-the-leader hypothesis.

These various concepts purporting to explain the growth and spread of multinational enterprises have stood up about as well as one could have hoped. The follow-the-leader hypothesis has been adequately confirmed in one or two solid studies.[3] As for the product-cycle hypothesis, there have been numerous confirming and elaborating studies,[4] as well as a few important qualifications, reservations, and demurrers.[5] On the whole, the concept seems to have had considerable utility in explaining past developments and predicting future ones.

However, what has changed—indeed, changed quite dramatically—is the applicability of the product-cycle hypothesis in explaining the present behavior and the likely future behavior of multinational enterprises based in the United States. As an explicator and predictor of U.S. performance, the product-cycle hypothesis had particular applicability to the conditions of, say, 1900 to 1970; this was a period in which the income levels of U.S. residents were higher than those in any other major market in the world, in which U.S. hourly labor costs were the highest in the world, and in which U.S. capital and raw materials were comparatively cheap. That set of unique conditions, it was posited, had been generating a stream of innovations on the part of U.S. firms responsive to their special environment. And as the income levels and relative labor costs in other countries tracked over the terrain previously traversed by the U.S. economy, U.S. innovations found a ready market in those other countries. These innovations were thought to provide an oligopolistic handhold that gave U.S. firms their dominant position in many markets of other countries.

But even as I went to press with *Sovereignty at Bay*, there were a few signs that the pattern might be losing its explanatory force for the United States. A section captioned "Toward Another Model" presented speculations about the consequences that might ensue as U.S. incomes and labor costs became more closely aligned with those of Europe and Japan. In that case, U.S.-based enterprises would no longer have the advantage of doing business in home markets under conditions that were precursors of those which eventually would appear in Europe and Japan. Accordingly, the innovational lead that the Americans had enjoyed in earlier decades could be expected to shrink.

I cannot say, however, that I had the prescience to realize how rapidly the factor cost configurations of the various national markets would be brought into alignment, speeded by the rise in raw material prices, by the increasing nominal cost of capital, and by the weakness of the U.S. dollar. In my speculation about the growth of European and Japanese investment in the United States, therefore, the tone was hypothetical; there was no sense of conviction that the trend would soon develop. Intellectually, readers were put on notice; glandularly, they were not forewarned.

It was only in the latter 1970s that the convergence in the factor costs of the principal exporting countries had developed sufficiently to prompt me to reappraise the relevance of the product-cyle concept as an explicator of U.S. behavior.[6] As a result of that reappraisal, I concluded that the product-cycle concept continued to have some utility, explaining some of the trade and investment patterns visible in various countries of the world; but its utility in explaining the behavior of the U.S. economy had measurably declined.

EFFECTS OF THE MULTINATIONALS

When *Sovereignty at Bay* was published in 1971, the advocates and the opponents of multinational enterprises were already locked in furious combat. Several dozen propositions about the consequences of the operations of these enterprises had been advanced by both sides. One of the objectives of *Sovereignty at Bay* was to test the leading propositions of the opponents with such data as could be mustered for the purpose.

The issues involved were too numerous and too diverse to be effectively reviewed here. At the time when *Sovereignty at Bay* was published, however, it seemed clear that both sides were grossly overreaching in their arguments; some cases were consistent with their sweeping hypotheses, some were not. Even more often, the asserted effects of the operations of these enterprises, whether benign or destructive, could not be supported by the evidence. The classic Scotch verdict—not proven—seemed more justified than any.[7]

By 1977, however, numerous researchers all over the globe had published a great many additional studies of the multinational enterprise. Some of these studies cast new light on the issues that had been dealt with tentatively in *Sovereignty at Bay*: typical of such issues, for instance, were those relating to the technological transfer activities of the multinationals. The piling up of such evidence moved me to publish a second book on multinational enterprises, which appeared under the title of *Storm over the Multinationals*.

The added evidence reviewed in that book went some way to confirm the fact that simpleminded propositions about the effects of multinational enterprises were as a rule highly vulnerable. On the basis of the new work, it was possible to speak with somewhat greater assurance about some of the economic and political effects of multinational enterprises; but those effects were not simple. The caution with which I had approached such questions as the balance-of-payment effects, income-distribution effects, and employment effects of multinational enterprises in *Sovereignty at Bay* seemed justified by the conclusions of *Storm over the Multinationals*. Generalizations on some points are possible; but they must be framed with due regard for the vast differences in the activities of multinational enterprises. Numerous variables determine the economic effects of the operations of individual firms, including for instance, their innovative propensities and their marketing strategies. Both the uninhibited broadsides of writers such as Barnet and Müller and the more restrained generalizations of scholars such as Robert Gilpin suffer from this lack of differentiation.

THREATS TO THE MULTINATIONALS

With the acuity that goes with hindsight, I might better have entitled my 1971 volume *Everyone at Bay*, in the spirit of its closing lines. But there would be some overreaching in such a title; I could hardly claim to have foreseen the spate of expropriations and nationalizations of the foreign properties of the multinational enterprises that occurred during the first half of the 1970s. My chapter on the raw materials industries, in fact, was written in a tone of complacency that must have been insufferable at the time to some of the worried managers of the international oil companies. The mood of that portion of *Sovereignty at Bay* is captured in the final paragraph of the raw materials chapter:

> Strong initiatives on the part of the governments of less developed countries to control the key factors in the exploitation of their raw materials are likely to continue. And as they do, the capacity of host governments to participate in management will increase. It is another question, however, whether the host countries will feel that their 'dependence' on the outside world has declined simply because their management role has increased. As long as the product requires marketing in foreign countries, dependence will presumably continue in some form.

Yet, as one reads the raw materials chapter with the hindsight of 1981, the argument for the increasing vulnerability of the oil companies is all there, carefully laid out under a heading dubbed "The Obsolescing Bargain." The oil-exporting countries, it was pointed out, no longer needed the oil companies as a source of capital; their taxes on the sale of crude oil were already providing a sense of independence on that score. Nor did the oil-exporting countries any longer feel shut away from access to the technology of oil exploration and exploitation; too many independent companies were bidding to provide that information and expertise. In the latter 1960s, the principal remaining source of vulnerability of the oil-exporting countries and the principal source of strength of the international oil companies was the companies' control over the channels of distribution.

What prevented me (and practically every other scholar at the time) from fully applying the lesson of the obsolescing bargain to the situation of the oil companies was our inability to appreciate that a profound shift in the supply-demand balance was taking place, which might reduce the need of the oil-exporting countries to rely on the marketing channels of the multinationals. Most of us took the chronic weakness of oil prices during most of the 1960s to mean that supplies were more than adequate. Accordingly, it was hard to contemplate that demand would soon grow so rapidly that the oil-exporting countries would feel free to cut their umbilical cord to the international oil marketers. Nor do I think that many analysts in the oil industry itself were aware of the dangers of an oil shortage at the time.

To be sure, by the latter 1960s, some thoughtful executives in the industry were deeply worried. Some were expressing alarm over the deterioration in their negotiating position, as Libya and other countries gleefully used the independent oil companies to leapfrog over one another in a continuous escalation of their terms. But so far as I know, nobody in the 1960s foresaw the great bulge in the demand for Middle East oil that would soon undermine the majors' position.

Looking back at the text of *Sovereignty at Bay* after ten years, I am frustrated by the fact that the analysis comes so close, while not quite drawing the key conclusion. The weakening of the international oil oligopoly during the 1960s is accurately enough portrayed; the appearance of the state-owned oil companies and the emergence of OPEC are appropriately chronicled. But it was not until a year or two later that I fully appreciated the key role played by the independent oil companies in weakening the position of the majors and in strengthening the negotiating hand of the oil-exporting countries. And it was a few years after that before it became evident that the period of weakening prices in the 1960s had been masking a shift in the supply-demand balance.[8]

No two persons will draw quite the same lessons from the experiences of the oil market during the 1960s and 1970s. The lessons that I draw, I suspect, will not be widely shared.

One of these is that any five-year projection of the supply-demand balance for world oil is inherently subject to gross margins of error, margins so large as to encompass both the possibilities of painful shortage and the possibilities of disconcerting glut. The importers of oil, of course, are justified in acting as if they expected an acute shortage, simply because the consequences of a shortage are so much more painful than those of a glut; prudence, therefore, demands that we act as if a shortage were inevitable. But whenever I review the various projections of supply and demand in the world oil market that are being circulated today, I am persuaded that today's projections are just as vulnerable as those of fifteen years ago.

A second conclusion, based as much on other raw materials as on oil, is that the concept of the obsolescing bargain does have a certain utility in analyzing the changing position of the multinational enterprises engaged in any given product line. Accordingly, wherever the conventional wisdom of any market turns from an expectation of shortage to an expectation of glut, I anticipate in accordance with the obsolescing bargain concept that the position of the multinationals will be somewhat strengthened.

And a third conclusion is that, for phenomena as complex as the role of multinational enterprises, scholars may be as vulnerable as laymen in speculating about the shape of future events. If scholars do their work well, their predictive models may be better crafted than those of the layman—more fully articulated, internally more consistent, more firmly based on earlier events. But scholars, perhaps more than laymen, must live with the risk of neglecting or overlooking what may prove to be the controlling factor that determines those future events.

The Problem of Multiple Jurisdiction

As the title *Sovereignty at Bay* suggests, the book was much more concerned with the interests and attitudes of governments than with the aspirations and fears of the multinational enterprises themselves. Insofar as the title was justified, the justification rested on the validity of three propositions: that most governments, reluctant to give up the advantages they perceive in inviting multinational enterprises into their jurisdictions, will continue to permit a significant part of their national output to be accounted for by the affiliates of such enterprises; that the policies of any affiliate of a multinational enterprise are bound to reflect in some degree the global interests of the multinational network as a whole, and hence can never respond singlemindedly to the requirements of any one national jurisdiction; and that the network of any multinational enterprise cannot escape serving as a conduit through which sovereign states exert an influence on the economies of other sovereign states.

After ten years, I see no strong reason to modify any of these propositions. During those ten years, some foreign affiliates of multinational enterprises were nationalized, while other foreign affiliates were liquidated or sold on the initiative of their parents. But, all told, these withdrawals were only a minor fraction of the new advances that multinational enterprises were making all over the globe. In 1979 alone, for instance, U.S.-based multinationals increased their foreign investment stake by $25 billion, of which $18 billion was in developed nations and $7 billion in developing countries. Indicative of the resilience of such enterprises to the buffeting they had received only a few years earlier was the fact that nearly $4 billion of the $7 billion build-up in developing countries was in the form of fresh money remitted by the U.S. parent, while the remainder consisted of the reinvestment of past earnings.

To be sure, there have been some changes during these ten years in the identity of the world's multinational enterprises. Those based in Europe and Japan have gained a little in importance relative to those based in the United States. Moreover, the world is beginning to see enterprises of this sort that have their home bases in Spain, Brazil, Mexico, India, Hong Kong, and other such locations.[9] But these changes simply add to the sense of vitality and durability of the multinational structures.

At the same time as there have been some marginal shifts in the identity of the multinational enterprises, there have also been some marginal alterations in their business practices. U.S.-based enterprises as a class have grown somewhat less reluctant to enter into joint ventures with foreign partners than had been the case in earlier decades. Multinational enterprises from all countries have proved increasingly flexible in taking on management contracts, acceding to so-called fade-out clauses, entering into partnerships with state-owned enterprises, and involving themselves in other ambiguous arrangements.

The proliferation of such arrangements raises the question whether the various affiliates of multinational enterprises continue to respond to a common global strategy and to draw on a common pool of resources to the same degree as in the past. The available signs point in many directions. Some observers insist, for instance, that when the subsidiaries of multinational enterprises enter into partnerships with state-owned enterprises, they often manage to increase the degree of their control in the local market rather than to diminish it.[10] The increased prevalence of joint ventures and other ambiguous arrangements suggests that the authority of the parents of the multinational networks over their affiliates is being diluted. But other developments seem to be pushing in the opposite direction. For instance, there has been a constant improvement of software and communication systems for the command and control of distant subsidiaries, a trend that places new tools in the hands of headquarters staffs. In addition, the multinational enterprises in some industries, including automobiles and machinery, have been pushing toward the development of world models for their products, a trend that requires increasing integration among the production units of the multinational enterprises concerned.

I anticipate that, in the end, the generalizations will be exceedingly complex. We may well find, for instance, that in many firms control over the finance and production functions has increased, even though the physical location of these activities has been dispersed. We may find, too, that in the selection of business strategies some multinational enterprises have opted to develop maximum flexibility and adaptation toward local conditions while others in the same general product line have opted for the maximum exploitation of global economies of scale.[11]

Still, I would be surprised if on balance multinational enterprises had greatly reduced the degree of central control over their global operations. For insofar as multinational enterprises have any inherent advantages over national enterprises, those advantages must rest on the multinational character of their operations, that is to say, on their multinational strategies and their common resources. Multinational enterprises, therefore, may have no real option; by giving up their multinational advantages, they may be destroying the basis for their competitive survival.

If multinational enterprises continue to pursue some elements of a global strategy and to draw on a common pool of financial and human resources, then the problems of multiple jurisdiction will continue to play a considerable role in their operations. At times, affiliates of such enterprises will be marching to the tunes of a distant trumpet being played from the ministries of another government or from the offices of another affiliate. Some cases of this sort are well enough known; the occasional forays of the U.S. government's antitrust division in attempting to break up international restrictive business practices that affect the U.S. economy have received particular attention. But these well-publicized cases are on the whole less important than those that are less transparent. Multinational enterprises with an affiliate in Germany, for instance, will have to entertain the demand of German unions for more output and more jobs, expressed through the hard-won rights of *Mitbestimmungsrecht*; responding to such pressures, the parent enterprise may be obliged to reduce the output of its Brazilian subsidiary, thereby exporting Germany's unemployment to Brazil. For multinational enterprises with an affiliate in Mexico, the insistence of the Mexican government that the local affiliates must import less and export more may lower the output of these networks in Barcelona and Detroit. And India's insistence that foreign parents should charge their Indian subsidiaries nothing for their technology could lower the income taxes and export earnings of the parents of those subsidiaries operating from their bases in other countries.

Since 1971, the problems of multiple jurisdiction generated by the existence of multinational enterprises have grown. More than ever before, governments are telling the affiliates of multinational enterprises what they must do or not do as the price for their right to continue in business. As the world's overt trade barriers have diminished, these commands have become a principal weapon of many governments for pursuing a beggar-my-neighbor economic policy. Accordingly, when I published *Storm over the Multinationals* in 1977, I developed the jurisdictional issue in considerably greater depth than in *Sovereignty at Bay*. But the second book was launched under the shadow of the first; whatever the second book had to say, it was commonly assumed, had already been said in *Sovereignty at Bay*.[12] The heightened emphasis on the jurisdictional issue in the second book, however, seems appropriate to current circumstances.

So far, jurisdictional conflicts have been contained by the fact that not all governments are systematically playing the beggar-my-neighbor game, and by the added fact that multinational enterprises have a strong incentive for muffling the effects of the game within their respective networks. My assumption has been, however, that the number of players and the intensity of the game will gradually increase. In that case, if multinationals are to avoid being the instruments through which national jurisdictions are brought into repeated conflict, the sovereign states must be willing to agree on some international regime that can reconcile their interests. Any such agreed regime would presumably do two things: it would specify the rights of multinational enterprises in and their obligations to the international community; and it would delineate and restrain the jurisdictional reach of the governments involved, wherever an important clash in national jurisdictions might be involved.

Since 1971, there have been dozens of projects for achieving international agreement with respect to the multinational enterprises. Most of them have included proposals to restrain the multinational enterprises in various ways; a few have proposed some guarantees for the multinational enterprises as well; but until very recently, most have neglected or avoided the pervasive problem of conflicting jurisdictions.

Indeed, some of the international actions and international proposals that have been launched since 1971 have seemed carefully designed to preserve the contradictions rather than to resolve them. The member countries of the OECD, for instance, have adopted a set of declarations proposing that each government should grant national treatment to foreign-owned subsidiaries in its jurisdiction, thus acknowledging the national character of such subsidiaries; at the same time, these governments have paid obeisance to the applicability of international law in the treatment of foreign-owned subsidiaries, whether or not such treatment conformed with national law, thus acknowledging the foreign element in the subsidiaries' identity. In a similar obfuscating mood, the developing countries, as a rule, have simultaneously insisted upon two propositions: that foreign-owned subsidiaries, being nationals of the host country, were subject to all the obligations of any other national; but that such subsidiaries, as the property of foreigners, could rightly be denied the privileges of other nationals.

I can find only one functional area in which governments have made a serious effort to reduce the conflicts or resolve the ambiguities that go with the operations of multinational enterprises.[13] The industrialized countries have managed to develop a rather extraordinary web of bilateral agreements among themselves that deal with conflicts in the application of national tax laws. Where such laws seemed to be biting twice into the same morsel of profit, governments have agreed on a division of the fare. Why governments have moved to solve the jurisdictional conflict in this field but not in others is an interesting question. Perhaps it was because, in the case of taxation, the multinational enterprises themselves had a major stake in seeing to the consummation of the necessary agreements.

So far, the world has managed to stagger on without effectively addressing the many facets of jurisdictional conflict and without directly acknowledging the inescapable fact that the behavior of any affiliate is unavoidably influenced by external forces. The various sovereigns direct their commands at a unit in the multinational network; the unit responds as it can, giving ground to the sovereign if it must; the other units in the network adjust their operations to the new situation, spreading the adjustment cost through the global system. As long as there is no overt acknowledgment of what is going on all the parties can pretend that the jurisdiction of each sovereign is unimpaired.

THE FUTURE OF THE MULTINATIONALS

Lincoln Gordon would agree, I think, that his one-time proposal for a tract entitled "Multinationals at Bay" would not arouse much interest today. The tumult of the 1970s over the multinational issue has lost some of its stridence. The incidence of nationalizations in developing countries has declined dramatically. Kolko, Williams, Barnet, and Müller seem somehow out of date, while the various scholars of *dependista* theory seem a bit jaded. The U.N. Centre on Transnational Corporations has developed a businesslike air, more akin to the professionalism of the Securities and Exchange Commission than to the prosecuting fervor of the Church Committee.

In retrospect, it appears that the numerous threats to the multinationals that were launched in the 1970s—the spate of nationalizations, the codes of conduct, the U.S. legislation against bribery, the demands and resolutions of the General Assembly—were fueled by a number of different elements. One of these was a manifestation of a much larger phenomenon, namely a pervasive revulsion in much of the world against the effects of industrialization, against the symbols of entrenched authority, and against the impersonal tyranny of big bureaucracies. Embodying all of these unfortunate attributes and burdened besides by the sin of being foreign, multinationals were inevitably a prime target of the period. A second factor that explained the attack on the multinationals, however, was the inexorable operation of the obsolescing bargain; as shortages appeared in various raw materials, multinationals lost the bargaining power that their marketing capabilities normally afforded.

The revulsion against bigness and bureaucracy that exploded in the late 1960s and early 1970s may have been ephemeral; but the process of the obsolescing bargain is not. From time to time, in the future as in the past, one foreign-owned industry or another will lose its defensive capabilities; and when that happens, some of those enterprises will be nationalized, joining the plantations, the power plants, and the oil wells that have been taken over by governments in years past.

But the future is no simple extrapolation of the past. Some forces seem to be speeding up the process by which the bargain between governments and foreign investors becomes obsolescent. At the same time, other forces seem to be diffusing and defusing the underlying hostility that gives the process of the obsolescing bargain some of its motive force.

The expectation that agreements between governments and investors will be breached even more quickly in the future than in the past is based on various factors. In reappraising their bargaining positions, governments are better informed and better equipped than they have ever been. Perhaps more to the point, opposition forces that are bent on embarrassing their governments have more information and more expertise. Besides, according to evidence presented in *Storm over the Multinationals*, governments are finding that in many lines of industry they have an increasing number of options for securing the capital, technology, or access to markets they require. Accordingly, although multinational enterprises taken as a class continue to account for a considerable share—even an increasing share—of the economies of most countries, individual multinationals have nothing like the bargaining position they sometimes held in the past.

Yet governments seem constrained to use their increased bargaining power in more ambiguous ways. Instead of outright nationalization, they seem disposed to settle for other arrangements, such as arrangements that make a gift of some of the equity to favored members of the local private sector or to an expanding state-owned enterprise, or contracts that allow the multinationals to manage their properties without formal ownership. Perhaps the increase in ambiguous arrangements is due to the decline in the power of the individual multinational enterprises; being less threatening, they are less to be feared. Perhaps, too, the ambiguity is due to the increasing power of the private industrialists in some countries who prefer to squeeze the foreign goose rather than to strangle it;[14] or to the unceasing struggle of the managers of some state-owned enterprises to weaken the control of their national ministries.[15] It may even be that the hostility of some countries to the multinational enterprises of others is being blunted by the growth of their own homegrown brand of multinationals.

Whatever the precise causes may be, I anticipate that business organizations with the attributes of multinational enterprises will not decline and may well grow in their relative importance in the world economy. Anticipating that development, I am brought back to what I regard as the central question. How do the sovereign states propose to deal with the fact that so many of their enterprises are conduits through which other sovereigns exert their influence?

Perhaps they will not deal with the problem at all. There is plenty of evidence for the proposition that nations are capable of tolerating ambiguity on a massive scale for long periods of time. And there are numerous cases in which scholars, peering into the future, have mistaken bogey men for monsters. But I am betting that the problem is real and its emergence as a political issue close at hand. In any event, it is this problem that invests the title *Sovereignty at Bay* with its real meaning.

NOTES

1. Robert Gilpin, *U.S. Power and the Multinational Corporation* (New York: Basic Books, 1975), p. 220. Be it said to Gilpin's credit that although he ascribes the phrase to me, he does not list me as one who subscribes to the model. Others, however, have been less careful in their attributions.

2. S. H. Hymer, *The International Operations of National Firms: A Study of Direct Foreign Investment* (Cambridge: M.I.T. Press, 1976), based on his 1960 thesis.

3. See F. T. Knickerbocker, *Oligopolistic Reaction and Multinational Enterprise* (Boston: Harvard Business School, 1973). His subsequent work on the hypothesis, unfortunately never fully published, went even further in confirming its utility.

4. The number of such studies by now is very large. Illustrations are: L. T. Wells Jr., ed., *The Product Life Cycle and International Trade* (Boston: Harvard Business School, 1972); J. M. Finger, "A New View of the Product Cycle Theory," *Weltwirtschaftliches Archiv* 3, 1, 1975; M. P. Claudon, *International Trade and Technology: Models of Dynamic Comparative Advantage* (Washington, D.C.: University Press of America, 1977); Seev Hirsch, "The Product Cycle Model of International Trade," *Oxford Bulletin of Economics and Statistics* 37, 4 (November 1975), pp. 305–17; Hiroki and Yoshi Tsumuri, "A Bayesian Test of the Product Life Cycle Hypothesis as Applied to the U.S. Demand for Color-TV Sets," *International Economic Review*, October 1980, pp. 581–95.

5. For instance: W. B. Walker, *Industrial Innovation and International Trading Performance* (Brighton, England: Sussex University, 1976); and Kiyoshi Kojima, "A Macroeconomic Theory of Foreign Direct Investment," *Hitotsubashi Journal of Economics* 14, 1 (June 1973).

6. Raymond Vernon, "The Product Cycle Hypothesis in a New International Environment," *Oxford Bulletin of Economics and Statistics* 41, 4 (November 1979), pp. 255–67; and Raymond Vernon, "Gone are the Cash Cows of Yesteryear," *Harvard Business Review*, November 1980, pp. 150–55.

7. For a review of many of these issues and a well-balanced critical appraisal of my views, see T. J. Bierstecker, *Distortion or Development? Contending Perspectives on the Multinational Corporation* (Cambridge: M.I.T. Press, 1979).

8. Those points are developed at some length in two later publications. See Edith Penrose, "The Development of Crisis" in Raymond Vernon, ed., *The Oil Crisis* (New York: W. W. Norton, 1976), pp. 39–57; and Raymond Vernon, *Storm over the Multinationals* (Cambridge: Harvard University Press, 1977), pp. 83–87.

9. A book on this subject will shortly appear under the authorship of Louis T. Wells, Jr.

10. This is a subject that is just beginning to be researched. For an analysis covering Brazil, see Peter Evans, *Dependent Development: The Alliance of Multinational, State, and Local Capital in Brazil* (Princeton: Princeton University Press, 1979).

11. Patterns of this sort are being researched by Yves Doz at INSEAD, Fontainebleau.

12. See for instance, C. P. Kindleberger's review of *Storm Over the Multinationals* in *Business History Review* 51, 4 (Winter 1977), pp. 95–97.

13. Nevertheless, there are glimmerings of some additional action eventually on the subject. Reference to the problem appears in a composite working draft of a code of conduct for multinational enterprises, prepared for consideration of an intergovernmental working group under the sponsorship of the U.N. Centre on Transnational Corporations; see Working Paper no. 7, November 1979, paragraph 56. But the prospects for action are not very great.

14. See for instance Evans, *Dependent Development.*

15. Yair Aharoni, "Managerial Discretion," in Aharoni and Vernon, eds. *State-Owned Enterprises in the Western Economies* (London: Croom Helm, 1980).

27. The Appropriability Theory of the Multinational Corporation

STEPHEN P. MAGEE*

ABSTRACT

The appropriability theory of the multinational corporation emphasizes the conflict between innovators and emulators of new technologies. Appropriability is "high," and innovators can protect their profits more easily for sophisticated technologies and on breakthroughs that can be transmitted worldwide through the innovator's own subsidiaries. Conversely, appropriability is "low," and multinationals find it less profitable to create simple technologies and ideas that require market transfer. This theory explains the limited role multinationals have played in the development of simple products and simple production technologies, both of which are important to the developing countries. The appropriability theory also predicts that products in Vernon's product cycle will move to stage II when developed countries start successful emulation of the product and to stage III when developing countries start successful emulation. The profit-maximizing price strategy an innovating multinational should follow is to sell new products at below the monopoly price and slowly cut the price of the product as appropriability mechanisms erode. In the long run, the multinational will be forced to sell at the perfectly competitive price. If the multinational has no long-run profit advantage over other producers, its long-run market shares should approach zero as the perfectly competitive price is approached.

It is said that Thomas Edison spent more on legal fees to protect his light bulb than he received in fees and royalties from that invention. A similar problem faces innovating multinational corporations. The pro-

* The author is indebted to the National Science Foundation, the University of Texas, and the University of Reading for financial support.

Stephen P. Magee is the Margaret and Eugene McDermott Professor and chairman of the Department of Finance at the University of Texas, Austin.

cess of protecting the returns from innovations has been explored in an appropriability theory of multinational corporation (MNC) behavior.[1]

The appropriability theory suggests that the most important consideration facing innovating multinationals is the possible loss of the technology to rivals and copiers. New ideas are public goods, which means that anyone who can figure out how to use them may do so without reducing the use by others. But unauthorized use of new ideas certainly reduces the profitability for innovators. The more difficult it is to protect the profitability of an innovation, the greater the appropriability problem. When applied to the multinational corporation, the appropriability theory suggests that it is more efficient to transfer high technology worldwide inside firms than through the market because there is less likelihood of it being copied and stolen by outsiders if it is under the control of a single firm. An innovating firm will invest resources to keep others from copying and stealing the idea. The appropriability theory suggests that mechanisms evolve to prevent the loss of high technology and that these form a central theme that can explain much multinational corporation behavior.

It will explain, for example, why MNCs create very sophisticated technologies rather than simple ones. Sophisticated ideas are hard to copy, while simple ideas are easy to copy. Therefore the appropriability problem is particularly severe for simple ideas. One implication of this hypothesis is that multinational corporations cannot be counted on to create the types of technology that are most useful for the developing countries. The developing countries need two types of technologies: simple production processes and simple products. However, the ability of private firms to capture the returns on these types of ideas is difficult.

The appropriability model generates results that both contrast with and help explain the Vernon product cycle.[2] In contrast, the appropriability model suggests that industry age—and not Vernon's product age—is the key to understanding international technology flows. This idea has been explored in the industry technology cycle.[3] Appropriability considerations complement Vernon's theory in explaining the length of each stage of his cycle. So long as the innovating firms in an industry maintain their technological lead over emulating firms, the industry will remain young and produce new products. When appropriability mechanisms break down (for example, when industry structure becomes less concentrated), emulators in the United States and abroad reduce the profitability of innovations so that the industry's product line shifts to older, more standardized products.

What price strategy will an innovating multinational pursue in the face of eroding appropriability?[4] Even if the multinational is the only producer early in a product's life, it should sell below the monopoly price—since the monopoly price encourages emulator production, which reduces the present value of future profits by more than is recouped in today's profits—and slowly cut the price as appropriability erodes until it hits the perfectly competitive price. The multinational's product market share hits zero just as the product becomes completely standardized. If the market share is still positive with standardization, the multinational has pursued too low a price strategy—that is, discouraged emulators more than was in its own profit interests.

This article reviews in some detail the three studies summarized. The first major section summarizes the appropriability theory and the industry technology cycle, while the second major section explores the profit-maximizing price strategy that multinationals will follow and how they will behave in the face of certain widely discussed (North-South type) policy changes.

ROLE OF APPROPRIABILITY IN THE CREATION AND DIFFUSION OF TECHNOLOGY

Consider the creation of technology by private firms. Technology is a durable good in that present resources must be devoted to its creation and its existence results in a stream of future benefits. Technology is also a public good in that once it is created, its use by second parties does not preclude its continued use by the party who discovers it. However, use by second parties does reduce the private return on information created by the first party. This last feature has been labeled the "appropriability problem."[5]

The appropriability theory of multinational corporate behavior is a natural outgrowth of the industrial organization approach to international direct investment developed by Hymer, Vernon, and Caves, as well as the views of Arrow, Demsetz, and Johnson on the creation and appropriability of the returns from private market investments in information.[6] The appropriability theory suggests that MNCs are specialists in the production of technology that is less efficient to transmit through markets than within firms; that MNCs produce sophisticated technologies because private returns are higher for these technologies than for simple ones; that the large proportion of skilled labor employed by the multinationals is an outgrowth of the skilled-labor-intensity of the production process for both the creation and the appropriability of the returns from technology; and that the relative abundance of skilled labor in the developed countries dictates that they have a comparative advantage in creating, exporting, and capturing private returns on new technologies.

The theory also suggests that the structure of industry and the creation of technology are jointly determined variables. The presence of a monopoly or oligopoly, *ceteris paribus*, encourages *R&D* and other investments in innovation because appropriability costs are lower for these industry structures. In turn, a major innovation encourages an increase in optimum firm size, so that industry structure becomes more concentrated. Thus, there is two-way causation between new technology and industry structure.

In the process of creating and carrying each product through its life cycle, multinationals must generate four distinct types of information—that is, new technology: product creation, product development, creation of the production processes, and creation of the markets. These four types of technology investments are described in the following paragraphs. Then the causes and consequences of appropriability are described. The welfare question of whether private markets or government agencies should produce new technology is examined briefly next, followed by a description of an industry technology cycle, paralleling Vernon's product cycle, which emerges from the appropriability theory.

Four Types of Technology Created by Multinationals

Each product goes through a life cycle with a lot of new information created in the early stages and less created as the product matures. Investments in information must be made for the discovery of new products, for their development, for the creation of their production functions, and for the creation of their markets.

First, investments are required to discover new products. While an increasing proportion of total *R&D* is done within large corporate organizations, many new ideas are still developed by small independent inventors. It is my impression that invention is not the focus of MNC activity: their *R&D* efforts are focused on innovation, which encompasses the next three types of information.

The second activity requiring large expenditures on scientists and engineers is in product development—that is, applied research, product specification, and prototypes. Mansfield finds that product development frequently requires five to ten years for major products.[7] These undertakings are the activities engaged in by multinational corporations at the beginning of each product's life cycle. MNCs develop a comparative advantage in moving products through Vernon's product cycle. MNCs are large because it is more efficient to transfer information on development from product to product within the firm rather than through the market. This explains the tendency of multinational corporations to carry more product lines than national firms.[8] Information on avoiding mistakes is usually more costly to transmit through the market than intrafirm.

The third piece of information required in the product cycle is the creation of the production processes. Economists have traditionally assumed the existence of "production functions"—provided by engineers. However, there is a growing awareness that the creation of the production processes is determined like other processes: by the supply and demand for production technology. Also, factor price structures differ between the developed countries (DCs) and the less-developed countries (LDCs).

Production occurs in LDCs so late in the product life cycle that discounting gives the importance of cheap unskilled LDC labor a small weight to the multinational. Another point is that industry structures become more competitive through the cycle as patents lapse, so that the production process becomes "frozen" or standardized at a more capital-intensive level than may be desirable for LDC production. The reason for the "freeze" is that increased industry competition erodes the private market appropriability of the private returns from developing unskilled-labor-intensive production techniques more fully. Still another reason for failure of MNCs to shift from capital-intensive to unskilled-labor-intensive production in the LDCs is quality control. For example, one firm that shifted from mechanized to hand-labor food canning in an LDC quickly regretted the decision after numerous cases of food poisoning developed.

Fourth, investments in information must be undertaken to create product markets. One interpretation of the multinational corporation is that they act like large retail stores in selling new technologies and new information.[9] Let us develop a framework for this theme. Information is closer to an "experience" good rather than a "search" good.[10] This distinction in the advertising literature explains why large retail stores have become important in prescreening for consumers. For example, if a person wishes to buy a very high-quality consumer product, he is more likely to go to Saks Fifth Avenue than to a bargain-basement discount store. "Experience goods" are those whose value to the purchaser cannot be established upon visual inspection and for whom the brand name of the good or the name of the retailer is an important signaling device. Search goods are those whose physical attributes can be examined and successfully compared with the claims of advertisers before purchase and for whom brand names are less important.

Causes and Consequences of Appropriability

Finally, there is an important fifth piece of information every multinational firm must have before it embarks on developing a particular product. This is appropriability itself.

There is considerable variation across products and processes in the extent to which a private firm can appropriate the returns from an investment in new information. For complicated ideas and technologies, it is relatively difficult for interlopers to steal the idea. For simple ideas, there is a larger sample of potential entrants who can steal the idea and reduce the returns on investments by an innovator. This is one reason for the lack of *R&D* in highly competitive industries. Loss of appropriability through time is analogous to depreciation; complicated ideas have slow depreciation rates, while simple ideas have high ones. Differential private appropriability leads to social underinvestments by private firms in simple and unskilled-labor technologies.

Coase points out that externalities can be efficiently handled by private parties—rather than the government—if the legal system clearly establishes property rights.[11] One implication of his article is that governmental intervention is not required in order to provide the optimum level of public goods, such as new information. However, the difficulty with the Coase argument when applied to new technology is that the legal costs to private firms of appropriating the returns on their *R&D* investments may be so high that only the government can provide certain types of information efficiently, for example, unskilled-labor-intensive technologies. Even "well-defined" legal rights do not guarantee a socially optimum level of appropriability.

The transactions and legal costs of establishing property rights for even sophisticated technologies are high. The irony is that private expenditures by individuals and firms to prevent the loss of appropriability are also public goods. The first firm in an industry may expend large sums to establish proprietary rights and establish legal precedents for property rights to complicated technologies used in the industry. Since subsequent innovators do not share in these investments but benefit from the appropriability protection they provide, they take a free ride on these legal investments. Thus, appropriability investments by MNCs may be low unless the industry is concentrated or some other consideration dictates that entrants pay "their share" of the appropriability costs.

There is ample evidence that the transactions costs of protecting new ideas are not trivial. This is true even for MNCs, which specialize in creating new technologies.[12] As a result, the company is forced to make costly variations in the patent on the same invention or process from country to country, making the descriptions wider or narrower, because of the local laws. Whenever a patent or licensing agreement is found invalid in one country, this upsets licensing agreements the company has worked out in other countries.

There are several implications of the appropriability theory for MNCs. Next we examine how it explains why technology-creating firms, such as MNCs, are large. After that, we examine the light appropriability sheds on the effects of dismantling large MNCs. Finally, we examine its consistency with the stylized facts of foreign direct investment.

Appropriability and Firm Size

Appropriability is the first reason why firms that develop new products became large. Innovating firms expand to internalize the externality which new information creates, namely, the public-goods aspect of new information. A U.S. MNC whose technology is being copied in Western Europe will be better able and more inclined to spot the interloper if it has a subsidiary in Western Europe than if it exports the good from the United States or if it sells it through a marketing licensee in Western Europe. A European licensee selling only in Europe is less likely than an MNC to expend funds to stop a European interloper from exporting to, say, South America, since the licensee derives no benefit from this expenditure.

Second, there is a tendency for new products to be experience goods and for standardized products to be search goods. Optimum firm size is usually larger for domestic retailers of non-brand-name experience goods. By analogy, subsidiaries of multinational corporations are more likely than licensing arrangements. Third, sales of many high-technology products must be accompanied by sales of service information. The firm's optimum size is expanded because of service subsidiaries, for example, IBM's servicing of computers. Fourth, the number of products produced by information-creating firms is large because of economies of scale within each of the four types of information; development, production, marketing, and appropriability. Fifth, for new and differentiated products, the spread between the buyer and seller valuation of new information is higher than when the products are older and more standardized. This again suggests that market transactions costs are relatively higher earlier in a product's life cycle so that optimum firm size will fall through the industry cycle.[13]

These five reasons explain why new technologies are correlated with concentrated industry structures, why international trade in technology occurs within large MNCs rather than through licensing agreements, and why older industries are more competitive and less innovative. The correlation between concentration and *R&D* early in an industry's life and competition with less *R&D* late in each industry's life is now explained, although the direction of causation is not. The empirical evidence shows that firm size is negatively related to the average age of industries.

Dismantling Large Innovating Firms

Given the interrelationships among the information needed for product creation, development, markets, appropriability, and related activities, the foregoing analysis suggests that dismantling large innovating multinationals might be very costly. The policy-maker must establish that there is an economic argument why the normal loss of appropriability and decline in optimum firm size through the technology cycle should be speeded up.

Appropriability and the Stylized Facts of Foreign Direct Investment

The previous discussion provides a framework within which to interpret recent discussions of the multinational corporation, direct investment, and technology transfers. The framework here emphasizes that multinational corporations generate new products requiring large investments in four complementary types of information and careful calculations of the appropriability of each type. It is fruitful to treat technology like any other tangible good and to think of the international operations of multinational corporations as international trade in this commodity.[14] The revenue from trade in information is the present value of the monopoly profit streams permitted by international patent agreements and trade secrets. The price of the information is the monopoly element in the price of the new product. What implications follow from this approach?

Since international trade in information is analogous to international trade generally, both exporters and importers will play optimum tariff games.[15] Importers will tax it—to push down the price paid to exporters—and exporters will restrict its flow in an effort to raise its price; for example, the opposition of the U.S. government to General Electric's sale of jet engines to France in 1972. Technology importers should realize that if they try to lower the price they pay to foreigners for their purchases of information, this will increase their welfare but will reduce the quantity of technology imported below free trade levels—that is, reduce the "transfer of technology."

What is a "technology gap?" It exists in any situation in which a country is a net importer of a product, since less is produced than is desired domestically at world prices. Some regions have comparative advantages in creating information and others have comparative disadvantages. The theory of comparative advantage applies to trade in information just as it applies to steel, autos, and textiles: countries that do not have a comparative advantage in creating it should import it. Thus a technology "gap" should not be judged equivalent to a welfare distortion.

The phrase "transfer of technology" must be refined. First, the connotation of a costless gift should be discarded: all information transfers entail some cost. There are many ways in which information is transmitted: intrafirm transmission through the multinational corporations, market transfer through licensing, and government transfers through aid. Second, for the multinationals, we have already emphasized that several types of information are created and transferable, and the type of information transferred should be specified. Third, the fact that existing information is a public good does not mean that speeding up its transmission is a welfare improvement. For example, a policy-imposed speed-up in the transfer of sophisticated production technology may cause its premature introduction into unskilled-labor-abundant LDCs.

Public versus Private Creation of New Technology

Debate continues over whether research and development should be done by private firms or by the government. Proponents of government *R&D* point to the results of agricultural research sponsored by the U.S. Department of Agriculture. New seed varieties and other discoveries are disseminated widely to farmers at low cost. If the same results were privately controlled by patents, the price charged for the breakthroughs would be higher, reducing their dissemination and utilization and the social benefit from the research would be lower. Proponents of *R&D* by private firms—and its protection by patents or trade secrets—note that the market provides a superior allocation of *R&D* and speed of research effort from many new products. It is apparent that *R&D* will be better allocated among hairdryers, razor blades, and steel-belted radial tires by private profitability considerations than by government agencies. To summarize, it appears that private firms have an edge in deciding the products on which to spend *R&D* funds, while free government dissemination of the fruits of *R&D* is superior after breakthroughs are found invalid in one country, this upsets licensing agreements the company has worked out in other countries.

There are several implications of the appropriability theory for MNCs. Next we examine how it explains why technology-creating firms, such as MNCs, are large. After that, we examine the light appropriability sheds on the effects of dismantling large MNCs. Finally, we examine its consistency with the stylized facts of foreign direct investment.

Appropriability and Firm Size

Appropriability is the first reason why firms that develop new products become large. Innovating firms expand to internalize the externality which new information creates, namely, the public-goods aspect of new information. A U.S. MNC whose technology is being copied in Western Europe will be better able and more inclined to stop the interloper if it has a subsidiary in Western Europe than if it exports the good from the United States or if it sells it through a marketing licensee in Western Europe. A European licensee selling only in Europe is less likely than an MNC to expend funds to stop a European interloper from exporting to, say, South America, since the licensee derives no benefit from this expenditure.

Second, there is a tendency for new products to be experience goods and for standardized products to be search goods. Optimum firm size is usually larger for domestic retailers of non-brand-name experience goods. By analogy, subsidiaries of multinational corporations are more likely than licensing arrangements. Third, sales of many high-technology products must be made. A solution utilizing the strengths of each would be to let private firms do the *R&D* and have the government buy up the most successful patents and make them available to all interested producers, not just the innovator. The latter would compete the price down from near monopoly levels with patents. Despite its reasonableness, this compromise is fraught with difficulties: it is hard for the government—or anyone else—to know the value of new discoveries; the presence of a single seller—the innovator—and a single buyer—the government—generates nontrivial haggling costs; and government procurement is plagued with influence peddling and lobbying.[16] Sales of new military technologies to the U.S. Department of Defense illustrate both problems.

From Vernon's Product Cycle to the Industry Technology Cycle

Vernon's product cycle suggested that the life of each product can be broken into three distinct stages: the new product, the maturing product, and the standardized product. He suggested that the locus of production would move from the originating developed country in the first stage to the LDCs in the third stage. Three considerations suggested why production would begin in the DCs for new products. On the demand side, high unit-labor costs generate demand for labor-saving investment goods and high incomes generate demand for sophisticated and differentiated new consumer products that save on household labor. On the supply side, the research intensity of new products is high, and the relatively large endowments of skilled labor—scientists, engineers, and so on—dictate that DCs have a comparative advantage in creating new products. Finally, demand and supply interact, since rapid changes in new products require swift and frequent communication between producers and consumers.

In Vernon's stage II, production expands from the originating DC to other DCs as foreign markets grow, as other DC import barriers rise, as international transportation costs become a larger proportion of the product price, and as the production process becomes more standardized. In Vernon's stage III—the standardized product stage—production shifts to the LDCs since little interaction is needed between producers and consumers, small inputs of research and development are required, and as the production technologies become routinized through assembly lining so that more unskilled labor can be utilized in the production process.

How do we make the transition from Vernon's product cycle to an industry product cycle? First, evidence that industries may also go through cycles is suggested by data showing that industry patents follow an S-curve over long periods of time. Second, the appropriability theory suggests that industry structure itself is affected by these forces and varies systematically through the life cycle. Industry structure and *R&D* have a two-way interaction: concentrated industry structures encourage *R&D*—product creation, development, production and marketing; but also successful inventions encourage expansion of firm size as innovators attempt to appropriate the returns on their *R&D*. The two-way causation suggests that young industries—those with new products—are concentrated, are associated with high *R&D*, and are more innovative while older ones are more competitive, spend less on *R&D*, and produce more standardized products.[17]

THE PRICE OF NEW HIGH-TECHNOLOGY PRODUCTS

Consider a multinational corporation that discovers a new product or a new technology that is embodied in a physical product. What price should it charge for this new product? If the innovating firm, such as IBM, charges a high price for the computer, it will experience high short-run profits but low long-run profits because of more rapid entry. Thus it gains short-run profits but gives away long-run profits. If it charges a low price in the short run, then it will have larger long-run profits but will earn low profits in the short run. It should be concerned about profits in both periods. The profit-maximizing firm will want to devise a pricing strategy that trades off short- and long-run profits appropriately. Such a strategy will be the one that maximizes the entire present discounted value of the monopoly profits on the new technology.

In a model more fully developed elsewhere, these elements and appropriability are integrated, producing the following propositions.[18]

1. The profit-maximizing price strategy for the innovating multinational is to set an initial price slightly below the monopoly price and continuously cut this price through time until the long-run competitive price is reached.

2. An ironic result is that a legally imposed reduction in the long-run market power of an innovating multinational raises today's price of technology and reduces the short-run flow of technology to the developing countries. This occurs because the restriction reduces the value of future profit to the MNC. It attempts to make more profits in the short-run by raising today's price. At the higher price, however, fewer high-technology products will be purchased by the LDCs, and hence less technology is transferred.

3. Revisions in the Paris Convention that relax the enforcement of patent laws in favor of emulators would do the following. Since the innovating firm's profit stream is hurt by this more rapid entry, it

becomes more concerned about its future profits. It will attempt to protect these profits by lowering today's price and all future prices in order to discourage the emulators. This results in an increase in short-run technology transfer and increases in the growth rate of technology transfer. However, there is no effect on long-run technology transfer by the policy of weakening patent enforcement, since the long-run price is unaffected.

4. There is a conflict between the level and the growth of technology exports. If the United States institutes a policy increasing the level of high-technology exports but policy-makers evaluate it by watching the growth rate of exports, following the initial increase in the level, they will think—erroneously—that the policy failed. For example, subsidizing the cost of computer technology transfer will increase the number of computers exported, for example, from 1000 to 1100 per year, but the yearly growth rate may fall from 7 percent to 5 percent, starting from the new level of 1100. The policy-maker should be aware of another important structural implication of the previous point. While the level of technology exports will be lower, the growth rate of technology exports will be higher, (1) to low-income countries for whom the innovating firm's costs of technology transfer are higher and to countries who have higher tariffs on technology imports, and (2) to high-risk countries to whom the innovating firm applies a higher discount rate.

POLICY QUESTIONS RAISED BY THE DEVELOPING COUNTRIES

The previous section enumerated several propositions related to the behavior of a profit-maximizing/technology-creating multinational corporation. We did not address the trade-off between the current supply of technology and the future supply of technology. If the developing countries attempt to tax technology imports, they should consider this trade-off. It is discussed in the following section. The next section addresses the restriction in developing countries on foreign ownership in MNC subsidiaries in their countries. Multinational corporation limitations on *R&D* in developing country subsidiaries are discussed in the subsequent section, and the final section deals with excessive pricing of technology.

Optimal Taxation of Technology Imports

The conflict between the pricing of existing technologies and the creation of future technologies can be illustrated by a discussion of the related question of expropriation. It is clear that any country that expropriates a foreign-held firm increases its short-run welfare—since profits on the existing operation are transferred from foreigners to the domestic government—but reduces its future welfare—there is a reduction in future investment by foreigners in the country. The same is true of technology. Countries cutting the prices they pay for existing technology—increased restrictions on profits and repatriation, and so on—gain in the short run, but they reduce the future supply of new technology to the country. The LDCs as a whole face a difficult decision on technology import tax policy.

What criterion should be used? There is some technology tax rate that will maximize LDC welfare. However, this tax will be less than the standard optimum tariff in international trade theory. That tax ignores the future and is determined by increasing the tax rate until the marginal increment to home welfare because of that part of the tax paid by foreigners—the price paid to foreigners falls as the tax rises—just equals the marginal increase in consumer welfare loss caused by the distorted higher domestic price—the technical term for the latter is the "consumer's deadweight loss." However, with technology imports the future supply is affected so that we must change the criterion to apply to present discounted values rather than current flows: the tax should be increased until the marginal present value of the gain—the tax paid by foreigners—equals the present value of the marginal consumer's surplus distortion. Supply falls through time as the foreign supply curve shifts to the left.

Majority Ownership of Foreign Affiliates

One of the most serious restrictions LDCs impose on multinational corporations attempting to set up subsidiaries in their countries, through either mergers or takeovers, is that foreign ownership not exceed 50 percent. The LDCs might benefit greatly if they permitted majority foreign ownership, at least 51 percent. This would still allow equity holders in the LDCs to capture nearly half of the profitability from the technology while overcoming the severe appropriability problem that is a key to much foreign direct investment in some high-technology industries. MNCs have a legitimate fear that if they do not control the operation, the other party to the agreement might "steal" the technology, sell it in third markets, and reduce the worldwide return on a given technology.

Limitations on R&D in LDC Subsidiaries

Two restrictions on LDC research and development documented in a UN study[19] are the limitations by multinationals on *R&D* done in LDC subsidiaries or affiliates and in "grant-back" provisions for *R&D* done in LDCs—that is, that the host country must provide the parent with the results of subsidiary *R&D* on a unilateral and frequently unremunerated basis. This allows modifications and adaptations of sophisticated *R&D* to developing countries to revert to the parent. This is socially wasteful, since it prohibits LDC subsidiaries from transforming sophisticated ideas into forms more useful to the LDCs. However, it is explainable, since the appropriability of the latter is low. The parent realizes that the simpler technology may undercut its profits on the more sophisticated technology. There is no easy solution to this problem; anything permitting the substitution of less appropriable technology reduces the long-run supply of sophisticated technology.

Excessive Pricing

A frequent complaint of technology importers is that the prices charged are "excessive." This could refer to attempts by technology exporters to extract the entire area under the technology import demand curve. If suppliers were completely successful in doing this, the quantity of technology transferred would equal that under free dissemination of technology. However, all of the economic benefit—technologists refer to this as the "economic surplus"—of the new technology is captured by the exporter rather than by the importer. The LDC obtains no welfare gain from the technology import, although he experiences no loss. One technique by which MNCs accomplish this is via a provision imposed on many technology importers in that the purchase of technologies be accompanied by an agreement to purchase—in some cases unrelated—raw materials, spare parts, intermediate products, and capital equipment from the technology supplier. A UN study showed that in four of the five importing countries, 66 percent or more of the contracts required tied purchase provisions.[20]

The "excessive pricing" problem is a normal consequence of the patent system: monopoly profits are the only reward of innovators, so that eliminating monopoly profits is an infeasible proposal if we expect private markets to create new technology. In fact, the case of the innovating firm capturing all of the benefits of a new technology cannot happen if there are active emulators. The model of optimal pricing by MNCs discussed earlier shows that an innovator will earn profits above production costs—otherwise it would have been foolish to extend the *R&D* funds—but these profits would be lower than those of a pure monopolist.

In the appropriability framework, innovators and emulators play important economic roles. Innovators reduce competition and charge high prices for new products, but they do innovate. Emulators steal technology and discourage innovation, but by cutting prices they make new technology available to us all. Private competition will provide for innovation and its dissemination properly only if the legal system and national policy balance appropriately the economic rights of innovators and emulators.

NOTES

1. The appropriability of an innovation is higher the larger the innovator's profits relative to the value to society of the innovation. The appropriability theory reviewed in this article is a summary and extension of the following three publications: Stephen P. Magee, "An Appropriability Theory of Direct Foreign Investment," in *The New International Economic Order: The North-South Debate*, ed. J. Bhagwati (Cambridge: MIT Press, 1977), pp. 317–40; "Multinational Corporations, the Industry Technology Cycle and Development," *Journal of World Trade Law*, 11:297–321 (July 1977); and "Application of the Dynamic Limit Pricing Model to the Price of Technology and International Technology Transfer," in *Optimal Policies, Control Theory and Technology Exports*, eds. Karl Brunner and Allan Meltzer (Amsterdam: North-Holland, 1977), pp. 203–224.

2. Raymond Vernon, "International Investment and International Trade in the Product Cycle," *Quarterly Journal of Economics*, 80:190–207 (May 1966).

3. See Magee, "Multinational Corporations."

4. See Magee, "Application of the Dynamic Limit Pricing Model."

5. See Kenneth Arrow, "Economic Welfare and the Allocation of Resources for Invention," in *The Rate and Direction of Inventive Activity: Economic and Social Factors*—a report of the National Bureau of Economic Research (Princeton, NJ: Princeton University Press, 1962), pp. 353–58.

6. Stephen H. Hymer, *The International Operation of National Firms: A Study of Direct Foreign Investment* (Cambridge: MIT Press, 1976). See also Vernon, "International Investment and International Trade in the Produce Cycle"; Richard Caves, "International Corporations: The Industrial Economics of Foreign Investment," *Economica* 38:1–27 (Feb. 1971); Arrow, "Economic Welfare and the Allocation of Resources for Invention"; Harold Demsetz, "Information and Efficiency: Another Viewpoint," *Journal of Law and Economics*, 12:1–22 (Apr. 1969); and Harry G. Johnson, "Multinational Corporations and International Oligopoly: The Non-American Challenge," in *The International Corporation*, ed. C. P. Kindleberger (Cambridge: MIT Press, 1970), pp. 35–56.

7. Edwin Mansfield, "Technology and Technological Change," in *Economic Analysis and the Multinational Enterprise*, ed. J. H. Dunning (New York: Praeger, 1974), pp. 147–83.

8. Raymond Vernon, *Sovereignty at Bay* (New York: Basic Books, 1971).

9. Lester Telser, "Comment," *Journal of Law and Economics*, 19:337–40 (1976).

10. Phillip Nelson, "Information and Consumer Behavior," *Journal of Political Economy*, 78:311–29 (Mar./Apr. 1970).

11. Ronald H. Coase, "The Problem of Social Cost," *Journal of Law and Economics*, 3:1–44 (Oct. 1960).

12. W. M. Carley, "Multinational Firms Find Patent Battle Consume Time, Money," *Wall Street Journal*, 24 June 1974, pp. 1, 17.

13. See Magee, "Technology and the Appropriability Theory of the Multinational Corporation."

14. G. K. Helleiner, "The Role of Multinational Corporations in the Less Developed Countries' Trade in Technology," *World Development*, 3:161–89 (Apr. 1975).

15. Carlos Rodriguez, "Trade in Technological Knowledge and the National Advantage," *Journal of Political Economy*, 83:121–35 (Feb. 1975).

16. William Brock and Stephen P. Magee, "The Economics of Special-Interest Politics: The Case of the Tariff," *American Economic Review*, 68:246–50 (May 1978).

17. Carley, "Multinational Firms Find Patent Battle Consume Time, Money."

18. See Magee, "Application of the Dynamic Limit Pricing Model."

19. United Nations Conference of Trade and Development, *An International Code of Conduct on Transfer of Technology* (New York: United Nations, 1975) TD/B/C. 6/AC. 1/2 Suppl. 1/Rev. 1, pp. 34–35.

20. United Nations Conference on Trade and Development, *Major Issues Arising from the Transfer of Technology to Developing Countries* (New York: United Nations, 1975), TD/B/AC. 11/10/Rev. 2, p. 16.

28. Multinationals and Developing Countries: Myths and Realities

PETER F. DRUCKER

I

Four assumptions are commonly made in the discussion of multinationals and the developing countries—by friends and enemies alike of the multinational company.[1] These assumptions largely inform the policies both of the developing countries and of the multinational companies. Yet, all four assumptions are false, which explains in large measure both the acrimony of the debate and the sterility of so many development policies.

These four false but generally accepted assumptions are: (1) the developing countries are important to the multinational companies and a major source of sales, revenues, profits and growth for them, if not the mainstay of "corporate capitalism"; (2) foreign capital, whether supplied by governments or by businesses, can supply the resources, and especially the capital resources required for economic development; (3) the ability of the multinational company to integrate and allocate productive resources on a global basis and across national boundaries, and thus to substitute transnational for national economic considerations, subordinates the best national interests of the developing country to "global exploitation"; (4) the traditional nineteenth-century form of corporate organization, that is, the "parent company" with wholly owned "branches" abroad, is the form of organization for the twentieth-century multinational company.

II

What are the realities? In the first instance, extractive industries have to go wherever the petroleum, copper ore or bauxite is found whether

Since 1971 Peter F. Drucker has been Clark Professor of Social Sciences and Management at the Claremont Graduate School in Claremont, California. From 1950 to 1971 he served as Professor of Management at the Graduate Business School of New York University.

in a developing or in a developed country. But for the typical twentieth-century multinational, that is a manufacturing, distributing or financial company, developing countries are important neither as markets nor as producers of profits. Indeed it can be said bluntly that the major manufacturing, distributive and financial companies of the developed world would barely notice it, were the sales in and the profits from the developing countries suddenly to disappear.

Confidential inside data in my possession on about 45 manufacturers, distributors and financial institutions among the world's leading multinationals, both North American and European,[2] show that the developed two-thirds of Brazil—from Bello Horizonte southward—is an important market for some of these companies, though even Brazil ranks among the first 12 sales territories, or among major revenue producers, for only two of them. But central and southern Brazil, while still "poor," are clearly no longer "underdeveloped." And otherwise not even India or Mexico—the two "developing" countries with the largest markets—ranks for any of the multinational companies in my sample ahead even of a single major sales district in the home country, be it the Hamburg-North Germany district, the English Midlands or Kansas City.

On the worldwide monthly or quarterly sales and profit chart, which most large companies use as their most common top-management tool, practically no developing country even appears in my sample of 45 major multinationals except as part of a "region," e.g., "Latin America," or under "Others."

The profitability of the businesses of these companies in the developing countries is uniformly lower by about two percentage points than that of the businesses in the developed countries, except for the pharmaceutical industry where the rate of return, whether on sales or on invested capital, is roughly the same for both. As a rule, it takes longer—by between 18 months to three years—to make a new operation break even in a developing country. And the growth rate—again excepting the pharmaceutical industry—is distinctly slower. Indeed, in these representative 45 businesses, 75 to 85 percent of all growth, whether in sales or in profits, in the last 25 years, occurred in the developed countries. In constant dollars the business of these 45 companies in the developed world doubled—or more than doubled—in the last 10 to 15 years. But their business in the developing countries grew by no more than one-third during that period if the figures are adjusted for inflation.

Published data, while still scarce and inadequate, show the same facts. Only for the extractive industries have the developing countries—and then only a very few of them—been of any significance whether as a source of profits, as loci of growth, or as areas of investment.

The reason is, of course, that—contrary to the old, and again fashionable, theory of "capitalist imperialism"—sales, growth and profits are where the market and the purchasing power are.

To the developing country, however, the multinational is both highly important and highly visible.

A plant employing 750 people and selling eight million dollars worth of goods is in most developing countries a major employer—both of rank and file and of management—and a big business. For the multinational parent company, employing altogether 97,000 people and selling close to two billion dollars worth of goods a year, that plant is, however, at best marginal. Top management in Rotterdam, Munich, London or Chicago can spend practically no time on it.

Neglect and indifference rather than "exploitation" is the justified grievance of the developing countries in respect to the multinationals. Indeed, top management people in major multinationals who are personally interested in the developing countries find themselves constantly being criticized for neglecting the important areas and for devoting too much of their time and attention to "outside interests." Given the realities of the business, its markets, growth opportunities and profit opportunities, this is a valid criticism.

The discrepancy between the relative insignificance of the affiliate in a developing country and its importance and visibility for the host country poses, however, a major problem for the multinationals as well. Within the developing country the man in charge of a business with 750 employees and eight million dollars in sales has to be an important man. While his business is minute compared to the company's business in Germany, Great Britain or the United States, it is every whit as difficult—indeed it is likely to be a good deal more difficult, risky and demanding. And he has to treat as an equal with the government leaders, the bankers and the business leaders of his country—people whom the district sales manager in Hamburg, Rotterdam or Kansas City never even sees. Yet his sales and profits are less than those of the Hamburg, Rotterdam or Kansas City sales district. And his growth potential is, in most cases, even lower.

This clash between two realities—the personal qualifications and competence, the position, prestige and power needed by the affiliate's top management people to do their job in the developing country, and the reality of a "sales district" in absolute, quantitative terms—the traditional corporate structure of the multinationals cannot resolve.

III

The second major assumption underlying the discussion of multinationals and developing countries is the belief that resources from abroad, and especially capital from abroad, can "develop" a country.

But in the first place no country is "underdeveloped" because it lacks resources. "Underdevelopment" is inability to obtain full performance from resources; indeed we should really be talking of countries of higher and lower productivity rather than of "developed" or "underdeveloped" countries. In particular, very few countries—Tibet and New Guinea may be exceptions—lack *capital.* Developing countries have, almost by definition, more capital than they productively employ. What "developing" countries lack is the full ability to mobilize their resources, whether human resources, capital or the physical resources. What they need are "triggers," stimuli from abroad and from the more highly developed countries, that will energize the resources of the country and will have a "multiplier impact."

The two success stories of development in the last hundred years—Japan and Canada—show this clearly. In the beginning, Japan imported practically no capital except small sums for early infrastructure investments, such as the first few miles of railroad. She organized, however, quite early, what is probably to this day the most efficient system for gathering and putting to use every drop of capital in the country. And she imported—lavishly and without restraints—technology with a very high multiplier impact and has continued to do so to this day.

Canada, in the mid-1930s, was far less "developed" a country than most American republics are today. Then the liberal governments of the 1930s decided to build an effective system for collecting domestic capital and to put it into infrastructure investments with a very high "multiplier" effect—roads, health care, ports, education and effective national and provincial administrations. Foreign capital was deliberately channeled into manufacturing and mining. Domestic capital and entrepreneurs were actually discouraged in the extractive and manufacturing sectors. But they were strongly encouraged in all tertiary activities such as distribution, banking, insurance and in local supply and finishing work in manufacturing. As a result a comparatively small supply of foreign capital—between a tenth and a twentieth of Canada's total capital formation—led to very rapid development within less than two decades.

There is a second fallacy in the conventional assumption, namely that there is unlimited absorptive capacity for money and especially for money from abroad. But in most developing countries there are actually very few big investment opportunities. There may be big hydroelectric potential; but unless there are customers with purchasing power, or industrial users nearby, there is no economic basis for a power plant. Furthermore, there is no money without strings. To service foreign capital, even at a minimal interest rate, requires foreign exchange. At that, loans or equity investments as a rule constitute a smaller (and, above all, a clearly delimited) burden than grants and other political subsidies from abroad. The latter always create heavy obligations, both in terms of foreign and domestic policy, no matter where they come from.

A developing country will therefore get the most out of resources available abroad, especially capital, if it channels capital where it has the greatest "multiplier impact." Moreover, it should channel it where one dollar of imported capital will generate the largest number of domestic dollars in investment, both in the original investment itself and in impact-investment (e.g., the gas stations, motels and auto repair shops which an automobile plant calls into being), and where one job created by the original investment generates the most jobs directly and indirectly (again an automobile industry is a good example). Above all, the investment should be channeled where it will produce the largest number of local managers and entrepreneurs and generate the most managerial and entrepreneurial competence. For making resources fully effective depends on the supply and competence of the managerial and entrepreneurial resource.

According to all figures, government money has a much lower multiplier impact than private money. This is, of course, most apparent in the Communist-bloc countries; low, very low, productivity of capital is the major weakness of the Communist economies, whether that of Russia or of her European satellites. But it is true also of public (e.g., World Bank) money elsewhere: it generates little, if any, additional investment either from within or from without the recipient country. And "prestige" investments, such as a steel mill, tend to have a fairly low multiplier impact—both in jobs and in managerial vigor—as against, for instance, a department store which brings into existence any number of small local manufacturers and suppliers and creates a major managerial and entrepreneurial cluster around it.

For the multinational in manufacturing, distribution, or finance locating in a developing country, rapid economic development of the host country offers the best chance for growth and profitability. The multinational thus has a clear self-interest in the "multiplier" impact of its investment, products and technology. It would be well advised to look on the capital it provides as "pump priming" rather than as "fuel." The more dollars (or pesos or cruzeiros) of local capital each of its own dollars of investment generates, the greater will be the development impact of its investment, and its chance for success. For the developing country the same holds true: to maximize the development impact of each imported dollar.

The Canadian strategy was carried on too long; by the early 1950s, Canada had attained full development and should have shifted to a policy of moving its own domestic capital into "super-structure" investments. But though the Canadian strategy is certainly not applicable to many developing countries today—and though, like any strategy, it became obsolete by its very success—nevertheless it was highly successful, very cheap and resulted in rapid economic growth while at the same time ensuring a high degree of social development and social justice.

What every developing country needs is a strategy which looks upon the available foreign resources, especially of capital, as the "trigger" to set off maximum deployment of a country's own resources and to have the maximum "multiplier effect." Such a strategy sees in the multinational a means to energize domestic potential—and especially to create domestic entrepreneurial and managerial competence—rather than a substitute for domestic resources, domestic efforts and, even, domestic capital. To make the multinationals effective agents of development in the developing countries therefore requires, above all, a policy of encouraging the domestic private sector, the domestic entrepreneur and the domestic manager. If they are being discouraged the resources brought in from abroad will, inevitably, be wasted.

For by themselves multinationals cannot produce development; they can only turn the crank but not push the car. It is as futile and self-defeating to use capital from abroad as a means to frighten and cow the local business community—as the bright young men of the early days of the Alliance for Progress apparently wanted to do—as it is to mobilize the local business community against the "wicked imperialist multinational."

IV

The multinational, it is said, tends to allocate production according to global economics. This is perfectly correct, though so far few companies actually have a global strategy. But far from being a threat to the developing country, this is potentially the developing country's one trump card in the world economy. Far from depriving the governments of the developing countries of decision-making power, the global strategy of the multinationals may be the only way these governments can obtain some effective control and bargaining leverage.

Short of attack by a foreign country the most serious threat to the economic sovereignty of developing countries, and especially of small ones, i.e., of most of them, is the shortage of foreign exchange. It is an absolute bar to freedom of decision. Realizing this, many developing countries, especially in the 1950s and early 1960s, chose a deliberate policy of "import substitution."

By now we have all learned that in the not-so-very-long run this creates equal or worse import-dependence and foreign-exchange problems. Now a variant of "import substitution" has become fashionable: a "domestic-content" policy which requires the foreign company to produce an increasing part of the final product in the country itself. This, predictably, will eventually have the same consequences as the now discredited "import substitution," namely, greater dependence on raw materials, equipment and supplies from abroad. And in all but the very few countries with already substantial markets (Brazil is perhaps the only one—but then Brazil is not, after all, "developing" any longer in respect to the central and southern two-thirds of the country) such a policy must, inevitably, make for a permanently high-cost industry unable to compete and to grow. The policy creates jobs in the very short run, to be sure; but it does so at the expense of the poor and of the country's potential to generate jobs in the future and to grow.

What developing countries need are *both*—foreign-exchange earnings and productive facilities large enough to provide economies of scale and with them substantial employment. This they can obtain only if they can integrate their emerging productive facilities—whether in manufactured goods or in such agricultural products as fruits and wine—with the largest and the fastest-growing economy around, i.e., the world market.

But exporting requires market knowledge, marketing facilities and marketing finance. It also requires political muscle to overcome strongly entrenched protectionist forces, and especially labor unions and farm blocs in the developed countries. Exporting is done most successfully, most easily and most cheaply if one has an assured "captive" market, at least for part of the production to be sold in the world market. This applies particularly to most of the developing countries, whose home market is too small to be an adequate base for an export-oriented industry.

The multinational's capacity to allocate production across national boundary lines and according to the logic of the world market should thus be a major ally of the developing countries. The more rationally and the more "globally" production is being allocated, the more they stand to gain. A multinational company, by definition, can equalize the cost of capital across national lines (to some considerable extent, at least). It can equalize to a large extent the managerial resource, that is, it can move executives, can train them, etc. The only resource it cannot freely move is labor. And that is precisely the resource in which the developing countries have the advantage.

This advantage is likely to increase. Unless there is a worldwide prolonged depression, labor in the developed countries is going to be increasingly scarce and expensive, if only because of low birthrates, while a large-scale movement of people from pre-industrial areas into developed countries, such as the mass-movement of American Blacks to the Northern cities or the mass-movement of "guest workers" to Western Europe, is politically or socially no longer possible.

But unless the multinationals are being used to integrate the productive resources of the developing countries into the productive network of the world economy—and especially into the production and marketing systems of the multinationals themselves—it is most unlikely that major export markets for the production of the developing countries will actually emerge very quickly.

Thus, the most advantageous strategy for the developing countries would seem to be to replace—or, at least to supplement—the policy of "domestic content" by a policy that uses the multinationals' integrating ability to develop large productive facilities with access to markets in the developed world. A good idea might be to encourage investment by multinationals with definite plans—and eventually firm commitments—to produce for export, especially within their own multinational system. As Taiwan and Singapore have demonstrated, it can make much more sense to become the most efficient large supplier worldwide of one model or one component than to be a high-cost small producer of the entire product or line. This would create more jobs and provide the final product at lower prices to the country's own consumers. And it should result in large foreign-exchange earnings.

I would suggest a second integration requirement. That developing countries want to limit the number of foreigners a company brings in is understandable. But the multinational can be expected to do that anyhow as much as possible—moving people around is expensive and presents all sorts of problems and troubles. Far more important would be a requirement by the developing country that the multinational integrate the managerial and professional people it employs in the country within its worldwide management development plans. Most especially it should assign an adequate number of the younger, abler people from its affiliate in the developing country for from three to five years of managerial and professional work in one of the developed countries. So far, to my knowledge, this is being done systematically only by some of the major American banks, by Alcan, and by Nestle. Yet it is people and their competence who propel development; and the most important competence needed is not technical, i.e., what one can learn in a course, but management of people, marketing and finance, and first-hand knowledge of developed countries.

In sum, from the point of view of the developing countries the best cross-national use of resources which the multinational is—or should be—capable of may well be the most positive element in the present world economy. A policy of self-sufficiency is not possible even for the best-endowed country today. Development, even of modest proportions, cannot be based on uneconomically small, permanently high-cost facilities, either in manufacturing or in farming. Nor is it likely to occur, let alone rapidly, under the restraint of a continental balance-of-payments crisis. The integration of the productive capacities and advantages of developing countries into the world economy is the only way out. And the multinational's capacity for productive integration across national boundaries would seem the most promising tool for this.

V

That 100-percent ownership on the part of the "parent company" is *the* one and only corporate structure for the multinational, while widely believed, has never been true. In so important a country as Japan it has always been the rather rare exception, with most non-Japanese companies operating through joint ventures. Sears, Roebuck is in partnership throughout Canada with a leading local retail chain, Simpson's. The Chase Manhattan Bank operates in many countries as a minority partner in and with local banks. Adela, the multinational venture-capital firm in Latin America, and by far the most successful of all development institutions in the world today, has confined itself from its start, ten years ago, to minority participation in its ventures, and so on.

But it is true that, historically, 100-percent ownership has been considered the preferred form, and anything else as likely to make unity of action, vision and strategy rather difficult. Indeed, restriction of the foreign investor to less than 100-percent control or to a minority participation, e.g., in the Andean Pact agreements or in Mexico's legislation regarding foreign investments, is clearly intended as restraint on the foreigner, if not as punitive action.

But increasingly the pendulum is likely to swing the other way. (Indeed, it may not be too far-fetched to anticipate that, a few years hence, "anti-foreign" sentiment may take the form of demanding 100-percent foreign-capital investment in the national company in the developing country, and moving toward outlawing partnerships or joint ventures with local capital as a drain on a country's slender capital resources.) The multinational will find it increasingly to its advantage to structure ownership in a variety of ways, and especially in ways that make it possible for it to gain access to both local capital and local talent.

Capital markets are rapidly becoming "polycentric." The multinationals will have to learn so to structure their businesses as to be able to tap any capital market—whether in the United States, Western Europe, Japan, Brazil, Beirut or wherever. This the monolithic "parent company" with wholly owned branches is not easily capable of. When companies, for example the West Europeans, raise money abroad, they often prefer financial instruments such as convertible debentures, which their own home capital markets, or the United States, do not particularly like and cannot easily handle. There is also more and more evidence that the capital-raising capacity of a huge multinational, especially for medium-term working capital, can be substantially increased by making major segments of the system capable of financing themselves largely in their own capital markets and with their own investing public and financial institutions.

But capital is also likely to be in short supply for years to come, barring a major global depression. And this might well mean that the multinationals will only be willing and able to invest in small, less profitable and more slowly growing markets, i.e., in developing countries if these countries supply a major share of the needed capital rather than have the foreign investor put up all of it.

That this is already happening, the example of Japan shows. Lifting restrictions on foreign investment was expected to bring a massive rush of take-over bids and 100 percent foreign-owned ventures. Instead it is now increasingly the Western investor, American as well as European, who presses for joint ventures in Japan and expects the Japanese partner to supply the capital while he supplies technology and product knowledge.

Perhaps more important will be the need to structure for other than 100-percent ownership to obtain the needed managerial talent in the developing country. If the affiliate in the developing country is not a "branch" but a separate company with substantial outside capital investment, the role and position of its executives become manageable. They are then what they have to be, namely, truly "top management," even though in employment and sales their company may still be insignificant within the giant concern.

And if the multinational truly attempts to integrate production across national boundaries, a "top management" of considerable stature becomes even more necessary. For then, the managers of the affiliate in a developing country have to balance both a national business and a global strategy. They have to be "top management" in their own country and handle on the local level highly complex economic, financial, political and labor relations as well as play as full members on a worldwide "system management" team.[3] To do this as a "subordinate" is almost impossible. One has to be an "equal," with one's own truly autonomous command.

VI

Domestically, we long ago learned that "control" has been divorced from "ownership" and, indeed, is rapidly becoming quite independent of "ownership." There is no reason why the same development should not be taking place internationally—and for the same two reasons: (1) "ownership" does not have enough capital to finance the scope of modern large businesses; and (2) management, i.e., "control," has to have professional competence, authority and standing of its own. Domestically the divorce of "control" from "ownership" has not undermined "control." On the contrary, it has made managerial control and direction more powerful, more purposeful, more cohesive.

There is no inherent reason why moving away from "100-percent ownership" in developing countries should make impossible maintenance of common cohesion and central control. On the contrary, both because it extends the capital base of the multinational in a period of worldwide capital shortage and because it creates local partners, whether businessmen or government agencies, the divorce between control and direction may well strengthen cohesion, and may indeed even be a prerequisite to a true global strategy.[4]

At the same time such partnership may heighten the development impact of multinational investment by mobilizing domestic capital for productive investment and by speeding up the development of local entrepreneurs and managers.

Admittedly, mixed ownership has serious problems; but they do not seem insurmountable, as the Japanese joint-venture proves. It also has advantages; and in a period of worldwide shortage of capital it is the multinational that would seem to be the main beneficiary. Indeed one could well argue that developing countries, if they want to attract foreign investment in such a period may have to *offer* co-investment capital, and that provisions for the participation of local investment in ownership will come to be seen (and predictably to be criticized) as favoring the foreign investor rather than as limiting him.

VII

The multinational, while the most important and most visible innovation of the postwar period in the economic field, is primarily a symptom of a much greater change. It is a response to the emergence of a genuine world economy. This world economy is not an agglomeration of national economies as was the "international economy" of nineteenth-century international trade theory. It is fundamentally autonomous, has its own dynamics, its own demand patterns, its own institutions—and in the Special Drawing Rights (SDR) even its own money and credit system in embryonic form. For the first time in 400 years—since the end of the sixteenth century when the word "sovereignty" was first coined—the territorial political unit and the economic unit are no longer congruent.

This, understandably, appears as a threat to national governments. The threat is aggravated by the fact that no one so far has a workable theory of the world economy. As a result there is today no proven, effective, predictable economic policy: witness the impotence of governments in the face of worldwide inflation.

The multinationals are but a symptom. Suppressing them, predictably, can only aggravate the disease. But to fight the symptoms in lieu of a cure has aways been tempting. It is therefore entirely possible that the multinationals will be severely damaged and perhaps even destroyed within the next decade. If so, this will be done by the governments of the developed countries, and especially by the governments of the multinationals' *home* countries, the United States, Britain, Germany, France, Japan, Sweden, Holland and Switzerland—the countries where 95 percent of the world's multinationals are domiciled and which together account for at least three-quarters of the multinationals' business and profits. The developing nations can contribute emotionalism and rhetoric to the decisions, but very little else. They are simply not important enough to the multinationals (or to the world economy) to have a major impact.

But at the same time the emergence of a genuine world economy is the one real hope for most of the developing countries, especially for the great majority which by themselves are too small to be viable as "national economies" under present technologies, present research requirements, present capital requirements and present transportation and communications facilities. The next ten years are the years in which they will both most need the multinationals and have the greatest opportunity of benefiting from them. For these will be the years when the developing countries will have to find jobs and incomes for the largest number of new entrants into the labor force in their history while, at the same time, the developed countries will experience a sharp contraction of the number of new entrants into their labor force—a contraction that is already quite far advanced in Japan and in parts of Western Europe and will reach the United States by the late 1970s. And the jobs that the developing countries will need so desperately for the next ten years will to a very large extent require the presence of the multinationals—their investment, their technology, their managerial competence, and above all their marketing and export capabilities.

The best hope for developing countries, both to attain political and cultural nationhood and to obtain the employment opportunities and export earnings they need, is through the integrative power of the world economy. And their tool, if only they are willing to use it, is, above all, the multinational company—precisely because it represents a global economy and cuts across national boundaries.

The multinational, if it survives, will surely look different tomorrow, will have a different structure, and will be "transnational" rather than "multinational." But even the multinational of today is—or at least should be—a most effective means to constructive nationhood for the developing world.

NOTES

1. The author acknowledges his indebtedness for advice and helpful criticism to Dr. Tore Browaldh, Chairman of Svenska Handelsbanken and recently a member of the U.S. Group of Eminent Persons studying multinationals, and to Dr. Ernst Keller, President of Adela Investment Co., S.A., Lima, Peru.

2. I have no data on Japanese-based multinationals; but in developing countries the Japanese are still mainly engaged in extractive and raw-material-producing business.

3. For a full discussion of this organization design, see my recent book *Management: Tasks; Responsibilities; Practices*, New York: Harper & Row, 1974, especially Chapter 47.

4. On very different grounds, Professor Jack N. Behrman, former Assistant Secretary of Commerce in the Kennedy Administration and a man with encyclopedic knowledge of how the multinational economy works, reached similar conclusions. See his *Decision Criteria for Foreign Direct Investment in Latin America*, New York: Council of the Americas, 1974.

VI. Rich Country–Poor Country Relationships

Traditional theory strongly implies that growing international trade is a powerful engine of development for all participating nations. Trade should reallocate factors of production towards more productive uses and raise incomes. In addition, it is generally thought that trade is a stimulus to technological advance and general economic progress, particularly when free movements of capital in the form of foreign investment occur.

It is exceedingly difficult to reconcile this roseate line of thinking with the continuing poverty of half the world's people following two centuries of deepening involvement in global patterns of trade and investment. This is not to say, of course, that this poverty is solely or even predominately a consequence of these patterns. In part, the income gap between rich and poor peoples may be a result of poor postindependence policy set by the countries themselves or of internal cultural and institutional patterns that are not conducive of growth. It is clear, too, that some less-developed countries such as Brazil, Pakistan, the Ivory Coast, Korea, and Taiwan have made rapid strides while more closely integrating their economies into the larger world economy.

Nonetheless, the wide differences in international standards of living and between theoretical expectation and reality contribute to a deep-seated frustration in many developing countries with the current structure of international economic relations. Some have rejected the outward-looking trade and open-door foreign investment policies called for by the standard theory. They have pursued inward-looking import-substitution strategies of development for long periods.

At its most extreme, the disappointment with the colonial and modern experience with trade and investment relations gives rise, largely among intellectuals in the Third World, to theories of imperialism, neo-imperialism, dependency, and exploitation. These argue, without much impact on western economic thought, that the rapid growth of the industrialized countries has actually caused and intensified the under-development of the poor nations. Prices of poor country exports are said to be kept low, wages are held down, excessively large profits are extracted, and overly high prices are demanded for industrial goods sold to poor countries. Although it is unclear whether all or any of these propositions are empirically valid, the ideas have immense appeal to ordinary people, students, and leaders throughout the Third World.

The negative reaction to existing international trade patterns and current multinational business activities has led to calls for a new international economic order (NIEO). The first selection in this section is the 1974 resolution of the General Assembly of the United Nations advocating the establishment of new international economic relationships. The declaration articulates principles of equality and equity as a basis for the NIEO. Twenty specific aims are listed and these are followed by policy suggestions. Stress is placed on fair pricing of the exports of developing countries. Access to rich-country markets is sought; use of buffer stocks to maintain stable and fair prices for primary products is desired; more development finance is hoped for, perhaps raised by issuance of more SDRs; more extensive transference of technology on equitable terms would be welcomed.

The next article, by Rachel McCulloch, describes recent United States proposals offering alternatives to NIEO-style reforms. The United States currently is reemphasizing reliance on free markets and open investment policies. This stance conflicts with Southern calls for special treatment of their exports, liberal foreign aid granted through international agencies, and regulated access of MNCs to developing country economies.

The United States is often the major market for a developing country's exports, which may comprise only a tiny fraction of United States imports. This asymmetry is also present in investment relations. Even small American businesses loom very large in overseas economies. The United States offers a favorite target for critics of the current international arrangements both because of its prominence in trade and investment connections and because of its expressed lack of sympathy for NIEO demands. American-Southern stresses have been exacerbated by the recent aggressive espousal by the U.S. of traditional free trade and investment logic. Previous policy had at least been non-confrontationist: warm agreement in principle with NIEO demands but inaction on implementation of specific instruments and mechanisms.

McCulloch points out that a test of the sincerity of the new U.S. policy will be American willingness to open the American market to developing nation imports, even when this means loss of American jobs in industries such as shoes, textiles, or steel. Further pressures on these trade-threatened industries, during a period of high domestic unemployment, may create sufficient political resistance to undermine any special treatment of developing country manufactured exports.

The last three papers represent different perspectives on the NIEO. Carlos Diaz-Alejandro believes that the call for a NIEO must be taken seriously by the rich countries. Without adopting the rhetoric of dependency or neo-imperialism, Diaz-Alejandro counsels orthodox economists to look closely at the assumptions and requirements of the standard trade model. A key fact is that most economists do not know in any real depth how commodity markets work. They do not know to what degree, if any, trade in primary commodities, each of which is so often of crucial importance to a few developing nations, is in fact controlled by a handful of large purchasers or marketers. Theory alone, in the absence of detailed study of individual countries, markets, commodities, and firm behavior may be a very poor guide to the best policy.

Paul Streeten's paper centers on the absence of effective international organizations to deal with trade, aid, investment, and technology relations between the rich and poor nations. He sees the NIEO proposals as one set of responses to the need for international cooperation in these fields. A crucial point, which the developing countries themselves often neglect, is that it is far from clear that all members of the Third World community have identical interests. The OPEC cartel, for example, illustrates that the gains of one group of less-developed countries, achieved through acquiring power over the marketing of a primary commodity, may harm others in the group. Streeten concludes with thoughtful statements of the constructive positions that the Third World and the rich countries may take on the NIEO and, more widely, outlines what is needed to build a healthy and more integrated world economy.

The final paper is by Herbert Grubel, who expresses reservations many economists have about the NIEO. He identifies a number of problems associated with the claim that primary commodities merit special treatment to stabilize their prices. He doubts that buffer stocks are a good way to attain that stability, if instability is indeed a problem.

Grubel criticizes the appeals for a code of conduct for MNCs and for use of newly-created SDRs as a source of development finance. He seeks to identify sources of political support for the NIEO and the increased number of international agencies and requisite bureaucrats it would entail. He argues that the Third World officials and intellectuals who push hardest for the NIEO would be the primary beneficiaries if high-paying and sometimes glamorous jobs were created in new international organizations. He concludes with the remark that his differences with advocates of the NIEO are not with respect to ends—enhancement of welfare in the Third World and removal of poverty—but over means.

29. Declaration on the Establishment of a New International Economic Order

UNITED NATIONS GENERAL ASSEMBLY

We, the Members of the United Nations,

Having convened a special session of the General Assembly to study for the first time the problems of raw materials and development, devoted to the consideration of the most important economic problems facing the world community,

Bearing in mind the spirit, purposes and principles of the Charter of the United Nations to promote the economic advancement and social progress of all peoples,

Solemnly proclaim our united determination to work urgently for the establishment of a new international economic order based on equity, sovereign equality, interdependence, common interest and co-operation among all States, irrespective of their economic and social systems which shall correct inequalities and redress existing injustices, make it possible to eliminate the widening gap between the developed and the developing countries and ensure steadily accelerating economic and social development and peace and justice for present and future generations, and, to that end, declare:

1. The greatest and most significant achievement during the last decades has been the independence from colonial and alien domination of a large number of peoples and nations which has enabled them to become members of the community of free peoples. Technological progress has also been made in all spheres of economic activities in the last three decades, thus providing a solid potential for improving the well-being of all peoples. However, the remaining vestiges of alien and colonial domination, foreign occupation, racial discrimination, *apartheid* and neo-colonialism in all its forms continue to be among the greatest

obstacles to the full emancipation and progress of the developing countries and all the peoples involved. The benefits of technological progress are not shared equitably by all members of the international community. The developing countries, which constitute 70 percent of the world's population, account for only 30 percent of the world's income. It has proved impossible to achieve an even and balanced development of the international community under the existing international economic order. The gap between the developed and the developing countries continues to widen in a system which was established at a time when most of the developing countries did not even exist as independent States and which perpetuates inequality.

2. The present international economic order is in direct conflict with current developments in international political and economic relations. Since 1970, the world economy has experienced a series of grave crises which have had severe repercussions, especially on the developing countries because of their generally greater vulnerability to external economic impulses. The developing world has become a powerful factor that makes its influence felt in all fields of international activity. These irreversible changes in the relationship of forces in the world necessitate the active, full and equal participation of the developing countries in the formulation and application of all decisions that concern the international community.

3. All these changes have thrust into prominence the reality of interdependence of all the members of the world community. Current events have brought into sharp focus the realization that the interests of the developed countries and those of the developing countries can no longer be isolated from each other, that there is close interrelationship between the prosperity of the developed countries and the growth and development of the developing countries, and that the prosperity of the international community as a whole depends upon the prosperity of its constituent parts. International co-operation for development is the shared goal and common duty of all countries. Thus the political, economic and social well-being of present and future generations depends more than ever on co-operation between all members of the international community on the basis of sovereign equality and the removal of the disequilibrium that exists between them.

4. The new international economic order should be founded on full respect for the following principles:

(a) Sovereign equality of States, self-determination of all peoples, inadmissibility of the acquisition of territories by force, territorial integrity and noninterference in the internal affairs of other States;

(b) The broadest co-operation of all the States members of the international community, based on equity, whereby the prevailing disparities in the world may be banished and prosperity secured for all;

(c) Full and effective participation on the basis of equality of all countries in the solving of world economic problems in the common interest of all countries, bearing in mind the necessity to ensure the accelerated development of all the developing countries, while devoting particular attention to the adoption of special measures in favour of the least developed, land-locked and island developing countries as well as those developing countries most seriously affected by economic crises and natural calamities, without losing sight of the interests of other developing countries;

(d) The right [of] every country to adopt the economic and social system that it deems to be the most appropriate for its own development and not to be subjected to discrimination of any kind as a result;

(e) Full permanent sovereignty of every State over its natural resources and all economic activities. In order to safeguard these resources, each State is entitled to exercise effective control over them and their exploitation with means suitable to its own situation, including the right to nationalization or transfer of ownership to its nationals, this right being an expression of the full permanent sovereignty of the State. No State may be subjected to economic, political or any other type of coercion to prevent the free and full exercise of this inalienable right;

(f) The right of all States, territories and peoples under foreign occupation, alien and colonial domination or *apartheid* to restitution and full compensation for the exploitation and depletion of, and damages to, the natural resources and all other resources of those States, territories and peoples;

(g) Regulation and supervision of the activities of transnational corporations by taking measures in the interest of the national economies of the countries where such transnational corporations operate on the basis of the full sovereignty of those countries;

(h) The right of the developing countries and the peoples of territories under colonial and racial domination and foreign occupation to achieve their liberation and to regain effective control over their natural resources and economic activities;

(i) The extending of assistance to developing countries, peoples and territories which are under colonial and alien domination, foreign occupation, racial discrimination or *apartheid* or are subjected to economic, political or any other type of coercive measures to obtain from them the subordination of the exercise of their sovereign rights and to secure from them advantages of any kind, and to neocolonialism in all its forms, and which have established or are endeavouring to establish effective control over their natural resources and economic activities that have been or are still under foreign control;

(j) Just and equitable relationship between the prices of raw materials, primary products, manufactured and semi-manufactured goods exported by developing countries and the prices of raw materials, primary commodities, manufactures, capital goods and equipment imported by them with the aim of bringing about sustained improvement in their unsatisfactory terms of trade and the expansion of the world economy;

(k) Extension of active assistance to developing countries by the whole international community, free of any political or military conditions;

(l) Ensuring that one of the main aims of the reformed international monetary system shall be the promotion of the development of the developing countries and the adequate flow of real resources to them;

(m) Improving the competitiveness of natural materials facing competition from synthetic substitutes;

(n) Preferential and non-reciprocal treatment for developing countries, wherever feasible, in all fields of international economic co-operation whenever possible;

(o) Securing favourable conditions for the transfer of financial resources to developing countries;

(p) Giving to the developing countries access to the achievements of modern science and technology, and promoting the transfer of technology and the creation of indigenous technology for the benefit of the developing countries in forms and in accordance with procedures which are suited to their economies;

(q) The need for all States to put an end to the waste of natural resources, including food products;

(r) The need for developing countries to concentrate all their resources for the cause of development;

(s) The strengthening, through individual and collective actions, of mutual economic, trade, financial and technical co-operation among the developing countries, mainly on a preferential basis;

(t) Facilitating the role which producers' associations may play within the framework of international co-operation and, in pursuance of their aims, *inter alia*, assisting in the promotion of sustained growth of world economy and accelerating the development of developing countries.

PROGRAMME OF ACTION ON THE ESTABLISHMENT OF A NEW INTERNATIONAL ECONOMIC ORDER

Raw Materials

All efforts should be made:

(a) To put an end to all forms of foreign occupation, racial discrimination, *apartheid*, colonial, neo-colonial and alien domination and exploitation through the exercise of permanent sovereignty over natural resources;

(b) To take measures for the recovery, exploitation, development, marketing and distribution of natural resources, particularly of developing countries, to serve their national interests, to promote collective self-reliance among them and to strengthen mutually beneficial international economic co-operation with a view to bringing about the accelerated development of developing countries;

(c) To facilitate the functioning and to further the aims of producers' associations, including their joint marketing arrangements, orderly commodity trading, improvement in export income of producing developing countries and in their terms of trade, and sustained growth of the world economy for the benefit of all;

(d) To evolve a just and equitable relationship between the prices of raw materials, primary commodities, manufactured and semi-manufactured goods exported by developing countries and the prices of raw materials, primary commodities, food, manufactured and semi-manufactured goods and capital equipment imported by them, and to work for a link between the prices of exports of developing countries and the prices of their imports from developed countries;

(e) To take measures to reverse the continued trend of stagnation or decline in the real price of several commodities exported by developing countries, despite a general rise in commodity prices, resulting in a decline in the export earnings of these developing countries;

(f) To take measures to expand the markets for natural products in relation to synthetics, taking into account the interests of the developing countries, and to utilize fully the ecological advantages of these products;

(g) To take measures to promote the processing of raw materials in the producer developing countries. . . .

General Trade

All efforts should be made:

(a) To take the following measures for the amelioration of terms of trade of developing countries and concrete steps to eliminate chronic trade deficits of developing countries:

(i) Fulfillment of relevant commitments already undertaken in the United Nations Conference on Trade and Development and in the International Development Strategy for the Second United Nations Development Decade [General Assembly Resolution 2626(XXV)];

(ii) Improved access to markets in developed countries through the progressive removal of tariff and non-tariff barriers and of restrictive business practices;

(iii) Expeditious formulation of commodity agreements where appropriate, in order to regulate as necessary and to stabilize the world markets for raw materials and primary commodities;

(iv) Preparation of an over-all integrated programme, setting out guidelines and taking into account the current work in this field, for a comprehensive range of commodities of export interest to developing countries;

(v) Where products of developing countries compete with the domestic production in developed countries, each developed country should facilitate the expansion of imports from developing countries and provide a fair and reasonable opportunity to the developing countries to share in the growth of the market;

(vi) When the importing developed countries derive receipts from customs duties, taxes and other protective measures applied to imports of these products, consideration should be given to the claim of the developing countries that these receipts should be reimbursed in full to the exporting developing countries or devoted to providing additional resources to meet their development needs;

(vii) Developed countries should make appropriate adjustments in their economies so as to facilitate the expansion and diversification of imports from developing countries and thereby permit a rational, just and equitable international division of labour;

(viii) Setting up general principles for pricing policy for exports of commodities of developing countries, with a view to rectifying and achieving satisfactory terms of trade for them;

(ix) Until satisfactory terms of trade are achieved for all developing countries, consideration should be given to alternative means, including improved compensatory financing schemes for meeting the development needs of the developing countries concerned;

(x) Implementation, improvement and enlargement of the generalized system of preferences for exports of agricultural primary commodities, manufactures and semi-manufactures from developing to developed countries and consideration of its extension to commodities, including those which are processed or semi-processed; developing countries which are or will be sharing their existing tariff advantages in some developed countries as the result of the introduction and eventual enlargement of the generalized system of preferences should, as a matter of urgency, be granted new openings in the markets of other developed countries which should offer them export opportunities that at least compensate for the sharing of those advantages;

(xi) The setting up of buffer stocks within the framework of commodity arrangements and their financing by international financial institutions, wherever necessary, by the developed countries and, when they are able to do so, by the developing countries, with the aim of favouring the producer developing and consumer developing countries and of contributing to the expansion of world trade as a whole;

(xii) In cases where natural materials can satisfy the requirements of the market, new investment for the expansion of the capacity to produce synthetic materials and substitutes should not be made.

(b) To be guided by the principles of non-reciprocity and preferential treatment of developing countries in multilateral trade negotiations between developed and developing countries, and to seek sustained and additional benefits for the international trade of developing countries, so as to achieve a substantial increase in their foreign exchange earnings, diversification of their exports and acceleration of the rate of their economic growth.

International Monetary System and Financing of the Development of Developing Countries

1. Objectives. All efforts should be made to reform the international monetary system with, *inter alia*, the following objectives:

(a) Measures to check the inflation already experienced by the developed countries, to prevent it from being transferred to developing countries and to study and devise possible arrangements within the International Monetary Fund to mitigate the effects of inflation in developed countries on the economies of developing countries;

(b) Measures to eliminate the instability of the international monetary system, in particular the uncertainty of the exchange rates, especially as it affects adversely the trade in commodities;

(c) Maintenance of the real value of the currency reserves of the developing countries by preventing their erosion from inflation and exchange rate depreciation of reserve currencies;

(d) Full and effective participation of developing countries in all phases of decision-making for the formulation of an equitable and durable monetary system and adequate participation of developing countries in all bodies entrusted with this reform and, particularly, in the Board of Governors of the International Monetary Fund;

(e) Adequate and orderly creation of additional liquidity with particular regard to the needs of the developing countries through the additional allocation of special drawing rights based on the concept of world liquidity needs to be appropriately revised in the light of the new international environment; any creation of international liquidity should be made through international multilateral mechanisms;

(f) Early establishment of a link between special drawing rights and additional development financing in the interest of developing countries, consistent with the monetary characteristics of special drawing rights;

(g) Review by the International Monetary Fund of the relevant provisions in order to ensure effective participation by developing countries in the decision-making process;

(h) Arrangements to promote an increasing net transfer of real sources from the developed to the developing countries;

(i) Review of the methods of operation of the International Monetary Fund, in particular the terms for both credit repayments and "stand-by" arrangements, the system of compensatory financing, and the terms of the financing of commodity buffer stocks, so as to enable the developing countries to make more effective use of them.

Transfer of Technology

All efforts should be made:

(a) To formulate an international code of conduct for the transfer of technology corresponding to needs and conditions prevalent in developing countries;

(b) To give access on improved terms to modern technology and to adapt that technology, as appropriate, to specific economic, social and ecological conditions and varying stages of development in developing countries;

(c) To expand significantly the assistance from developed to developing countries in research and development programmes and in the creation of suitable indigenous technology;

(d) To adapt commercial practices governing transfer of technology to the requirements of the developing countries and to prevent abuse of the rights of sellers;

(e) To promote international co-operation in research and development in exploration and exploitation, conservation and the legitimate utilization of natural resources and all sources of energy. . . .

Regulations and Control over the Activities of Transnational Corporations

All efforts should be made to formulate, adopt and implement an international code of conduct for transnational corporations;

(a) To prevent interference in the internal affairs of the countries where they operate and their collaboration with racist régimes and colonial administrations;

(b) To regulate their activities in host countries, to eliminate restrictive business practices and to conform to the national development plans and objectives of developing countries, and in this context facilitate, as necessary, the review and revision of previously concluded arrangements;

(c) To bring about assistance, transfer of technology and management skills to developing countries on equitable and favourable terms;

(d) To regulate the repatriation of the profits accruing from their operations, taking into account the legitimate interests of all parties concerned;

(e) To promote reinvestment of their profits in developing countries. . . .

Special Programme

The General Assembly adopts the following Special Programme, including particularly emergency measures to mitigate the difficulties of the developing countries most seriously affected by economic crisis, bearing in mind the particular problem of the least developed and land-locked countries:

The General Assembly,

Recalling the constructive proposals made by His Imperial Majesty the Shahanshah of Iran [U.N. Doc. A/9548, annex], and His Excellency Mr. Houari Boumediène, President of the People's Democratic Republic of Algeria [U.N. Doc. A/PV.2208, pp. 2–50];

1. *Decides* to launch a Special Programme to provide emergency relief and development assistance to the developing countries most seriously affected, as a matter of urgency, and for the period of time necessary, at least until the end of the Second United Nations Development Decade, to help them overcome their present difficulties and to achieve self-sustaining economic development;

2. *Decides* as a first step in the Special Programme to request the Secretary-General to launch an emergency operation to provide timely relief to the most seriously affected developing countries, as defined in subparagraph (c) above, with the aim of maintaining unimpaired essential imports for the duration of the coming 12 months and to invite the industrialized countries and other potential contributors to announce their contributions for emergency assistance, or intimate their intention to do so, by 15 June 1974 to be provided through bilateral or multilateral channels, taking into account the commitments and measures of assistance announced or already taken by some countries, and further requests the Secretary-General to report the progress of the emergency operation to the General Assembly at its twenty-ninth session, through the Economic and Social Council at its fifty-seventh session;

3. *Calls upon* the industrialized countries and other potential contributors to extend to the most seriously affected countries immediate relief and assistance which must be of an order of magnitude that is commensurate with the needs of these countries. Such assistance should be in addition to the existing level of aid and provided at a very early date

to the maximum possible extent on a grant basis and, where not possible, on soft terms. The disbursement and relevant operational procedures and terms must reflect this exceptional situation. The assistance could be provided either through bilateral or multilateral channels, including such new institutions and facilities that have been or are to be set up. The special measures may include the following:

(a) Special arrangements on particularly favourable terms and conditions including possible subsidies for and assured supplies of essential commodities and goods;

(b) Deferred payments for all or part of imports of essential commodities and goods;

(c) Commodity assistance, including food aid, on a grant basis or deferred payments in local currencies, bearing in mind that this should not adversely affect the exports of developing countries;

(d) Long-term suppliers' credits on easy terms;

(e) Long-term financial assistance on concessionary terms;

(f) Drawings from special International Monetary Fund facilities on concessional terms;

(g) Establishment of a link between the creation of special drawing rights and development assistance, taking into account the additional financial requirements of the most seriously affected countries;

(h) Subsidies, provided bilaterally or multilaterally, for interest on funds available on commercial terms borrowed by the most seriously affected countries;

(i) Debt renegotiation on a case-by-case basis with a view to concluding agreements on debt cancellation, moratorium or rescheduling;

(j) Provision on more favourable terms of capital goods and technical assistance to accelerate the industrialization of the affected countries;

(k) Investment in industrial and development projects on favourable terms;

(l) Subsidizing the additional transit and transport costs, especially of the land-locked countries;

4. *Appeals* to the developed countries to consider favourably the cancellation, moratorium or rescheduling of the debts of the most seriously affected developing countries, on their request, as an important contribution to mitigating the grave and urgent difficulties of these countries;

5. *Decides* to establish a Special Fund under the auspices of the United Nations, through voluntary contributions from industrialized countries and other potential contributors, as a part of the Special Programme, to provide emergency relief and development assistance, which will commence its operations at the latest by 1 January 1975. . . .

30. U.S. Relations With Developing Countries: Conflict And Opportunity

RACHEL MCCULLOCH

ABSTRACT

The United States has proposed a new approach to the problems of developing nations that reserves aid for the very poorest countries and stresses the role of free markets in stimulating Southern growth through expanded trade and private investment. Because the new policy rests upon opportunities for mutual gain, it may enjoy greater support in the North than past proposals to aid poor nations. However, expansion of North-South trade is central to the prospects for market-guided development. The new approach can succeed only if the United States and other Northern nations can adjust their own industrial structures to accommodate a new global division of labor.

Transactions with the United States dominate North-South economic relations.[1] Whether in terms of commercial ties—goods and services trade, foreign investment, technology transfer—or concessional loans and grants, the sheer size of the U.S. economy means that Southern transactions with the United States are often larger in absolute magnitude than those with all other Northern nations combined. Likewise, the United States is by far the largest financial supporter of the multilateral agencies that channel resources to Southern nations and has a major voice in determining the policies of those institutions.[2] A natural consequence is that the United States is usually the focus of Southern discontent with the individual and collective roles of developing nations in the world economy.

Rachel McCulloch is Professor of Economics at the University of Wisconsin, Madison.

FROM "NORTH-SOUTH DIALOGUE" TO "GLOBAL NEGOTIATIONS"

For a period during the 1970s, economic relations with the South were catapulted to the top of the U.S. policy agenda by the unprecedented actions of the Organization of Petroleum Exporting Countries (OPEC). Other primary commodity producers soon openly contemplated similar price-raising arrangements, and a worldwide commodity boom lent credence to their threats of "commodity power." In the United Nations and other international forums, the South engaged the North in a protracted and acrimonious "dialogue." Acting as a bloc, the Southern nations voiced their dissatisfaction with past progress, demanded redistribution of world wealth, and pressed for restructuring of the international economy to better meet the needs of poor countries.

The North-South dialogue of the 1970s has been supplanted by calls for United Nations-sponsored "global negotiations" on a similar set of proposals, but the economic and political climate is now vastly different. Commodity power no longer appears to pose an imminent threat, and the issues raised by Southern nations have been pushed aside by concerns more urgent to U.S. policymakers—persistent inflation and unemployment at home and ominous political and military developments abroad. Even before the election of President Reagan the political consensus necessary to maintain U.S. commitments to international agencies was badly frayed, thanks to the perceived ineffectiveness of official development assistance—aid—in achieving either the humanitarian or strategic goals of the donors. In the eyes of many Americans, the billions of U.S. aid dollars spent over past decades did little but enrich Southern elites quick to denigrate capitalism and to accuse the United States of indifference to the plight of the world's poor.

Now the Reagan administration has announced a new U.S. policy on Southern economic problems. The new approach explicitly rejects massive transfer of resources from North to South as necessary or even desirable to promote development in poor nations. Reserving official development assistance for the "poorest of the poor" nations,[3] President Reagan has stressed the role of free markets in stimulating the growth of Southern nations through trade and private investment.

Reagan's critics at home and abroad have greeted with a mixture of horror and disbelief the president's call for greater Southern reliance on "the magic of the marketplace."[4] Implicit in the critics' response is that the proposed U.S. policy represents an important departure from past practice. Yet the Reagan formula may be less a change in the substance of U.S. policy than in its rhetoric. Past aid has played at best a minor role in economic development, while foreign investment and export orientation have been the typical concomitants of sustained per-capita income growth.[5] If the Reagan administration is actually prepared to carry through on its promise to facilitate market-guided development, the result may be to widen and deepen the one documented channel for "transferring" wealth to Southern nations.[6] But the willingness and, perhaps more important, the ability of the administration to create the conditions necessary for successful export-led economic development in the South cannot be taken for granted.

BEYOND THE NEW INTERNATIONAL ECONOMIC ORDER

The Southern rallying cry of the 1970s was "the New International Economic Order" (NIEO). The list of specific Southern demands associated with the establishment of the new order was long and subject to frequent revisions, but three basic themes emerged from the succession of stormy confrontations. The first of these was the demand for massive resource transfers—specifically, automatic, multilateral, and unconditional transfers—from North to South. Sometimes described in value-laden terms as reparations for past Northern exploitation, these transfers were seen as a direct and immediate measure to reduce the income gap between North and South. The second theme was a demand for increased Southern representation and power in the major institutions that set ground rules for international transactions. This new role was to ensure adequate representation of Southern interests in the international decision-making process and, equally important, to serve as a public affirmation of the equal status of Southern nations in the world economy. Finally, Southern demands called for broad preferential treatment of developing nations in their commercial transactions with the North. By virtue of their less-developed status, Southern nations argued that special and preferential treatment in trade, investment, and technology transfer was required to produce equitable outcomes.

In the North-South dialogue of the 1970s, the United States adopted a largely defensive but conciliatory stance.[7] U.S. negotiators typically worked to slow down or dilute changes demanded by the South, acceding explicitly or implicitly to the principles while minimizing their practical consequences. This foot-dragging approach meant that many Southern goals were achieved in some fashion, but almost always in a smaller and less effective manner than envisioned by their advocates.

The Reagan administration has chosen to break with past practice in a spectacular fashion.The abrupt change in U.S. policy toward Southern demands has been clearly visible in recent United Nations confrontations on issues ranging from infant formula to Law of the Sea, as well as in important noneconomic areas such as human rights and freedom of the press. In a series of public addresses, President Reagan and other

U.S. officials have outlined the administration's market-oriented approach to the problems of developing nations. The details of the Reagan formula remain to be supplied, but several important principles have already been laid down:

1. *Aid.* Conventional economic aid will be reserved only for the poorest nations.
2. *Lending.* Private capital flows to finance development will be encouraged. The World Bank and International Monetary Fund (IMF) will be urged to restore stringent conditionality in lending and to adopt practices that support rather than supplant private markets.
3. *Trade.* Export-led development will be promoted through expanded trade opportunities for Southern nations.

These principles are in obvious conflict with the tenets of the South's proposed NIEO. The Reagan formula is diametrically opposed to the Southern goal of automatic and unconditional multilateral transfers to developing nations. After a period of tactful lip service to the Southern quest for national sovereignty, the older notion that would-be recipients ought to shape their policies in accord with the values of aid donors is clearly reemerging. Furthermore, there is a strong suggestion of "workfare" on an international level in Reagan's appeal to Southern nations to take maximum advantage of trading opportunities.

Implicit in Reagan's signals to the World Bank and the IMF is that the expansion of the South's role in setting policies of these institutions has gone too far. However, the Reagan plan may leave room for some preferential treatment of developing nations, albeit with strict provisions for "graduation" of countries that have already achieved considerable progress. Special status has already been promised for the very poorest countries, and the administration is apparently willing to consider an expansion of the Generalized System of Preferences(GSP), under which developing nations gain preferential access to tariff-protected U.S. markets for their manufactured and semimanufactured exports.[8]

IMPLEMENTING THE REAGAN PLAN

Can the new approach be implemented? If it is implemented, can it succeed? Tightening up on aid and on the activities of the World Bank and IMF should be politically easy for Reagan to accomplish, with public sentiment and congressional votes solidly behind him. Indeed, the president has already been accused of political expediency in this area. Budgetary stringency has made cuts in official development assistance almost inevitable, so that Reagan's stand makes a virtue of necessity. Even leaders of other Northern nations, beset by domestic economic problems similar to those of the United States, may welcome an excuse to scale down their own commitments to the international agencies.[9]

The proposed cuts in U.S. aid may have only a minor impact on global development prospects, especially of the very poorest nations, whose poverty is trotted out regularly by Reagan's ideological and political foes. Past U.S. economic aid has gone mainly to serve the nation's strategic objectives, rather than to ameliorate the lot of the world's neediest inhabitants;[10] U.S. food aid has been motivated primarily by the needs of domestic agriculture. And, although the World Bank has accomplished much of value in its past activities, some officials there privately doubt that the poorest nations can usefully "absorb" even as much development aid as they are already receiving, while the more advanced developing countries will be able to finance needed investments from private sources. In any case, past development assistance in the form of loans at highly subsidized interest rates may have distorted Southern investment patterns, providing labor-abundant poor nations with perverse incentives to adopt the newest capital-intensive technologies.[11]

Encouragement of private capital flows to the South should also present no important obstacles. The Overseas Private Investment Agency, an official U.S. agency that guarantees U.S. private investments abroad, has already emerged from obscurity to aid in this function, and the Reagan administration is talking about a similar agency on an international level to insure against risks incurred by private Northern investors. However, provision of this type of insurance on a large scale may be complicated, politically and economically, and will surely require a sizable staff of bureaucrats to perform the task. The end result may be a less "private" form of investment than the president appears to envision.[12]

Furthermore, given the host of market "distortions" that impede the efficient functioning of Southern markets, old doubts remain as to whether private capital will necessarily flow to the regions and projects that are most desirable from the social standpoint.[13] In theory this problem is solved by the nonmarket process that currently performs most investment allocation in developing nations. However, when economic decision-making power is highly centralized and objectives lofty but vague, there is ample opportunity for error or corruption. In many developing nations this is the unfortunate rule rather than the exception.

PROSPECTS FOR NORTH-SOUTH TRADE

Expansion of North-South trade is central to the president's plan for harnessing market forces to promote development. Here lie the greatest potential benefits to Southern nations, but also—and not coincidentally—the most formidable obstacles to the Reagan approach. Few Southern countries would dispute the key role of exports in promoting economic development. However, the political feasibility of maintaining and even expanding Northern markets for the goods and services Southern nations can offer is far from obvious. The Northern nations, which together account for more than 80 percent of Southern export earnings, have been experiencing persistent domestic economic problems. In the current environment of low growth and high unemployment, protectionism is enjoying new respectability.

Some developing nations have already followed the route recommended by President Reagan and have achieved remarkable success in expanding both the volume and the range of their exports to Northern markets. The rapid growth of these imports, ranging from textiles and shoes to sophisticated electronic gear, has been an important factor in the sectoral adjustment problems now affecting most Northern nations. Unwilling to take politically difficult steps to promote adjustment, the industrial nations have instead moved to protect their domestic industries with new trade barriers, especially nontariff barriers such as "voluntary" export restraints (VERs) and orderly marketing agreements (OMAs). These barriers are aimed particularly at labor-intensive manufactured goods, the chief area of comparative advantage for the developing countries, and at the most dynamic exporting nations.

Past Southern efforts to spur development through trade with the North have been concentrated in two areas: proposals to raise and stabilize the prices of primary exports and proposals to gain preferential access to Northern markets for manufactured exports under the Generalized System of Preferences(GSP). In the commodity area, little of substance has been achieved and the Reagan plan so far has nothing to offer.[14]

Southern efforts to gain preferential treatment of their manufactured exports have achieved some success; every Northern nation has enacted a version of the GSP. However, the consequences for North-South trade have been too small to satisfy the South, yet too large to escape the wrath of competing Northern producers. Despite the name, existing preferential arrangements are far from generalized and effectively exclude many of the goods in which Southern producers can claim a true comparative advantage, for example, textiles, apparel, and shoes. Furthermore, the most industrialized and wealthiest of the developing countries have gained considerably from the plan, while the GSP offers little, at least in absolute terms, to the truly poor nations. Import-competing producers in the United States have questioned the rationale of a scheme that provides benefits primarily to exporters such as Taiwan, Hong Kong, Korea, Mexico, and Brazil, countries whose ability to compete over a broad range of industrial activities is well established.

A politically attractive step for the Reagan administration would be to change the GSP rules to broaden product coverage for the poorest and least-developed nations and to terminate eligibility for relatively wealthy and established exporters. This would reserve preferential access for the countries that need help most, while protecting domestic producers from established competitors in the South. Under this arrangement, the middle-income nations, with per capita incomes still far below those of the North, would pay much of the price of continued protection for U.S. import-competing producers, with the remainder of the cost borne by consumers "protected" from low-cost imports.

TARGETED MOST-FAVORED-NATION TRADE LIBERALIZATION[15]

A less likely step, but one in keeping with President Reagan's avowed free-trade philosophy, would be to reduce trade barriers on a most-favored-nation (MFN), that is, nondiscriminatory, basis, concentrating on goods and services of greatest importance to Southern exporters. However, with their own producers eager to retain or even increase protection from imports, the United States and other Northern nations have been understandably slow to offer unilateral tariff cuts targeted to Southern exports.

Past reductions in trade barriers have been achieved primarily through rounds of multilateral trade negotiations under the General Agreement on Tariffs and Trade (GATT). Using a system of reciprocal bargaining, Northern nations have achieved major reductions in their average tariff levels. In the Tokyo Round that concluded in 1979 the negotiators also made a start toward setting rules to limit the use of nontariff barriers. But the GATT rounds have so far accomplished little to further the particular interests of exporters in developing countries. Even the Tokyo Round, which began with a pledge of special attention to the needs of developing countries, did little to address the most important problems facing developing country exporters, notably, the proliferation of Northern nontariff barriers aimed specifically at their fast-growing exports of manufactured goods.[16]

An important reason that GATT negotiations have failed to produce much improvement in Southern exporters' access to Northern markets is the passive role that most developing countries have played in past negotiations. In the GATT, developing countries are allowed to benefit from negotiated tariff reductions without making their own reciprocal concessions. As a result of this special status, Southern nations have made little attempt to exercise their substantial collective bargaining power as present and potential importers.[17] The active negotiators—especially the United States and the European Community—have quite naturally concentrated their efforts on the barriers of greatest importance to their own exporting industries. Yet a quid pro quo in the form of enhanced export possibilities for the Northern nations could go far toward shifting the internal political balance in the North on trade issues of interest to the South. And given the South's rapid growth rates, potentially important reciprocal concessions could in many cases be accommodated without displacing existing Southern production.

Multilateral trade negotiations along the lines of the Kennedy and Tokyo rounds may not be the most effective means of achieving targeted MFN liberalization of U.S. trade with Southern nations. An alternate approach would entail bilateral talks between the United States and Southern nations, individually or in groups. In such negotiations, the United States could offer increased access to the U.S. market for important developing country exports such as textiles, apparel, footwear, and other labor-intensive manufactures, while seeking an expanded Southern market for its own exports of capital goods, high-technology consumer goods, and agricultural products.[18] Services, which have received little attention in past negotiations, offer additional opportunities for mutually beneficial trade expansion.

Even with reciprocal concessions from Southern nations, a proposal to liberalize U.S. trade with developing nations will meet resistance in the Congress. Like other Northern nations, the United States has experienced persistent difficulty in adjusting to changes in international comparative advantage. The recent proliferation of U.S. trade barriers aimed specifically at products of developing nations and Japan is a good indication of lagging adjustment in many import-competing sectors. Trade liberalization along lines of comparative advantage would mean still more pressure on some Northern industries already in trouble. However, unlike other proposed policies to meet Southern needs, trade expansion does hold out, at least in the longer run, the potential for important mutual benefits. Expanded Southern markets for U.S. exports would draw resources into the nation's most productive sectors.

A LOOK AHEAD

Development in the South means new commercial opportunities for the United States, but also new competition. Rapid market-guided development can succeed only if the United States and other Northern nations are willing and able to adjust their own industrial structures to accommodate a new division of labor worldwide. Given the past record of sectoral adjustment problems in the North and the current depressed state of Northern economies, this will not be easily achieved. However, in contrast to most other programs advanced under the NIEO banner, successful market-oriented development could mean more rapid growth and productivity improvement worldwide, not just in the South. The political and economic obstacles are obvious, but so are the rewards.

NOTES

1. Following recent usage, "North" here denotes the industrialized market economies, located mainly in the Northern Hemisphere. Synonyms include rich nations or "haves." Likewise, the less-developed—or developing or poor—nations, located mainly in the Southern Hemisphere, are collectively designated the South, or Third World, or "have-nots."

2. Developing nations, international agencies, and other aid donors often down-play the absolute level of U.S. contributions by citing statistics for the ratio of aid to gross national product (GNP). This ratio is about 0.2 for the United States and over 0.7—the United Nations target for all Northern donors—for the Netherlands and the Scandinavian countries. See *World Development Report 1981* (Washington, DC: The World Bank, 1981), pp. 164–65. It is noteworthy in this connection that U.S. trade with the South, as a share of GNP, is larger than for most other industrial countries.

3. As defined by the World Bank, these are the 36 nations with per-capita incomes below $370.

4. This much-quoted phrase was used by President Reagan in his September 1981 speech opening the annual meeting of the World Bank and IMF.

5. However, direction of causation cannot always be inferred. Some nations with ample foreign investment and trade ties have nonetheless grown slowly or not at all.

6. Because market transactions rest on mutual benefits, it is more accurate to say that new wealth is thereby created, rather than existing wealth transferred.

7. The Algiers summit conference of "nonaligned" nations—mainly the same nations as the South, but excluding a few with strong U.S. military ties—marked the start of a two-year cycle of open North-South confrontation and escalation in the United Nations and elsewhere. Although the internal U.S. position on the NIEO issues softened gradually, the shift to a conciliatory official posture was denoted in Secretary of State Henry Kissinger's speech for the Seventh Special Session of the United Nations General Assembly in September 1975. For a detailed evaluation of North-South negotiations during the 1970s, see Rachel McCulloch, "North-South Economic and Political Relations: How Much Change?" *Carnegie-Rochester Conference Services on Public Policy*, 10:253–82 (1979).

8. On the history and mechanics of the GSP, see Tracy Murray, *Trade Preferences for Developing Countries* (London: Macmillan, 1977).

9. *The Wall Street Journal*, 13 Oct. 1981, p. 30.

10. In 1980, more than one-third of total U.S. bilateral economic assistance went to Israel, Egypt, and Turkey, all middle-income countries by World Bank standards. In 1981, aggression from Libya suddenly boosted the U.S. aid prospects of Sudan, whose $370 per-capita income puts the country just within the World Bank's low-income category.

11. The incentives may not be perverse, however, from the viewpoint of Northern exporters eager to provide the required capital equipment, construction services, and technical assistance.

12. A true supporter of free enterprise might ask why private markets have failed to provide the required insurance.

13. See, for example, G. K. Helleiner, "World Market Imperfections and the Developing Countries," in *Policy Alternatives for a New International Economic Order*, ed. William R. Cline (New York: Praeger, 1979), pp. 357–89. A frequently expressed reservation concerning the adequacy of private capital flows as a means of promoting development concerns needed investments in infrastructure. Although private investors often provide some infrastructure to make their own projects feasible, a pure market approach would lead to systematic underinvestment in social overhead capital.

14. On Southern proposals for commodities trade, see McCulloch, "North-South Economic and Political Relations," pp. 266–69.

15. The feasibility of MFN trade liberalization targeted to Southern exporters is discussed in detail in Rachel McCulloch,"Gains to Latin America from Trade Liberalization

in Developed and Developing Nations," in Werner Baer and Malcolm Gillis, eds., *Export Diversification and the New Protectionism* (Champaign: National Bureau of Economic Research and University of Illinois, 1981), pp. 231–57.

16. On the implications of the Tokyo Round for developing countries, see Rachel McCulloch, "The Tokyo Round and the Future of the GATT," *Portfolio* (forthcoming).

17. For both the United States and the European Community, the South has become the largest and fastest-growing export market.

18. Bilateral U.S. trade negotiations with developing nations are proposed in Robert Baldwin, "Some Aspects of Multilateral Trade Negotiations" (Paper prepared for the National Science Foundation Workshop on the Politics and Economics of Protection, Spring Hill Conference Center, Minneapolis, 29–30 Oct. 1981.

31. International Markets for LDCs—The Old and the New

CARLOS F. DIAZ-ALEJANDRO

Within even the narrowest purview of the most abstract model of competitive economy, efficiency requires public actions to deal with externalities, public goods, pervasive economies of scale, and incentives to destroy competition.*

Who is responsible for such public actions in international transactions and markets? Who enforces contracts and settles disputes over property rights in the international area?

Throughout history, powerful nations have tried to create international economic systems according to their own tastes and in harmony with their own interests. If the leaders of such great nations have thought about the subject at all, they have had no great difficulty in persuading themselves that the systems they were promoting also served the interests, if not the tastes, of the rest of mankind. In the past few decades, one power that has been pressing hard for the creation of an international system in its own image has been the United States.

The international economic system that prevailed roughly from the end of World War II until the beginning of the 1970's was characterized by the unprecedented prominence of international economic institutions

Carlos F. Diaz-Alejandro is Professor of Economics at Yale University.

* Edmar Bacha and Gerald K. Helleiner have been crucial partners in the preparation of this paper. Benjamin I. Cohen, Jorge Braga de Macedo, Gustav Ranis, Louka Papaefstratiou, and Ernesto Zedillo made helpful comments on an earlier draft.

and by a strong dose of hegemonial leadership by the United States, which not only placed its unmistakable stamp on international institutions but also enjoyed substantial leadership in the management of economic relationships.

But perhaps international economic relationships could be said to be characterized by a strong tendency toward competition, so that hegemonial leadership may be limited to a benign concern for enforcing contracts, correcting externalities and supplying public goods. The mid-ocean auctioneer and atomistic merchants could then fruitfully carry on their tasks.

The hypothesis that unorganized markets, with prices made by merchant intermediaries, had been the dominant market form throughout most of history may work fairly well, up until this century. But such markets surely have markedly declined. They have been largely replaced by fix-price markets, in which prices are set by the producers themselves (or by some authority); so they are not determined by supply and demand. It is of course granted that cost conditions, and sometimes also demand conditions, affect the prices that are fixed; but when these change, prices do not change automatically. Decisions, which are influenced by many other things than the simple demand-supply relationships, have to be made about them. That modern national and international markets are predominantly of the fix-price type hardly needs to be verified. It is verified by the most common observation.

Calls for a New International Economic Order (NIEO) have focused attention on the issues raised above, which can be summarized in the following questions: Who sets the rules of the game for international transactions and markets? Who has the power to initiate changes in such rules? Which international transactions are encouraged and which discouraged by the rules? How efficient and competitive are international markets?

The basic hypothesis is that the institutional framework within which international transactions take place has been historically rigged in favor of economic agents from the politically powerful countries, that is, on the whole rigged against economic agents from the less developed countries (LDCs). At least from a scholarly viewpoint, it is a virtue of the call for a NIEO that it tries to examine the nature of the whole system of international economic relations, besides raising more specific proposals for reform.

The debate over the NIEO has witnessed an unusual amount of sound and fury, including the cool fury of some economists who dismiss all LDC positions as the babbling of economic illiterates seized by a fit of passion. Particularly at the journalistic level, the picture is often drawn of an efficient, competitive, and liberal international order threatened by cartelizing or bureaucratizing pretensions of emotional, greedy, or ignorant LDC agents. This is why I have relied in this introductory section on extensive (hidden) quotes from the writings of four distinguished economists to state what I regard as the basic case for taking the call for a NIEO quite seriously, both at the academic and policy levels.[1]

What follows will discuss some of the *prima facie* in efficiencies and asymmetries of the international economic system, naturally stressing a few of special interest to LDCs. A modest pretension is to convince the reader to question the assumption that international markets and arrangements are as efficient, competitive and liberal as they can be. If such a view were accepted, a more fruitful dialogue between the North and the South could ensue.

I

It is a fair guess that to a Martian observer of our planet's economy, the most striking puzzle would be why a person growing cocoa in the tropics makes one-tenth of the wage a man making aluminum ingots in cooler regions. After all possible explanations are given for this phenomenon, the suspicion remains that the world's labor force is not allocated in a Pareto optimal fashion. Large disparities seem to persist between different parts of the world in the returns to unskilled labor, much larger than disparities in the returns to capital, or to skilled labor.

The Martian observer may be told that the postwar liberal international economic order has encouraged a tendency toward a narrowing of the unskilled wage differential by promoting freer trade in commodities as well as freer capital movements. Beautiful Hecksher-Ohlin-Samuelson diagrams will help the Martian understand how a freer movement of goods and capital work toward such a purpose. Indeed, it may be suggested that insofar as wage gaps persist between the tropics and the cool regions this could be due to foolish tropical barriers to commodity trade or to inflowing capital.

Being naive, our Martian may ask: Would it not be simpler to allow unskilled labor to move from where its marginal product appears low to where it seems to be high, thus making everybody potentially better off? After all, during the nineteenth century there were massive and persistent movements of unskilled white labor from Europe to "regions of recent settlement." A possible answer to this query is to tell the Martian that he is being impractical and that he should go back to where he came from. Alternative answers could express concern about an apparently unconquerable tropical incontinence, or to complications arising from the existence of public property.

Given the ingenuity of our profession, it is conceivable that models could be built in which gaps in wages between the tropics and cooler regions would be compatible with an optimal allocation of world resources. What is remarkable is how quietly our profession, otherwise so intolerant of bureaucratic limitations on the freedom of economic agents, accepts and takes for granted governmental barriers to the free flow of unskilled labor across artificial national boundaries. An economist working for the U.S. government, for example, may have to simultaneously argue for the desirability of nondiscriminatory or national treatment for U.S. direct foreign investment in Mexico, for the importance of freer emigration of skilled labor from Eastern Europe and for the necessity for the Mexican government to force its unskilled masses to stay on their side of the river. Matters may even be more complicated for that economist's professional conscience: he or she may have to urge Mexicans to export oil and gas but to go easy on their exports of steel. A comparison of the legislation and practice of industrial countries regarding immigration with that regulating their merchandise imports reveals that they mercantilistically prefer their commodity imports raw and their immigrants polished.

The relative prices and income distribution which would exist in a world of no interference with the free flow of unskilled labor are very likely to be different from those which were generated under the international economic system of the last thirty years. A plausible conjecture is that this counterfactual situation would have been more favorable to many economic agents in LDCs. Hence it is not surprising that some LDC spokesmen regard the international economic system as rigged against their interest, and tending to keep the value of tropical labor below that of cooler regions' labor. They may attempt using countervailing power to offset Northern monopsony power. Without *laissez-passer* for unskilled labor, the case for *laissez-faire* is weakened.

II

One group of economists believes that all prices quickly approach marginal social costs regardless of apparent impurities in real world markets, whether national or international, and in spite of public or private efforts to thwart what they regard as spontaneous economic forces. Another group prefers to take more seriously the apparent departures from the assumptions necessary for generating purely competitive results, and to explore the consequences of oligopoly, oligopsony, and quasi rents. Those in the first group, for example, regard the OPEC or the diamond and nickel cartels as transient phenomena, unimportant in the long run. Such departures from competition are doomed to failure, they argue, and presumably the quasi rents they capture in the short run will not influence significantly long-run values or the distribution of income and wealth. Economists of that persuasion will find little interest in what follows.

Just like the farmers and the miners from the Midwest and the West of the United States late in the last century, LDCs feel that the markets for what they sell and what they buy are manipulated by economic agents they do not control, and who tilt market results against them. The populist suspicions about middlemen, the railroads, the banks, and of remote concentrations of economic power in general, are echoed in the calls for a NIEO, which therefore may be said to be as much of a "cooperativism of the poor" as a "trade unionism of the poor." The same issues, of course, reappear within LDCs, between town and country, and between the informal and the organized sectors.

Crucial complexities in international markets for tropical products are far from fully captured by standard demand and supply schedules and assumptions about the instantaneous clearing of markets. Since the last century it has been observed that while production of those commodities was often in the hands of not far from atomistic LDC producers, the marketing, storing, grading, and processing was handled by non-LDC economic agents of nonatomistic dimensions with privileged access to credit, and who carefully controlled market information. For example, in 1888 the association of Cuban sugar producers had to set up a system of daily telegraphic reports from New York and London to learn not only the commodity prices, but to receive estimates of Cuban sugar production. It is said that all such information was controlled by the Willett and Gray firm, a member of the U.S. sugar trust, was sent by Western Union, and was distributed in Cuba by the Associated Press.[2] More recently, the U.S. Justice Department has alleged that the New York Coffee and Sugar Exchange, Inc., which many thought a reasonable example of an auction or flexprice market, and various coconspirators were artificially influencing sugar prices, while an E.E.C. commissioner charged that a few companies had indulged in "grave and scandalous speculation" in sugar markets.[3] One may entertain a reasonable doubt as to whether it is correct to interpret LDC efforts to extend an international sugar agreement as nothing more than the replacement of efficient competitive markets by a cartel run by UNCTAD bureaucrats. One may also add that sugar is a product for which the presumed concern of the cooler countries for a rational allocation of resources, free from artificial distortions, shines not too brightly in historical perspective. More generally, with agricultural sectors in industrialized countries so plagued with departures from *laissez-faire*, one marvels at their fervent advocacy of *laissez-faire* in international agricultural markets.

In the case of LDC mineral exports, production as well as marketing and processing has been controlled by non-LDC economic agents, of a size only the hopelessly myopic could call atomistic. Vertically integrated, transnational corporations internalized most markets between mines and the consumer of finished products, leaving the auctioneer in mid-ocean to amuse himself with thin, residual and unstable markets. It is bizarre to hear warnings of how Jamaica is cartelizing the bauxite market from economists who hardly mention the organization of the aluminum industry nor the ghostly nature of "the bauxite market," more the creation of aluminum company accountants than the domain of auctioneers.

It may be useful to conceptualize many historical international mineral markets as having been organized by a few transnational corporations, which ran species of commodity stabilization schemes, where unexpected changes in economic conditions were reflected not on price movements but first of all in changes in the levels of the buffer stocks controlled by those corporations and/or in changes in the speed with which different types of customers were serviced. Besides subtle "customers' relationships" those corporations have maintained links with governments, particularly those of parent and host countries. Corporate central planning boards decided on investment projects on the basis of long-term forecasts, rather than just on the basis of present market conditions (futures' markets were also internalized). It can be argued that such arrangements were often economically superior to anything the mid-ocean auctioneer and a mob of atomistic economic agents could have wrought. This may be so, but to analyze such situations standard demand and supply schedules provide limited insights.

The blunt fact is that scientific knowledge about the operation of international commodity markets is very scanty. The hypotheses that these markets function as if they were competitive and with desirable properties such as informational efficiency have been seldom put to rigorous test. Sheer repetition of hypotheses should not be confused with established fact, and helps little when making the difficult choice between imperfect buffer stock arrangements and imperfect unregulated markets.

III

It may be a good thing that there are economists with whom one has to argue at some length the thesis that international markets are far from competitive, that the international economy has room for improving both its efficiency and its equity, and that political power can be translated into favorable rules of the game and the privilege of initiating changes in those rules. Space allows only a few more examples of such propositions, which many will find bland.

The macroeconomic management of the capitalist world economy has been in the hands of representatives of a few industrialized countries. Other nations, particularly the LDCs, have been forced to be passive spectators, even though world economic conditions can influence their welfare significantly. The record of the macroeconomic managers over the last few years is not a spectacular one. The massive unemployment and idle capacity of the industrialized countries are not just monumental wastes in themselves, but by directly and indirectly discouraging international specialization they also impose waste on the rest of the world. Surely issues such as the smooth servicing of LDC debt cannot be discussed in isolation from those of world macroeconomic management and outbreaks of protectionism in industrialized countries. At least some LDCs must increasingly participate in world macroeconomic management.

Advocates of the flexibility and resourcefulness of a decentralized international market can point with pride to the mushrooming of international private lending to LDCs over the last ten years or so. But a curious thing seems to be happening here. Orthodox voices are being increasingly heard arguing that this stronghold of *laissez-faire* is in need of regulation. International lenders, it appears, compete too much and a paternalistic International Monetary Fund may be needed to insure "orderliness" in that market. A credit cartel to such orthodox observers may be required to correct market failures (of an unspecified sort); the same observers would undoubtedly scorn proposals to regulate direct foreign investment by transnational enterprises. Finally, it may be interesting trying to explain to a Martian observer of the world economy the rationale for the continuing U.S. trade embargo against countries such as Cuba and Vietnam.

However it is time to turn to an obvious question: Is it that the NIEO seeks the establishment of international markets resembling those of a neoclassical textbook? The answer, of course, is no. Several of the LDCs which have spearheaded the drive for a NIEO, and the public and private economic agents behind that drive may best be conceptualized as new oligopolists, trying to break into world markets dominated by old oligopolists. The new oligopolists want to exercise a greater share of market power, whether in the markets for their raw material and primary product exports, or in those for their new manufactured exports, or in those for their imports of machinery and technology. The new oligopolists will set up their own transnational corporations for this purpose, or will try to manipulate existing ones. The incentive is not just a cut in declared oligopolistic profits and rents, but also a share in the "perks" attached to control of hierarchical bureaucratic organizations, which under standard accounting conventions are recorded as business costs.

While this may not be their intention, the eruption of new oligopolists into world markets could in fact lead directly and indirectly to greater competition and a closer approximation to textbook ideals, at least in some markets, and for a while (for example, copper). Populist agitation, economic historians remind us, helped to bring about antitrust legislation, a more rational control over money in the United States and contributed to ambiguous forms of contervailing power and to regulations stabilizing oligopolistic market situations. In short, the call for a NIEO may be interpreted partly as a call for adjusting to "two, three, more Japans" within the world capitalist economy. The LDCs such as Algeria, Brazil, and the Philippines, with a growing industrial might and high capacities to absorb capital and technology, are interested neither in wrecking international markets nor in shutting themselves off from them; they seek first to gain a greater share of the action in those markets, and then to participate in "organizing" trade in them. Wise old oligopolists will understand such motivation, even as their anxieties increase over their possible loss of industrial and technical hegemony.

Where does that leave the poorest LDCs, or the poorest groups within most LDCs? One should not rule out the possibilities that in some cases those groups may benefit from the NIEO. The new oligopolists need political legitimation and votes at the United Nations. A given policy proposal can benefit countries with very different social systems, leading to startling alliances, such as the close Brazilian-Cuban cooperation in the negotiations for an international sugar agreement. But even a total acceptance of NIEO proposals, taken by itself, is unlikely to significantly improve in the short run the welfare of the poorest half of LDC families, nor to significantly worsen, one may add, the welfare of the poorest families in the North. While the economist should be skeptical of claims by some of the new would-be oligopolists to represent and work for the poor, he or she should also not take as self-evident the pretension of old oligopolists to be helpless minions of The Market Force, nor the embodiment of The National Interest.

During the last one hundred years latecomers to industrialization, such as Germany, Italy, and Japan, were not smoothly integrated into the world economy. Even today, deep suspicions remain in Europe and the United States as to whether Japan plays fair, a suspicion which is no doubt reciprocated. For the sake of world peace one hopes that the process of adjusting to late-late-comers will be less painful.

NOTES

1. The first paragraph has been lifted directly from Arthur M. Okun, p. 32. The third paragraph is also lifted completely from Raymond Vernon, p. 12. The fourth paragraph paraphrases Marina v.N. Whitman, p. 7. The sixth paragraph also paraphrases John R. Hicks, pp. x–xi. I beg the indulgence of these authors, especially of the last two.
2. See Manuel Moreno-Fraginals, p. 20.
3. See the *Wall Street Journal*, p. 2; and *The (London) Economist*, p. 66.

REFERENCES

John R. Hicks, *Economic Perspectives; Further Essays on Money and Growth,* Oxford 1977.

M. Moreno-Fraginals, "Cuban-American Relations and the Sugar Trade," mimeo., Oct. 1977.

A. M. Okun, "Further Thoughts on Equality and Efficiency," in Colin D. Campbell, ed., *Income Redistribution,* Washington 1977.

Raymond Vernon, *Storm Over the Multinationals; The Real Issues,* Cambridge, Mass. 1977.

M. v.N.Whitman, "Sustaining the International Economic System: Issues for U.S. Policy," in *Princeton Essays in International Finance,* No. 121, June 1977.

The (London) Economist, Sept. 24, 1977.

Wall Street Journal, Oct. 18, 1977.

32. Approaches to a New International Economic Order

PAUL STREETEN

1. THE LAG OF INSTITUTIONS BEHIND TECHNOLOGY

I should like to make a few suggestions as to how to construct a basis for more imaginative and constructive responses to the call for a New International Economic Order (NIEO) than those that have been forthcoming in the past. I regard the main problem as a lag between appropriate global institutions and the evolution of the global reality. As Frances Stewart points out in her paper, 'Framework for international financial cooperation', an efficient world order depends on the co-ordination of three or four functions: first, the generation of balance-of-payments surpluses; second, the existence of financial institutions to invest these surpluses in developing countries; third, the existence of industries that produce and sell capital goods needed for development, on which the money is spent; and fourth, the military power to back the economic power derived from the previous three functions. Until

Paul Streeten is Director of the World Development Institute and Professor of Economics at Boston University.

about 1970 these four functions had been combined and co-ordinated in one dominant country. Until 1914 this country was Great Britain, which imposed upon the world the *Pax Britannica.* After the Second World War, for a quarter of a century, it was the USA which imposed the *Pax Americana.* But since 1970 the functions have been fragmented and dispersed. The single dominant power has been replaced by a pluralism without co-ordination. The surpluses in the balance of payments are generated by a handful of capital surplus OPEC countries, and occasionally by Germany and Japan. The financial institutions are still largely in London and New York, but increasingly also in Hong Kong, Singapore and Beirut. The industries supplying capital goods at competitive prices are in some OECD countries, such as Germany and Japan. And military power in some cases seems to weaken economic power. The USA and the Soviet Union, while militarily strong, have suffered economically from the high level of their arms expenditure, while Germany and Japan have profited from low levels of defence spending. The new task consists in creating institutions that co-ordinate the four functions so that the financial surpluses of the OPEC countries, the productive capacity of the OECD countries and the under utilized labour surpluses of the developing countries can be brought together for the purpose of development, instead of lying idle and provoking mutually destructive responses.

We hear nowadays a good deal about interdependence, one world and the emerging global village. The international dissemination of cultural influences has increased enormously. Its ultimate cause is the advance of technologies in transport and electronic communications and the growing urbanization. Popular songs, styles in dress and hair styles, attitudes to divorce, abortion, homosexuality, drugs, even crimes, are spreading rapidly across the globe. While in previous ages the common culture was confined to a thin layer of the upper class, today it has reached the mass culture in many countries. In the huge underdeveloped regions of the South, however, the masses of people live in extreme poverty and cultural isolation, though a small upper class has become part of the international culture. Even among the élite, there are now moves to assert indigenous cultural values and to establish national and ethnic identities. It is partly a reaction against the rapid spread of the mass culture of the West.

International relations have grown not only in the cultural but also in the economic sphere. This growth is usually measured by the rapid growth of world trade in the last two or three decades, a growth that was substantially faster than the growth of GNP, so that the ratio of exports to GNP has also grown. World trade has increased from over $100 billion in 1960 to over $1 trillion in 1977, and the ratio of exports to GNP has risen from 13.7% in 1960 to 21.8% in 1976.

Taking a longer historical perspective, the ratio of trade to GNP for the main industrial countries is not much higher now than it was in 1913.[1] But there has been a large increase in the trade share of the private sector. The aggregate ratio conceals this because of the large increase in the public sector and the relative rise in prices of those services that are not internationally traded.

It is useful to draw a distinction between integration and interdependence.[2] International integration was probably greater in the 19th century, when national governments adhered to the gold standard, fixed exchange rates, and balanced budgets, than today, when domestic policy has set up targets for employment, growth, price stability, income distribution, and regional policy, among other objectives, while at the same time rejecting the constraints which integrated the world internationally.[3] Greater economic interdependence consists in greater international mobility and substitutability of goods, services and capital, and greater mobility across frontiers of management and technology.

But in trade, as in culture, the poorest countries did not share in this expansion. The share of the low-income countries, excluding the petroleum-exporting countries, fell from 3.6% in 1960 to 2.2% in 1970, and to 1.5% in 1977. Of the total exports of the industrial countries 17.3% went to the non-oil-exporting developing countries in 1970, but only 15.8% in 1977.[4] The notion that we have become one interdependent world has, therefore, to be qualified in at least three respects. First, much of the growth of trade is a return to the pre-1914 situation which had been disrupted by two world wars and a severe depression. Second, the poorest countries and the poorest people have been left out of this growing cultural and trade interdependence (though they are dependent on aid flows). A third aspect in which it has to be qualified is discussed later on p. 511. It refers to the importance of the trade volumes and the losses that would be suffered if the trade were eliminated. The importance is illustrated by a thought experiment suggested by Sir Arthur Lewis: how much would one group of countries, developing or developed, lose, if the other group were to sink under the sea?

While cultural dissemination and economic interdependence between countries have grown, international co-operation between governments has lagged and in some cases grossly failed. The gap of our times is not so much, as is often said, that between science and morality, as that between our soaring technological imagination and our inert institutional imagination. While our scientific and technological imagination has leaped ahead, putting man on the moon, deciphering the genetic code, discovering new subatomic worlds, and probing the recesses of inner space, and the farthest reaches of outer space, our institutional and social imagination has lagged inertly behind. The most flagrant failure of international co-operation is the arms race and the $450 billion annually devoted to military expenditures, which has increased violence in the world.

International co-operation for meeting the impending energy crisis has also failed. There is a need for a global energy programme for conservation and exploration of alternative sources of energy.

National policies to fight the evils of pollution have been successfully designed, but the solution of problems of global pollution (like that of the oceans or air across national boundaries) have been much less effective. The same is true of policies to prevent excessive depletion of non-renewable resources.

There has been almost no international co-operation in fighting the world-wide crisis of unemployment, accompanied by inflation and sagging growth. National policies are being pursued in isolation, the balance-of-payments surpluses of a few countries are kicked around from country to country, Japan and Germany are exporting their unemployment, and what each country does often increases the difficulties of others. There is no exchange of information on investment plans, hence we lurch from excess capacity to shortages in steel, fertilizers and shipbuilding.

International co-operation for development—our main concern here—has also lagged behind the challenge to eradicate world poverty. Insufficient attention has been paid by analysts to this discordance between the (partial) success of interdependence and our failure to co-operate and use it for our joint benefits.

The failure in co-operation has been accompanied by a growth of intergovernmental organizations, forums and conferences charged with tackling these issues. The call for the exercise of our institutional imagination must not be confused with its opposite: the growth of bureaucracies that oppose new ideas and only spawn obstructionist bureaucrats. Even though practical solutions are proposed, the resistance, often on some minor point, by one or two governments, prevents joint action. This resistance to global action on the part of governments is in stark contrast to the successful co-ordination of international action by big business—by the transnational corporations and by the banks in the Eurocurrency market. We have the framework for intergovernmental action, but it is largely unused.

There are two opposite forces at work. National integration has contributed to international disintegration. The rejection of the gold standard, of fixed exchange rates, and of balanced budgets has liberated national policy to pursue a growing range of national objectives, but has contributed to international disintegration. The rejection of irrational constraints by each state has produced world-wide irrationality. At the same time, the integration of the upper classes of developing countries into the international system has contributed to national dualism, national division and national disintegration in some developing countries. Hence the call for 'delinking' and the assertion of a national identity, based on indigenous values.

There are, however, some instances of successful intergovernmental co-operation, usually in specialized, technical fields: The Universal Postal Union (more than 100 years old), the International Telecommunication Union, the International Civil Aviation Organization and the World Meteorological Organization are examples of outstanding successes in international co-operation. The World Health Organization and UNICEF have also been successful. Stressing the technical, non-political aspects of co-operation helps to prevent issues from becoming politicized. Functional solutions at the global level work. I shall return to this theme and the lessons to be learned at the end of this paper.

2. ORIGINS OF THE CALL FOR AN NIEO

The developing countries' call for an NIEO has many diverse sources, some going far back in history. At the root of this call lies the dissatisfaction with the old order which, it is felt, contains systematic biases perpetuating inequalities in power, wealth and incomes and impeding the development efforts of the developing countries. Three recent phenomena can be singled out that gave the demand for an NIEO special impetus: the disappointment with aid, the disappointment with political independence, and the success of OPEC.

Development aid, on which so many hopes had been pinned in the 1950s and early 1960s after a vigorous beginning, partly inspired by the Cold War, was regarded as inadequate in amount and poor in quality. A target for official development assistance to the developing countries of 0.7% of the gross national product of the developed countries had been set up. But the net official development assistance given by the DAC members fell from 0.42 in 1964–1966 to 0.35 in 1978. Intergovernmental aid negotiations led to pressures, frictions and acrimony. Although it was correctly seen that for aid contributions to be effective a country's whole development programme had to be scrutinized, developing countries found it intolerable that donors who contributed only 1–2% of the national income of the recipients should meddle in their economic and political affairs. Performance criteria and political, as well as economic, strings produced tensions and recriminations, which led to a plea for a 'quiet style in aid'. By this was meant a transfer of resources that would be automatic or semi-automatic, hidden, or at least unconditional. The inefficiencies and inequities (as a result of the capricious impact) of commodity agreements, trade preferences, debt relief, SDR links etc., were regarded as a price worth paying for a hoped-for larger volume of transfers and a defusing of diplomatic tensions.

The second source of the call for the automatic, concealed, unconditional transfers of the NIEO is the disappointment with political independence that has not produced the hoped-for economic independence. True, most Latin American countries have been independent for a long time, but it is precisely from there that the doctrine of *dependencia* has emerged. It explains the demand for 'sovereignty over resources' and the hostility to some features of the transnational corporations and, more generally, to the international rules of the game as they had evolved after the war.

The third cause is the success of OPEC (and a few other mineral exporters), which appeared to offer an alternative to the appeal to the conscience of the rich. This success was accompanied by a change to a sellers' market and to world shortages of food and raw materials. These events encouraged developing countries to explore the scope for similar actions on other fronts, to emphasize joint bargaining, the use of 'commodity power', and the exercise of power in other areas, such as the treatment of transnationals.

3. INTERPRETATIONS OF THE NIEO

The NIEO means different things to different people. Under its banner, a great variety of interpretations have been gathered. Three distinctions are useful in clarifying some of the ambiguities.

Some have interpreted the NIEO as a demand for exemptions from established rules. Non-reciprocal preferences for manufactured exports, debt relief, more concessionary aid fall under this heading. Others have interpreted the NIEO as a radical change in the rules.

A second distinction is between those who seek a few more concessions from the developed countries, more aid, more trade preferences, contributions to commodity agreements, better access to capital markets, cheaper technology transfer, debt relief etc., and those who want fundamental structural change, in the form of new institutions and a shift in power relations.

A third distinction is that between those who interpret the NIEO as being essentially about rules and restraints, like those laid down at Bretton Woods and the GATT, whether the demand is for exemptions from old or for new rules, and those who interpret the restructuring to refer to the totality of economic, political and even cultural relations. This second interpretation sees in the post-colonial power structure the continuation of domination and dependence, caused not only by rules, procedures and institutions designed by the powerful, rich countries, but also by numerous other factors, such as the thrust of science and technology, the priorities in research and development, the cumulative nature of gains, the structure of markets, the influence emanating from the mass media, the educational systems and the values they impart etc.

The discussion about appropriate rules for international economic relations has suffered from a long-standing confusion. It is the confusion between *uniform* (sometimes also called *general*) principles or rules (the opposite of specific ones, and therefore necessarily simple) and *universal* principles or rules (which may be highly specific and complicated, provided that they contain no uneliminable reference to individual cases). Further confusion is caused if a third characteristic of rules is added: *inflexibility* over time, and confused with either uniform, i.e. simple, or universal, i.e. may have a lot of 'exceptions' written into it. The 'equal' treatment of unequals is not a principle of justice, and a general rule commanding it is an unjust rule. In order to prevent partiality and partisanship, rules have to be universal, i.e. not contain references to individual cases. They may, and indeed should not be uniform. They should pay attention to the varying characteristics and circumstances of different countries.

Those who charge the developing countries with asking for exemptions from rules are guilty of this confusion between *uniform* and *universal* rules. Thus a differentiated system of multi-tier preferences according to the level of development of the exporting countries, may be best and most just for a group of trading countries at different stages of development. A fair system of rules also points to the differentiation in responsibilities and rights according to circumstances. Middle-income countries would not have the responsibility to give aid, but neither would they receive it. They would not have to give trade preferences, but neither would they receive them. Even finer differentiation would be possible. A country like Saudi Arabia might be asked to contribute to loans because of its foreign exchange earnings, and to aid because of its income per head, but might receive trade preferences, because of its low level of industrialization. The 0.7% aid target would be replaced by a system in which those below a certain income per head are exempted, and the percentage target rises with income per head.

There is, of course, a practical and tactical case for *simple* rules which might overrule the case in fairness for universal (though complex) rules: they are less open to abuse and easier to police. And there may be a tactical case for uniform rules: they may be easier to negotiate. It is for such pragmatic reasons rather than on theoretical grounds that one may advocate that rules should not be too complex, and should not be changed too often.[5]

Any specific proposals, like non-reciprocity in trade concessions, or trade preferences would, of course, have to be examined on their merits. But the distinction between 'exemption from rules' and 'drawing up new rules' is logically untenable, to the extent to which the call for exemption is really a call for a set of *universal* rules that pays attention to the different characteristics and circumstances of different countries, just as income tax allowances for dependants or lower rates on earned than on unearned income, are not 'exceptions' but reflect our notions of fairness.

Those who are concerned with changing the rules of international relations are aiming partly at removing biases in the present rules, partly at the exercise of countervailing power where at present the distribution of power is felt to be unequal, and partly at counteracting biases that arise not from rules but from the nature of economic processes, such as the cumulative nature of gains accruing to those who already have more resources, and the cumulative damage inflicted on those who have initially relatively little (polarization or backwash effects).

In so far as the NIEO is about strictly economic relations, there is scope for positive-sum games. But in so far as it is about national power relations between sovereign states with different aims, power is by its very nature a *relative* concept, and what is at stake are zero-sum games. Greater participation in the councils of the world and corrections in the biases of the international power distribution are bound to diminish the power of the industrialized countries.

It is part of the weakness of the poor countries and of the syndrome of underdevelopment that they have not succeeded in articulating these pleas altogether convincingly. An unsympathetic approach can always find faults and criticize specific proposals and the manner in which they are presented. A more imaginative approach would attempt to understand the underlying grievances, even though often badly expressed and poorly translated into concrete proposals. An entirely adequate approach would require a well-staffed, highly qualified secretariat of the Third World, which would muster the evidence, prepare the case for international negotiations, and propose feasible reforms, worked out in detail.

4. HETEROGENEITY OR HOMOGENEITY OF THE THIRD WORLD?

The NIEO has been acclaimed by *all* developing countries, but the diversity of their interests is reflected in the long list of the UNCTAD Agenda, by the strains caused by specific proposals, such as debt relief, by the inconsistency of some of the targets, and by the OPEC oil price rise. Concern with reforming the international system has, at least in the rhetoric, been closely linked with concern for the world's poor. But the poor are largely in what is sometimes called the Fourth World: South Asia, sub-Saharan Africa and a few islands. Their need is mainly for additional financial and technical assistance. The more advanced countries of the Third World need better access to capital markets, to markets for their manufactured exports and to modern technology.

The cohesion between these two groups of countries has been maintained largely because OPEC has used its petropower to press for other reforms on the agenda, such as the inclusion of non-energy issues in the Paris Conference on International Economic Co-operation (CIEC), initially intended to be devoted solely to energy. It has succeeded in the liberalization of IMF credits, and the liberalization of the compensatory finance facility. OPEC has also given substantial aid.

The cohesion of the Third World may also be threatened by the formation of North–South blocs: Europe forging special ties with Africa through Lomé, Japan (and Australia and New Zealand) with East Asia through ASEAN, and some non-oil Arab countries with the Arab members of OPEC. It would not be surprising if, in default of global progress, developing countries were to attempt to strike bargains with specific developed countries, or groups of them. Some of the weaker and poorer countries are bound to suffer, inequalities to be increased, and the cry of neocolonialism to be raised again. Such fragmentation of the world into regional blocs is not in the interest of development or of the developed countries.

In spite of heterogeneity and diversity of interests, there are strong common interests in the Third World, which can provide a basis for collective action. These countries are, by and large, poorer than the developed countries (the existence of borderline cases with small populations does not destroy the distinction), many have been colonies and they benefit and suffer from the impulses propagated by the advanced, industrial countries in similar ways.[6]

In answering the question whether homogeneity or heterogeneity is stronger among the countries of the so-called Third World, we would have to begin by listing criteria for a typology of countries, relevant to the dimensions of what might constitute the 'Third World'. These might include income per head, growth rates, inflation rates, indicators of economic structure (such as proportion of the labour force in agriculture, trade ratios), human and social indicators (life expectancy, infant mortality, literacy), water supply, indicators of inequality, population growth, indicators of dependence such as concentration of exports by commodities and by destination, statistics of brain drain, political indicators etc. If we find that on the whole the same countries cluster round each end of these scales, the division will be found to make sense. If, on the other hand, groupings cut across the conventional North–South division, we may have to revise our typology and the notion of a homogeneous 'Third World'.

But it may be both tactically wiser and in the service of truth to acknowledge that many problems of the developing countries are not just the problems of a block, but are common to us all: there are rich and poor among the OECD countries, there are relations of dominance and dependence between developed countries, and even between regions within one country, there are biases and imperfections in the system of international relations that discriminate against members of the First World and there are important interest alignments that cut across national frontiers. On the other hand, many of the objectionable features of the relations between the industrial and the developing countries are replicated in those among the stronger and weaker developing countries. If 'delinking' of the Third World were to become a reality, much the same phenomena would arise in the relations between Brazil and Bolivia as now arise in the relations between the USA and Latin America as a whole.

Moreover, there is another danger for the fate of the poor within what has been called the 'trade union of the Third World'. This danger is that, as in the original trade union movement, the benefits from joint action may be reaped by the stronger members, who wield the power, and the weakest and poorest get left out.

For reasons such as these, emphasis on the homogeneity of the Third World may be both mistaken and misguided, and an appeal to universal principles and globally shared problems may be wiser.

5. CRITICISMS OF THE NIEO

There has been no shortage of criticisms of the proposals under the NIEO. Very often these have taken the form of evaluations by professional economists, in the light of the objectives of efficiency and equity commonly accepted in the profession. Yet, a proper evaluation ought to start from the objectives of the developing countries themselves (or specified groups within them), and distinguish between criticisms of the objectives and criticisms of the proposed means of achieving these objectives. There is also the danger that we may impute objectives to the developing countries that they do not share with us. One difficulty is that in the discussions ends and means have been confused, so that greater self-reliance, larger shares in income, wealth or power, larger shares in industrial production or trade, earnings stabilization, price stabilization of particular commodities, and price stabilization of all exported commodities, have been debated at the same level. An appraisal of the NIEO is likely to come to different conclusions according to whose objectives are chosen, according to the degree of generality at which the instruments for these objectives are discussed, and according to whether we are discussing ends or the appropriateness of instruments.

Another source of confusion is the fact that criticisms often compare the proposals with some 'ideal' solution, when in fact they should be compared with the most likely alternative. Thus, transfers through commodity agreements may, by some criteria, be thought to be worse than direct transfers through unconditional, untied, grants, which can be related to the needs of the recipients and the capacity to pay of the donors. SDR creation that should be guided by the world's liquidity requirements should, ideally, be separated from increases in development aid, not fused together in a 'link' etc. But the NIEO proposals have to be seen in the context of a world which is not 'ideal' but very imperfect. The alternative to doing things badly is often not doing them at all.

Another question is whether NIEO proposals should be assessed individually or collectively. It is possible to raise criticisms against each individual item on the Agenda, some of which at least would be answered by accepting certain packages. The Common Fund has been criticized for its inequitable impact on distribution between countries; debt relief, on the other hand, which benefits the poorest countries, has been criticized for its impact on capital markets, of concern mainly to middle-income countries. A package of the Common Fund, debt relief to the poorest and soft ODA might meet the needs of both middle- and low-income countries.

Criticisms have also been directed at the objectives and motivations of the NIEO. It has been easy to disprove the argument that reparations are due for the exploitation in the colonial era. But the disproval is irrelevant, because the case for progressive redistribution of income and wealth and for international contributions to poverty eradication does not depend on the infliction of past damage. Few believe that colonial rule was necessarily harmful, though it would be difficult to prove that it was necessarily beneficial. It should be plain that internal measures are crucial for both growth and domestic advance.

A more fundamental criticism of the NIEO has been along the following lines. Moral imperatives apply only to individuals, not to governments. If international transfers are to be justified on moral grounds, donors must ensure that the moral objectives are attained. This implies highly conditional, targeted transfers for basic human needs, poverty alleviation, reduction of unemployment etc. The proposals of the NIEO do not meet this condition, since the distribution of benefits between countries and within countries is capricious. Only strict control and monitoring by donor countries can insure that the target groups are reached.

The first point to be made in reply to this criticism is that in a complex, interdependent world institutions have to be used as vehicles for achieving moral objectives, even if it were agreed that only individuals are the appropriate ultimate targets of moral action. Up to a point, these institutions have to be trusted to concern themselves with the intended beneficiaries. The risk of some leakage has to be accepted. Family allowances intended to benefit children are paid to mothers and fathers who might spend them on gambling and drink. Local governments receive grants, intended for their citizens, from central governments, or states and provinces in a federation from the federal government. It is therefore perfectly legitimate to apply moral rules to states, the necessary conduits for channelling funds to individuals in the world order as its exists. (That this principle is accepted even by the advocates of the view that only individuals are appropriate moral targets can be seen when these same advocates demand debt service from countries whose governments have changed since the debts were incurred, or when they demand that multinational companies should be treated as 'moral persons'.) Of course, funds accruing to governments through commodity agreements and debt relief can be spent on the wrong purposes and may benefit the rich in poor countries, but so may aid funds. The best method to make it probable that donor objectives of poverty alleviation are achieved is not to rule out institutional intermediaries, nor to attach strict performance criteria to all transfers and monitor meticulously expenditure, but to select governments committed to anti-poverty policies and support them. Such selection is, to some extent, consistent with the proposals of the NIEO.

But a dilemma remains. Developing countries insist on national sovereignty in the use of resources, while the supporters of larger transfers in the developed countries through official development assistance, the SDR link, debt relief, the integrated commodity programme or any other vehicle, stress the need for monitoring performance and internal reforms to benefit the poor. The resolution of this dilemma can be found in moves towards the 'global compact', or the 'planetary bargain' which Mr. McNamara, the Aspen Institute, Mahbub ul Haq and others have advocated. But as the positions of the North and South are defined at present, we are still some way from such a global compact. The North is not prepared to transfer the additional resources, the South is not prepared to give the necessary undertakings.

A final criticism of the call for an NIEO is that it is rigid, because relations between states and institutions needed to support them are constantly changing. But this is not a valid objection to constructive responses, because an order can incorporate rules and procedures for orderly change and adaptation to new circumstances.

It is unfortunate that the developing countries have chosen a set of ill-designed measures to translate worthy objectives into reality. Generalized debt relief (now dropped) and commodity schemes in so far as they are concerned with more than price stabilization, are regarded by many professional economists as inefficient and inadequate ways of achieving the objective of significant transfers of income, wealth and power, and of achieving a radical restructuring of the international system. In addition, the conflict over the demand by the developing countries for sovereignty over the use of resources, and by the developed countries for careful targeting and internal reforms, adds a serious obstacle in the way of reaching agreement. On the other hand, it is at least equally unfortunate that the developed countries have not responded more constructively and imaginatively to the pleas of the developing countries.

6. ALTERNATIVE RESPONSES BY THE THIRD WORLD TO THE CURRENT IMPASSE

The responses of the Third World to the current impasse in the dialogue can be discussed under the following headings:

(a) self-reliance, in the sense of doing desirable things for themselves and for each other, whether on the basis of an individual country, a group of countries or the Third World as a whole;
(b) exercise of joint bargaining power to counter biased income, wealth and power distributions;
(c) exploration of areas of common and mutual interests between the South and North;
(d) evolution of rules, procedures and institutions to avoid mutually damaging confrontations and conflict.

(a) Self-reliance: What Can the Developing Countries Do by and for Themselves?

This area overlaps with the subsequent two. Greater self-reliance will increase bargaining power and make it more likely that adjustments in imperfections and inequities will be brought about. If self-reliance raises incomes and purchasing power, it will give rise to new common interests. But self-reliance is not in need of these secondary justifications. In the longer term, most of the things developing countries need they can produce for themselves, and most of the things they can produce they themselves need.

Reduced dualism and a more poverty-oriented approach will tend to create greater intra-Third World trade opportunities. Various forms of joint multinational enterprises will give rise to opportunities of investment co-ordination. Monetary co-operation can encourage trade expansion, and growing trade, e.g. through Third World preferences, can be financed by intra-Third World financial co-operation, such as clearing or payments unions. Mutual aid and technical assistance in rural development, family planning, technology, is often more effective between countries that are not at too dissimilar levels of development than when inappropriate methods are transferred from highly advanced countries. Joint activities could be developed in professional associations, in research, in the exchange of information, in education and training, in transport and communications, in food and energy policy. In these ways, the developing countries could make themselves less dependent on concessions from the rich countries and, at the same time, evolve their own styles of development.

Such a strategy calls for new types of institutions. A strong Third World secretariat, with a first-class staff and Third World loyalties has been proposed. Institutions in other fields, like a bank capable of creating monetary assets for Third World trade, or a board co-ordinating investment decisions, or a community of developing country governments monitoring each other's basic needs policies,[7] are possibilities.

(b) Exercise of Joint Bargaining Power

In addition to such actions of self-reliance, the developing countries could use joint action in certain spheres to strengthen their power in bargaining with the developed countries. The debate over the course of the terms of trade has been shunted onto the wrong track, by disputing the question as to whether they had deteriorated historically. The relevant question is not what are the terms of trade compared with what they were, but what are they compared with what they should and could be. Producers' associations in some instances might take the place of commodity agreements on which consuming countries are represented. The fact that current price rises might speed up the process of inventing substitutes is not necessarily an argument against them, for the greater short-term receipts could be used for diversification funds. The question is complicated not only by the difficulty of estimating short- and long-term elasticities of demand and their interdependence, but also by the possibility of the developed countries retaliating by raising their export prices. But it might be easier to get agreement of purchasing countries on nonretaliation than on commodity agreements.

Joint action *vis-à-vis* multinational corporations could replace or reinforce a generally agreed upon code. Developing countries could agree not to erode each other's tax base by giving competitive tax concessions and to apply similar rules and guidelines. Bargaining power can be used also in other spheres, such as overflying rights for airlines, narcotics control, patent law etc. The main obstacle is that some differences among developing countries are as great as those between them and the developed countries, and joint action is difficult to achieve without a much stronger system of incentives to form and adhere to these agreements. Producers' associations are notorious for their instability, for the more successful the agreement is in raising the price, the stronger the incentive for individual members to defect. And the fear that others may operate outside the agreement, or that all may have to operate without the agreement, is itself a powerful destabilizing force. More thought should be devoted to mechanisms to create incentives to penalize outsiders and defectors, and to reward adherents, as well as to strengthen solidarity, in order to increase the stability of joint action.

Successful co-operation among developing countries may not be possible in all areas but may be feasible in some, e.g. in improving the terms of technology transfer, in bargaining with multinationals, in controlling migration of professionals, in reaching joint action on taxation of foreign investment.

Topics (c) and (d)

Much has been written recently on the importance of exploring mutual interests. Clearly, this is a promising area because it provides a firmer basis for action than unilateral, unrequited concessions. Since reform in this area is in the interest of both the developing and developed countries, it will be discussed in the next section that deals with the response of the developed countries.

7. A CONSTRUCTIVE RESPONSE BY THE DEVELOPED COUNTRIES

Although some of the developing countries' proposals for an NIEO have not been well designed, the response of the developed countries has not been constructive or imaginative. If the package proposed at present were to be the only one on which developing countries could agree, this would be an argument for supporting it, in spite of its deficiencies. It is, however, worth considering modifications of this package (it has already been modified by the abandonment of the demand for general debt relief and the scaling down of the Common Fund) and alternative packages. It would require a separate paper to map out such alternatives but it is possible to lay down certain principles on the basis of which progress may be made.

There are three areas in which more thought should be devoted to the design of appropriate policies:

(1) First, there is the area where developed and developing countries have common or mutual interest. (The two, though often confused, are clearly not the same. The former refers to objectives pursued by co-operation, the latter by exchange.) This covers the exploration of positive-sum games.

(2) Second, there is the area of the avoidance of negative-sum games. Other countries can be not only sources of positive benefits, but also of threats that we must try to avert. Coexistence in an interdependent world can give rise to the production of goods;

but it can also give rise to the production of 'bads', which have to be combatted by 'anti-bads'. The exploration of areas of joint action for 'anti-bads' may be even more important than the search for goods.

(3) Third, there are areas where existing biases, discriminations and imperfections in the international economic order work against the interests of the developing countries and where we have to explore joint methods of correcting them. This looks like an area of zero-sum games, although long-term benefits to all may accrue. Under this heading would also fall more 'voice' for the developing countries and concessional, gratuitous transfers.

The three areas are related to Kenneth Boulding's exchange system, threat system, and integrative or love system. In the exchange system partner A does something good to another partner (B) in return for B doing something good to A. In the threat system A threatens to do something bad to B, unless B does something good for A. The integrative or love system is a system in which the individual comes to identify his own desires with those of others. Exchange systems are the basis of economics, threat systems of politics. Exchange systems are based on the transfer of goods, threat systems on the transfer of 'bads'.

Clearly, the three areas overlap, and each overlaps with self-reliance on the part of the developing countries. Where there is common interest and harmony, so that reforms yield joint gains, there remains the division of these gains between rich and poor countries which can give rise to conflict. Self-reliance by the poor may be in the short- and long-term interest of the rich countries. They may prefer Korea to sell its shoes in Lahore, and Taiwan its textiles in Indonesia, to having their own markets swamped. And the correction may impose short-term losses on rich countries but benefit them in the long run.

Following on from the work in these areas is the question of the links between restructuring the international system as it affects relations between governments, and the consequential domestic measures required in both developing and developed countries to ensure that the benefits accrue to the poor, and that the costs are borne fairly.

Trade liberalization involves both restructuring in developed countries, so that the whole burden is not borne by the dismissed workers in depressed areas, and in developing countries, so that the gains from liberalization do not wholly accrue to big exporting firms, possibly even multinationals. In reaching commodity agreements, there should be some safeguards that the higher prices do not fall exclusively on poor consumers in rich countries, and that the restrictions that quota schemes involve are not largely borne by small farmers in poor countries, so that the big plantations benefit from both higher prices and unrestricted sales. And when we agree on debt relief, we want to be sure that it is more than relief for bankers in rich countries, whose loans are serviced out of aid funds. Such consequential domestic measures are necessary both inside developed and inside developing countries, if the ultimate impact of the reforms of the NIEO is to be on improving the lot of the poor.

8. COMMON AND MUTUAL INTERESTS

Until 1973, issues of economic interdependence and development belonged to largely separate areas. Development was dealt with by development assistance and trade preferences of varying generosity. Interdependence was dealt with in the OECD. It was a matter for the rich.

The validity of this dichotomy has been questioned in the last 7 years. The developing countries' shares in world population, in world trade and in world production have increased. Some developing countries have now large international reserves, others large international debts.[8] They supply raw materials, especially metals, on which the developed countries increasingly depend. The one-way dependence of the South on the North has now become a two-way interdependence.

International inter*dependence* should be distinguished from international *relations*. The test of the difference is this: if relations were cut off, ready substitutes could be found so that not much damage would be done. Inter*dependence* means that if relations were cut off, substantial damage would result. To illustrate: much trade between industrial countries is conducted in similar finished consumer goods and caters for slight differentiation in tastes. A smaller volume of trade (and a less rapidly growing one) with the developing countries consists of vital food and raw materials. In technical language, it is consumers' (and producers') surpluses that count, not trade volumes (values) and their growth.

Trade is not an end in itself, but a means to a more efficient allocation of resources and to greater consumers' satisfaction. The long-term importance of trade is, therefore, measured not by its total value or its rate of growth, but by: (a) the difficulty in *production* of substituting domestic goods for imports by shifting resources employed in exports, and (b) the sacrifice in *consumption* of shifting from imports to domestic import substitutes, if the products are not identical, or of doing without them altogether.[9] A vast and ever-growing exchange of Volkswagen for Morris Minors reflects small importance, a small exchange of coffee or copper (not to speak of oil) for engineering goods reflects vital dependence (or interdependence). Americans would not suffer much hardship if they had to drive Fairmonts instead of Volvos, but might if they had to drink Almadén instead of Château Margaux, and certainly would if they had to do entirely without manganese, tin or chromium imports. Total trade figures are, of course, relevant to other issues, such as changes in the balance of payments, which in turn may affect consumption and welfare. But these sequences would have to be spelled out.

The most generally accepted area of mutual interest is trade liberalization and liberalization of the flow of the factors of production, capital and labour. On trade, it could be argued that already fairly rich developed countries should weigh the costs of adjustment, probably repeated and painful adjustments, against the gains from further additions to income. Affluent countries, or at any rate their governments, might decide that it is in their national interest to forego at the margin further income rises for the sake of a quieter life, and greater industrial peace.

The difficulty with this position is that the security of employment is not necessarily guaranteed by protection, for jobs in export trades are endangered, and that the costs of such a form of a quiet life can be very high indeed, particularly for a country dependent on foreign trade. Moreover, if several countries adopted such a position, the mutual impoverishment could be substantial.

Not only may the costs of adjustment be high, but the benefits from additional trade may be low. Sir Arthur Lewis invited us to imagine the consequences upon the remaining group of countries if either the rich countries of the North or the poor countries of the South were to sink under the sea. His argument is that, after a period of adjustment, the losses would be negligible. If this were so, the large and, until 1973, rapidly growing trade volumes are no indication of genuine inter*dependence*.

There are also mutual gains from the flow of capital. Here, special attention should be paid to measures which, without being identified with aid, could have a leverage effect on aid, such as guarantees, co-financing, improved access to capital markets and markets for manufactured exports etc.

Movement of goods and of capital and labour would not only register all the mutual benefits expounded by the theory of comparative advantage, but would also accelerate growth, reduce inflation, generate unemployment, expand choice and support the international system of trade and debt service.

The most powerful argument for international trade is not one based on the doctrine of comparative advantage, which assumes constant costs (Ricardo) or increasing costs (Heckscher-Ohlin), but one based on economies of scale, increasing returns, learning-by-doing and decreasing unit costs, as elaborated by Allyn Young. Adam Smith already had pointed out that the 'division of labour is limited by the extent of the market'. He thought mainly of the geographical extent. Allyn Young added the reverse proposition, that the extent of the market, not only in the geographic sense, but also in the sense of the size of the income, depended on the division of labour. Production, productivity and incomes rise as specialization proceeds. It is on the interaction between these two—the division of labour and the extent of the market—that economic progress depends. To widen the market, to raise incomes in the South, makes greater international specialization possible, which in turn contributes to raising productivity and incomes. It has, of course, been questioned whether this style of development, relying on large-scale production and increasing specialization, is consistent with the desire for diversity, human dignity, self-reliance and respect for the environment.

Two specific issues under the heading of international trade are worth exploring. The first is the reform of tariff structures which now tend to cascade with successive stages of processing. Such de-escalation would improve the international location of industries and would permit developing countries to benefit from the external economies of learning effects from a primary product-based form of industrialization. They might also be able to make better use of waste products, now discarded by the richer countries.

The second area is that of stabilization of commodity prices. The large fluctuations that occur now benefit neither producers, who are discouraged from investing, nor consumers, who find it difficult to plan production.

On present evidence and theoretical considerations, there is not much in the argument that *general* flows of ODA to developing countries—what is sometimes called a Marshall Plan for the Third World—can regenerate growth in the developed countries. For the Third World to be an 'engine of growth' for the industrialized countries, the quantities are too small (though they can make a contribution), and domestic measures (tax reductions and public expenditure increases) can do the same with higher political and economic returns, if the national interest were the only guide and if fuller employment were really desired. Some of the demand created in the North is from arms sales. If these were to be reduced, another source would have to replace them. Moreover, the greatest need for ODA is in the poorest countries, the trade share of which is small and only slowly growing, whereas the best 'investment' of such aid would be in the middle-income developing countries, which are already earning much foreign exchange through their exports.

The argument that *specific* exports can be supplied from underutilized capacity at low, zero or negative costs, and that *specific* imports can contribute to bottleneck busting, and hence to the resumption of orderly growth without premature inflation, deserves closer examination.

Aid from surplus capacity has certain drawbacks. If, in the long run, the surplus capacity should be scrapped and the workers retrained, this process is delayed and an inefficient production structure is perpetuated. This can be particularly damaging if the surplus capacity competes with imports from the developing countries. If the production could have been used at home, or could have been exported at a commercial value, the costs of the aid are correspondingly higher. Nor is it always the case that recipients need or want the surplus production, when it is available, although the rapid growth of exports in the past has left certain industries, such as steel, chemicals and building materials, underutilized more than the average.

There remain, however, sectors and industries, especially those where indivisibilities are important, in which the temporary (cyclical) emergence of surplus capacity could be harnessed to the aid effort. Steel plant manufacturing capacity, shipbuilding capacity, or other heavy capital goods sectors are for technical reasons subject to fluctuations in utilization, and periods of underutilized capacity might be used for aid-financed exports to developing countries in need of steel plants, ships or other capital goods. Even where the case is strongest, aid from surplus capacity reduces the costs for the donor; it does not add to his profits.

As far as *imports* are concerned, developed countries wishing to resume growth are liable to run into *bottlenecks* before full employment for the economy as a whole is achieved. Imports from developing countries can help to break these bottlenecks and thereby enable developed countries to resume higher levels of activity with less inflation.

The removal of certain world-wide scarcities, which now prevent countries from resuming non-inflationary, full-employment growth, may be against the interests of small groups benefiting from these scarcities, but is clearly in the interest of all countries and humanity at large. Normally, resources devoted to one sector deprive other sectors of resources. But bottleneck-busting investment in the bottleneck sector *increases* the utilization of resources in other sectors and provides a stimulus for further investment. There is a multiplier effect. More specifically, energy and certain minerals fall into this category. Investment that raises the world supply of energy is bound to benefit all people in the long run. (The case for investment in raising world food production, often mentioned in this context, is a different one: it is that at small cost to the developed countries the major evil of hunger and malnutrition can be removed.)

These bottlenecks can be either of a short-term nature, or they can represent long-term scarcities. In the latter case, investment by the North in the South, in order to overcome these global scarcities, can make a contribution to the resumption of long-term orderly growth without inflation. But in the long-term interdependence is likely to be less than in the short term, because substitutes for and economies in the use of the scarce materials are possible. With technological advance, it is doubtful whether, in the long run, any country or group of countries can be said to be wholly dependent on some other countries. This is true both for the North and for the South. It greatly reduces the alleged significance of global interdependence.

Institutional innovation in the field of minerals and energy requires resolution of the present conflicts between companies and governments. Exploration is a risky business in which one lucky strike has to pay for numerous unlucky strikes. This type of risk is borne more efficiently by an intergovernmental organization, which would also add to available information and reduce friction in negotiating contracts. A new institution could also supply finance for host country equity in new developments and for processing facilities in developing countries.

An area of positive-sum games is policies towards transnational corporations and direct private foreign investment. In the past, fears of expropriation, restrictions on repatriation or remittances, price controls and other policies reducing profitability or leading to losses have caused uncertainty and have raised the required rate of return on foreign investment. This high rate of return has, however, often led to the very measures that the investor feared, for host governments felt that companies were taking out of the country more than they were putting in.

There is a specific dilemma for developing countries. If the rate of reinvestment of foreign profits is lower than the rate of return on the capital invested, remission of profits presents a drain on foreign exchange. If, on the other hand, the rate of reinvestment of foreign profits exceeds the rate of return, on plausible assumptions about the rate of growth of national income and the capital-output ratio, a growing proportion of the stock of capital is going to be owned by foreigners. This dilemma between foreign exchange losses and alienation of assets has led some countries to expropriate foreign enterprises. A reduction in the uncertainty about such measures would reduce both the rates of return required by the companies and incentives to take measures by host governments that raise risks for companies. Well-designed measures to reduce uncertainty can increase the flow of foreign investment, induce companies to take a longer-term view, alleviate fears of host governments, and thus benefit both firms and host countries.

Among such measures would be investment guarantees, agreements on arbitration procedures, sell-out and buy-out options after agreed periods of prices to be determined by agreed procedures, model contracts, investment codes, joint ventures, and new public-private hybrid institutions, combining the virtues of private initiative and enterprise with those of a commitment to development.

Another area of mutual interest for policies toward multinational firms is the application of anti-trust action to the international behaviour of these companies. It is just as much in any industrial country's interest that its companies should not act like cartels or monopolies internationally, as it is that foreign companies should not monopolize its domestic market. There is now an asymmetry in that anti-trust action and restrictive practices tend to be outlawed for domestic activity but permitted (or even encouraged) for international ones.

The conclusion that these considerations lead to is the need for a new international institution which would comprise some of the areas now covered by GATT, some of those covered by UNCTAD, and some not covered at all. Such a new International Trade and Production Organization (as Miriam Camps[10] has called it) would be concerned with laying down rules and principles not only for tariff and non-tariff barriers to trade, but also for intra-firm trade (which now escapes these rules), for state trading (increasingly important also in mixed economies), for restrictive business practices, agricultural products and raw materials (now under UNCTAD), for services and for investment. The multilateral trade negotiations have not solved the problems of structural adjustments that a new, changing international division of labour calls for, nor have they touched on the investment wars that have tended to arise from the attempts of national governments to capture for themselves taxes and other benefits from private investment, thereby eroding the potential gains from investment. (Institutional arrangements to prevent these wars fall under the subsequent heading, 'avoiding negative-sum games'.) It may be argued that it is better to build on existing institutions and procedures, but, as Gerald Helleiner has reminded us, Clausewitz said 'a small jump is easier than a large one, but no one wishing to cross a large ditch would cross half of it first'.

Common interests can also be established through co-operation in the management of the global commons: ocean fisheries, air and sea pollution, radio frequencies, civil air and merchant shipping routes and world monetary conditions. The already mentioned success of some international institutions devoted to technical aspects of international co-operation, like the Universal Postal Union or the International Telecommunication Union or the World Meteorological Organization bear witness to the possibility of successful international co-operation if strictly defined technical areas are at stake. As a by-product of this global management, revenues might be raised from some of these activities, like ocean fisheries or international travel.

9. AVOIDING NEGATIVE-SUM GAMES

The essence of interdependence is that members of the world community are capable, by unilateral action, of inflicting harm on others. The fear that others may take such action can be a sufficient condition for defensive, detrimental action of this kind.

The prime example in this field is the arms race which absorbs scarce resources and, beyond a certain critical point which we have long ago exceeded, breeds violence. Between 1946 and 1976, 120 wars were fought, 114 of them in the Third World. The number of people killed is somewhere between those killed in the First and Second World Wars. It has often been noted that economic growth has not abolished poverty. It is less often noticed that large defence expenditure has actually bred violence. The Laffer curve, whatever may be true for taxation, seems to apply to expenditure on arms. Three percent of the total annual expenditure of $450 billion now devoted to armaments would double the annual resources now spent by the OECD countries on official development assistance. But such arguments do not cut any ice until it can be established that the expenditure at present levels is counter-productive and that we would get better security from a reduced volume of expenditure.

In the economic area protectionism and deflation to protect the balance of payments are instances of negative-sum games. In the area of private foreign investment, actions by both parent and host governments to tilt the advantages from private foreign investment in their direction have similarly destructive effects. Large incentives are offered to bid for these investments in 'investment wars', like the trade wars of the 1930s. Overfishing, the pollution of the sea and the global atmosphere, and the excessive exhaustion of non-renewable resources are other examples. Co-ordination of policies and international institutions for co-operation are needed to avoid such mutually destructive actions.

The institutional responses might be illustrated by internationally co-ordinated action. In order to avoid the self-defeating and mutually destructive actions arising from attempts to correct balance-of-payments deficits imposed by a few persistent surplus countries, an international central bank, with power to create liquid assets, is necessary. It has been argued that the system of flexible exchange rates has restored full autonomy for national monetary policies. But this is by no means as obvious as is often thought. Hardly any government would permit completely 'clean' floating, and 'dirty' floating may well require larger rather than smaller reserves to counter speculative attacks. For the creation of these an international central bank is necessary.

A second institutional reform would be a mechanism for some form of co-ordination of investment decisions, so as to avoid the swings between over-capacity and shortages of capacity from which we have suffered in the past. Opponents of such co-ordination fear lest this is the entry of market-sharing agreements and cartels, but in many national plans co-ordination of investment decisions has proved entirely compatible with maintaining competition.

Other illustrations would be agreements to refrain from trade and investment wars and the already mentioned establishment of international firms that would combine the virtues of private enterprise and freedom from bureaucratic controls with the objective of promoting development. Another area would be taxes on activities where independent national actions now lead to the deterioration of the world environment: a tax on overfishing, on polluting the sea and atmosphere, or on mining nonrenewable natural resources.

10. ZERO-SUM GAMES

Exploration of areas of zero-sum games, that is to say actions where a sacrifice is required on the part of the developed countries in order to benefit the developing countries, comprise three fields. First, the correction of imperfections and biases in the existing world order which work against the developing countries. Second, transfers of resources from the rich to the poor. And third, more 'voice' for the developing countries in the councils of the world.

(a) Existing Biases, Imperfections and Discriminations in the International System and How To Correct Them[11]

An international economic order that discriminates systematically against one group of countries can give rise to confrontations and conflicts and to negative-sum games in which all lose. But the appeal to correcting inequities need not be wholly to national self-interest. There is an independent moral case for a just world order.

Countries should be willing to co-operate in correcting biases in market structures and government policies that are damaging to the developing countries. Such corrections would contribute to a more equitable and therefore acceptable world order and, by reducing frictions and conflicts, can be seen to be also in the long-term interest of the developed countries.

A response along such lines would meet the demands of both efficiency and distributive justice. Not only are the specific proposals more in line with the canons of economic efficiency, but, by accommodating the developing countries' call for a fairer international order, they would prevent the recriminations and conflicts that are bound to cause international disorder, one of the greatest sources of inefficiency.

At the national level, governments attempt to provide macroeconomic stability through monetary and fiscal policies, to redistribute income through progressive taxes and social services, to guarantee farmers an adequate income, to correct for the worst features of free competitive markets, and to cushion victims against the damage of change. All these government actions are in the nature of public goods. There is no international government to do any of these things on a global scale.

In the 19th century Great Britain, and for about 25 years after 1945 the USA, provided a power centre that fulfilled some of the functions of an international government, such as providing compensating capital movements, financial institutions and being a lender of last resort. Since about 1970 such a centre has been lacking. The international organizations have been too weak to fulfil the required functions. International institutions are needed to provide internationally the 'public goods' of stability and equity that civilized national governments provide as a matter of course for their citizens. The implementation of such reforms would be a contribution to the foundation of a stable, equitable and prosperous world order.

Whatever our motivation for correcting imperfections or biases in the present international economic order, such biases occur in various fields. The division of the gains from trade may be very unequal because a few large buying companies from rich countries confront many weak sellers from developing countries, and the demand for the final product is fairly inelastic. Or the bulk of the processing of raw materials from developing countries may be done in the developed countries, who reap the large value added, not because they enjoy a comparative advantage but because of market power and policies, such as cascading tariffs, or discrimination in shipping or credit. Or the distribution of the gains from productivity growth between exporters and importers may be uneven, so that improving commodity terms of trade are consistent with deteriorating double factoral terms of trade.

In this context, thought should be given to what reforms are needed, by creating new or changing old institutions, rules, policies and other measures to change the location of economic activities and to improve the developing countries' bargaining power, so as to reduce the bias in the distribution of gains from trade.

There are imperfections in the export markets of developing countries. There are also imperfections in the supply of imports. Developing countries are often faced with import prices that are higher than those charged to industrial countries and often suffer from price discrimination, restrictive trade practices, export cartels, inter-firm arrangements for the allocation of markets, etc. There exists evidence that small countries pay higher prices for imported machinery, chemicals, iron and steel than large countries. The USA prohibits cartels internally, but specifically exempts export cartels. Should there not be an antitrust law internationally, just as there is one to protect US citizens?

There are imperfections in access to market information. The ability to buy cheap and sell dear depends upon full market information. The large transnational firms possess this but poor developing countries do not. The disadvantage is cumulative: ignorance about how to acquire information about production processes reinforces the absence of information about these products or processes themselves. There are imperfections in access to knowledge and technology. Several measures have been proposed to correct this bias. They involve reforms of the patent law, in the market for technology and in the thrust of research and development expenditure. There is a bias in the developing countries' access to capital markets. There may be no shortage of finance in Eurocurrency markets, suppliers' credits or through the World Bank, but there may be a bias in the issues and bond markets. Much needs to be done in order to reduce imperfections and other obstacles in the way of access to the world's capital markets.

Imperfections in labour markets are reflected in the present bias in the admission and encouragement of certain types of professional manpower, often trained by the developing countries (brain drain), and the considerably less free movement of unskilled labour. The world's division into nation states, each monopolizing the physical and technical assets within its boundaries for its own benefit, is not consistent with a rational or moral or acceptable world order.

Does the international monetary system discriminate against developing countries? Monetary restrictions have an important impact on unemployment. The SDR-aid link is probably dormant for a while, but there should be a gold-aid link. As central banks sell gold to the IMF for SDRs, the IMF can sell the gold and use the receipts for contributions to IDA.

Transnational corporations also introduce imperfections. How can we strengthen the bargaining position of developing countries in drawing up contracts with TNCs; how can we enlarge the scope for 'unbundling' the package of capital, management, know-how and marketing; what is the role of public-sector enterprises in negotiating with private TNCs?

An analysis of the distribution of gains arising from much-touted 'outward-looking' foreign investment, where the quasi-rents and monopoly profits accruing to capital, management and know-how go to the rich countries, while the near-subsistence wages for semi-skilled labour go to the developing countries would be useful. The world in which we live corresponds to neither of two popular models: it is neither a truly 'liberal' world in which all factors are completely mobile across frontiers, so that they can seek their highest rewards; nor is it the world of the textbooks in which all factors are completely immobile internationally and trade is a substitute for factor movements. Some factors of production, such as capital, management and know-how, are fairly mobile internationally, and earn high rewards, whereas unskilled and semi-skilled labour are immobile internationally, though in abundant supply domestically, and earn low rewards. This has important implications for the distribution of gains from trade, technology and investment, and for the attitudes towards multinational firms.

There may be biases in information on political news coverage. Are the media biased in the scope and content of their news coverage? Is there a need for additional press agencies representing the point of view of developing countries?

Should reforms in all these areas take the form of restoring genuine competition, to reduce market power concentrations in rich countries, or should they take the form of mobilizing countervailing power, like organizing numerous poor producers (as the trade unions did in the 19th century), or should they take the form of changes in rules, institutions or legislation? Should there be reforms in the accumulation, selection and dissemination of information and knowledge? Many current recommendations are based on the false premise that existing markets are competitive and efficient, and spread the benefits of economic progress speedily and widely. This assumption is quite unrealistic for the world as a whole.

(b) Resource Transfer

An NIEO calls for a substantial increase in the amount of resources to be transferred to the developing countries, with the primary objective of eliminating the worst aspects of poverty within the lifetime of a generation. The specific forms this transfer takes is a secondary question. It has been proposed that developed countries should commit themselves to a total, but that each country should be free to decide in what form it wishes to make its stipulated contribution, whether through commodity agreements, preferences, debt relief, additional ODA etc. Such an approach would prevent differences among developed countries over specific instruments blocking the achievement of an agreed objective.

The rational way would be an international, progressive income tax, with a lower exemption limit and a rising aid/GNP ratio as income per head rises. Other tax proposals have been made, such as a tax on overfishing, on global pollution, on seabed resources, on international travel, on armaments etc. But an international income tax would be the most rational way towards automaticity in contributions and fair sharing.

Monitoring of the objective, poverty eradication, can be done in a way that would avoid the intrusion of donor-country performance criteria, with all the suspicions to which this would give rise, and without the abuse of funds received by developing countries. Harlan Cleveland has proposed a system like that under the Marshall Plan, in which the developing countries themselves would examine and monitor each other's performance in reducing poverty. Accepted extranational secretariats are another possibility.

(c) 'Voice'

The demand of the developing countries for greater participation in the international decision-making process calls for a reform in the membership and voting system of international institutions. More 'voice' for the developing countries is likely to remove some of the frustrations that spring from the perception of powerlessness. But greater participation by the developing countries would be pointless if it were accompanied by reduced contributions from the industrial countries.

The demand for 'more voice' is, of course, ultimately a demand for a different power distribution. Power to achieve common objectives can be a positive-sum game, in the sense that joining others can strengthen this power. But where objectives conflict, power is a zero-sum game. If there were a harmony of interests, more voice would not be needed. The demand for 'more voice' implies that certain objectives of the claimants have not been met. What is ultimately at stake is a restructuring of power relations.

11. THE RELATION BETWEEN NARROW AND 'HIGHER' NATIONAL SELF-INTEREST

We can build on areas of common national interests, emphasizing mutual benefits to be derived from, for example, resumption of orderly and equitable growth in the world economy, forswearing self-defeating protectionism, exploring ways of increasing the resources in globally scarce supply etc. But while there is considerable scope for positive-sum games in exploring areas of common and mutual interests and of avoiding self-defeating, mutually destructive policies, there is also a 'higher' interest in a world order that both is, and is seen to be, equitable, that is acceptable and therefore accepted, and that reduces conflict and confrontation.

All societies need for their self-regulation and for social control a basis of moral principles. Individuals are ready to make sacrifices for the communities they live in. Can this principle stop at the nation state? A belief in the harmony between self-interest and altruism is deep-seated in Anglo-Saxon thought and action. One is reminded of the 18th century Bishop Joseph Butler: 'When we sit down in a cool hour, we can neither justify to ourselves this or any other pursuit, till we are convinced that it will be for our happiness . . .' The only question is why it appears to be easier to identify, or at least harmonize, individual happiness with the national interest than with that of the world community. It is odd that a moral, disinterested concern by rich countries with the development of the poor is hardly ever conceded. As hypocrisy is the tribute vice pays to virtue, so professions of national self-interest in the development of poor countries may be the tribute that virtue has to pay to vice. Let us, in the present fashion for stressing common and mutual interests, not underestimate the power of moral appeals. Holland, Sweden and Norway, which have put international co-operation squarely on a moral basis, have hit the 0.7% target. It is the countries in which aid has been sold to the public as in the national self-interest where the effort is sadly lagging.

The common interests must also be defined in terms of different time horizons: the next year, the next 5 years, the next 20 years. There may be conflicts and trade-offs between these different time spans. For example, concessionary aid to the poorest may involve economic sacrifices in the near future but, by laying the foundations for a world in which all human beings born can fully develop their potential, it contributes to the long-term interest of mankind.

One difficulty is that in democracies adults have votes, but children and the unborn have no votes. The fight is not only against powerfully organized vested interests, but also against all our own short-term interests, that neglect the interests of future generations.

The 'higher' interest in an acceptable world order can be defined either in moral terms or in terms of the desire to avoid negative-sum games, to avoid breakdown and wars. Whatever the definition and justification, its aim is to transform adversary relationships into cooperation. When interests diverge or conflict, the task of statesmanship is to reconcile them. This is a task quite distinct from, and more important than, that of exploring areas of common or mutual interest. It is in this light that co-operative action to eradicate world poverty and to restructure the international economic order have to be seen.

NOTES

1. The ratio of exports to GNP was: for the UK 19.3% in 1913 and 20.7% in 1976; for the USA 6.5% in 1913 and 6.8% in 1976; and for Germany 20.5% in 1913 and 22.3% in 1976.

2. For another distinction, viz. that between interdependence and international relations, see p. 511.

3. To say that the world was more integrated in the 19th century than it is today implies using a definition of 'integration' which does not comprise equal opportunities for all citizens. Clearly, the opportunities were very unequal. But the world resembled more a single country than it does today.

4. In the low-income developing countries exports were 13.8% of GNP in 1960 and 15.7% in 1976. Low-income countries are those with an income per head of less than $300 in 1975.

5. Of this long-standing confusion between universal and uniform, or general rules, even such a clear-headed thinker as David Hume is guilty. Hume contrasts the highly specific reactions when we are seeking our own self-interest with the 'universal and perfectly inflexible' laws of justice. He seems, like many others (including GATT), not to make a necessary distinction between general principles (the opposite of specific ones and therefore necessarily simple) and universal principles (which may be highly specific and highly complicated, provided that they contain no uneliminable reference to individual

cases). Thus, Hume says, in one place 'universal and perfectly inflexible', but lower down 'general and inflexible'. And the use of the word 'inflexible' conceals a confusion between a principle being able to be altered (which has nothing to do with its universality or generality) and its having a lot of exceptions written into it (which is consistent with universality but not with generality). Hume evidently thinks that the rules of justice have to be simple, general ones. He argues that unless the rules are general, people will be partial in their application of them and 'would take into consideration the characters and circumstances of the persons, as well as the general nature of the question . . . the avidity and partiality of men would quickly bring disorder into the world, if not restrained by some general and inflexible principles'. But this is fallacious. In order to prevent people from being partial, the principles have to be universal, i.e. not contain references to individuals; they may, and indeed should, not be general; surely our judgements based on them ought to 'take into consideration the characters and circumstances of the persons, as well as the general nature of the question'.

6. For a valiant attempt to demonstrate common factors in the Third World, see Ismail-Sabri Abdalla, 'Heterogeneity and differentiation—the end of the Third World?', *Development Dialogue*, No. 2 (1978).

7. See Harlan Cleveland, *The Third Try at World Order* (New York: 1976).

8. The share in total world trade of all developing countries has increased from 21.4% in 1960 to 24.6% in 1976 (though excluding major oil exporters the share declined from 14.8 to 10.2%); their share in international reserves has increased from 17.8% in 1960 to 45.9% in 1976 (excluding OPEC from 13.8 to 20.2%); their share in population from 72% in 1960 to 76% in 1976; and their share in production from 18.2% in 1960 to 22.6% in 1976, measured at constant 1975 dollars.

9. Irma Adelman, in private correspondence, has suggested that the major influence of international trade on development is that it enables a country to decouple production from consumption, and thereby presents more options for development policy.

10. *The Case for a Global Trade Organization* (Council on Foreign Relations, 1980).

11. This subject is well treated in Gerald K. Helleiner, 'World market imperfections and the developing countries', Overseas Development Council, Occasional Paper No. 11 (1978).

33. The Case against the New International Economic Order

HERBERT G. GRUBEL

In this paper I am presenting the case against the New International Economic Order (NIEO hereafter).* In Part I the political origins of

Herbert G. Grubel is Professor of Economics at Simon Frasier University, Vancouver, Canada.

I acknowledge the receipt of useful comments on an earlier draft of this paper by G. Helleiner and my colleagues, D. Devoretz, M. Khan and K. Okuda, who do not all share my distrust of the wisdom of bureaucrats, national and international. The arguments were sharpened by my participation at a conference on the New International Economic Order held in December 1976 at the Institut für Weltwirtschaft in Kiel, Germany.

the demand for the NIEO are presented and the detailed proposals for reform are listed. In Part II, I analyse the shortcomings of the proposed commodity program, drawing mainly on the history and analysis of past attempts to manage commodity markets. Part III presents arguments against changes in regulations governing the international transfer of technology and the distribution of Special Drawing Rights (SDRs) by the International Monetary Fund. In Part IV, I sketch a program of positive steps which should be taken to alleviate the problem of poverty in developing countries.

The historic and analytical case against the NIEO is very powerful and raises the question why the proposed reforms enjoy such strong support from many sources. In Part V, I attempt to answer this question by considering likely motives of politicians and bureaucrats in developing countries and international agencies and of intellectuals in industrial countries. The paper closes with a summary and conclusions.

I. THE NEW INTERNATIONAL ECONOMIC ORDER AND ITS POLITICAL ORIGINS[1]

In 1955 the United Nations had 59 members, as of mid-1975 it had 141. Of these 141 members about 110 are so-called non-aligned and less-developed countries. Recently it has become fashionable to refer to this group of countries as the South, the industrial countries with market economies as the North and the Communist countries as the East. The South coalition consists mostly of countries with exceedingly small populations, territories and productive capacity, though they include also India, Indonesia, Egypt, Brazil, Nigeria and the Arab countries which through their size and natural resource basis are potentially rich and powerful nations.

The South coalition in the United Nations General Assembly has an overwhelming voting majority based on the one country, one vote principle. It has been using this voting power to transform the U.N. General Assembly into a progressively more militant and vocal forum for articulating demands for policies aimed at narrowing the income gap between the North and the South. In this debate, the East has been supporting the South with votes. However, it should be noted that the U.N. General Assembly has no real power and an extremely limited budget. Decisions leading to significant collective international political and military actions are made in the U.N. Security Council where the big nations have veto power and economic policies of importance are made in the International Monetary Fund, World Bank, and the General Agreement on Tariffs and Trade where voting power is in proportion to members' financial commitments.

The South coalition of countries pursued the strategy of articulating and propagandizing demands for the equalization of North-South incomes through the passing of resolutions in the General Assembly, the creation of a number of new agencies and the organization of international conferences whose resolutions and reports are dominated by the same distribution of voting patterns as the General Assembly. Thus, in 1964 the first U.N. Conference on Trade and Development (UNCTAD) was held and thereafter was made into a permanent institution with a staff in Geneva, Switzerland, and periodic meetings, the last one in May 1976 in Nairobi, Kenya, known as UNCTAD IV. In 1966, the U.N. Industrial Development Organization (UNIDO) was created and in 1970 the United Nations announced an International Development Strategy for the Second Development Decade.[2] Large conferences concerned officially with such topics as Environmental Pollution, Population, Women's Rights and Habitat have been held.

In all of these agencies and conferences during the 1960s demands for the narrowing of the North-South income gap were dominated by two specific proposals, the granting of tariff preferences to LDCs by industrial countries and foreign aid transfers targeted at 1 percent of GNP of the industrial countries. The first demand has been met to a substantial degree. At least partially as a result of tariff preferences granted by the United States, exports of manufactures from the LDCs, mainly to the industrial countries, grew at annual rates of over 20 percent in real terms during the period 1969–73, while overall world trade manufacturers grew at only 12 percent annually.[3] The aid target of 1 percent of GNP was achieved only by very few countries and actual aid transfers measured in this manner have fallen continuously in recent years and in 1975 reached about 0.35 percent.

During the 1970s the Southern coalition in the United Nations began to shift its tactics away from demands for concessions on tariffs and for more aid to demands for changes in existing economic institutions, which were alleged to have been designed for the perpetuation of existing inequities in the world. The World Bank, the IMF and GATT were denounced as instruments of Northern domination. Equally important were the denunciations of the very basic features of the Northern economic system, market determined prices for manufacturers and raw materials and the international transmission of capital and technology through private, often multinational, corporations.

Specific proposals for changes in the economic system were advanced at the "Summit Conference of Non-Aligned Nations" held in Algiers in September 1973 shortly after the successful formation of the Organization of Petroleum Exporting Countries (OPEC) by some of the members of the South coalition and the dramatic increase in petroleum prices. In the mood created by the success of OPEC, the Sixth Special Session of the U.N. General Assembly was called hastily for April 1974.

This session adopted, without a vote, a manifesto entitled "Declaration and Program of Action of the New International Economic Order." In December 1974 the General Assembly approved the "Charter of Economic Rights and Duties of States".[4]

The most important proposals in the resolution calling for a New International Economic Order were as follows:

1. adoption of an "integrated" approach to price supports for an entire group of LDC commodity exports;
2. the "indexation" of LDC export prices to tie them to rising prices of developed countries' manufactured exports;
3. the attainment of official development assistance to reach the target of 0.7 percent of GNP of the developed countries;
4. the linkage of development aid with the creation of SDRs;
5. the negotiated "redeployment" of some developed countries' industries to LDCs;
6. the lowering of tariffs on the exports of manufactures from LDCs;
7. the development of an international food program;
8. the establishment of mechanisms for the transfer of technology to LDCs separate from direct capital investment.

The Charter of Economic Rights and Duties of States included two basic and controversial propositions:

1. It affirmed each state's "full permanent sovereignty" over its natural resources and economic activities, which was specifically set out to include the right to nationalize foreign property in disregard of existing international laws.[5]
2. Primary product producers have the "right" to associate in producers' cartels and other countries had the "duty" to refrain from efforts to break these cartels.[6]

Both of these U.N. documents affix blame for the low incomes in the South on past "exploitation" under "colonialism" and "neocolonialism." These terms came from the socialist-Marxist literature in economics and simply define as exploitation commercial activities in which business firms retain any part of net revenue as profits or return to invested capital rather than paying it all in the form of wages to labor employed by the firms. This proposition follows directly from the Marxist proposition that any net income not going to wages is "surplus value." Under colonialism the instruments of exploitation were the colonial administration and under neo-colonialism they are the modern multinational enterprises.

Confronted by the far-reaching demands for reform of the economic and social systems of the world, the North responded by calling for the Seventh Special Session of the U.N. General Assembly held in September 1975, in order to negotiate compromises on these demands. The session resulted in the issue of Resolution 3362, which was adopted by consensus. This resolution basically endorsed the demands for a New International Economic Order, the ideas for price indexation, the 0.7 percent aid target, the SDR aid link and many other provisions originating with the South coalition. The United States and other Northern delegations attached detailed reservations to the resolution, but its passage remains a symbolic victory for the South. The negotiations leading to the resolution had the main effect of changing slightly the militant tone of the preceding documents and led to the incorporation of some demands for changes and programs proposed by H. Kissinger.

These U.S. proposals[7] were centered on the basic principle of maintaining the existing economic system and the provision of development assistance through increased trade liberalization, the transfer of aid and technology through international organizations outside the direct control of the United Nations and the creation of some programs for the stabilization of commodity prices and the creation of some buffer stocks, of a fund to stabilize export earnings of LDCs and of agreements on coffee, cocoa and sugar. It is perhaps characteristic of the nature of the negotiations at the Seventh Special Session that they led to the acceptance of those of Kissinger's proposals which involve a transfer of resources from the North to the South, while demands for a basic change of the existing world economic system were retained and at best worded less offensively.

At the UNCTAD IV conference in Nairobi in May 1976, the proposals for the establishment of a New International Economic Order were reworded slightly in some instances, but in their essence remained unchanged when they were adopted as resolutions, with only the United States and the Federal Republic of Germany voting against them. Most significantly, the conference laid out a time-table for the study and implementation of one of the most controversial proposals involving the integrated program for commodities, giving them a bureaucratic life of their own and raising expectations about their ultimate adoption.

II. APPROPRIATE RESPONSE TO DEMAND FOR COMMODITY POLICIES

The most important provisions in the program designed to establish the NIEO deal with the management and pricing of at least 10 "core" commodities: cocoa, coffee, tea, sugar, hard fibres, jute, cotton, rubber, copper and tin and 7 other commodities with slightly lower priority: bananas, wheat, rice, meat, wool, iron ore and bauxite. Specifically, the objectives of the commodity program are:

1. reduction of excessive price and supply fluctuations;
2. establishment and maintenance of commodity prices which, in real terms, "are equitable to consumers and remunerative to producers."

To achieve these, and some other, rather unobjectionable goals, the following "integrated" measures are proposed:

1. the establishment of international buffer stocks,
2. the creation of a common fund to finance these stocks,
3. the signing of multilateral trade commitments,
4. the arrangement of improved compensatory financing to stabilize export earnings.

Similar proposals presumably will also emerge eventually from efforts to develop a program for food products, especially basic staples, such as grains.

The reaction of governments in developed countries to these proposals will influence international economic relations and the future of world trade and welfare very importantly. In my judgment, these proposals should be rejected totally and should not even be given any increased status by the acceptance of plans for "further study" and negotiation by officially constituted committees of UNCTAD or any other world-wide bodies. My recommendation for this reaction is based on my understanding of a large stock of theoretical and empirical evidence concerning the operation and welfare effects of efforts to manage commodity markets.[8] The conclusions of these studies may be summarized in the following three major points.

Price against Income Stability

First, the real source of welfare losses to producers of primary commodities is not price but income instability, but, as can be seen above, the proposed commodity program calls for the stabilization of prices as one of the prime objectives. However, it is a simple economic fact that in markets where demand is stable and supply fluctuates as a result of random influences such as weather, the maintenance of stable prices tends to increase income instability above what it would be with flexible prices.

The validity of this proposition can be seen readily by considering the example of a perfectly stable price for cocoa maintained through the operation of a buffer stock. In a period of short harvests producers' incomes fall equi-proportionately to the reduction in output. However, if during this bad harvest period the price of cocoa had risen, then incomes of the farmers would not have fallen as much since their income is the product of quantity times price. By analogy, with flexible prices during periods of bumper harvests the farmers' income rise is smaller than it would be under a fixed price.

It is the latter fact, of course, which motivates the demand by so many farmers in nearly all countries for price stabilization schemes. However, if such schemes are run strictly such as to even out fluctuations in supply, then it follows as a matter of logical necessity that the income benefits during periods of bumper crops must be compensated for by income reductions during periods of harvest shortfalls; and there are no average increases in earnings and the variance of producers' income raised.

In the analytically opposite case where supply of a commodity is stable while demand fluctuates, as for example in the case of copper or tin, the creation of buffer stocks and stable prices has the disadvantage of reducing average incomes of producers. This result is due to the fact that during periods of global boom and excess demand generally, the elasticity of demand for these products is low because of the reduced availability of substitutes, so that producers can exploit this low elasticity and raise their incomes through higher price. By analogy, during periods of excess capacity and lower product prices, the elasticity of demand tends to be high and producers' incomes fall less. Fixed prices to consumers over the full cycle prevent the exploitation of this asymmetry in elasticities and lower average incomes.[9]

These disadvantages of price stabilization schemes could be combatted by the direct stabilization of producers' incomes, as is demanded by the U.N. resolutions calling for the NIEO. However, as the preceding arguments show, income stabilization is made more difficult by the operation of price stabilization schemes and if the former were in effect there would be no need for the latter.

Random Changes and Trends

The second class of problems relating to both price and income stabilization efforts is that there exists no method for distinguishing in practice whether a given price or income change is merely a random event or whether it reflects a fundamental trend. In the former case stabilization efforts may be justified since, ceteris paribus, there are welfare gains from the elimination of random shocks netting to zero over a certain time period. In the latter case, however, resistance to relative price and income changes caused by technological innovations, changes in consumer tastes or the discovery of new sources of supply leads to inefficiencies. The proposed "indexing" of commodity prices to some measure of cost of other goods implies that relative prices of these commodities will be pegged regardless of long-run trends concerning their real value in exchange.

In the absence of methods for identifying operationally and in advance random and fundamental price trends historically nearly all price stabilization schemes, whose operation tends to be dominated by producers' representatives or in which the prices of stabilized goods are determined by some form of indexing, have erred on the side of overestimating the price at which buffer stocks remain constant in the longer run. As a result, buffer stocks typically have grown so large and expensive to operate that all agreed-upon financing plans proved inadequate and the programs have been abandoned. At such times, the sale of the accumulated stocks tended to depress prices and producers' incomes, offsetting the gains made during the periods of artificially high prices. Typically, the fluctuations of prices and incomes of producers have been larger with than they would have been without the temporary operation of the buffer stocks.

Pure income stabilization programs are subject to another shortcoming, the risk of inefficiency and overall economic stagnation. The history of national policies intended for income stabilization shows that typically such programs evolve into permanent subsidies to inefficient producers and industries. The reason for these developments is again that it is impossible to know whether given producers' troubles are due to random short-run or fundamental long-run trends and that the producer-dominated administrations of schemes have every incentive to treat all problems as temporary ones. As a result, such income stabilization programs on average pay producers' incomes which are higher than the value at market prices of the output they produce. These subsidies represent a net drain on society's real output capacity and they tend to grow as more sectors of the economy demand such income stabilization programs and it becomes politically impossible to dismantle any of them. Eventually, these programs would reduce economic growth so much that even the subsidized producers end up with lower incomes than they would have in the absence of such programs.

Fair Consumer against Remunerative Producer Prices

The third problem with the proposed commodity program arises from the innocuous-sounding but practically most difficult idea that prices for commodities should be set such that they are "fair to consumers and remunerative for producers." Unfortunately setting the price for a commodity involves a zero sum game, a little more fairness to consumers means a little less remuneration for producers. In all past national and international attempts to determine prices through collective decision involving consumers and producers, such as national marketing boards for agricultural products of the Common Agricultural Policy of the EEC, producers dominate the proceedings and set the price at a level where it results in excess supplies.

This result is not surprising and is readily explained by the fact that consumers individually do not suffer greatly from excessive prices for agricultural products and they have no incentive to engage in strong collective action to oppose the officially set prices. Producers, on the other hand, are only a relatively small number and for every one of them the benefits are substantial, generating strong incentives for effective organization and political lobbying. There is every reason for believing that a similar process would take place in international agencies setting prices for commodities.

It could be argued that commodity prices favoring their producers in developing countries at the expense of consumers in developed countries is exactly what is necessary to equalize incomes in the world and therefore is desirable. However, unfortunately the setting of high commodity prices does not achieve this objective because at these prices competition among producers leads to the condition where each earns only normal returns to invested capital and other factor inputs. This competition takes many forms, such as increased output by producers in business when the plan is put into operation, the entry of new producers and the development of substitutes for products whose prices have been raised.

The most visible effects of setting commodity prices at a level above long-run equilibrium is the accumulation of surplus stocks. It is important to realize that, in order to provide the benefits desired by the producers there must be a continuous *flow* of excess production and goods must never be sold from the stockpile. As a result, the *stock* of commodities held by the authorities must grow continuously and without limit. Eventually, such stocks must become very large, simply through the operation of the principle of compound interest. This analysis shows clearly the irrationality of attempting to provide development assistance through the maintenance of excessively high prices for commodities: the world community as a whole devotes increasingly large resources to produce goods which are then perpetually locked into stockpiles, where they are subject to spoilage and additional resources have to be devoted to keeping them safe, while depletion of reserves increases the cost of these goods to current users. It is obvious that these resources have better use in current consumption, capital formation and direct income assistance to low income people and countries.

A less visible, but in the longer run potentially very important effect of permanently raised commodity prices is the induced development of substitutes by consumers and competitive producers. As has been observed in the case of higher petroleum prices, cars are being built smaller, insulation in structures is increased and many other innumerable small changes resulting in lower demand are induced. Combined with the development of energy substitutes, there exists the possibility that in the longer run the demand for petroleum is lowered so much that the present value of reserves in 1973 will have turned out to have been smaller with than without the price increases which took place that year. Only time will tell the correctness of this analysis, but there is little doubt that similar such substitution processes would be at work against the longer-run interests of producers of the commodities suggested for inclusion in the proposed program, especially since for most of them substitutions appear technically to be much easier than in the case of petroleum.

The adverse effects of raised prices for producers just sketched can be prevented in principle if free markets and competition were eliminated. The demand for the signing of multilateral trade commitments as part of the proposed commodity program may be interpreted as being an attempt to force developed countries into taking such steps in their own economies. In my view, such a sacrifice of free market institutions would not be in the interest of either the developed or the developing countries for the following reason. Historically, one of the most important sources of increased productivity in the world has been technological and product innovations originating with free market economies, whose incentive structure encourages them, while the bureaucracies of planned economies discourages them. Thus, if developed market economies switched to a system of central planning to maintain demand for certain commodities, the growth of world productivity would be slowed and eventually, even the producers of these commodities in developing countries would be worse off than without the higher prices and the abandonment of market economies.

Price theory suggests that there is only one price for every commodity, which is both fair to consumers and remunerative for producers. This is the price established in competitive markets. For most of the commodities in the proposed program world-wide competition has been very strong. In cases where competition is constrained, the optimal method for assuring the desired pattern of prices is to encourage competition, often through changes in domestic policies of the developing countries, but if shown to be necessary, it may require collective action through some agency of the United Nations.

The history of national and international attempts to stabilize commodity prices and incomes or to raise permanently the incomes of producers through higher commodity prices, buffer stocks or direct production subsidies does not augur well for the success of similar programs undertaken globally by the United Nations. The analysis of the causes of the failure of past schemes summarized above suggests that the U.N. schemes would also have to fail, not because of ideology or lack of sympathy for the plight of developing nations, but because these schemes are an indirect and wasteful method for dealing with the basic problem of poverty and lack of economic development. It makes no sense for either the developing or developed countries of the world to set aside resources for the production of goods ending up in permanent hoards. If developed countries are willing to take away any resources from their own use in consumption or capital formation, then they should be made available to developing countries in the form of purchasing power to be used as they determine to be in their best interest.

III. PROPOSALS ON CAPITAL FLOWS AND THE SDR-AID UNITS

Transmission of Knowledge Capital

The proposals for changes in the rules guiding the transmission of knowledge capital are as follows:[10]

1. the negotiation of a new international patent convention;
2. the development of a code of conduct on the transfer of technology;
3. the development of better means of controlling restrictive business practices and of reining in the multinational firms through fiscal cooperation.

In my judgment, there is no need for the revision of international or most national patent conventions because economic analysis has shown that there exists a basic and unavoidable conflict between static and dynamic efficiency in the production and use of knowledge. The existing limit on the life of patents is a reasonable compromise aimed at obtaining for society the maximum net benefits from losses due to restrictions on the use of existing knowledge on the one hand and gains from the maintenance of incentives for the creation of new knowledge on the other. Demands for changes of the laws are motivated either by a failure to understand these principles, by a desire to obtain short-run gains for LDCs at the expense of long-run technological progress for the world as a whole or by an attempt to change the basic principles of a free market economy which requires private ownership of patents. To change the laws in order to accommodate people acting from any of these three motives, in my judgment, would not be in the interest of either the developed or developing countries.

Closely related to the demand for changes in international patent laws are the demands for new "codes of conduct" (read methods) for the transfer of technology and controls over the operation of multinational firms. Stripped of all technicalities, these demands for changes boil down to the desire to obtain the technology and capital of the West at a lower price than it is available under current conditions. As a result, the ultimate question is whether or not the current price is efficient and required to maintain an optimum level of technological development and real capital formation in the longer run and to the benefit of the entire world or whether the multinational firms are in strong monopoly positions and are extracting excessively high prices from LDCs.

The answer to this question given by some analysts, mostly from the LDCs and international organizations, is that multinational firms are indeed monopolists and exploiters of LDCs. However, most economists from the North do not share this view and argue that competition assures that prices charged by multinationals for their goods, capital and technology by and large do not contain significant elements of monopoly. There is strong competition among multinationals from many countries in the same industry and there is competition among multinationals and local firms producing substitute products, which limits the strength of any potential monopoly. Moreover, it should be realized that the most important welfare effects from foreign investment result from the ability of LDCs to tax the incomes of multinationals, which because of international double taxation agreements, and high rates of taxation in the North, actually have an incentive to report profits in LDCs. The benefits from the taxation of the profits of multinational corporations in LDCs tend to dominate the negative welfare effects of instances where competition is insufficiently strong and some elements of monopoly remain.[11]

These propositions about the basic tendency of competition among multinational firms to force them into charging competitive prices for their technology and capital, of course, do not preclude the possibility that there exist documented instances where competition has failed to work. However, close examination of most such instances reveals that they have been created by the policies of LDCs' governments themselves, granting tax concessions and monopolies to a limited number of multinational firms.

From the preceding view of the role of global competition among multinational firms it follows that the appropriate action for the world community of nations and LDCs is the encouragement of competition through the dismantling of existing national controls and regulation and not the establishment of new international ones. As the modern theory of regulation argues and the empirical evidence shows, regulatory and control agencies cause not only waste and inefficiencies but inevitably lead to the establishment and maintenance of strong monopolies.[12]

It should be noted that the failure to establish an international bureaucracy for the control and regulation of multinational firms does not prevent individual or groups of LDCs from passing laws which end abuses which they feel are perpetrated by multinational firms in their countries. Especially, if they wish, they can demand separation of technology, financial capital and ownership, as Japan has done. Such a decentralized approach to the solution of problems as and where they are perceived is more efficient and equitable than is a global solution through the construction of sets of rules and regulations covering all possible contingencies and conditions in the world.[13] Some countries, such as Canada, might offer their expertise in dealing with foreign investment to individual developing countries wishing to devise their own national control legislation.

THE LINK PROPOSAL

The linkage of development aid to the creation of SDRs by the IMF has been discussed widely in the literature and involves some sophisticated principles of monetary and political theory. [14] In my view the essence of the arguments can be summarized by the following analogy. In nation states central banks produce money in the form of bills and coins, which the public needs in order to run the business of growing economies. This money is put into circulation by governments by paying for services or transfer payments without having to raise taxes or creating inflationary pressures. In individual countries the spending of the money is part of the general budgetary process and controlled by legislatures reflecting the entire spectrum of the constituents' interests. The quantity of money issued is determined as part of overall economic demand management. Consequently, there are ample safeguards against the creation of inflationary quantities of money for the benefits of certain interest groups.

In the case of the creation of international liquidity through SDRs, there exists a similar opportunity to finance expenditures and transfers because nations have a growing demand for international reserves. However, in the case of SDRs there is no general budgetary process undertaken by a representative legislature. In fact, the demands are that the resources be distributed as the analytical equivalent of social welfare payments to certain governments of the world. Presumably, this fact by itself would not give rise to any problems.

The real difficulties with the proposed scheme are that the decisions on the proper quantity of liquidity to be created are made by the IMF and are subject to the kind of political bargaining characteristic of international organizations not subject to direct control by an electorate. There exists therefore the great danger of confrontation between those countries wishing to create efficient and non-inflationary quantities of SDRs and countries wishing to create SDRs in quantities maximizing the transfers to them. Such confrontations would create uncertainties and inefficiencies in the international monetary system and, if countries receiving transfer payments and their ideological allies obtained a majority of votes on the governing body of the IMF, would lead to a situation equivalent to the amalgamation of national central banks and finance ministries, with control over the quantity of money created and used for welfare programs in the hands of the welfare recipients.

The benefits accruing to the world from the efficient and non-inflationary operation of the IMF independent from global welfare expenditures in the long run are very large and the dangers that they may be lost through the Link scheme so great, that I believe it is not in the interest of developing or developed countries to pursue this proposal.

IV. SOME POSITIVE RESPONSES TO THE DEMANDS

The demands for the NIEO just discussed have their basic economic origin in the unfortunate gap in income between people in the industrial and developing countries. I believe that industrial countries have a moral obligation to enact policies to narrow this gap. Policies, which will have this effect and none of the serious flaws connected with the proposals for the NIEO just discussed are as follows.

First, the industrial countries should encourage operation of market forces and the development of world trade. For this purpose, trade restrictions should be removed on industrial countries' imports of textiles, clothing, shoes, processed foods and many other manufactured articles in which the poor countries are developing productive capacity. The domestic adjustments in industrial countries made necessary by the removal of such trade barriers should be facilitated economically and politically through public adjustment assistance.

Second, the governments of industrial countries should continue to support the operation of international organizations such as the IMF, World Bank and GATT, which are designed to internalize the global negative externalities arising from the operation of free market forces alone. There are undoubted world benefits from the provision of a stable international monetary system through the IMF, the pooling of risks from investment in developing countries through the World Bank and the efforts to remove trade barriers through GATT.

Third, the industrial countries should continue to provide foreign official aid, raising the volume to 0.7 or more percent of GNP and making the funds available without restrictions.

The investment of resources by industrial countries in the three areas outlined would serve not only to raise incomes in developing but also in industrial countries. Furthermore, they are fully in the tradition of market economies, where private and public income transfer have been used to help those who are in need.

It has been argued that the NIEO is necessary because the nature of the political process in democracies, public ignorance or lack of compassion in industrial countries have restricted the enactment of the kinds of policies recommended here. I believe that this conclusion is not warranted, any more than it makes sense to give a patient medicine which will aggravate his illness just because there is not available enough of the correct medicine. Under such conditions, the only proper policy is to strengthen efforts to obtain the proper medicine, whatever the obstacles may be.

V. THE DEMANDS IN PERSPECTIVE

In the light of the preceding analysis it is perhaps surprising to find that the demands for the NIEO have found so many supporters in both developing and some industrialized countries. Therefore it may be useful to provide some perspective on the motives underlying this support for the NIEO. Such an analysis of motives must of necessity be speculative and general and is likely to do injustice to many individuals. But such are the risks of the undertaking, worth incurring in the expectation that it provides a useful perspective on the nature of the support for the NIEO.

Developing Countries

The support for the NIEO in developing countries comes from the bureaucrats and politicians in control of the planning and control systems of these countries. These bureaucrats and politicians are convinced that economic development and a desirable income distribution can be achieved only by the continuation of planning and control in their own countries and expansion of the system internationally and to the existing market economies.[15]

These bureaucrats and politicians are not dissuaded from their views by the fact that[16] in developing countries growth has been retarded by bureaucratic nightmares of regulation and control, the stifling of personal initiatives and the misallocation of resources through mistakes in planning, all accompanied by restrictions on personal liberty and freedom of expression. The retardation of growth is blamed instead on past exploitation through colonialism by Western governments, current exploitation through neocolonialism of multinational corporations and the failure of the international economy to perform as expected.

The proposals for the NIEO essentially represent efforts to deal with these alleged obstacles to economic development of the LDCs through the extension of bureaucratic control over the international economy and the economies of industrial countries. Underlying the interpretation of the causes of failure of economic development under bureaucratic control and the push for the expansion of this control are the natural reluctance of the bureaucrats and politicians to admit that they have made mistakes or that the very system is inappropriate. It is much easier to blame failures on sinister forces from abroad and to argue that any mistakes made are simply a matter of learning and will be avoided next time. Such views are even more understandable if it is realized that bureaucrats and politicians in LDCs have a strong vested interest in the maintenance of a system which is providing them with employment, high income and status.

International Agencies

The strongest support for the NIEO originates with the international bureaucracies of the United Nations. These bureaucracies are staffed predominantly with people from developing nations who qualified for their positions through technical expertise or past meritorious service in national politics or bureaucracies. These international civil servants live in some of the best cities of the world, such as Geneva, Rome, Vienna, New York and Washington and they enjoy incomes that often exceed those of national bureaucrats with similar responsibilities in the civil service of the United States and other industrial countries.[17] Their incomes are many times above those they could earn in their native countries. One of the shortcomings of working as an international bureaucrat is that most agencies of the United Nations have little or no power and executive responsibilities. Consequently, a very large proportion of the time of these international bureaucrats is spent in writing reports for other U.N. agencies and generally keeping going a dialogue among countries of the world on a wide range of topics.

The preceding analysis of the role of international bureaucrats working for the U.N. agencies does not imply that their work has low social productivity or that the bureaucrats' incomes are too high. The analysis merely suggests a reason why international bureaucrats would tend to push the NIEO in spite of the problems associated with it: the NIEO would provide them with increased power and status and since it would lead to an expansion of the bureaucracy, lead to greater demand and income for their services. International bureaucrats' support for the NIEO therefore is not entirely free of some selfish motives.

Industrial Countries

The demands for the establishment of the NIEO have received support also from certain groups within industrial countries. The first of these groups are the bureaucrats and politicians in foreign ministries. Their professional concern is with the maintenance of good relations with other countries and support of demands which would improve these relations is to be expected.

The second group consists of intellectuals in universities, governments and the media. Many of these intellectuals are in favor of more government intervention in economies generally and their support of the NIEO is consistent with this attitude. However, there are also many influential intellectuals who support calls for the NIEO and who would not have done so at other times. These intellectuals were influenced in their attitudes by the developments of the late 1960s and early 1970s, inflation, scarcities, the population explosion and pollution, which seemed to suggest that the world had changed fundamentally and was in need of new institutions to deal with unprecedented problems of mankind.[18]

The case against the NIEO made above will be strengthened in the minds of these influential intellectuals if it can be shown that in fact the troubles of the late 1960s and early 1970s were not symptomatic of a radically different world, but only of a passing episode of bad economic policy making. For this reason it is useful to provide the following perspective on recent events.

During the 1950s the most influential idea of economics in the North was that unemployment existing even during boom times in market economies was a very serious social evil, that moderate inflation had few undesirable welfare effects and that unemployment could be reduced permanently by the pursuit of inflationary monetary and fiscal policies. The intellectual victory of this idea came in the early 1960s when the United States and thereafter nearly all other industrial nations began to increase their money supplies at rates greater than consistent with price stability and, in perversion of Keynesian ideas of demand management, ran deliberate budget deficits when the economy was running at what previously had been considered full employment. As a result of these policies during the 1960s the world economy boomed and real growth proceeded at unprecedented rates. Unemployment fell, government revenues increased very rapidly. Intellectuals were warning the public of the consequences of excessive leisure time, the United States started "wars" on poverty, the polluted environment, the corporations ripping off the consumers, a traditional war on "aggression" in Vietnam, all simultaneously and without tax increases. The prosperity spilled over even into LDCs whose export earnings rose but whose expenditures rose even faster.

The bubble of unsustainable prosperity broke through simultaneous events on three fronts. First, the iron laws of economics reasserted themselves. The creation of money and running of budget deficits does not generate permanent wealth and output. Initially, these policies can create economic euphoria, as they have done at numerous instances in history, because they led to the depletion of inventories, temporarily higher demand for labor and wages and greater capacity utilization. But eventually, the purchasing power and demand for goods created without any counterpart of real output led to inflation and a falling of real wages. By 1973 the inflation caused such serious harm to most market economies that it was considered to be a greater evil than unemployment. Monetary and fiscal brakes were applied and welfare programs were cut back. The inflation led to income redistribution to strongly organized and unionized sectors of the economy and encouraged more workers and other interest groups to organize and protect their interests through strikes. The results of these events were anguished cries about the failure of the free market system and an intellectual climate generally favorable to criticism of the system[19] and tolerance of attacks from the South in the United Nations and elsewhere.

Second, one of the consequences of excessive money creation has been a disruption of the traditional process of discovery and opening up of mineral and energy sources, which historically had always produced an average of about fifteen years' future supply, and increased demand for food, especially in the form of proteins, in the LDCs. As a result, the prices of minerals, energy and food rose very sharply during the late 1960s and early 1970s. This phenomenon attracted the attention of the famous Club of Rome, which includes some intellectual and business men who had had great success in operating the system or understanding and putting to use the laws of nature, but who showed a deplorable lack of understanding of how the economic system works and what role prices play.[20] Like Malthus and numerous other intelligent people since him, the members of the Club of Rome were overwhelmed by the discovery that anything growing at compound rates of interest must eventually become infinitely large. While the Club of Rome eventually retracted its alarmist predictions about the dangers of an unplanned system[21] its naive ideas together with those of ecologists and conservationists had created an atmosphere of crisis and doubts about the merit of economic systems based on free markets. It also created tolerance for and interest in the kinds of ideas embodied in the proposals for a NIEO.

Third, in the midst of rising raw material prices and developing scarcities, the OPEC countries formed their cartel and effectively tripled the price of petroleum. The effects of this action on the economies and intellectual climate of the North were traumatic and reinforced the view that, as the population experts, conservationists, ecologists and Club of Rome had argued, the nature of the world had changed fundamentally during the 1960s.[22] The spread of nuclear weapons to India and Israel added to the sense of coming doom. In this atmosphere intellectuals and leaders of the North were more tolerant than ever of ideas critical of democratic systems based on free markets and ready to support demands for a NIEO.

The dramatic inflation and commodity scarcities of the period finally forced the governments of the world into contractionary economic policies which produced a severe economic slump and falling commodity prices. Capacity and reserves returned to normal and in 1976 there are many indications that the world economy has returned to the basic properties it had possessed before the recent inflation. However, the intellectual and political movements which had developed in response to the inflation and abnormal conditions have their own momentum and if history is any guide for the future, they will experience the same fate as other such movements in the past. With a lag, they will die like the concerns over the dollar shortage, dollar glut, cybernetics, permanent economic depression (as during the 1930s), population decline (in Europe during the 1930s), permanent changes in climate (the prairie dust storms), imminent extinction through atomic holocaust during the Cold War and many others remembered only by historians.

However, the great risk is that institutional changes proposed during the period of world crisis will be enacted simply because they have taken on a life of their own. One can only hope that the influential intellectuals of the North who have supported the NIEO initially will change their views and oppose the proposals before it is too late.

VI. SUMMARY AND CONCLUSIONS

In this paper I have attempted to show that the demands for a NIEO have originated with a group of non-aligned and developing countries which have formed the South Alliance in the United Nations. There they have used in recent years their numerical voting strength to formulate and propagandize demands for the adoption of international economic institutions which would replace market mechanisms by planning and control through international bureaucrats.

I have argued that such institutional changes are not in the interest of the world, including that of the people living in the LDCs, if one can judge from the performance of the completely planned economies of the Soviet bloc or the economies of the LDCs encumbered by vast bureaucratic networks of controls and regulation. The bureaucrats of the LDCs are in favor of such institutional changes because they appear not to understand how market economies work; because they are opposed to market economies on idealogical grounds; because the new system provides them with power, status and income not possible under a free market system; or a mixture of all of these reasons.

The most objectionable institutional change involves the proposed bureaucratic management of commodity markets through the creation of buffer stocks and the fixing of prices. Such management has too many inconsistent objectives and problems of forecasting that it has never worked in the history of the world and typically has resulted in the creation of greater price fluctuations and welfare losses to producers and consumers than did the system of free markets. Arguments that the world has changed fundamentally in recent years to make such management both necessary and possible were shown to be based on a misinterpretation of the causes of recent price instabilities, capacity shortages and reserve depletions. These were caused by excessive demand inflation and not by discontinuities or threshold effects in nature or economic development of the world.

In conclusion I must make a point which should be obvious but may not be. The case made against the NIEO and the resultant bureaucratization of the international economy emanates not from a lack of concern for the welfare of people in the LDCs, the effort to maximize the industrial countries' advantage from international trade or some attempt to obtain personal gains. Like supporters of the NIEO, I believe that the world would be a better one for all men if the problem of poverty in the LDCs could be relieved. The disagreement is not over motives but the methods for best achieving the same objective.

NOTES

1. This section draws heavily on an excellent study by R. McCulloch and K. Brunner. See R. McCulloch, *Economic Policy in the United Nations: A New International Economic Order?* A paper presented at the Carnegie-Rochester Public Policy Conference, April 23–24, 1976; [Karl Brunner, "The New International Economic Order, A Chapter in a Protracted Confrontation," *Orbis*, Vol. 20, Philadelphia, Pa., 1976, pp. 102 sqq.] The former contains references to recent studies of the United Nations.—For a broader perspective on the issues, including demands for control over multinational enterprises, see F. Hirsch, *Is there a New International Economic Order?* Inaugural Lecture, University of Warwick, Department of International Studies, 23rd February, 1976, mimeo.

2. Canada's L. Pearson produced a study which provided much of the factual and intellectual background for the formulation of the International Development Strategy. See Lester B. Pearson, *Partners in Development: Report of the Commission on International Development,* New York, 1969.

3. These figures were cited by J. Tumlir, *Adjustment Cost and Policies to Reduce It,* A Paper Presented at an MIT Workshop, May 17–20, 1976, mimeo.

4. The original proposals are found in a number of U.N. General Assembly resolutions especially 3201 (S–VI), 3202 (S–VI) and 3281 (XXIX) and the publications of the ad hoc Committee of the Seventh Special Session (A/AC. 176/2.3, and Add. 1–7), New York, September 14, 1975.

5. The precise wording of the document is "to nationalize, expropriate or transfer ownership and that compensation disputes should be decided upon by domestic tribunals."

6. The precise wording of the document is "that all states have the duty to co-operate in achieving adjustments in the prices of exports of LDCs in relation to the prices of the imports."

7. The sources of these proposals are *An Integrated Programme for Commodities: Specific Proposals for Decision and Action by Governments,* Report by the Secretary-General of UNCTAD, TD/B/C.1/193, October 28, 1975, and supporting documents TD/B/C.1/194 to 197, Geneva.—For another critical analysis of these proposals see Harry G. Johnson, *Commodities: Less Developed Countries' Demands and Developed Countries' Response,* A Paper Presented at an MIT Workshop, May 17–20, 1976, mimeo.—For a more sympathetic view see M. Sakellaropoulo, *The Controversy on Commodities: The Present and Prospects for the Future,* A Report and Some Notes on a Seminar Held in La Mainaz (France), Centre for Research on International Institutions, Geneva, March 1976.

8. For a sympathetic review see Chapter 5 of G. K. Helleiner, *International Trade and Economic Development,* Penguin Modern Economics Texts, Development Economics, Harmondsworth, Middlesex, 1972.—Two of the best-known studies critical of the need for and effectiveness of stabilization efforts are Alasdair I. MacBean, *Export Instability and Economic Development,* Forew. by Edward Mason, University of Glasgow, Social and Economic Studies, N.S., 9, London, 1966; Benton F. Massell, "Export Instability and

Economic Structure", *The American Economic Review*, Vol. 60, Menasha, Wisc., 1970, pp. 618 sqq.

9. This argument has been made in Herbert G. Grubel, "Foreign Exchange Earnings and Price Stabilization Schemes", *The American Economic Review*, Vol. 54, 1964, pp. 378 sqq.—A complete analysis of the relationship between price, income and expenditure fluctuations should also take account of the realistic cases where demand and supply vary simultaneously. See the references cited in the footnote, p. 290, for such a general analysis.

10. See G. K. Helleiner, "Canada and the New International Economic Order", *Canadian Public Policy*, Summer 1976, p. 463.

11. Empirical support for this proposition is found in Herbert G. Grubel, "Taxation and the Rates of Return from Some U.S. Asset Holdings Abroad, 1960–1969", *The Journal of Political Economy*, Vol. 82, Chicago, Ill., 1974, pp. 469 sqq.

12. See George J. Stigler, "The Theory of Economic Regulation", *The Bell Journal of Economics and Management Science*, Vol. 2, New York, N.Y., 1971, pp. 3 sqq.—Sam Peltzman, "Toward a More General Theory of Regulation". *The Journal of Political Economy*, Vol. 84, 1976.

13. The last decade saw efforts to solve through global international agreements the solution of the problems of disequilibrium exchange rates and transnational pollution. Negotiations for the solution of both programs could not be concluded successfully because of the basic inability to write laws covering all possible contingencies perceived by individual countries as involving their national interest. On the exchange rate problem finally a general rule about appropriate national behavior was accepted and all hopes to devise specific rules of behavior were abandoned. A. D. Scott argues for a similar solution to the problem of reaching agreement on treaties dealing with transnational pollution. See Anthony Scott, "Transfrontier Pollution and Institutional Choice", in: *Studies in International Environmental Economics*, Ed. by Ingo Walter, New York, 1976, pp. 303 sqq.

14. For a more detailed discussion, with references to opposing viewpoints, see Herbert G. Grubel, "Basic Methods for Distributing Special Drawing Rights and the Problem of International Aid", *The Journal of Finance*, Vol. 27, Worcester, Mass., 1972, pp. 1009 sqq.

15. See Brunner, *op. cit.*, for elaboration on this view.

16. For a discussion of the evidence see Johnson and Meier, where references to other works are found: Harry G. Johnson, *Economic Policies Toward Less Developed Countries*, The Brookings Institution, Washington, D.C., 1967; Gerald M. Meier, *Leading Issues in Economic Development*, Studies in International Poverty, 2nd Ed., New York, 1970.

17. The salary structure of international bureaucracies has been indexed to inflation and in recent years produced such high pay scales that national governments, including that of the United States, find that their civil servants in equivalent positions are earning considerably less than their international counterparts. The U.S. Congress has repeatedly, but unsuccessfully, attempted to bring about a less rapid rise in the salaries of some international bureaucracies.

18. As a case study of how the government of an industrial country has responded to the demands for the NIEO we might consider the case of Canada. At the Prime Ministers' Commonwealth Conference in May 1975, Prime Minister Trudeau stated "that Canada will not only support international stockpiles of grain and other essential commodities but will surrender to an international body the degree of control necessary to manage and apportion these reserves; that Canada will index or begin to negotiate a consumer-producer agreement of a specified list of commodities which are deemed essential in order that both raw and labor-intensive manufactured commodity prices are in just relationship to imports and exports." Cited by A. E. D. MacKenzie "Canada and the New Economic Order", *Cooperation Canada*, Ottawa, 1975, No. 21, p. 11.

In his speech to the U.N. General Assembly in September 1975, the Canadian Minister for External Affairs, Allan MacEachen, again endorsed the general program of buffer stocks and a common fund, but the support for price fixing was more circumspect: "We recognize that commodity prices cannot be determined without reference to market forces. At the same time, we are well aware that no one's interest is served by commodity prices that are so low as to discourage production." A. J. MacEachen, "The Challenge of Change", Speech Delivered at the Seventh Special Session of the U.N. General Assembly, September 3, 1975, *Statements and Speeches*, No. 75/26, Department of External Affairs, Ottawa, 1975, p. 4. The two sentences cited are an interesting example of diplomatic double-talk. If market forces are allowed to operate prices may well have to be low to discourage production of commodities in excess supply for whatever reason.

19. This period saw the development of The Economics of the New Left whose contents have been examined critically by Assar Lindbeck, *The Political Economy of the New Left, An Outsider's View,* Forew. by Paul A. Samuelson, New York, 1971.

20. Solow quotes Jay Forrester, one of the authors of the Club of Rome Report: "'Above all, it [i.e., a group of gifted people to solve world problems] shouldn't be mostly made up of professors. One would include people who had been successful in their personal careers, whether in politics or business or anywhere else. We should also need radical philosophers, but we should take care to keep out representatives of the social sciences. Such people always want to go to the bottom of a particular problem. What we want to look at are the problems caused by interactions'." Robert M. Solow, "Is the End of the World at Hand?" *Challenge,* Vol. 16, White Plains, N.Y., March/April 1973, p. 39.

21. For a review of the latest, much more balanced view of the future accepted by the Club of Rome, see A. King, "The Club of Rome, An Insider's View", *The Center Magazine,* repr. in: *Economic Impact,* Washington, D.C., 1975, No. 12.

22. C. Fred Bergsten ("The New Era in World Commodity Markets", *Challenge,* Vol. 17, September/October 1974, pp. 34 sqq.) articulated the view held by a number of economists that conditions in the world's commodity markets had changed fundamentally.

"State on U.S. Aims at the World Trade Minister's Meeting: A Labor View" by Rudy Oswald. Reprinted from the U.S. Approach to 1982 Meeting of World Trade Ministers on the GATT, Before the Subcommittee on International Trade, Senate Committee on Finance, March 1, 1982.

"The GATT Ministerial: A Postmortem" by Jeffrey J. Schott. From *Challenge,* May–June 1983, pp. 40–45. This article is reprinted with the permission of publisher, M. E. Sharpe, Inc., Armonk, New York, 10504.

"The 1980s: Twilight of the Open Trading System?" By C. Michael Aho and Thomas O. Bayard. Reprinted by permission from *The World Economy*, 5:4, December 1982.

III. THE UNITED STATES IN THE WORLD ECONOMY: ISSUES OF THE 1980s

"The United States in the World Economy: Strains on the System" by the Council of Economic Advisers. Reprinted from the *Economic Report of the President* together with the *Annual Report of the Council of Economic Advisers,* 1982. Statistical tables omitted.

"American Foreign Economic Policy: Challenges of the 1980s" by John Adams. Reprinted from the *Journal of Economic Issues* (18:1, March 1984) by special permission of the copyright holder, the Association for Evolutionary Economics.

"Incorporating the Gains from Trade into Policy" by J. Michael Finger. Reprinted by permission from *The World Economy* 5:4, December 1982.

"Wage Competitiveness in the U.S. Auto and Steel Industries" by Modechai E. Kreinin. Reprinted from *Contemporary Policy Issues,* No. 4, 1984 by permission of Western Economic Association International.

"Is Industrial Policy the Answer?" by Martin Feldstein. Speech by Martin Feldstein, Chairman, Council of Economic Advisers, to the Commonwealth Club of California, October 28, 1983, San Francisco, California.

IV. THE INTERNATIONAL MONETARY SYSTEM: OPERATION AND MANAGEMENT

"Balance-of-Payments Concepts—What Do They Really Mean?" by Donald S. Kemp. Reprinted from *Federal Reserve Bank of St. Louis Review,* July 1975. The author acknowledges the helpful comments on earlier drafts from Allan H. Meltzer and Wilson E. Schmidt.

"Fixed and Flexible Exchange Rates: A Renewal of the Debate" by Jacques R. Artus and John H. Young. Reprinted by permission of the International Monetary Fund from *Staff Papers,* 26:4, December 1979.

"Unexpected Real Consequences of Floating Exchange Rates" by Rachel McCulloch. From *Essays in International Finance,* No. 153, August 1983. Copyright © 1983. Reprinted by permission of the International Finance Section of Princeton University.

"The Case for Managed Exchange Rates" by John Williamson. Reprinted by permission of the MIT Press from *The Exchange Rate System.* Copyright © 1983 Institute for International Economics. All rights reserved.

"Techniques of Exchange Rate Management" by John Williamson. Reprinted by permission of the MIT Press from The Exchange Rate System. Copyright © 1983 Institute for International Economics. All rights reserved.

"Evolution of the SDR" by William J. Byrne. Reprinted from *Finance and Development,* September 1982.

"International Debt: Conflict and Resolution" by James R. Barth and Joseph Pelzman. Reprinted by permission from Fairfax, VA: Department of Economics, George Mason University, January 1984. The authors gratefully acknowledge the very helpful discussions with Michele Fratianni and Robert Kelcher and are heavily indebted to the earlier research on this issue conducted by Robert Weintraub.

V. THE MULTINATIONAL CORPORATION IN THE INTERNATIONAL ECONOMY

"Multinational Corporations and Foreign Investment: Current Trends and Issues" by Jane Sneddon Little. Reprinted from volume No. 460 of THE ANNALS of the American Academy of Political and Social Science. THE ANNALS © 1982 by the American Academy of Political and Social Science.

"The Product Cycle Hypothesis in a New International Environment" by Raymond Vernon. Reprinted by permission of Basil Blackwell from *Oxford Bulletin of Economics and Statistics,* 41:4, November 1979.

"Sovereignty at Bay, Ten Years After" by Raymond Vernon. Reprinted from *International Organization,* 35:3 by permission of the MIT Press, Cambridge, Mass. © 1981 by the World Peace Foundation and the Massachusetts Institute of Technology. "The Appropriability Theory of the Multinational Corporation" by Stephen P. Magee. Reprinted from volume no. 458 of THE ANNALS of the American Academy of Political and Social Science.

"Multinationals and Developing Countries: Myths and Realities" by Peter F. Drucker. Reprinted by permission of the author from *Foreign Affairs,* vol. 53 (October 1974).

VI. RICH COUNTRY–POOR COUNTRY RELATIONSHIPS

"Declaration on the Establishment of a New International Economic Order," United Nations General Assembly. Reprinted from the United Nations General Assembly Resolutions 3201 (S–VI) and 3202 (S–VI), May 1, 1974.

"U.S. Relations with Developing Countries: Conflict and Opportunity" by Rachel McCulloch. Reprinted from volume no. 460 of THE ANNALS of the American Academy of Political and Social Science. THE ANNALS © 1982 by the American Academy of Political and Social Science.

"International Markets for LDCs—The Old and the New" by Carlos F. Diaz-Alejandro. Reprinted by permission of the American Economic Association from *American Economic Review,* vol. 68 (May 1978).

"Approaches to a New International Economic Order" by Paul Streeten. Reprinted with permission from *World Development,* vol. 10, no. 1. Copyright 1982, Pergamon Press, Ltd.

"The Case Against the New International Economic Order" by Herbert G. Grubel. Reprinted by permission from *Weltwirtschaftliches Archiv*, Bd. 113, No. 2 (1977) pp. 284–306.